Administrative Implementation of
CIVIL RIGHTS

Administrative Implementation of

CIVIL RIGHTS

JOSEPH PARKER WITHERSPOON

UNIVERSITY OF TEXAS PRESS

AUSTIN & LONDON

Library of Congress Catalog Card No. 66–15708

Type set by G&S Typesetters, Austin
Printed by The Steck Company, Austin
Bound by Universal Bookbindery, Inc., San Antonio

To My Wife and Sons

CONTENTS

Administrative Implementation of
CIVIL RIGHTS

PART I

The Challenge of Federal Civil-Rights Policy to Our Federal System

THE CIVIL-RIGHTS REVOLUTION

As an economic and social crisis of unprecedented proportions continued to engulf their ethnic group of approximately twenty million persons, Negroes initiated in 1963 a series of widespread nonviolent actions to protest their unbearable situation. One of their principal leaders, Reverend Martin Luther King, based his espousal of this type of protest action upon his "great hope" that the Negro masses to whom he appealed would continue to utilize that method rather than violence.[1] He believed that this method would be efficacious in moving the white majority group to moderate the discrimination and other harmful action directed against Negroes that constituted the principal cause of the economic and social crisis affecting them. But James Foreman, as executive secretary of the Student Nonviolent Coordinating Committee which was spearheading the civil-rights struggle in the rural Deep South, in 1963 warned that a large percentage of Negroes did not favor the nonviolent approach because they did not believe that it would work.[2] The riots by Negroes in major cities across the country during the summers between 1964 and 1966—especially in New York and Philadelphia in 1964, Los Angeles in 1965, and Cleveland in 1966 —seemed to confirm his judgment. After the summer of 1967 there could be no doubt that Foreman had been more accurate in his assessment of the Negro viewpoint. The riots in Newark, Detroit, Minneapolis, and numerous other major cities demonstrated that the techniques

---

[1] Martin Luther King, Jr., "The Case against Tokenism," *The New York Times Magazine* (August 5, 1962), pp. 49, 52–53.

[2] Claude Sitton, "Not Token Freedom, Full Freedom," *The New York Times Magazine* (June 9, 1963), p. 80.

of a brutal and bitter violence have been added to the nonviolent techniques of the Civil-Rights Revolution.

Negroes are not the only ethnic group sorely afflicted by unprecedented economic and social crisis. In some respects the nation's six million Latin Americans, principally drawn from Mexican and Puerto Rican stock, may be even more grievously affected.[3] Their plight, moreover, results from the same kinds of actions by the majority group that have been directed against the Negroes. Long accustomed to accept what seemed to be an ineradicable part of their existence, Latin Americans have been deeply impressed by the nonviolent and violent protest actions of Negroes. The California grape strike of 1965 and the Texas melon-pickers strike of 1966 represented the Latin Americans' entry into the Civil-Rights Revolution. The violent overtones of recent disturbances in Latin American ghettos in Chicago and New York simply demonstrate that forces similar to those operating in the Negro ghettos cannot be contained. There are, moreover, Latin American leaders who suggest that techniques of violence may become necessary for attaining the justice so long denied their people.

There are other disoriented groups in our nation's cities besides their Negroes and Latin Americans. Both in urban and rural areas there are many more millions of non-Latin white persons who are mired in a poverty or near-poverty status than there are Negroes and Latin Americans.[4] The participation of white persons alongside Negroes in the Detroit riots has a significance that should not be overlooked. It seems fair to say that close to fifty million persons in this country—Negro, Latin American, and other white persons having a very low income status—suffer in the same economic and social crisis caused by substantially the same kinds of actions on the part of a white majority group which tightly controls access to all goods, services, and fields of endeavor.

This nation consists of people of many different races, colors, religions, ancestries, and national origins. Indeed, many have boasted that

[4] *Poverty in the Affluent Society*, edited by Hannah H. Missner (New York: Harper and Row, 1966), pp. 43–67; Herman P. Miller, "The Dimensions of Poverty," and S. M. Miller and Martin Rein, "The War on Poverty: Perspectives and Prospects," in *Poverty as a Public Issue*, edited by Ben B. Seligman (New York: The Free Press, 1965), pp. 20–51; Dwight MacDonald, "Our Invisible Poor," and Oscar Ornati, "Poverty in America," in *Poverty in America*, edited by Louis A. Ferman, Joyce L. Kornbluh, and Alan Haber (Ann Arbor: The University of Michigan Press, 1965), pp. 8–10, 25–39.

the strength of this nation is traceable to this diversity. It is essential to the public welfare, peace, and continued progress that this diversity serve to strengthen individual and collective efforts to achieve man's enduring goals and that it not be used to weaken these efforts. This latter result occurs when members of one group through discrimination and similar practices prevent members of another group from obtaining access to the important opportunities and goods of community life merely on account of their race, color, religion, ancestry, national origin, sex, age, economic status, or other normal group characteristic. Pursued ruthlessly and relentlessly enough against enough people, these harmful practices by the group in power can destroy the integrity of our free society and the acceptance of its authority by the people harmed. These practices can also destroy the nation's capacity to provide leadership in the free world and among the uncommitted underdeveloped nations.

The riots of the summers between 1964 and 1967 demonstrate that substantial numbers of the nation's fifty million Negroes, Latin Americans, and other whites of very low income have lost hope in the face of their long unrelieved and increasingly desperate situation as human beings.[5] Substantial numbers of these groups have concluded that the techniques of reasoned argument, nonviolent direct actions of protest, and prayer cannot produce the change toward more just treatment which they have so long been promised and for which they have waited and worked. This loss of hope by so many of its people—in the context of the crowded society in which we live today—presents the United States with the most serious problem it has confronted since its birth. This nation has long since been known as the most lawless society in the world with its continually growing network of organized crime syndicates and rackets.[6] One shudders to think of the opportunities for organized crime as our society comes apart at the seams in our cities and our national and local governments fumble in employing temporary expedients to deal with the crisis.

No thoughtful person or institution should fail to assess the degree of the discontent entertained by members of the Negro and Latin American communities concerning discrimination against them in all its

---

[5] *Cf.*, *The New York Times* (July 16, 1967) sec. 4, p. 12; (July 30, 1967), sec. 4, p. 8; *America* (July 29, 1967), p. 105.

[6] Max Lerner, *America as a Civilization* (New York: Simon and Schuster, 1957), p. 661; Gus Tyler, *Organized Crime in America* (Ann Arbor: The University of Michigan Press, 1962).

forms, and especially in its economic aspects. They desire to be admitted *now* into the whole of community life, its dialogue, and its processes of decision. They desire to have their problems frankly faced by all leaders in the business, political, educational, and other aspects of community life. They want to participate as equal members in proposing and disposing. As a result of better educational opportunities in both the North and the South, they have come to understand the meaning of the American credo, the differences between its promises and its realization for themselves, and they seek to have it given substantial meaning for themselves through their participation in the whole of community processes. Both groups now conceive of discrimination in all its forms as an intolerable social cancer that they must seek vigorously to eliminate through all forms of social, economic, and political self-help. They see our nation as a house divided against itself and they believe not only in their personal right to have that division eliminated but in their duty, as Americans, to seek its elimination before it destroys the remaining integrity of the nation. It is inevitable that these groups will concentrate upon and be successful in participating more effectively in the electoral and political processes at all levels. It is inevitable that they utilize the various group processes of speech, publication, boycott, picketing, and other forms of economic and social persuasion to obtain what others have obtained before them by the same means. It is also inevitable that when these processes of persuasion prove inefficacious in changing the attitudes and actions of the majority group, they resort to techniques of violence. The Civil-Rights Revolution—particularly with the advent of the urban riots such as those of 1967—presents the nation with the immediate necessity for truly understanding the civil-rights problem of its minority groups and its poor and for taking effective remedial action to resolve it on a permanent basis.

Many different approaches looking to a solution of the civil-rights problem are needed. In this book we will focus upon but one of these, the use of law to regulate or to promote human relations in such a way that the conflicts and tensions between different social groups will be ameliorated, their causes removed, and positive action taken to relieve unjust conditions and to eliminate unjust actions affecting members of one or more groups. We have had considerable experience with this form of law during the past twenty years. It is essential that we examine this experience with a view to evaluating it and to determining how it can be made more effective than it presently is in contributing to the solution of the nation's civil-rights problem.

THE NATURE OF THE CHALLENGE

The federal civil-rights policy established between 1957 and 1968, despite its many remedial imperfections and substantive inadequacies, constitutes one of the great monuments of American social legislation. The principal piece of this policy is the Civil Rights Act of 1964.[7] Like the Interstate Commerce Act of 1887 and each major component of the massive economic and social legislation enacted since that date, this statute established an important permanent policy for the entire nation. It proscribed several forms of the discrimination that today prevent numerous minority groups and other disadvantaged persons from participating on equal terms with other persons in vital areas of our public life. It reached discrimination practiced by private persons and institutions as well as by public officials. The Civil Rights Act of 1957,[8] as amended by the Civil Rights Act of 1960,[9] had applied only to deprivations of the right to vote, suffered primarily by Negroes in the Deep South, and, in actual practice, caused by public officials.

The 1964 act also authorized federal officials to utilize many forms of government action to promote in an affirmative way the elimination of the discrimination prohibited by the act. This included the use of a government suit for injunctive relief against discriminatory practices (a technique which had been utilized in the 1957 act), as well as several types of administrative process. The statute thus assured that modern governmental processes and techniques would now be used to protect the vital interests of members of minority and disadvantaged groups as equal participants in our democratic society, just as these processes had long since been used to protect the interests of consumers, competitors, workers, shippers, investors, passengers, depositors, and many other interest groups in the nation. Its healing principles are broadly stated, following the classic mode of our major federal statutes. Its provisions consequently provide considerable latitude for agencies and courts to apply them wisely and justly to the endless variety of situations that will occur. More important, the statute provides

[7] 42 U.S.C. §§ 1971, 1975a–1975d, 2000a–2000h (1964), *as amended* (Supp. II, 1965–1966).
[8] 42 U.S.C. §§ 1971(a)–(d), (g) (1964), *as amended* (Supp. II, 1965–1966).
[9] 42 U.S.C. §§ 1971(c), (e) (1964), *as amended* (Supp. II, 1965–1966).

a firm nucleus around which future legislation can be constructed for strengthening or extending its operation. The proposed Civil Rights Act of 1966, which was eventually defeated in the Senate, and its counterpart of 1967, are examples of such construction.[10] The 1966 proposed act would have amended Titles III and VI of the 1964 act so as to strengthen the administration of prohibitions of discrimination in public education and other public facilities and in programs receiving federal financial assistance. It would also have added new provisions prohibiting discrimination in housing and in the financing of housing. Another proposed act, H.R. 10065, that also was passed by the House of Representatives, would have greatly extended the scope and strengthened the administration of Title VII of the 1964 act relating to discrimination in employment.[11] The Age Discrimination in Employment Act of 1967 and the historic Civil Rights Act of 1968, creating among other things a fair housing policy, are further examples of the Congress building around the nucleus of the concepts embodied in the Civil Rights Act of 1964.[12]

The Civil Rights Act of 1957 had been the first major step in the direction of establishing a federal civil-rights policy. It authorized the Attorney General to institute a suit for injunctive relief against any action or practice depriving any person of his right to vote as defined

---

[10] The proposed 1966 act was introduced by identical bills in the House of Representatives and the Senate: H.R. 14765 and S. 3296 [*Hearings on S. 3296, etc. before the Subcommittee on Constitutional Rights of the Senate Committee on the Judiciary*, 89th Cong., 2nd Sess. (Washington, D.C.: U.S. Government Printing Office, 1966), pt. 1, p. 10]. A contemporary bill, S. 2923, which would have expanded the coverage of Title VII of the 1964 act relative to employment discrimination, redefined the term "employer" to include a state or a political subdivision of a state [*Id.*, p. 35]. H.R. 14765 passed the House of Representatives on August 9, 1966, by a vote of 259 to 157 [*Congressional Record*, Vol .112 (Washington, D.C.: U.S. Government Printing Offices, daily ed., August 9, 1966), p. 17916]. The proposed 1966 act was definitively defeated in the Senate by the failure of two-thirds of its members to support a motion for cloture on September 14 and again on September 19, 1966. The vote on the latter date was 52 to 41 [*Congressional Record*, Vol. 112 (daily ed., September 19, 1966), p. 22114].

[11] H.R. 10065, which is set out in 62 *Labor Relations Report* No. 1 (Special Supp., May 2, 1966), was almost identical with the provisions of H.R. 8998 introduced in the first session of the 89th Congress [*Hearings on H.R. 8998 and H.R. 8999 before the General Subcommittee on Labor of the House Committee on Education and Labor*, 89th Cong., 1st Sess. (Washington, D.C.: U.S. Government Printing Office, 1965), p. 1]. For an analysis of the late 1967 status of similar proposed legislation see *Congressional Quarterly Weekly Report*, Vol. XXV, No. 41 (October 13, 1967), pp. 2065–2067.

[12] P.L. 90-202 (Dec. 15, 1967), and P.L. 90-284 (April 11, 1968), respectively.

in two provisions.[13] One of these was the right to vote at any election, without distinction of race, color, or previous condition of servitude. The other was the right to vote in any election for federal office.[14] Prior to this time the only remedies provided by statute for deprivation of the right to vote were a suit by the person injured[15] or a criminal action by the government.[16] Moreover, these remedies were available only against action affecting the right to vote that was "under the color of law" (*i.e.*, action primarily by public officials). These remedies possessed only limited effectiveness in providing protection for the civil right in question. The great advance made by the Civil Rights Act of 1957 was that it authorized civil actions by the government, actions that could, presumably, encompass continuing, broad-scale judicial control of discriminatory conduct by state and local government that adversely affected the exercise of the right of Negroes to vote. This device had been used with great effectiveness by the federal government previously, for example, in implementing federal antitrust policy protecting the principle of competition in the market place. The device, however, proved relatively ineffective in protecting the right to vote despite efforts of Congress to strengthen it in the Civil Rights Acts of 1960 and 1964. This ineffectiveness was due, in large part, to the fact that individual lawsuits, without the aid of other enforcement techniques, are not an adequate way of dealing with the widespread violations of law existing in the civil-rights field.[17] Congress finally recognized its error in expecting this device alone to protect the right to vote, and enacted the Voting Rights Act of 1965.[18] This act established certain criteria for designating states in which the registration of voters for all elections is to be done by federal examiners.[19] Upon their designation by the Attorney General, the Civil Service Commission appoints examiners who then prepare a list of qualified voters for the state in which they are authorized to operate. State authorities, when they receive this list, must place the names of the listed voters in the official voting records.[20]

---

13 42 U.S.C. § 1971(c) (1964), *as amended* (Supp. II, 1965–1966).

14 *Id.*, § 1971(a) (1), and (b).

15 *Id.*, § 1983.

16 18 U.S.C. § 242 (1964).

17 See the statement by officials of the U.S. Commission on Civil Rights supporting this proposition. [*Hearings on S. 3296*, p. 364].

18 42 U.S.C. §§ 1963–1974 (Supp. II, 1965–1966).

19 *Id.*, § 1973(b) (Supp. II, 1965–1966).

20 *Id.*, § 1973e(a)–(b).

The 1964 act authorized the Attorney General, under certain conditions, to file a suit for preventive relief against actions violating prohibitions of discrimination against persons because of their race, color, religion, national origin, or sex, in connection with certain types of activities.[21] The prohibitions related to certain public accommodations, any governmental facility including the public schools, any program or activity receiving federal financial assistance, employment practices by employers and unions engaged in an industry affecting interstate and similar commerce, and employment practices by employment agencies serving an employer covered by the act.[22] The act also created the federal Equal Employment Opportunity Commission (EEOC) to employ some of the techniques of the modern administration process to deal with discrimination in employment practices.[23] It also directed the numerous administrative agencies providing financial assistance to various programs and activities to formulate administrative regulations prohibiting discrimination in the programs on the basis of race, color, or national origin.[24] After satisfying certain conditions, these agencies were to enforce these regulations by terminating or refusing to grant or to continue financial assistance or by other means authorized by law.[25] The United States commissioner of education was authorized to render technical assistance to public schools in implementing plans for desegregation and to provide training for school personnel designed to prepare them for dealing with problems occasioned by desegregation.[26] A special administrative agency, the Federal Community Relations Service, was created to provide assistance to communities and persons in resolving difficulties relating to discrimination against minority groups.[27] It was also provided that the Attorney General might intervene in suits brought by private persons injured by violations of the act.[28] Beyond these authorizations for official action to deal with discrimination, private persons filing these suits were given

[21] *Id.*, §§ 2000a-5, 2000(a) (1964).

[22] *Id.*, §§ 2000a–2000a-2 (public accommodation); 2000b–2000b-3 (governmental facilities); 2000c, 2000c-6–2000c-9 (public schools); 2000d–2000d-1 (programs receiving federal financial assistance); 2000e-2(a), -2(c) (employment practices by employers and unions); 2000e-2(b) (employment practices by employment agencies).

[23] *Id.*, §§ 2000e-4–2000e-5(e), 2000e-5(i).

[24] *Id.*, § 2000d-1.

[25] *Ibid.*

[26] *Id.*, §§ 2000c-2–2000c-5.

[27] *Id.*, §§ 2000g–2000g-2.

[28] *Id.*, §§ 2000a-3(a), 2000e-5(e), 2000h-2.

various types of assistance to facilitate their filing and prosecution of suits to enforce the act. These included the right to appointment of an attorney to represent the plaintiff, commencement of suit without payment of fees, costs, or security, and payment of attorney's fees.[29]

Five of the titles of the 1964 act are directed primarily against discriminatory practices occurring in the Southern states. These titles concern discriminatory practices relative to voting rights, public accommodations, government facilities, public education, and programs receiving federal financial assistance (primarily programs involving matters other than housing). These practices were so deeply entrenched in the social fabric of many of these states that nothing short of federal intervention would have been likely to change them in the reasonably foreseeable future. The forms of discrimination actually reached by these titles are either practically nonexistent in the Northern and Western states, or, if existent to a substantial degree—as in the case of public accommodations—can be effectively controlled by local and state laws already generally available in these areas. The one title of the act actually directed to a problem confronting minority groups throughout the whole country is Title VII, which covers discrimination in employment. The prohibition of this form of discrimination was limited to a maximum coverage, as of July 2, 1968, of employers and unions with twenty-five or more employees or members, in industries affecting interstate commerce. Further, state and local governments were expressly exempted from the prohibition.[30] This limited coverage of private employers and exclusion of governmental employers meant that the overwhelming majority of employers throughout the country, including some of the largest, were exempt from the prohibition against discrimination in employment established by Title VII.[31]

If the limited coverage of discriminatory employment practices by the 1964 act is understandable in light of political considerations at work prior to its enactment, it is less easy to understand the ineffective remedies chosen by Congress to implement the new civil-rights policy it established. The basic method adopted to eliminate discrimination against minority groups, except in the case of programs receiving fed-

[29] *Id.*, §§ 2000a-3(a), 2000e-5(e).
[30] *Id.*, § 2000e(b).
[31] Fewer than 8 per cent of all employers in businesses affecting interstate commerce are covered and only 29 per cent of all employers with 8 or more employees in businesses affecting interstate commerce are covered. Out of a total of 3,440,000

eral financial assistance, was, as previously stated, a suit by the Attorney General in a federal court for preventive relief. This was true
even with regard to employment discrimination under Title VII. The
EEOC is an enforcement agency only in the broadest sense of the
term. Its five-man bipartisan board is authorized to investigate charges
of unlawful employment practices filed either by individuals aggrieved by these practices or by a member of the commission.[32] When
the board finds reasonable cause to believe such charges are true, it is
authorized to resolve the underlying disputes through informal methods of conference, conciliation, and persuasion. If the board is unable
to obtain voluntary compliance with the prohibitions of employment
discrimination against minority groups, however, its work is substantially over. Further enforcement of the prohibition is left either to the
person aggrieved by the alleged unlawful practice, or, under certain
circumstances, to the Attorney General. By 1964, it was quite evident,
upon the basis of the experience of states and municipalities having
civil-rights legislation, that the reliance upon administrative techniques of persuasion and conciliation to secure voluntary compliance
with prohibitions against discrimination in employment were most
certainly doomed to failure.[33] The availability of an administrative
trial and an effective civil sanction in case conciliation does not suc-
ceed has been a *sine qua non* to progress in enforcement of civil
rights. By 1964 it was equally evident, in light of federal experience
with the 1957 Civil Rights Act and amendments made to it by the
1960 Civil Rights Act, that a suit for preventive relief by the Attorney
General as the sole means for enforcement was a cumbersome, time-
consuming, and thoroughly unsatisfactory way of dealing with a widespread form of law violation in the civil-rights field.[34] Two years after
enactment of the 1964 act experience with its administration had confirmed what was evident at the outset about the ineffectiveness of the
type of remedies chosen to eliminate employment discrimination. The
EEOC had received in its fiscal year ending June 30, 1966, a total of
8,854 complaints. In nearly 25 per cent of these the commission had

---

employers, only 258,000 are presently covered; 21,093 state, county, and municipal
government employers with a total of 6,586,000 employees are exempted from the
act [*Hearings on H.R. 8998 and H.R. 8999*, p. 108; U. S. Department of Commerce,
Bureau of the Census, *Statistical Abstract of the United States: 1965* (Washington,
D.C.: Government Printing Office, 1965), pp. 436, 441].

[32] 42 U.S.C. §§ 2000e-5(a), -5(e), -6(a) (1964).

[33] See Chapter 4, below.

[34] *Hearings on S. 3269*, p. 364.

made no effort whatsoever to deal with the discrimination charged. The reason given by the EEOC for rejecting these cases was "lack of jurisdiction." For an agency that had no enforcement power anyway this would appear to be an extraordinarily unseemly, if not lame, excuse. Nothing precluded the EEOC from utilizing its good offices to resolve cases of employment discrimination although it lacked "jurisdiction," where its help was sought by complainants. Many state and local agencies having the authority to apply sanctions to violators of civil-rights legislation have operated in this fashion with regard to cases as to which they did not have this authority. In doing so they have sometimes achieved quite good results. EEOC did not reveal how many employers, unions, and employment agencies were charged with discrimination in the 8,854 complaints filed. The agency did complete investigations of 1,659 cases during 1965–1966. It found that in 704 of these cases involving 214 employers, unions, and employment agencies, probable cause existed for believing discrimination in employment had occurred. At the end of the fiscal year only 45 of these respondents had agreed to cease their discriminatory practices. This was only 20 per cent of the 214 respondents whom the EEOC believed had probably discriminated in employment. On the assumption that the same ratio obtained between total complaints and total respondents, conciliation has been successful with regard to fewer than 2 per cent of all respondents charged with discrimination; 80 per cent of respondents believed by the EEOC to have discriminated had either refused to comply with the act as urged, refused to comply fully with it, or else were undergoing the process of conciliation. The cases in which investigation of discrimination charges had been completed made up only 10 per cent of those that had been filed. It is generally recognized that complaints filed with human-relations commissions represent a very small proportion of the discriminatory transactions actually occurring. For this reason the percentages reported so far are indicative of an even smaller impact upon discrimination in employment. Moreover, the EEOC in 1965–1966 had recommended to the Attorney General that he file a suit for injunctive relief against persons charged with employment discrimination in only 10 of the 6,133 cases it had docketed during that year. This recommendation was made only in cases in which the EEOC considered there was a pattern or practice of discrimination involved.[35] This is the only type of case

---

[35] *EEOC Newsletter*, Vol. 1, No. 5 (July–August 1966), p. 1.

in which the Attorney General is authorized to seek injunctive relief under Title VII. By any standards of performance, EEOC had accomplished very little in its first year of operation.

In evaluating the performance of EEOC it is important to note that almost all of its enforcement activity had concerned the Southern and border states (55 per cent) along with ten heavily industrialized states primarily in the Middle West and East (41 per cent). Enforcement activity in nearly one-half of the states located in the North and West has been negligible and considerably reduced from a full enforcement load in the other half. For example, in North Carolina 709 complaints were filed with the EEOC as against 190 in New York, one of the Eastern states in which the agency has carried on substantial enforcement activity.[36]

The EEOC faces a huge problem of law enforcement and necessarily has to choose some part or parts of the total problem for emphasis in its enforcement effort. In most of the states of the North and West, such as Massachusetts, New York, Michigan, Minnesota, Colorado, Washington, and Oregon, state human-relations commissions already exist, which continue to handle employment-discrimination cases. In most of these states the EEOC is foregoing the exercise of its full jurisdiction and is instead relying upon these human-relations commissions to enforce a state policy against this form of discrimination. What is not generally recognized is that most state human-relations commissions in the North and West are not currently making, nor can they make as presently constituted and operating, any substantial headway in eliminating employment discrimination.[37] The reasons for this difficulty will be examined in this book. Due to its greatly reduced operation in states of the North and West, the EEOC has not made and is not likely to make much of an impact upon employment discrimination in these areas. It seems even more certain that discrimination in employment in the South and Southwest, where the EEOC is directing its greatest efforts at enforcement, will not be substantially altered as a result of the application of Title VII. There are no adequate state and local civil-rights laws or agencies in the states of these areas. As already indicated, the EEOC is far weaker in authority and structure than many of the state and local commissions in the North and West. It has no power to compel obedience to the

[36] *Ibid.*
[37] See Chapters 4 and 5, below.

prohibition against employment discrimination. Moreover, the civil action for injunctive relief available to the Attorney General in cases where there is a pattern or practice of employment discrimination is a wholly inadequate tool for dealing with the widespread violation of the civil-rights law that exists in the South and Southwest. As a matter of fact the Attorney General filed but one suit under Title VII in 1965–1966.[38] The experience in enforcing Titles II, III, and IV through the only available remedy of a suit by the Attorney General for injunctive relief has been somewhat the same as the experience in enforcing Title VII. It was not until September 1966 that the Attorney General filed his first suit under Title III relating to discrimination in governmental facilities other than public schools.[39] As of the same date he had filed only some fifty suits under Title II relating to discrimination in public accommodations[40] and only about eighty suits under Title IV relating to discrimination in public schools.[41] Enforcement of Title VI relating to discrimination in programs receiving federal financial assistance had been considerably more effective. It is significant that the enforcement method utilized in this title is one of the well-established forms of administrative process backed up with legal sanctions. Even here, as studies of the U.S. Commission on Civil Rights show, there is considerable room for improvement in the application of what is basically a sound enforcement method.[42]

The lack of adequate coverage of employment discrimination by Title VII, coupled with the ineffective method of enforcing its prohibitions and the de-emphasis upon enforcement in the North and West by the EEOC, could only be regarded by Negroes in these areas, who constitute 48 per cent of their whole ethnic group,[43] with a great sense of frustration and disillusionment. The Civil-Rights Revolution of

[38] Department of Justice, News Release, February 4, 1966; 1 *Lab. Rel. Rep.* (61 *L.R.R.M.*) 102 (February 14, 1966).

[39] Department of Justice, *News Release*, September 1, 1966.

[40] Department of Justice, *News Release*, July 22, 1966.

[41] Department of Justice, *News Release*, August 22, 1966.

[42] See, U.S. Commission on Civil Rights, *Title VI . . . One Year After* (Washington, D.C.: U.S. Government Printing Office, 1966); U.S. Commission on Civil Rights, *Survey of School Desegregation in the Southern and Border States: 1965–1966* (Washington, D.C.: U.S. Government Printing Office, 1966): U.S. Commission on Civil Rights, *Equal Opportunity in Farm Programs: An Appraisal of Services Rendered by Agencies of the United States Department of Agriculture* (Washington, D.C.: U.S. Government Printing Office, 1965).

[43] Charles E. Silberman, "The City and the Negro," *Fortune*, Vol. 70 (March 1962), p. 89.

1963–1964 in these areas resulted in large measure from the dissatisfaction of Negroes with the employment opportunities available to them.[44] Discrimination by employers and unions kept most of them confined to low-paid work requiring little skill and to a median wage approximately one-half that paid to white persons. Negroes in these areas already had legal and actual access to voting rights, public education, governmental facilities, and, if they could earn enough to afford them, to most public accommodations denied to Negroes in the South. One of the chief things they lacked was a similar access to employment opportunities. It was their demand for an end to discrimination in allocating these opportunities that heavily contributed to the decision of Congress to enact the Civil Rights Act of 1964. Similarly, the exemption of governmental employers from Title VII has been a galling matter to Negroes and Latin Americans in the South and Southwest, where government still is a primary factor in the maintenance of the whole system of discrimination by the majority group against minority groups. Negroes in the South and Southwest, who were the civil-rights activists of that area during 1963–1964, were especially concerned with discrimination in employment by state and local governments. Negroes had sought for years to move the power structure to open the gates of government employment to members of their ethnic group. Securing elimination of this form of discrimination was one of the goals of Southern Negroes in making their demands for remedial legislation.[45] They could only view the exemption of government employers from Title VII, therefore, as a refusal by Congress to deal with one of their major problems. Since enactment of the 1964 act Negroes and Latin Americans in the South and Southwest have also begun to seek an opening of opportunities for private employment and union membership. Like their counterparts in the North and West, they have encountered a great deal of resistance to change on the part of private employers and unions. For this reason the sense of frustration and disillusionment that had earlier entered the ranks of Negroes in the North and West because of the incapacity of the 1964

[44] See, *Hearings on H.R. 405 and Similar Bills before the General Subcommittee on Labor of the House Committee on Education and Labor*, 88th Cong., 1st Sess. (Washington, D.C.: U.S. Government Printing Office, 1963), pp. 26–39, 136–147; *Hearings on Miscellaneous Proposals Regarding Civil Rights before Subcommittee No. 5 of the House Committee on the Judiciary*, 88th Cong., 1st Sess. (Washington, D.C.: U.S. Government Printing Office, 1963), pp. 1336–1337, 2341–2345, 2050–2051.

[45] *Ibid.*

act to respond to their needs for employment opportunities has now spread to the ranks of Negroes and Latin Americans in the South and Southwest.

What is true of Title VII is even more true of Title VI, which covers programs receiving federal financial assistance. Many housing programs have received this assistance for more than three decades.[46] The housing and home-finance industries since 1935 have been greatly assisted in the conduct of their operations by insurance contracts of the Federal Housing Administration and by loan guaranties of the Veterans Administration. Through these devices the federal government has insured private lending institutions against loss and, as a consequence, greatly facilitated the entire housing market. In addition, under other programs the federal government charters and insures the accounts of private lending institutions that make a large proportion of all residential mortgage loans. Indeed, over 80 per cent of all outstanding home loans by private institutions have been substantially assisted by the federal government through insurance of loans, guaranties of loans, charters, and insurance of deposits. All of this has been done, at least since 1935, to the accompaniment of a federal policy either of actively promoting discrimination in housing against Negroes and other minority groups by builders, lenders, and realtors, or of supporting this discrimination as they practiced it. Until 1947 the FHA officially sanctioned racially restrictive covenants which were being promoted by real estate operators throughout the country. It also sought to promote stability of neighborhoods through securing occupancy of property within them by the same social and racial group. After 1947 it abandoned its advocacy of a "model" racially restrictive covenant but continued the real substance of its policy by the artifice, among others, of substituting the term "incompatible groups" in its directives for naked references to racial groups. It was not until early 1950, eighteen months following the decision in *Shelley v. Kraemer*[47] striking down judicial enforcement of racially restrictive covenants as unconstitutional, that FHA stated it to be its policy not to insure loans where these covenants were utilized in the underlying transaction. Even then FHA took no affirmative steps to

---

[46] This review of administration of this assistance is largely based upon data presented in hearings on the proposed Civil Rights Act of 1966 relative to its Title IV concerning discrimination in housing [*Hearings on S. 3296*, pp. 82–88, 362–365, 1401–1436].

[47] *Shelley v. Kraemer*, 334 U.S. 1 (1948).

eliminate discrimination in housing against minority groups by the builders, lenders, and realtors it was assisting.

The situation concerning FHA policies was paralleled by the Veterans Administration which supported a home-construction program for white veterans while leaving Negro veterans to search for homes in limited developments near existing Negro ghettos. The Public Housing Administration also followed a policy of constructing separate-but-equal facilities for minority groups so that today over 80 per cent of the low-rent public housing units in the country are racially segregated. In addition, the Urban Renewal Administration has supported the wholesale removal of Negroes from their homes in urban-renewal areas and their placement either in segregated public-housing units or in segregated residential areas. Often Negroes affected by urban-renewal or highway-building programs have had to leave integrated areas and move to segregated areas because the latter provided the only available housing. These federal policies of promoting or supporting discrimination against minority groups in housing were developed by key officials drawn from the financial and real-estate interests which were the prime movers in getting these policies adopted. As the United States Commission on Civil Rights stated recently, "prior to the issuance by President Kennedy of Executive Order No. 11063, none of the Federal agencies concerned with the extension of housing and mortgage credit took significant action to assure that the institutions they assisted—builders, mortgage lenders, and realtors— made their service available to all persons on equal terms." Even this order has had relatively little effect upon housing discrimination due to its prospective operation and to subsequent administrative action exempting owner-occupied one- and two-family houses from its coverage.[48]

Title VI of the 1964 act left this mass of federally supported housing discrimination almost completely intact by its exemption of all programs enjoying government contracts of insurance and of guaranty. It also failed to cover the operations of lending institutions chartered by the federal government. While Title VI does reach new public housing receiving federal financial assistance, this coverage can do little to rectify the segregation resulting from the location of existing units decided upon under the old dispensation.[49] This and other cover-

---

[48] *Hearings on S. 3296*, p. 363.

[49] U.S. Housing and Home Finance Agency, *18th Annual Report* (Washington, D.C.: U.S. Government Printing Office, 1964), pp. 28–33.

age of discrimination in housing programs receiving federal financial assistance is certainly salutary. Nevertheless, the fact remains that Title VI did nothing about the overwhelming mass of discrimination in housing programs receiving this assistance.

The Civil Rights Act of 1968,[50] enacted as a result of the nation's shock and remorse over the killing of the Reverend Martin Luther King, has added, among other things, a direct prohibition against discrimination in housing. While its coverage under its Title VIII will extend to approximately 80 per cent of all housing by December 31, 1969, the 1968 act unfortunately continues the policy of the 1964 act in relying only upon court actions for enforcement of its prohibitions of this form of discrimination.

Beyond these deficiencies either in coverage of discriminatory transactions or in enforcement methods is the fact that the federal civil-rights policy, as formulated in the 1964 act, does not speak at all to many serious problems currently plaguing minority groups in this country. It is inapplicable to discrimination by operators of most types of businesses soliciting the patronage of the general public for their goods and services. It is inapplicable to discrimination by professional groups in admitting persons to membership. The act expressly makes its prohibition of discrimination in public schools inapplicable to the knotty and serious problem of *de facto* segregation in public schools, a problem currently plaguing the North and West and already beginning to plague the South and Southwest as well.[51] The act does not deal with the failure of municipal officials to deal with the wholesale violation of local law by landlords in the upkeep of their premises in slum areas, now occupied largely by Negroes, Latin Americans, and other minority groups. These premises are often rat-infested firetraps and sources of disease and suffering. The act does not provide for handling complaints, frequently although not exclusively made by members of minority groups, of police brutality and other forms of police maladministration. It does not provide protection for persons participating in the direct-action efforts of civil-rights groups. It does not deal with discrimination in jury selection in state and federal courts. It does not provide for removal of criminal cases from state to

[50] P.L. 90-284 (April 11, 1968).
[51] John J. Doyle II and Christopher M. Little, "Widening the Field of Vision: De Facto Segregation in Southern Public Schools" (unpublished civil-rights seminar paper, The University of Texas School of Law, March 8, 1966).

federal courts when prosecution of state offenses in a federal district court is necessary to assure equal protection of the laws.

One reason the 1964 act did not provide more effective remedies for the discrimination it prohibited or more extensive coverage of discriminatory transactions was the political impossibility in 1964 of enacting a more stringent federal civil-rights act. The defeat of the proposed Civil Rights Act of 1966, which would have strengthened and extended the 1964 act, re-emphasized the potency of the resistance to effective implementation of the principle of equal opportunity for minority groups. Another important reason for the limited coverage of discrimination against minority groups in the 1964 act was the conviction shared by legislators and the public that the primary role in the solution of the civil-rights problem, in all its aspects, should and could be performed by local and state governments rather than by the federal government.[52] This conviction is the reason that the act was designed to operate almost exclusively in those areas of the South where local and state governments had long since demonstrated their utter lack of responsibility and their unwillingness to deal fairly with local problems relative to minorities. This design is reflected in many provisions of the act. Thus, some provisions in the act direct that in areas having state or local laws prohibiting public-accommodations discrimination identical with that covered by the act, complaints of this discrimination shall be referred to the appropriate state or local authority for disposition before the aggrieved person may bring a civil action under the act. Even in areas not having this state or local law, the federal court in which a complaint of public-accommodations discrimination is filed may refer the matter to the Federal Community Relations Service; that agency would then assist local or state authorities to resolve the dispute and obtain voluntary compliance.[53] For areas of the country having state or local laws prohibiting employment discrimination identical with that covered by the act, similar provisions are made for handling the reference of complaints to local or state authorities before they may be filed with the EEOC. In addition, this new federal commission may enter into cooperative agreements with state and local agencies charged with administration of

[52] This conviction is apparent from the Senate Judiciary Committee's desire to rely on state remedies wherever possible [*Senate Report* (Judiciary Committee) No. 872, 88th Cong., 2d Sess. *U.S. Code Congressional & Administrative News*, Vol. 12 (1964), p. 2368].
[53] 42 U.S.C. §§ 2000a-3(c), -3(d) (1964).

state fair-employment-practices laws under which the federal commission in effect relinquishes to these agencies on a continuing basis its jurisdiction over complaints of employment discrimination.[54]

The limited advances secured in federal civil-rights policy by the Age Discrimination in Employment Act of 1967 and the Civil Rights Act of 1968 demonstrated once again how potent is the political opposition to effective legislation in this field. Their provisions calling for referral of complaints to state or local agencies under certain circumstances also demonstrated again the strong disposition to rely upon state and local governments for performing the primary role in solving the civil-rights problem.

The underlying philosophy of the 1964, 1967, and 1968 acts presents a serious challenge to the concept of our federal system which allocates to local and state government the function of resolving local and state problems. By and large, denials of equal opportunities to members of minority groups occur in the course of transactions which are wholly local in nature or in which there is a very substantial local interest. Moreover, the discrimination causing these denials is certainly the type of action to which local and state government can direct practicable remedial measures. The public problem involved in discrimination against minority groups is, therefore, one to which valid local and state governmental action may be readily directed as well as one likely to respond favorably to careful official efforts to eliminate it. It is part of our commitment to our federal system that public problems like this one should be handled by our local and state governments. These acts reaffirm that commitment. They insert the federal government into the regulation of a problem that could be handled by local and state governments only to the extent that legislators deemed absolutely necessary. On the other hand, these acts are also reaffirmations of the belief that the federal government should take action on problems that have become national in scope, whatever their intrinsic nature. In the past eighty years, the federal government has dealt with many problems that local and state governments either could not or would not deal with effectively. This federal action has resulted, as we know, from a vital, profound shift in the real structure and dynamism of our pluralistic society, and it has produced a fundamental change in our federal system. By and large this change was necessary and salutary, although frequently caused by the gross and

54 *Id.*, §§ 2000e-5(b), -5(c), -8(b).

foolish injustices of private centers of power. In the case of the civil-
rights problem involving minority groups, federal legislation is not
intrinsically necessary. During the past twenty years, however, the
problem has emerged as a major national issue, and our federal government, responding to various pressures, has increasingly moved to
implement the civil rights of minorities by judicial, administrative,
and, more recently, legislative action. The fact that the federal government has been increasingly called upon to act testifies clearly that
in this area our private holders of power and our local and state governments have failed to perform effectively their essential functions
in our federal system. The chief significance of the 1964–1968 acts
may be that they now affirm the national character of certain basic
aspects of the civil-rights problem. They are, in effect, a warning to
our private holders of power and to our local and state governments.
If they persist in dealing ineffectively with the various aspects of the
civil-rights problem, the implications for our federal system will be
clear. The federal government will then have to respond to the problem by substituting effective federal for ineffective local and state governmental institutions, officials, and procedures, and by substantially
limiting the exercise of discretion by private holders of power.

The present status of local and state governmental efforts in dealing
with the many aspects of the civil-rights problem is not encouraging.
Prior to 1963, some twenty states and twenty local governments had
established reasonably effective human-relations commissions to deal
with discrimination in employment, public accommodations, education, and housing.[55] A large part of this book will be devoted to analyzing and criticizing this governmental experience. Despite solid progress attained by these commissions prior to 1963, since that time they
have been increasingly bypassed by civil-rights organizations which
have become impatient with the slowness of official progress in opening equal opportunities to minority groups. The reaction to this lack of
progress on the part of the masses of the poorer Negroes in our large
urban ghettos is manifest to all. It is essential that the hand of these
pioneering local and state commissions be strengthened so that they
may do their work as effectively as possible.

Since 1963 many additional communities and a number of states
have responded favorably to local pressure by acting to create the first

[55] See Appendices of this book.

official agencies for dealing with the civil-rights problem.[56] Undoubtedly this response reflects a growing and commendable appreciation of the responsibility of local and state governments. Nevertheless, in contrast to the earlier, reasonably well-established commissions, most of the local agencies established since early 1963 are primitive, *ad hoc* constructions. From the outset they were doomed to be ineffective expedients because they were created without regard to prior experience in the field. Disenchantment with them is already developing. The new state commissions have tended to follow the model of the earlier-established state commissions and thus to perpetuate weaknesses in their authority, structure, and procedures. It is essential that the new local and state agencies be rapidly reorganized if they are to deal effectively with the civil-rights problems in their areas. Moreover, it is essential that the twenty-odd states and many hundred major communities across the country that have as yet taken little or no action whatsoever to create human-relations commissions or to deal otherwise with the civil-rights problem assume their responsibilities. As pressure resulting from the civil-rights problem continues to mount, unless effective remedial action is taken not only in states and local communities having reasonably effective human-relations commissions but also in those that do not now have them, the question will inevitably be raised whether the major civil-rights effort should not be made by the federal government rather than by local and state governments. It is quite conceivable that civil-rights organizations, frustrated by the small fruits produced through their efforts on local scenes, will cease efforts to obtain or strengthen local and state human-relations commissions and instead will seek to make the federal government the principal instrument for the enacting and administering of civil-rights laws for all levels of our federal system. Any relaxation of efforts by civil-rights groups to obtain local and state civil-rights legislation, when viewed against the background of increasing federal civil-rights

[56] See the Appendices of this book. A survey was conducted by a national organization in 1964 relative to the 589 cities having over 30,000 population. This survey revealed that 225 of these cities had established human-relations commissions with 120 of them having acted in 1963. It also revealed that one-third of the 128 cities in the Southern region, one-half of the 187 cities in the Midwest region, three-quarters of all cities over 100,000 population, and more than one-quarter of all cities under 100,000 population had these commissions in 1964 [U.S. Conference of Mayors, *Community Relations Service* (Washington, D.C.: U.S. Conference of Mayors, 1964) § 1].

legislation, may operate to move the "establishments" controlling local and state governments to discontinue giving serious consideration to creating or strengthening their own human-relations commissions and programs. As one who has been in the middle of the civil-rights fray on the Southern scene, I believe leaders of civil-rights organizations and of the local and state establishments would be making a grave error of judgment if they permitted this to happen.

THE THESIS OF THIS BOOK

The federal government must obviously perform a major and vigorous role in any practicable effort to resolve the nation's problem with the civil rights of minority groups. This is true for two central reasons. One is that there are some civil-rights problems which the federal government has helped to create and others which only it can effectively resolve. The other reason is that the federal government is currently the only government in the federal system from which it is possible to obtain relief for pressing civil-rights problems in many localities and states. Recognition of the necessity for the involvement of the federal government in efforts to resolve the nation's civil-rights problem is just the beginning of wisdom relative to civil-rights policy. The federal government must obviously extend the coverage of its existing civil-rights laws and provide greatly improved judicial and administrative remedies for enforcing prohibitions of discrimination. The question remains, however, concerning the appropriate interim and long-term roles of each government in our federal system in the civil-rights field. The underlying thesis of this book is that the approach to legislative implementation of the civil rights of minority groups which promises the most in early and wide-scale accomplishment is one which accords a major role to local and state governments. Whatever emergency approaches the federal government takes for dealing with the civil-rights problem in the Deep South and whatever permanent nationally administered civil-rights law is required, I vigorously assert that the permanent underlying policy of the federal government should be principally oriented to moving and assisting local and state governments—and their citizenry—to assume and to perform their appropriate and all-important roles in creating equal opportunities for persons belonging to minority groups. The civil-rights problems of minority groups are too pressing, their continuing existence too dangerous, and the problems of their adequate resolution too complex for us to rely upon the usual pattern of federal regulation. We cannot afford to wait thirty or more years—as we did in the case of federal antitrust policy enacted in 1890—for the federal government to become effective, if it ever does, in implementing a federal civil-rights policy through the device of the typical Washington-based independent regulatory agency. The cost of the delay in effectively implementing our federal antitrust policy was an increase in concentration of economic power so overwhelming that we have never since been able to overcome the result. One can readily surmise what a similar delay would mean in implementing federal civil-rights policy in an effective way. For these reasons, three purposes shape the content of the discussion that follows.

The first purpose of this book is to examine the nature of the civil-rights problem and the relatively successful experience of the few well-organized local and state human-relations commissions. An attempt will be made to determine what aspects of their organization, functions, personnel, and techniques have enabled these commissions to deal as effectively as they have with this problem. They have been established during the past twenty years as the result of efforts of civil-rights organizations to secure effective legislation implementing the civil rights of minority groups. The new legislation enacted because of these efforts replaced ineffective earlier forms that relied upon criminal prosecutions and private suits for their enforcement. Analysis of the human-relations commission established by such legislation will indicate that it is an administrative agency employing a new concept of the regulatory function, one peculiarly adapted to resolving the civil-rights problem and one that may well be a forerunner of many future administrative agencies. When organized along certain lines and employing programs and techniques proven by experience, these agencies have attained a considerable degree of effectiveness in accomplishing the purposes of their institution: the creation and improvement of opportunities for members of minority groups to exercise their various civil rights. Analysis of this new type of administrative agency will first focus upon its use by state governments. The 1964, 1967, and 1968 acts each borrowed somewhat from state government experience in allocating to an administrative agency (the EEOC, Secretary of Labor, and Secretary of Housing and Urban Development, respectively) a function of receiving complaints of discrimination, investigating them, and utilizing conciliation to eliminate discrimination believed to exist. Moreover, these acts provide for referring complaints of discrimination, under specified circumstances, by federal authority to state and local commissions having jurisdiction over them. Also, the

EEOC in dealing with employment discrimination is authorized in effect to relinquish its jurisdiction by entering cooperative agreements with state commissions having similar jurisdiction. These three facts make it utterly essential to ferret out weaknesses in existing state civil-rights statutes and in their administration. By pointing out these weaknesses and developing remedies for them, we may show how both the federal and state acts may be made more effective. We may also demonstrate how the federal acts need to be modified in order to provide for their enforcement through administrative-agency hearings and sanctions. We finally may offer some guidance for other states which have yet to enact their first civil-rights legislation.

Analysis of the human-relations commission here will also focus upon its use by local governments. This analysis will subserve two objectives. It will permit us, as in the case of our analysis of state commissions, to perceive weaknesses in local law and administration and to seek adequate remedies for these. It will also permit us to evaluate the special role that has been performed in the human-relations field by the few well-organized local commissions.

Throughout the twenty years of experience with human-relations commissions, most of the Northern and Western states having these commissions have operated under the theory that the state human-relations commission should be the only or principal agency in the state for administering civil-rights laws at the local level. Local governments have either been legally precluded or officially discouraged from establishing their own human-relations commissions for administering either local or state civil-rights legislation in their communities. The second purpose of this book is to demonstrate that local rather than state governments should be the principal administrators of civil-rights law at the local level. The primary framework for this administration should be a local human-relations commission. While this commission should have authority to hear and determine individual complaints of discrimination and to apply civil sanctions to resolve them, its most effective tools for implementing the civil rights of minority groups are neither adjudicative nor mediative in nature (although the achievements of local commissions with enforcement power by use of techniques of conciliation and persuasion have been quite good). Rather, the most effective tools of implementation are certain "constructive" techniques developed by these agencies in recent years—techniques designed to produce those attitudes, actions, and conditions in the community essential to moving its majority group to provide and its minority groups to seek, prepare for, and take advantage of equal opportunities to exercise civil rights. Use of these "constructive" techniques by a specially trained professional staff of human-relations workers under the guidance of carefully selected agency members can achieve remarkable results over a period of time in creating equal opportunities for members of minority groups in a community and in moving these persons to prepare for and utilize the opportunities. In essence, the local human-relations commission should be an official agency to provide leadership in the community, both within and without its government, for the purpose of organizing the maximum efforts possible on the part of all elements in that community and all community leaders to deal constructively with the problem of majority-minority-group relations.

For a number of reasons later to be developed, the state government is much less able than the local government to provide the kind of "tailored" local administration of civil-rights legislation essential for successfully handling the civil-rights problem. The same reasons operate far more powerfully upon the federal government and render even more difficult federal efforts to administer civil-rights legislation at the local level. A state government should first of all provide a minimum code of law providing for the protection of the civil rights of minority groups. It should also establish a state human-relations commission having as its principal function the encouragement of local governments to establish effective local human-relations commissions. These, in turn, should serve as the primary agencies for administration of civil-rights laws in their respective communities and should perform the various "constructive" functions appropriate to local commissions. As part of its function the state commission should provide services, programs, assistance, personnel, financial aid, and supervision to insure that the local commission performs its work in the best possible way. Only where a local community does not provide and maintain an effective commission, or does not provide one having the full jurisdiction deemed essential, should the state agency provide the primary administration of civil-rights legislation in that community. There are, of course, some problems of human relations which can be adequately handled only by a state human-relations commission. Discrimination by state agencies or by private concerns having statewide operations, for example, is inherently beyond local control and thus is a problem for the state commission to handle. Moreover, both the state human-relations commission and other state agencies and officials can perform important roles in creating the climate within state government and throughout the state in which solution of human-relations problems may proceed most advantageously. Perhaps the most important example of the latter is negotiation by state officials with financial, industrial, commercial, and union leaders to provide improved opportunities for members of minority groups. Outside of state-level problems like these, I contend that the state human-relations commission can greatly increase the effectiveness of civil-rights-law administration by eliciting, assisting, and overseeing local governmental administration of those laws.

The third purpose of this discussion is to suggest that the underlying thesis concerning the optimum roles of local and state government in the civil-rights field has far-reaching implications concerning the optimum role of the federal government in the same field. It has already been suggested that the federal government must obviously extend the coverage of its existing civil-rights laws and provide greatly improved judicial and administrative remedies for enforcing prohibitions of discrimination against minority groups. It must obviously deal with civil-rights problems that transcend the normal realm of local and state governments. It is also evident that these governments are currently falling very short of performing their optimum roles in the federal system relative to the civil-rights problem. The federal government cannot afford to wait any longer for local and state governments in the South and Southwest to initiate substantial efforts to perform their responsibilities. Nevertheless, when all of this has been said and the complex and difficult nature of the civil-rights problem has been properly assessed, we must recognize that the federal effort to deal with this problem must not merely follow the traditional pattern of other federal regulatory legislation, with a central agency and field offices. The federal government must develop additional techniques for restoring the effectiveness of local and state government. One of these techniques involves the use of the "carrot" of federal financial help and other types of assistance to move local and state governments and their citizenry to improve or to initiate efforts to deal with the civil-rights problem. In the South and Southwest another technique must be devised for many if not most communities and states. This book suggests that the technique of a federal-local human-relations commission is an essential tool for administration of federal civil-rights policy in these and similar areas. Such a policy should not stop with laws that prohibit various forms of discrimination against minority groups. It should also extend to the full range of laws that deal with community relations at the local and state levels. A federal-local human-relations commission would be located in each of the communities in the nation, principally in the South and Southwest, that has not yet seen fit to establish its own local human-relations commission. Its members would be drawn from the local community if it is possible to find local leaders of understanding and courage to serve as commission members. Commissioners would have the assistance of an able staff of professional human-relations specialists, lawyers, and additional necessary personnel. The federal government would provide all the necessary funds and assistance to operate and protect the commission and its personnel. The federal-local commission would proceed to enforce all federal law bearing upon discrimination through the most advanced forms of administrative process. Its orders would be enforceable in the federal courts. Where it seems feasible, a federal-state human-relations commission should be organized along the lines of existing well-organized state human-relations commissions. The essential purpose of these federal-local and federal-state human-relations commissions would be to develop a new leadership within the localities and states in which they operate—a leadership that could become effective in dealing with civil-rights matters. Details concerning these proposals are examined later in this book. Analysis of their content will indicate that a new round of federal civil-rights legislation is necessary and that this legislation must be radically different from the 1964–1968 acts or the civil-rights legislation proposed during the period between their enactment. Necessary as this legislation was and important as it is to strengthen it in ways similar to those included in recently proposed civil-rights acts, much more and different legislation is required to strike at the heart of the civil-rights problem of minority groups.

The main proposals of this book are set forth in Chapters 5 through 7. To provide for their implementation a series of "Alpha Model Civil Rights Acts" have been developed. These are set forth in Chapters 8 through 11. Each model act is accompanied by a commentary indicating the reasons for the underlying policy choices. Two model acts pertain to the states. One sets up a state human-relations commission and establishes the law to be administered by it. It is compared with the "Uniform" Model State Antidiscrimination Act adopted by the National Conference of Commissioners on Uniform State Laws in 1966[57] and with the "Harvard" Model State Civil Rights Act prepared by the Harvard Student Legislative Research Bureau of Harvard Law School in 1965.[58] The other state model law pertains to the creation and operation of local human-relations commissions. Following these are set forth a model federal civil-rights act and a model local human-relations ordinance.

[57] National Conference of Commissioners on Uniform State Laws, "Model [State] Anti-Discrimination Act," *Harvard Journal of Legislation*, Vol. 4 (1967) pp. 224–278.

[58] Harvard Student Legislative Research Bureau, "A Proposed Model State Civil Rights Act," *Harvard Journal of Legislation*, Vol. 3 (1965), pp. 63–102.

2

The Civil-Rights Problem from the Legislator's Point of View

In order to evaluate success or lack of success in administration of local, state, and federal civil-rights legislation, we must understand the real nature of the civil-rights problem. This understanding is also essential if we wish to ascertain the roles appropriate to each of the several governments in our federal system in dealing with this problem, and to propose improvements in the legislative formulas used by these governments for this purpose. The nature of the civil-rights problem of minority groups is, of course, to be viewed as it confronts the legislator who must devise a basic policy to resolve it. From his point of view the problem has two aspects. One involves the majority group of each community as the primary cause of the problem. The other focuses upon the minority group as the recipient of majority-group action.

From the first approach, the legislator must inevitably see the civil-rights problem as essentially one resulting from the defective character of the majority group. This group, however heterogeneous its elements may be in other respects, holds views concerning one or more minority groups—for example the Negro—that cause these elements to act in a more or less common way toward these minorities. One such solidifying view may maintain that the Negro is, by nature, an inferior human being, not entitled to participate equally in the life of the community. This is probably the dominant view in many parts of the Deep South.[1] It is generated by irrationalisms of various kinds and by considerations of self-interest.

A second view is that immediate integration of the Negro into the life of the community will unjustifiably upset existing social, eco-

[1] Gunnar Myrdal, *An American Dilemma: The Negro Problem and Modern Democracy*, 2 vols. (New York: Harper & Bros., 1944), I, 26–122.

nomic, and political conditions.[2] The *status quo* which strongly favors the majority white group is considered to have paramount value among other considerations. The various leadership echelons of the majority group attained their status in society as the result of strong intragroup competition, either during the present or a prior generation. This status is vital to well-being and those who have it are not willing to have it impaired. Frequently, holders of this view concede in theory the claim of the Negro as a human being to full integration into community life. Nevertheless, they assert that admission to this life must be obtained only on the payment of two prices. In the first place, the Negro must as an individual prepare himself adequately for this admission. In the second place, the Negro must move the majority group to accept him as an equal, even when he is fully prepared for admission. This is the "approved" position among Southern business and political leaders in the more advanced areas.

Closely associated with the high value placed by holders of this second view upon the *status quo* and its protection is an actual fear of the Negro entertained by this group. In the South the Negro has been increasingly isolated by the white majority just as he had been previously isolated in the North and West. This isolation prevents the white majority from knowing and understanding him, his current plight, and his determination to change his status in society. The whites know generally that among Negroes unemployment, crime, illegitimacy, school drop-outs, and dependence on relief are high, but do not know and apparently do not care to discover the real reasons for this. These conditions are frequently explained as evidence of basic group characteristics. Some of the majority group simply fear that integration will mean the loss of existing social and economic benefits. Some fear, for example, that when a Negro family moves into a white neighborhood the social structure of the neighborhood will deteriorate and the value of property will fall. With others the fear covers the entire spectrum of possible community change. In many communities of the South, democratic process is not very effective. Many white persons do not register or vote, and effective control of political power is held by a relatively small group. One gets the impression that an overriding fear of such entrenched establishments is that emergence of the Negro into the life of the community will seriously impair their political power. This fear is not confined to areas where the Negro constitutes a large

[2] *Id.*, pp. 462–466.

percentage of the population. In other areas the Negro leadership has shown facility for aligning the Negro section of the community with certain white occupational and nationality groups. If this process of alignment is extended into political arenas, as it probably will be, it would mean a considerably changed political picture.

A third view or position is simply an outgrowth of the malady of apathy toward the suffering or plight of another person or group, intensified by the fact that the suffering person or group is Negro and, as in the second view, is largely unknown and feared.[3] This view frequently obtains in a society whose majority group has supported the enactment of legislation recognizing and protecting the Negro as an equal in that society. In this type of society, the Negro usually has long since possessed the rights to vote and to attend unsegregated public schools. In more recent years he has been admitted more fully to the use of public accommodations. Nevertheless, the majority group in these societies views the Negro apathetically, whatever his suffering, if assistance may involve consequences like panic sales of property when a Negro family moves into a formerly all-white neighborhood, painful readjustments in the current availability of neighborhood schools, or loss of domination over the better jobs made possible through long years of vigorous labor-union efforts and current labor-management arrangements. The third view is, of course, the view that is prevalent in the North and West. The attitude of the majority group in these areas toward the Negro minority is often similar to its attitude toward the Puerto Rican, the Latin American, the Indian, and the Jew.

Each of the three views to some extent overlaps the other two. Moreover, each of these three views may obtain with varying degrees of force among members of the majority group in the same community. Each has proceeded from basic defects in the character of the majority group and in turn has helped to shape the character of the group and its individual members. This character, in the course of time, has been translated into numerous actions, habits, customs, and official and private arrangements that have produced the conditions adversely affecting the minority groups within the community—now principally the Negro. To insist that the civil-rights problem must be viewed from the standpoint of the legislator and administrative official who must deal with it and that so viewed it is at its core a problem of regu-

[3] *Id.*, pp. 383–394. A more accurate description is contained in Gertrude Samuels, "Even More Crucial than in the South," *The New York Times Magazine* (June 30, 1963), p. 12.

lating and adjusting the defective character of the majority group is not to overlook the obvious accompanying problems of regulating overt conduct on the part of the community or on the part of individuals and groups within that community. It is simply to insist that the most basic element of the civil-rights problem, the specific difference which distinguishes it from other public problems of a society, is the necessity for achieving an adjustment in the defective character of the majority group of an entire society.

If one examines each of the hundreds of major public problems to which government has applied its official regulatory processes in this century, he will discover how difficult it is to describe any of these regulatory problems as calling for adjustment of the character of those regulated and particularly of the ruling class of a whole community. It has usually been sufficient for the legislator to direct legislation to the overt conduct of those who had by that conduct precipitated the public problem. The character of the local or state community or of its majority group has not been implicated in or formed part of the public problem. Rather it has been the character of the community, and the sense of justice prevailing in it, that has been responsible for its enactment of new legislation to strike at the wrongful overt acts of the few who have wounded its public interest.[4] By way of contrast, a city or a state with a major civil-rights problem is quite a different community from the usual one. It is a society whose majority group has a defective character. It is a society that, because of this defective character, has created conditions of discrimination and disadvantage to which the Negro and other minority groups have been subjected. It is a society in which, to a greater or lesser degree, the majority group has lost the virtue of listening and responding justly to the petitions for redress of grievances presented by a part of its citizens or members. Where the character of its majority group is grossly deficient, the society lacks much more than effective leadership concerned with helping its majority group confront and resolve fairly its civil-rights problems. It also lacks any effective loyal opposition within or without the establishment to provide constructive criticism of the *status quo*. In the more gross examples of deficiency in majority-group character, an entire system composed of a defensive philosophy, an etiquette, and sanctions has developed within the majority group for totally excluding from its

---

[4] See Thomas V. Smith, *The Legislative Way of Life* (Chicago: The University of Chicago Press, 1940), pp. 14–16, 73–84.

official and private dialogue any genuine consideration of changes in the existing order of intergroup relations. Of course no real dialogue obtains between the majority and minority groups. Few dictatorships have ever achieved the effectiveness of thought and action control produced by the defense system of the majority in many parts of the Deep South. In a community of this sort it is evident that initial development and administration of any kind of civil-rights policy for protection of minorities must come from without. The principal purpose of the 1964 federal Civil Rights Act was to provide a minimal civil-rights policy for the South. On the other hand, the civil-rights policy developed by an "outside" authority for that community must, in order to be effective, be directed at much more than preventing overt acts of discrimination against the Negro by the government of that community and by members of its majority group. There are countless ways in which local officials, individuals, and private groups bent on noncompliance can successfully frustrate the effectiveness of a legal program for preventing or penalizing overt discriminatory conduct. Ultimately an effective regulatory program by an "outside" authority operating in Southern or any other communities, whether state or federal, must be directed toward creating a local leadership that can effectively cause the majority group in these communities to change in character and to take steps on its own initiative to recognize and deal justly with the grievances of its chief minority groups. This has been, as we shall see, the secret of what progress has been made in the North and West. The 1964 federal Civil Rights Act has only a very few provisions that deal even indirectly with this central facet of the civil-rights problem. One of these is directed toward facilitating registration of Negro voters.[5] The other principal one is directed toward preventing discrimination in activities and programs receiving federal financial assistance.[6] The former is intended to compel the majority group on Southern scenes, as a matter of self-interest, to confront and to resolve fairly its civil-rights problem with the Negro. The latter is designed to serve the same purpose throughout the country. Neither of these approaches, however, and certainly none of the remaining techniques of the 1964 federal act, is adequate for meeting what is unquestionably the core of the civil-rights problem either in the Deep South or in the rest of the country. While the Civil-Rights Act of 1968 now reaches a vital area

[5] 42 U.S.C. § 1971 (1964).
[6] *Id.*, §§ 2000d–2000d-1.

of housing discrimination, neither it nor the 1965–1967 acts remove the basic inadequacies of the 1964 act.

The well-informed person has a reasonably accurate idea of the problem of human relations in the Deep South. It is doubtful, however, whether there is general appreciation of the problem of human relations in the more advanced areas of the South. In many respects, the civil-rights problem in these areas does not fundamentally differ from the problem in the North and West. In the communities of the South where a loyal opposition does operate with some effectiveness within the majority group and some degree of dialogue is occurring between that group and the minority group, there is an on-going local confrontation of sorts with the civil-rights problem. Examination of this confrontation in a particular context will, I think, demonstrate the nature of the problem beyond serious doubt and illustrate the difficulties in dealing with it and the requirement for effectuating any real solution to it. The city of Austin, capital of the state of Texas, will serve as a good example.

One would think that Austin should provide one of the most felicitous social contexts in Texas or, indeed, in the entire South for the solution of human-relations problems. Its business and political leaders and those of the entire state have worked very hard and with considerable success for several decades to place their area in the mainstream of the nation's agricultural, industrial, commercial, financial, political, and educational life.[7] As a result of this leadership, the state is now a leading producer of many agricultural and industrial products. The capital city with its key state government offices and private association headquarters has become a mecca for persons, both in and out of the state, who seek to secure their interests by influencing official action.[8] Austin is also the home of a school of national distinction, The University of Texas, which with its nearly thirty thousand students, half a billion dollars endowment, and excellent legislative and private support, has long been the chief training ground for the state's political, business, and professional leaders.[9] The city also is a growing com-

---

[7] Rubert N. Richardson, *Texas: The Lone Star State*, 2nd ed. (Englewood Cliffs, N.J.: Prentice-Hall, 1958), pp. 296–306, 338–440.

[8] Austin Chamber of Commerce, *Austin's Opportunities* (Austin, Texas). This brochure was distributed to businesses considering a location in Austin during 1966 and 1967. The description of Austin contained in the next two paragraphs is largely based upon data contained in it.

[9] The University of Texas, *Official Notice of Sale and Prospectus for Board of Regents of the University of Texas, Permanent University Fund Bonds, Series 1966*

mercial and industrial center serving a large trade territory with a population of over 500,000. Its research and development industry has achieved national importance since World War II. A 222 mile chain of seven artificial lakes links the city with an area having excellent potential for future industrial and population growth due to the copious supply of water and electric power provided by their dams. The activist character of this bustling metropolis is reflected by its numerous local business, professional, educational, social, and religious organizations capped by its 250 different churches, including 16 Roman Catholic and 2 Jewish.

Despite these many fine features the city of Austin in 1967 faced serious human-relations problems whose causes were inflicting grievous harm upon its minority groups. Neither local nor state leaders were directing adequate efforts toward solving these problems. Progress in solving earlier human-relations problems relative to discrimination in public accommodations and governmental facilities had been obtained only as a result of vigorous action by members of Austin's minority groups. There still remained despite their efforts, the general practice of discrimination in employment by governmental and private employers, in union membership and apprentice-training programs, in the sale and rental of private housing, in public housing, in a number of business services, such as financing, as well as in a few public accommodations. Successive efforts between 1963 and 1966 to get the City Council to enact a comprehensive human-relations ordinance administered by an official human-relations commission had each failed. In late 1966 minority group employees of the city's garbage disposal department had protested working conditions. Upon being dismissed for absence and failure to return to work by a stated deadline, some of the former employees, it was reliably reported, began talking of undertaking extraordinarily vigorous self-help measures as a means of protest. A series of private efforts succeeded, perhaps by a very narrow margin, in averting open conflict. Also in late 1966 Latin American farm workers from the Rio Grande Valley staged a march all the way from the farms to the steps of the State Capitol Building to dramatize their protest against working conditions and their demands for a minimum wage law. In 1967 a growing restlessness among Negro and Latin American youths was evident. While

---

(brochure, 1966), p. 9; The University of Texas, *The University of Texas* (brochure, 1965).

the status of human relations had not reached the boiling point already attained in Houston, Newark, Detroit, and many other cities of the nation, Negro and Latin American leaders privately expressed fears that it was just a matter of a year or two until a serious intergroup conflict situation would probably occur. An understanding of the city's human-relations impasse in 1967 and the possibilities for effectuating a change for the better may be obtained only through examining the plight of its minority groups and the attitudes and actions of its majority group.

In Austin, as in most of the major cities of Texas, there are two principal minority groups: Negroes and Latin Americans.[10] The latter group is also referred to as Mexican Americans because most of its members trace their derivations ultimately from Mexico. This group refers to the majority group in the Southwest as Anglo Americans or simply "Anglos." Other groups are rapidly accepting this designation. Negroes of Texas and Austin are primarily descendants of slaves freed in the state after the Civil War. Prior to 1910 most Negroes in Texas earned their living as self-employed sharecroppers raising the bulk of the cotton crop.[11] When landlords rendered this operation unprofitable through various unconscionable practices and when other economic factors and war intervened, Negroes began to move to Southern and Northern cities in search of a better life.[12] By 1960 more than 75 per cent of Texas Negroes lived in urban areas.[13] Most Latin Americans in Texas have come to the state or are descendants of persons who came to Texas after 1910 as emigrants from Mexico, in three successive waves of immigration.[14] The newcomers, who sought to escape from a

[10] Harvey L. Browning and S. Dale McLemore, *A Statistical Profile of the Spanish-Surname Population of Texas* (Austin: The University of Texas Bureau of Business Research, 1964); U.S. Commission on Civil Rights, "Spanish-Speaking Peoples," staff paper (Washington, D.C.: February 5, 1964), Appendix A, Table 2, pp. 3–5 (mimeographed).

[11] Richardson, *Texas: The Lone Star State*, pp. 162, 216, 404; Carey McWilliams, *Ill Fares the Land: Migrants and Migratory Labor in the United States* (London: Faber and Faber, 1945), pp. 208–229; Carey McWilliams, *North from Mexico: The Spanish-Speaking People of the United States* (Philadelphia: J. B. Lippincott & Co., 1949), p. 70.

[12] Richardson, *Texas: The Lone Star State*, p. 278; Myrdal, *An American Dilemma*, pp. 185, 193–197; McWilliams, *Ill Fares the Land*, pp. 251–254; Charles Silberman, "The City and the Negro," *Fortune*, Vol. 70 (March 1962), p. 88.

[13] Browning and McLemore, *A Statistical Profile*, p. 18.

[14] Leo Grebler, *Mexican Immigration to the United States: The Record and Its Implications* (Los Angeles: Mexican-American Study Project, 1966), pp. 7–11, 17–41, 51; H. T. Manuel, "The Mexican Population of Texas," *The Southwestern So-*

dismal poverty, have been mainly unskilled persons heavily concentrated in low-grade occupations.[15] They provided needed manpower to support the economic growth of the Southwest by building its railroads, working its mines, and laboring on its farms. Increasing mechanization of farm production has, however, forced a large movement of this ethnic group to the cities where over 78 per cent of its members lived in 1960.[16] Despite this change many Latin Americans still serve as migrant farm workers.

In 1960 Negroes and Latin Americans represented 26,072 and 27,224, respectively, or 25 per cent of the total 212,136 population in the metropolitan Austin area.[17] Statewide in 1960, these same two groups constituted 1,204,846 and 1,417,510 persons, respectively, or 27 per cent of the total 9,579,677 population. In the Southwest region, consisting of Texas, New Mexico, Colorado, Arizona, and California, the same two groups amounted to approximately 2,200,000 and 3,465,-000, respectively, or 19 per cent of the total 29,304,012 population. Thus, while the percentage of Austin's Negro population was less than that in East Texas urban areas and the percentage of its Latin American population was less than that in South Texas urban areas,[18] the minority-group population in Austin was a microcosm of the situation in the state and in the Southwest.

What are the actual relationships between Austin's ethnic groups: between the majority Anglo group and the two principal minorities, on the one hand, and between Negroes and Latin Americans themselves, on the other? In the first place, there is very little actual contact between the masses of each of these ethnic groups. The social processes of each of these groups take place almost exclusively in isolation from those of the other two groups. This isolation is largely facili-

---

cial Science Quarterly, XV (1934–1935), 35; Lamar B. Jones, "Mexican-American Labor Problems in Texas" (unpublished Ph.D. dissertation, The University of Texas, 1965), p. 8.

[15] Grebler, *Mexican Immigration*, pp. 45–50.

[16] Jones, "Mexican American," pp. 102–103, 156–157; Walter Fogel, *Education and Income of Mexican-Americans in the Southwest* (Los Angeles: Mexican-American Study Project, 1965), pp. 20–21; Browning and McLemore, *A Statistical Profile*, p. 18; Ruth P. Connor, "Some Community, Home, and School Problems of Latin-American Children in Austin, Texas" (unpublished master's thesis, The University of Texas, 1949), p. 12; McWilliams, *North from Mexico*, p. 170; McWilliams, *Ill Fares the Land*, pp. 231–243.

[17] U.S. Commission on Civil Rights, "Spanish-Speaking Peoples," Appendix A, Table 2, p. 3.

[18] Browning and McLemore, *A Statistical Profile*, pp. 11–12.

tated by the fact that the great bulk of each of these groups lives in separate areas of the city. A freeway runs north and south through the center of the city. Most Negroes and Latin Americans live east of this highway. Within this area Negroes and Latin Americans live primarily in distinctly separate sections. Additional members of these two groups live in a southeast and central portion of the city south of the river. There is also one "satellite slum" area northeast of the city occupied by Negroes. Anglos of Austin thus live in largely all-white residential areas although some Latin Americans live in most school districts of the city.

The residential pattern of Austin's ethnic groups leads to a second observation about the status of relations between them. This pattern has resulted from two causes: (a) discrimination against both minority groups in the sale and rental of housing and real property, and (b) the much lower income earned by minority-group families.[19] Discrimination is the principal reason Negroes are confined to their east-side area. About five hundred of Austin's five thousand Negro families earn enough to purchase at least a modest home anywhere in the city. Two hundred of these families could purchase moderate- to high-priced homes anywhere in the city. In fact, however, only a very few have been able to purchase homes in Anglo areas. Most real-estate firms find means of avoiding sale of property in Anglo areas to Negroes. A study made in 1961 revealed that Latin Americans also encounter difficulty in purchasing or renting modest homes in Anglo areas through certain real-estate firms. Like most Negroes, most Latin Americans do not have sufficient earnings to purchase or rent other than very modestly priced homes.[20]

[19] Terry Gardner and Burrell D. Johnston, "A Study of Human Relations in Austin, Texas" (unpublished civil-rights seminar paper, The University of Texas School of Law, December 16, 1965), pp. 18–22; Henry B. Gonzalez, "Poverty and Discrimination in the Southwest," *Congressional Record*, Vol. 112 (Washington, D.C.: U.S. Government Printing Office, daily ed., May 12, 1966), p. 9990; Doris Barr Stanislawski, "A Study of Leadership in a Spanish-Speaking Community" (unpublished master's thesis, The University of Texas, June, 1961), pp. 59–61.

[20] U.S. Department of Commerce, Bureau of the Census, *Census of Population: 1960. General Population Characteristics: Texas* (Washington, D.C.: U.S. Government Printing Office, 1960), Vol. I, Part 45–439. Approximately five hundred nonwhite families in Austin had incomes in excess of $6,000 per year in 1960. The median income of all families with two children under eighteen years of age was $6,088 in the same year [*Id.*, Part 45–421]. In 1960 an Anglo family with $6,000 income could purchase a home under the FHA program in the $12,000–13,000 range with a downpayment of $360 to $400 [Interview with Mr. Dixie Rice, Rice Real Estate Company, Austin, Texas, by Mr. Burrell D. Johnston, my research assistant (October, 1966)]. Approximately two hundred nonwhite families in Austin had incomes

The third facet of the relations between Austin's majority group and its minority groups is that residential segregation resulting from both discrimination and low income produces *de facto* segregation in the public-school system.[21] Over half of the Negro children attend one *de facto* segregated high school and a large number attend another high school attended chiefly by minority-group children. The same is approximately true of Latin American and Negro children attending junior high schools. Both Latin American and Negro children attend almost exclusively *de facto* segregated elementary schools. Thus, although Austin's schools have been legally open to all children within each school district since 1963, residential segregation largely continues the situation that obtained before legal integration. It is fortunate that several high schools and junior high schools now have a significant proportion of minority-group children not previously in attendance. For the remainder of the children the cumulative effect of *de facto* segregation, very low family incomes, and discrimination in employment and housing has adversely affected their motivation. The drop-out rate is far higher among them than among Anglo children.[22] In 1960, in Austin, the median years of school completed by Latin Americans and Negroes were 4.4 and 8.6 as compared with 12.3 for Anglos. This lower educational level has a serious adverse impact upon the ability of the minority groups to compete with Anglos in the labor

in excess of $9,000 in 1960 [U.S. Department of Commerce, Bureau of the Census, *Texas*, Vol. I, Part 45–439]. An Anglo family with $9,000 income could purchase a home under the FHA program in the $18,000–19,000 range with a down payment of $1,000 in 1960 [Interview with Mr. Dixie Rice]. The building of many new homes would have been required annually in the 1960's if nonwhites in the income group from $4,000 to $7,000 living in Selected Standard Metropolitan Statistical areas had been able to purchase homes at the same rate as whites in these same income brackets. As it was, many homes built for white occupancy went unsold for considerable periods of time [*Hearings on S. 3296, etc. before the Subcommittee on Constitutional Rights of the Senate Committee on the Judiciary*, 89th Cong., 2d Sess. (Washington, D.C.: U.S. Government Printing Office, 1966), p. 1419]. Several studies have reported on discrimination in housing in Austin against the Negro [Gardner and Johnston, "A Study of Human Relations," pp. 9–14, and Gerald R. Colen and Michael Harshman, "The Negro Family in Austin, Texas" (unpublished civil-rights seminar paper, The University of Texas School of Law, December 17, 1965), p. 20], and against the Latin American [Stanislawski, "A Study of Leadership," p. 61].

[21] Gardner and Johnston, "A Study of Human Relations," pp. 9–14; John J. Doyle II and Christopher M. Little, "Widening the Field of Vision: De Facto Segregation in Southern Public Schools" (unpublished civil-rights seminar paper, The University of Texas School of Law, March 8, 1966), pp. 12–17; Colen and Harshman, "The Negro Family," pp. 19, 21, 23–24.

[22] Browning and McLemore, *A Statistical Profile*, pp. 30, 32, Table 13.

market. In addition, that inadequate education is obtained under circumstances previously mentioned that fail to bring members of the majority and minority groups together. For this reason, *de facto* segregation in Austin not only is operating in a way that fails to provide adequate education for minority groups but also is preventing the continuous contact between majority and minority groups that would be so helpful in enabling both to work together for the common good.

The fourth characteristic about relations between Austin's majority group and its minority groups has to do with income and employment. If there were no other walls between these groups, the factors of income and employment patterns of both minority groups would keep them largely excluded from participating in community processes and the decision-making that determines the outcome of those processes. They would still be excluded from enjoying most of the things and experiences commonly enjoyed by Anglo families. Families whose total earnings are less than $3,000 annually are generally characterized as poverty stricken.[23] In 1960 the median incomes of Negro and Latin American families in Austin were $2,723 and $3,219, respectively.[24] Approximately 80 per cent of Negro and Latin American families earned less than $5,000. Most of the families in two of the city's satellite slums earned incomes in 1966 that were well below the poverty level. The existence of widespread poverty and generally lower incomes among minority groups in Austin serves in many ways to erect a wall between them and the Anglo majority group. The consequences of the ghetto life produced by these incomes are the usual ones: housing units that are three times more dilapidated and deteriorated, poorer public facilities, *de facto* segregated schools, poorer school attendance and greater drop-out rates, more breakdowns in family units, greater dependency upon relief and welfare assistance programs, inadequate clothing and food, greater susceptibility to oppressive credit practices, and far greater delinquency and crime rates.[25]

The fifth characteristic about relations among Austin's ethnic

[23] U.S. Department of Commerce, Bureau of the Census, *Current Population Characteristics* (Washington, D.C.: U.S. Government Printing Office, June 11, 1965), Series P-20, No. 139, p. 5.

[24] Browning and McLemore, *A Statistical Profile*, pp. 50, 53; Frank L. Wright (executive of the University YMCA–YWCA of Austin, Texas), letter to author of July 27, 1966 concerning information obtained by him from the City Planning Department of the City of Austin, not generally circulated, relating to St. John's community; Census of Montopolis Neighborhood, Austin, Texas (Reverend Fred Underwood, pastor of Dolores Catholic Church and supervisor of census, 1966).

[25] U.S. Commission on Civil Rights, "Spanish-Speaking Peoples," Appendix A,

groups is the discrimination in employment generally practiced by governmental and private employers and by unions against both Negroes and Latin Americans. A study of employment in Austin in 1947–1948 revealed the following comparative figures concerning the distribution of all workers in each ethnic group among the principal work categories:[26]

| Work Categories | Percentage | | |
	Of All Negro Workers	Of All Latin Am. Workers	Of All Anglo Workers
Professional, managerial, official	1	1.8	10
Clerical, sales	1	4	27
Blue-collar	2	6	18
Unskilled (construction, railroad section, canning)	34	41	10
Domestic, personal, building maintenance services	43	18	8
Semiskilled	19	29	27

Table 18, p. 2; Gardner and Johnston, "A Study of Human Relations," pp. 9–18; Colen and Harshman, "The Negro Family," pp. 11, 22. In Texas there are over two times as many Latin American and three times as many Negro families earning less than $1,000 than there are Anglo families in this category. These families cannot subsist without welfare assistance [U.S. Commission on Civil Rights, "Spanish-Speaking Peoples," Appendix A, Table 13]. Many Negro and Latin American families in Austin earning as much as $3,000 annually must obtain assistance from public and private organizations regularly for clothing and food for their children. In 1965 there were 9,601 actual offenses committed and 9,128 arrests made in connection with them in Austin, Texas. Of these arrests, 2,519 involved Negroes and 2,783 concerned Latin Americans [Austin Police Department, *Annual Report: 1965*, pp. 15, 42]. The great bulk of each of these two minority groups lives, as earlier indicated, in a segregated area in the eastern part of the city. A 1955 survey of the city's Negro and Latin American slum areas—census tracts 8, 9, and 10—showed that while they constituted only 10 per cent of the whole city area, they accounted for 55 per cent of all juvenile-delinquency cases, 51 per cent of all tuberculosis cases, 88 per cent of home fire deaths, 30 per cent of police calls, and 43 per cent of service costs [Stanislawski, "A Study of Leadership," p. 18]. Several studies report upon the special problems of Latin Americans in the public schools [Stanislawski, "A Study of Leadership," pp. 62–63; Isabel W. Cromack, "Latin-Americans: A Minority Group in the Austin Public Schools" (unpublished master's thesis, The University of Texas, August, 1949), pp. 48–49, 64–96]. One study reports that welfare agencies in Austin actually encourage the break-up of minority-group families. The city hospital clinic will not give a clinic card to a woman who is working unless she can show she is separated from her husband. The only proof that the clinic will accept is the filing of a divorce petition. When women seeking the assistance of the Legal Aid Clinic at The University of Texas School of Law were asked the reason they desired divorces, many of them answered that they wanted the divorces in order to obtain clinic cards [Colen and Harshman, "The Negro Family," pp. 21–25].

[26] Forrest Burr Crain, "The Occupational Distribution of Spanish-Name People in

Very, very few of either the Negro or Latin American workers group were members of the first three preferred work categories while the bulk of Anglo workers group were clustered in these categories. Most Negro and Latin American workers performed in the unskilled construction and service categories. Even in the unskilled and semiskilled categories Anglos served in the preferred jobs. For this reason Negroes and Latin Americans seldom advanced to become skilled workers. Those who served in the first three preferred categories usually performed their work in segregated contexts.

The author of the 1947–1948 study of Austin's employment pattern concluded that education levels and discrimination in employment operated to cause the difference between the favorable position of Anglos in the job classifications and the far less favorable positions of Latin Americans and Negroes.[27] He pointed out that the lower educational level of the minority groups was itself the result of discrimination and prejudice. At the time Negroes were still segregated by law in the public schools and some school districts in the metropolitan area still followed discriminatory practices toward Latin Americans. Discrimination in employment against Negroes was so widespread that the author considered the value of the experience of the ethnic group as a basis for comparative study of discrimination against Latin Americans had been destroyed. Few employers, according to Texas State Employment Agency interviewers, would consider Negroes for sales and clerical jobs.[28] For this reason, the interviewers deemed it pointless even to classify Negroes for these jobs. Moreover, practically all Negro men were referred by the agency for unskilled work without regard to the job classifications they had been given. A Negro veteran, who was a carpenter, was told that Anglos would not employ him.[29] Before Latin American women were referred to employers seeking clerical help the agency would call the employer to determine if he would accept an applicant of that ethnic group.[30] Some agency interviewers took the position that the only jobs open for Latin American women were in

---

Austin, Texas" (unpublished master's thesis, The University of Texas, August, 1948), pp. 13, 26–28, 29, 32.

[27] *Id.*, pp. 58, 73, 76, 79; Harry K. Wright, *Civil Rights U.S.A.: Public Schools . . . Southern States—1963: Texas*, Staff Report for U.S. Commission on Civil Rights (Washington, D.C.: U.S. Government Printing Office, 1964), p. 1.

[28] Crain, "The Occupational Distribution," pp. 55, 57.

[29] Interview with Mr. Rufus D. White, Negro contractor, Austin, Texas, by author (September, 1966).

[30] Crain, "The Occupational Distribution," pp. 55, 58, 65, 69, 74.

the laundry even when faced with a person who could type 60 words per minute. They were openly critical of business schools which trained Latin Americans for positions that were not open to them (these same schools did not admit Negroes to their classes). By and large Latin Americans and Negroes were excluded from union membership. Even where they held the same jobs, there was a substantial wage differential between Anglos on the one hand, and Latin Americans and Negroes on the other.

Bureau of Census figures for 1960 indicate that there has been only small to moderate improvement in the employment patterns of Austin's minority groups.[31] In 1960 over 65 per cent of Latin American and over 78 per cent of Negro males were still in the lower-paid, relatively unskilled occupations. Of Negro female workers 75 per cent were still employed as domestic and service workers. Although Austin's high schools are annually turning out numerous Negro and Latin American graduates and although a considerable number from each minority group are attending or have attended schools of higher education, there are no current signs that a substantial change in employment patterns will soon take place. Based upon statewide figures for male workers no more than 6 per cent and as little as 1 per cent of all carpenters, electricians, machinists, masons, painters, plumbers, welders, policemen, or firemen were Negroes.[32] As of December 1965 there were no Negroes or Latin Americans participating in twelve of thirteen apprentice-training programs conducted by building-trades unions; none employed as tellers or loan officers, or in similar positions by banks; two Negroes enrolled as members of the 650-member carpenter's local union; few of either group employed in sales positions in department stores; and few Negroes employed in Anglo-area grocery stores.[33]

A study of employment agencies in Austin in 1965 revealed that they had concluded that 98 per cent of Austin employers strongly preferred Anglo clerical workers.[34] They felt that a more favorable employer attitude was developing toward Latin Americans but not toward Negroes. Language problems, appearance, and inability to get

[31] Browning and McLemore, *A Statistical Profile*, p. 41.

[32] Bureau of the Census. *Census of Population: Texas*, Vol. I, Part 45–869.

[33] Gardner and Johnston, "A Study of Human Relations," pp. 36–37, 44; Ada Cecile Collins-Anderson, "Race and Ethnic Origin as a Determinant of Acceptability for Employment in Austin, Texas" (unpublished master's thesis, The University of Texas, August, 1965), p. 8.

[34] Collins-Anderson, "Race," pp. 56–57.

along with other workers were reasons given by employers for not employing Latin Americans. Lack of experience, fear of customer reaction, and fear of employee reaction were common reasons stated for not employing Negroes. Most of the agencies asserted that there was practically no opportunity to place Negroes in sales positions. They were able to place Negroes in drive-in groceries in or near Negro neighborhoods. Most employers, it was said, rejected Negroes for managerial positions, while some would employ Latin Americans.

In 1965 two studies were made of employers inserting classified ads listing employment opportunities in the *Austin American-Statesman* with a view to determining their willingness to employ Negroes and Latin Americans for the positions advertised.[35] Both studies revealed that Latin Americans and Negroes were rarely considered for positions in the higher categories, but that Latin Americans were given greater access to them than Negroes. One of these studies showed that 75 per cent of the employers utilizing classified ads were unwilling to consider Negro applicants. The other study indicated that over half of the employers would make race or ethnic origin a factor in employing one of a group of applicants including Anglos, Latin Americans, and Negroes.

The city government of Austin is one of the largest employers in the city, with some 3,700 employees.[36] It is estimated that approximately 20 per cent of these are Negroes. A somewhat smaller per cent are Latin Americans. Very few members of these minority groups serve in white-collar or skilled blue-collar positions. Most of them serve in street jobs or jobs in the open, such as garbage collecting. There are very few Negroes employed as secretaries. A police force of nearly 270 included only 10 Negroes and 4 Latin Americans in 1963 although together these groups constitute 25 per cent of the population.[37] The fire department in the same year employed 7 Negroes and 2 Latin Americans on a force of 300.[38] In 1965 there were no Negroes filling positions above the middle of the hierarchy. Minority-group persons

[35] Collins-Anderson, "Race," pp. 31–54; Gardner and Johnston, "A Study of Human Relations," pp. 37–39, 45–50.

[36] Gardner and Johnston, "A Study of Human Relations," p. 34; E. W. Bizic and W. W. McNeal III, "Negro and Latin-American Employment in Austin, Texas" (unpublished civil-rights seminar paper, The University of Texas School of Law, November 19, 1963), pp. 16–21.

[37] Austin Police Department, Interview with employees of Personnel Office by Burrell D. Johnston (October, 1966).

[38] Austin Fire Department, Interview with employees of Personnel Office by Burrell D. Johnston (October, 1966).

held positions such as general nurses and supervisors at the city hospital, electricians, social workers, and similar positions. Out of 2,179 teachers employed by the Austin Independent School District in 1965–1966 approximately 12 per cent were Negroes and 2 per cent were Latin.[39] These were largely deployed in the minority-group communities. One of the studies previously mentioned reported an interview with the city's assistant personnel manager.[40] He indicated that if the supervisor of a given department requests the personnel office not to send a Negro applicant for a job interview, this office complies. The city official conceded in the interview that some departments are segregated, and that if a qualified Negro were placed by his office in one of these departments, the supervisor would fire the new worker within a week on the ground that his work was "unsatisfactory." The official took the position that final decision upon employment of applicants must be left up to department supervisors in order to maintain proper control over and harmony within the departments.

The sixth and final characteristic to be noted concerning relations among Austin's ethnic groups is the lack of any substantial contact and cooperation between Negroes and Latin Americans.[41] The two minority groups live apart from each other. Their community processes take place without any substantial contact or interpenetration. Negroes are almost wholly Protestant in faith while Latin Americans are largely Roman Catholic. The social, fraternal, political, civil-rights, and other organizations in the minority-group communities largely follow ethnic lines. This physical and social separation between the two minority-group communities has been promoted by politicians. Congressman Henry B. Gonzales from Texas has described the operations of the political broker. This type of operator first acquires a reputation as a spokesman for a particular ethnic group by talking about the needs of "his" group, but without really helping to solve the basic problems:

Soon he is recognized as a "leader," and is asked to join in meetings with local politicos and officials. But the trouble with his leadership is that typically his demands in behalf of the downtrodden group turn out to be demands for jobs or political appointments. Who needs a job, the "Anglo"

[39] Austin Independent School District, *Directory of Austin Public Schools 1965–66* (Austin, Texas: 1965); Gardner and Johnston, "A Study of Human Relations," p. 15.
[40] Gardner and Johnston, "A Study of Human Relations," pp. 34–35.
[41] Stanislawski, "A Study of Leadership," pp. 23–30, 43–48, 54, 58, 66–67.

official might ask. Why, I do, says the "leader." So the leader and his friends get a handful of jobs, and the politicos have quieted some unpleasant noise about bad housing, poor schools and unemployment. This has been the technique used in Texas for many years. The capital of the political broker is the poverty and misfortune of others. But his authority is questionable, if not illegitimate, his methods are morally bankrupt, and he sells the people out.[42]

The very nature of the political broker's operations tends to keep his ethnic group from cooperating with another minority group having similar problems and needs.

Mr. Arthur Dewitty, a Negro who has taken a leading part in Austin's local politics for many years, has described another phenomenon that is probably more fundamental in keeping the minority-group communities separated.[43] For many years he has contended, in opposition to the political brokers, that Negroes and Latin Americans confront basically the same problems in dealing with the Anglo majority group. He has continually urged that the two minority groups unite in their efforts to obtain the social justice due them. He suggests, however, that both Anglo and Latin American leaders have consistently opposed this alignment, although for somewhat different reasons. Anglo politicians fear a union of Negro and Latin American efforts would make them far more effective at the polls. They have, therefore, played Negro against Latin American and vice versa whenever possible. Latin American leaders have felt that they had more to gain for their ethnic group by negotiating separately with the Anglo hierarchy. This feeling has usually been encouraged by Anglo politicians. There is no question but that a substantial number of Latin Americans have a prejudice against association with Negroes.[44] One Latin American leader has stated that there is a four-foot fence between the Negro and the Latin American as compared with the one-foot fence between the Latin American and the Anglo.[45]

The separateness of the two minority groups in Austin has been

[42] Gonzalez, "Poverty and Discrimination," p. 9989.

[43] Interview with Mr. Arthur Dewitty in August and September 1966.

[44] Separate interviews with numerous Austin Negro citizens having long experience with the Austin situation confirm this. While Austin Latin American leaders usually deny the discrimination, some candidly admit that it exists. Dr. Hector P. Garcia, founder of the American G.I. Forum, suggested at a meeting of this organization in Austin in early 1967 that Latin American prejudice against Negroes is unworthy of the Mexican tradition and something learned during the American experience.

[45] Stanislawski, "A Study of Leadership," p. 54.

most evident with regard to their efforts to secure human rights.[46] In 1939 Austin's Anglo group generally practiced segregation against both Negroes and Latin Americans in places of public accommodation, government facilities, employment, union membership, housing, credit facilities, membership in all forms of organizations, and education. Between 1939 and 1947 Latin American leaders engaged in a major effort through negotiation, protests, and court actions to eliminate segregation and discrimination against members of their ethnic group, focusing mainly upon public accommodations and governmental facilities. By and large they did not seek assistance of Negro leaders in this effort nor did they make any effort to assist Negroes in obtaining relief from similar discrimination.

While Latin American leaders achieved moderate success in opening up public and governmental accommodations, they were far less successful in opening up employment, union membership, housing, and credit or in obtaining representation in government or other powerful decision-making institutions for their group. The latter problems were far more complex and difficult to resolve and called for a high order of leadership, organization, and collective action in the Latin American community as well as cooperation with the Negro community. Unfortunately, there has been a paucity of knowledgeable, trained, and financially secure persons to provide leadership.[47] Lack of education and of time to do more than earn a living has greatly handicapped both potential leaders in the community and those who might respond to their leadership. There has been little interest in politics in the Latin American sector of the city. The better-educated Latin Americans frequently move out of this sector and lose their identification with it. Those who have some leadership status in the ethnic group exhibit jealousy of each other and have not been able to work together on a consistent basis. What leaders there are can be characterized mainly as politically oriented. They maintain only *ad hoc* political organizations to get out the vote at election time. They bargain with the Anglo politicians for jobs for their followers as well as for material improvements to the community. They have never at-

[46] The information about the conditions of minority groups in Austin between 1939 and 1962 was obtained through interviews between January and October 1966 with Mr. Paul Reyes, Mr. Mack G. Martinez, Mr. Roy Velasquez, Mr. Arthur DeWitty, Mr. and Mrs. M. J. Anderson, Mr. Jasper Glover, Mr. Calvin Lynch, Mrs. James H. Means, Mrs. J. M. Holloway, and others. All have sought to provide leadership within their minority groups in Austin for many years.

[47] Stanislawski, "A Study of Leadership," pp. 74–77.

tempted to get their ethnic group organized to work as a whole on its many problems. The picture of Latin Americans in Austin is one of diffused leadership, lack of organization, lack of education, self-isolation, apathy in politics, and disunity. Little progress in obtaining equal opportunities has been achieved since 1950.

Between 1946 and 1962 Negro leaders engaged in a fairly continuous separate effort to obtain an end to segregation and discrimination against members of their ethnic group. Their efforts, like those of the Latin American leaders, were primarily directed toward discrimination in public accommodations and government facilities, and were organized and directed by two institutions: the local branch of the National Association for the Advancement of Colored People and the Travis County Voters League. The first was conceived as a "legal arm" and the second as a "political unit" for obtaining an end to segregation and discrimination. Between 1946 and 1948 the principal efforts of the NAACP were concerned with a case filed by Heman M. Sweatt seeking a mandamus to compel University of Texas officials to admit him to the University School of Law. These efforts were successful as a result of a decision by the Supreme Court in *Sweatt v. Painter*.[48] After this decision Negro leaders initiated a systematic attack upon the entire dual system. On the one hand, their political unit conducted annual poll-tax campaigns to increase the number of all voters in the city and especially in the Negro and Latin American communities. The public-relations unit of the NAACP set out to state and interpret the goals of Negro leaders in order to win friends for their point of view throughout the city and to obtain support for their goals and policies at the polls. Through negotiation, protests, and threatened court action they attacked segregation in local and intrastate transportation. They secured an end to the requirement that Negroes enter through the back doors of buses and sit at the rear. Through the same methods they desegregated water fountains, restrooms, and seating within the Travis County Court House. They also obtained entrance for Negroes to the main city library and to city-owned parks and swimming pools. They attacked discrimination in the city-owned hospital with less effective results. They forced an end to a policy of excluding Negroes from the fire department although as late as 1963 all Negroes employed, a total of nine, were assigned to one station.[49] After the decision of the Supreme Court in

[48] 339 U.S. 629 (1950).
[49] Bizic and McNeal, "Negro and Latin-American Employment," p. 18.

Brown v. Board of Education,[50] Negro leaders moved quickly for integration of the public-school system. In 1955 the board of education responded by establishing a grade-a-year plan starting in the twelfth grade.[51]

Despite the progress that had been made by the two largely separate drives by Latin American leaders and by Negro leaders for ending discrimination against their respective ethnic groups between 1939 and 1962, a whole host of major problems of discrimination and disadvantages still remained to be solved. For the Negro there were still numerous forms of public accommodations and some government facilities that remained segregated. For both the Negro and the Latin American discrimination in employment by both private and government employers and by unions continued largely unabated. Discrimination in housing affected primarily the Negro, although also, to some extent, the Latin American. The disadvantages of poverty and near poverty for a majority of families in each minority group continued to doom their children to a future not greatly better than that of their parents.

In the early 1960's a new coalition seemed to be emerging for dealing with the problems just mentioned. Various Negro groups directed efforts toward integrating a number of businesses affording public accommodations. They were joined in their efforts by a number of individual Anglos drawn from such groups as the University YMCA-YWCA, religious-worker groups, churches in the University area, the Austin Council of Churches, two theological seminaries, and the University faculty and student body. The first businesses approached were the theaters in the University area, and later the downtown area theaters, restaurants, and lunch counters. Picketing and sit-in techniques succeeded in opening their facilities to Negroes although the largest department store and a principal drug store elected to close down their luncheon facilities rather than to integrate them.

As 1963 opened, Austin's hotels, motels, restaurants, hospitals, bowling alleys, business schools, and a number of other public-accommodations businesses remained segregated in their normal operations.[52] It was also generally believed by knowledgeable Negroes

[50] 347 U.S. 438 (1954).

[51] Wright, *Public Schools . . . Southern States–1963: Texas*, p. 29.

[52] Austin downtown hotels were open to Negroes attending conventions as well as special events held in them. These cracks in the generally solid front of public accommodations businesses had resulted from negotiation and protest actions of Negroes in 1961–1962.

that the city-owned hospital remained segregated in its assignment of rooms. A small group of Negro and Anglo citizens formed the Citizens' Committee for a Human Relations Ordinance[53] to organize efforts to deal with some of the remaining aspects of discrimination of this type. They were members of the Austin Council on Human Relations, a private organization made up mainly of Anglos who talked extensively about the need for improvement in human relations in Austin but followed the strict policy of not acting to do anything about it.[54] The Negro members of the Citizens' Committee were all members of the United Political Organization,[55] a statewide political organization almost wholly composed of Negroes committed to the policy of providing political support to candidates who would promise to provide jobs for Negroes. Among its members are the business and professional men of the Negro communities throughout the state. UPO bound itself to support John Connally, a political conservative, in his first race for governor of the state in 1962 and was instrumental in obtaining widespread Negro support in the Democratic primary. This resulted in defeat for the more liberal candidate and caused dissension in UPO ranks and some disaffection. The Citizens' Committee counted among its Negro members the state president of UPO and grand master of a multistate Negro fraternal organization, the pastor of the largest and most affluent Negro Baptist church, the pastor of the leading Negro Methodist church, a teacher in the public schools who had organized picket lines, and an insurance man. Among its Anglo members were the president of the Austin Council of Churches, a Jewish businessman who was president of one of the principal downtown businessman's

[53] A series of interviews and conversations with Mrs. M. J. Anderson and Mrs. James H. Means are the main sources of information concerning the foundation and operation of the Citizens' Committee prior to March 1, 1963, and between February and March, 1964. Mrs. Anderson served as chairman of the Citizens' Committee. Early in March 1963 I became a legal consultant to this committee and much of the Austin story subsequent to this date is reported as a matter of personal experience.

[54] This statement is based upon personal observation of the performance and statements by this ten-year-old organization during the period between 1963 and 1967. Its Negro members were largely drawn from the upper-income brackets of their ethnic group. A study confirms this view [Gardner and Johnston, "A Study of Human Relations," pp. 60–61].

[55] Arthur Schechter, "Private Groups: Their History, Effect, and Means of Implementation in the Civil Rights Movement" (unpublished civil-rights seminar paper, The University of Texas School of Law, December 20, 1963), pp. 19–21, 49; United Political Organization of Texas, *Newsletter*, Vol. I, No. 1 (Spring, 1963), p. 2.

organizations, a lawyer-investor who was president of the Austin Council on Human Relations, and the pastor of the leading Anglo Baptist church.

In early March deliberations by the Committee resulted in a consensus in favor of asking the Austin City Council to enact a civil-rights ordinance similar to the one adopted in El Paso, Texas, in June 1962.[56] It applies only to discrimination by operators of hotels, motels, and restaurants when based upon race, color, or religion. It is enforceable only through criminal process. I was asked, as a member of The University of Texas School of Law faculty, to act as legal consultant to the Committee. I advised its members that the criminal mode of enforcement of civil-rights ordinances had not proved effective in other areas and advised elimination of this feature of the contemplated proposal. I urged the substitution of a provision creating a human-relations commission with authority to issue cease and desist orders against discriminatory practices and to obtain their enforcement in the courts. The Committee agreed and I was asked to prepare a draft of an ordinance similar to the one adopted by El Paso.

Subsequently the Citizens' Committee decided, in light of suggestions received in the course of several meetings with leading citizens, to extend the proposed ordinance to all recreational and amusement facilities. Still later, the Committee determined to extend the draft ordinance to include all business and professional men who sought the trade of the public generally and all city government agencies. During the summer and early fall several informal or "workshop" meetings were held with members of the City Council to discuss the provisions and merits of drafts of the proposed ordinance. These meetings were of great importance for, as it turned out, they were the only forums in which it was possible to raise most of the arguments for and against the ordinance and to secure a genuine exchange of ideas concerning it. The purpose of the meetings, from the Committee's viewpoint, was to assess the attitude of the City Council and to make any changes in the ordinance, without sacrificing principle, that might enhance its chances for passage. One of the five members of the City Council did not attend these meetings. Ironically, this member had consistently received support from the "liberal" section of the community at election time.

56 El Paso, Tex., Code Ch. 15, Sec. 15-2.1.

The arguments made against the proposed ordinance by some of the City Council members included the following:

(1) The problem of segregation and discrimination against minority groups is a moral problem and does not admit of legal solutions. The only real solution is a change in personal moral attitudes and law cannot change these.

(2) The use of law to compel businessmen or professional men serving the public generally to deal with the Negro is an unwarranted interference with the right of these people to conduct their affairs and to use their private property as they see fit. To use law here is to favor the private moral right of members of minority groups over the private legal rights of property owners.

(3) This city has made considerable progress in integrating various public facilities including city-government facilities, the city schools, and many restaurants, hotels, motels, and theaters. Voluntary integration is working in this city and there is, therefore, no real need for civil-rights legislation.

(4) While the Negro faces a most difficult situation in obtaining employment and union membership, the city government is ready to consider any qualified Negro for employment and already has some Negroes employed in responsible positions. The principal problem is the Negro's lack of qualifications for the jobs available. The City Council has been very active in dealing with human-relations problems in the past and will continue to be so in the future. A commission could not have accomplished more than the City Council has.

(5) Enactment of this ordinance will mean that businessmen, professional men, and city agencies will be faced with a flood of complaints that they have been discriminating. They will lose much valuable time in having to appear at public administrative hearings. The subpoena power will be used by the human-relations commission to search into private business matters and to conduct witch hunts. Businessmen and others will constantly be forced to go to court to protect themselves.

(6) Legislation in this sensitive area should not be enacted until we have very nearly universal support for it and we are a long way from having that kind of support.

(7) Legislation of this sort should be uniform throughout the state and nation. For this reason the proper government to legislate in this field is the state or federal government. Since the federal government is likely to enact civil-rights legislation, we should not enter this field.

(8) The Police Chief has informed the Mayor that in Philadelphia a commission of this sort caused great difficulty for the city police department and wasted much valuable time of police officers. With each arrest of a Negro or Latin American, we can expect a complaint that the police discriminated against him because of his race or nationality. The whole process of law enforcement will be hamstrung.

The Committee devoted its participation in the workshop meeting to replying to these arguments and pointing out instances of discrimination by city government and private firms that were especially resented by minority groups. The Committee stated that the overt behavior of discrimination could be dealt with by law and that in other areas the conduct of businessmen and others had been subjected to regulation when the common good had been adversely affected. It also pointed out that many areas in which discrimination was occurring had not been changed by voluntary efforts and a law and a commission with authority was essential to achieving progress. The Committee also suggested that the experience of other cities with commissions demonstrated that public administrative hearings were not usually required. Rather, this experience showed that mediation was usually successful in adjusting a complaint of discrimination found to be well-grounded.

At the last workshop meeting, Mayor Lester Palmer gave the general impression that he had been favorably inclined toward the proposed ordinance. He suggested that the Citizens' Committee must now contact various civic and other organizations throughout the community and obtain their support for the ordinance. He indicated that the City Council could only vote in favor of the ordinance in the context of a demonstration by the Committee that there was widespread public support for it. One Council member, Mrs. Emma Long, stated that she was favorably inclined toward voting for the ordinance.

The Citizens' Committee immediately set out to elicit resolutions from various organizations in support of its proposal. Its members appeared at various public and private meetings to explain the ordinance and to meet various arguments. One particularly interesting meeting was held at The University of Texas School of Law by the Austin Council on Human Relations. Three persons spoke at this meeting. One was Mr. Harry Akin, a leading Austin restaurateur and president of the National Association of Restaurateurs, who had been active in moving many local restaurant owners to integrate their facilities. Another was the pastor of the leading Negro Methodist church. The third was myself. Mr. Akin took the position that it was futile to attempt to solve the problem of discrimination against the Negro by legislation, asserting that the real problem was lack of necessary qualifications by many members of that ethnic group. He also contended that the proposed ordinance set down detailed and arbitrary rules that were bound to operate unfairly. The Negro minister replied that if legislation could be used to exclude the Negro from the public life of the community, it could also be used to include him. I simply reviewed the experience of other cities with the kind of legislation being proposed and indicated that that experience demonstrated that it was both well-conceived and practicable. It is significant that in the daily newspaper report of this meeting the following day mention was made only of Mr. Akin's remarks. The presence of the other two speakers was not even mentioned.

The City Council of Austin held its first public hearing on the proposed ordinance on October 17, 1963. It lasted three hours. The Council chamber was filled to overflowing. During the hearing twenty-seven local organizations either made or filed statements in favor of the ordinance. Members of the Citizens' Committee made a series of statements in favor of the proposed ordinance. As legal consultant I was called upon to explain its provisions and the positive values to be realized through creation of an official human-relations commission with effective enforcement authority to deal with discrimination in public accommodations and governmental facilities. Numerous persons not affiliated with the Citizens' Committee also expressed their support of the ordinance. Only three persons, speaking as individuals, opposed its enactment. They relied upon the kinds of arguments previously summarized.

When all discussion from the assembled persons had concluded, the Mayor indicated that if a vote were to be taken at the meeting, he would vote against the ordinance. He felt that the vast majority of Austinites were opposed to enactment of the ordinance. He also pointed to the progress made in integrating various facilities in the Austin area by voluntary action. He did not attempt to answer specifically the various arguments that had been made in favor of the ordinance during the public hearing or to state any other reasons that had moved him to oppose the ordinance. He inquired if the group seeking the ordinance would be willing to wait for a period of some six months while the process of private voluntary action toward integration was given a further trial. He suggested, as reported in *The Houston Chronicle*, that "the 'lawyers' and 'even some of the ministers' ought to withdraw from the ordinance movement and let things be worked out on an informal basis. . . . I think you lawyers have a way of complicating things and you wind up in the courthouse and you can't agree on what to do."[57]

Council member Emma Long indicated that she was inclined to vote for the ordinance, although she insisted that before she would consider doing this, another public meeting must be held. The three other members of the Council, all businessmen like the Mayor, manifested little enthusiasm for the presentations in favor of the ordinance but declined to state their positions. When the president of the Negro Huston-Tillotson College expressed his hope that the Council would continue to consider the ordinance most carefully, the Mayor agreed that a second hearing would be set shortly at which those opposed to the ordinance could present their views.

At the second City Council meeting held on December 19 opponents of the ordinance were present in force. These were chiefly businessmen. One of them, a former member of the City Council and an insurance man, had been busy before the meeting contacting fellow businessmen, particularly in the downtown area, with a view to moving them to defeat the ordinance effort. Announcing that the purpose of the meeting was to give an opportunity to those opposed to the ordinance to be heard, the Mayor called upon the City Attorney for an opinion concerning the constitutionality of the ordinance. Prior to the first City Council meeting on the ordinance, the City Attorney had informed me through an intermediary that his office would not take a position on the constitutionality of the ordinance. At that meeting this official had stated that while he had not examined the proposed ordinance, the problem of its constitutionality was of such a nature that it would be best to leave decision on that matter to the courts. At this December meeting, however, he read a prepared brief in which he expressed the view, based principally on substantive due process grounds, that the ordinance was unconstitutional. Copies of this brief had not been furnished to proponents of the ordinance nor were they made available at the hearing. Following the City Attorney's presentation, three civic leaders spoke for the business community against the ordinance. Their arguments were basically the same as those presented at the 1963 workshop meetings with the Council, previously summarized. Some of the arguments were presented with ridicule and

[57] *The Houston Chronicle* (October 18, 1963), Sec. 1, p. 1.

sarcasm. The opponents warned that the requested ordinance was but
the proverbial foot in the door.

Reverend Robert Rowe served as coordinator for the Citizens' Committee presentation. After summarizing the arguments for the ordinance, he called upon me for comments on new matters that had developed since the last Council meeting. I discussed the following
points: (a) that the City Attorney had cited none of the numerous
decisions that, since the 1880's, have regularly sustained the constitutionality of state and local civil-rights legislation on due process and
other grounds that have been urged against it; (b) that the city attorney of San Antonio had recently advised the city commissioners of
that city that an antidiscrimination ordinance relying upon administrative process for its enforcement would be valid;[58] and (c) that the
city attorney of El Paso had drafted the civil-rights ordinance recently
enacted by that city and that he obviously considered it constitutional.[59] I presented the Council a copy of the extensive brief of the city
attorney of Tulsa who had ruled constitutional a proposed Tulsa ordinance quite similar to the proposed Austin ordinance.[60] In addition, I
indicated the strong probability that federal civil-rights legislation
would, in effect, give cities and states the option either of operating
under federal regulation of discriminatory practices in business affecting interstate commerce or of operating under local and state agencies
with effective authority to deal with these matters. I also presented the
Council with a letter from a former Texas businessman of note, Mr.
Earl B. Schwulst, who knew about human-relations commissions and
was favorably inclined toward them. Then chairman of the board of
one of the country's largest savings banks located in New York City,
he prepared the letter, containing his views on the merits of human-
relations commissions,[61] at my request especially for use on the Austin
scene. In answer to charges that the procedures of the proposed commission were arbitrary in nature, I stated that they had been modelled
closely upon the Federal Administrative Procedure Act,[62] and the

[58] Letter to me dated November 27, 1963, from Mr. Crawford B. Reeder, San Antonio city attorney.

[59] Letter to me dated November 8, 1963, from Mr. Travis White, El Paso city
attorney.

[60] Charles S. and Brice W. Rhyne, *Civil Rights Ordinances* (Washington, D.C.:
National Institute of Municipal Law Officers, 1963), Report No. 148.

[61] Letter to me dated December 3, 1963, from Mr. Earl B. Schwulst, Bowery Savings Bank.

[62] 5 U.S.C. §§ 552–559 (Supp. II, 1965–1966).

New York Civil Rights Act,[63] both of which have been highly praised for their procedural fairness over the past decade.

Subsequently, to the surprise of proponents of the ordinance, two leading Anglo businessmen spoke in favor of enacting either it or some similar ordinance. These were Mr. Akin, previously mentioned, and a prominent local builder. Both made the point that we live in changing times and that these demand an improved solution to the problem of human relations. Mr. Akin reaffirmed his strong belief in the necessity for continued use of private efforts at voluntary integration, but also stated that these need to be supplemented by an official body, such as the one contemplated by the ordinance. He supported the proposed ordinance on two conditions: (1) that able citizens having the confidence of all be appointed to the new commission, and (2) that the commission give primary emphasis to methods of education, persuasion, conciliation, and mediation set forth in the ordinance. He later indicated that the statement of the New York banker, mailed to him before the meeting, had been most persuasive. Ministers or lay leaders of the three major faiths again spoke in favor of the ordinance. One of them reminded the Council that the ordinance was important for the protection not only of Negroes but also of Jews and Latin Americans, among others.

Toward the end of the four and one-half hour meeting, the Council unanimously voted to create a committee to study the feasibility of establishing a commission on human relations and to make recommendations based upon its study. Prior to this vote it was made quite evident that the Council would not then vote in favor of the proposed ordinance. Two members expressed their definite opposition. The Mayor, who had already stated his opposition, closed the meeting with the statement that the problem of human relations was one that the community must face and solve. It was not, he said, a problem that would simply go away. He expressed the hope that enactment of the ordinance could still be avoided as a result of voluntary integration, but he thought that the committee could render a useful function by studying the situation and making proposals for dealing with it.

A seven-member committee on human relations was appointed by the Council. This committee, under the chairmanship of Mr. Akin, began its studies of the Austin situation in February 1964 with the first of a series of hearings. The mere existence of this committee and

[63] See Appendix A of this book.

its hearing had several values. It showed an official concern with the local civil-rights problem. It also involved many more persons officially with the problem than had ever before been involved. It confirmed facts about the status of human relations in the city that had previously been asserted as facts only by the Citizens' Committee and other private civil-rights groups. It caused the persons who might be subject to an ordinance to examine their affairs and to state their positions in opposition to the ordinance. It assured, finally, that the local newspaper and radio and television stations would give more adequate coverage to discussions of the civil-rights problem. These were real gains for the Austin community.

The hearings revealed that somewhat more than 50 per cent of the 256 eating establishments and 50 per cent of the motels in the city remained unintegrated, although all 8 of the larger hotels and motor hotels had integrated. They also indicated that there was discrimination in employment by the city government despite a stated policy of nondiscrimination. Moreover, qualified Negroes and Latin Americans were generally being denied opportunity for private employment of many types. Beyond this, Negroes could not obtain adequate business vocational training. On March 12 the committee stated its conclusion that despite progress in human relations in Austin, "much room for further progress remains, particularly as regards discrimination on the basis of race, color, or national origin."[64] It proposed, with but one dissenting vote, adoption of an ordinance, which it had drafted, creating an Austin human-relations commission without, however, giving it any authority to enforce civil-rights law. The function of this commission would be to promote mutual understanding and respect among all economic, social, religious, ethnic, and racial groups; to act as conciliator in controversies involving intergroup relations; and to cooperate with federal, state, and other city agencies in dealing with intergroup problems. Particularly significant was the committee's proposal for an adequate budget and the employment of an executive director to assist the commission.

After hearing the nearly unanimous recommendations of the study committee it had appointed, the City Council rejected them and by resolution reaffirmed its original position. At this point, the Citizens' Committee, convinced at long last that its efforts to persuade the Council to support an effective human-relations commission ordinance had

---

[64] *The Austin American* (March 13, 1964), p. 28.

failed, withdrew from further efforts. Its place was taken by the NAACP, which had grown increasingly restive since early January over the lack of progress. The NAACP president had made it known privately that he favored an "El Paso" type of ordinance employing only criminal sanctions and dispensing with the idea of a human-relations commission. In late March his organization proposed this type of ordinance to the City Council. Following the short shrift given this proposal by the Council, the NAACP, on April 2, began a two-week marathon filibuster or "speak-in" in the City Council chambers to protest the failure of the Council to deal effectively with the city's civil-rights problem. This filibuster, made possible by a Council rule permitting unlimited speeches by citizens, succeeded in completely stopping the processing of usual city business by the Council. Soon a plethora of new proposals for ending the protest emerged. One of these, which had been originally proposed in 1963 by the Mayor to the Citizens' Committee and was now offered by the City Attorney, suggested the extraordinary step of authorizing a private organization rather than an official agency to handle complaints of discrimination for the city government.

Finally on May 12, 1964, the City Council enacted an ordinance that fell considerably short of its study committee's proposal and that was but a sad shadow of the proposal made by the Citizen's Committee in late 1963.[65] A human-relations commission was created, but it was given no effective authority to investigate complaints of discrimination and none of the usual and important authority to study and report upon conditions adversely affecting human relations in the community and to promote better intergroup relations through affirmative action. Still more telling was the fact that the City Council failed to provide the commission with either a staff or funds with which to operate. As was to be expected, no law proscribing discrimination against minority groups was enacted and the commission was given no authority to eliminate it.

The new commission was never put into operation. This one official gesture toward solving the civil-rights problem was rendered nugatory when all but one of the original members resigned in a body shortly following their appointment. Ostensibly, these mass resignations occurred as a result of a statement by liberal Councilwoman Long questioning the representative character of the appointees. Perhaps the

---

[65] Austin, Tex., Ordinance 640512-A, May 12, 1964.

most telling comment about the commission and the conception of its role was made by one of the appointees, a retired minister. He stated that he had agreed to serve on the commission to help solve the civil-rights problem, not to become a part of it. A more probable reason for the mass resignation was a reaction of the Anglo power structure to the City Council's "moment of weakness" in acting to create the commission following the "speak-in" conducted by NAACP. Although little change, if any, in the status of human-relations problems could be produced by action of this weak commission, the power structure apparently thought the City Council had grievously erred by acting at all favorably toward those asking for much stronger action. Another reason was, unquestionably, the fact, evident to all, that the NAACP lost much support both within Negro and Anglo circles as a result of its "speak-in" and some of the circumstances surrounding its conduct. As the emotion and fear the speak-in had stimulated faded away and the *ad hoc* nature of the NAACP and other organizational efforts became more evident, the power structure apparently decided that there was no need for a weak commission.

Following the demise of the newly created commission, the Anglo and Negro members of the Citizens' Committee ceased to function as an effective, on-going group. Most of the Anglo members of this group, ill-trained in practical politics, probably felt they had sufficiently discharged their moral duties as concerned citizens. The Negro UPO leaders, some of whom were never really persuaded that the Citizens' Committee efforts were worth making, decided that it was futile to seek to persuade the present members of the City Council to enact a civil-rights ordinance. They returned to their main emphasis upon conduct of their private businesses and of obtaining jobs for UPO members from the Connally state organization in return for political support. The NAACP local branch resumed performance of its earlier role in the community. This consisted largely in making interstitial, frequently misdirected, and largely ineffective efforts to improve human relations for Negroes in Austin. The great bulk of Austin's Negroes knew and cared little about the NAACP local branch which had no programs and promoted no measures to relieve their many problems. Its Negro leaders were "weak" and heavily dependent upon a small group of Anglo liberals for ideas and financial support. Few talented Negroes participated in its management or activities even when they held membership cards. The UPO and NAACP leaderships, which had not worked together in the civil-rights efforts, were farther apart than ever before. Neither the UPO nor the NAACP had recruited a membership from the Latin American group. The Citizens' Committee also failed to include any Latin Americans in its work. Moreover, at no time during the previous two years had any Latin American group actively inserted itself into the Civil-Rights Revolution that had begun to reach Austin. While the Political Association of Spanish-Speaking Organizations, a very weak group, had endorsed the ordinance proposed by the Citizens' Committee at the last moment, neither of the two leading Latin American civic organizations—the League of United Latin American Citizens (LULACS) and the American G.I. Forum—had extended a hand to the Citizens' Committee, the NAACP, or the UPO in the efforts they had made to obtain a civil-rights ordinance.

No significant development in the Austin civil-rights dialogue occurred between the demise of the new commission in June 1964 and May 1965. Following earlier conferences, Mr. Volma Overton, president of the local branch of NAACP, at my suggestion and with the approval of his organization, obtained a place on the City Council agenda. A number of persons, including The University of Texas basketball coach and myself, appeared to present arguments in favor of reactivating or strengthening the defunct commission on human relations.[66] Continuing the hostile approach he had manifested in earlier sessions of the Council on civil-rights matters, Mayor Palmer required each person seeking to speak to state whether he or she was a member of the NAACP. After hearing the arguments, the Council determined not to appoint new members to the official commission to replace those who had resigned nearly twelve months earlier.

Shortly following this meeting Mayor Palmer appointed a committee to consider some compromise method for dealing with complaints of discrimination in the city. A subcommittee was also designated to prepare a draft proposal for consideration by the whole committee. This subcommittee consisted of Mr. Overton; Mr. Kenneth Lambkin, a Negro attorney; and the City Attorney. The understanding of the committee appointed was that the subcommittee would in due course submit a proposal and that the committee would study it and make its recommendations to the City Council.

In October 1965 I was informed by a member of the City Council through an intermediary that the subcommittee had drafted a proposal

[66] *The Daily Texan* (May 7, 1965), p. 1.

and that it would submit the proposal directly to the City Council for adoption. The Council member also sent me a copy of the current draft of the proposal. It called for creation of a nonprofit corporation by private citizens with the board of directors to be selected by the City Council. It was contemplated that the corporation would enter into a contract with the city to handle all complaints of discrimination filed by members of minority groups within the city. The corporation would not be an official arm of the city government nor even a city-government corporation, and it would have neither substantive law prohibiting discrimination to enforce nor any procedural powers to assist it in investigation and disposition of complaints. Moreover, it would have no active role in promoting integration in the community. It would simply sit in an office and wait for minority-group members to come to it. This notion, as earlier noted, had first been advanced by the Mayor in the 1963 workshop sessions with the Citizens' Committee.

The proposal presented a great danger to future progress in human relations in Austin. In the first place, the city was proposing to abandon its responsibility in civil-rights matters and to turn that responsibility over to a private corporation having no responsibility to the people. In the second place, this abandonment of responsibility represented a large step backward from the 1964 ordinance creating an official city human-relations commission, an ordinance that had not yet been put into effective operation. Wherever progress of a substantial kind had been made in other cities and states in human-relations matters, it had been achieved through the creation of a strong official human-relations commission. Private efforts had never been sufficient to meet the hard core of discrimination. In the third place, the private corporation would not have the authority necessary to enable it to become an effective instrument in resolving legitimate complaints of discrimination filed by Negroes or Latin Americans. It could only make weak efforts to persuade businessmen and government officials to stop discriminatory practices. In the fourth place, the proposal undercut the Civil Rights Act of 1964. That act was, in effect, a challenge to local and state governments, particularly in the South, to undertake the performance of their responsibility in civil-rights matters. If a local government created an official commission and gave it authority to administer law prohibiting discrimination in public accommodations and in employment covered by the federal statute, then that government would be permitted in effect to displace federal courts and agencies in dealing with that discrimination. Moreover, under Title VII of the federal statute there was a provision authorizing agreements between the federal Equal Employment Opportunity Commission and official local and state agencies operating in the same field. Under these agreements the federal agency could reimburse the local and state agencies for utilizing their services in enforcing the federal statute. The federal agency could also agree to turn over administration of the federal act to local and state official agencies in the case of discrimination in employment. The Mayor's proposal would be a complete obstacle to carrying out this basic policy of the new federal statute.

Additional objections to the proposal were most apparent. The private corporation could not be representative of the people of Austin and, most particularly, of minority groups. It was not proposed as a private corporation with members who voted to elect its board of directors. It was to be a private corporation tightly controlled by the City Council. The proposal did not stipulate that a certain number of representatives from the minority groups were to sit on it. Past appointments to various committees and to the official commission on human relations by the City Council had indicated that only persons who were closely oriented to the present political leadership would be appointed. The private corporation proposal also held the promise of monopolizing the field of private action for advancing civil rights. The fact that the City Council backed the new corporation with city funds would give it a special blessing and authority. This might make it difficult for bona fide private organizations, such as the NAACP and the Citizens' Committee, to obtain a sympathetic ear in talking with businessmen and government officials. They could always respond that they would be guided by decisions of the city's contract partner, the new private corporation. Bona fide private organizations in the civil-rights field might be made to appear as mere interlopers. In view of these and other considerations the minority groups of Austin would find it difficult to respect the proposed private corporation or to have confidence that it would fairly handle their complaints of discrimination or to attack in a vigorous, affirmative manner the many human-relations problems in the city. Without their respect and confidence the new corporation would not only be an ineffective expedient but also delay efforts to obtain the inevitable and needed official governmental assumption of its responsibility in civil-rights matters.

The UPO and NAACP leaderships, in a series of separate meetings, discussed these and other difficulties about the Mayor's proposal of a private corporation.[67] Eventually the UPO leadership determined against another effort to influence the City Council. Its president took the position that the present membership on the City Council made it impossible to obtain any beneficial action.[68] He also felt that the inadequacy of the private corporation idea would show up in practice and that its failure in operation would prepare the way for appropriate action. He also thought that UPO could not work effectively with the NAACP due to the attitude of its president, Mr. Volma Overton, and of its members toward the UPO, an attitude of suspicion about the latter's objectives and policies. He suggested that, as a result of its support of Governor Connally, UPO had achieved what no other Negro organization had ever achieved, the opening of nearly five hundred jobs to Negroes within the state government. He took the position that the movement of the Negro into positions of power in the business community was the only way that significant change in human relations could be effectuated. It seemed clear that UPO was not likely to become involved again in any significant effort for a local civil-rights ordinance.

As a result of the conferences previously mentioned,[69] Mr. Overton determined to rescind his support of the Mayor's proposal which he had given it as a member of the subcommittee appointed in early 1965. He was not, however, at all enthusiastic about initiating another NAACP general effort before the Council. His health was not good and he felt very discouraged with the Austin situation. He did, however, agree to call a meeting at which a new organization might be formed to oppose the Mayor's proposal and to work for a better day in civil-rights matters in Austin.

At the first meeting called by NAACP on January 4, 1966, I was asked to present the arguments against the Mayor's plan in public as they had been earlier presented in the closed meetings of the NAACP leadership and the proposal for a new organization of interested organizations to work in the field of civil rights. Mr. Lambkin, one of the members of the Mayor's subcommittee, was present but declined to answer the arguments in detail. He repeated a statement earlier publicized in the mass media that he had a letter from the Federal Com-

[67] *The Austin American* (October 28, 1965), p. A16; *The Austin-American Statesman* (Nov. 6, 1965), p. 4; *The Austin American-Statesman* (November 7, 1965), p. A26.

[68] Conversation with Mr. M. J. Anderson, president of the UPO, in December, 1965.

[69] The author participated in these conferences.

munity Relations Service indicating that the Mayor's proposal for a private corporation involved the type of agency contemplated by the Civil Rights Act of 1964 for promoting federal-local cooperation. This statement was highly misleading and capable of damaging local civil-rights efforts. To counter it, I had obtained, with the concurrence of the NAACP president, a letter ruling from the general counsel of the Equal Employment Opportunity Commission stating that the Mayor's proposal would not enable the city to undertake the local functions contemplated by Title VII (employment) of the Civil Rights Act of 1964.[70] This letter was read to the assembled group. Although an able, indeed prizewinning, reporter of the *Austin American-Statesman* was present, either he did not report this important ruling or the report of it was deleted from his story that appeared the following day.[71] Only *The Daily Texan*, a University student newspaper, reported upon this letter.[72] The idea of an organization of local organizations to promote human rights having been presented, the group resolved to meet weekly until some new organization might be set up to begin a new effort to obtain effective official action in this area.

During the next four weeks of meetings it became apparent that neither Mr. Overton nor the other members of NAACP were willing to spend time at meetings looking to a new human-rights organization cutting across ethnic group lines. Very few Negro members of NAACP attended the organizational meetings. At times only a handful of Anglos and one or two Negroes were present. No Latin Americans attended. Most of those in attendance appeared to be a small and fairly close-knit group of Anglos and a few Negroes associated with an organization known as the Liberal Democrats of Travis County. Many of this same group also regularly participated in the work of the

[70] Letter to me dated December 3, 1965, from Mr. Charles T. Duncan, general counsel of the Equal Employment Opportunity Commission. As a result of a similar letter request to Mr. John Doar, assistant attorney general in charge of the Civil Rights Division of the Department of Justice, the Federal Community Relations Service repudiated the interpretation of its letter by Mr. Lambkin. [*The Austin American* (January 25, 1966), p. 23]. Mr. Doar also issued a letter ruling to the same effect as the one issued by Mr. Duncan concerning the ineffectiveness of the Mayor's plan to create a local agency contemplated by Titles II (public accommodations) and VII of the 1964 act as the basis for federal-local cooperation in the enforcement of civil-rights law [Letter to me dated April 11, 1966, from Mr. John Doar, assistant attorney general, Civil Rights Division, U.S. Department of Justice].

[71] Chris Whitcraft, "Human Rights Plan Advanced," *The Austin American* (January 5, 1966), p. 1.

[72] *The Daily Texan* (January 6, 1966), p. 1.

NAACP, the University YMCA-YWCA, and the Friends Meeting of Austin. During the first four weeks of organizational meetings, the basic concept was hammered out for a new organization that, the group hoped, could become more effective in advancing human relations than earlier organizations had been.[73]

I proposed, in light of the earlier failures by other organizations, the utilization of the nonprofit corporation device in order to give more stability and continuity to the new effort. The Citizens' Committee had been an *ad hoc* organization with few lines drawn concerning decision-making and certainly without any inclination to obtain widespread participation in its operations by members of the two minority-group communities. To avoid duplicating the latter result I proposed that the new corporation consist of individual and organizational members, who would select its board of directors and determine its fundamental purposes and policies and that the central goal of the new corporation should be to promote equality of opportunity for all persons in Austin through active cooperation among Negro, Latin American, and Anglo citizens, their churches, and other organizations.

The new group decided that it not only would oppose the Mayor's proposal but also would make a counterproposal for a new comprehensive civil-rights ordinance and present it to the City Council at a hearing to be requested for that purpose. I was directed to draft an ordinance that would prohibit discrimination in public accommodations, governmental facilities, and employment against any person on the basis of his race, color, religion, or national origin. The group laid plans for publishing an ad in the local newspaper telling of the new organization, its opposition to the Mayor's proposal, and its own proposal for a new civil-rights ordinance, and inviting readers to a mass meeting at a large city-owned auditorium in the Negro community to discuss the new organization's objectives and projects.

Definite efforts were made to obtain support from minority-group organizations for the new "umbrella" organization which called itself the Citywide Committee of Organizations for Human Rights (CCOHR). A few of the younger Latin American leaders attended the organizational sessions. Eventually, the NAACP, the American G.I. Forum, and the Political Association of Spanish-Speaking Organizations agreed to become organizational members of CCOHR and to join in the project to propose a new civil-rights ordinance. The UPO also

[73] *The Austin American-Statesman* (April 23, 1966), p. 6.

became an organizational member but this membership proved to be a nominal one mainly designed to give CCOHR moral support. A deputy state director of the League of United Latin American Citizens attended the organizational sessions, but he was unsuccessful in his attempt to obtain the agreement of the local branch of LULACS to join CCOHR and to support the ordinance proposal. It was highly significant that for the first time several Latin American leaders were actively participating with a few Negro leaders and Anglo citizens in a joint effort to advance human rights in Austin.

In early February CCOHR received a report that the Mayor might shortly present his proposal to the City Council for turning over the handling of civil-rights matters to a private corporation. CCOHR determined to publish its ad, previously mentioned, in the *Austin American-Statesman* with a view to informing the general public about the nature of the Mayor's proposal, which had never been released to the public, and about the difficulties involved in implementing it. The ad was constructed to occupy one-half page of copy. One part was entitled "Why the Mayor's Proposal is Unacceptable"; a second was entitled "Does Discrimination Exist in Austin?" a third was labeled "How the City Council Has Failed"; a fourth had the heading "Why the 1964 Human Relations Ordinance is Inadequate"; and a fifth summarized the concept of the CCOHR, its purposes, and its first project—the attempt to obtain enactment of a comprehensive civil-rights ordinance.[74] It stated that CCOHR had learned that the Mayor's proposal would be taken up on February 17th and urged citizens to be present to state their views on it. After having been quoted a fixed sum for publication of the ad, CCOHR submitted it for publication. When its representatives sought to pay that sum for the ad, a newspaper employee in charge of the ad desk would not accept a proffered check. He stated that the newspaper's lawyers objected to that part of the material under the title "Does Discrimination Exist in Austin?" When asked to state the reasons for not accepting the ad with this material, he declined to state them. When asked if he would accept a check for any larger sum that might be necessary to pay for the ad on the theory that it was, as he had suggested, a political ad, he declined to accept a check for any amount.

The material contained in the objected-to part of the ad simply summarized the conclusions reached by two senior law students at The

[74] Citywide Committee of Organizations for Human Rights, "A Statement on Austin's Major Problem" (circular, February 14, 1966).

University of Texas in a civil-rights seminar paper. The principal part of the material to which objection was raised stated that the city of Austin was still discriminating against Negroes in employment in a number of departments due to the decisions of their supervisors. It also pointed out how few Negroes and Latin Americans were employed in positions beyond the menial level and gave the data supporting the charge of discrimination. It was later learned that the newspaper's lawyers based their objection upon the ground that the statement charged city officials with violating the criminal provisions of the Civil Rights Act of 1964 and that its publication would thus, as a libel, subject the newspaper to legal liability under state tort law. The lawyers apparently did not know that the Civil Rights Act of 1964 did not apply, relative to employment discrimination, to cities and their officials, nor even create any criminal liability. They also were apparently not familiar with the recent case of *New York Times Company v. Sullivan*,[75] which made it clear that neither a newspaper nor individuals who insert an advertisement in it criticizing public officials for the way they perform their functions could be held for a libel where the criticism is made without knowledge of its falsity or without reckless disregard of whether it was false or not. Of course, CCOHR believed its charge that the city was discriminating in employment to be true and had extraordinarily cogent evidence for so believing. When the *Sullivan* case and the facts concerning the 1964 federal law were brought to the attention of the *Austin American-Statesman*, its officials refused either to reply to the letter transmitting the information or to the request to publish the ad. The failure to obtain publication of the ad or adequate coverage of its activities greatly hampered CCOHR in its efforts to focus the public's attention upon civil-rights issues. The group did circulate twenty thousand copies of the ad by handbills but these reached relatively few citizens.

Mr. Roy Wilkins, executive director of the National Association for the Advancement of Colored People, spoke in Austin shortly after the *Austin American-Statesman* had refused to print the ad of CCOHR. He stated: "It's incredible that in the capital of Texas there should be a debate on establishing a human-rights commission. Austin has a lot of problems. One of the greatest seems to be your newspaper. I understand the newspaper refused to publish an ad on a new committee to organize for human rights. The editors . . . said take out this and that

[75] 376 U.S. 254 (1964).

paragraph, no censorship, of course."[76] In an angry response the news-paper accused me of having "accompanied [Wilkins] during much of his Austin stay,"[77] as if this should be enough to discredit an Austin white citizen among his peers. The paper stated, also quite falsely, that it had conveyed to me and other CCOHR representatives the legal objections its attorney had to its printing the CCOHR ad.

During February and March CCOHR perfected its proposed civil-rights ordinance. It also elected three co-chairmen. One was Mrs. James H. Means who had served with the Citizens' Committee. Closely associated with the small group of Anglos who had assisted in the for-mation of CCOHR, she had severed her connection with the UPO. The second was Mr. Robert Canino, the energetic and politically minded president of the local branch of the American G.I. Forum. The third was myself. The idea in the selection of these three was to involve as equally as possible each of the three major ethnic groups in the leader-ship of the organization. CCOHR also determined to incorporate un-der the Texas nonprofit corporation statute and its co-chairmen were elected members of its board of directors. It also slightly changed its name to become the Citywide Committee of Individuals and Organiza-tions for Human Rights (CCIOHR). Late in March the organization requested a hearing before the City Council in which to present its arguments against the Mayor's proposal and to advocate adoption of the civil-rights ordinance it had drafted. The City Council set the hear-ing for May 5th but refused to schedule a night meeting in order to make it easier for minority-group members to be present.

Throughout the remainder of March, April, and early May, CCIOHR conducted its weekly meetings in different churches in both minority-group communities. In these meetings the nature of its pro-posed civil-rights ordinance was explained and new persons attending the meetings were urged to join the group at the City Hall on May 5th. CCIOHR members were also active in contacting various civic, religious, university, and other organizations seeking endorsement of the proposed ordinance. A number of CCIOHR members fanned out into the Negro and Latin American communities to obtain signatures on a petition requesting the City Council to reconsider CCIOHR's re-quest for a night meeting in order to make it possible for more minor-ity-group persons to be present. By April 29 CCIOHR had gathered

[76] *The Austin American-Statesman* (February 16, 1966), p. 3.
[77] *Id.*, p. 1.

nearly six thousand signatures, most of them from Negroes and Latin Americans. The City Council, despite the submission of this petition, still refused to schedule a night session. It was later learned that members of the Council were fearful that a large gathering of minority-group members would "get out of hand." By scheduling the session at 3:00 P.M., while most of the minority-group members were still at work, it was expected that only a small turnout would occur.

On May 5th, CCIOHR went to its session with the City Council with more support for official action on its civil-rights ordinance proposal than had ever before been manifested in the civil-rights struggle in Austin. Despite the daytime session and the rain, over five hundred persons turned out for the session. Most could not get into the Council chamber and many had to stand on the steps and sidewalk outside City Hall in the rain. Many had given up part or all of a day's work in order to be present. Reflecting the City Council's view of the assembled citizens, the Chief of Police, in an unprecedented action, informed CCIOHR's board of directors that he had stationed plain-clothes men in the Council chamber. CCIOHR proceeded to conduct a careful, responsible, and vigorous presentation in behalf of its proposed ordinance. It first presented letter endorsements of its proposal obtained from twenty-nine different local organizations and groups. Missing from the list of groups endorsing the proposed ordinance were the Austin Chamber of Commerce, every major professional and business organization (other than the pastors' associations), the Negro Ministerial Alliance of Austin, and all but three of the local unions. A number of individuals either wrote letters or personally appeared in favor of the ordinance. These include, most significantly, six of the most outstanding Latin American businessmen and civic leaders, twenty-two members of the faculty of the School of Law of The University of Texas, the pastor of the second largest Negro Baptist church, the pastor of the largest Latin American Methodist church, and the chaplain of the Catholic Student Center. Mr. Overton, president of the local branch of the NAACP, read a letter from the general counsel of NAACP in New York City praising the ordinance and its adoption. Rabbi Clyde Sills of the Hillel Foundation stated that "the continued existence of discrimination within our community not only dehumanizes the victims and the perpetrators, but is a shameful disgrace to our great city of Austin."[78] He urged adoption of the CCIOHR proposal.

[78] Letter to me dated May 2, 1966, from Rabbi Clyde T. Sills, who repeated this in substance at the City Council hearing.

The Most Reverend Robert Lucey, Archbishop of the Roman Catholic Archdiocese of San Antonio, whose letter concerning the work of an organization like CCIOHR was presented to the Council, stated: "the twentieth century has caught up with those citizens of our country who try to be neutral, uncommitted and uninvolved in the presence of human degradation. The world has just about caught up with those ... who pretend to believe that if they look the other way, social problems will somehow be dissipated."[79]

The City Council had set a time limit of two hours for hearing CCIOHR in spite of the fact that in 1963, 1964, and 1965 when similar presentations had been made, it had permitted far more time to proponents of civil-rights legislation. When the two hours allotted it had expired, CCIOHR had called up fewer than half of the persons it had scheduled to speak to the City Council. Before relinquishing the floor, CCIOHR indicated to the City Council that the organization had heard that the Council had already made up its mind in private to adopt the Mayor's private corporation proposal and had even selected the persons to sit as the first members of its board of directors. CCIOHR asked if this report was true, and requested, if it was, that the Council set a hearing upon the proposal after first making the Mayor's proposal public so that it could be studied and subjected to public debate.

The Mayor categorically denied that the Council had privately decided upon the adoption of his plan. Councilman Louis Shanks also stated he knew nothing of such a decision. The Mayor then stated that CCIOHR had had its opportunity to speak and that now his plan would be discussed. He called upon Mr. Lambkin, the Negro lawyer who had sat on the Mayor's subcommittee to draft the plan. Mr. Lambkin compared the private corporation idea to the private human-relations organizations like the NAACP. The City Attorney, upon being asked to speak, took the position that the city, although operating under a home-rule authority, could not regulate human relations through the proposed civil-rights ordinance. Councilwoman Emma Long asked that the City Attorney read the Mayor's proposal saying that it had been several months since she had read it and that she did not remember its provisions in detail. At this point, Mr. Richard Brown, publisher of the *Austin American-Statesman*, asked for the floor. He had been sitting with a group of prominent businessmen who had been observing the meeting. He indicated that the newspaper's

[79] Letter to me dated September 7, 1965, from the Most Reverend Robert E. Lucey, archbishop of the Archdiocese of San Antonio, Texas.

lawyers had been asked to examine both the Mayor's and the CCIOHR proposals and that they recommended the former. He urged the Council to come to grips with that proposal and to adopt it without further delay. In response to a question from Councilwoman Long, CCIOHR referred to the two letters previously mentioned from the Department of Justice and the Equal Employment Opportunity Commission ruling that the Mayor's proposal did not involve an agency to which the federal courts or the Commission could defer in the enforcement of the Civil Rights Act of 1964. When this Council member again insisted upon a reading of the Mayor's proposal, Councilman Louis Shanks laughingly said: "Let's pass it first and read it later."

Since it had become evident that the Council would shortly vote unanimously to adopt the Mayor's proposal and would not further consider CCIOHR's proposed civil-rights ordinance or hear arguments from CCIOHR or others against the Mayor's proposal, it requested and was granted the opportunity to make a closing statement. In behalf of the organization I stated:

Our business community as a whole, in contrast to business communities all over the country outside the South, has demonstrated that neither it nor its political representatives are willing to study and resolve through official action the city's human-relations problems. The business community has not gone, as has CCIOHR, to the minority-group communities and listened to people telling about their problems. The Negroes and Latin Americans who sit before the businessmen and council members, and other members of their ethnic groups who could not attend the day session, can have but one reaction to what has gone on this day. This is to believe that they have not received a hearing from the Anglo community or the City Council. We leave here tonight persuaded more than we ever have been during the past three years of effort for improvement of human relations in Austin that we have not been able to touch your hearts, much less your minds. We in CCIOHR are very fearful of the distress with which we are coming into contact in the minority-group communities. There is an almost overwhelming sense of frustration at large in these communities. It is time for people who are Jews, Catholics, and Protestants in the Anglo community to stop and ask the question: "Is this true?" It is time for them to take some time and to spend some money to find the answer to this question. We now know that we have not accomplished anything by our presentation. We know we leave this chamber without having been heard. You have listened, but you have not heard. I find it difficult to take pride in our community. I can only feel sadness, a very deep sadness, that we cannot find it in our hearts to do what most states and cities outside the South have been able to do in dealing with human-relations matters.[80]

The Council then voted unanimously in favor of the Mayor's proposal. A number of weeks later the contemplated private corporation, the Equal Citizenship Corporation (ECC), was formed. The Council appointed a group of able citizens to its board of directors, but only one was a Negro and one a Latin American and they were persons who were closely aligned with the city's power structure. Both were, or had been, members of the conservative Negro organization, UPO. Neither had participated actively in the four-year struggle in Austin since 1962 to achieve an amelioration of its human-relations problems. The ECC established an office in an upper floor of a downtown office building and waited for members of minority groups to come to it with any complaints of discrimination. Despite the good intentions and eminence of its board members and despite the grant to it of $25,000 of city funds, the ECC barely functioned during its first year of operation. People did not in fact take their complaints to the corporation, with the result that it received only seven complaints in all. Most did not even know of its existence, much less its location. The organization did not insert inself into the social fabric of the city. It did not employ any experienced human-relations specialists or an executive director. It did not go out into the community to find out what its human-relations problems were, to study them, to formulate policies and means for resolving these problems, and to promote the adoption of these policies. It developed no positive programs for promoting progress in widening opportunities for minority groups and the poor.

The City Council in the fall of 1966 directed the ECC to investigate charges that the city sanitation department was discriminating against Negro and Latin American garbage collectors, thirty-nine of whom had been dismissed due to their failure to return to their posts after a work absence in protest of working conditions. Its first investigation and report that it found no evidence of discrimination was based only upon conversations with the Anglo supervisors of the department.[81] Although directed by the City Council to investigate the matter further, the ECC found itself unable to obtain evidence from the ex-

[80] Transcript of Hearing on May 5, 1966, before Austin City Council, record 16, supplied to a CCIOHR representative by Mr. C. B. Smith, a prominent Austin businessman.

[81] *The Austin American-Statesman* (October 25, 1966), p. 1.

garbage collectors without the subpoena power.[82] These ex-employees had been advised by their counsel not to discuss their grievances with ECC, pending trial of a suit against the city charging it with illegal action. Relying principally upon city employment records, the ECC again found no substantial evidence of discrimination against minority groups although it did recommend some changes in personnel policies. From every point of view, the ECC had proved to be a substantial failure in its first year of operation. It had earned no respect from minority groups. The NAACP local branch urged members of these groups not to use it. As the head of the city-county health unit observed: "It's not surprising people haven't flocked to a new Commission [sic] headed by whites."[83]

By way of contrast the Citywide Committee for Human Rights, since presenting its ordinance proposal to the City Council, has made a major contribution to the betterment of human relations in Austin.[84] It established a Human Rights Center in the summer of 1966 in a well-equipped older building formerly used as a hospital, deep in the heart of the Negro ghetto on the near east side, only a few blocks from the northernmost tip of a large area occupied by Latin Americans. Through this center it has conducted an extensive educational program, a social case-work program, a public forum program, a public-affairs program, and a welfare-assistance program. Operating on the theory that the current problems of human relations are created at and must be solved primarily at the local level, CCHR has constantly urged that there are vast human and material resources at the local level, now largely untapped, which can be used to promote better human relations in Austin. It has asserted that these resources are far greater than anything the state or the federal government can be expected to devote to improvement of human relations in the local area for the foreseeable future. It has sought to promote equality of opportunity for all citizens in Austin through active cooperation of its three major ethnic groups, their churches, and other organizations.

CCHR has conducted its various programs without federal, state, or local government money. It has raised the necessary funds for its programs, small in comparison with the $25,000 given the ECC by the city government, through solicitation of its members and friends in

[82] *The Austin American* (January 12, 1967), p. 1.
[83] *The Austin American* (July 28, 1966), p. A6; (September 15, 1966), p. A50.
[84] Letter to the Austin City Council dated July 6, 1967, from the Board of Directors of CCIOHR.

the local community. Its educational program, for example, has consisted of a tutorial program for adults seeking their high school diploma equivalent, a tutorial program for school-age children in need of remedial help, a typing and business-English class, and several special classes. Over 125 persons are regularly enrolled in these programs. Some 75 persons have voluntarily contributed from one to two hours a week of their time to serve as tutors or teachers of these students. Drawn principally from such organizations as the Lutheran Student Center, the Catholic Student Center, Hillel Foundation, Concordia Lutheran College, Huston-Tillotson College, the First English Lutheran Church, and The University of Texas, these persons have operated on a 1-to-1 basis primarily. Many adult students have already obtained their diplomas and others have passed several of the required tests. Many children have been enabled to pass courses they would have failed. A number of adults have been trained to perform secretarial duties.

CCHR has also handled over 300 cases in its social and legal casework program during its first year of operation. This was made possible through the contributed time of nearly 25 students at The University of Texas School of Law under the supervision of myself, a young Austin lawyer, and a member of the CCHR board of directors. Cases handled consisted of those in which trouble was encountered in obtaining assistance from the established agencies.

CCHR has also sought out jobs to be opened for the first time to members of the minority groups. It has felt that the Texas Employment Commission local office does not perform this function in an adequate manner. As a result of its efforts, it was able to locate around 60 persons in adult training programs or jobs.

Through its public forum program CCHR has kept in intimate contact with members of the minority-group communities. These forums are held about twice a month in different churches, upon subjects of deep interest to these citizens. One of these forums, for example, focused upon the conditional sales contract used for sale of real estate to Negroes and Latin Americans in over 90 per cent of all transactions involving them. This contract is written so as to permit forfeiture of the property upon nonpayment of a single installment even though the purchaser may have placed substantial improvements upon the property and have paid considerable sums toward its purchase over the years. Speakers at the forum informed those in attendance of other methods of purchasing property and of means of avoiding the situation of forfeiture. These forums demonstrate to the minority-group communities that an organization does exist that is willing to discuss their problems in an honest and candid way. Members of the two minorities have an opportunity to hear able presentations concerning their problems and to engage in a give-and-take discussion of them. The forums also serve to educate members of the Anglo power structure about the people and problems in the minority-group communities. Both majority- and minority-group members attend these forums and experience, many for the first time, the kind of community living that must increasingly take place.

CCHR has had reasonably good success in finding Negroes and Latin Americans with significant leadership potential and in helping them to work effectively in the field of human relations. This, as previously mentioned, was a central goal underlying formation of the organization. While there are many Negroes and Latin Americans with leadership potential in human relations, few of them had in fact exercised it in the Austin community. By and large the existing leaderships in the Negro and Latin American communities have concerned themselves with other matters. The finding of new Negro and Latin American leaders to fill the gap created by failure of the existing leaderships to focus upon human-relations problems may be the greatest single contribution of CCHR.

In its first two years of existence CCHR has had a great impact upon community relations. Negroes and Latin Americans in need of various kinds of assistance have turned to this organization to obtain it. They look upon it increasingly as *their* organization. Many organizations and individuals previously without opportunities to contribute toward improved human relations have found CCHR to be the kind of operation through which they can contribute. Its performance has not gone unnoticed by the Anglo power structure. Night sessions of the City Council, first requested by and denied to CCHR, have quietly been inaugurated, with the result that Negroes and Latin Americans can and do attend these sessions far more readily. Two Council members were elected who let it be known that they were very much in favor of real progress in human relations. While CCHR is and has remained a nonpolitical organization, its leaders as individuals did give a great deal of help to these two new council members when they were seeking election. In an appearance in July 1967 before the new City Council, CCHR opposed continuation of the City Council's arrangement with the old City Council's private corporation, the ECC, and again asked for creation of an official human-relations commission. Understating its accomplishments before the Council to achieve a greater effect, CCHR was surprised by the compliment paid it by a new Council member other than the two just mentioned.[85] This member stated that CCHR did not know how widely its work was respected or how much good it had accomplished. He also stated that he was going to make a personal contribution to CCHR and to solicit contributions for it from his friends.

However, Austin was not yet ready, in the early fall of 1967, to consider in a serious way the creation of an effective official human-relations commission, or to consider other measures to solve its enormous human-relations problem. On October 5 of that year the City Council, again with little consultation—if any—with civil-rights groups, enacted an ordinance creating an official human-relations commission of the weakest type, without law concerning discrimination to enforce, without the subpoena power and most of the other devices needed to assure its effective operation. The reasons were not hard to find. Despite the elections of more enlightened Council members, Austin was still a city whose professional, business, and union leaders, all drawn from the ranks of the Anglo majority group, were not ready to confront the manifold human-relations problems of their city. It was a city whose Anglo leaders had not yet taken the time or trouble to discuss the reasons for the depth of the suffering and degradation in which the bulk of their Negro and Latin American fellow citizens lived. It was a city in which many of its ministers sought, as one of them put it, to preserve their "effectiveness" by not asking their congregations to involve themselves meaningfully in relieving the suffering of their brothers in the minority groups. It was a city whose Negro and Latin American business and professional men were failing to provide any substantial leadership in human-rights matters for members of their respective ethnic groups. It was a city in which the federal poverty program, as then conducted, could not even begin to touch the heart of the city's troubles. It was a city, like most cities of the North and West, whose employment patterns had not yet been touched substantially by the Civil Rights Act of 1964. It was a city in which no national organization in the civil-rights field was hazarding any significant effort to assist the masses of Negroes and Latin Americans. It was a city that was still wasting the most important resources

[85] *The Austin Statesman* (July 6, 1967), p. 1.

it had. It was a city headed for the deepest of troubles in human relations that had engulfed so many other cities in the four previous summers.[86]

The failure of Austin, as one of the more advanced of our Southern communities, to begin to deal in the 1960's in an adequate way, through official action, with its civil-rights problem raises the question of whether its failure is likely to be repeated in other cities in the state and in the South and Southwest. In late 1967 it is correct to say that most of Texas' twenty-one urban centers and most of its smaller towns and cities either have not yet reached or have not progressed beyond the point that Austin has reached, of actually debating concrete legislative proposals for dealing with human-relations problems. By and large, the same is true throughout the South and Southwest where the Negro and Latin American ethnic groups are in the numerical minority. This failure in other sites of confrontation with human-relations problems, plus the fact that substantially the same or even worse conditions in human relations obtain in these localities, indicates that the experience in Austin contains valuable lessons not only about the probable course of events when the confrontation does take place, but also for the action persons should take in seeking progress in human relations in these and, indeed, in other areas as well.

Another Texas city, Corpus Christi, in 1964 became the first government at any level in the states of the old Confederacy to enact a civil-rights ordinance prohibiting discrimination against minority groups that was enforceable through an official human-relations commission and the courts.[87] The experience of this city confirms the lessons indicated by the experience of Austin. Despite the good beginning in Cor-

---

[86] On August 15, 1967, the Austin City Council held its first informal "workshop" session with representatives of most significant civil-rights and ethnic-group organizations in the city that had been active in seeking improvements in human relations and various kinds of opportunities. Mayor Harry Akin expressed his concern that justice be done by the city government in its dealings with minority groups and that opportunities be opened to them throughout the community. On May 17, 1968, the Council adopted, by a three to two vote, a fair housing ordinance substantially similar to Title VIII of the Civil Rights Act of 1968. Opponents, through a petition signed by 26,000 citizens, immediately forced a referendum (yet to come at this writing) on the ordinance. Just as a principal reason for enactment of the late 1967 ordinance was the spreading conflagration of the urban riots, so the enactment of the 1968 ordinance was deeply influenced by the nation's, and the city's reaction to the report of the President's Advisory Commission on Civil Disorders and to the killing of the Reverend Dr. Martin Luther King. [*The Austin American* (August 15, 1967), p. 1].

[87] See Appendix C of this book.

pus Christi, a University of Texas School of Law civil-rights seminar study in December 1964 revealed that the city human-relations commission had seriously failed in its efforts to resolve underlying human-relations problems.[88] While discrimination in public accommodations had been almost completely eliminated—in the main without the necessity for commission action—no substantial progress had been accomplished in other pressing areas of discrimination. The existence and the work of the commission received almost no publicity in the daily papers. Several members of the commission had not been actively discharging their duties. The remaining members of the commission were making no efforts to move the city council to strengthen the hand of the commission by grants of needed procedural authority, a more adequate budget, and authority to employ a full-time staff of human-relations specialists. Latin Americans had begun to turn to other organizations to obtain the needed leadership in human relations. Commission members had lost their enthusiasm for their work. They had established no goals for the community in human relations nor worked out policies and a timetable for realizing them. They had held no public hearings upon problems of discrimination although authorized to do this under their constitutive ordinance. By and large, the Negro and Latin American ethnic groups were lacking in leaders who could organize effective group action for the amelioration of the discrimination and disadvantages being suffered by these groups. Meanwhile, the Anglo group, despite the well-meaning efforts and intentions of some of its members, had made little more effort than its counterpart in Austin to confront and resolve the human-relations problems of Corpus Christi.

The failure of Austin and Corpus Christi, two of the more advanced Southern communities, to deal in an adequate way through official action with their civil-rights problem indicates that each community facing a serious problem of discrimination against minorities passes through a kind of social thought process. At first the community is generally unaware or unmindful of the terrible social costs of discrimination. Some members of that community are made aware of that problem and seek to eliminate it by voluntary means. They attain some degree of success, but the knottier and larger problems of discrimination remain unsolved. Eventually leaders representing all ele-

[88] Robert A. DeWitt and Frank G. Jones, "A Study of the Corpus Christi Human Relations Commission," (unpublished civil-rights seminar paper, The University of Texas School of Law, September 17, 1965), pp. 22–58.

ments in the community come to see that the use of law to deal with
discrimination is no different from the use of law to deal with other
modern public problems. They then develop indigenous forms of law
calculated to deal more effectively with this especially sensitive and
different area of public problems. The first step is usually the creation
of an official human-relations commission to conciliate grievances
growing out of discrimination and to study the problem and its possible remedies. The next step is to strengthen the hand of the commission so as to put the authority of government into the effort to eliminate discrimination and create equal opportunities for minority
groups. The process by which a community matures and addresses itself effectively to its civil-rights problem takes time and the speed with
which it moves depends upon the kind of leadership that is brought to
bear both from outside and from within the community.

The Civil Rights Acts of 1964–1968 are examples of leadership
provided to communities from without. The same is true of state
civil-rights legislation for communities within the enacting state.
When the 1964 act was enacted, Austin and Corpus Christi already
had a considerable degree of integration in public accommodations.
The act hastened a change, already partially completed, in the character and action of the majority group. It elicited a response from
each community that was simply waiting to be elicited. This illus-
trates one type of situation in which civil-rights legislation by an authority outside a local community can be most useful: the situation in
which some of the majority still discriminate and in which the majority as a whole is not yet capable of enacting a just law to deal with the
problem.

There are other areas of discrimination in communities that do not
respond as well to the enactment or even enforcement of civil-rights
legislation by the government of the state or of the nation. In Austin,
for example, almost all private employers and the city, county, and
state governments continued in 1967 to discriminate in employment
against both Negroes and Latin Americans. Only certain private employers are covered by the 1964 federal act and, by and large, they
have made no move to comply. The willingness of the community to
abide by law, in the case of employment, amounts to no more than
waiting for the law to be invoked against individual employers who
will then comply to the extent necessary. In order for this federal law
to be effective, it will have to be invoked by those affected by discrimination in employment and applied by the federal agency and courts

charged with its enforcement to individual employers. The process of enforcement will be a long and tedious one.

What is true of Southern and Southwest cities relative to the 1964 federal act prohibiting employment discrimination is true of Northern and Western cities relative to state laws prohibiting discrimination in employment, housing, home financing, unions, and other fields. As will be seen in subsequent discussion in this book, discrimination in these fields continues substantially unabated in Northern and Western cities although modern state legislation covering all or some of the discrimination has been in force from five to twenty years. Most Negro and Latin American children in these cities attend schools that are all Negro or all Latin American—*de facto* segregation resulting from housing, employment, and other forms of discrimination. These schools frequently are older and less well-equipped to prepare their students for the future than are other schools in the community. Moreover, the resulting isolation of Negro and Latin American children from Anglo children prevents the adequate preparation of all for integration of these minorities into community life. Living conditions of the Negro and Latin American groups in their Northern and Western urban ghettos are the worst in these areas. Landlords frequently fail to comply with local building and sanitary regulations so that the health, safety, and welfare of their minority-group tenants are badly prejudiced, and, despite complaints, local officials do not enforce these regulations. Underlying all this is the havoc created by unemployment and underemployment (generally at lower incomes), for a very large percentage of families, the poverty status forced upon minority groups by the discrimination and disadvantages encountered by them.

With respect to the discrimination in employment, housing, financing, unions, and similar fields throughout this country—discrimination that has proved impervious to federal and state legislation—if a change for the better is to be achieved in the foreseeable future, it will come only because the local leadership is moved to seek improvement in the defective character of the majority group so that it will begin to recognize and to deal justly with the civil-rights problem of minority groups created by its action. Any legislative or executive civil-rights program by a government extrinsic to a local or state community will be grossly deficient if it does not recognize and build upon this fact. Substantial change in the character and action of the majority group in a community will result only from a force that moves from within that community. This change from within can be elicited, encouraged, assisted, and perhaps even prodded from without. But the dialectic by which it is accomplished depends in essence upon the awakening of the social conscience of the community itself and upon the development of an active local minority as well as an effective local leadership within the majority group to guide the process and to maximize the concrete local opportunities for improving majority-minority group community relations. The 1964–1968 federal acts provide no substantial means at present for meeting the civil-rights problem in Southern communities any more than it does in Northern and Western communities. The same is true of state legislation relative to the latter communities. This is due to the fact that neither the federal acts nor any state act concerning civil rights focus upon development of effective leadership within the majority group at the local community level relative to human-relations problems.

We have observed that the legislator concerned with solving the civil-rights problem of minority groups must attack the first major aspect of this problem—the majority group as its cause—by seeking an adjustment in the character as well as the actions of that group. He must also focus upon a second major aspect of the problem: the minority group that suffers from the discrimination and disadvantages imposed upon it by the majority group. In regarding the minority group, the legislator meets a whole array of needs, difficulties, and deficiencies to which he must in some adequate way respond. In the case of our Negro and Latin American minorities, decades upon decades of discrimination have deeply marred the capacity of each as a group to achieve a readjustment of its lot in our society without substantial assistance. Legislative action must be directed toward enabling each minority to make a satisfactory adjustment of its status. As in the case of the majority group, this legislative action must be directed at the local level where the necessary adjustment of the majority- and minority-group relations must take place.

The needs, difficulties, and deficiencies of our Negro and Latin-American minorities are sixfold. First, each minority requires current protection from specific discriminatory acts and disadvantages which he is suffering because of his race or nationality. This discrimination involves denial of opportunities—irrespective of personal merit or capacity—for employment, housing, financing, public accommodations, education, and other basic requirements for decent living. Unless the current widespread discrimination against these minorities is eliminated, they cannot even begin to achieve a satisfactory readjustment of their status in our society. Of course, the need for elimination of some forms of this discrimination is more pressing than the need for eliminating other forms, as in the case of employment discrimination. Secondly, these minorities require an official agency or body that will receive and fairly dispose of complaints of discrimination. Unless there is an effective official body of this sort, the discrimination that is currently most widespread and harmful will continue to proliferate its effects upon both the majority and minority groups. The vicious circle has to be broken by enactment of a law which prohibits the discrimination and by its effective enforcement by an official agency of government. Furthermore, such an agency should provide a societal safety valve by which the tensions that are building up in the minority group can be vented and the majority group made to confront the civil-rights problem it has produced. Indeed, these latter two effects of an official agency may outweigh in value the first one. This agency should be a local one if it can be constituted so as to operate effectively in dealing with discrimination on the local scene. A local agency over the long haul can be more responsive to local complaints and can achieve greater effectiveness with the local majority group. In any event, the policy of the state and federal governments should eventually be to promote the establishment of local agencies to subserve the function just outlined.

A third need of the Negro and Latin American minorities is for someone to represent their interests actively and vigorously before the holders of public and private authority when they are making decisions affecting the public. These holders of authority presently belong overwhelmingly to the majority group. Their decisions can vitally affect the opportunities available to members of a minority group. Even if, as by a sudden stroke of societal good fortune, overt discrimination against the Negro and Latin American were to be eliminated, there would still remain the countless ways in which subtle discrimination could be practiced and go untouched because not susceptible to proof. More important than this, however, are the countless ways in which a sympathetic decision-maker can act affirmatively to improve opportunities available to these minorities and to communicate this availability to them. These minorities desperately need an official agency which, because constituted by and having an entree to the majority group, will seek actively and vigorously to place before its decision-makers the needs of these minority groups and the societal gains to be produced by subserving these needs fairly and capaciously. This function is very difficult, if not impossible, for these minorities presently to perform because of the small degree of communication that is possible between them and the majority group. An official agency to perform this function has well been called a "bridge" between the two groups. Obviously, here again, a local agency is in a far better position to be effective than either a state or a federal agency. It is more likely to understand the particular local opportunities that can be opened to these minorities and it can be more effective in moving the leadership of the majority group to make them available.

A fourth need of the Negro and Latin American minorities is the attainment of greater solidarity and effectiveness in both intragroup and intergroup actions aimed at presenting demands for fairer treatment to the majority group. A concomitant need is protection of these minorities from hostile elements of the majority group when they engage in these actions. Despite what has been called its new racial solidarity, the Negro minority still lacks at the crucial local levels the developed capacity for effective group action to promote group interests. This is even more the case with the Latin American minority. The greatest assurance of fair treatment of a group in a community is its effectiveness in putting its case before that community and in bringing various kinds of legitimate pressure to bear to ensure that a favorable response will be forthcoming. Legislation truly responsive to the civil-rights problem must seek to develop a method by which wise and vigorous leadership among the members of the minority at local levels can be encouraged and assisted. Here we find a very close parallel with the previously discussed problem of developing leadership within the majority group. Unless there is an able leadership within the Negro and Latin American minorities at each local level, one of the truly important ingredients for changing the status of that minority will be missing. A group that is lethargic about its status and treatment in a community achieves very little for itself. Within the Negro and Latin American minorities on local scenes are a large number of people who are fearful and timid, and have little hope of changing the present state of affairs. With many the reluctance to join in group actions comes from lack of experience and knowledge about group actions and the long-ingrained habit of accepting the *status quo*. Many also are justifiably fearful that involvement in the civil-rights controversy will cause them to lose their jobs or will otherwise prejudice their economic future. In some areas of our country many are justifiably fearful of physical violence, visited upon themselves or their homes and churches. Whether the fear be of economic reprisal or of physical violence, however, large numbers of the Negro minority are kept from joining more vigorously in group actions for the advancement of group interests by intimidation. The development of effective group leadership and action is to that extent greatly hindered. For this reason legislation that seeks to subserve the fourth need of these minorities now being considered must also aim at assuring protection of Negroes, Latin Americans, and others who engage in action designed to present minority claims for fair treatment to the majority group. Again, preferably, this protection should come from a local source. It certainly must, however, be provided from some official source.

A fifth need of the Negro and Latin American minorities is assistance for individuals of the groups who become involved in tension incidents. At first sight this appears to be a problem similar to the protection of minority persons who engage in group actions to advance group interests. While at times a tension incident may bear the possibility for widespread intergroup conflict, it does not, as defined here, result from an effort by minority persons to engage in group action. It arises in a more mundane way. A Negro family moves into a white neighborhood. A Negro boy is accused of stealing a book at an integrated school. A Negro neighborhood, on hearing of a rodent-control campaign with house-to-house inspection, fears that this is a prelude to movement of families out of the area and the necessity for finding other housing (something that is always difficult for Negroes to do). These are occasions when tensions are likely to rise with fear, anguish, and anger coming to dominate the relations between individuals of the majority and minority groups. If not adequately resolved, these tensions can lead to serious violence and further tensions in cumulative fashion. Moreover, as in the last example, the tension may arise as a result of lack of understanding by minority individuals about the purposes of the majority group. To deal with tension incidents the only practicable instrument is a local agency with intimate knowledge of the community and the leadership in both majority and minority groups. This local agency by assisting these two groups to work together in resolving each tension incident calmly and rapidly can prevent these matters from developing into dangerous community problems.

A sixth need of the Negro and Latin American minorities is assistance in obtaining employment, union membership, education, skills training, housing, use of public accommodations, political status, and the opportunity to become owners and managers of business concerns. At the present time these groups especially need assistance in obtaining opportunities for employment and in preparing to take advantage of these opportunities when they are made available. Today these groups face an acute economic crisis throughout the country. The precise nature of this crisis will be developed at a later point when an evaluation is made of the work of state human-relations commissions in attempting to eliminate the barriers to equal employment opportunities. It suffices here to say that the crisis for the Negro and the Latin American is one of widespread unemployment with public relief for the unemployed; concentration in the lowest-skilled and lowest-paid jobs in the economy for those who are employed, with a median pay that is only about one-half that earned by Anglos; constant elimination of the lowest-skilled jobs (largely held by Negroes and Latin Americans) due to automation; absence of Negroes and Latin Americans from training programs conducted by business and union managers for the higher skills; difficulty even for those with the necessary skills in obtaining memberships in unions and employment in the higher-skilled jobs in business concerns; and, on top of all of these economic disadvantages, higher prices and rentals produced by a booming economy.

The task of facilitating the movement of these minorities into training and jobs and the reception of them by businesses and unions is truly gargantuan. A substantial start with this job must be made. It must be performed on thousands of local scenes across the country and by many persons and groups, both public and private. While, undoubtedly, substantial public funds must be expended to support the process of training and assistance, this will be far from sufficient to bring change in the degree of skills training generally possessed by these minority workers or to secure their entrance into jobs requiring the higher skills. A variety of problems will be encountered. Apprenticeship programs are sponsored by unions and employers. Negroes and Latin Americans are reluctant to apply for admission to these programs and to many types of jobs: since they have long been excluded from such programs and jobs because of their race or nationality, they are fearful of rejection and doubtful of obtaining fair treatment. Moreover, many Negroes and Latin Americans are not aware of the nature and crucial value of apprenticeship programs. Information is not readily available to them about what apprenticeship programs exist and their comparative value, or about where and by whom they are offered. Information programs need to be established in each local area to publicize apprenticeship programs and job opportunities as they are opened to these minorities.

When minority-group persons do apply for apprenticeship programs or jobs, many are likely to be handicapped in qualifying, for a number of reasons. Frequently, they have received poor counseling in their schools and homes which keep them from making the best possible presentation of their qualifications. In addition, because applicants have lacked information about the entrance requirements for these programs, many of them have failed to observe preliminary training essential to admission. Still further, many minority youth, simply because they have come from slum areas and undergone slum influences, have had trouble with the police or have developed emotional problems which keep them from getting along with others. They may have manners or ways of speaking that are different than those of the majority group. These youth, when properly handled during a period of probation, can develop skills and adjust to their new environments as well as other youth. Still, their past records and their personal qualities will weigh heavily against them with unions and employers considering their applications. It seems clear that if large numbers of minority youth are to be moved into apprenticeship programs and the higher-skills jobs, unions and employers must be persuaded to establish a probationary status for those with these. Still further, most minority youths will require much better counseling than they have received concerning how to apply for training and jobs, and what preliminary training to seek to achieve their objectives. These and many other related practical problems confront those attempting to assist the Negro and Latin American to prepare for and to obtain the training and jobs essential to their enjoyment of equal opportunity in our society.

In this chapter we have looked at the civil-rights problem of the nation concerning its minority groups from the standpoint of the legislator who must eventually address legislation to this problem in a meaningful way. There is another important viewpoint beyond that of the legislator or, for that matter, of any official of government. This is the viewpoint of persons in private life and of organizations interested in effectively dealing with the civil-rights problem of minority groups. Only limited success by private groups can be expected in most of the Deep South where the Negro is a minority numerically. Here the federal government must provide the essential momentum and direction in efforts to resolve the civil-rights problems of minority groups. The efforts of private groups at the outset have had to be that of serving as "shock troops" in this area. But in the more advanced communities in the South and Southwest and in the rest of the country persons in private life and private organizations may and should take upon themselves an important role in the solution of the civil-rights problem of minority groups. The mere existence of local and state civil-rights law is not enough to assure the necessary change that must be effectuated in the treatment and conditions of minority groups. There must be a structure and momentum within the community itself that is conducive to the effectuation of civil-rights policy.

Each of the more advanced communities of the South and Southwest and of the rest of the country has a majority group that strongly resists change in the treatment and conditions of minority groups in some important respects. On the other hand, there is great potential in these communities for immediate and long-range change in the treatment and conditions of minority groups. The enactment of appropriate civil-rights laws at all levels of government is, of course, essential for effectuating this change. But there is just as much, if not more, need for careful organization and direction of the majority and minority groups for the purpose of dealing with human-relations problems until this law is enacted, for promoting the enactment of this law and its gradual extension to all facets of these problems, for insuring the adequate administration of this law, and for dealing with a wide spectrum of human-relations problems that law does not or cannot adequately resolve. The organization and direction of these private efforts calls for organizational, legal, and leadership skills of the highest order. The work of the Citywide Committee for Human Rights in Austin is indicative both of the great potentiality and the difficulty in organization and direction of these organizations. The work of this and similar organizations should be carefully studied and lessons drawn in order to provide guidance for other communities.

CHAPTER

3

The Emergence of Modern Civil-Rights Legislation

In order both to ascertain the role appropriate to each type of government in our federal system in implementing, by legislation, the civil rights of minority groups and to propose statutory formulas in this field, we have examined the real nature of the civil-rights problem. It is also necessary, for accomplishing these purposes, that we look to the experience of these governments. Until very recently the bulk of the legislation had been enacted by state and local governments.[1]

Prior to 1945, legislation designed to implement the civil rights of minority groups was directed mainly to protecting their members as customers of business institutions.[2] It did not protect them against discrimination in employment, housing, union activities, governmental facilities and services, and many other areas. Moreover, this legislation was enforceable primarily through criminal adjudication and private suits for damages. It is universally conceded that judicial enforcement of this early form of civil-rights legislation was a dismal failure. In 1961, for example, although Ohio's statute prohibiting discrimination in public accommodations had been on the statute books for seventy-eight years, the state civil-rights commission found that the legislation, which was enforceable only through judicial action, was virtually ignored by most businesses.[3]

[1] See the Appendices of this book.
[2] See Appendix V to the opinion of Mr. Justice Douglas in *Bell v. Maryland*, 378 U.S. 226 at 284–285 (1964) and William Graves, *Fair Employment Practice Legislation in the United States: Federal-State-Municipal* (Washington, D.C.: U.S. Government Printing Office, 1951), pp. 15–22.
[3] Ohio Civil Rights Commission, *Third Annual Report* (1962), p. 9.

The principal reason advanced for the failure of this legislation is the heavy load of enforcement activity which has made prosecutors slow to file criminal actions of this type. Another reason offered is the fact that criminal enforcement of legislation is a spotty proposition with the borderline or sophisticated type of violations going largely unquestioned. Underlying both reasons, however, is the fact that criminal enforcement of civil-rights legislation is inherently incapable of providing the necessary tools for continuous supervision and adjustment of the sensitive problems of human relations. Private suits as a mode of enforcement of this legislation failed largely due to lack of funds by minority plantiffs to pay for bringing them and the futility of attempting to prove substantial pecuniary damages.

The modern civil-rights problems first emerged as a pressing public issue during World War II, in two different ways. The war created a tremendous need for using all available manpower in the defense effort, due to the vast expansion in our production.[4] Despite this need, the many new jobs created in war industries were given primarily to white workers who had been either unemployed or employed in less-well-paid jobs.[5] Employment of white workers continued to be the rule during the first two years of our defense effort, even when acute shortages of labor developed in these industries.[6] A widespread resistance to employment of Negroes had formed throughout the North and West, partly because of the movement of Southern white workers into the war industries.[7] The result was that Negroes were prevented from profiting from the war boom as much as white workers had. Indeed, unemployment among Negroes increased due to reduction during the war of the types of jobs they performed and their exclusion from war production industries. Even when Negroes were admitted to these industries they were relegated to the lower-paid jobs. There was, however, no discrimination in inducting Negroes into the armed forces. Although treated as second-class citizens on the home front, they were

---

[4] Louis Ruchames, *Race, Jobs, and Politics: The Story of the F.E.P.C.* (New York: Columbia University Press, 1953), pp. 11–21; Duane Lockard, "The Politics of Anti-Discrimination Legislation," *Harvard Journal of Legislation*, Vol. 3 (1965), p. 1. The first of these contains an excellent summary statement of the conditions leading to establishment of the first Federal Fair Employment Practice Committee.

[5] Ruchames, *Race, Jobs, and Politics*, p. 12.

[6] U.S. Fair Employment Practice Committee, *First Report* (Washington, D.C.: U.S. Government Printing Office, 1945), pp. 89–90.

[7] Gunnar Myrdal, *An American Dilemma: The Negro Problem and Modern Democracy*, 2 vols. (New York: Harper & Bros., 1944), I, 410; II, 736–926.

required to risk their lives like first-class citizens on foreign shores. The situation, particularly after our entry into the war, presented a golden opportunity for the Negro protest movement which had become institutionalized for the first time early in this century.

In 1941 Negro organizations demanded with renewed vigor that the Negro be accorded full equality in community life.[8] The principal target of their efforts was discrimination in employment by war industries and federal agencies. Negro leaders formed a March-on-Washington Committee in January 1941 to plan a march on the nation's capital to protest this discrimination and urge remedial measures. Earlier governmental measures during the defense effort had proved inadequate. Finally on June 25, 1941, President Roosevelt, faced with the imminent threat of the projected march, issued an executive order reaffirming the federal policy against discrimination in employment by employers and unions in defense industries and by federal governmental agencies on the basis of race, creed, or national origin.[9] This order also established a Committee on Fair Employment Practice to implement this policy. By this and a subsequent order[10] the Committee was authorized to receive and investigate complaints of discrimination covered by the order, to hold public hearings, to make findings of fact, and to take appropriate steps to eliminate discrimination when it was found to exist. While the Committee had no authority to enforce its determinations in the courts, it was able to employ with good effect the technique of reasoned argument in mediation of disputes, as well as publicity concerning the facts of discrimination.

During the five years of its existence the Committee received around 12,000 complaints of discrimination in employment; 80 per cent of these involved allegations of discrimination against Negroes and 10 per cent against Jews. During the critical period from July 1943 to January 1945 the Committee received 7,245 complaints.[11] Of these,

---

[8] Ruchames, *Race*, pp. 11, 13–21; Myrdal, *An American Dilemma*, I, 414–415; II, 850–852.

[9] Exec. Order No. 8802, *Federal Register*, Vol. 41 (Washington, D.C.: U.S. Government Printing Office, June 25, 1941), p. 4544.

[10] Exec. Order No. 9346, *Federal Register*, Vol. 43 (May 27, 1943), p. 8652.

[11] U.S. Fair Employment Practice Committee, *First Report*, p. 2. There were 1,052 cases pending on July 1, 1943, representing a carry-over from the first committee's operations [*Id.*, p. 16]. In 1944 the second committee docketed 3,458 additional cases [U.S. Fair Employment Practice Committee, *Final Report* (Washington, D.C.: U.S. Government Printing Office, 1947), p. iii]. This plus the complaints referred to in the text indicate that a total of at least 11,782 complaints were re-

1,442 or 20 per cent were not placed on the case docket because the Committee's staff considered that the Committee had no jurisdiction over them. These complaints undoubtedly involved many actual situations of discrimination that went uncorrected. Including the cases carried over from the Committee's earlier operation, 6,855 cases were on the docket during this period. Of these, 4,801 cases were closed by official action. Of the cases closed, 45 per cent were dismissed by the examiner or staff on the basis of an investigation which revealed either a lack of merit in the complaint or insufficient evidence to support it. In 7 per cent of the cases the complainant withdrew the complaint before official action was taken. In 36 per cent of the cases closed, the examiner or staff determined that discrimination did exist but was able by conciliation and persuasion to adjust the matter satisfactorily through obtaining an agreement of the respondent to cease the discrimination and to implement a fair-employment-practices program. In the remaining approximately 12 per cent of cases closed, the examiner or staff dismissed the cases for lack of jurisdiction or for some other reason, such as death of the complainant or closing of the business of the party charged. In many of these cases discrimination undoubtedly had occurred and was not remedied. In forty-five of all the cases it handled, the examiner or staff was unable to secure a satisfactory adjustment by mediation of discriminatory practices that had been determined to exist.[12] In these cases a public hearing was then held and upon a formal finding that discrimination had been practiced by the respondent, the Committee issued a directive to the respondent to cease and desist from these practices. When thirty-six of the forty-five respondents refused to comply with the directive, the Committee was powerless to compel obedience.

Preceding and paralleling the federal action, the governor of New York in March 1941 appointed a Committee on Discrimination in Employment within the New York State Council of Defense.[13] This agency, also acting without enforcement authority, was able to adjust satisfactorily over 95 per cent of the approximately 1,000 cases of discrimination in employment presented to it. Despite the limited nature of

---

ceived by the two committees. Undoubtedly additional complaints were received but not docketed due to lack of jurisdiction prior to July 1, 1943, and in 1945.

[12] John Huddle, "Fair Practice in Employment," *Editorial Research Reports,* I (1946), 43.

[13] Graves, *Fair Employment Practices,* p. 28.

their operations and the difficulties in dealing with recalcitrant employers and unions, the federal and New York Committees had a salutary effect upon the employment of members of minority groups. Negro employment in the war industries increased substantially in many urban areas after the middle of 1942.[14] Undoubtedly the technique of persuasion utilized by these committees combined with other forces to produce this result. The other factors were the acute wartime labor shortage and the employer's patriotism or dislike of exposure through publicity. The experience of these committees proved that implementation of either a national or state policy against racial and religious discrimination in employment could be satisfactorily accomplished only through legislation providing an administrative agency with effective authority to enforce that policy.[15]

The modern civil-rights problem also emerged as a pressing public issue in another way during World War II. As employment opportunities for Negroes in war industries began to open, after mid-1942, many Negroes in the South moved to the great urban production areas of the North, Midwest, and Far West. In 1940 some 24 per cent of all Negroes lived in Northern urban centers as a result of earlier migrations beginning with World War I and the depression of the thirties.[16] During the war approximately 700,000 additional Southern Negroes migrated to Northern as well as Western urban areas.[17] By 1960, as a result of the new migration, nearly 48 per cent of all Negroes lived outside the South, chiefly in the twelve largest urban areas.[18] During the war Los Angeles had a 78 per cent and San Francisco a 227 per cent increase in Negro population.[19] The Chicago-Gary area and Cleveland each had 18 per cent increases.

Detroit was one of the chief centers receiving this Negro migration and as a result its Negro population grew by 45 per cent.[20] Attracted by high wartime wages, some 300,000 Southern white persons and

[14] U.S. Fair Employment Practice Committee, *First Report*, pp. 88–91.

[15] U.S. Fair Employment Practice Committee, *Final Report*, p. 5.

[16] Myrdal, *An American Dilemma*, I, 183.

[17] U.S. Fair Employment Practice Committee, *Final Report*, pp. 50–83, 92–93; *Encyclopedia Britannica Book of the Year* (1945), p. 486; Davis McEntire, *Residence and Race* (Berkeley: University of California Press, 1960), p. 11.

[18] Charles Silberman, "The City and the Negro." *Fortune*, Vol. 70 (March, 1962), p. 88.

[19] U.S. Fair Employment Practice Committee, *Final Report*, p. 93.

[20] *Ibid.*

Negroes came to Detroit between 1940 and 1943.[21] In all there were some 500,000 white Southern-born persons and 210,000 Negroes in this city of 1,500,000 in 1943.[22] Housing was almost unavailable to Detroit's wartime newcomers and particularly to Negroes. The latter had to live crowded together in a filthy, smelly, dive-ridden district called Paradise Valley, described at the time as the most intensely crowded urban area in the country. With their pockets filled with war wages, Negroes became determined to overcome the discrimination that confined them largely to the Paradise Valley area. In need of recreation, Negroes also began to use one of the only two major parks then existing in the city. A large segment of the white population resented their use of the park and determined to prevent Negroes from moving into other areas of the city. White opposition to the Negro was enflamed by the Ku Klux Klan which had been organized some twelve years earlier in the city. Negroes were unable to use taxicabs in the city and very few were employed on the city's large police force. Some 2,500 white evangelists, many of whom were members of the Klan, held forth in the city, typically advocating, in and out of their pulpits, that the Negro be kept in his accustomed place in society. In February 1942 the federal government prepared to open a new housing project designed to relieve the housing shortage being encountered by Negroes. At one time due to white pressure, the project had been rescheduled for use by whites but this plan was dropped as a result of counter-pressure from Negroes. On opening day a mob of 1,200 white persons with knives, clubs, and guns gathered before the project ready to fight to prevent Negro tenants from entering. As the new tenants approached, shots rang out. Some eighteen persons were injured in the melee that followed.

During the next fifteen months tensions continued to mount in Detroit between the white and Negro groups as hate organizations continued their efforts. It was generally recognized that the situation was a tinder box of racial passion likely to go up in flames at any time. In early 1943 a series of anti-Negro hate strikes were staged by white workers. On the 25th of March a strike was held at the Vickers plant when 2 Negroes were promoted. On the 27th of May, 20,000 white workers at Packard Company struck to protest the upgrading of 3

---

21 *Encyclopedia Britannica Book of the Year* (1944), p. 580.

22 George Brown, "The Truth about the Detroit Riot," *Harpers*, Vol. 187 (November, 1943), p. 488. The report that follows concerning the conditions leading to the Detroit race riot of 1943 is based largely upon this article.

Negroes. Finally, on Sunday, June 20, a mixed crowd of nearly 100,000 gathered at Belle Isle Park, located on an island in the Detroit River, to enjoy a day of recreation. A fight broke out between a Negro and a white man. Soon the fighting spread. Some 200 white sailors joined in the fighting against Negroes. False rumors spread among each of the racial groups to the effect that certain abhorrent criminal acts had been committed by the other group. This stimulated further violence. Incited by persons who allegedly belonged to the Klan, white persons formed into mobs of 800 to 1,000 persons. They roamed the streets attacking Negroes riding in their automobiles and on street cars. Negroes were pulled from cars and assaulted. Their automobiles were overturned and burned. By 3:00 A.M. Monday morning, the mobs were breaking into the fronts of stores and looting shelves. Fighting continued throughout Monday. By 4:00 P.M., when the high schools were dismissed, bands of Negro and white boys fought with each other. At 6:30 P.M. 4 white boys shot a middle-aged Negro who was waiting for a street car. The governor declared limited martial law shortly thereafter. Finally, at 11:55 P.M. President Roosevelt issued a proclamation dispatching federal troops to assist local and state officials in restoring order. By morning 6,000 troops had arrived and moved into position in the critical areas. With this the race riot was ended. In all 34 persons had been killed of whom 26 were Negroes.[23] Nearly 700 persons were injured. Some $2,000,000 in property damage had been inflicted.

Many of the conditions that obtained in Detroit also existed in other urban centers.[24] In the period between July 1943 and December 1944 there were some forty strikes over racial issues affecting 286,000 employees throughout the country.[25] In addition there were many labor disputes involving racial issues that did not culminate in strikes. Negroes typically were confined to crowded ghettos. Despite the passing of the depression many Negroes were on relief rolls. In 1941, for example, about 46 per cent of all Negroes in Chicago received direct relief.[26]

In Los Angeles, prior to the Detroit riot, soldiers and sailors had

---

[23] *Newsweek*, Vol. 22 (July 5, 1943), pp. 35–36.

[24] Turner Catledge, "Behind Our Menacing Race Problem," *The New York Times Magazine* (August 8, 1943), p. 7.

[25] U.S. Fair Employment Practice Committee, *First Report*, pp. 79, 83.

[26] U.S. Fair Employment Practice Committee, *Final Report*, p. 65; Myrdal, *An American Dilemma*, II, 755.

attacked young Latin Americans and Negroes who were wearing what were then called "zoot-suits."[27] Rioting, which began on June 3, 1942, continued for six days. Two hundred Anglo sailors had decided to take the law in their own hands after a group of eleven sailors had been set upon by a gang of boys in a Latin American neighborhood. Police made no serious efforts to stop the marauders who went about the city threatening Latin Americans with violence if they did not remove their zoot-suits. In the early stages they simply set upon individual young Latin Americans leaving them lying on the pavement, beaten and injured. Los Angeles newspapers heralded the work of the servicemen as dealing with roughnecks. They warned that the Mexican zoot-suit wearers were planning to retaliate as a group. On the evening of June 7th a mob of several thousand Anglo servicemen and civilians marched through the streets of downtown Los Angeles. They forced their way into numerous movies theaters and dragged Mexican Americans and Negroes into the streets. Similarly, they halted street cars and pulled Mexican Americans and Negroes into the streets, beating them badly and stripping off their clothes. The mob started for the Negro community but decided to go to the Mexican American community when they learned members of the former would provide resistance. They continued the process of beating up Latin American youths. The police rarely interfered. Rioting by Anglo youths continued for two more days in the suburbs. The Los Angeles City Council adopted a resolution prohibiting the wearing of zoot-suits. A careful scholar has documented how the police department and the press of this misguided city and the servicemen temporarily present within it deliberately combined their efforts to produce this disgraceful outbreak.[28]

In August of the same year New York City experienced a race riot in which 5 Negroes were killed and 561 persons injured.[29] This riot was touched off when a New York policeman shot a Negro military policeman who had interefered with the arrest of a Negro woman in a hotel. Additional large-scale and smaller outbreaks, often related to the zoot-suit wearer, occurred throughout the country.[30] It was, however, the Detroit riot that chiefly prompted local authorities to do

[27] *Britannica Book of the Year* (1944), p. 580.
[28] Carey McWilliams, *North from Mexico: The Spanish-Speaking People of the United States* (Philadelphia: J. B. Lippincott Co., 1949), pp. 223–258.
[29] *Britannica Book of the Year* (1944), p. 580.
[30] McWilliams, *North from Mexico*, p. 256.

something about the tension in their communities between members of the majority and minority groups.

Although the Detroit mayor set up a committee to study the causes of his city's riot and to recommend measures to prevent future outbreaks, the first city to establish a committee to deal with the problem of tensions in relations between the majority and minority groups on a permanent basis was Chicago. Mayor Kelly appointed a Mayor's Committee on Race Relations in November 1943.[31] Los Angeles County and Detroit followed in that order in January 1944, with New York City acting the following month.[32] By August 1944 thirty-one cities had established official interracial committees or commissions.[33] Most of these were brought into existence by the chief executive of the local government. They were poorly financed. Chicago and Detroit appropriated only $25,000 and $15,000, respectively, at the outset. These figures had been increased only to $50,000 each by 1951.[34] Many of these cities appropriated no more than $10,000 for the operations of their agencies. The agencies also were given no enforcement authority to deal with individual cases of discrimination in employment, public accommodations, housing, or other matters. Thus while many of the agencies investigated complaints of discrimination in employment and public accommodations, they rather uniformly took the position that they could not be effective in eliminating this discrimination unless legislation was enacted to provide them with effective enforcement authority.

By and large, with their limited funds, these agencies have performed a fact-finding and educational function designed to acquaint their communities with the extent and nature of the discrimination and tensions existing in the area. Frequently they have been able to make recommendations for useful action on the part of municipal authorities with respect to recreational facilities and police departments.[35] In this way additional personnel were provided for under-

[31] Los Angeles County Commission on Human Relations, "Notes on the History and Activities of the Human Relations Commission," Los Angeles, July, 1963 (mimeographed); Sister Claire Marie, "A Study of the Department of Civil Rights of the Chicago Commission on Human Relations from 1943 to 1954" (unpublished master's thesis, Loyola University, Chicago, Illinois, 1956).

[32] Graves, *Fair Employment Practices*, p. 89.

[33] *American City* (August, 1944), p. 74.

[34] Pamela H. Rice and Milton Greenberg, "Municipal Protection of Human Rights," *Wisconsin Law Review* (1952), pp. 698, 701, 708–710.

[35] *Id.*, pp. 702–704.

staffed parks and trained to deal with tension situations. In Detroit, upon the Commission's recommendation, the number of Negroes on the city's police force was increased.[36] A number of the commissions, faced with complaints about police brutality and unfair court actions, arranged conferences between the municipal officials concerned and members of minority groups.[37] Although originally established to deal with race relations these commissions and committees soon discovered that the tensions which develop between various groups in a community extend well beyond racial groups. To comprehend these broader areas of concern, the committees were given more comprehensive names and functions. Within a short time, the Los Angeles County Committee for Interracial Progress became the Committee on Human Relations.[38] In 1945, when Buffalo acted by ordinance to strengthen its committee, it chose to call the committee the Board of Community Relations.[39] Pittsburgh called its first official agency, created in 1947, the Civic Unity Council.[40] Chicago, by ordinance in 1947, followed the Los Angeles example.[41] In 1955 New York City by a local law established a Commission on Intergroup Relations.[42]

Despite the broadening of their names and functions, local governmental agencies organized along the lines of committees and commissions on human relations just reviewed produced prior to the mid-fifties little substantial change in the civil-rights problem of minorities in the communities they served. Appropriately given the function of ameliorating intergroup frictions and tensions in their communities, the agencies were given inadequate tools for getting at the causes of these frictions. They lacked the authority to compel elimination of the various types of debilitating discrimination that formed one broad area of causes for these frictions. Lacking adequate staffs and budgets they were unable to develop and administer programs adequately designed to resolve the civil-rights problem in light of its underlying dual nature.

As we have seen, this nature involves, from the standpoint of the

---

[36] William Granger, "Hopeful Sign in Race Relations: Interracial Committees in the United States," *Survey Graphic*, Vol. 33 (November, 1944), p. 476.

[37] Rice and Greenberg, "Municipal Protection," p. 704.

[38] Los Angeles County Commission on Human Relations, "Notes on the History."

[39] Graves, *Fair Employment Practices*, p. 90.

[40] Louis Mason, Jr., "Equal Opportunity and the Law," Pittsburgh Commission on Human Relations (1962), p. 1 (mimeographed).

[41] Chicago, Municipal Code Ch. 21, Sec. 49–52.

[42] New York City, Administrative Code, B1-5.0, Art. 9.

majority group, basically a problem of developing a leadership within that group that can awaken the social consciousness of the community to the problem of its minorities and guide the process of maximizing upon concrete local opportunities for bettering majority-minority-group relations in the community. From the standpoint of the minority group it is a question both of developing a leadership within the group and providing assistance in enabling the group to become effective in achieving a satisfactory adjustment of its status in the community.

A recognition of the ineffectiveness of the early local and state governmental agencies organized along the lines of the committees just reviewed as well as the possibilities of fair-employment-practices legislation at these levels led to the first important modern development in the legislative implementation of civil rights of minority groups. The modest achievements of the Federal Committee on Fair Employment Practice stimulated efforts to obtain establishment of a permanent, well-financed federal agency, equipped with effective enforcement authority, to carry on its work. These efforts, beginning in 1944, continued without success in each succeeding Congress until 1964.[43] When it became evident in 1944 that these efforts would not bear early fruit, civil-rights organizations began to focus their efforts to obtain this legislation at the state level and, where state action appeared unlikely, at the local level. In March 1945, as a response to these efforts, New York State enacted a statute popularly known as the Fair Employment Practices Commission Law.[44] Using this statute as their model, twenty-nine other states enacted similar legislation between 1945 and 1965. About twenty large cities adopted similar FEPC ordinances during the same period. Minneapolis was the first city to act, in 1947. It was followed by Philadelphia (1948); Cleveland, Gary, and Youngstown (1950); Pittsburgh and River Rouge (1952); Duluth (1953); Erie (1954); St. Paul and St. Louis (1955); Baltimore (1956); Des Moines and San Francisco (1957); Canton (1958); New Haven (1964); and Louisville and South Bend (1965). The virtue of these statutes and ordinances was that they established administrative

---

[43] Will Maslow and Joseph B. Robinson, "Civil Rights Legislation and the Fight for Equality: 1862–1952," *University of Chicago Law Review,* Vol. 20 (1953), pp. 394–398; Will Maslow, "F.E.P.C.: A Case History in Parliamentary Maneuver," *University of Chicago Law Review,* Vol. 13 (1946), p. 407.

[44] See Appendices A–D of this book for citations to the legislation referred to in this paragraph.

agencies with effective enforcement authority to compel elimination of discrimination in employment against members of minority groups.

Before we attempt to assess the value of the contribution these agencies have made in implementing civil rights, we should note four general facts. In the first place, partly because the first even moderately effective work in resolving the modern civil-rights problem had been accomplished in 1942–1945 at the federal and state level, civil-rights organizations committed themselves early to the notion that a state, and ultimately a federal, agency was the ideal agency for administering civil-rights laws. The possibility that local government should have a significant, or indeed, the most significant role in solution of the civil-rights problem was hardly conceived, much less carefully investigated. The result was that the effort to obtain state agencies and their establishment operated to inhibit the creation of local agencies with effective authority to deal with the civil-rights problem. Sometimes the new statutes precluded local governments from creating agencies of this kind.[45] In other instances, state agencies as a matter of policy effectively discouraged the creation of local agencies.[46]

In the second place, because the federal agency was the model for local and state fair-employment-practices commissions, most of the new agencies were created with a view to their utilizing as almost their sole tool in eliminating discrimination in employment the tech-

---

[45] California and Michigan. See Appendix A for citations to this legislation.

[46] The New York State Commission, for example, had relied, prior to 1962, only upon "advisory councils" and had not followed the example of the Pennsylvania Commission in actively assisting local governments in setting up or expanding local human-relations commissions with enforcement authority [New York State Commission against Discrimination, *Report of Progress* (1960), pp. 85–87]. By 1962 the same Commission recognized a need for "reaching out to the people of the state," not by encouraging local governments to form local commissions with enforcement authority, but by creating additional regional offices to decentralize the work of the Commission. Citizen "advisory committees" for these regional offices were also formed. The Commission stated: "Subsequent appearances of members of the [Upper Manhattan] committee in the community, both formally and informally, were a valuable asset to the effectiveness of the local office" [New York State Commission for Human Rights, *Annual Report, 1962*, p. 51]. The Commission noted that its increase in complaint activity in the Greater New York area in 1962 was due to the opening of new branch and regional offices within the area [*Id.*, p. 3]. It also noted that its work with local governments was primarily confined to New York City [*Id.*, p. 30]. In June 1965 the New York State Legislature corrected this situation in part by making the jurisdiction of the New York City Commission on Human Rights concurrent with that of the New York State Commission for Human Rights [N.Y. Gen. Munic. Law § 239-s (Supp. 1967)]. By 1965 the State Commision was actually promoting local commissions [New York State Commission for Human Rights, *Annual Report, 1965*, p. 25].

nique of processing individual complaints of discrimination. They proceeded against discrimination only by the case method utilizing mediation and, where necessary, the formal processes of adjudication to eliminate it. In the third place, because the state agencies proved successful in handling individual complaints of discrimination in employment, state legislatures were moved, as the civil-rights problem became more pressing, to expand the jurisdiction of state agencies to cover other areas of discrimination in public accommodations, housing, and education. Again, few questioned the wisdom of relying upon a state agency rather than a local governmental agency as the primary administrator of civil-rights laws within a state. Moreover, few doubted the wisdom of using the case method as the primary technique for eliminating discrimination against minorities and creating equal opportunities for them. Thus in New York, Massachusetts, New Jersey, Oregon, Pennsylvania, and Washington the state commissions were subsequently given jurisdiction to compel by this method elimination of discrimination in public accommodations, housing, and education.[47] Many additional states have extended the original jurisdiction of their commissions to one or two additional areas of discrimination. To reflect their broader concerns these agencies were often named civil-rights or human-relations commissions. These agencies simply applied their case-method technique, without substantial modification, to resolving controversies about discrimination in the additional areas.

In the fourth place, in states where state legislation appeared unlikely at an early date, cities which were moved by civil-rights groups to enact fair-employment-practices commission ordinances often gave their commissions the function of carrying on the much broader work of earlier city human-relations committees, in addition to the function of eliminating discrimination in employment on a case basis. This additional authority was sometimes granted initially, as in the case of the Pittsburgh Commission,[48] and sometimes subsequently, as in the case of the Baltimore Commission.[49] The New York City Commission was a carry-over from an older city commission and received its first enforcement authority in the field of housing rather than in the field

[47] See Appendix A of this book.
[48] Pittsburgh, Penn., Ordinance No. 479 (1946); *Id.*, Ordinance No. 465 (1952); Mason, "Equal Opportunity," pp. 1–3.
[49] Baltimore, Md., Ordinance No. 379 (1956), *Race Relations Law Reporter*, Vol. 1 (1956), p. 1113; *Id.*, Ordinance No. 103 (1964), *Race Relations Law Reporter*, Vol. 9 (1964), p. 354.

of employment.[50] All of the city commissions in this group, around ten in number, were consequently given the function of bettering the relations in general between the majority and minority groups, of relieving community tensions, and of creating equal opportunities for minority groups, in addition to dealing with specific complaints of discrimination in employment or housing. Due to the broad scope of their functions and their closeness to the civil-rights problem, these agencies early confronted very nearly the whole spectrum of this problem. They encountered problems involving police–minority-group relations; tension incidents between members of different groups in the community; orientation of immigrant minorities to city life; adaptation of public educational and other governmental facilities to minority needs; difficulties involving housing, hospital, and medical services; and lack of leadership within both majority and minority groups. The case method of the state agencies was simply not adapted to providing a practicable or adequate mode for dealing with these problems. In light of their earlier confrontation with the whole of the civil-rights problems, a few of our major city agencies were forced, as state agencies were not, to break with the case-processing approach and to develop more adequate methods for resolving various aspects of the civil-rights problem. For this reason, the activity of these few local agencies represents in many ways a significantly different experience in dealing with the civil-rights problem of minorities from that of the states. The four facts just noted make it necessary not to rely unduly upon prior state experience in evaluating the possibilities or lack of them for resolving the civil-rights problem of minorities through use of administrative process. They also suggest that we may have much to learn about these possibilities by examination of the experience of the few well-organized local agencies that have dealt with the civil-rights problem.

---

[50] New York City, Charter and Code, Vol. 5, Tit. X, Secs. x41-1.0 to -4.0 (1962–1963 Williams Cum. Supp.).

CHAPTER

4

Commission Experience in Processing Complaints of Discrimination

While thirty-two states had by January 1968 established human-relations commissions to enforce prohibitions against discrimination directed toward minority and other disadvantaged groups, only about fifteen of these have had extensive experience with this modern form of civil-rights legislation.[1] It is extraordinarily important to study this experience in order to determine how this legislation and its administration can be made more effective. The status of majority-minority-group relations since 1963 throughout the nation emphasizes the significance of this study.

The principal weapon used by experienced state commissions for eliminating discrimination due to race, color, religion, national origin, sex, or older age, over which they have jurisdiction, is the processing, case by case, of individual charges of discriminatory practices.[2] It is evident that the civil-rights laws administered by these state commissions are designed primarily to assist people who already have the requisite ability, education, training, experience, money, facilities, and qualifications to take advantage of various kinds of opportunities generally available to members of the majority group in employment, housing, unions, training programs, public accommodations, public education, governmental facilities, and programs receiving govern-

[1] See Appendix A of this book for a complete listing of these states and citations to their legislation. Appendix E contains a table listing by states the times at which the different forms of civil-rights law enforced by human-relations commissions were enacted.

[2] Note, "The Right to Equal Treatment: Administrative Enforcement Legislation," *Harvard Law Review*, Vol. 74 (1961), p. 526; Paul H. Norgren and Samuel E. Hill (assisted by F. Ray Marshall), *Toward Fair Employment* (New York: Columbia University Press, 1964).

mental assistance. These laws are designed to assist members of minority and other disadvantaged groups who, having the requisite qualifications and means to warrant their consideration by those controlling the access to these opportunities, are being denied them because of their race, color, religion, national ancestry, sex, or older age. The number of persons in a given minority or disadvantaged group who possess these necessary qualifications or means varies, of course, with the nature of the opportunity in question. In housing, for example, the percentage of minority-group members who possess the qualifications and means is relatively high. In employment, the percentage will be relatively lower due to the employer's or union's requirement that employees or members have developed certain skills and professional qualifications. Even here, however, there is a great need for protection of employees with lesser qualifications.[3] If the minority-group employees receive less pay than majority-group employees, from the same employer for the same type of work, the damage to the former and to the community can be incalculable. If the lesser-skilled and lower-paid minority-group employees of an employer are never given an opportunity to receive the on-the-job training or promotions made available generally to majority-group employees, the damage to the former and to the community is of the same nature. If minority-group members are rarely considered for employment by or membership or participation in businesses and unions because majority-group members who are concentrated in decision-making positions turn to friends and relatives in their own group for these purposes, both the individuals affected and the community suffer greatly. With regard to many opportunities, such as public accommodations, public education, governmental facilities, welfare-assistance programs, and governmental services, the percentage of minority-group members who are qualified or have the need to obtain or to be admitted to them may be very much higher than that of the majority group. Admission to many of these opportunities on a nondiscriminatory basis can be for many minority-group persons the difference between some minimally acceptable existence and personal tragedy. Thus it is clear enough that in order for civil-rights legislation to be worth its salt it must deal with discrimination against individuals of a minority or other disadvantaged group through processing and resolving, case by case, individual complaints that allege unlawful discriminatory practices by employ-

---

[3] Norgren and Hill, *Toward Fair Employment*, pp. 17–39.

ers, governments, home owners, real-estate firms, bankers, builders, and the whole array of discriminators in the majority group. What needs to be determined, however, is the effectiveness of this device, necessary and useful as it may be, for turning back the tide of discrimination against minority and other disadvantaged groups. This is the question pursued in this chapter. What also needs to be determined, even if this device is not in itself sufficient for combating discrimination, is what improvements can be made in its use so as to make it as effective as it can be made. That question is pursued in the next chapter. Finally, the question remains concerning what other principal devices or techniques are needed to make human-relations commissions at all levels of the federal system more effective in eliminating discrimination. This question is discussed in the latter part of this book.

In order to analyze the effectiveness of case-by-case processing of individual complaints of discriminatory practices in the civil-rights field, it is essential to understand how this mode of proceeding has been accomplished by the experienced state and local human-relations commissions. It is also necessary to examine the results obtained in disposing of these complaints. Finally, it is incumbent upon us to determine the overall impact of these dispositions upon existing patterns of discrimination.

State human-relations commissions in processing complaints of discrimination in any field over which they have jurisdiction proceed basically in the same way that the wartime Federal Committee on Fair Employment Practice proceeded.[4] The central difference between their procedures and those of this first federal civil-rights agency is, of course, the availability, where conciliation measures fail, of a formal hearing procedure, the authority to issue subpoenas and orders to cease and desist from discriminatory practices, and the right to obtain judicial enforcement of these orders.

In one-third of the states having human-relations commissions as of January 1968 complaints may be filed only by the person affected by an alleged discriminatory practice.[5] In fewer than one-half of these

---

[4] U.S. Fair Employment Practice Committee, *First Report* (Washington, D.C.: U.S. Government Printing Office, 1945), pp. 18–22; Note, "The Right to Equal Treatment," *Harvard Law Review*, pp. 526–555.

[5] These states are the following: Arizona, Illinois, Indiana, Kansas, Maryland, Michigan, Nebraska, Nevada, and Utah. In a number of additional states the attorney general is also authorized to file a complaint, but, in actual fact, he has almost never exercised this authority so that the aggrieved person is the only person able

jurisdictions a complaint may also be filed either by the commission or one of its officials. When a complaint is filed, it is investigated for the purpose of developing the relevant facts essential to making an official determination of whether there is probable cause for believing the allegations of a complaint, for example, that an employer has discriminated against the individual complainant or other person because of his race, religion, national origin, or other specified basis.[6] Either a field representative of the commission's staff or a commissioner with the aid of a staff member usually conducts the investigation. The investigator first interviews the complainant and others to determine the chronological sequence of events, and the identity of persons involved in the alleged violation, the personal and educational background and employment record of the complainant, and his appearance and attitudes. The investigator next visits the employer against whom the complaint has been made. He seeks to determine whether the complainant's application for a specific job or activity is on file, whether a job opening existed at the time the application was made, what the requirements of the job are in terms of training and qualifications, what procedures are used in verifying the training and experience claims of the complainant and the person who obtained the job, whether the employer considers the complainant qualified for the job and what the basis was for his decision not to employ the complainant. The investigator also determines, in investigating the employer's overall employment policies, the number of minority-group members employed, their distribution in the various job classifications utilized, and the methods used in recruiting new workers. Many commissions consider the investigation stage in processing a complaint as a first opportunity to effectuate an immediate settlement of the case where the investigator believes it is likely that discrimination has occurred. Much of the discrimination against minorities in employment occurs as a result of misinformation and lack of understanding of the problem presented by this discrimination. The investigating official seeks, in his second role, to acquaint the employer with the fair-employment-

---

to exercise this function. These additional states include California, Hawaii, Missouri, New Hampshire, and Oregon. See Appendix A of this book for references to the laws of these states.

[6] Pennsylvania Fair Employment Practices Commission, *First Annual Report* (1957), pp. 12–14; Norgren and Hill, *Toward Fair Employment*, pp. 102–103; Note, "The Right to Equal Treatment," *Harvard Law Review*, pp. 533–540. The first reference describes in considerable detail investigational procedures rather universally employed by similar agencies.

practices provisions of the civil-rights law and the operations of the commission in administering them. Most of the cases filed with many commissions are resolved at the investigation stage. The typical case investigation of a complaint of employment discrimination will involve twelve personal interviews, letters, telephone calls, record checks, conferences, and meetings.[7] Some cases require forty or more of these investigative steps.

When the investigator files his report and if a prior settlement has not been made, the next step is the official determination of whether probable cause exists for crediting the allegations of the complaint. Usually this determination is made by a single commissioner who has been assigned responsibility for the case.[8] If he determines probable cause does not exist, he dismisses the case. If he determines that probable cause exists for crediting the allegations of the complaint, he initiates a process of conciliation by which he seeks to move the employer to eliminate the discriminatory practice relative to the individual complainant and, where appropriate, to adjust his general employment policies to preclude discrimination against minority-group members so as to provide equal opportunities for them to obtain employment.[9] The commissioner in meeting with an employer informs him that his discriminatory practice is in violation of the law and seeks to persuade him to eliminate the practice. If the employer indicates that he expects difficulties in integrating his workshop or plant, the commissioner is prepared to refer to examples of employers, including those in the same line of business, who have not encountered the supposed difficulties in integrating in compliance with the law or have met them successfully. The commissioner informs the employer that it is the commission's policy to rely heavily upon conciliation to resolve complaints and that it has established a fine record of conciliation which it wants to maintain. Every effort is made to establish an attitude of friendly understanding of the employer's problems while insisting upon some satisfactory adjustment of the complaint. The employer learns that the commission is prepared, if necessary, to take the case to a public administrative hearing, to make findings of fact, and to issue an administrative order to prevent the discriminatory practice. Most cases

[7] Pennsylvania Fair Employment Practices Commission, *Second Annual Report* (1958), p. 2.

[8] A more detailed analysis of the determination relative to probable cause appears in Chapter 5, below.

[9] A more detailed analysis of the conciliation process appears in Chapter 5, below.

involving a finding, whether informal or formal, that discrimination in employment has occurred are satisfactorily adjusted.

A typical case of alleged discrimination in employment is exemplified by the following situation:

A young, qualified Negro electrician applied for a position as an equipment installer with a large and nationally known electric company in Pittsburgh. The applicant had had considerable experience in this field. When interviewed by the crew supervisor of the company, the applicant felt he was being subjected to evasive and purposefully discouraging personnel techniques. He was told he might be unable to work with other crew members or to find housing in the Southern states in which he would have to travel extensively. When he was not employed, the applicant filed a formal complaint with the Pittsburgh Commission on Human Relations. Commission staff members then interviewed the personnel manager, district superintendent, and the branch manager of the company. They discovered that although the company was located in a substantially Negro community, fewer than 1 per cent of its employees were nonwhite. The district superintendent revealed that the company abided by a policy of honoring "customer preference" which, in Southern states, required use of all-white installation crews. When informed that this practice violated a city ordinance, the official replied it was not the intention of the company to discriminate. As the investigation proceeded, the complainant was hired by the company in a position other than that of equipment installer. He was informed, however, that he would be able to transfer to a position more related to his qualifications when he had fulfilled seniority requirements.

Although the individual grievance was satisfactorily settled during the investigation of the complaint, a finding of probable cause was made that the hiring policies of the company, as revealed by the investigation, violated the city ordinance prohibiting discrimination in employment. In the conciliation stage, the Commission proposed that the company extend its general policies of nondiscrimination in employment to that part of the organization responsible for installing office equipment. The management of the company executed a conciliation agreement by which it agreed to comply with the Commission directive.[10] A follow-up review of compliance efforts of the company indicated that its initial fears concerning the attitude of fellow crew

---

[10] *Pittsburgh Human Relations Review,* Vol. 5, No. 1 (February, 1962), p. 3.

members and the possible problems of the lone Negro employee had not materialized. Indeed, several additional qualified Negro applicants had since been employed without incident.[11]

Basically the same approach utilized by human-relations commissions in processing complaints of discrimination on the part of employers is utilized by them in processing complaints of discrimination by unions, employment agencies, operators of public-accommodations businesses, owners and other purveyors of housing, and educational institutions.

The record of the well-established state and local human-relations commissions in obtaining satisfactory adjustment of employment cases in which a finding of discrimination has been informally or formally made appears to be excellent. The experience of the Pennsylvania and Pittsburgh Commissions is typical. Almost all of the complaints of discrimination filed with them with respect to which a finding has been made that the alleged discrimination probably exists have been satisfactorily adjusted either at the stage of investigation or of conciliation without the necessity of holding a public administrative hearing or invoking the assistance of the courts. This statement applies both to the adjustment of the grievances of individual complainants and to the revision of illegal general policies of employers, unions, and employment agencies. Between 1956 and 1965 the Pennsylvania Commission processed 2,050 complaints of employment discrimination.[12] In 844 of these cases a finding of probable cause was made. In almost all of these cases a satisfactory adjustment was obtained of the problem of discrimination presented through the process of conciliation. As earlier indicated the problem resolved may have been discrimination in a particular transaction, in general employment policies and practices, or in both respects. The agreement to eliminate the discrimination was obtained in each of these cases without the necessity for holding a public administrative hearing or the issuance of a cease and desist order. Instead the conciliation technique of providing information and utilizing various types of persuasion proved effective. Of the conciliation agreements, 80 per cent executed were with employers,

[11] This sentence is a reflection of the frequent result in other actual cases. Ohio Civil Rights Commission, *Third Annual Report* (1962), pp. 21–22; Ohio Civil Rights Commission, *Fourth Annual Report* (1963), p. 12; Norgren and Hill, *Toward Fair Employment*, pp. 118–122.

[12] Pennsylvania Human Relations Commission, *Tenth Annual Report* (1965), p. 27.

8 per cent with employment agencies, and 4 per cent with unions.[13] In only a very few cases was it necessary to hold a public administrative hearing and to issue a cease and desist order. In addition to resolving satisfactorily by conciliation most of its cases of employment discrimination, about 41 per cent of its 2,050 case load, the Commission dismissed another 48 per cent of its cases on the ground that the complaint of discrimination had not been established. In this way the Commission, while serving the purpose of a sounding board and a safety valve for the airing and resolution of grievances, also appeared to have protected employers from unwarranted or mistaken charges that they had discriminated. Of the remaining 11 per cent of the total cases, half were dismissed for lack of jurisdiction and half were dismissed because the complainant failed to proceed or withdrew his complaint. Currently the Commission is handling about 324 cases of alleged employment discrimination annually and is satisfactorily adjusting by conciliation almost all of the approximately 124 cases in which it finds there is probable cause to believe discrimination exists.[14]

To the accomplishments of the Pennsylvania Commission must be added those of cities having comparable local commissions. In Pittsburgh and Philadelphia, for example, these commissions handle annually about 50 and 110 complaints of employment discrimination, respectively.[15] Since 1948 the Philadelphia Commission has satisfactorily adjusted by conciliation all of the cases in which it has found probable cause existed for believing discrimination had occurred, about 25 per cent of its total case load.[16] It has dismissed about 65 per cent of all its cases on the ground that the evidence did not establish the allegation of discrimination. Pittsburgh has had a comparable case-disposition experience. The New York State Commission disposes of approximately 800 employment-discrimination complaints annually.[17] In about 10 per cent of these cases, on the average, it finds probable cause exists for believing discrimination has occurred. Over the fifteen-year period, 1945–1960, the Commission has deemed it necessary to hold public hearings and to issue cease and desist orders

---

[13] *Id.*, p. 22.

[14] *Id.*, p. 27.

[15] *Pittsburgh Human Relations Review*, Vol. 5, No. 6 (December, 1962), pp. 1–2; Philadelphia Commission on Human Relations, *Annual Report* (1962), p. 53.

[16] Philadelphia Commission on Human Relations, *Annual Report* (1963), p. 32; *Annual Report* (1964), p. 39; *1965 Annual Report*, p. 22.

[17] New York State Commission for Human Rights, *Annual Report, 1962*, p. 14; *Annual Report, 1965*, pp. 14, 11.

in only a very few cases.[18] While 15 hearings were ordered in 1965 in employment-discrimination cases that were eventually closed, 14 of these were either not held or terminated with a conciliation agreement being executed. In light of the few public hearings it has held, the Commission similarly has been only rarely required to resort to the courts.

The experience just reviewed of these state and local commissions in dealing with employment discrimination does not differ from their experience in dealing with discrimination occurring in public accommodations, education, housing, and other areas. Moreover, their experience is typical of that of all of the thirty state and about twenty-five city commissions having enforcement authority. Almost all grievances found to be justified are resolved through conciliation agreements to eliminate the discrimination of which complaint has been made.

Perhaps the most significant factor contributing to the typical ability of a human-relations commission to dispose through the techniques of conciliation of almost all violations brought to its attention is its possession of ultimate authority to enforce compliance with the law if conciliation fails. This authority consists of the right to hold a public hearing, to compel attendance of witnesses and production of evidence through issuance of subpoenas, to issue orders to cease and desist from discrimination in appropriate cases, and to obtain judicial enforcement of its orders. The experience of human-relations commissions without this enforcement authority supports this conclusion. Kansas, for example, in 1953 enacted a statute prohibiting discrimination against minority groups,[19] but it did not provide its newly created Commission on Civil Rights with enforcement authority. For several years the Commission attempted to eliminate discrimination through education and conciliation. It encountered what its executive director described as a complete indifference and lack of cooperation on the part of businessmen. In 1961 the Commission urged the legislature to grant it enforcement authority. This request was granted. In operating under the new authority, the Commission found that most of its earlier frustrations had been removed. Its executive director reported that it now obtains almost voluntary cooperation from businessmen.[20] The Indiana Civil

[18] New York State Commission for Human Rights, *Annual Report, 1962*, pp. 49–52; *Report of Progress* (1963), p. 13; *Report of Progress* (1964); *Annual Report, 1965*, p. 11.

[19] See Appendix A of this book.

[20] Indiana Civil Rights Commission, *Toward Equal Opportunity* (1962), p. 15.

Rights Commission had much the same experience.[21] In 1962 it received 145 complaints of discrimination in the areas of employment, public accommodations, housing, and education. It obtained satisfactory adjustment in 27 of these cases but in 28 other cases in which it found discrimination had occurred it was confronted by an uncooperative respondent who completely ignored Commission proceedings and findings because he knew the law could not be enforced. In 1963 the Commission urged that it be given enforcement authority similar to that given to commissions whose experience has already been reviewed. It referred to the fact that four hundred leading citizens from thirty-three Indiana communities attending the Governor's Civil Rights Conference in 1963 had indicated that Indiana's greatest need in the civil-rights field was an enforceable law. The Indiana legislature granted the requested authority in 1963.[22]

The experience of local commissions without enforcement authority has paralleled that of the Kansas and Indiana state commissions. The Louisville Board of Aldermen in 1963 granted enforcement authority to its human-relations commission because of the inability of the commission, despite its extensive efforts to obtain voluntary integration, to persuade 35 per cent of the city's restaurants, all but one of its bowling alleys, many of its theaters, and most recreational facilities to integrate.[23] The Baltimore Equal Opportunity Commission had much the same experience in operating under its original ordinance.[24] In its 1959 annual report the Commission indicated that it had processed since its creation in excess of one hundred complaints and after investigation, had found one third of these to be valid. It characterized its record of conciliation as fair but pointed out that use of conciliation techniques without the backing of an enforcement authority did not often result in producing employment for the complainant or for the minority group of which he was a member. It stated that some employers alleged to have discriminated in employment refused to attend hearings or to obey cease and desist orders issued after a finding that they had discriminated. In 1960 the Commission requested and in 1961 was granted enforcement authority. As a result of this new au-

---

[21] *Id.*, pp. 12–15.

[22] See Appendix A of this book.

[23] Louisville [Kentucky] Human Relations Commission, *1962–3 Annual Report,* pp. 20–21, 25, 28–29.

[24] Baltimore Equal Employment Opportunity Commission, *Third Annual Report* (1959), pp. 1–12; *Annual Report* (1961), p. 7.

thority the number of complaints filed with the Commission during the next year doubled. Despite this fact the Commission was able to obtain all information it requested from employers as well as to confer with them in investigating complaints without a single refusal to co-operate. Indeed, the mere filing of a complaint moved a number of employers to act on their own initiative to resolve the complainant's grievance concerning discrimination. The Commission reported that the grant of enforcement powers to it had had many salutary effects and that the attitude of a great many of those affected by the law had been changed.

The experience so far of the Equal Employment Opportunity Commission, which was given no authority to issue cease and desist orders or to enforce them in the courts against employers, unions, and employment agencies found to have discriminated, has been similar to that of state and local commissions lacking this authority. Persons and institutions which the EEOC has determined are probably engaging in discriminatory practices are not frequently moved to discontinue these practices by the fact that they are subject to civil actions for injunctive relief by the persons aggrieved by their actions or, where there is a pattern or practice of discrimination, by the Attorney General. The great bulk of the respondents in these cases have either refused to comply with the act, refused to comply fully, or have not yet responded to attempts at conciliation. Both the Attorney General and the U.S. Commission on Civil Rights have recommended that the EEOC be given authority to hold hearings on complaints of discrimination, to issue cease and desist orders, and to obtain enforcement of them in the courts. They take the position that the EEOC's lack of enforcement power is not aided by the fact that civil actions may be filed in the courts because this remedy cannot be effective where there is widespread violation of civil rights.[25]

So far we have focused upon the ability of a human-relations commission to obtain "satisfactory adjustments" of alleged grievances, found to be probably justified, concerning discrimination. Of course, the value one ought to attach to the commission action reviewed earlier depends upon a number of factors not yet examined. One of these relates to what a "satisfactory adjustment" of a justified grievance means. Moreover, even if a "satisfactory adjustment" of a complaint of discrimination can be viewed as truly satisfactory at the time it is

---

[25] See text at notes 11–12, Chapter 1 above.

made, its ultimately satisfactory quality depends heavily upon its effect in the period subsequent to the immediate disposition of the complaint. A third factor to be considered is the wisdom of a commission in relying upon the technique of processing complaints of discrimination filed by or on behalf of individual aggrieved persons as the primary means for eliminating discrimination that is admittedly widespread in nature. Modifications of this technique and alternative techniques are available. One modification is greater reliance by the commission upon the holding of public hearings in individual grievance cases and upon the issuance of cease and desist orders, either of a consent or imposed type, that are enforceable in the courts. An alternative technique is an industry-wide approach utilizing a whole array of modern administrative methods designed to produce broad compliance throughout each industry. Even the side-effects of these techniques may well outweigh by far the direct effects upon discrimination produced by the primary technique of administration now in vogue. A fourth factor to be considered focuses once again upon the technique of processing complaints of discrimination filed by or on behalf of particular individuals. It will be recalled that the overwhelming bulk of these cases are disposed of through a commission determination that "no probable cause" exists for crediting the allegations of discrimination contained in the complaints which initiated these cases. If these determinations are well-grounded, both in law and in fact, no criticism can be made of them. On the other hand, if these determinations are not well-grounded in either law or in fact, then to the extent this is true a commission is failing to deal with cases of alleged discrimination as it should and its record of "satisfactory adjustments" becomes unrealistic. The questions just raised concerning the value of the usual method for processing complaints of discrimination utilized by state human-relations commissions will be discussed in the next chapter. Alternative methods will be examined and their value assessed. In this chapter our purpose is to examine the extent to which the total situation of discrimination in a state has been and is being changed by the action of its human-relations commission in utilizing the usual method for processing complaints of discrimination.

There is no question that the well-established state and local commissions with enforcement authority have slowly been producing some solid progress in opening up opportunities for minority groups to obtain employment, public accommodations, education, and housing to the extent of their jurisdiction in these fields. Some of these commissions have been more successful than others as a result of a number of factors to be reviewed in a subsequent section of this paper. In particular, the New York and Pennsylvania Commissions, at the state level, and the New York City, Philadelphia, and Pittsburgh Commissions, at the local level, have achieved more results than other commissions.

Continuing studies by the New York State Commission concerning the impact of its work upon employment patterns of employers involved in "satisfactorily adjusted" cases indicates that there have been substantial increases in the number of Negroes employed in professional, technical, skilled, and semiskilled categories by 85 per cent of these employers.[26] In three industries that have traditionally excluded Negroes from employment—banking, department stores, and insurance—the Commission found that over a thirteen-year period most employers previously involved in "satisfactorily adjusted" cases have substantially increased both the number of Negroes they employ and the number of occupations to which they admit Negroes.[27] In the New York public-utilities industry, which also has traditionally excluded Negroes, the employment of Negroes increased from less than 2 per cent of the industry's total work force in 1950 to 5 per cent in 1960. Negroes in this industry were also employed in a large number of semiskilled and skilled jobs. The recent Norgren-Hill private study of human-relations commissions dealing with employment discrimination regards the achievements of the New York State Commission "as a major landmark in the chronology of governmental efforts to eliminate job discrimination."[28]

In Pennsylvania a decade ago the Governor's Commission on Industrial Race Relations conducted a study of discrimination in employment. It summarized its principal findings as follows:

(1) in hiring unskilled workers four out of ten firms discriminated against a minority group;

(2) in hiring semiskilled workers five out of ten firms discriminated against a minority group;

(3) in hiring skilled workers about seven out of ten firms discriminated against a minority group;

---

[26] New York State Commission against Discrimination, *1951 Annual Report*, pp. 7–8.
[27] Norgren and Hill, *Toward Fair Employment*, pp. 119–122.
[28] *Id.*, p. 102.

(4) in hiring persons for engineering and sales positions nine out of ten firms discriminated against a minority group;

(5) while most of the discrimination in employment was directed against Negroes, there was significant evidence of similar discrimination against Jews and members of other religious groups, and against nationality groups;

(6) nearly all firms discriminated in hiring against one specific minority group citing "tradition" or "company policy" as the principal reasons;

(7) nine out of ten firms discriminated against a minority group in either hiring, apprenticing, upgrading, or promoting workers.

(8) seven out of ten establishments employing apprentices limited apprenticeship opportunities for minority-group workers.[29]

In 1961 the Pennsylvania Fair Employment Practices Commission, now called the Human Relations Commission, reported the results of its study of the impact of its work upon employers during the previous five-year period.[30] It stated that it had been able to achieve significant changes in the employment of Negroes in retail and wholesale trades, heavy industry, public schools, government agencies, the garment industry, the communications industry, and the restaurant trade. These changes related both to the number of Negroes employed and the number of skilled, sales, clerical, semiprofessional, and professional jobs in which they were employed. The Norgren-Hill study confirms that the work of the human-relations commissions in this and three other states has achieved material abatement of employment discrimination since their establishment although the achievement fell considerably short of that attained in New York.[31] The Pennsylvania Commission itself, in setting its goals for the future, in 1961 indicated the scope of the discrimination in employment still occurring in that state.[32] It stated its goals to be the elimination of obstacles in the way of job upgrading and promotion for persons of minority status. It indicated that arbitrary limits still are imposed by business concerns upon opening supervisory and administrative levels of employment to Negroes.

Another indication of the results of the work of well-established

[29] "Employment Practices in Pennsylvania," Condensed Report of the Governor's Commission on Industrial Race Relations (September, 1954), pp. 6–7.

[30] Pennsylvania Fair Employment Practices Commission, *Fifth Annual Report* (1961), p. 11.

[31] Norgren and Hill, *Toward Fair Employment*, pp. 122–124.

[32] Pennsylvania Fair Employment Practices Commission, *Fifth Annual Report* (1961), p. 11.

state and local human-relations commissions with enforcement authority is found by comparing the improvement in nonwhite employment between 1950 and 1960 in states having these commissions with the situation in states not having them.[33] While in New York, Negroes in managerial and official's positions increased by 164 per cent in this decade, in Indiana, Illinois, and Missouri—all states without state or local commissions with enforcement authority—Negroes enjoyed only a 6 per cent increase in these positions. The comparable increases in retail-sales positions were 41 and 15 per cent; in construction craftsmen, 46 and 8 per cent; and in manufacturing operatives, 65 and 20 per cent. In all employment categories, employment of Negroes in New York increased, on the average, 75 per cent, while in the other three states under consideration employment of Negroes in the same categories increased 34 per cent. The Norgren-Hill study of other states which have had well-established commissions with enforcement authority for a considerable number of years indicates that Negro employment both in total numbers and in occupations filled has shown improvement comparable to but smaller than the gains made in New York State although larger than gains made in states without commissions. Of particular significance in this regard is the fact that as of June 1962 in New York City one quarter of all Negro workers were employed in managerial, professional, technical, sales, and office positions in establishments holding federal contracts. This was five times more than the proportion of Negroes in these categories in similar establishments in Chicago and seven times more than the proportion in Indianapolis and St. Louis. None of the latter cities had a local commission with enforcement authority, nor did Indiana. Illinois and Missouri had created commissions with enforcement authority only in 1961 and, of course, these commissions had not had time by June 1962 to change the employment patterns within their states significantly.

In all, there have been thirty state human-relations commissions operating mainly in the North and West prior to January 1968 with jurisdiction to compel elimination of discrimination in employment against members of minority groups and to take other action designed to create employment opportunities for these persons. Half of these commissions had been operating for a decade or more. Despite their

---

[33] Norgren and Hill, *Toward Fair Employment*, pp. 126–130. This book is the source of the information summarized in this paragraph.

work, the Negro in the North and West, as elsewhere, according to a recent Bureau of Census study, "still ranks among the poorest of the poor and . . . his economic status relative to whites has not improved for nearly 20 years."[34] There have been some absolute employment gains by Negroes, as previously reported in this section, but the over-all employment status of Negroes relative to white persons remains substantially unchanged. What improvement has occurred in the occupational status of the Negro since 1940, according to the Bureau of Census study, has resulted from the movement of the Negro from the rural South to the urban industrial areas.[35] There has not been, however, any significant improvement in job opportunities for the Negro in Northern and Western industrial areas during the period in which state human-relations commissions have been operating. Instead of being concentrated, as formerly, in sharecropping and farm labor, Negroes have entered into the area of unskilled and semiskilled factory jobs. Some have also gained white-collar employment. While this absolute improvement has been occurring for Negroes, however, white persons have been enjoying a similar upgrading in the jobs they hold. There have been, as a consequence, few significant changes in the occupational distribution of Negroes relative to whites during the past twenty years. Negroes are still concentrated in the lowest-paid occupations. The median wage or salary income for Negroes is still almost identical with what it was in 1947, 54 per cent of that received by whites. The rate of Negro unemployment is still double that of white unemployment.[36] In some areas (Chicago, for example), the rate of Negro unemployment is four times that of white unemployment. Among Negro young people, the unemployment rate is as high as 70 per cent.[37] A new and frightening factor affecting the Negro's economic status is the accelerating pace at which the kinds of low-paid, low-skilled jobs largely held by Negroes are being eliminated due to the

[34] *Hearings on S. 773, S. 1210, S. 1211, and S. 1937, Equal Employment Opportunity, before the Subcommittee on Employment and Manpower of the Senate Committee on Labor and Public Welfare,* 88th Cong., 1st Sess. (Washington, D.C.: U.S. Government Printing Office, 1963), p. 321.

[35] *Id.*, p. 322.

[36] Matthew A. Kessler, "Economic Status of Nonwhite Workers 1955–62," *Monthly Labor Review,* Vol. 86 (1963), p. 782; John D. Pomfret, "Economic Factors Underlie Negro Discontent," *The New York Times* (August 18, 1963), Sec. 4, p. 10, col. 1; Samuel E. Hill, "Twenty Years of State Fair Employment Practice Commissions," *Buffalo Law Review,* Vol. 14 (1964), p. 31.

[37] Charles E. Silberman, "The City and the Negro," *Fortune,* Vol. 70 (March, 1962), p. 139.

inexorable process of automation.[38] Some estimates place the rate of job elimination resulting from automation as high as two million jobs a year.[39] Beyond this is the fact that although the Negro needs training for the higher skills as never before because of this disappearance of low-skilled jobs, he is still not participating to any substantial extent in union and management programs for providing training in these skills.[40] Finally, while he bears the cross of all these economic disadvantages despite the efforts of human-relations commissions during the past twenty years, the Negro must contend with higher prices and rentals in a booming economy.

Many factors account for the continuation without substantial abatement of the Negro's concentration in the lowest-paid jobs, with low median pay, unemployment, absence from training programs for the higher skills, nonmembership in unions, and nonemployment in the higher-paid jobs. It is generally agreed, however, that a major factor is widespread discrimination against Negroes by employers, unions, and employment agencies.[41] Another major factor is discrimination in housing against Negroes and the concomitant effects of this discrimination to be seen in the poorer schools of the Negro ghettos and the various conditions in these areas tending to undermine the opportunities of Negroes to prepare for and obtain better forms of employment.[42] Still a third factor is the inertia of employers in continuing to follow employment practices the natural impact of which is to exclude the Negro from employment opportunities.[43] It seems reasonably clear that the thirty state human-relations commissions have not been able to deal sufficiently effectively with these causative factors and to produce any substantial changes in the North and West in the

[38] U.S. Commission on Civil Rights, *1961 Report: Book Three, Employment* (Washington, D.C.: U.S. Government Printing Office, 1961), pp. 2, 95, 153.

[39] *Barron's* (December 9, 1963), p. 1, col. 3.

[40] U.S. Commission on Civil Rights, *1961 Report: Book Three, Employment*, pp. 97–111; U.S. Commission on Civil Rights, *Hearings Held in Cleveland, Ohio* (April 1–7, 1966), pp. 389–510; George Strauss, "How Management Views Its Race Relations Responsibilities," *Employment, Race, and Poverty*, edited by Arthur M. Ross and Herbert Hill (New York: Harcourt, Brace, & World, 1967), pp. 261–289; Herbert Hill, "The Racial Practices of Organized Labor: The Age of Gompers and After," *Employment, Race, and Poverty*, pp. 290–307; and John E. Hutchinson, "The AFL-CIO and the Negro," *Employment, Race, and Poverty*, pp. 365–431.

[41] Norgren and Hill, *Toward Fair Employment*, pp. 17–55; F. Ray Marshall, *The Negro and Organized Labor* (New York: Wiley, 1965), pp. 53–132.

[42] See text at note 72 and following in this chapter.

[43] Charles E. Silberman, *Crisis in Black and White* (New York: Random House, 1964), pp. 242–248; Marshall, *The Negro and Organized Labor*, pp. 133–176.

availability of employment opportunities for the Negro relative to white persons during the past twenty years. Indeed, the racial unrest between 1964 and 1968, as contrasted with that of 1963, has largely centered in the North and West. At its center has been the concern over lack of adequate employment opportunities and the economic crisis this has precipitated for the Negro. A great sense of frustration has swept over the Negro community in the North and West. It has become disenchanted with the performances of state human-relations commissions and is now largely by-passing them in its efforts to find new and better solutions for the problem of unequal employment opportunities and its causes.

The Norgren-Hill study of the work of state human-relations commissions with employment discrimination has pointed out a number of deficiencies in the operations of these agencies. To remedy these deficiencies, the makers of this study propose that the operation of the New York State Commission against Discrimination be taken as the model to be emulated by other state and local human-relations commissions.[44] They selected this Commission as the model for others upon the ground that it has achieved substantial progress in eliminating employment discrimination as a result of its twenty-years' work in this field. In elaborating their proposal, these authors suggest that other commissions adopt the main procedural provisions of the New York statute administered by the New York State Commission as well as certain administrative policies utilized by it. They also propose that other commissions be provided with budgets comparable to that provided the New York State Commission on the well-grounded theory that what that Commission has accomplished has in large part been due to its reasonably ample financing and the administrative staff and staff work this has made possible. Finally, these authors proposed the creation of a federal agency comparable to that of the New York State Commission in its authority to administer substantive prohibitions relative to employment discrimination, as well as in its procedures, administrative policies, and budget.[45] The difficulty with these proposals is the limited nature of their usefulness. The performance of the New York State Commission is, when carefully examined, hardly an adequate standard by which to judge what should be done by states and political subdivisions in opening up employment opportunities

---

[44] Norgren and Hill, *Toward Fair Employment*, pp. 148, 230–233, 246–258, 275–278.
[45] *Id.*, pp. 258–265.

for minority groups, and especially the Negro. Excellent as the work of this Commission has been in comparison with the work of most other state commissions, the Negro still confronts basically the same economic facts in New York as he confronts in Northern and Western states generally. The recent Bureau of Census study previously mentioned demonstrates that in New York, despite the gains mentioned in the Norgren-Hill study, the Negro has not improved his occupational status relative to whites during the past twenty years. The Negro still has substantially the same occupational distribution relative to whites in New York that he had in 1940 and 1950. The other facets of the Negro's economic crisis exist in New York as elsewhere. The reasons for this continuing situation are the same in New York as in other states of the North and West having state human-relations situations. These reasons, as summarized earlier, are discrimination by employers, unions, and employment agencies; discrimination in housing and the disabling effect it has upon members of minority groups; and the inertia of employers and unions in continuing to follow practices which though not overtly discriminatory, operate in fact to exclude the Negro from employment opportunities.

The small overall impact of the work of the New York State Commission upon discrimination in employment may readily be discerned by an examination of its processing of complaints of discrimination filed by aggrieved individuals. In 1960, this Commission received 652 complaints of employment discrimination: 563 of these were complaints against employers and employment agencies; 67 involved complaints against unions.[46] In 1965 the total number of complaints of employment discrimination filed was 761.[47] In processing and disposing of a total of 798 complaints of employment discrimination in 1965 (some of which had been filed prior to that year), the Commission found that some unlawful discriminatory practice had been committed in 95, or 12 per cent, of these cases. This compares with the 45 per cent recorded in the 1945–1960 period.[48] Since it is universally agreed that the number of complaints of discrimination filed with a commission each year is only a small percentage of the total discriminatory

[46] New York State Commission against Discrimination, *Report of Progress* (1960), p. 39.
[47] New York State Commission for Human Rights, *Annual Report, 1965*, pp. 12, 14.
[48] New York State Commission against Discrimination, *Report of Progress* (1960), pp. 39–40.

transactions occurring during that year,[49] it is clear that in New York discrimination in employment continues to be a widespread practice on the part of employers, employment agencies, and unions. This is further borne out by the fact that when the Commission proceeds to initiate an investigation of employment practices on its own motion, rather than to wait for complaints to be filed by aggrieved persons, it finds a much higher percentage of the situations investigated to involve unlawful discriminatory practices.[50] In 1960 its investigations demonstrated that 78 per cent of the situations investigated involved unlawful discrimination as compared with 28 per cent of the cases investigated on the complaint of aggrieved persons. Moreover, in its first nineteen years of operation, it had been able to effectuate agreements to revise general employment practices adversely affecting minority groups, with only some 2,000 employers in the entire state. These are employers who have been involved in cases initiated by complaint of an aggrieved person in which there was evidence of discriminatory practices affecting others besides the complainant. These 2,000 employers represent only a very small percentage of all those employing six or more persons over whom the Commission has jurisdiction.[51] One is forced to observe that the Negro's failure to achieve any substantial progress in his occupational distribution relative to white persons during the past twenty years in New York is closely paralleled by the small overall impact upon employment discrimination which has been obtained through the efforts of the New York State Commission. Indeed, civil-rights leaders and many other responsible citizens in New York have vigorously criticized the work of the New York State Commission in recent years.[52] They take the position that the

[49] New York County Lawyers Association, Committee on Civil Rights, "Time for a Change: A Reexamination of the New York State Law against Discrimination in Employment and Its Operation" (December, 1963) (committee report), pp. 4–5, 9–10; Minnesota Commission against Discrimination, *1959 Annual Report* (1960), p. 9; Minnesota Commission against Discrimination, *1962 Annual Report* (1963), p. 21; Michigan Fair Employment Practices Commission, *1962 Annual Report*, p. iii; New Haven Human Rights Committee, "Special Report to the Mayor of New Haven," (1964), pp. 35–36.

[50] New York State Commission against Discrimination, *Report of Progress* (1960), pp. 25, 29, 40.

[51] Norgren and Hill, *Toward Fair Employment*, p. 117; Hill, "Twenty Years of State Fair Employment Practice Commissions," p. 55.

[52] New York County Lawyer's Association, Committee on Civil Rights, "Time for a Change"; Hill, "Twenty Years of State Fair Employment Practice Commissions," pp. 52–69.

Commission has failed to utilize in an adequate way its powers of investigation and enforcement. Members of minority groups who bear the brunt of the widespread discrimination in employment have questioned the effectiveness of the New York law against discrimination and the good faith of the Commission administering it. Their feelings of cynicism and frustration with the failure of the Commission to do more than it has to end discrimination in employment have been reflected in the public demonstrations, riots, and violence that have swept over New York, particularly in 1964. One must conclude that the proposal of the Norgren-Hill study to extrapolate upon the experience, policies, and procedures of the New York State Commission in dealing with employment discrimination so as to extend these, as a model for other states and local governments, is unacceptable.[53]

Turning to the modern experience in dealing with housing discrimination, one discovers that as of January 1968 out of the thirty-two state human-relations commissions with jurisdiction to compel elimination of discrimination of some form or other against members of minority groups, only eighteen had jurisdiction to eliminate housing discrimination.[54] Several local commissions possessed this jurisdiction also.[55] Most of these commissions have had this jurisdiction only during the past five to ten years. By and large, as earlier indicated, these commissions are relying primarily upon the same technique for eliminating housing discrimination that they have used in dealing with employment discrimination: the processing, case by case, of individual complaints of discrimination filed by aggrieved persons, the use of conciliation to promote "satisfactory adjustment" of any grievance found to be justified, and, where necessary, the holding of hearings and issuance of cease and desist orders. When one examines the knotty problem of opening housing opportunities for minority groups, one recognizes even more readily than in the case of employment oppor-

---

[53] The New York State Commission has itself stressed in recent years that "there are substantial areas in the field of employment in which equal opportunity without reference to race, creed, color or national origin cannot be assured by sole or even major reliance upon the individual complaint case process" [New York State Commission for Human Rights, *Annual Report, 1965*, pp. 15–16]. On the other hand, the Commission has as yet projected no major change in its usual modes of operation.

[54] See Appendix A of this book.

[55] See Appendix C of this book.

tunities how inadequate the individual case approach is, as a principal or sole weapon, for enabling state human-relations commissions to deal adequately with the problem.

It seems clear that for Negroes the situation in the North and West concerning housing opportunities, despite the work of state and local human-relations commissions, is not substantially different from what it was twenty years ago. In 1940 the "Black Belts" of the cities followed one of four general patterns: either a single, central belt extending into surrounding areas; two or more major belts; several major belts and many minor ones; or a single major belt and a minor one.[56] In 1960 the cities of the North and West still were characterized by a principal ghetto area in which Negroes were concentrated.[57] This area typically included a segregated core surrounded by a cluster of zones in which Negroes were concentrated to a greater or lesser extent depending on a number of factors. If a city had more than one of these areas, it tended to resemble the principal area. The only change in the housing situation for Negroes during the past twenty years appears to be one simply of the size and shape of the areas in which they are concentrated. Thus, in 1960, 90 per cent of the Detroit Negro population was concentrated within twelve closely related communities which simply enclosed the smaller area of concentration that had existed in 1940.[58] As Negroes have entered white areas adjacent to their ghettos, the white persons in them usually have moved out. Thus, while 18,758 Negroes were moving into Pittsburgh between 1950 and 1960 and occupying a larger area of the city, 91,232 whites moved out of the city to the suburbs.[59] Between 1960 and 1964, 400,000 majority-group whites, most of them belonging to younger families, left New York City for the suburbs while their places were being taken by Negroes and Puerto Ricans. Between 1960 and 1965 Negro occupancy in one of the Los Angeles communities adjacent to the ghetto area, Green Meadows, had increased from 59 to 79 per cent. It appears that by

[56] Robert Clifton Weaver, *The Negro Ghetto* (New York: Harcourt and Brace, 1948), p. 100.

[57] Davis McEntire, *Residence and Race*, Final Comprehensive Report to Commission on Race and Housing (Berkeley: University of California Press, 1960), p. 34; Karl E. and Alma F. Taeuber, *Negroes in Cities* (Chicago: Aldine Publishing Co., 1965), pp. 28–64, 99–125, 256–275.

[58] Detroit Commission on Community Relations, *Report on Racial Characteristics of the Detroit Area Population* (June, 1963), p. 2.

[59] Pittsburgh Commission on Human Relations, *Report on the Status of Housing of Negroes in Pittsburgh* (May, 1962), pp. 3–4.

1980 many of our major urban centers will be more than 50 per cent Negro. In New York City, the two principal minority groups, Negro and Latin American, may be a larger per cent of total population than this figure by that time.

The segregation of Negroes into ghettos results from a number of factors.[60] One, of course, is the low economic status of Negroes, a condition itself due in substantial part to discrimination in employment. Another factor is the low cultural attainment of many Negroes and the desire this creates in them to congregate in the same area. The third reason is the stronger degree of discrimination exercised by the white majority group in housing—particularly in the suburbs—than is exerted relative to most other matters.[61] This discrimination both excludes the Negro and provides a haven for whites fleeing from our center cities. It is universally recognized that this discrimination is the major cause of the residential segregation of Negroes, many of whom are financially prepared to move out of the ghetto and desirous of doing so. In Detroit, for example, it is estimated that 27 per cent, or more than 33,000, of all Negro families receive income sufficient to allow them to purchase housing outside the areas in which Negroes are concentrated.[62] Nevertheless, widespread discriminatory practices in housing prevent them from moving. Most property owners in white neighborhoods over the country will refuse to sell their homes to Negroes.[63] Businessmen who build, finance, and market housing also act

[60] McEntire, *Residence and Race*, pp. 67–87.

[61] "The truth of the matter is that the racial ghetto results from an all-encompassing system of discrimination, and more directly, from discrimination in the housing market. Negroes live in ghettos, despite their expressed wishes to the contrary, because white Americans keep them there and away from their own (white) residential areas" [*Hearings on S. 3296, etc. before the Subcommittee on Constitutional Rights of the Senate Committee on the Judiciary*, 89th Cong., 2nd Sess. (Washington, D.C.: U.S. Government Printing Office, 1966), Pt. 1, p. 1410]. The statement is that of Edward Rutledge, executive director of the National Committee against Discrimination in Housing, an affiliation of 41 major religious, civil rights, labor, and civic organizations, concerned with removing housing restrictions based on race, creed, or national origin in the United States. A recent comprehensive study, examining the relationship of Negro poverty to housing segregation, concluded: "the net effect of economic factors in explaining residential segregation is slight. . . . Clearly, residential segregation is a more tenacious social problem than economic discrimination. Improving the economic status of Negroes is unlikely by itself to alter prevailing patterns of racial residential segregation" [Taeuber and Taeuber, *Negroes in Cities*, pp. 94–95].

[62] Detroit Commission on Community Relations, *Report on Racial Characteristics*, pp. 2, 6.

[63] McEntire, *Residence and Race*, pp. 73–77.

in numerous discriminatory ways that promote segregation of the Negro.[64] We have previously reviewed how various housing programs of the federal government have either promoted or supported segregation policies by these business interests. Turning from Detroit to Los Angeles, we find that between 1950 and 1960 only about 1,400 Negro citizens out of more than 334,916 were able to find residences outside the central city ghetto or other nearby segregated areas.[65] This city, however, normally has about 70,000 to 80,000 vacancies, and in 1966 had 150,000 vacancies, enough to accommodate all Negroes living in Watts. In Pittsburgh in 1960, as in 1950, only a small proportion of Negroes lived in neighborhoods that were not known as Negro residential areas.[66]

A comparison of the situation in residential segregation and the results attained by a particular human relations commission in processing individual complaints of housing discrimination will demonstrate the small efficacy of this technique in opening housing opportunities for Negroes. The situation in Pennsylvania may be taken as an example.[67] In 1960 this commonwealth had approximately 750,000 Negro citizens. Over 500,000 of these citizens lived in Philadelphia and over 100,000 lived in Pittsburgh. Thirty cities in all had more than 1,000 Negro residents. Negroes in all these cities are residentially segregated. A recent study reports that the chief controlling factor in this segregation is housing discrimination. Many Negroes now have jobs and incomes which would enable them to move out of their present neighborhoods but they are prevented from doing this. The state Commission and the Pittsburgh and Philadelphia Commissions have exercised jurisdiction over housing discrimination since 1960, 1958 and 1963, respectively.[68] The state Commission had, by the end of 1965, disposed of a total of 606 complaints of housing discrimination;[69] 372 of these dispositions involved a finding of probable cause that discrimination had occurred. Almost all of these latter cases were "satisfactorily ad-

[64] *Id.*, pp. 75, 175–198, 218–250.

[65] Los Angeles County Commission on Human Relations, "Report on Population and Housing in Los Angeles County" (revised March, 1963), p. 1 (mimeographed).

[66] Pittsburgh Commission on Human Relations, *Report on the Status of Housing*, pp. 3–4.

[67] Commonwealth of Pennsylvania Department of Labor and Industry. *Report of the Governor's Committee on Discrimination in Housing* (January, 1959).

[68] See Appendices A and C of this book.

[69] Pennsylvania Human Relations Commission, *Tenth Annual Report* (1965), p. 27.

justed" by conciliation. The Philadelphia and Pittsburgh Commissions closed approximately 100 cases satisfactorily in the same year.[70] It is evident, even if no more than 25 per cent of Pennsylvania's 750,000 Negro citizens could afford housing outside their ghettos that the opening of housing accommodations to Negroes in about 475 instances in 1965 through Commission action represents very small progress, even taking account of the recent date that two of the commissions obtained jurisdiction over housing discrimination. In New York in 1965 where the state and New York City Commissions have had this jurisdiction since 1955 and 1957 respectively, these commissions were disposing of complaints concerning housing discrimination at the rate of 825 per year.[71] In 350 of these cases, the commissions found that discrimination existed, and they were able to obtain "satisfactory adjustments" by concilation in almost all instances. Nevertheless in relation to the total Negro population of 1,417,511 in 1960, this rate of opening housing accommodations to Negroes represents very small progress. Even granting that there have been substantial increases in case loads handled in the early 1960's by these and other human-relations commissions operating in this field, it is evident that little change is being produced or likely to be produced relative to housing discrimination against the Negro by the methods currently employed by these commissions in the North and West. Indeed, the situation concerning housing opportunities has probably worsened.

We may say, in summary, that while somewhat more progress has been made in eliminating discrimination in employment, the Negro's position has not improved relative to whites during the past twenty years with regard to either employment or housing opportunities. No state or local commission has demonstrated that its existing statutory framework and administrative policies, which almost universally emphasize the processing of individual complaints of discrimination, are yet sufficient to ensure substantial progress in eliminating most forms of discrimination suffered by minority groups. Negroes in Northern and Western states, despite the work of state and local human-relations commissions, are confronted with the two central facts—a widening economic depression in a time of increasing white affluence, be-

[70] *Pittsburgh Human Relations Review*, Vol. 5, No. 6 (December, 1962), pp. 1–2; Philadelphia Commission on Human Relations, *1965 Annual Report*, p. 19.

[71] New York State Commission for Human Rights, *Annual Report, 1965*, p. 14; New York City Commission on Human Rights, *Annual Report for 1965*, p. 21.

cause they are excluded from employment and housing opportunities and confined to central city ghettos by white prejudice.

The consequences of residential segregation of the Negro have been well documented.[72] This segregation, and the discrimination which enforces it, are the foundation stones upon which rest all other segregation, discrimination, and disadvantages suffered by the Negro. Prices for goods and services are generally higher and quality is generally lower in stores of the ghettos than in the stores located in the higher economic areas of our cities. Unemployment, particularly among the young, is very high relative to unemployment among whites. Public services, such as garbage collection and street repairs, are often inadequate. Public facilities of Negro neighborhoods are poorer than those of other neighborhoods. School buildings and facilities are frequently older and teachers less able. The U.S. Commissioner of Education, Francis Keppel, has remarked that education in a Negro ghetto is characterized by a massive deterioration.[73] Parks and playgrounds in a Negro ghetto are also often less well equipped and fewer in number. Enforcement of zoning and building laws is less adequate. The housing available to Negroes is both much smaller in amount and inferior in quality. Of the 330,000 new housing units built in Detroit between 1950 and 1960, for example, only 3 per cent were made available to Negroes.[74] Moreover, the units made available were mainly public-housing units. Although Negroes obtain poorer housing than white persons and have only about one-half their median income, they pay approximately the same rentals or purchase prices. Negroes have great difficulty in obtaining mortgage credit and, when they obtain it, they usually are given shorter periods for repayment than others are given. The older housing available to Negroes in their ghettos does not provide enough space for them and has usually reached the point that it is costly to maintain. For these reasons many of the olders residences are subdivided and shared by many more families than they were designed properly to hold.

The crowded conditions of the ghettos have a severe impact upon the vitality and unity of family life. The lack of privacy and difficulty in maintaining a clean and orderly home under these conditions tend

[72] McEntire, *Residence and Race*, pp. 88–101; Silberman, *Crisis in Black and White*, pp. 36–67, 249–307.

[73] Silberman, *Crisis in Black and White*, p. 257.

[74] Detroit Commission on Community Relations, *Report on Racial Characteristics*, p. 2.

to create tensions. Rather than homes in which good family life nurtures the character and personality of the occupants, these residences are often little more than stopping places for individuals wandering along a lonely path without the hope of escaping to a better existence. In Harlem, it has been reported, over half of the Negro young people under eighteen do not live with both of their parents.[75] Shut up in their ghettos, Negroes are not really known as individuals by most white persons. Instead, they are regarded as all of a type according to the mold in which current myths and prejudices cast them. The other side of the coin is the fact that Negroes are prevented, as a result of their residential segregation, from obtaining the experiences needed to prepare them for advancing in community life. The young Negro needs to know the values and customs of the majority group in order to compete in its sphere of operations. He can obtain this knowledge only through good education, family life, and associations cutting across the whole community. Life in the ghetto frequently means, moreover, that the Negro family loses control over its children very early in their life. It also means that the young Negro must attend an all-Negro school where he encounters other young people, who, like himself, have only limited backgrounds. Each can learn little from the other, unlike the child in a school society that is open at least to white children of highly diverse backgrounds. Living in a Negro ghetto as well as attending a ghetto school appears to "dull rather than stimulate achievement."[76] Set apart from children of the majority group and aware of the limited future opportunities available to them, young Negroes are likely to develop in their second-rate ghetto schools either feelings of inferiority and hopelessness or the desire to reject the values and customs of the majority group and to turn to activities that are delinquent and criminal in nature in order to obtain the things that seem important to them. The breakdown in family control over rebellious Negro young people that occurs in the ghetto facilitates the latter development. Charles Silberman has observed: "The disorganization of the family is reflected in a disorganization of Negro life itself—an absence, in too many individuals, of the inner strength and self-discipline necessary if one is to be the master rather than the servant of his environment in a competitive society."[77] Ultimately, the effect of the Negro ghettos is to prevent their inhabitants from obtain-

[75] Silberman, *Crisis in Black and White*, p. 228.
[76] *Id.*, p. 46.
[77] *Id.*, p. 231.

ing the opportunities that would enable them to fulfill their potential for self-achievement and to contribute their human resources to the service of their country and the common good. Beyond this is the cost in national and local unity. To be a Negro in the United States usually involves living in a Negro ghetto, becoming angry with the situation, and hating white persons.

Since 1963 Negroes have almost universally expressed general dissatisfaction with conditions affecting their opportunities in employment, housing, public education, governmental facilities and services, public accommodations, financing, professional organizations, unions, and other important areas. Since 1965 Latin Americans, the nation's second largest minority group, have been voicing the same dissatisfaction.[78] Both groups have asserted that a major cause for their difficulties in obtaining equal opportunities is discrimination against them both by government and by private persons and institutions. The marches, sit-ins, boycotts, picketing, and similar types of non-violent protests utilized by Negroes have been matched more recently by the *huelgas* (strikes), *marchas*, walk-outs, vigils, and other demonstrations of Latin Americans.[79] Leaders of the latter group constantly point to the gains obtained by Negroes through their protest actions and are determined to follow the same pattern. Labor unions have begun at long last to enter the former province of civil-rights organizations by supporting efforts of Mexican American farm workers in striking for better wages, working conditions, and collective-bargaining guarantees.[80] But as Mexican Americans have entered the fray in the Southwest, the center of the civil-rights battleground for the Negro has moved to the North.[81] All know that in the Negro ghettos of our major urban centers there is greater frustration, bitterness, and hatred for

[78] *The Forumeer*, Vol. XIII, Nos. 5 and 10 (May and October, 1966). This organ of the American G.I. Forum, one of the leading organizations of Mexican Americans, reviews events in the Mexican American community of the Southwest from September, 1965, when Mexican American grape pickers went on strike in the Delano area of California, to early September, 1966, when Mexican American farm workers from the Rio Grande Valley concluded their three hundred mile march to Austin, Texas, to protest working conditions and to seek a state minimum-wage law. These events have also been reported in other publications [*America* (April 23, 1966), pp. 589–590].

[79] *Congressional Record*, Vol. 112 (U.S. Government Printing Office, daily ed., May 12, 1966), pp. 9997–10,002.

[80] *The National Observer* (August 22, 1966), p. 9; (August 29, 1966), p. 1.

[81] "New Tactics for Civil-Rights Movement," *The National Observer* (May 16, 1966), p. 1.

the white man than ever before.[82] Life in these ghettos is almost inconceivably bad and the Negro desperately wants to remedy the situation. Each year the ghettos in Northern and Western cities grow by another half million as additional Negroes, Mexican Americans, and Puerto Ricans move into them from the South, Southwest, and Puerto Rico, respectively, seeking to escape conditions of poverty and discrimination. Increasingly, the latter two groups have become restive as they confront the same conditions that have plagued the Negro for so long in these cities.

Many studies have been made of the modern urban ghettos. An authoritative study made in 1965 of a now well-known ghetto revealed that there was a deep and long-standing hostility between much of the Negro population and the police department, with no independent effort of a substantial nature on the part of the city government to correct the situation. Only 4 per cent of the police department's commissioned officers were Negroes. Unemployment was two to three times as much as in the white (Anglo) sections of the city. There was widespread discrimination by both employers and unions against Negroes. Three-fourths of the students attending schools conducting double sessions were from areas that were predominantly Negro or Mexican American. Many elementary schools in these districts did not have school cafeterias and those that had them had no system for providing free or reduced-price lunches for children from needy families. Reading performance of children in ghetto schools was three to four times less effective than that of children in "advantaged areas." Higher prices were regularly charged ghetto families than those charged families in other areas. These families often had to buy spoiled meat or produce or old bread at the same price as fresh provisions. They also had to buy goods made of shoddy materials at high interest rates in ghetto stores run by white merchants. There were no alternative sources of supply since there was no adequate public transportation available to enable ghetto families to get outside the ghetto. For the same reason inhabitants of the ghetto found it difficult to get outside of it to seek and to hold jobs, attend schools, go to the hospital, and do many other needed things. The hospitals available to ghetto families were grossly inadequate in quality and in quantity of facilities. By and large, the residential segregation of Negroes was the

---

[82] Jerrold K. Footlick, "A New Look at the North's Ghettos," *The National Observer* (July 30, 1966), pp. 5–6.

product of an almost universal discrimination against them by home-owners and realtors, lending institutions, and builders.[83]

The ghetto just described was Watts in 1965. It was inevitable that unless conditions like these in our urban ghettos were alleviated and their causes effectively removed, we should encounter violence from their inhabitants when they finally lost hope that their desperate and tragic situation would be relieved by the majority group. The riots in Harlem in 1964 and in Watts in 1965 failed to persuade much of the country of this fact. Only those who do not want to understand could fail to see the import of the riots in some 104 large cities during the summers of 1966 and 1967.[84]

The real significance of the riot in Watts is now clear. The riot has become a symbol to the Negro poor of all our major urban centers: North, West, and South.[85] It is a symbol of their rejection of all the conditions under which they have lived so long. It is their way of characterizing as the white man's crime against humanity his delib-erate creation of the conditions that have produced the Negro ghetto. Watts and the technique of riot are matters of pride to the Negro poor. More than anything else—as both they and Latin Americans have been quick to point out—the riots have caused the nation, the states, and the cities finally to focus upon the inhumanity of the Negro ghetto and to begin to do something about changing it.[86] The tension in the Puerto Rican ghettos of New York City and Chicago indicates that their poor also may share this condition. Mexican Americans speak with admiration of the progress Negroes have made through various nonviolent techniques and now ponder the appropriateness of using more forceful techniques.[87]

---

[83] State of California, Governor's Commission on the Los Angeles Riots, *Violence in the City: An End or a Beginning?* (Los Angeles: December 2, 1965) (commis-sion report).

[84] William F. Soskin, "Riots, Ghettos, and the 'Negro Revolt'," *Employment, Race, and Poverty*, edited by Arthur M. Ross and Herbert Hill (New York: Har-court, Brace & World, 1967), pp. 205–233; Michael Harrington, "The Economics of Protest," *Employment, Race, and Poverty*, pp. 234–257.

[85] Footlick, "A New Look," pp. 1, 15; Thomas A. Johnson, "Watts: Anger, Fright and Shame in a Tense Ghetto," *The New York Times* (May 22, 1966), Sec. 1, p. 70.

[86] *Congressional Record*, Vol. 112 (May 12, 1966), pp. 9997–10,002.

[87] "With Violence, A Minority Makes Its Presence Known in Chicago," *The National Observer* (June 20, 1966), p. 9; Jonathan Randal, "Brownsville: Neighbor-hood of Poverty and Strife," *The New York Times* (July 17, 1966), Sec. 1, p. 59. Negro gains as a result of their various forms of protest have unsettled the pattern of hopeless acceptance of existing conditions by Mexican Americans [Peter Bart,

For the majority group the significance of the riots in Watts and over a hundred cities in the following two summers is also clear. The United States faces the greatest internal crisis since the Civil War.[88] The formation of the Urban Coalition on July 31, 1967, confirms the recognition of this fact by one thousand of the nation's industrial, labor, educational, religious, civil rights, and city government leaders.[89] Meeting in Washington, D.C., in late August of that year, this group moved to promote the realization of a set of far-reaching principles in the day-to-day operation of American life. Basically, these principles called for short- and long-range programs in both the private and public sectors to create "a new political, social, economic, and moral climate that will make possible the breaking of the vicious cycle of the ghetto." Typical of the principles adopted was the one calling for the private sector to recruit, train, and hire the hard-core unemployed and for the government to assume this responsibility when the private sector is unable to carry it out. Another called for providing every American family with a decent home, a suitable living environment, and guarantees of equal access to housing, employment, and all other important opportunities of Americans generally.[90]

It also is abundantly clear that every effort must be made to improve the effectiveness of law designed to assure equality of opportunities for all persons. The existing law of this type has not, as this chapter has indicated, made a substantial contribution toward achieving this goal. It is essential to discover what changes can be made both in the existing law and in its administration to render both as effective as they may possibly be. An absolute first step in this direction is the investigation of ways to improve the individual-case approach for dealing with unlawful discriminatory practices.

"Negro Gains Vex Coast Mexicans," *The New York Times* (October 17, 1965), Sec. 1, p. 82; *Congressional Record*, Vol. 112 (May 12, 1966), pp. 9997–10,002]. As one who has worked closely on the Southwest scene with Mexican American leaders, I can report that tension and resentment is very high among many members of their ethnic group and has been rising throughout 1967 as improvements in the availability of employment and other important opportunities have been slow in developing.

88 *The New York Times* (July 16, 1967), Sec. 4, p. 8.
89 *The Washington Post* (August 25, 1967), p. 1.
90 *Ibid.*

The Need for Effective Law and Law Enforcement

General Considerations

As of January 1968 thirty-two states had established human-relations commissions with enforcement power over some form of discrimination.[1] Thirty of these had enforcement power over employment discrimination, twenty-five over public-accommodations discrimination, and twenty-one over housing discrimination. Approximately thirty-five local governments also had human-relations commissions with enforcement power over one or more forms of discrimination.[2] The experience of about half of the state and local commissions extends over a period of a decade or more.[3] Their experience has demonstrated that discrimination against minority and other disadvantaged groups by government officials and private persons and institutions can be dealt with effectively. That is, this experience demonstrates that individual persons aggrieved by discrimination can be effectively assisted and that persons found to have engaged in discriminatory practices can be effectively prevented from continuing them. The essential device for accomplishing this effectiveness in eliminating individual instances of discrimination is the utilization of modern administrative process with the backing of judicial process to enforce administrative orders when this becomes necessary. To say that the experience of these state and local governments proves that discrimination against individual members of minority and other disadvantaged groups can be effectively prevented does not mean, however,

[1] See Appendix A of this book.
[2] See Appendix C of this book.
[3] See Appendix E of this book.

that that experience proves that the overall incidence of discrimination against minority groups is being significantly reduced. The purpose of the last chapter was to demonstrate that the current methods of case-by-case processing of individual complaints of discrimination by human-relations commissions having enforcement power was not accomplishing the latter result. It remains to be discerned how government can become effective in reducing substantially the overall incidence of discrimination. In this chapter we will examine what kind of civil-rights law and what kind of enforcement of that law is needed to achieve this goal to the extent possible. In subsequent chapters we will examine other means of increasing the effectiveness of government in dealing with discrimination against minority groups.

The federal Equal Employment Opportunity Commission,[4] most local human-relations commissions (several hundred in number),[5] and a few state human-relations commissions[6] have not been granted the authority to enforce administrative prohibitions against discrimination and other action that seriously harm minority and other disadvantaged groups. These commissions are in the situation either of having no law prohibiting discrimination to enforce—as is the case with most local and some state commissions—or of having some duties to administer law of this kind but no authority to enforce it administratively—as is the case with the federal Equal Employment Opportunity Commission. The result is the same in either case; neither type of human-relations commission can be effective in eliminating individual instances of discrimination.[7] Experience has also shown that allocation of enforcement power only to aggrieved individuals or to attorney generals or similar law-enforcement officials is not an effective way to enforce civil-rights law.[8] The *sine qua non* to dealing effectively with individual instances of discrimination is the existence of some form of civil-rights law prohibiting discrimination against minority and other

[4] 42 U.S.C. §§ 2000e–2000e-15 (1964); see text at notes 32–33, Chapter 1, above.
[5] See text at note 56, Chapter 1, above; also see Appendix D of this book.
[6] See Appendix B of this book.
[7] Note, "The Right to Equal Treatment: Administrative Enforcement Legislation," *Harvard Law Review*, Vol. 74 (1961), pp. 526, 581–582; Pamela H. Rice and Milton Greenberg, "Municipal Protection of Human Rights," *Wisconsin Law Review* (1952), p. 678; Sanford Jay Rosen, "Division of Authority under Title VII of the Civil Rights Act of 1964: A Preliminary Study in Federal-State Interagency Relations," *George Washington Law Review*, Vol. 34 (1966), p. 846.
[8] Note, "The Right to Equal Treatment," p. 526; *Hearings on S. 3296 etc., before the Subcommittee on Constitutional Rights of the Senate Committee on the Judiciary*, 89th Cong., 2nd Sess., p. 364 (1966).

disadvantaged groups and the availability of a human-relations commission with ample authority to enforce that law administratively
against officials and private persons and institutions who violate it.
The existence of these two factors has been the reason for the degree
of success attained so far by the state and local human-relations
commissions referred to in the last paragraph.

If the federal Equal Employment Opportunity Commission, the
several hundred similar local human-relations commissions, and several similar state human-relations commissions now in existence are
to become at all effective in disposing of individual instances of discrimination, they must be given a law to administer that prohibits
discrimination and the power to compel individual violators to obey
the law through cease and desist orders enforceable in the courts.
Moreover, if the federal government is to become effective in administering the remainder of its civil-rights law—such as the Civil Rights
Acts of 1871, 1964 (Titles II, III, and IV), and 1968 (Titles I, VIII,
and IX)—it must create or designate a federal human-relations
commission or agency to administer that law and it must give that
commission effective power to enforce it. The same thing is true of the
few states which have civil-rights laws on the books that are enforceable only through judicial process and the application of either criminal or civil sanctions. *A fortiori*, the same thing is true of the approximately twenty states and over two thousand local governments with
serious problems concerning discrimination[9] that still have not enacted any civil-rights laws or created any human-relations commissions
to administer them. But as the federal, state, and local governments
act to establish human-relations commissions with enforcement power,
they must regard the experience of state and local governments that
have had these commissions during the past twenty years. They must
adopt measures that will make the newly created and empowered
human-relations commissions more effective than their predecessors
have been.

The Need for Full Coverage of Discriminatory Transactions

We have observed that while the best-organized state and local
human-relations commissions with enforcement powers have been
able to deal effectively with individual instances of discrimination,
they have not yet been able to make substantial progress in reducing

---

[9] See text at notes 11–16, Chapter 6, below.

the overall incidence of discrimination. The failure of these commissions in the latter respect is grounded upon basic flaws in their jurisdiction, underlying structure, procedure, concept of operation, and funding. In the first place, the civil-rights statutes creating these commissions frequently do not cover or else exclude large numbers of discriminatory transactions occurring within the states and localities in which they operate. It really is impossible for a human-relations commission to make much headway against discrimination directed toward minority groups unless it is given jurisdiction over most instances of the most harmful forms of discrimination. As we saw in the last chapter, discrimination in housing and in home financing are the principal factors producing our Negro ghettos. They are the backbone upon which rests all other segregation, discrimination, and disadvantages suffered by the Negro. Improvement of the economic status of Negroes will have little effect upon their residential segregation. The same is largely true of the Puerto Rican and Mexican American, who are the principal components of our Latin American ethnic group. Failure to deal effectively with discrimination in housing and home financing simply means that the fundamental causes of our minority-group ghettos will continue to operate and to cause the other forms of discrimination and disadvantage flowing from the intrinsic characteristics of ghetto life. It may be politically more expedient to initiate civil-rights legislation that deals with other forms of discrimination than discrimination in housing and home financing, but it does not make much sense at all with regard to accomplishing the goal of a state or a locality becoming really effective in eliminating discrimination against minority groups. Until we begin to deal effectively with the full range of discrimination in housing and in home financing, we are not likely to make much overall progress with other difficult forms of discrimination. If this is correct, it is easy to see why we have made so little progress in turning the tide of discrimination against minority groups.

Twenty-nine states, as of January 1968, had no commission-enforced laws dealing with discrimination in private housing[10] and thirty-six had no similar laws dealing with discrimination in home financing.[11] Moreover, only nine of the eighteen states with well organized human-relations commissions exercising jurisdiction over housing could reach

[10] See Appendix A of this book.
[11] *Ibid.*

substantially 100 per cent of the discrimination in residential property advertised for sale, in rental housing, and in home financing.[12] Prior to 1965 the Rhode Island Commission had jurisdiction only over discrimination in public housing.[13] As of January 1968 the California Commission[14] had jurisdiction primarily, and, prior to June 8, 1967, the Washington Commission had jurisdiction only, over publicly assisted housing. The California Commission had only limited jurisdiction over housing that was not publicly assisted. Both commissions could exercise their jurisdiction over publicly assisted housing only so long as the public assistance continued. The Washington Commission's jurisdiction over publicly assisted housing was relatively unlimited while that of the California Commission attached only to housing that consisted of three or more dwelling units or of a single dwelling occupied by the owner. The latter's jurisdiction covered no other publicly assisted dwellings and little commercial property, whether publicly assisted or not. Its jurisdiction also extended to the owners of dwellings which did not receive public assistance if there were five or more dwelling units within the dwelling. This is also a fairly typical provision in city civil-rights ordinances dealing with housing discrimination. The number of dwelling units required in order for a dwelling to be covered is often five, as in Ann Arbor, Michigan,[16] and Oberlin, Ohio.[17] Section 501 of the Harvard Model State Civil Rights Act also restricts coverage of housing accommodations to those that are publicly assisted or multiple or contiguously owned.[18] The latter two types of housing accommodations are defined to mean those having five or more dwelling units in the same dwelling or located on land that is contiguous and owned by one person.[19]

An example of what exceptions of the kind included in the California statute and Ann Arbor and Oberlin city ordinances can mean

[12] *Hearings on S. 3296*, pp. 1401–1436.

[13] *R.I. Gen. Laws, Ann.*, §§ 11-24-2 to -3 (1956).

[14] Cal. Health & Saf. Code, §§ 35700–35744, *as amended* (Supp. 1966).

[15] Wash. Rev. Vode Ann. §§ 49.60.010–.320 (1962). On June 8, 1967, a law dealing with discrimination by real estate brokers and salesmen went into effect [Wash. Laws 1967 ch. 22].

[16] Ann Arbor, Michigan, Ordinance No. 16-62, *Race Relations Law Reporter*, Vol. 8 (1963), p. 1677.

[17] Oberlin, Ohio, Ordinance No. 235, *Race Relations Law Reporter*, Vol. 8 (1963), p. 256.

[18] Harvard Student Legislative Research Bureau, "A Proposed Model State Civil Rights Act," *Harvard Journal of Legislation*, Vol. 3 (1965), pp. 63–102.

[19] *Ibid*. See Subsections (f)–(i) of Section 201.

is provided by the statute under which the Connecticut Commission operated until 1961. The statute prohibited discrimination in public accommodations, which were defined to include publicly assisted housing accommodations consisting of five or more housing accommodations located either on a single parcel of land or on contiguous parcels of land and under the ownership or control of a single person.[20] Between 1959 and 1961 the Connecticut Commission had jurisdiction over approximately 100,000 rental units under this statutory formula.[21] In 1961 the Commission's jurisdiction was expanded to cover three or more units under the previously stated formula.[22] This additional jurisdiction doubled the number of rental units covered by the law.[23] The majority of the additional units were three-family houses from twenty-five to fifty years in age, located in middle or lower economic-class areas in cities where the bulk of the Connecticut Negro population resides. This housing included moderate- and low-rent housing where it was most needed. Prior to the amendment, therefore, Negroes could not obtain relief from discrimination by owners of these additional units. In 1963 the Connecticut General Assembly expanded its commission's jurisdiction to include most housing for sale and the bulk of housing for rent.[24]

In order to get at the very heart of discrimination against minority groups it is essential to reach the great bulk of real-estate transactions involving housing accommodations. Certainly there is no justification for permitting owners of real property to practice discrimination in housing that is receiving any form of public assistance. There are many forms of public assistance for housing including government construction, ownership, or operation of housing; government tax exemption for housing; sale of land below cost for housing; government acquisition or assembly of land for housing; community redevelop-

[20] Conn. Gen. Stat. Rev. §§ 53-35 to -36 (1960).

[21] Connecticut Commission on Civil Rights, *Annual Report to the Governor* (1960–1961), p. 1 (Reprint from 1961–1962 Digest of Connecticut Administrative Reports to the Governor).

[22] 1961 Conn. Pub. Act. 472, Conn. Gen. Stat. Rev. §§ 53-35 to -36, *as amended* (Supp. 1963).

[23] Connecticut Commission on Civil Rights, *Annual Report* (1960–1961), p. 1. Similarly in New York prior to the 1961 amendment to the state law against discrimination the state Commission had jurisdiction over discrimination relative to only 5 per cent of the total housing supply in the state [New York State Commission against Discrimination, *Report of Progress* (1960), p. 5].

[24] 1963 Conn. Pub. Act 594, Conn. Gen. Stat. Rev. §§ 53-35 to -36(d), *as amended* (Supp. 1965).

ment projects touching land for housing; and any form of government financial assistance for housing, including the guaranty or insurance by government of loans covering the financing of any matter related to housing accommodations.[25] Once property has been substantially aided by public assistance of these types other than tax exemption, there seems little justification for cutting off the coverage of discrimination in transactions involving that property. The public assistance has made possible the existence of the housing on that property and the benefit conferred upon the owner continues in the fact of the very existence of the housing. Moreover, there is little justification for exempting the owner of publicly assisted housing from coverage where only a few dwelling units are involved. The principle of covering housing for the purpose of opening up accommodations to minority groups because it has been publicly assisted should make irrelevant the degree of public assistance granted. In Chapter 8 is set forth the Alpha Model State Civil-Rights Act.[26] The comment to Section 842 of this act contains a provision for dealing with discrimination in publicly assisted housing that follows the ideas developed in this chapter. The provision relative to publicly assisted housing accommodations is, however, considered only a minimal coverage of discrimination in housing and is suggested only as an alternative to a more adequate coverage.

The jurisdiction of federal, state, and local human-relations commissions should be extended to housing accommodations that do not receive public assistance. Much housing of crucial importance to minority groups falls into this category, including both old and new housing.[27] The provision of the Harvard Model State Civil Rights Act dealing with this type of housing is wholly unacceptable since it restricts coverage to transactions involving dwellings on land that is contiguous and owned by one person.[28] Experience shows that this provision would exempt as much as one-half of the housing capable of subserving the needs of minority groups. A far more preferable and useful provision is the type utilized in the Alaska, Michigan, and New

[25] Martin Meyerson, *Housing, People and Cities* (New York: McGraw-Hill, 1962), pp. 219–241, 262–266, 291–313.

[26] The term "ALPHA" has been selected simply to permit an easy way of distinguishing the model legislation suggested by this book from other similar model legislation.

[27] *Hearings on S. 3296*, pp. 1401–1436.

[28] §§ 501 and 201(g)–(i). See note 18 above.

York civil rights laws;[29] the proposed federal Civil Rights Act of 1966 that failed of passage;[30] and the Uniform Model State Anti-Discrimination Act (adopted in 1966 by the National Conference of Commissioners on Uniform State Laws).[31] The Alaska and Michigan laws cover, and Title IV of the proposed federal Civil Rights Act of 1966 covered, all dwellings designed for residential use by one or more individuals or families. The New York civil-rights law and Sections 602–603 of the Uniform Model State Anti-Discrimination Act cover all such dwellings with exceptions for rentals of an owner-occupied dwelling containing no more than two dwelling units and of rooms in private residences. The Alpha Model State Civil-Rights Act[32] adopts in its Section 842 the formula used in the Alaska and Michigan acts, one more extensive than the Title VIII formula of the Civil Rights Act of 1968.

The jurisdiction of federal, state, and local human-relations commissions should also extend to discrimination in commercial space. By this term reference is made to space in any building that is used or designed to be used for the manufacture, sale, resale, processing, reprocessing, displaying, storing, handling, garaging, or distribution of personal property or to space that is used or designed to be used as a separate business or professional office in any building.[33] The opportunity for qualified members of minority groups to practice their professions or to open and operate businesses in the general business areas of a city is a crucial one to their attainment of success in their professions or businesses. So long as they are confined by discriminatory practices to commercial space in ghetto areas, their opportunities for success are extraordinarily limited. Similarly, the jurisdiction of federal, state, and local human-relations commissions should also extend to discrimination by persons engaged in the business of providing financial assistance for the purchase, acquisition, construction, rehabilitation, repair, and maintenance of any housing accommodations or commercial space. Discrimination in the financing of housing accom-

---

[29] See Appendix A of this book.

[30] *Hearings on S. 3296*, pp. 19–30.

[31] National Conference of Commissioners of Uniform State Laws, "Model [State] Anti-Discrimination Act," *Harvard Journal of Legislation*, Vol. 4 (1967), pp. 224–278; Norman Dorsen, "The Model [State] Anti-Discrimination Act: Introduction," *Harvard Journal of Legislation*, Vol. 4, p. 212.

[32] See Chapter 8.

[33] This concept of commercial space is based upon the definition contained in the New York civil-rights law [N.Y. Exec. Law § 292(13) (McKinney Supp. 1967)].

modations and commercial space are equally as effective as discrimination in real-estate transactions for accomplishing the purpose of excluding members of minority groups from needed opportunities to obtain housing and commercial space. It does little good to reach the latter without also reaching the former because most people require financing in order to acquire housing or commercial space. While both the Harvard State Civil Rights Act[34] and the Uniform Model State Anti-Discrimination Act[35] apply to discrimination in the provision of financial assistance for housing accommodations, only the latter applies to discrimination in commercial space or in financial assistance for it. The Alpha Model State Civil-Rights Act covers all of these forms of discrimination in Sections 842 and 843.[36]

Another form of seriously harmful discrimination against minority groups, as our review of the Austin and national situations has well demonstrated, is that practiced by employers, unions, and employment agencies. The *sine qua non* to improvement of many conditions affecting minority groups is improvement in their economic status. While improvement in this status will not significantly affect the problem of discrimination in housing or in home financing against minority-group families, it will significantly affect their opportunities to provide better education, more adequate food and clothing, and better housing for their children. It will contribute significantly to the abilities of these families to secure good and prompt medical attention. It will provide the minimal conditions in which family life can subsist on a normal basis. Beyond this it will prepare the way for knocking down the various barriers to full integration of our minority groups— principally our Negroes and Latin Americans—into all the processes of community life. Just as it is important for this purpose to protect the full range of housing opportunities by civil-rights law so is it important to protect the full range of employment opportunities. By and large, existing civil-rights law does not do this. The Harvard Model State Civil Rights Act applies only to employers of eight or more employees.[37] The Uniform Model State Anti-Discrimination Act defines "employer" to include contractors performing work for the state and other employers of several employees.[38] It neither stipulates the number of employees required for coverage nor makes any suggestions as

---

[34] § 503. See note 18, above.
[35] § 604. See note 31, above.
[36] See Chapter 8.

[37] § 201 (b). See note 18, above.
[38] § 301 (1). See note 31, above.

to what number would be appropriate. The federal Civil Rights Act of
1964 covers, at its maximum coverage to be reached on July 1, 1969,
employers of twenty-five or more employees in an industry affecting
interstate commerce.[39] This means that fewer than 8 per cent of all
employers in businesses affecting interstate commerce and only 29 per
cent of all employers with eight or more employees in businesses of
the same type are covered.[40] Out of a total of 3,440,000 employers,
258,000 are presently covered by the federal act.[41] In addition, 21,093
state-, county-, and municipal-government employers,[42] with a total
of 6,937,000 employees as of October 1965, are exempted from the
act.[43] This exemption involves more employees than are employed by
all employers in industries affecting commerce, who employ between
fifty and ninety-nine employees each.[44] As of January 1968, states
having laws enforced by human-relations commissions covered discrimination by employers who employed the following number of
employees:[45]

Illinois (25 or more effective July 1, 1968)	50 or more
Maryland, Missouri, Nebraska, Utah, and West Virginia	25 or more
Nevada	15 or more
Kentucky, Michigan, and Washington	8 or more
Colorado, Indiana, Massachusetts, New Hampshire, Oregon, and Pennsylvania	6 or more
California	5 or more
Kansas, Iowa, New York, Ohio, and Rhode Island	4 or more
Connecticut	3 or more
Wyoming	2 or more
Alaska, Hawaii, Minnesota, New Jersey, New Mexico, and Wisconsin	1 or more

The exclusion of employers from coverage in Illinois meant that in

---

[39] 42 U.S.C. § 2000e(b) (1964).

[40] *Equal Employment Opportunity 1965: Hearings before the General Subcommittee on Labor of the House Committee on Education and Labor,* 89th Cong., 1st
Sess. (Washington, D.C.: U.S. Government Printing Office, June 15–July 21, 1965),
p. 108.

[41] *Ibid.*

[42] U.S. Department of Commerce, Bureau of the Census, *Statistical Abstract of
the United States 1965* (Washington, D.C.: U.S. Government Printing Office, 1966),
p. 419.

[43] U. S. Department of Commerce, Bureau of the Census, *Public Employment in
1965* (Washington, D.C.: U.S. Government Printing Office, 1966), Table 5, p. 10.

[44] *Equal Employment Opportunity 1965,* p. 108.

[45] See Appendix A of this book.

this state 98 per cent of all employers and 93 per cent of all employers of four or more employees are free, under state law, to discriminate in employment against members of minority groups.[46] The exclusion of employers from coverage in Maryland, Missouri, Nebraska, and Utah meant that 92 per cent of all employers and 80 per cent of all employers of four or more employees are likewise free, under state law, to discriminate against members of minority groups.[47] In ten states at least 75 per cent of all employers are excluded from coverage by civil-rights laws.[48] Six states have found it feasible to administer civil-rights legislation with respect to employers of four or more employees and have not found discrimination in this larger area of coverage to be any less. In Ohio, for example, the state human-relations commission in 1966 processed 919 cases of employment discrimination to rack up one of the highest case loads in the country.[49] Six states, including some of our large industrial states, now cover employers with one or more employees.

In light of the experience of these states and the need for the widest possible coverage of discrimination in employment, the Alpha Model State Civil-Rights Act has defined the term employer in its Section 821 to include an employer with one or more employees.[50] The suggestion by the Harvard Model State Civil Rights Act for coverage of employers of eight or more employees[51] is rejected as wholly unrealistic in light of the urban crisis throughout the nation. Moreover, the Uniform Model State Anti-Discrimination Act does not specify clearly that it covers political subdivisions as employers.[52] As we have seen, government employment is a very significant area of employment due not only to the number of employees affected but also to the fact that discrimination in employment by government sets a very poor example for other employers. Moreover, discrimination in employment by governments against minority groups is a denial of equal protection of the laws. For this reason, the Alpha Model State Civil-Rights Act adopts

---

[46] U.S. Department of Commerce, Bureau of the Census, *Historical Statistics of the United States, Colonial Times to 1957* (Washington, D.C.: U.S. Government Printing Office, 1960), p. 571. The national percentages supplied by this source are taken in the text as uniformly applicable to these states.

[47] *Ibid.*

[48] *Ibid.*

[49] Ohio Civil Rights Commission, *Seventh Annual Report* (1967), p. 20.

[50] See Chapter 8.

[51] § 201(b). See note 18, above.

[52] §§ 301(1) and 201(5). See note 31, above.

the approach of most states having civil-rights acts enforced through human-relations commissions, and, through its Section 821, covers as an employer not only the state but also any political subdivision of the state.[53] Moreover, it covers all unions and employment agencies without limitation.

In the field of public accommodations, only one state commission has as yet reported the substantial elimination of this form of discrimination against minority groups. This is the Rhode Island Anti-Discrimination Commission.[54] Other states having human-relations commissions with enforcement authority still experience substantial discrimination in public accommodations. Furthermore, considering the overall scene only twenty-four of the thirty-one existing state commissions with enforcement authority have any jurisdiction over public-accommodations discrimination.[55] Between 1952 and 1965, the New York State Commission processed 1087 complaints of public-accommodations discrimination with 587 of these occurring in the last five year period.[56] The 1960 report of this Commission indicated substantial incidents of discrimination in resort areas against Jews and Negroes.[57] It also referred to discrimination against Negroes by barber shops. More recent reports of other agencies state that substantial discrimination against Negroes is being practiced by New York hospitals.[58] The sister states of Ohio and Pennsylvania in 1961 granted jurisdiction to their human-relations commissions over public-accommodations discrimination.[59] Ohio's commission reported that the statute prohibiting this discrimination had been virtually ignored by business concerns prior to 1961.[60] In its first five years of administration

---

[53] See Chapter 8.

[54] Rhode Island Anti-Discrimination Commission, *1959 Annual Report*, as reported in *Race Relations Law Reporter*, Vol. 4 (1959), p. 468.

[55] See Appendix A of this book.

[56] New York State Commission against Discrimination, *Report of Progress* (1960), p. 40; New York State Commission for Human Rights, *Report of Progress* (1963), p. 14; *Report of Progress* (1964), p. 11; *Annual Report*, 1965, p. 14.

[57] New York State Commission against Discrimination, *Report of Progress* (1960), pp. 77–83.

[58] New York State Advisory Committee to the United States Commission on Civil Rights, *Report on Buffalo: Health Facilities* (Washington, D.C.: U.S. Government Printing Office, 1964), pp. 10–19, 24–25; New York State Advisory Committee to the United States Commission on Civil Rights, *Report on New York City: Health Facilities* (Washington, D.C.: U.S. Government Printing Office, 1964), pp. 11–12, 15.

[59] See Appendix A of this book.

[60] Ohio Civil Rights Commission, *Second Annual Report* (1961), p. 5.

of this prohibition, the Ohio Commission processed about 425 complaints.[61] The Pennsylvania Commission in its first five years of administering a similar provision processed 398 complaints of public-accommodations discrimination.[62] Both the Ohio and Pennsylvania Commissions reported that substantial discrimination was occurring in the conduct of skating rinks, taverns, swimming pools, dance halls, fishing lakes, barber shops, golf courses, motels, and restaurants.[63] Two major cities in Pennsylvania in 1963 granted their human-relations commissions their first jurisdiction over public-accommodations discrimination.[64] This legislative action shows that this form of discrimination is still a major problem in the North. Other states either have public-accommodations legislation enforceable through court actions which have proved to be an ineffective remedy or they have no legislation at all covering public-accommodations discrimination.[65]

Even among the thirty-five states having, as of January 1968, human-relations commissions with enforcement power over discrimination in public accommodations, there is a great variance in coverage. With regard to their jurisdictional coverage, commissions in these states can be classified in three groups: those having complete coverage, including Alaska, Connecticut, Indiana, Massachusetts, Ohio, Pennsylvania, and Washington; those having broad coverage although limited to specified areas, including Colorado, Delaware, and New York; and those whose coverage is, at best, limited, including Kansas, Maryland, and Oregon. An extreme example of this wide variance is shown by comparing the jurisdiction of the Massachusetts and Kansas Commissions. The Massachusetts statute provides that "a place of public accommodation, resort or amusement . . . shall be deemed to include any place whether licensed or unlicensed, which is open to and accepts or solicits the patronage of the general public . . ."[66] In con-

---

[61] Ohio Civil Rights Commission, *Seventh Annual Report* (1967), p. 25.

[62] Pennsylvania Human Relations Commission, *Tenth Annual Report* (1965), pp. 27–29.

[63] Ohio Civil Rights Commission, *Fourth Annual Report* (1963), pp. 16, 17–18; Pennsylvania Human Relations Commission, *Seventh Annual Report* (1963), pp. 9–10.

[64] Erie, Philadelphia. See Appendix C of this book.

[65] See Appendix F of this book.

[66] Mass. Gen. Laws Ann. ch. 272, §§ 92A, 98, *as amended* (Michie Supp. 1966), as enforced under Mass. Gen. Laws Ann. ch. 151B, §§ 5–6, *as amended* (Michie Supp. 1966).

trast, the Kansas Commission only has jurisdiction over "discrimination, segregation or separation in hotels, motels, cabin camps and restaurants."[67] Many of the twenty-three states do not have provisions in
their civil-rights statutes applicable to discrimination by professional
men and by businessmen who render services rather than sell goods.
Other states have provisions in their statutes that leave the matter of
coverage in this respect doubtful. Since these business and professional
men either solicit or welcome the patronage of the general public, they
should be subject to civil-rights law administered by human-relations
commissions. Similarly, most states do not have provisions in their
civil-rights laws applicable to business and professional men who have
formed business and professional associations.[68] Membership in these
organizations is often necessary in order for one to be able to operate
successfully in a given business or profession. All of these business and
professional organizations should be prohibited from discriminating
in their admissions policy on the basis of race, color, religion, sex, or
national origin. Most states do not have any specific provision enforced
by a human-relations commission or similar agency applicable to discrimination by state and local government in the operation of public
facilities or provision of public services. Some, like Massachusetts,
New York, and Pennsylvania, have specific provisions directed toward discrimination by educational institutions.[69] These, however, are
principally concerned with private educational institutions. The provisions contained in Titles III and IV of the federal Civil Rights Act
of 1964 directed toward discrimination in governmental facilities and
public schools are very salutary ones and should be included in state
and local civil-rights legislation administered by human-relations
commissions.[70]

Both the Harvard Model State Civil Rights Act[71] and the Uniform
Model State Anti-Discrimination Act[72] are deficient in much the same
way that most state civil-rights laws are in dealing with discrimination in public accommodations against minority groups. Both apply

[67] Kan. Gen. Stat. Ann. §§ 44-1001 to -1013, *as amended* (Supp. 1965).

[68] Connecticut is an example of the exception to this proposition [See, Conn. Gen.
Stat. Rev. §§ 53-35(a) to -36, *as amended* (Supp. 1965)].

[69] See Appendix A of this book.

[70] 42 U.S.C. §§ 2000b, 2000c (1964). The Alpha Model State Civil-Rights Act
proscribes these forms of discrimination in its Subsection (a) of Section 813; see
Chapter 8.

[71] § 201(c). See note 18, above.

[72] § 401. See note 31, above.

apparently only to "business" establishments thus failing to cover the operations of professional persons and firms, as well as those of government, in providing facilities, services, and public education. Neither speaks to discrimination against minority groups in admissions policies of business and professional organizations. The Alpha Model State Civil-Rights Act through its Section 831 retains the wide coverage of the more advanced state acts now in existence and widens this so as to include discrimination by business and professional men rendering any kind of service, and, through its Section 851, by business and professional organizations.[73]

If existing state and local human-relations commissions are to become effective in eliminating discrimination against minority groups, it is clear that, whatever other changes in their operations must be made, these changes can have little impact unless their jurisdiction to compel elimination of discrimination extends to all forms of this discrimination that are seriously harmful to minorities and to the fullest practicable extent over each form of this discrimination. For this reason every existing state and local human-relations commission should be given jurisdiction to the fullest extent practicable over discrimination in employment by employers, unions, and employment agencies, in housing and commercial space by all those responsible for it in a direct or indirect way, in home and commercial-space financing, in public accommodations inclusive of all business and professional services, in business and professional organizations, and in all governmental facilities and services including the public schools. Each of these commissions now has sufficient experience to warrant the extension of its jurisdiction to each of these areas of seriously harmful discrimination. Most, if not all, of these commissions have established a reputation for fairness and wisdom in the processing and adjustment of grievances and have become recognized as essential institutions in the legal order. They have helped the principle of equal opportunity in employment to become accepted not only within their states but also at the federal level, even though their implementation of this principle has fallen far short of producing substantial changes in the Negro's occupational status relative to white persons. By extending the jurisdiction of state and local commissions both within and beyond the field of employment discrimination, state and local governments will assure an eventual acceptance of the principle of equal opportunity in

[73] See Chapter 8.

all these areas. Moreover, when changes in the structure and concept of operation utilized by these commissions, as suggested below, are made in order to cause them to be more effective in their work, their increased jurisdiction over discrimination against minorities will enable them to achieve far more meaningful results than ever before.

When a state or local government not now having a state human-relations commission moves to establish one, it would be wise to grant the commission jurisdiction to deal with all types of seriously harmful discrimination against minorities, at least by way of initiating and receiving complaints, investigating them, and employing the technique of conciliation with a view to obtaining a satisfactory adjustment of grievances found to be justified. The state or local government should also authorize its new commission to hold a public hearing on a complaint when conciliation proves ineffective. Although a state or local commission having only this authority would not be able to compel elimination of discrimination through issuance of a cease and desist order enforceable in the courts, it would be able to accomplish a great deal. It would serve as a safety valve in the state or locality through which just grievances could be aired and the compulsion of publicity and official intervention could be brought to bear upon persons not willing to implement the principle of equal opportunity. The commission would also gain valuable knowledge and experience in dealing with concrete cases of discrimination and would be enabled to counsel the state or local legislature and chief executive more wisely. Chapter 8, as previously stated, sets forth the Alpha Model State Civil-Rights Act. Chapter 11 contains the Alpha Model Local Civil-Rights Ordinance. Chapter 9 contains the Alpha Model State Act for authorizing local governments to establish human-relations commissions and regulating to some extent their operation. Parts VI and VII of these model acts relate to the powers, and duties and procedures respectively, of a human-relations commission. These parts provide a minimum authority for human-relations commissions to proceed along the lines just described as desirable for a state and local human-relations commission. Part VII of each model act authorizes the commission to employ the subpoena power either in the conduct of an investigation following the filing of a complaint of discrimination or the conduct of a public hearing instituted following a failure to obtain a satisfactory adjustment of the complaint through conciliation. The experience of human-relations commissions indicates the great value of the subpoena power whether or not these commissions are also given the authority to issue cease and desist orders enforceable in the courts. These and other sections of the model acts are discussed thoroughly in subsequent chapters.

When a state or local government not now having a state human-relations commission moves to establish one, it would also be wise to confer jurisdiction upon its commission to compel elimination of some of the discrimination against minority groups when use of conciliation fails to accomplish this result. As earlier indicated, the universal experience of these commissions has been that their hand is greatly strengthened in conciliation of grievances by the availability of this authority. Moreover, the fact that a commission has once been granted enforcement authority and has wisely exercised it in one area of discrimination becomes a most effective argument in favor of extending that authority to new areas of harmful discrimination when this extension becomes a public issue. Since enforcement authority is ultimately needed in all of these areas, it is important to grant a state or local commission at least some limited form of this authority as early as this can practicably be done. It is also important to select carefully the initial area or areas of discrimination to be reached by a civil-rights law. In Southern and border states it has usually been conceived that discrimination in certain public accommodations is the most appropriate area for initial regulation by a human-relations commission. In Northern states the initial area usually selected was employment discrimination. Passage of the Civil Rights Acts of 1964–1968 provides a new context for examination of this problem by the eighteen states and many hundreds of communities across the country which, as of January 1968, have yet to create a commission with enforcement authority. It would now be wise for each of these states and localities to confer jurisdiction upon its commission, when first created, to compel elimination of discrimination at least to the extent of the discrimination covered by Titles II (public accommodations) and VII (employment) of the 1964 act and Title VIII (housing home financing) of the 1968 act. Discrimination in these areas will, in any event, be subject to processing by the federal courts in the case of public accommodations and by a federal agency and federal courts in the case of employment and housing. If human-relations commissions were granted jurisdiction over these areas, they would be able under these titles to exercise this jurisdiction and to gain valuable experience. Having jursdiction over employment discrimination at least to the extent of the coverage under Title VII, a state or local commission could then seek cooperative agreements with the federal Equal Employment Opportunity Commission under Section 709(b) of the act.[74] This section permits the federal agency to relinquish its jurisdiction to process complaints of employment discrimination covered by the act within a state to a state or local agency having jurisdiction to compel elimination of that discrimination under its governing statute. Having jurisdiction over public-accommodations discrimination at least to the extent of the coverage of Title II of the act, a state or local commission would be assured that written notice would have to be given it by a person wishing to file a civil action in a federal court complaining of a violation of that title. Section 204(c) of this act precludes the filing of this civil action until written notice is given to a state agency having authority to grant or to seek relief under state law from this discrimination and until thirty days after the giving of this notice.[75] Even after the filing of the civil action upon a complainant's compliance with Section 204(c), a federal court in which the action is filed may stay the proceeding pending termination of enforcement proceedings undertaken by a state agency relative to the subject matter involved in the action. Meanwhile, the state or local agency, when properly authorized, may act to investigate the complaint, utilize the techniques of conciliation, and, if these fail, proceed to a public hearing and issuance of a cease and desist order enforceable in the state courts or request the appropriate enforcement official to institute proceedings for enforcement of the state or local act. Sections 706(b) and (c) of the 1964 federal statute are designed to operate in a way similar to Section 204(c) in regard to a complaint of employment discrimination filed either by an aggrieved person or by a commissioner of the federal Equal Employment Opportunity Commission.[76] While the act has no provisions similar to the three just mentioned that are applicable to complaints of discrimination in governmental facilities and in public schools, it is clear that if a state or local human-relations commission were authorized to eliminate this discrimination through issuance of cease and desist orders enforceable in state courts or otherwise, federal authorities would want to allow ample time for the state commission to exercise its authority relative to any given complaint of discrimination.[77] Indeed, both Titles III and

[74] 42 U.S.C. §§ 2000e-8(b) (1964).
[75] 42 U.S.C. §§ 2000a-2(c) (1964).
[76] 42 U.S.C. §§ 2000e-5(b)–(c) (1964).
[77] In his remarks on December 4, 1964, before the Practising Law Institute

IV of the 1964 federal act provide that the Attorney General, as a condition precedent to instituting a civil action in a district court of the United States relative to discrimination in governmental facilities or public education, must certify that the signer or signers of a complaint of this discrimination are unable, in his judgment, to initiate and maintain appropriate state legal proceedings for relief.[78] The availability of the procedures of state or local human-relations commissions with ample authority to compel elimination of discrimination in governmental facilities or public education would permit a person contemplating the filing of a complaint of this discrimination to initiate and maintain appropriate state or local legal proceedings for relief. Of course, the state or local commission would need to exercise its authority expeditiously and effectively in order for its proceedings to be considered "appropriate" under the federal act. Probably the state and local commissions should also be authorized to obtain protection in the courts for persons filing complaints with them relative to their personal safety, employment, and economic standing, as well as for their families and their property. Similarly, it would be wise for a local or state government which has not done so to confer upon its human relations commission jurisdiction over housing, home financing, and brokerage service discrimination, at least to the extent covered by the Civil Rights Act of 1968.[79] Section 810(c) of this act provides that when a state or local fair housing law provides rights and remedies substantially equivalent to those provided under that act, the Secretary of Housing and Urban Development is to refer to the appropriate state or local official any complaint filed with him, and to take no further action if that official conducts the proper proceedings. Moreover, Section 812(a) provides that the United States district court in which a civil action is filed under Title VIII of the act may continue the case while conciliation efforts are pursued by a state or local agency.

The provisions of the 1964–1968 acts constitute an implied directive to state and local governments to begin to exercise their responsibility

---

Forum, on "The Community and Racial Crises," Mr. Harold H. Greene (chief, Appeals and Research Section, Civil Rights Division, United States Department of Justice), agreed with this view [*The Community and Racial Crises,* edited by David Stahl, Frederick B. Sussmann, and Neil J. Bloomfield (New York: Practising Law Institute, 1966), pp. 28–71]—this reference only partially reflects his remarks.

[78] 42 U.S.C. §§ 2000b(a)(b), 2000c-6 (1964).

[79] P.L. 90-284 (April 11, 1968).

to deal effectively with the civil-rights problem. Discrimination by private action in several areas having been prohibited by these acts, it is now only a question of which element in our federal system is to administer the law in these areas. Surely prudence and commitment to the maintenance of our federal system as we have known it demands that this element be our state and local governments. Discrimination by governmental action relative to governmental facilities and public education has also been prohibited by the 1964 federal act. There have never been any adequate arguments against legislation to preclude this discrimination. The issue has finally been resolved. As in the case of discrimination by private action, it is now only a question of which element in our federal system is to administer law in these areas. It is high time that state and local governments in the South and elsewhere establish the legal framework for discharging their responsibility.

One area of employment discrimination not covered by the 1964 federal act, as previously noted, is that practiced by state and local governments. This is surprising in view of the fact that those who have opposed this discrimination, even on Southern scenes, have generally fared reasonably well in securing official support for their position. Numerous local governments have adopted resolutions indicating that equal opportunity in government employment was their policy, although the subsequent implementation of these resolutions has left much to be desired. One of the Southwestern states has indeed set up its first human-relations commission to deal with this matter.[80] Even if a state or a local government setting up its human-relations commission in the future does not choose to grant that commission jurisdiction to enforce elimination of discrimination covered by the 1964 federal act, it should consider carefully the wisdom of at least granting the commission jurisdiction to compel elimination of discrimination in governmental employment and in employment by government contractors. This area of discrimination is one in which a state and a local government is especially well placed to act with evident justification and to set a model of behavior for employers generally. The state government also has sanctions to apply that are particularly effective in securing compliance with the law.[81] Moreover, since the

[80] Oklahoma. See Appendix B of this book.
[81] *E.g.*, withdrawal of the privilege of becoming a government contractor and cancellation of a license to do business.

federal government has largely not dealt with this area, the need for state and local governmental regulation is especially great.

Another area of discrimination that appears a likely one to choose for granting a commission initial jurisdiction to compel its elimination is discrimination in some or all of public accommodations. In many parts of the South, substantial progress has been achieved in eliminating this form of discrimination by voluntary action.[82] The grant of authority to a state commission to compel elimination of this type of discrimination would in many areas simply reinforce a process already largely completed and reach the more difficult situations in which efforts to secure voluntary compliance with the principle of equal opportunities have failed.[83]

THE PAUCITY OF COMPLAINTS BY MINORITY GROUPS

It has already been suggested that extension of the jurisdiction of state human-relations commissions to additional areas of harmful discrimination against minority groups will not in itself improve the effectiveness of these commissions. It will simply prepare the way for a commission to have a greater impact upon this discrimination when and if its effectiveness can in some way be increased. A second point about these commissions, therefore, relates to a central evidence concerning their ineffectiveness. In the midst of a sea of discriminatory transactions involving minority groups, state human-relations commissions are receiving at best only a trickle of complaints about discrimination from members of these groups. Complaints of discrimination have been so few in relation to the extensive discrimination occurring that some commissions have come to the point of advertising for complaints to be filed through statements at public meetings and through pamphlets, billboards, and ads.[84] Most complaints filed by aggrieved persons result from their having been in personal communication with a member or employee of the commission or some private

[82] *The New York Times* (September 1, 1963), sec. 4, p. 1, cols. 2–3; *The Wall Street Journal* (January 6, 1965), p. 1, col. 6.

[83] This is the purpose underlying enactment of recent ordinances proscribing discrimination in all types of public accommodations by Louisville, Kentucky, and Corpus Christi, Texas [Louisville Human Relations Commission, *1962–3 Annual Report*, pp. 20–1, 25, 28–9, and "Report of Corpus Christi Human Relations Committee to the Mayor, City Council, and City Manager of Corpus Christi, Texas," pp. 6–7 (June, 1964) (mimeographed)].

[84] New York County Lawyers Association, Committee on Civil Rights, "Time for a Change: A Reexamination of the New York State Law against Discrimination in Employment and Its Operation" (December, 1963) (committee report), p. 4.

agency with a civil-rights interest.[85] Moreover, it is now generally recognized that the complaint pattern in employment cases is inversely related to the actual pattern of discrimination.[86] One reason for this seeming anomaly is that minority-group members usually apply for employment with concerns which already employ members of that person's racial, religious or nationality group.[87] They seek employment with these firms because they judge that they are more likely to be accepted by them than by other firms. Nevertheless, a person applying to one of these concerns may encounter discrimination or what he reasonably judges to be discrimination. The complaints filed, therefore, tend to be from individuals applying to these firms.

There are only three likely reasons that can be offered for the relatively few complaints that are being filed with human-relations commissions by minority-group members who have encountered discrimination in employment or in some other field. The first reason may be that persons simply do not know about the existence and facilities of state human-relations commissions. Negroes and Puerto Ricans and Mexican Americans, for example, are minority groups in which large numbers of persons do not read well or extensively. While civil-rights organizations have been especially active in recent years in the sections of the communities in which Negroes and Puerto Ricans live, these minority groups are not so organized that information about these commissions and their functions would be brought home to their members in a thoroughgoing way. The commissions themselves feel that the problem of the paucity of complaints results from the lack of adequate communication lines between the commission and minority groups.[88] This is the reason the commissions have devoted so much effort in recent years to publicizing the nature of their work and attempting to persuade minority-group members to file complaints. A second reason for the small number of the complaints filed

---

85 Minnesota Commission against Discrimination, *1959 Annual Report* (1960).

86 *Ibid.*; Philadelphia Commission on Human Relations, *Annual Report* (1962), pp. 19–20; New York State Commission for Human Rights, *Annual Report, 1965*, pp. 15–16.

87 Minnesota Commission against Discrimination, *1959 Annual Report* (1960); and Philadelphia Commission on Human Relations, *Annual Report* (1962), pp. 19–20.

88 New York County Lawyers Association, Committee on Civil Rights, "Time for a Change," p. 4. The trend among the commissions toward opening regional offices is based upon this judgment [New York State Commission for Human Rights, *Annual Report* (1962), pp. 3, 44, 51; Pennsylvania Human Relations Commission, *Eighth Annual Report, 1963*, p. 19; Paul H. Norgren and Samuel E. Hill (assisted

with the commissions may well be that members of minority groups do not have any confidence that these commissions will provide them with effective and prompt remedies against the discrimination they have suffered. Civil-rights groups have been very critical of the work of most state and local human-relations commissions. These commissions have been rejected by members of minority groups because they have proved ineffective instruments for producing equal opportunities in employment and other areas.[89] They assert that more complaints will be filed with the commissions only when necessary changes in their structure and concept of operations have been made and they have demonstrated a new effectiveness in handling complaints of discrimination.[90]

A third reason for the small volume of complaints of discrimination filed with state and local human-relations commissions by members of minority groups may well be the remoteness of these commissions from local community and neighborhood affairs and the difficulty which these persons have in utilizing the facilities of these commissions. It must be remembered that members of minority groups most affected by discrimination by and large belong to the lowest economic groups in their communities and states. They are bowed down by poverty, ill-educated, poorly motivated, and fearful. On the other hand, the state human-relations commission is a state agency rather than a local one. In most states the commission is wedded to the notion of a centralized administration of the law under which it operates.[91] No matter how many local advisory committees are utilized by a state commission so committed, it remains aloof and remote from local affairs. It is not sufficiently accessible to the ordinary person. It does not really involve the leadership of the majority and minority groups in each community in the administration of the basic law. Under these circumstances, it is wholly unrealistic to expect that members of minority groups will often resort to the facilities of a state human-rela-

---

by F. Ray Marshall), *Toward Fair Employment* (New York: Columbia University Press, 1964), p. 145].

[89] New York County Lawyers Association, Committee on Civil Rights, "Time for a Change," pp. 1, 5, 7, 9; Samuel E. Hill, "Twenty Years of State Fair Employment Practice Commissions: A Critical Analysis with Recommendations," *Buffalo Law Review,* Vol. 14 (1964) pp. 23, 68–69.

[90] New York County Lawyers Association, Committee on Civil Rights, "Time for a Change," pp. 13–16; Hill, "Twenty Years of State Fair Employment Practice Commissions," pp. 40, 55–56, 66–68.

[91] Norgren and Hill, *Toward Fair Employment,* p. 145.

tions commission. All three reasons given above have probably been operative in causing minority-group members to refrain from filing complaints of discrimination with state human-relations commissions. The first two reasons have also operated to cause the same result with local commissions. On the other hand, the position is taken that no amount of advertising of the wares of these commissions is likely to establish the necessary communications lines with members of minority groups and to move them to begin to file these complaints more readily. The three major difficulties with the operation of state and local human-relations commissions call for more fundamental changes. One difficulty relates to weaknesses in the technique which they utilize in processing complaints of particular discriminatory transactions. A second difficulty flows from the reliance by these commissions almost exclusively upon the processing, case by case, of individual complaints as the basis for producing equal opportunities for minority groups. A third difficulty relates to the failure of the state commissions to decentralize their operations and of the local commissions to reach into the heart of minority-group ghettos.

THE NEED FOR COMPLAINTS FILED BY COMMISSIONS

Turning to an examination of the first difficulty with state and local human-relations commissions, it is evident from what has been said that one major weakness in their structure is the requirement for many of them that they first receive a complaint from a person aggrieved by an allegedly discriminatory transaction before they can initiate their official processes looking to the use of enforcement power, if necessary, to end discrimination found to be occurring. While these commissions may initiate investigations of persons and concerns covered by the statutes they administer, they are not authorized to file complaints for the purpose of instituting enforcement proceedings to eliminate discrimination found to exist.[92] Surely no more disabling requirement could have been imposed upon these agencies or could be less consistent with their mission once it is understood why minority-group persons are not filing complaints of their own volition. One of the central facets of modern administrative process is its capacity to shape the nature of the litigation by which form is given to the stat-

---

[92] This was true of the New York State Commission between 1945 and 1965 [New York State Commission for Human Rights, *Annual Report, 1962*, pp. 2, 5]. In subsequent years this Commission has begun to encourage local efforts [New York State Commission for Human Rights, *Annual Report, 1965*, p. 25].

utes administered and to regulate the emphasis and momentum to be developed in enforcement actions.[93] The National Labor Relations Board is an example of an agency administering a statute in which only an official can file a complaint instituting the adjudicative processes of the board.[94] The Federal Trade Commission in administering Section 5 of the Federal Trade Commission Act provides another example of this.[95] When private persons aggrieved by alleged violations of statutes administered by administrative agencies are permitted to set in motion the adjudicative process of these agencies, this is typically permitted as an alternative to these agencies instituting this process upon their own motion. This is the arrangement typically employed in the case of the Interstate Commerce Commission.[96] It has also been utilized in the Civil Rights Act of 1964 so far as the federal Equal Employment Opportunity Commission is concerned.[97] Unless state and local human-relations commissions are granted the authority to investigate for the purpose of determining if violations of the statutes they administer are probably occurring and, upon finding that this is the case, to file complaints initiating their enforcement processes, it is clear that these commissions will remain seriously incapacitated in reaching the bulk of the discriminatory transactions that are occurring. This authority is especially needed with regard to concerns and unions which have not yet opened employment or other opportunities to any minority-group members. As earlier indicated, few complaints are being filed with state and local agencies regarding these concerns and unions. This authority is also needed for dealing with those areas of discrimination in which it is very difficult for the one discriminated against to know whether discrimination has occurred. This is particularly true of discrimination by employment agencies which, by and large, are continuing to honor requests by employers for personnel belonging to the white race only.[98] These requests are readily kept secret by these agencies and the minority-group person seeking a job through them usually has no way of knowing whether discrimination has occurred. Obviously, in these circumstances, a complaint is not filed by that person. The only remedy in this situa-

---

[93] Kenneth Culp Davis, *Administrative Law Text* (St. Paul, Minnesota: West Publishing Co., 1959), pp. 13–17.

[94] 29 U.S.C. §§ 153(d), 160(b) (1964).

[95] 15 U.S.C. §§ 45(b) (1964).

[96] 49 U.S.C. §§ 13, 15(1), (1964).

[97] 42 U.S.C. § 2000e-5(a) (1964).

[98] Norgren and Hill, *Toward Fair Employment*, pp. 35–39, 131–132.

tion is an investigation by the human-relations commission and the filing by it of complaints in appropriate cases. The Alpha Model State Civil-Rights Act through its Section 702 authorizes the state commission, as well as a person aggrieved by discrimination, any civil-rights organization chartered to combat discrimination, and the attorney general, to file complaints concerning alleged discrimination.[99]

It must be observed that a commission's concept of its operation may cause it not to utilize authority, when it is granted, to file complaints. This is indicated by the fact that although some state human-relations commissions have been granted the authority to file complaints initiating enforcement proceedings, they have, by and large, used this authority only sparsely. The Massachusetts Commission, for example, rarely uses this authority. Mrs. Mildred H. Mahoney, who, prior to 1965, served for many years as chairman of the Massachusetts Commission, stated that her opposition to using the authority extensively was based upon the ground that this use is inconsistent with the Commission's function of seeking to obtain adjustment of complaints through a process of conciliation.[100] By way of contrast, the Pennsylvania Commission has always made a substantial use of its authority to file complaints of violation after an investigation. In its first year of operations it initiated 52 per cent of the complaints it processed.[101] In the second and third years it initiated 40 per cent or better of the complaints it processed.[102] For the ten-year period ending December 31, 1965, the Commission had initiated 32 per cent of all complaints of employment discrimination processed by it.[103] Similarly it had initiated 28 and 18 per cent, respectively, of all complaints of discrimination in housing and public accommodations processed by it by the end of 1965. The Pennsylvania Commission has as excellent a record of "satisfactory adjustments" of complaints through conciliation as has the Massachusetts Commission.[104] This indicates that the Massachu-

[99] See Chapter 8.

[100] Interview with Mrs. Mildred H. Mahoney conducted by Mrs. Judith G. Shepard, my research assistant, in April, 1964.

[101] Pennsylvania Fair Employment Practices Commission, *First Annual Report* (1957) p. 16.

[102] Pennsylvania Fair Employment Practices Commission, *Second Annual Report* (1958), p. 3; *Third Annual Report* (1959), p. 3.

[103] Pennsylvania Human Relations Commission, *Tenth Annual Report* (1965), p. 17.

[104] Pennsylvania Commission as of December 31, 1962: 53 per cent of all cases [*Id.*, pp. 21, 27]; Massachusetts Commission as of December 31, 1962: 71 per cent

setts Commission is not justified in its failure to make extensive use
of its authority to file complaints.

THE NEED FOR BETTER COMPLAINT-FILING PROCEDURES

Three remaining points may be profitably made about the initiation
of complaints by a commission when it has been given this authority.
One refers to the kinds of complaints a commission should seek to file.
The second concerns the percentage of all complaints processed which
a commission should be initiating. The third involves the question of
whether a single commissioner should be permitted to file a complaint.
As to the first point, a commission should seek to emphasize the "big
cases" in its filing of complaints. If it is doing its work well, a commission is likely to receive an ample supply of complaints of particular
discriminatory transactions from persons aggrieved by them. For this
reason, the peculiar virtue of commission-initiated complaints is that
they can be directed to concerns and persons responsible for large
numbers of discriminatory transactions. When the commission initiates an investigation of this type, it should primarily be seeking to discover whether that concern is in any of its divisions or departments
following a general practice of discriminating against members of minority groups. This does not mean that a commission would not be
concerned with discovering and providing remedies for particular instances of discrimination involving isolated individuals. It simply involves the matter of primary emphasis and objectives underlying use
of commission-initiated complaints. The second point to be discussed
concerns the extent to which a commission should be initiating complaints. The experience of the Pennsylvania Commission indicates that
a commission can readily handle a load of complaints 35 to 50 per cent
of which it is initiating itself. It would appear that all state and local
human-relations commissions without the authority to file complaints
should, upon receiving this authority and with appropriate budgets
and staffs, increase their caseloads until complaints filed by them represent at least 35 per cent of their total caseloads. Moreover, in view of
the usefulness of commission-initiated complaints, each commission
should attempt to increase its filings of complaints to the maximum extent possible beyond this figure. A final point relating to commission-

---

of all cases [Massachusetts Commission against Discrimination, *Annual Report*
(1965), p. 27]. One half of the Massachusetts cases were concerned, however, with
age discrimination while almost all Pennsylvania cases were concerned with discrimination based upon race, religion, national origin, and similar grounds.

initiated complaints concerns whether or not a single commissioner or a member of the commission staff should be permitted to file a complaint. Eight of the existing thirty state commissions, as of January 1967, were permitted to file complaints only when a majority of its members voted in favor of filing the complaint.[105] The state and local human-relations commissioners have a wide variety of functions to perform both collectively and individually in the work of the commission.[106] It is important that no function be assigned the whole commission for which there is not a strong justification. Usually, single commissioners are designated to investigate, with the help of the commission's staff, complaints of discrimination, to make findings as to whether probable cause exists for believing the allegations of discrimination, and to attempt to obtain elimination of discrimination by conciliation and persuasion. To file a complaint initiating this process is of the same order as the functions already allocated to a single commissioner. If it is important that the authority to initiate complaints be lodged somewhere in the commission, as has already been amply demonstrated, the usual nature of the functions of a single commissioner argues strongly that this additional function be added to them. Spreading the authority to initiate complaints among each of the several commissioners will serve to expedite the filing of complaints. Of course, the authority to file a complaint accorded individual commissioners should be limited to situations in which they have good reason to believe an unlawful practice has been committed. Section 702 of the Alpha Model State Civil-Rights Act contains a provision granting this authority to a single commissioner.[107] Much can be said for granting this authority also to the executive director of a human-relations commission. He has general supervisory authority over the staff of the commission which conducts investigations of complaints. He is thoroughly familiar with the work of the staff and frequently advises individual commissioners or the whole commission about decisions they the investigation of a complaint, a fact which helps assure the exercise of an impartial judgment. He is the chief officer of the commission

[105] Connecticut, Massachusetts, Minnesota, New York, Ohio, Pennsylvania, Rhode Island, and Washington. See Appendix A of this book.

[106] Elizabeth Salk, "The Commissioners," *Pittsburgh Human Relations Revised* (October, 1962), Vol. 5, No. 6, p. 1, col. 2. This note contains a useful brief discussion of the role of commissioners of human-relations commissions and the relationship between them and the commission staff.

[107] See Chapter 8. This follows the practice that has been adopted in Colorado, Iowa, Kentucky, and Wyoming. See Appendix A of this book.

an impartial judgment. He is the chief officer of the commission charged with translating its general policies into effective action by members of the staff. Probably for these and perhaps other reasons, Alaska[108] and New Haven, Connecticut,[109] in recently establishing their human-relations commissions granted the executive director authority to file complaints. The experience of these commissions with this new device should be closely watched.

THE NEED FOR A LONGER PERIOD FOR FILING COMPLAINTS

A fourth point about the ineffectiveness of human-relations commissions relates to the short period allocated for filing a complaint of discrimination after the occurrence of the allegedly unlawful act. As of January 1968, Utah[110] and Baltimore, Maryland,[111] permitted only thirty days; most states[112] and the federal government[113] permitted only ninety days for filing a complaint relative to employment discrimination, while five states[114] permitted six months, and New York[115] and California[116] one year. Since the principal remedy available for discrimination by a business house, union, property owner, or government agency is injunctive in nature, there is far less reason for brief limitation periods than for ordinary civil causes of action. The principal objective of administrative action is to stop a continuation of discriminatory action, and to provide the complainant with the thing or opportunity he was seeking which the discriminatory action precluded him from obtaining. The mere fact that an injury was done to the complainant for which he may obtain some form of compensation or damages from the respondent in the same administrative or separate court action should be no peculiar reason for insisting upon a short limitation period in which complaints may be filed. Statutes of limitation for asserting civil causes of action, particularly for torts to

[108] See Appendix A of this book.

[109] See Appendix C of this book.

[110] Utah Code Ann. 1953 § 34-17-7(15) (1966).

[111] See Appendix C of this book.

[112] Connecticut, Hawaii, Indiana, Iowa, Kansas, Michigan, Nebraska, New Hampshire, Pennsylvania, and Wisconsin. See Appendix A of this book.

[113] 42 U.S.C. § 2000e-5(d) (1964). However, a longer time is permitted when a complainant has first sought relief under a state or local law as required by 42 U.S.C. § 2000e-5(b) (1964). See Rosen, "Division of Authority under Title VII of the Civil Rights Act of 1964," pp. 860–865.

[114] Colorado, Massachusetts, Minnesota, Ohio, and Washington. See Appendix A of this book.

[115] N.Y. Exec. Law § 297(3), *as amended* (McKinney Supp. 1967).

[116] Cal. Labor Code § 1422 *as amended* (Deering's Supp. 1966).

which unlawful discrimination most nearly corresponds, rarely set a period less than one year and frequently allow a longer period.[117] The "short, short" period of limitation contained in most civil-rights statutes simply means that society places a very low value on the right we permit to be vindicated under these statutes. The practical effect of such limitations is to cut off all practical remedies from discrimination for many members of minority groups and to cut down the effectiveness of administration of civil-rights statutes.

There are special reasons for not restricting complainants under civil-rights statutes too severely in filing complaints of discrimination. One is the fact that it is difficult to discover whether discrimination has been practiced when employment, housing, financing, admission to a union, or referral by an employment agency has been denied.[118] In many instances the ascertainment of whether discrimination has been practiced is beyond the capacity of most persons refused some opportunity. If discriminatory practices in these instances are to be discovered, they must be ferreted out as a result of regular inspection and investigation conducted under government auspices. This inspection and investigation are of necessity often conducted long after discriminatory practices have occurred. It seems highly unjust to preclude a person from filing a complaint upon the basis of data discovered in a government investigation that could not possibly have been accessible to him earlier, just because 30, 90, or even 330 days have elapsed since the discrimination occurred. Another reason that counsels against a short period of limitation in the human-rights field is the nature of the complainant, particularly when the only complaint that may be filed is one of the person aggrieved by discrimination. The minority-group complainant is often unfamiliar with the existence of a human-relations commission and may be reluctant or even afraid to approach the commission even if he does know about it. A person aggrieved by discrimination must usually be counseled by a civil-rights organization, a church, a friend, or a member of a human-relations commission that he should file a complaint with the commission in order to protect his rights.

[117] New York, for example, has established a three-year limitation period for actions for personal injuries except in the case of actions for assault, battery, false imprisonment, malicious prosecution, libel, slander, or violation of the neglect of privacy where the limitation period is two years [N.Y. Civ. Proc. Law §§ 214–215 (1963)].

[118] See Norgren and Hill, *Toward Fair Employment*, pp. 17–55.

The Utah limitation period of thirty days probably precludes the filing of more justified claims of discrimination than it permits. The ninety-day period presents the same kind of difficulty for many members of minority groups, differing only slightly in effect from the thirty-day limitation period. The only practicable thing a member of a minority group can do is to file a complaint upon each refusal of an opportunity or thing desired. This is, of course, most undesirable. The New York legislature in 1965 dropped the ninety-day period in favor of a period of one year.[119] This legislative change came after the New York Commission had worked with the ninety-day period for twenty years. The Harvard Model State Civil Rights Act allows six months for filing a complaint.[120] The Uniform Model State Anti-Discrimination Act allows one year except in the case of employment discrimination.[121] Little or no justification can be adduced for allowing a different period of time for filing a complaint depending upon the kind of discrimination that is involved. The one-year period is justified as against shorter periods of time in light of the special difficulties in discovering the existence of discrimination encountered both by members of the minority group affected and by the commissions themselves. For this reason the Alpha Model State Civil Rights Act, through its Section 703, has adopted the uniform period of one year for filing a complaint with regard to all forms of discrimination.[122]

THE NEED FOR EXPEDITING THE PROCESSING OF COMPLAINTS PRIOR TO THE HEARING STAGE

A fifth point to be made about the ineffectiveness of existing state and local human-relations commissions focuses upon their processing of complaints of discrimination once they have been filed. Even if the jurisdiction of these commissions is extended to the widest practicable reaches of discrimination, if their lines of communications with minority groups are improved, and if authority is granted them to initiate complaints, these changes will achieve very little if these commissions fail to process complaints in an effective manner. It is the position of this book that these commissions are performing this function in a very unsatisfactory manner and that this is the reason members of minority groups regard them today with great cynicism and refuse

---

[119] N.Y. Exec. Law § 297(3), *as amended* (McKinney Supp. 1967).
[120] § 707(a). See note 18, above.
[121] § 703(a). See note 31, above.
[122] See Chapter 8.

to make extensive use of their facilities. It has already been pointed out that state and local commissions rely almost exclusively upon a three-step procedure for processing each complaint: an investigation of the complaint, a determination on the basis of this investigation whether probable cause exists for crediting the allegations of discrimination, and an attempt through conciliation to persuade the person believed to be discriminating to cease from his unlawful practice. The statistic which state and local human-relations commissions cite most frequently as evidence of their accomplishments is the high percentage of "satisfactory adjustments" obtained through conciliation of complaints which they have found to be probably justified after investigation. They point with great pride to the fact that they conducted only a negligible number of public hearings and issued even fewer orders in disposing of these complaints. These commissions place a very high value upon the conciliation process and they have worked very hard to make it very nearly their exclusive method for producing compliance with the law they administer.

In maintaining their commitment to the conciliation process, state and local human-relations commissions have, however, sacrificed a number of values of very great importance. It is clear that, due to this commitment, these commissions, in comparison with other administrative agencies, usually devote an extraordinarily long time to their performance of the steps of investigation, "probable cause" determination, and attempt to obtain a settlement of complaints through conciliation. It is not unusual that these commissions take a year or more to complete these three steps.[123] Meanwhile, the complainant who had encountered the alleged discrimination in the course of seeking a job, union membership, or housing, has long since been forced to take a substitute for what he originally was seeking, or to do without it. By the time the commission has finally obtained its "satisfactory adjustment" the complainant in the case will in most instances have substantially changed his position from what it was when he filed his complaint. It is not difficult to see that the remedy, if any, provided a complainant one or more years after he has encountered a discriminatory transaction is usually not very helpful to that complainant, whatever its value as a "satisfactory adjustment" in other respects. As soon as the minority-group communities become aware that this is not an

[123] State of New York, Staff Report to the Joint Legislative Committee on Industrial and Labor Conditions. *Discrimination in Employment and the Operation of the New York State Commission for Human Rights* (December, 1964), pp. 7–11.

unusual plight for a person filing a complaint of discrimination with a state or local commission, that awareness will inevitably move them to bypass the commission and use other means than filing complaints for attempting to increase their opportunities for obtaining employment, housing, and other vitally needed things. Perhaps this, more than any other one factor, has affected adversely the lines of communications between state and local commissions and minority groups. It also demonstrates that state and local commissions are victims of their own practices. The Colorado Commission has recently recognized the facts of life about the obstructionism of respondents and delays produced by its commitment to the use of conciliation process as the primary means for producing compliance with the law. It has proposed that the state legislature amend the civil-rights law administered by it so as to permit the assessment of penalties against respondents for the purpose of remunerating complainants "for the delays and hardships suffered by them" after the Commission has determined that probable cause exists for crediting the allegations of their complaints.[124] This is a striking and candid admission of a problem created by the universal commitment of state human-relations commissions to the almost exclusive use of conciliation process for obtaining compliance with civil-rights law. While the proposal obviously has merit for delays that cannot be avoided by a commission, it also suggests the question whether the obstructionism and delays being created through the present method of using conciliation process are not in themselves so unreasonable as to demand a stringent modification of this method. It is the position of this book that these effects of the conciliation process are grossly unreasonable. An examination of the work of several state commissions will amply support this conclusion.

Prior to 1965, the New York State Commission had no authority to initiate complaints although it could request the industrial commissioner or the attorney general of the state to file a complaint, both of whom were authorized to do this.[125] The Commission did not utilize this latter alternative, preferring to process complaints filed by aggrieved persons or to conduct informal investigations without a complaint having been filed.[126] During 1960 the Commission received 652

[124] Colorado Anti-Discrimination Commission, *Eighth Annual Report* (1961–1962), p. 10.

[125] N.Y. Exec. Law § 297, *as amended* (Supp. 1964).

[126] New York State Commission against Discrimination, *Report of Progress* (1960), p. 18; New York State Commission for Human Rights, *Annual Report, 1962,*

complaints of employment discrimination filed by aggrieved persons.[127] At the beginning of 1960 it had on hand 653 similar complaints which had not been closed during the previous year either by dismissal, execution of a conciliation agreement, or issuance of a cease and desist order following the calling or holding of a public hearing. The total cases of employment discrimination in the state Commission's hands during 1960 were, therefore, 1,305 in number. By the end of 1960 the Commission had disposed of 710 of these 1,305 cases. It consequently had approximately 600 cases left which it had not been able to close during the year, representing a little less than one-half of its entire case load and a little less than the number of cases falling in the same category at the beginning of the year. If 1960 is to be taken as typical of the Commission's operations, this indicates that in a very substantial number of cases of employment discrimination processed each year, the Commission has taken at least one year to complete the stages of investigation, probable cause determination, and conciliation. The figures for the Commission's 1962 operations indicated that this was still true.[128] Moreover, when it is considered that 470 out of the 710 cases closed in 1960 were closed on the ground that no probable cause existed for crediting the allegations of the complaint, it is not improbable that in many, if not a majority, of the cases in which probable cause was determined to exist, the Commission takes longer than one year to complete the investigation, probable cause determination, and the additional step of conciliation that is involved in disposing of them. Indeed, the Commission reported in 1960 upon cases in which it had ordered a public hearing.[129] These were cases in which the three steps of processing the usual complaint had not sufficed to move a respondent to agree to cease what was believed by the Com-

---

pp. 1–2. But in *Lefkowitz v. Farrell*, C-9287-63 (N.Y. State Comm. for Human Rights, 1964), *Race Relations Law Reporter*, Vol. 9 (1964), p. 393, the Commission held that a union had excluded Negroes from membership throughout its existence, after hearing a complaint filed by the Civil Rights Bureau of the State Attorney General's Office. Its remedial order was enforced [*State Commission for Human Rights v. Farrell*, 262 N.Y.S. 2d 526 (Sup. Ct., N.Y. Co., 1965); 263 N.Y.S. 2d 250 (Sup. Ct., N.Y. Co., 1965)].

[127] New York State Commission against Discrimination, *Report of Progress* (1960), p. 29.

[128] New York State Commission for Human Rights, *Annual Report, 1962*, p. 9; State of New York, Staff Report to the Joint Legislative Committee on Industrial and Labor Conditions, "Discrimination in Employment," pp. 7–11.

[129] New York State Commission against Discrimination, *Report of Progress* (1960).

mission to be an unlawful practice. In four employment-discrimination cases involving airlines reported upon in 1960, the Commission had taken a period of approximately two years to complete the three-step process it usually follows. In two steamship-line cases, this process had taken two and four years, respectively, to complete. In all six instances, the Commission had not scheduled a hearing date by the end of 1960 although the public hearing had been ordered to be held in each in 1959. Consequently the period between the filing of the complaint and final Commission action could not have been less than three years in five of these cases nor less than five in one of them. In its 1962 report, the Commission indicated that 140 of the 519 complaints of employment discrimination that had not been closed by December 31, 1962, had been received in earlier years.[130] This figure was equivalent to 70 per cent of the cases in which satisfactory adjustments of discriminatory practices were achieved in 1962, the cases in which it is usual that all three steps for processing complaints are taken. This more precise information reinforces the conclusion drawn upon the basis of the earlier figures noted. In 1965, despite having received 150 more employment complaints than in 1964, the Commission succeeded in reducing the number of cases left open in all categories of alleged discrimination from 580 to 469.[131] This indicates that the Commission is making progress in cutting down the processing time.

The Ohio Commission has a similar record. This Commission reports on its activities on a fiscal year basis ending on May 31. In June 1962, the Commission had 156 complaints of employment discrimination under investigation carried over from the previous fiscal year.[132] It received 203 complaints of this type during the fiscal year ending May 31, 1963. The total complaints sufficiently alleging discrimination in employment that were on hand for processing during the 1963 fiscal year were, therefore, 359 in number. Of these complaints 91 were still under investigation at the end of the year. Another 41 complaints had been processed through the stage of conciliation but were being kept open while the quality of compliance was being checked. Thus, during the 1963 fiscal year, in processing about 35 per cent of the complaints of employment discrimination filed with it, the Ohio

---

[130] New York State Commission for Human Rights, *Annual Report, 1962*, p. 2.

[131] New York State Commission for Human Rights, *Annual Report, 1965*, p. 12.

[132] Ohio Civil Rights Commission, *Fourth Annual Report* (1963), p. 10. This figure was obtained by deducting total invalid and valid new complaints from total cases processed in the fiscal year reported upon.

Commission spent on the average at least one year in completing the stages of investigation, probable cause determination, conciliation, and checking on compliance before closing a case. By the 1966 fiscal year, this percentage had increased to 42 per cent.[133] In its 1961 report, the Commission refers to one employment-discrimination case in which the investigation stage alone was described as having taken many months to complete.[134] This, incidentally, was a case in which the Commission found that there was no probable cause for crediting the allegations of the complaint. In 1962 the Minnesota Commission reported a case of employment discrimination in which its investigation covered a period of three years.[135] The case was then referred back to the Michigan Commission with which it had originated. In the fourth year following the filing of the complaint by the aggrieved person, the latter Commission made a finding that probable cause existed for crediting the allegations of the complaint. Subsequently in that year the complainant was employed as an airline hostess by the respondent involved in the case. The Minnesota Commission then voted to categorize the case as "satisfactorily adjusted."

The Pennsylvania Commission has a better record than have the New York and Ohio Commissions. At the beginning of its 1965 reporting year, the Commission had on hand 149 cases of alleged employment discrimination.[136] By the end of this period it had received 260 additional complaints of this form of discrimination. Out of the 409 complaints of this type it had under consideration in the 1965 reporting period, the agency closed 324 cases, leaving 86 cases still in the process of investigation, probable cause determination, or conciliation. In 124 cases it found unlawful discrimination and obtained a satisfactory adjustment of it. Unlike the performances of the New York and Ohio Commissions, the Pennsylvania Commission takes less than one year to complete its processing through the stage of conciliation of almost all complaints found to be justified.

The case disposition statistics of the New York, Ohio, and other commissions are all indicative that the filing of a complaint in a large number of cases involving an allegation of employment discrimina-

---

[133] Ohio Civil Rights Commission, *Seventh Annual Report* (1967), p. 20.

[134] Ohio Civil Rights Commission, *Second Annual Report* (1961), p. 17.

[135] Minnesota Commission against Discrimination, *1962 Annual Report* (1963), p. 4.

[136] Pennsylvania Human Relations Commission, *Tenth Annual Report* (1965), pp. 21–29.

tion is the prelude to a long, drawn-out process of investigation, probable cause determination, and conciliation in which these commissions spend a year or more seeking to avoid bringing to trial a respondent believed by them to have violated the law. As we shall see shortly, this means for many complainants the loss of a substantial remedy they might have obtained if the commission had brought the case to trial at an earlier date following a reasonably short period for the usual three-step processing of complaints. While the situation in processing housing-discrimination complaints is somewhat less obvious than in the case of employment-discrimination complaints, it is clear that the New York and Pennsylvania Commissions are carrying forward from each year's operations a substantial number of complaints for disposition in the following year. As we shall see, delay in settling a complaint of housing discrimination even for a fairly short period can result in the loss of a substantial remedy for the complainant.

The Right to a Hearing

One effective solution to the problem presented by the tendency of state commissions to prolong the period of processing a complaint unduly and not to call for a public hearing of it is to accord to the complainant the right, upon request, to obtain a hearing of his charges after the commission or one of its authorized officers has determined that probable cause exists for crediting those charges. In order to preserve the commission's role in attempting to obtain compliance by conciliation, the commission should be granted a period of no more than thirty days following the determination that probable cause exists to use the technique of conciliation for this purpose. If the commission has not obtained a settlement of the case within that period and the complainant has requested a hearing, the commission should be required to conduct a hearing in the same way that it is required to conduct hearings ordered by it or by a commissioner assigned to process a complaint. Section 711 of the Alpha Model Civil Rights Act contains a provision embodying this solution.[137] The formula incorporated in this provision is very similar to the one utilized in Section 706(e) of the Civil Rights Act of 1964.[138] The latter provision authorized the federal Equal Employment Opportunity Commission to extend the original thirty-day period for conciliation purposes not more than

[137] See Chapter 8.
[138] 42 U.S.C. § 2000e-5(e), (1964).

sixty days upon a determination that further conciliation efforts were warranted. This modification has been rejected in the suggested statute as not necessary in view of the fact that conciliation efforts can be continued by a commission until the hearing date or even beyond that date. The proviso of Section 706(e) permits a period of delay in commission procedure that does not appear justified.

The solution suggested may not be sufficient to eliminate the tendency of state commissions to take an inordinate time in investigating a complaint and in determining whether probable cause exists for crediting it. The problem presented by delay at the point of these earlier steps is, however, believed to be due to the manner in which they are being performed rather than to the agency's commitment to use conciliation instead of holding public hearings. This problem will be discussed immediately below and a solution suggested for it.

The Harvard Model State Civil Rights Act does not speak to the problem of undue time taken by a human-relations commission in conducting the process of conciliation or to any related problem.[139] The Uniform Model State Anti-Discrimination Act does attempt to do this as well as to speak to the problem of the commission's failure "to act seasonably on a complaint" in so far as the investigation and probable cause determination is concerned.[140] It tries to do this through one provision, Section 704.[141] Under this section if, within sixty days after a complaint is filed or within thirty days after an application is filed for review of a determination that no probable cause to credit a complaint exists, the commission has not issued an order dismissing the complaint or stating the terms of a conciliation agreement, the commission shall set a hearing on the complaint. This formula, it is suggested, is too rough and inflexible a solution for the several problems involved. A commission may have very good reason for taking considerable time to make an investigation. No two cases are alike. The Uniform Model State Act takes no account of the need for according discretion to an able and diligent commission at this stage of the proceedings. The second problem is one concerned with the commission's determination that probable cause does or does not exist for crediting the allegations of a complaint of discrimination. The time for making

---

[139] See note 18, above.
[140] National Conference of Commissioners on Uniform State Laws, "Fourth Tentative Draft: Uniform State Anti-Discrimination Act," comment to Section 704, p. 51 (mimeographed).
[141] See note 31, above.

this determination should not and does not greatly vary from case to case. The difficulty with regard to these determinations has not been one of time consumed in making them but, as will shortly be demonstrated, with the quality of these determinations and the guidelines for making them. A time limit is a poor substitute here for the right kind of remedy for this type of problem. The third problem is, as previously suggested, the undue time that has been taken by commissions in attempting to move a recalcitrant employer, union, or employment agency voluntarily to comply with the act. Here it seems a time limit is appropriate. But the remedy of a time limit should be applied *from the time that conciliation begins* which is precisely when the problem of undue time is likely to be presented. It is inappropriate to set a time limit on processing a complaint dating from any point in time prior to the initiation of conciliation proceedings. It is this distinction of problems that is wholly overlooked by the drafters of Section 704 of the Uniform State Anti-Discrimination Act. The solution adopted in Section 711 of the Alpha Model State Civil-Rights Act[142] appears eminently better suited for solving the problem of a human-relations commission "failing to act seasonably on a complaint." It is designed to leave to the discretion of the commission the time for conducting an investigation. Any tendency of the commission to litigate *ex parte* the complaint at this time can be taken care of through a specific provision directed to this problem. This particular problem will shortly be discussed. This model act also is designed to take care of the poor quality of probable cause determinations. That problem will be discussed next. Finally this model act is designed to cut down on the undue time spent in conducting conciliation looking to voluntary cessation of unlawful practices of which complaint has been made. The solution has been discussed in the last few paragraphs and involves a time limit tailored to the incidence of the problem.

In order to obtain maximum effectiveness for the conciliation process after the determination that probable cause exists for crediting a complaint, it is suggested further that the commission be permitted to use its discretion in publicizing the fact that a complaint has been filed and the nature of its endeavors to obtain a settlement of it. Most state and local statutes governing human-relations commissions as well as the Harvard Model Civil Rights Act[143] and the Uniform Model State

---

[142] See Chapter 8.
[143] § 707(b). See note 18, above.

Anti-Discrimination Act[144] preclude this publicity. The Alpha Model State Civil-Rights Act in Chapter 8 has omitted this usual provision and leaves the matter to the discretion of the commission.[145] Publicity can do a great deal of good in moving a respondent to comply with the act. If compliance is forthcoming quietly, it need not be used. With the shortening of the time for conciliation, the weapon of publicity is an appropriate one.

THE NEED FOR IMPROVED DETERMINATION OF PROBABLE CAUSE

A sixth weakness of human-relations commissions relates to the fact that in processing complaints of discrimination these commissions are disposing of a large percentage of these complaints by determining that no probable cause exists for crediting the allegations of discrimination contained in them. Since most of these commissions have no authority to file complaints, this statement has reference almost exclusively to complaints filed by persons who have alleged they have been subjected to discrimination. The New York State Commission in 1962 dismissed upon this basis 588, or 70 per cent of a total of 843 complaints of employment discrimination finally disposed of by it.[146] Over a period of seventeen years ending in 1962, this Commission had finally disposed of 51 per cent of all complaints of employment discrimination by ruling no probable cause existed for crediting their allegation. This percentage has been consistently at or above 80 since 1962.[147] The Pennsylvania Commission in 1962 disposed of 77 or 60 per cent of a total of 126 complaints of employment discrimination by this type of ruling.[148] This percentage was only slightly less in 1965.[149] The experience of the New York Commission with complaints of housing and public-accommodations discrimination indicates that they are also dismissing a large number of these for lack of probable cause to credit them. In 1962 the New York Commission dismissed upon this

---

[144] § 703(d). See note 31, above.

[145] A similar solution has also been recommended by a special commission appointed by the governor of Massachusetts [*Report of the Special Study Commission to Review the Functions and Policies of the Massachusetts Commission against Discrimination* (December 30, 1964), p. 16].

[146] New York State Commission for Human Rights, *Annual Report, 1962*, p. 14.

[147] New York State Commission for Human Rights, *Report of Progress* (1963), p. 14; *Report of Progress* (1964), p. 11; *Annual Report, 1965*, p. 14.

[148] Pennsylvania Human Relations Commission, *Seventh Annual Report* (1963), p. 14.

[149] Pennsylvania Human Relations Commission, *Tenth Annual Report* (1965), p. 27.

basis 146 or nearly 40 per cent of the 372 housing discrimination complaints closed by it that year.[150] This percentage had increased to 46 in 1965. It also dismissed in 1962 upon this basis 89 or 52 per cent of 170 public accommodations complaints closed by it during this same year. This percentage was only slightly less in 1965. During the same period the Pennsylvania Commission had a much smaller, although substantial, percentage of complaints in these two areas dismissed upon this basis.[151] It will be recalled that the Pennsylvania Commission files about 35 per cent of the complaints that it processes each year while the New York Commission did not have authority to do this prior to 1965. This fact would certainly tend to result in many more valid complaints on the average being filed and fewer that could be dismissed upon the ground of lack of probable couse to credit them. Despite this fact, in 1965 the Pennsylvania Commission dismissed 57 or 26 per cent of 220 housing-discrimination complaints upon this basis. The Massachusetts Commission dismissed upon this basis 16 per cent and Ohio only 10 per cent of all forms of complaints processed and closed by them in 1965.[152] In employment-discrimination cases that have been closed, most of the other state commissions have a higher percentage of dismissals for lack of probable cause: for example, Illinois, 44 per cent; Connecticut, 60 per cent; Minnesota, 45 per cent; Indiana, 58 per cent; Michigan, 72 per cent; and New Jersey, 65 per cent.[153]

There would be no cause for alarm regarding these statistics concerning dismissals of complaints for lack of probable cause to credit them if there were adequate safeguards for assuring that these determinations were being correctly made at the administrative level or if at least judicial review of these determinations could be obtained by complainants. Unfortunately, neither these adequate safeguards nor this judicial review are usually available. The determination of whether probable cause exists for crediting the allegations of a com-

[150] New York State Commission for Human Rights, *Annual Report, 1962*, p. 14.
[151] Pennsylvania Human Relations Commission, *Seventh Annual Report* (1963), p. 25.
[152] Massachusetts Commission against Discrimination, *Annual Report* (1965), p. 27; Ohio Civil Rights Commission, *Seventh Annual Report* (1967), p. 20.
[153] Illinois Fair Employment Commission, *1962 Annual Report*, p. 4; Connecticut Commission on Civil Rights, *Annual Report* (1964–1965), p. 1; Minnesota Commission against Discrimination, *Ninth Annual Report* (1965), p. 6; Indiana Civil Rights Commission, *1965 Report*, p. 16; Michigan Civil Rights Commission, *1964 Annual Report*, p. 14; New Jersey Division on Civil Rights, Civil Rights Commission, *Fiscal 1961 Annual Report*, p. 17.

plaint is designed to be only a tentative determination of whether a respondent had committed an unlawful discriminatory practice if it was adverse to him. Its function, relative to the respondent, is simply to provide a reasonable condition to be satisfied by a commission before it resorts either to conciliation in an effort to persuade the respondent to cease the practice tentatively determined by the commission to be unlawful or to a public hearing on the complaint. The determination that probable cause exists for crediting a complaint does not bind a respondent named in it. If he wishes to stand on his rights, the respondent may insist upon a public hearing and have a full opportunity to demonstrate that he has not violated the statute. Commissions have, however, handled the step of determining whether probable cause exists to credit a complaint not as a tentative adjudication but as a final adjudication. They have done this, on the one hand, by rarely proceeding to a public hearing of complaints and then only after a long drawn-out process of conciliation has failed. They have also done this by the very method used in making the probable cause determinations. The objective of commissions in making this determination has not been, as one would suppose was the case, to ascertain simply whether there is reasonable evidence for believing that a violation of the statute may have occurred. Rather their objective has been one of weighing all the evidence gathered in the investigation, usually of a conflicting nature, and then determining whether a violation has in fact occurred.

The Ohio Commission, for example, reported that its investigation in 1961 in one employment-discrimination case covered a period of many months during which "testimony" was received from twenty-six persons. This Commission described the nature of its own thought process in this case: *"the Commission had to sift the facts as they related to the charge. Was the man dismissed because of race? Or was the employee dismissed because of disciplinary actions or for some other reason, just or unjust? After much investigation, and much weighing of evidence, the Commission determined that the employee was not dismissed because of race,* and found no probable cause to credit the charge and the case was dismissed."[154] In a more general characterization of its concept of the "probable cause" determination, the Commission stated that it "conducts its investigations of allegations of employment discrimination to determine whether the specific com-

[154] Ohio Civil Rights Commission, *Second Annual Report* (1961), p. 17.

plainant had been subjected to unlawful employment discrimination."[155] It seems clear that the Ohio Commission examines the evidence gathered in its investigation of complaints with a view to determining, after sifting and weighing it, whether an unlawful act has in fact been committed. When this determination has been made, then and only then does the Commission assign the value to it that "probable cause" does or does not exist. In short, the Commission proceeds like any court or administrative tribunal finally adjudicating the merits of a controversy before it. A recent study of the work of the New York State Commission concluded that it had been doing precisely the same thing that the Ohio Commission did in making the "probable cause" determination.[156]

This method of making the tentative adjudication of violation is not prejudicial to respondents charged with unlawful discrimination. If the result is adverse to them and they are dissatisfied with it, they may still insist upon a public hearing with all its safeguards for assuring an accurate final adjudication of liability. On the other hand, if the determination is that "no probable cause" exists for crediting the allegations of a complaint, the statutes direct the commission to dismiss the complaint. The complainant may not insist, as the respondent may when the determination is adverse to him, upon the holding of a public hearing by the commission after this determination is made. When, therefore, the commission makes the determination relative to the existence of probable cause by sifting and weighing all the evidence to determine if a violation has occurred in fact rather than simply ascertaining that a prima facie case is made out by the evidence, it has greatly cut down the complainant's chances of causing a public hearing to be held to verify his allegations while in no way prejudicing the respondent's right to insist upon a public hearing. Although the determination that no probable cause exists for crediting a complaint is a final one for the complainant, it is not made under the safeguards required of other administrative agencies when they engage in a final adjudication of a controversy. It is not reached by the commission following a public hearing in which evidence of violation is carefully developed on a record under the testing fire of adversary process and its various tools for getting at the truth of the matter. Moreover,

---

[155] *Id.*, p. 19.

[156] New York County Lawyers Association, Committee on Civil Rights, *Time for a Change: A Reexamination of the New York State Law against Discrimination in Employment and Its Operation* (December, 1963) (Committee Report), pp. 14–15.

the complainant, who has the greatest interest in seeing that adequate evidence of violation is developed, is in no way permitted to participate in the procedure which ends in a determination of whether probable cause exists. The procedure is wholly that of an *ex parte* investigation usually conducted by a staff member of a commission. This investigation is shrouded with secrecy because of a statutory requirement that it be shielded from public view. The determination relating to the existence of probable cause is usually made by a single commissioner. It also is an *ex parte* decision. The complainant can neither appeal this determination to the whole commission nor to the courts. Thus, although the determination that probable cause does not exist (which in actual operation means a determination on the weighing of evidence that no discrimination was in fact practiced) is a final one for all purposes so far as the complainant is concerned, it is made in the course of a process that is lacking in all of the procedural safeguards usually deemed essential in Anglo-American jurisprudence for final adjudication of controversies. On the other hand if the determination is that probable cause exists (which in actual operation means a determination on the weighing of evidence that discrimination was in fact practiced), that determination is not a final one so far as the other party to the controversy, the respondent, is concerned. A serious question of procedural due process is presented because of the nature assigned in practice to these determinations of probable cause by state human-relations commissions.[157] If they were in fact no more than a determination that the evidence did not make out a prima facie case of violation, this question of procedural fairness could not be reasonably raised. The determination would then be analogous to that of a court in determining that the plaintiff's evidence was insufficient to warrant submission of his case to the jury, a determination of a question of law. In fact, however, these determinations are full assessments

---

[157] *Cf.*, J. Black's statement in the majority opinion in *Griffin v. People of the State of Illinois*, 351 U.S. at 18–19 (1956): "Statistics show that a substantial proportion of criminal convictions are reversed by state appellate courts. Thus to deny adequate review to the poor means that many of them may lose their life, liberty, or property because of unjust convictions which appellate courts would set aside." By way of a strong analogy we may properly say that statistics show that a substantial proportion of "no probable cause" determinations would never have stood had the complainant been permitted to participate in the procedure leading to the determination or, in lieu of this, to obtain a hearing on his complaint as the respondent in these cases may. In fact, many complainants in these cases are poor and the only way they can defend their right to equal opportunities in these cases is to secure and participate in a hearing on the merits of their complaints.

of the weight of all the evidence, which is usually conflicting in nature, and each of them constitutes a judgment that the respondent did or did not violate the statute. This judgment involves the determinaion of questions of fact and of the proper application of law to the facts determined. Despite the actual nature of the proceeding, relative to the complainant, as a final adjudication of the merits of his complaint, he is accorded no opportunity to obtain a fair hearing or trial. Even if it is determined that procedural due process is not being denied the complainant under these circumstances, the procedure certainly appears to present a serious question concerning whether the complainant is being denied equal protection of the laws.[158] The stake of a complainant in a controversy is surely to be equated to that of a respondent, particularly when this controversy turns upon a statute that grants a right to the complainant and imposes a correlative duty upon the respondent. Nevertheless, the procedure just reviewed provides the respondent a full hearing if the probable cause determination is adverse to him but denies a full hearing to the complainant if this same determination is adverse to him. Surely this is a distinction in procedure without a rational justification for the determination of rights and duties that are correlative to each other.

It certainly seems necessary to conclude that state and local human-relations commissions have erred grossly in interpreting their function in making determinations relative to whether probable cause exists for crediting the allegations of a complaint. The error is somewhat analogous to, although more gross than, that committed by those who sought to convert the probable cause concept involved in arrest or search and seizure cases from one requiring ascertainment of whether a substantial basis exists for concluding a violation of law is occurring to one that requires ascertainment of whether there is an evidentiary basis for acting that would be competent evidence upon trial to prove a violation of law. To this proposed conversion, the Supreme Court of the United States replied that it

goes much too far in confusing and disregarding the difference between what is required to prove guilt in a criminal case and what is required to show probable cause for arrest or search. It approaches requiring (if it does not in practical effect require) proof sufficient to establish guilt in order to substantiate the existence of probable cause. There is a large difference between the two things to be proved, as well as between the tri-

---

[158] *Cf., Skinner v. Oklahoma,* 316 U.S. 535 (1942).

bunals which determine them, and therefore a like difference in the quanta and modes of proof required to establish them.[159]

The Court went on to say that if the standards for determining whether probable cause existed for making an arrest or for search and seizures were those required in formal adjudication of law violation, "few indeed would be the situations in which an officer, charged with protecting the public interest by enforcing the law, could take effective action toward that end."[160] By way of explaining the positive meaning of the probable cause concept in these cases the Court continued:

In dealing with probable cause, however, as the very name implies, we deal with probabilities. These are not technical; they are the factual and practical considerations of everyday life on which reasonable and prudent men, not legal technicians, act. The standard of proof is accordingly correlative to what must be proved. "The substance of all the definitions" of probable cause "is a reasonable ground for belief of guilt." And this "means less than evidence which would justify condemnation" or conviction. Probable cause exists where "the facts and circumstances within their (the officers') knowledge and of which they had reasonably trustworthy information (are) sufficient in themselves to warrant a man of reasonable caution in the belief that" an offense has been or is being committed.[161]

The Court explained that the concept of probable cause in these cases was a "practical, nontechnical conception affording the best compromise that has been found for accommodating (two) often opposing interests." On the one hand is the citizen's right to be safeguarded "from rash and unreasonable interferences with privacy and from unfounded charges of crime." On the other hand is the interest in providing "fair leeway for enforcing the law in the community's protection . . . Requiring more [than probable cause] would unduly hamper law enforcement. To allow less would be to leave law-abiding citizens at the mercy of the officers' whim or caprice."[162]

There is much to be said in favor of applying the definition of probable cause utilized in search and seizure cases to the function of human-relations commissions in determining whether probable cause exists for crediting the allegations of a complaint. Almost nothing can be said for the alternative, which these commissions have, in fact, chosen, of examining not only the evidence supporting the complainant's

[159] *Brinegar v. United States*, 330 U.S. at 172–173 (1949).
[160] *Id.*, p. 174.
[161] *Id.*, pp. 175–176.
[162] *Id.*, p. 176.

position but also the evidence supporting the respondent's position and, after weighing the evidence, making a finding that the respondent either has or has not violated the law. There is very good reason in this field for seeking to emphasize the process of conciliation in obtaining compliance with the law. The assurance that a substantial case against a respondent has been developed is a mighty force for moving him to agree to a settlement in this process. On the other hand, commissions should not be permitted to overemphasize the value of conciliation. The complainant member of a minority group cannot long sustain a failure of government to try his claim of discrimination. Moreover, an overlong process of conciliation may discourage members of minority groups from relying upon the processes of law for securing their interests. A good compromise in the civil-rights field appears to be an approach that considers probable cause to be satisfied when the evidence in support of a complaint developed in the course of an investigation is sufficient to constitute a prima facie case of violation. Prima facie case in this context should mean that, when considered by itself and without regard to evidence to the contrary, the evidence is of a substantial nature in support of the allegations of the complaint. In light of the practice that has grown up concerning the procedure for determining whether probable cause exists for crediting a complaint, a civil-rights statute administered by a human-relations commission should also express the admonition that this determination is not to be made by weighing all the evidence gathered in the investigation. This approach more nearly resembles the standard for judging when the court should submit an issue of fact to the jury in a civil case than it does the standard for determining whether a warrant of search or arrest should be issued. The Alpha Model State Civil-Rights Act adopts these two approaches to the probable-cause determination in its Section 705.[163] The Harvard Model State Civil Rights Act attempts to deal with this problem by providing that conciliation process shall begin if it is concluded "after investigation that facts exist which tend to substantiate the allegations of the complaint."[164] Although this provision is an improvement over existing law establishing human-relations commissions, it is susceptible, without further specification, of being applied as the term "probable cause" has been applied in the past. The Uniform Model State Anti-Discrimination Act, using the

---

[163] See Chapter 8.
[164] § 707 (b). See note 18, above.

term "reasonable cause," does not define it or attempt to specify the procedure to be utilized in this initial determination.[165] These approaches are rejected in the Alpha Model State Civil-Rights Act in favor of the most explicit specification of appropriate procedure due to the well-ingrained practice of many commissions previously described.[166]

THE NEED FOR AGENCY AND JUDICIAL REVIEW OF NO-PROBABLE-CAUSE DETERMINATIONS

A seventh point about the weakness of human-relations commissions concerns still another matter that seriously impeaches the assurance that determinations relative to probable cause for crediting complaints are being carefully made. By and large, commissions have not spelled out the legal criteria being applied by them in making these determinations. Moreover, the commissions do not disclose the particular data which moved them to their determination that no probable cause exists for crediting the allegations of a complaint. Until the legal criteria underlying probable-cause determinations are expounded and the particular data to which they are applied are made available to test a state commission's determination that no probable cause exists for crediting the allegations of a complaint of discrimination, the issue covering the content of the criteria being applied is a crucial one since the overwhelming bulk of the cases are disposed of through this form of determination. It is interesting to note that in late 1963 a commissioner of the Massachusetts Commission against Discrimination, which was established in 1946, found it necessary to request an opinion from the attorney general's office concerning the meaning of the phrase "probable cause."[167] Under the Massachusetts statute, as in many states, probable-cause determinations are made by the single commissioner assigned to process each case.[168] Assistant Attorney Gen-

---

[165] § 703(b). See note 31, above. The draftsman of the Uniform Act explained in his comment on this section that the term means "the complaint lacks sufficient merit to warrant the case going forward to the conciliation and the National Conference of Commissioners on Uniform Laws, and hearing stage" ["The Model [State] Anti-Discrimination Act: The Comprehensive Act," *Harvard Journal of Legislation*, Vol. 4 (1967), p. 254].

[166] See Chapter 8.

[167] Letter dated January 3, 1964, to Massachusetts Commission against Discrimination from Assistant Attorney General Lee H. Kozol, chief of the Division on Civil Rights and Liberties.

[168] Mass. Gen. Laws Ann. ch. 151B, § 5, *as amended* (Michie Supp. 1966).

eral Lee H. Kozol, chief of the Division of Civil Rights and Liberties, advised the commission in January 1964 that it was not necessary for the investigating commissioner to determine which of two conflicting stories offered by a complainant and an employer is true.[169] In order for the investigating commissioner to determine that probable cause exists, it is only necessary for him to prove that the hearing commissioners, as reasonable fact finders, could believe either story. On the other hand, Mr. Kozol took the position that if the investigating commissioner determined that no reasonable man could credit the complainant's allegations of discrimination, a no-probable-cause determination was required. An interview with Commissioner Batson of the Massachusetts Commission, who had requested the opinion just mentioned, revealed that she was in accord with it.[170] On the other hand, an interview with Chairman Mahoney of the Commission indicated that she and Commissioner Batson disagreed at a number of points about the factors that are to be considered indicative of probable cause for crediting a claim of discrimination.[171] Commissioner Batson, for example, takes the position that for a landlord to make a credit check upon a Negro seeking a rent premises although the landlord does not usually do this in the case of white persons is sufficient evidence that a subsequent failure to rent to the Negro was probably discriminatory. Chairman Mahoney took the position that the landlord's making of a credit check upon a Negro applicant in these circumstances is no evidence that a subsequent failure to rent to the Negro is probably discriminatory. Mr. Kozol stated that the result in any probable-cause determination depended largely upon the particular commissioner assigned to handle a particular case and the philosophy of administration of the statute to which he adhered.[172] Mr. Kozol indicated that each of the four Massachusetts commissioners can be roughly categorized as falling either into a "conservative" or a "liberal" camp. A conservative commissioner is much less likely to find that probable cause exists to credit the allegations of any given complaint of discrimination after investigation than a liberal commissioner. At the time he spoke the four commissioners were equally divided between the two camps. In

---

[169] Letter dated January 3, 1964, to Massachusetts Commission against Discrimination from Assistant Attorney General Lee H. Kozol, chief of the Division on Civil Rights and Liberties.

[170] Interview by Mrs. Judith G. Shepard, my research assistant, in May, 1964.

[171] Interview by Mrs. Judith G. Shepard, my research assistant, in May, 1964.

[172] Interview by Mrs. Judith G. Shepard, my research assistant, in April, 1964.

this situation it is self-evident that the concept of probable cause is one of those fuzzy legal concepts which admits of varying interpretations and that the Massachusetts Commission has not, even after eighteen years of operation, been able to settle upon objective criteria for applying it or to apply these criteria consistently from case to case.[173] For this reason, the Commission's record of "satisfactory adjustments" of cases in which probable cause to credit allegations of discrimination has been found to exist becomes much less persuasive or remarkable than appears at first sight. A very large number of cases, often the greater bulk, are disposed of by the route of the determination that no probable cause exists for crediting the complaint and many of these would have been determined to involve probable cause had different commissioners been assigned to process them. It is clear from this that it is absolutely essential that a careful study be made concerning the legal criteria being used generally by human-relations commissions in making their determinations relative to probable cause and concerning the types of applications being made of these criteria. Only then will it be possible to evaluate the validity of the large percentage of their total case dispositions that are based upon this kind of determination. It certainly appears necessary also that the statutes administered by human-relations commissions be amended to provide that a no-probable-cause determination made by a single commissioner or staff official is subject to review by the entire commission or by one of its panels, as well as by the courts. In this way, there will be some assurance that an objective interpretation of the probable cause concept will be developed and its application made more uniform. The Alpha Model State Civil-Rights Act adopts this approach in its Section 704.[174] It authorizes the chairman of a commission to designate a single commissioner to make an investigation of a complaint. Experience has shown that a single commissioner with the aid of the commission staff can handle this function well. It is clear that a panel of commissioners or the entire commission would prove considerably less effective than a single commissioner particularly in the conduct of the conciliation process. On the other hand, the function should be the responsibility of a commis-

[173] Mr. Kozol's view has been confirmed by a study commission appointed by the governor of Massachusetts. [*Report of the Special Study Commission to Review the Functions and Policies of the Massachusetts Commission against Discrimination* (December 30, 1964), pp. 7–10].

[174] See Chapter 8; the Massachusetts statute was amended in 1967 to adopt this approach. See Appendix A.

sioner rather than of a member of the commission staff in order to demonstrate to a respondent the weight the commission gives to the initial complaint, investigation, probable-cause determination, and the effort at conciliation. This consideration is likely to be of less importance when a commission has gained widespread local acceptance. The commissioner, moreover, is not required to perform this function personally in all its respects. He simply is to have responsibility for its performance. This commissioner is charged under Section 705 of the act with making a prompt investigation of the complaint and with determining whether probable cause exists to credit the allegations in it. Section 707 also provides that if the investigating commissioner determines after his investigation that no probable cause exists for crediting the allegations of the complaint, he shall cause to be served upon the complainant or the person aggrieved by an alleged violation, where a commissioner filed the complaint, written notice of the determination. This notice is required to state that the complaint will be dismissed unless the complainant or aggrieved person files with the commission a request for a review hearing within ten days of service of the notice. If the review hearing is requested, the commission is directed under Section 708 to provide a hearing either before the commission, or a member or staff representative of the commission. At this hearing the complainant or aggrieved person may present any additional information that may be available to support the allegations of the complaint. The section makes reviewable in the courts a determination after the review hearing that no probable cause exists as in the case of other commission orders. This solution should go far to remedy the problem of lack of standards or their nonuniform application in probable-cause determination. Since it permits a complainant to present information in support of the complaint for consideration of the whole commission and, ultimately, the courts, it assures that few dismissals of complaints for no probable cause to credit them can stand if the complainant can make out a prima facie case of violation.

The Harvard Model State Civil Rights Act[175] does not provide for a review by the commission of a determination by itself or by a single commissioner or by the commission staff that no probable cause exists to credit a complaint. It also apparently precludes a judicial review of this determination. Section 707(d) of that model act provides that "No order [of the commission] shall be issued which is based upon a com-

---

[175] See note 18, above.

plaint . . . on which the respondent has not had a hearing." Section 708(a) of this act authorizes judicial review only of final orders of the commission. Since dismissals of complaints occur without the commission hearing the respondent, it would appear that Section 707(d) precludes the dismissal from being an "order"; therefore, it is not a commission action reviewable by the courts under Section 708(a). While the latter section accords a complainant the right to judicial review, this is limited to a "final order" of the commission and, thus, would seem to point, in light of Section 707(d), to issuance of an order after a hearing either dismissing a complaint or directing the respondent to cease and desist from unlawful discrimination. The approach of the Harvard Model Act is unacceptable since it continues the current situation with respect to many commissions and does not respond to the necessity of providing both agency and judicial review of a commission determination that no probable cause exists for crediting a complaint. The Uniform Model State Anti-Discrimination Act does provide for review of these determinations both by the commissions and by the courts.[176] There is, however, one difficulty presented by its Sections 703(b) and (c) which specify the procedure for review of these determinations by the commission. Section 703(b) permits the commission to issue an order dismissing a complaint immediately upon the making of the determination by the commission, a commissioner, or the commission staff that no probable cause exists. Section 703(c) provides that the complainant may within thirty days after receiving a copy of the dismissal order, file for reconsideration of the order. This section does not provide that the complainant may adduce new evidence of discrimination. While the Uniform Model State Act provision is a great improvement over the Harvard Model State Act in this respect, it places an undue burden upon the complainant by requiring him to overcome a formal decision of dismissal by the commission.[177] It also fails to specify that one of the purposes of the new hearing is to examine any additional evidence that the complainant may have. The Alpha Model State Civil-Rights Act, set out in Chapter 8, remedies both of these defects.[178] Under its Section 707 no formal order of dismissal of the complaint may be issued after the no-probable-cause determination has been made until an opportunity has been accorded to complainant to present his case and any additional evidence to the

[176] See note 31, above.
[177] *Cf., Asbacker Radio Corp. v. FCC*, 326 U.S. 327, 330–333 (1945).
[178] See Sections 707 and 720, pp. 356, 367.

whole commission or to a review board or staff member designated by it. Moreover, like the Uniform Model State Act, Section 720 of the Alpha Model State Act in Chapter 8 makes any order of the commission disposing of a complaint reviewable by the courts.

THE NEED FOR AUTHORITY TO OBTAIN
TEMPORARY RESTRAINING ORDERS

An eighth weakness of most state and local human-relations commissions is that they are without authority to preserve intact the job or housing facility about which it has received a complaint of discrimination having been practiced while it goes about the necessary process of investigating and otherwise disposing of the complaint.[179] Meanwhile, the person against whom the complaint is filed is free to give the job or housing facility to someone else and frequently does. This means that the commission often has no adequate remedy to provide a complainant whom it later finds has a justified grievance relative to the job or housing facility lost. Nevertheless, commissions in cases of this sort persist in classifying the remedies they effect through conciliation agreements as "satisfactory adjustments." A close examination of the greater bulk of these adjustments, particularly in housing-discrimination cases, reveals that they are far from being satisfactory either from the standpoint of the minority-group member filing the complaint found to be justified or of the public interest in producing and maintaining a competitive market for jobs, housing, or other things as to which discrimination is proscribed. In view of this fact, the lack of authority in a commission to preserve intact the job or housing facility sought by the complainant while it processes his complaint prevents the commission from effectuating meaningful and useful dispositions of complaints through conciliation. Since a conciliation agreement is almost the only disposition most commissions are willing to make use of in dealing with justified grievances, the impact of their lack of authority to preserve the job or housing in issue is often devastating.

A good example of this eighth point is provided by the operation prior to April 1962 of the New York City Commission on Human Rights, the first commission to be given jurisdiction over discrimina-

---

[179] *Report of the Special Study Commission to Review the Functions and Policies of the Massachusetts Commission against Discrimination* (Submitted to Governor Endicott Peabody, December 30, 1964), pp. 13–14.

tion in private housing accommodations.[180] This Commission had annually reported the usual high number of "satisfactory closings" of housing-discrimination cases achieved by conciliation. Yet only one of the eight categories of satisfactory closings involves an offer by the respondent to the complainant of the dwelling unit the latter had been seeking.[181] The remaining categories, embracing roughly 73 per cent of all cases satisfactorily closed, were cases in which the original dwelling unit sought by the complainant is no longer available because rented or sold to another applicant for it. In 16 per cent of the New York City Commission cases satisfactorily closed, the only remedy is a signed or oral policy commitment obtained from the respondent that he will not discriminate in the future. In Massachusetts, the state Commission utilized this remedy in disposing of 35 per cent of its satisfactorily closed cases.[182] In an additional 25 per cent of the New York City Commission's cases, an alternate dwelling unit was offered to the complainant.[183] Of the complainants receiving this offer, 65 per cent rejected it. This percentage of those rejecting an offer of an alternate unit is considerably higher than that of those rejecting an offer of the original unit sought. Other things being equal, such as the factor of the complainant being unable to accept because he had been forced to take other housing before administrative action had been completed, the higher percentage of rejection tends to indicate that alternate units are inherently less satisfactory to complainants than the original housing sought. This probable condition is especially understandable in the case of a complainant who was seeking to buy a house since a house may have individual characteristics hard to duplicate in another random house offered. Obviously, the offer of a waiting list status or an offer to process an application for housing, the only remedy granted in another 30 per cent of the cases deemed satisfactorily closed, is far less satisfactory to the complainant than the remedy of an offer of the original dwelling sought by the complainant. Both of these remedies

---

[180] United States Commission on Civil Rights, *1961 Report: Housing,* (Washington, D.C.: U.S. Government Printing Office, 1961), p. 121.

[181] New York City Commission on Intergroup Relations, *1961 Annual Report,* p. 49.

[182] United States Commission on Civil Rights, *Massachusetts Advisory Committee Report on Massachusetts: Housing in Boston* (Washington, D.C.: GSA, 1963), p. 40.

[183] New York City Commission on Human Rights, *1961 Annual Report,* pp. 43, 49.

may mean an unreasonably long wait by the complainant before another satisfactory housing opportunity becomes available. Moreover, other normal factors may intervene to prevent the consummation of a housing transaction when these opportunities do develop. The fifth category of satisfactorily closed cases, representing 27 per cent of all such cases, involves an offer by the respondent to the complainant of the dwelling unit he had originally sought. If this offer is made soon after the earlier refusal to make the dwelling unit available, this is usually a closing that is fully satisfactory. Since the complainant is still looking for housing and this is the housing he wanted, he is likely to accept the offer. In fact, 60 per cent of the complainants offered the original premises accepted the offer. The other 46 per cent did not accept, usually due to the fact that they had already contracted for other and often less satisfactory premises. Similarly, some 65 per cent of the complainants offered alternative premises refused to accept the offer. Many of these also had already taken other premises and thus could not benefit from the remedial action provided in the conciliation agreement. A review of these five forms of remedial action indicates that for the most part they are either unacceptable or offer no remedy whatsoever to at least 52 per cent of the complainants in cases "satisfactorily closed." In another 32 per cent of the cases, there is no information of whether the remedy that was initially accepted actually was productive of a dwelling unit for the complainant. In only 16 per cent of the cases was this actually proven to be the case, those in which the original dwelling unit was offered by the respondent and accepted by the complainant.[184] Our review of the five major forms of remedies in satisfactorily closed housing cases reveals that unless the respondent in these cases can be prevented from disposing of the dwelling unit at issue in them while the commission processes it and unless the commission acts expeditiously in doing so, many and perhaps most complainants will receive no adequate relief through conciliation agreements. Moreover, there is no assurance that the respondent in these cases will change his ways of dealing with future members of the complainant's minority group.

The materials now available do not permit one to assess fully what the effect is upon complainants in employment and other types of discrimination cases when the respondents in those cases dispose of the opportunity to another concerning which complaint has been made. It

[184] *Ibid.*

seems clear, however, that the effect will be in many instances as drastic as in the housing cases previously reviewed. Apprentice-training programs, for example, have only limited openings available during the period of enrollment.[185] If a Negro complains of discrimination because of his race in a union's conduct of an apprentice-training program, it seems clear that the union's awarding of an opening or enrollment he sought to a white person before the commission has acted on the complaint disposes of the opportunity to the great prejudice of the complainant. Even if the union is found to have discriminated against the complainant and is directed to cease and desist from the discrimination, the complainant will probably be forced to wait a considerable period of time until further openings in the training program develop. In many instances this will mean that the Negro will be forced to seek other training opportunities and perhaps to forego permanently seeking opportunities of the type originally sought. This results from the straitened circumstances in which most Negroes find themselves. Similarly, if one is seeking employment as a company physician from a company that hires but one physician and suffers discrimination because of his race or religion, he can receive no real relief from favorable commission action and a cease and desist order if meanwhile that company has employed a physician of a favored race or religion. An order to cease and desist from discrimination in these circumstances simply means that some years hence, if the physician employed in his stead resigns or dies, the complainant will be able to insist upon the company considering his application in compliance with the administrative order issued years previously. More generally, the situation just described is likely to occur among employers of relatively few employees, which constitute the great bulk of employers covered by these statutes. Many of the state acts cover employers of as few as six employees. Depending upon employee turnover, an employer of few employees who discriminates may have no new opening to offer a complainant against whom he has discriminated until a considerable period of time has elapsed. These examples indicate the importance of preventing a respondent from disposing of an employment or job-training opportunity until a commission has finally disposed of a complaint charging that respondent with discrimination.

[185] See, *e.g.*, United States Commission on Civil Rights, *Advisory Committees' Reports on Apprenticeship* (Washington, D.C.: U.S. Government Printing Office, 1964), pp. 96–99, 104.

Several ways are available for remedying the situation just described. One of these is the grant of authority to a commission to file an action for a temporary restraining order and injunction, pending its disposition of a complaint, which would direct the respondent not to dispose of any protected opportunity of which complaint has been made. Another remedy is the grant of authority to a commission to stipulate in conciliation agreements and in cease and desist orders that the respondent pay damages to a complainant who has been injured by the loss or withholding of a particular opportunity due to the respondent's discrimination. The first authority should be used wherever feasible since it makes possible the best possible remedy, in the usual case, for the complainant subjected to unlawful discrimination. On the other hand, there will be cases in which the use of this authority would work an unusual hardship or be impossible. In these cases, the second authority would have a special office to perform.

It may well be that a human relations commission has an inherent authority to obtain a temporary restraining order and injunction in order to preserve its jurisdiction over the subject matter of a case properly before it for conciliation and, where necessary, adjudication.[186] If a commission does possess this authority, it is not necessary to consider granting this authority by statute. Commissions have not, however, asserted this authority. Several commissions have relied upon or sought statutory authority to obtain judicial assistance when faced with the situation under discussion. In recent times the New York State Commission has utilized a provision authorizing the state attorney general, upon its request, to institute a civil action which is necessary for effective enforcement of the state law against discrimination.[187] The attorney general has, upon request of the Commission relative to a housing case before it, filed an action seeking a temporary restraining order and an injunction requiring the respondent in that case to refrain from

---

[186] Comment, "Interim Injunctive Relief Pending Administrative Determination," *Columbia Law Review*, Vol. 49 (1949), p. 1124. The authority of a court to preserve the *status quo* by injunction pending trial or judicial review is well established [*United States v. UMW*, 330 U.S. 258 (1947) and *Scripps–Howard Radio, Inc. v. FCC*, 316 U.S. 4 (1942)]. The implied authority to preserve the *status quo* by injunction pending administrative determination has also been recognized. [*Board of Governors of Federal Reserve System v. Transamerica Corp.*, 184 F. 2d 311 (9th Cir. 1950), *cert. denied*, 340 U.S. 883 (1950); West India Fruit and Steamship Co. v. Seatrain Lines, 170 F. 2d 775 (2d Cir. 1948) *cert. dismissed on motion of petitioner*, 336 U.S. 908 (1948); *Public Utilities Commission of District of Columbia v. Capital Transit Co.*, 214 F. 2d 242 (D.C. Cir. 1954)].

[187] N.Y. Exec. Law § 63(9), *as amended* (McKinney Supp. 1967).

disposing of the housing in question to one other than the complainant prior to the Commission's final disposition of the case. This authority was utilized in 1964 in only a very few of the many housing cases being processed by the New York State Commission.[188] In 1961 the Massachusetts Commission was granted specific statutory authority, through an investigating commissioner, after making a probable-cause determination to file a petition in equity seeking an injunction against the respondent in that case to restrain him from selling, renting, or otherwise making unavailable to the complainant any housing accommodations with respect to which complaint had been made.[189] In 1963 this authority was extended to include complaints of discrimination in public accommodations.[190] Prior to late 1967 the Commission was, however, subject to one severe limitation in using this authority. No court authorized to issue the requested injunction might do this except upon hearing both parties fully and upon the commissioner's giving the respondent three days notice of this hearing. In four out of five cases filed under the new statutory authority in 1963 the dwelling unit had been rented or sold before the expiration of the three-day period between the giving of notice of hearing and the hearing on the petition for an injunction.[191] In these cases, until this statutory requirement was deleted late in 1967, the Commission was placed in the same position as it was before passage of the 1961 amendment. The New York City Commission was granted authority in 1962 that avoided the pitfall of the Massachusetts statute.[192] It was specifically authorized to direct the corporation counsel to file an action for a temporary restraining order according to the usual procedures as well as an injunction in the supreme court of a county in which the violation occurs or in which the respondent resides or transacts business. The experience in 1964 in getting temporary restraining orders in housing cases in New York indicates that it takes no more than twenty-four hours to

---

[188] Remarks on December 4, 1964, by Mrs. Shirley A. Siegel, assistant attorney general of New York in charge of the Civil Rights Bureau of the Office of the Attorney General of the State of New York, before the Practicing Law Institute Forum on "The Community and Racial Crises" [*The Community and Racial Crises*, pp. 211–212].

[189] Mass. Gen. Laws Ann. ch. 151B, § 5, *as amended* (Michie Supp. 1966).

[190] *Ibid.* In late 1967 the limitation discussed below was deleted from the provision [Mass. Gen. Laws Ann. ch. 151B, § 5, *as amended* (Michie Supp. 1967)].

[191] Interview in April, 1964, of Mr. Lee H. Kozol, assistant attorney general in charge of the Division of Civil Rights and Liberties, Commonwealth of Massachusetts, conducted by Mrs. Judith G. Shepard, my research assistant.

[192] N.Y. City Charter and Code, Sec. X41-4.

obtain them.[193] The results of the new authority have been gratifying. In 1965, 48 per cent of the Commission's satisfactory adjustments involved an offer to the injured part of the dwelling place at issue.[194]

One state, Oregon, amended its civil-rights statute in 1963 to provide that prior to a final administrative determination on the merits of a complaint of discrimination filed under it, a respondent is prohibited from taking any action, with intent to defeat the purpose of the statute, to make unavailable to the complainant any services, real property, employment or employment opportunities sought by that complainant.[195] The statute also gives a complainant a cause of action for actual damages resulting from a respondent disposing of the property or other thing sought by a complainant and an additional reasonable amount as exemplary damages.[196] The Oregon statute is to be commended for its broad coverage of opportunities denied a person because of discrimination which it seeks to keep open or available to that person pending final administrative action upon his complaint. It is a legislative judgment that supports the thesis already stated in favor of statutes granting broad authority to commissions to obtain temporary restraining orders and injunctions to preserve their jurisdiction to provide an effective remedy to complainants. On the other hand, it would seem more appropriate to permit the commission to award a complainant an amount as back wages or, in other cases of discrimination, an amount as restitution for the loss suffered due to the unlawful act of discrimination by the respondent. If the commission does not elect to seek a temporary restraining order and injunction in a particular case, because of its peculiar circumstances, it does not appear justified to authorize the recovery of special damages from a respondent for his disposition of the opportunity sought by a complainant prior to the commission's final action. It should be sufficient that the commission is authorized to assess damages for the unlawful discriminatory act of the respondent. Several states have given this authority to their commissions.[197] In some states, due to state constitutional provisions, this will not be possible and a cause of action for damages will have to be created.

The Alpha Model State Civil-Rights Act in Chapter 8 contains

193 See *The Community and Racial Crises*, p. 212.
194 New York City Commission on Human Rights, *Annual Report for 1965*, p. 23.
195 Ore. Rev. Stat. § 659.055 (1965).
196 Ore. Rev. Stat. § 659.105 (1965).
197 See, *e.g.*, Ohio Rev. Code Ann. § 4112.05 (G), *as amended* (Page's Supp. 1966).

provisions implementing the suggestions just made. Section 706 of the statute authorizes the chairman of the commission, once the determination has been made that probable cause exists to credit a complaint, to direct its attorney to commence an action for injunctive relief, including temporary restraining orders, to prevent the respondent from disposing of the job, housing accommodation, or other thing with respect to which complaint of unlawful discrimination has been made, pending final administrative determination of the proceedings under the statute. A court of competent jurisdiction in which the action is brought may issue temporary restraining orders upon terms and conditions it deems just and proper. Within thirty days of the effective date of the court order, the commission is required to render its decision in the case unless the time for doing this is extended by the court. Subsection (c) (10) of 716 authorizes the commission, if it determines a respondent has engaged in an unlawful practice to order him to take affirmative action that includes restitution to the complainant for losses suffered as a result of the unlawful practice.

The Harvard Model State Civil Rights Act has no comparable provision relating to injunctive relief pending final administrative determination under a complaint.[198] The Uniform Model State Anti-Discrimination Act does have a comparable provision of this sort.[199] Subsection (c) of Section 706 of the Alpha Model State Civil-Rights Act in Chapter 8 adds a thirty day time limit within which the commission must render its decision in the case unless it obtains an extension of this time from the court.[200] This time limit seems salutary since the remedy is an extraordinary one and may involve considerable hardship for the respondent. This subsection of the Alpha Model Act also follows the Uniform Model State Act in protecting the respondent when the commission dismisses the complaint by a final order or a court directs the dismissal of the complaint. The protective formula accords the respondent the right to recover from the state or local government damages and costs sustained by reason of the injunctive relief in an action in the court which granted that relief. The Alpha Model Act does not stipulate, as does the Uniform Model State Act, when a court granting temporary injunctive relief to a commission must accord a hearing to the respondent before permitting the relief to continue, nor does it indicate on what basis the continuance may be

[198] See note 18, above.
[199] § 703(f) (1) (2). See note 31, above.
[200] See pp. 326–327.

permitted. This would seem to be a matter to be handled wholly in accordance with local law in similar situations.

Like the Alpha Model State Act, both the Harvard Model State Civil Rights Act[201] and the Uniform Model State Anti-Discrimination Act[202] provide that a commission cease and desist order may contain a provision requiring the respondent to pay the complainant damages for an injury caused by the discriminatory practice and costs. The latter act adds the requirement for payment of a reasonable attorney's fee. Both of these acts also provide for payment of at least $500 for each violation. The Alpha Model State Civil-Rights Act adopts these additional formulas in its Section 716.[203]

THE NEED FOR REVIEW OF COMPLIANCE
WITH CONCILIATION AGREEMENTS

A ninth weakness of state and local human-relations commissions relates to their postconciliation procedures. Most commissions do not conduct with any regularity or thoroughness any check-ups on the extent of compliance with conciliation agreements achieved in satisfactorily closed cases.[204] Some commissions, as previously pointed out, seek to obtain an effective agreement relative not only to adjustment of the grievance of the individual complainant but also to revision of general employment policies and practices of the company. Perhaps the principal value of individual complaint cases is the opportunity presented to the commission to deal with the general policies of the respondent reflected in the case and to obtain an agreement from him to effectuate long-range and wide-scale adjustments of these policies. Yet unless these agreements are adhered to by those making them, little is accomplished. There is good evidence for believing that these agreements are widely disregarded by respondents in housing cases. While the contrary has been asserted relative to agreements in employment cases, it seems clear that one necessary assurance that agreements will be honored is regular and thorough check-ups on the degree of compliance. There are strong pressures at work that are likely to

---

[201] § 707(g). See note 18, above.
[202] § 706(a)(b). See note 31, above.
[203] See Chapter 8.
[204] Norgren and Hill, *Toward Fair Employment*, p. 118; *Report of the Special Study Commission to Review the Functions and Policies of the Massachusetts Commission against Discrimination*, pp. 17–18; National Conference of Commissions on Uniform State Laws, "Second Tentative Draft: Uniform State Civil Rights Act," comment, pp. 71–72 (mimeographed).

move these respondents not to comply. Unless check-up procedures are utilized by commissions, these pressures may prove too strong to withstand. Of course, it is quite possible that a mere check-up on compliance with conciliation agreements will not produce compliance in many cases. This leads to a tenth point concerning the weakness of state human-relations commissions.

THE NEED FOR AUTHORITY TO ENFORCE CONCILIATION AGREEMENTS

Only a very few commissions currently have authority to enforce conciliation agreements upon which such heavy reliance is placed in enforcing civil-rights legislation.[205] If the commission without this authority does discover that a conciliation agreement is not honored by a respondent and he persists in his recalcitrance, the commission can proceed against him only on the basis of a fresh complaint of discrimination. Where the commission must rely upon the filing of complaints of others, its ability to proceed against the violator of an agreement may be very limited. If it does receive a complaint against one who has signed a conciliation agreement or, as a few commissions may, it files a complaint against that person on its own motion, the commission should not, if it ascertains that probable cause exists, resort to conciliation but should hold a public hearing in the case and, if appropriate, proceed to the issuance of an enforceable cease and desist order. Since commissions are so prone to rely upon conciliation agreements to settle cases, it appears that one salutary improvement in the individual case method could be effectuated by granting commissions the authority to obtain judicial enforcement of these agreements. This would both protect what value there is in commission emphasis upon the use of these agreements and make these agreements more effective in the long run for achieving elimination of discrimination.

The Alpha Model State Civil-Rights Act contains provisions (Sections 709 and 710) regulating the making of conciliation agreements or settlements of complaints.[206] These sections are modeled upon the settlement procedure developed after much experience by the Federal Trade Commission.[207] The Harvard Model State Civil Rights Act[208]

---

205 Ky. Rev. Stat. §§ 344.200(4), 344.240(i) (Cum. Supp. 1966); Md. Ann. Code, art. 49B, §§ 13(c), 15 (1964); Ore. Rev. Stat. §§ 659.050(2), 659.070 (1965); Wash. Rev. Code Ann. §§ 49.60.240, 260 (1962).

206 See Chapter 8.

207 Rule 2 (formerly Rule 3.25) of the Rules of Procedure of the Federal Trade Commission. [16 CFR 2.1–2.4 (Supp. 1966)].

208 See note 18, above.

does not and the Uniform Model State Anti-Discrimination Act[209] does contain a provision relating to conciliation agreements and their enforceability. The latter does not provide any guidelines for the procedure to be followed in negotiating an agreement or for its content. Of course, the value of a conciliation agreement depends upon what is in it. There should be a certain minimal content to an agreement in order to eliminate all questions as to its enforceability and its effectiveness, when enforced, to assure attainment of the goals of the act. Subsection (b) of Section 709 of the Alpha Model State Act places the burden upon a respondent to request, at any time after the filing of a complaint, a reasonable delay to permit negotiation of an agreement, and leaves the permitted duration of negotiation up to the appropriate commission official. This is a salutary arrangement because it acts as a stimulant or at least a suggestion to a respondent to seek a settlement even before the commission has made its probable-cause determination. By way of contrast, the Uniform Model State Act speaks of the relevancy of conciliation agreements only after referring to the initiation of the conciliation process by the commission. Also under Section 710 of the Alpha Model State Act, each agreement must contain, among other things, an admission of the jurisdictional facts, a provision that the consent order shall have the same force and effect as if entered after full hearing, a waiver of findings of fact and conclusions of law, a waiver of further procedural steps before the commission or any official of it, and a waiver of any right to challenge or contest the validity of the order. The inclusion of these matters assures the enforceability of all orders. For the protection of both parties, the conciliation agreement may also contain a provision that the agreement shall not become a part of the official record of the proceeding until it becomes a part of the decision of the commission. For the protection of the respondent, the agreement must contain a statement that the signing of the agreement is for settlement purposes and not an admission by a respondent that he has violated the law as alleged in the complaint.

THE NEED FOR GREATER USE OF HEARING PROCEDURES

In the eleventh place, most state and some local commissions have relied far too much upon the technique of processing complaints of discrimination against particular individuals as their basic method for

---

[209] § 703(d). See note 31, above.

producing equal opportunities in employment, union membership and activities, education, housing, public accommodations, and other areas over which they have jurisdiction. It is true that these agencies have also performed an "educational" function. They have distributed tons of literature to business concerns covered by civil-rights legislation and their commissioners and staff directors have delivered hundreds of talks before civic groups of all kinds. Nevertheless, it remains true that most commissions primarily depend upon their processing of individual complaints case by case to turn the tide of discrimination. There are, however, far more effective techniques available to commissions for speeding up the process of creating equal opportunities in all the needed areas. One group of these techniques would be negotiating with broad sections of the business community and of the government for securing from them effective action toward improvement of opportunities available to minority groups. While use of a process of education is essential to the commission's performance of this negotiating function, its key ingredient is more especially the affirmative use of the subtle powers of government to compel the institution of positive improvements in available opportunities for minority groups. One of these powers is the conduct of industry-wide or government-wide investigations to determine the degree to which minority groups are participating in the workshops and offices of private and government employers as well as their general employment policies and arrangements with unions or employment agencies affecting adversely the employment of minority-group members. These investigations are conducted on the premises of the affected employers. Another power is the use of public hearings similar to those conducted by legislative committees to reduce to a public record the general facts in an industry or the government concerning how discrimination is purposely effectuated in employment, union activities, housing, public facilities and services, education, and other crucial areas. The artful use of publicity in disseminating the facts discovered in investigations and public hearings and of hints that individual complaints will be filed unless changes are made are frequently sufficient to provide the climate in which industry groups and government agencies will agree to commission proposals for concrete remedial measures to be undertaken by all in the group concerned. The aim of this negotiation function is not merely the elimination of the more overt or gross types of discrimination but the removal of all unreasonable obstacles to minority groups in their effort to obtain employment, union membership and services, housing, use of

public facilities and services, education and other needed things. Another group of techniques involves giving broad assistance to minority-
group members in preparing themselves for taking advantage of available opportunities and for engaging in effective self-action designed to
increase the availability of these opportunities. Only two state commissions, those in New York and Pennsylvania, have performed to any
considerable extent these "constructive-action" functions. The primary agencies performing these functions have been local commissions, of which the Philadelphia Commission is the prime, successful
example.

Since 1960 the Philadelphia Commission has invested most of its
time, energy, and resources in its new techniques of negotiating broad-
scale adjustments in favor of minority groups.[210] So far its efforts in
this new direction have focused upon the problem of employment.
Prior to 1960 this Commission used the individual case method almost
exclusively (as most state commissions still do) in dealing with this
problem. From 1960 to the present, by way of contrast, the Philadelphia Commission has conducted a plant-inspection program.[211] As part
of this on-premises program the Commission in 1962 examined the
policies and practices of seventy-one different business concerns which
employed a total of 21,258 persons. It similarly checked, on seventy
occasions, upon employers having contracts with the city and upon
unions associated with performance of these contracts. In 1965 it conducted 300 plant inspections in the small loan and consumer industry
and in the trucking industry.[212] It also inspected the operation and
selection procedures of apprenticeship programs using city school facilities. In both report years the Commission discovered that the recruiting practices of many firms and unions limited members of
minority groups in obtaining employment opportunities. This Commission, one of the few possessing the authority to initiate complaints
on its own motion, was able by negotiation to persuade many employers to institute affirmative "merit employment programs" and to expand recruiting programs so as to reach additional minority-group
persons.[213] It was also able to secure commitments on nondiscrimina-

[210] Philadelphia Commission on Human Relations, *Annual Report* (1962), pp. 3,
26–7.
[211] *Id.*, pp. 3, 20–26.
[212] Philadelphia Commission on Human Relations, *1965 Annual Report*, p. 9.
[213] Philadelphia Commission on Human Relations, *Annual Report* (1962), pp.
20–26.

tion that would bring into compliance numerous firms in a given industry. When these agreements are once negotiated, the Commission follows them up by counselling on employment patterns and policies, investigations, and efforts to obtain agreements from individual firms in the industry. In 1965, for example, the Commission reported upon its agreement with the Printing Industries of Philadelphia. As a result of this agreement, further inspection showed that many Negroes were employed as journeymen and as apprentices.[214]

Of course, where plant and similar investigations conducted upon an industry- or area-wide basis are not sufficient, along with a reminder of the Commission's power to invoke or obtain formal proceedings, to eliminate discrimination and other harmful practices, the Commission must be more forceful. Thus, in 1965, it moved the procurement commissioner of the city to remove twenty-three firms from the approved bidders' list.[215] The Commission also filed twenty-nine complaints of discrimination against other firms and unions. Twenty-eight of the respondents agreed thereafter to eliminate their discriminatory practices. The Commission also secured action from the appropriate public agencies suspending the right of an apprentice program to use school premises until, or warning of other withdrawal of rights unless, its sponsors brought it into compliance with the fair practices or other law relating to selection procedures.

The Commission has also used the technique of industry-wide public investigative hearings and industry-wide surveys without hearings. In 1960, following public investigative hearings into the employment practices and policies of the hotel and restaurant industry, the Commission was able to negotiate a consent order with the Greater Philadelphia Restaurant Operators Association.[216] This order called for elimination of discrimination against minority groups, promotion of minority-group personnel then employed, modification of seniority requirements, development of written job specifications, and affirmative action toward integration of employee referral lists. By 1962 the Commission was able to report that follow-up investigations to these hearings had noted the employment of nonwhite workers in several job categories from which they had previously been excluded. Obvi-

---

[214] Philadelphia Commission on Human Relations, *1965 Annual Report*, p. 7.
[215] *Ibid.*
[216] Philadelphia Commission on Human Relations, *Annual Report* (1962), pp. 20–26.

ously, the public investigative hearing has values for inducing agreements that are lacking in connection with other techniques.

The industry-wide survey of employment patterns has been frequently used by the Commission. After making a survey of the banking industry in 1962, the Commission held a series of conferences with members of that industry. As a result of the negotiations conducted, the Commission secured an agreement that, when effectuated, produced a substantial increase in the nonwhite persons employed in that industry.[217] It also, however, reported lack of success with an industry-wide survey and negotiations with the insurance industry. Obviously, other techniques will have to be applied to this industry which employs only 2 per cent nonwhite persons in a community in which they constitute 29 per cent of the whole population.

As a whole, the city Commission has concluded that the three techniques of plant and similar on-the-premises inspections, industry-wide public investigative hearings, and industry-wide surveys—combined with follow-up negotiations and inspections—have together "become far more productive than the case by case approach as vehicles for improving employment opportunities."[218] The Commission emphasizes in the use of these techniques that the basic concept of its plan of operations is to produce "compensatory opportunity" for minority-group persons who, like culturally deprived students in public education, have suffered great losses and require special adjustments in existing arrangements to facilitate more adequately their entry into better employment.[219]

There is great promise in the use by human-relations commissions of negotiation with broad sections of the business community and of government for opening up needed opportunities for minority groups. The central impetus for achieving results through this technique is the ultimate ability of the commission to take the business section, union, or government agency "to the country" through press releases, public investigations, and public enforcement proceedings. All of the proposals so far for expanding commission jurisdiction over discrimination and for improving the effectiveness of commission handling of individual complaints of discrimination are important in their own right— that is, in making commissions more effective instruments for accom-

---

[217] *Ibid.*

[218] *Id.*, p. 21.

[219] Philadelphia Commission on Human Relations, *Annual Report* (1963), pp. 3–4, 7–11; *Annual Report* (1964), pp. 24–27.

plishing the objects of the statutes they administer through processing of individual complaints. But these proposals are far more important for the bargaining strength they bring to the commission as it approaches representatives of a whole profession, a broad section of the business community, or government with a view to negotiating improvements in opportunities for minority groups. Each of the thirty state and approximately twenty-five local commissions having enforcement powers already have the authority to utilize what has been described here as the broad-spectrum negotiation power. In order to stimulate human-relations commissions to utilize this power extensively, the Alpha Model State Civil-Rights Act provides in its Sections 502 and 503, that it is the sense of the legislature that the state human-relations commission should seek to devote a considerable part of its total administrative effort to promoting through negotiation, backed up by industry-wide investigations, surveys, and public hearings, the taking of positive action by each industry and profession as a whole, their organizations, and government agencies, designed to open up greater opportunities for members of minority and other disadvantaged groups.[220]

We have observed that the Philadelphia Commission has sought agreements from businessmen to take action that is more than merely corrective of violations of existing law against discrimination. These agreements have stipulated for the taking of action that removes unreasonable impediments in the way of minority group persons obtaining various needed opportunities. An example of this sort of action would be the institution by an employer of an affirmative program of recruiting Negroes and providing them with training in order to build up a pool of qualified persons for jobs that the employer is regularly filling. The lack of a program of this sort could well be viewed as an unreasonable impediment to Negro's obtaining jobs for which they are not presently qualified because of past discrimination on the part of unions, employers, and education programs. The failure to provide this program could probably not, however, be considered unlawful discrimination by the particular employer. To strengthen a commission's hand in negotiating for improvement of minority group opportunities in this situation, it is essential that it be backed up by a new principle of law, one differing considerably from the current law against specific acts of discrimination. What is needed is the establishment of a legal

[220] See Chapter 8.

principle not unlike the legal principle established by the Federal Trade Commission Act of 1914 against unfair methods of competition in commerce.[221] The principle to be established should be one prohibiting any method of conducting a business, profession, or government agency that unreasonably restricts a person of any race, color, religion, sex, national origin, or age in obtaining employment, housing, home financing, public accommodations, education, or otherwise participating in any phases of community life. It is impossible to spell out the specific kinds of unreasonable restrictions employed by businesses, professional men, and government agencies that bear prejudicially and unreasonably upon minority and other disadvantaged groups. The Alpha Model State Civil-Rights Act incorporates this prohibition into its Section 811 dealing with unlawful discriminatory acts in general.[222] The concept of "unreasonable restriction" here advanced will, however, take on more specific meanings in the course of efforts by the commission in processing particular cases and in negotiating with broad sections of the business community, unions, and government agencies, in particular instances. The underlying formula, in light of its purpose, will provide a sufficient guide for analyzing and judging individual situations just as the broad formulas of our federal antitrust laws have proved to be highly practicable in operation. Under Section 811 a commission is authorized to find that a violation of this principle is committed when the action of several businessmen, professional men, or government officials, creates the unreasonable restriction, although the action was not concerted in nature and although the action of no one person taken by itself would constitute an unreasonable restriction. In this situation the commission is authorized to order all members of the particular business or businesses affected to take affirmative corrective action either jointly or severally.

The Need for More Adequate Budgets and Staffs

In the twelfth place, state human-relations commissions have not been as effective as they could have been for lack of adequate budgets and staffs. Until these commissions are as well-financed and staffed as other commissions having comparable work loads, they cannot be expected to accomplish the results of which they are capable. While the New York State Commission has certainly been one of the better state

---

[221] 15 U.S.C. sec. 45(a)(1) (1964).
[222] See Chapter 8.

commissions, even that commission, as earlier indicated, has failed to generate more than a fraction of the complaints that should be filed relative to the total discriminatory transactions that have been occurring. Nevertheless, an examination of its budget in relation to what it has been doing permits us to make some useful calculations of the budget it would need in order to do the job it should be doing. In 1960 the jurisdiction of the New York Commission extended to less than 25 per cent of all employers.[223] They employed, however, about 80 per cent of all employees.[224] The Commission also had jurisdiction over all unions and employment agencies but only over 5 per cent of all housing accommodations in the state.[225] In the same year the Commission operated on a budget of $950,000.[226] It allocated 70 per cent of this amount, or $665,000, to its administration of the prohibition of discrimination in employment:[227] 84 per cent of its enforcement actions were concerned with employers, 10 per cent with unions, and 6 per cent with employment agencies.[228] Despite the wide coverage over discrimination by unions and employment agencies and the high incidence of discriminatory activity by them, the Commission in fact was examining in 1960 only "a small proportion" of these activities by employment agencies and only a "meager" amount of these activities by unions. The importance of employment agencies in effectuating discrimination is indicated by the fact that nearly 25 per cent of all hiring in the country is done through employment agencies. In light of the fact that the Commission had jurisdiction over less than 25 per cent of employers, as well as the numerous deficiencies in its operation previously noted, it also seems unlikely that more than 10 to 15 per cent of all discriminatory transactions by employers were in 1960 being processed by it. Probably less than 1 per cent of all discriminatory transactions in housing were being reached by it in that year. The Commission had no jurisdiction in 1960 over discrimination in commercial space or by financial institutions providing financing for the purchase, construction, rehabilitation, or repair of housing and commercial space. It seems obvious that the Commission's budget of $950,000 in 1960 was enabling it to reach only a small portion of the

[223] See text at notes 46–48, above.
[224] *Ibid.*
[225] New York State Commission against Discrimination, *Report of Progress* (1960), p. 5.
[226] Norgren and Hill, *Toward Fair Employment*, p. 100.
[227] *Id.*, p. 276.
[228] *Id.*, pp. 132–142.

discriminatory transactions over which it had jurisdiction. If it had had jurisdiction in 1960, as it now does, over nearly 100 per cent of discrimination in housing, commercial space, financing of housing and commercial space, public accommodations, and activities of all unions and employment agencies, as well as discrimination in employment relative to most employees, it seems obvious that the $950,000 budget would have been grossly inadequate for enabling the commission to deal with the great mass of discrimination against minority groups in 1960. It seems fair to say that this budget was surely no more than 5 to 10 per cent of the amount the New York Commission needed in 1960 to deal with the problem of discrimination in all these fields. Assuming $10,000,000 was the amount needed by the New York Commission to handle adequately this discrimination in 1960, we discover that this was only 3 per cent of all the money expended at the state and local level in New York for police protection.[229]

There are very good reasons for using a proportion of the amount spent on police protection in a state for determining the amount that should be spent by that state for resolving human-relations problems through a human-relations commission. In the first place crime, juvenile delinquency, family difficulties, and intergroup tensions and conflicts are extraordinarily high in the minority-group communities as compared with the majority-group community. The police direct a very large proportion of their activities in dealing with these matters toward members of minority groups located in city ghettos. The work of the police is largely defensive with regard to these matters. Human-relations commissions are also concerned with minority groups and deal not only with the causes of these conditions but also, in the case of intergroup tensions and conflicts, directly with them. At the local level human-relations commissions, as we shall shortly see, also handle a large number of problems that bring them in direct contact with minority groups and conditions affecting their ability to cope, on a somewhat more equal basis, with government—including the police—and business. The work of commissions, in contrast to that of the police, is largely prophylactic and remedial. There should be a considerable amount of money devoted to this type of government activity, dealing with minority groups, just as there is toward the defensive

---

[229] U.S. Department of Commerce, Bureau of the Census, *Census of Government: Compendium of Governmental Finance*, Vol. IV, No. 4 (Washington, D.C.: U.S. Government Printing Office, 1962).

activity of the police bearing upon minority group areas. Moreover, there are large areas of activity where there must be close liaison between the work of the police and the work of human-relations commissions. One would think that at least half as much money should be spent getting at the causes of minority-groups tensions, frustrations, and adverse conditions as is spent defending the community against the crime and juvenile delinquency which is so heavily centered in minority-group neighborhoods. Certainly the devotion of only 5 per cent of the total spent on police protection would seem to be a minimal figure for supporting the work of a state human-relations commission. Using this as a fair index of what the budgets of human-relations commissions should minimally be, we see that they are in fact grossly insufficient. In 1960 New York had a budget, as we have mentioned, of only $950,000, when it should have had, under the suggested index, a budget of $16,211,000.[230] The comparable actual and needed budget figures for 1960 in other key states were as follows: California, $203,-000—$18,710,000; Massachusetts, $100,000—$3,645,900; Michigan $148,000—$4,674,000; New Jersey, $148,000—$5,280,700; and Ohio, $100,000—$4,727,650.[231] One wonders if the needed amount had been spent in these states on the activity of human-relations commissions whether some of the excesses that have occurred in their ghetto areas —such as Watts, Newark, and Detroit—might have been avoided. The 1965 budgets of these and similar states were still well below the figures needed even in 1960: California, $585,381; Massachusetts, $634,-441; Michigan, $390,000; New Jersey, $250,146; New York, $1,963,-010; and Ohio, $211,750.[232]

It is entirely possible that the changes proposed earlier in the jurisdiction of state and local human-relations commissions, in their mode of processing individual complaints of discrimination, in their greater use of the public hearing rather than prolonged conciliation efforts, and in their employment of broad-scale negotiation with sections of the business community will substantially increase even the higher budget figures already indicated to be essential on the basis of their current jurisdiction and modes of operation. Moreover, proposals made

[230] *Ibid.*
[231] *Ibid.*
[232] U.S. Commission on Civil Rights, "Summary Fact Sheets for State Public Agencies With Jurisdiction Over Discrimination in Employment" (August 1965) (mimeographed).

later in this book for giving additional functions to state commissions will, if adopted, further increase the budgets needed by state human-relations commissions.

THE NEED FOR A FEDERAL HUMAN-RELATIONS COMMISSION

A thirteenth feature concerning the weakness of state and local human-relations commissions is the absence of an overall federal human-relations commission to deal with discrimination and other action causing serious harm to minority and other similarly disadvantaged groups in obtaining various opportunities in community life. We have seen the utter necessity for having a human-relations commission with enforcement power to deal effectively with these forms of harmful action at the state and local level. We have also studied various needed changes in the jurisdiction, structure, methods of operation, and funding of state and local agencies. But when all this has been done, these agencies will still lack authority to deal effectively with many forms of conduct affecting minority and other disadvantaged groups within the jurisdiction of the particular localities and states being served. One of the most obvious of these situations is presented by a federal government agency that discriminates in employment. Despite the existence of Presidential executive orders this form of discrimination does exist in some parts of some federal agencies.[233] Another type of situation is presented by businesses and unions that operate across state lines. A state or local human-relations commission is hampered in dealing effectively with local offices or units of interstate concerns or unions.[234] A problem of discrimination in a local office of a concern having headquarters and plants outside the city or state frequently is but part of a much larger problem of discrimination or disadvantage suffered by minority groups at the hands of that concern. Certainly the performance of the broad spectrum negotiation function with the units of an industry by state and local commissions can be meaningfully done by

[233] The head of the Austin office of a major federal agency informed me in August, 1966, that he would not place Negroes in certain positions that required them to go on the land of ranchers and farmers although he would employ them in other positions. Also see, statement of Herbert Hill, labor secretary of The National Association for the Advancement of Colored People, *Equal Employment Opportunities, Hearings on H.R. 405 and Similar Bills before the General Subcommittee on Labor of the House Committee on Education and Labor* (Washington, D.C.: U.S. Government Printing Office, April 22–June 6, 1963), pp. 140–141, 142.

[234] *Id.*, p. 138. An example of this is the textile industry which is the largest and most important manufacturing industry of the South [*ibid.*].

a human-relations commission usually only with the respect to entities of the industry located in the state or city. Still another type of situation that is difficult for state and local human-relations commissions to handle is the promotion or toleration of discriminatory conduct by federal-government agencies. The most obvious example has been the utilization of financial assistance by federal agencies to promote discrimination against minority groups in the housing and home-finance industries reviewed in the first chapter.[235] Even if the overt promotion of this discrimination by federal agencies has ended, the momentum of past overt discrimination still is having a very large impact. The federal agencies responsible for this discrimination are not acting to stamp out the continuing discrimination in the housing and home-finance industries with respect to homes benefiting from government insurance or guarantees of loans entered into prior to the President's executive order of 1962 or with respect to homes currently receiving the benefit of loans made by federally chartered institutions.[236] Finally there are areas of business dealings in interstate commerce involving discrimination against minority groups that state and local government cannot hope to regulate adequately. In all these instances, the only adequate solution is the creation of a federal human-relations commission along the lines suggested in this chapter for state and local human-relations commissions. The failure of the federal government to deal with discrimination that should be handled by a federal commission simply makes more difficult the work of state and local commissions, which already is difficult enough.

It is clear that none of the agencies created or empowered by the 1964–1968 acts are organized in an adequate way to perform the role of a federal human-relations commission. In the first place, they have no administrative enforcement power since it cannot issue and enforce in the courts cease and desist orders and other orders that are essential for ending discrimination and other harmful action against minority groups and similar disadvantaged groups.[237] The existing system of federal enforcement through civil actions for injunctive relief by either the aggrieved person or, under limited circumstances, by the Attorney General is wholly inadequate for enforcing the existing prohibitions against discrimination in public accommodations, govern-

[235] See text of Chapter 1 at notes 46–50 above.
[236] *Ibid.*
[237] See text of Chapter 1 at notes 31–42.

mental facilities, employment, and housing.[238] Moreover, the existing system of federal enforcement of prohibitions against discrimination in programs receiving federal financial assistance is inadequate.[239] Although these prohibitions are enforced by administrative agencies, these agencies are not primarily human-relations agencies. They have other programs that are more central to their work. Their function in the human-relations field is simply an auxiliary function and is likely to receive less attention than their main functions. The experience of these agencies in enforcing the prohibitions of discrimination in programs receiving federal financial assistance is far from encouraging. It seems wise to create a single federal human-relations commission and to assign to it all the typical enforcement functions that have been performed by state and local human-relations commissions.

In the second place, the federal Equal Employment Opportunity Commission has very limited jurisdiction in the human-relations field. Its limited coverage of discrimination by employers has already been mentioned. No more than 8 per cent of all employers in industries affecting interstate commerce are covered by the Civil Rights Act of 1964.[240] Considerably less than all unions and employment agencies are covered. But beyond this, the agency has no jurisdiction whatsoever over other areas of discrimination covered by the Civil Rights Act of 1964. Still further, as previously indicated, the federal government has not even begun to deal with many forms of discrimination against minority groups that only the federal government can effectively reach or that it can greatly assist in eliminating along with the work of state and local commissions.[241]

In Chapter 10 there is set out the Alpha Model Federal Civil-Rights Act designed to create a new federal human-relations commission to prohibit all forms of discrimination and other seriously harmful conduct affecting minority and other disadvantaged groups properly within federal cognizance, and to empower the new commission to uti-

---

[238] *Ibid.*

[239] See Chapter 1, note 42.

[240] See, *Equal Employment Opportunity, Hearings on H.R. 8998 and H. R. 8999 before the General Subcommittee on Labor of the House Committee on Education and Labor, House of Representatives,* 89th Cong., 1st Sess. (Washington, D.C.: U.S. Government Printing Office, June 15–July 21, 1965), pp. 7, 108.

[241] See text of Chapter 1 between notes 29 and 51.

lize all the modern array of authority necessary to make its work effective. The suggestions of this chapter relative to better structure and procedures for enforcement of prohibitions of discrimination and certain other harmful action have been incorporated into this model act. So far as substantive law, the model act covers discrimination in housing; financing of housing with one or more dwelling units; the operation of federally chartered financial institutions; employment practices by employers and unions of one or more employees or members in an industry affecting interstate commerce and by employment agencies serving them; employment practices by federal government agencies, states, and political subdivisions of states; in governmental facilities; in public education; in programs receiving any form of federal financial assistance; and in public accommodations by establishments of any type whose operations affect interstate commerce or are supported by state action.

This model federal act also contains a new concept of implementing the relation between the federal government and state and local governments in the human-relations field. The discussion of this chapter has proceeded along lines that have assumed that the existence of state and local human-relations commissions is essential for any adequate resolution of the manifold human-relations problems of our day. The discussion that follows in the immediately succeeding chapters will explore this assumption and seek to demonstrate that a human-relations commission operating at the local level, although not necessarily a local government human-relations commission, is the *sine qua non* for accomplishing significant results in overcoming the overall incidence of discrimination and other action seriously affecting minority and other similar disadvantaged groups. If this is true, it is necessary that the existing concept of both federal and state civil-rights legislation undergo radical changes. The reasons for these changes are discussed in Chapter 6. The form of the necessary changes is discussed in Chapters 7, 8, 9, and 10.

In Chapter 11 there is set out the Alpha Model Local Civil-Rights Act designed to create a local government human-relations commission, to prohibit all forms of discrimination and other seriously harmful conduct affecting minority and other disadvantaged groups properly within local cognizance, and empowering the local commission, like the federal and state commissions, to utilize all the modern array of authority to make its work effective. The suggestions of this chapter relative to better structure and procedures for enforcement of prohibitions of discrimination and other harmful conduct have been incorporated into this model act. It also covers commission operations not usually performed by state commissions due to the special office that is appropriate to local commissions. These operations will be explained in Chapter 6. Special problems of coordinating the work of a local commission with the work of the state and federal commissions are presented. These will be explored in Chapters 7 through 9.

CHAPTER

$\boxed{6}$

Dealing Effectively with Intergroup Relations at the Local Level

General Considerations

Discrimination against minority groups is but one of the many difficult problems of relations between the majority group and minority and other disadvantaged groups in our communities. These additional problems of intergroup relations are always closely related to problems of discrimination. Their elements either support, result from, or cause discrimination. The experience of several cities with well-established human-relations commissions demonstrates very forcibly that attempts to solve these additional problems of intergroup relations cannot wisely be either neglected or separated from attempts to solve problems of discrimination. Moreover, all problems of intergroup relations both arise and have their principal impact at the local level—in our cities, towns, villages and counties. The experience of several cities with well-established human-relations commissions also clearly demonstrates that solution of all these problems must take place at the local level, whether the agency that attempts to provide the solution be a local, state, or federal government human-relations commission. This latter fact condemns the method that has almost universally been adopted by states and by the federal government in creating and administering civil-rights law. The creators of this method have conceived that the sole focus of civil-rights law should be discrimination against minority groups and that this law should be administered from a central agency that neither operates in nor really involves the citizenry of each community affected by its operations. No conception of civil-rights law and law administration could be more erroneous.

The extraordinary influence of each community's approach to intergroup relations is demonstrated by an examination of how "outsiders" coming into a community typically react to its approach to these relations.

Frequently, a major company or a federal or state agency with its headquarters located far away from a given city will pursue a double standard in its relations with minority groups. In the state of its headquarters and in other states seeking to protect the economic opportunities of minority groups, a large company may be an exemplary employer and pursue a merit employment policy. But in Dallas, Baton Rouge, or Los Angeles, it may do the very opposite by conforming meekly to the local mores about employment, housing, and public accommodations for minority groups.[1] Similarly, the national or state headquarters of a great international union may talk vigorously in its plush offices about the need for respecting human rights of minority groups but pursue a Milquetoast policy toward discrimination by its well-named "locals" in Buffalo, Denver, or Chicago.[2] A federal agency with a well-stated and even well-implemented merit employment policy may in Texas exclude Negroes from certain "contact" positions simply because they "fear" that Negroes holding these positions would be subjected to bodily harm or that its patrons would be offended.[3] Negroes will be employed by such an agency but they will be placed in the agency's laboratory or other "inside, non-contact" jobs. In short, the "outsider" company, union, government agency, professional or business organization, school, institution, or person coming into a community is very much more concerned with "fitting-in" and "getting the business" than it is with doing simple human justice, maintaining proper human relations, and obeying the law. There is little statesmanship employed by "outside" businesses, professions, associations, or government agencies when they confront the fact that a majority group in a community is mistreating or neglecting the needs of its minority and other disadvantaged groups. They frequently, if not usually, conform to local practices and support the whole local program of discrimination and other harmful activity directed toward

---

[1] *Equal Employment Opportunity, Hearings on H.R. 405 and Similar Bills before the General House Subcommittee on Education and Labor* (Washington, D.C.: U.S. Government Printing Office, 88th Cong., 1st Sess., April 22–June 6, 1963), pp. 138–139; Munro S. Edmonson and David R. Norsworthy, "Industry and Race in the Southern United States" *Industrialization and Race Relations,* edited by Guy Hunter (London: Oxford University Press, 1965), pp. 52–53; Ray Marshall, "Industrialization and Race Relations in the Southern United States," *Industrialization and Race Relations,* pp. 73–76.

[2] Paul H. Norgren and Samuel E. Hill, *Toward Fair Employment* (assisted by F. Ray Marshall) (London: Oxford University Press, 1964), pp. 40–55.

[3] See note 233, Chapter 5, above.

minority and other disadvantaged groups by the local majority group. If "outsiders" react to each community's approach to its intergroup relations in ways similar to those just described, it is no wonder that inhabitants of a community largely continue to maintain the status of intergroup relations that were handed down to them.

In Chapter 2 it was suggested that the civil-rights problem must be regarded as essentially one resulting from the defective character of the majority group in each community and state.[4] This group, depending upon where it is located, holds one or more erroneous and unfair views concerning the nature and character of minority and other disadvantaged groups in the community. However heterogeneous these views may be they all are translated into various kinds of typical majority-group actions, habits, customs, and official and private arrangements that have produced the conditions affecting so seriously the minority and other disadvantaged groups within the communities—such as the Negro, the Latin American, the Jew, the Indian, the poor white, and others. At the same time, these disadvantaged groups have serious internal group problems.[5] Some of the problems are the result of cultural heritages and others are the result of long-continued discrimination practiced by the majority group. Any effort to raise the status and improve the opportunities of minority groups must take cognizance of these internal group problems. Almost always the bulk of the minority groups are poor, poorly educated, poorly trained, holders of lower-paid jobs, and relatively more in debt than others. There is also among them greater incidence of illness, unemployment, crime, juvenile delinquency, and family disorganization. Within the minority or disadvantaged group there is frequently little or no effective leadership relative to promoting the interests of the group vis-à-vis the majority group. There are usually some well-educated and able Negroes, Latin Americans, and other members of minority groups in each community. These, however, are very few in number relatively and by and large they have not provided effective leadership for their people with regard to improving their relations with the majority group or improving their ability to assist themselves in obtaining and qualifying for various opportunities. We are familiar with the term "ghetto mentality." It stands for many things. With regard to a minority group one meaning has reference to the intense and often un-

---

[4] See text of Chapter 2 between notes 7 and 13.
[5] See text of Chapter 2, pp. 49–52, 88–91.

just competition within that group for what is minimally available to its members at any particular time. Another is the political misleadership of the persons characterized as "political brokers" by Congressman Henry Gonzalez of Texas.[6] There is no more hateful and unneeded participation in a community than that provided by the minority-group politician or businessman who primarily seeks to aggrandize the local situation for his own personal benefit and that of his close political and business associates. In each community, fortunately, there are other members of the minority groups who are a minority themselves within their group. They may be teachers, real-estate brokers, salesmen, contractors, plumbers, or carpenters. They are not likely to be ministers or large businessmen. They possess a deep commitment to their people and a desire, as well as a capacity, to be of help to them. On the other hand, they are inexperienced in matters of group leadership. They lack the essential contacts with the majority group to voice their knowledge of minority-group conditions and their suggestions for dealing with them. Indeed, they may be lacking in the know-how for solving these problems simply because they have not had that kind of experience or do not have the kind of available organization through which to begin to work with human relations problems. They certainly are lacking in both time and material resources for this purpose.

The Constructive Action Function in Intergroup Relations at the Local Level

The great task that must be performed in each community with serious problems of intergroup relations is the reorganization of the human and material resources of that community that can contribute to resolving those problems and bringing those resources to bear upon these problems in the most effective way. The majority group of each community must be made to realize that its various actions, habits, customs, and arrangements bearing upon minority groups are seriously damaging both the latter and the whole community. Persons within the majority group must be found who will provide leadership within that group so as to move it to begin to confront and to resolve its intergroup problems. Similarly, within the minority groups leaders must

---

[6] Henry B. Gonzalez, "Poverty and Discrimination in the Southwest," *Congressional Record* (Washington, D.C.: U.S. Government Printing Office, daily edition, May 12, 1966), p. 9989.

be found who will help these groups to perform the kinds of actions that are calculated to start and facilitate the process of dialogue and negotiation between the majority and minority groups looking to an improvement in their relations and in the opportunities available to minority groups. If leaders of the kind just described do not presently exist within the majority and minority groups, then it is essential that potential leaders be found and trained and motivated to perform the needed leadership roles in their communities. Most communities outside of the Deep South and even some communities within this unhappy area have to a greater or lesser degree the necessary human and material resources for resolving their intergroup problems. What is lacking essentially in most communities throughout the nation is the leadership, commitment, organization, and appropriate legal and private arrangements for organizing and redirecting these human and material resources. We have already seen the necessity for the establishment of a human-relations commission with power to enforce prohibitions against all discrimination that seriously harms minority and other disadvantaged groups. We have examined some of the weaknesses in existing local, state, and federal agencies in performing this first function of a human-relations agency and how these weaknesses may be remedied. We have also examined a second function of these agencies in conducting negotiation with large sectors of the business, union, professional, and government agency worlds for the purpose of getting them to open up opportunities to minority groups. We now need to focus upon the third major function of human-relations agencies: the performance of a whole series of related functions which we may designate as the taking of constructive—more properly, "reconstructive"—action designed to produce the attitudes, conditions, and actions essential for enabling a community to solve its serious intergroup problems. This function has only been performed by local human-relations commissions and it has been performed well by only a very few of those which have undertaken it.

During the past twenty years a few major cities have developed comprehensive official programs for accomplishing each of the three principal functions of a human-relations commission just described through a local official agency. Among these cities are Philadelphia, Pittsburgh, New York City, Erie, Detroit, Baltimore, St. Louis, and perhaps one or two others.[7] These cities and particularly the first five

[7] See Appendix C of this book.

mentioned, whose programs began at least by the late 1940's, provide us with excellent examples or promise of what can be accomplished at the local level through well-rounded official programs dealing with problems in intergroup relations. In performing the first function of processing individual complaints of discrimination, these local human-relations commissions basically resemble the state and local commissions earlier studied and the federal human-relations commission that has been proposed in this book. They have the power to hold hearings, when attempts to obtain voluntary compliance with the law fail, and to issue, when appropriate, cease and desist orders that are enforceable in the courts through injunctions. In performing this first function, these local commissions have done as well as, and in some instances somewhat better than, the state commissions.[8] A local commission was the originator of the second human-relations commission function involving the negotiation with wide sectors of business, unions, professions, and government for improved opportunities for minority groups.[9] Very few state commissions have even attempted to perform this function. These local commissions have also been the originators of the third human-relations commission function described earlier and have accomplished some very remarkable results in performing it. State commissions have seldom attempted to perform this last function.[10]

The reason for the failure of most state commissions to perform the first two functions of a human-relations commission as well as have the few exceptional local commissions just mentioned is not merely the gross inadequacy of their budgets and staffs and the need for improvement in their jurisdictional coverage, structures, procedures, and operating concepts. The reason is rather the immense scope of discriminatory practices throughout each state and the fact that most state commissions have sought to utilize the single, state-wide commission with its typical "long-distance," out-of-the-community approach to the human-relations problems of each community. No single, state-wide commission can possibly deal with more than a fragment of the dis-

---

[8] The Pittsburgh Commission is an example of a local commission that has done an outstanding job of performing this function.

[9] See text of Chapter 5, at note 210 and following.

[10] An exception to this general rule is presented by the intervention of the Pennsylvania Human Relations Commission in the dispute between Negroes and the Chester, Pennsylvania, School District concerning *de facto* segregation [*Pennsylvania Human Relations Commission v. Chester School District*, 224 A. 2d 811 (Pa. Super. Ct., 1966)].

crimination at local levels throughout a state with this mode of administration. Moreover, even if it could physically manage to process most of the discriminatory transactions occurring within the state through some notion of decentralization of its functions, this still would leave the typical state-wide commission far from being prepared to handle successfully the problem of discrimination in each community. Aside from the fact that state human-relations commissions have not looked favorably upon a decentralized operation, a state agency built along the usual lines, simply because it is a state agency, is greatly impaired in its ability to respond to the subtle nature of the civil-rights problem of minority groups at the local level. A state agency finds even more difficulty in performing the second function of negotiating in each community with wide sectors of its local businesses, unions, professions, and government agencies for improvement of opportunities of minority groups. A state agency organized along the usual lines cannot even perform the third task of human-relations commissions. The state agency is an "outsider" and its professional personnel and agency heads are "outsiders." The latter lacks the insight, leadership, special influence, and subtle controls that local leaders can bring to bear upon their community as well as the flexibility and breadth of action that is available to them for effectuating the basic task that has to be performed in human relations in their community. The solution of the civil-rights problem of minority groups demands that that problem be recognized by each community as its own problem—both by its majority and by its minority groups—and that each community and each of these groups within it direct both official and unofficial efforts toward solution of that problem. It is essential that the leaderships of both the majority and minority groups become involved in these local efforts and that they become the agencies for awakening the social conscience of the community to the civil-rights problem within it and for causing that community to take effective steps toward resolving it. Until this occurs all efforts of state and federal commissions remain peripheral to the central civil-rights problem in each community and advance its solution only in minimal ways.

Even if a state or a federal commission might overcome the handicap of being an outsider in dealing with intergroup problems within a community, there remains the unavoidable obstacle of the overwhelming magnitude of the effort needed in dealing with intergroup problems at the local level. Human-relations commissions, whether they be established by the local, state, or federal governments, should at least be operating at the local level in each city and county having a population which includes 1,000 or more Negroes or Latin Americans. Experience indicates that these local governments generally have serious human-relations problems concerning these and other minority groups.[11] Using this figure as a criterion, we find that human-relations commissions should be established to operate in 425 out of the 675 cities with 25,000 or more population, 535 counties having less than 25,000 populations, and 400 cities with less than 25,000 population which are located in large counties.[12] These are localities having 1,000 or more Negroes in them. Moreover, even in the 250 cities with 25,000 or more population having fewer than 1,000 Negroes in them there is reason to believe that human-relations commissions should be established now in order to handle human-relations problems before they assume the difficulty of management found in other cities.[13] Latin Americans of Mexican extraction are heavily concentrated in the states of the Southwest, particularly in Texas and California.[14] In Texas alone there are 95 counties and 219 cities and towns having substantial Latin American populations and relatively small numbers of Negroes present.[15] In Arizona, California, and New Mexico there

[11] Commonwealth of Pennsylvania Department of Labor and Industry, *Report of the Governor's Committee on Discrimination in Housing* (January, 1959), p. 4. This report states: ". . . at least thirty cities of the Commonwealth now have over 1,000 nonwhite citizens." And the evidence gathered by the Committee indicates that patterns of discrimination and segregation are no less severe in the smaller cities than in the largest. In some respects, the smaller cities are even more restrictive. (Michael Culling and David W. Raven, "Discrimination and the Small Town" [unpublished civil-rights seminar paper, The University of Texas School of Law, December 17, 1966]) in their study of discrimination against minority groups in two central Texas towns near Austin, Texas, amply demonstrate this fact. In one of these, San Marcos, Latin Americans constitute 47 per cent of the total population which, in 1960, was 12,713. In the other, Taylor, Negroes constitute 22 per cent of the total population which, in 1960, was 9,434.

[12] These totals were obtained by author's count from tables included in U.S. Department of Commerce, Bureau of the Census, *County and City Data Book: 1962* (Washington, D.C.: U.S. Government Printing Office, 1963).

[13] *Ibid.*

[14] Lee Grebler, *Mexican Immigration to the United States: The Record and Its Implications* (Los Angeles: Mexican-American Study Project, January, 1966), pp. 51–53.

[15] Harvey L. Browning and S. Dale McLemore, *A Statistical Profile of the Spanish-Surname Population of Texas* (Austin: The University of Texas Bureau of Business Research, 1964), Table A-1, pp. 69–79; *The Dallas Morning News Texas Almanac, 1964–65*, pp. 185–284. These totals were obtained by author's count from these two sources and by having reference only to counties, and cities within them, in which Latin Americans heavily predominate relative to Negroes and in which Negro population is less than 1,000.

are 387 smaller towns and cities in which the predominating minority group is likely to be Latin American rather than Negro.[16] In each of these areas a human-relations commission should also be operating. There are, therefore, well over 2,000 cities, towns, and counties throughout the nation in each of which a human-relations commission is needed.

Before exploring how the administration of civil-rights law must be changed to permit the operation of a human-relations commission in each of these more than 2,000 local governments, it is important to understand the way in which the third important function of these commissions is now being performed by a few well-established human-relations commissions. This will enable us to see the utter necessity of including the performance of the third function within any local, state, or federal program relating to civil-rights of minority groups. It will also show us the necessity for each program to be focused upon the local level where intergroup problems subsist and must be solved.

PROMOTING INTERGROUP COMMUNICATION: NEED FOR AN OFFICIAL HUMAN-RELATIONS COMMISSION

The third function of a human-relations commission is concerned with the causes, effects, conditions accompanying, and means of overcoming the various disadvantages, including discrimination, to which a majority group in a community subjects one or more minority groups. The first two functions are concerned with specific harmful actions such as discrimination and unreasonable impediments to the enjoyment of equal opportunities. A human-relations commission begins its performance of the third function by initiating a process of communication between the majority and minority groups.[17] The pur-

---

[16] In Colorado and New Mexico the Latin American population is three or more times the Negro population. In Arizona the Negro population is heavily rural while Latin Americans are concentrated in urban areas. In California the two groups are more evenly balanced with Latin Americans predominating in most urban areas such as Fresno, Ontario, Riverside, San Bernardino, San Diego, San Jose, Santa Barbara, and Stockton [U.S. Commission on Civil Rights, "Spanish-Speaking Peoples," staff paper (February 5, 1964), Appendix A, Table 2].

[17] George Schermer, *Guidelines: A Manual for Bi-Racial Committees* (New York: Anti-Defamation League of B'nai B'rith, 1964), pp. 15–18. It is unfortunate that this fine pamphlet is marred by having a title referring to "bi-racial" committees. The term is most offensive to many Negroes who see this notion as divisive and separatist in connotation. Moreover, a human-relations commission is concerned with relations between many kinds of groups of which one is Negro. Many other

pose of the communication process initiated is to bring these groups into contact with each other, to enable them to develop a spirit of friendliness and concern about the views and problems of each group, and to move them to work out a series of programs to be directed toward the causes, effects, conditions accompanying, and means of eliminating the various disadvantages under which minority groups labor, and to involve as many people in the community as possible in carrying out these programs. Regard for these purposes shows why it is essential to have an official human-relations commission to perform in a community the third function of which we have been speaking.

It is fairly obvious, in light of the universal experience of our society in dealing with pressing public problems, that both law and an official agency of government to enforce it are essential for eliminating conduct that is harmful to society. Despite the protests of local power structures to the contrary, so far as discrimination against minority groups is concerned the judgment indicated by this universal experience is increasingly being adopted by cities and states in dealing with discrimination against minority groups. It is not, however, as obvious that an official agency of government is needed to deal with the many other aspects of intergroup problems in a community. Many cities and states that have been willing to adopt programs directed at discrimination against minority groups have not yet undertaken the official performance of the third function now under discussion. Mr. George Schermer, one of the leading experts in the field of human-relations, has stated that the experience of the last twenty years indicates that neither federations and councils of organizations nor voluntary committees or councils can carry on a successful program directed toward the performance of this third function.[18] The former must engage in a process of decision-making that is too cumbersome. It is difficult to get separate organizations to coordinate their efforts and to allocate responsibility. The voluntary committees tend to represent too limited a sector of the overall spectrum of community interests and concerns. They do not usually enjoy the support or the confidence of the power structure. They also do not enjoy the support of minority groups. Mr. Schermer tends to emphasize the lack of the former support. I would

---

minority groups, including Mexican Americans, Puerto Ricans, American Indians, and poor Southern whites, suffer in much the same way as Negroes and often subject each other to harmful action as well. Most communities have two or more social groups within them to which this term "bi-racial" is not at all responsive.

[18] *Id.*, p. 16.

suggest that lack of the latter support is just as damaging. A good example of both points is the Equal Citizenship Corporation of Austin, Texas, set up at the behest of the City Council by a number of influential citizens of the city.[19] Although the members of its board of directors included such people as the publisher of the *Austin American-Statesman*, the corporation was given very little support by either the city administration or by the Anglo community in general.[20] But far more significant for its success, the corporation was given practically no support whatsoever by the two minority-group communities. It did not enjoy their confidence. The minority-group communities judged that the corporation was representative of the power structure only. No communication process had been initiated by the creation and operation of that corporation. Mr. Schermer emphasizes that in order for an agency concerned with improvement of intergroup relations in a community to be successful, experience indicates it must

a. be established by and serve as the creature of the local government;

b. have fairly specific responsibilities and powers delegated to it by a council ordinance or the mayor's executive order;

c. be manned by a board of persons having prestige and respect, truly representative of the responsible racial, religious, business, labor, and civil elements and organizations;

d. be independent of any particular group in the city;

e. receive an appropriation or have some other assured source of financial support;

f. employ an executive staff to assure the continuity of the program.[21]

One can disagree with Mr. Schermer's conclusion that establishment of a human-relations commission by local government is essential while agreeing with the underlying reason for his conclusion. It is better for local government to establish an official human-relations commission, but in all events an agency to deal with human-relations problems in a community should be established by government. If the local government fails to perform its duty in this respect, then the

[19] See Chapter 2, above.

[20] It had no official status as part of the government, no government authority, no government staff, and no government quarters. It was eventually allocated $25,000 under a contract with the city to support its operations.

[21] Schermer, *Guidelines*, p. 17; also see National Association of Intergroup Relations Officials, *A Memorandum to Municipalities: Guidelines for Municipal Relations Committees* (Washington, D.C.: pamphlet, 1964), pp. 11–19, 22–23.

state government should establish a commission in each community. On the other hand, all of the other needs for a successful operation can be met even though the government establishing the local commission be the state or the federal government. It is too important that Americans begin in earnest to deal with intergroup relations to postpone that action until local communities establish effective human-relations commissions. Only 20 per cent of 249 cities surveyed in a recent study had established human-relations commissions by ordinance and no more than ten of these had truly comprehensive statutory structures and programs. When measured against the current need for more than 2,000 such local government commissions, this is a very limited response by local government.

Securing Reliable Information about Intergroup Problems

One of the first steps in the communication process that must take place in each community with serious intergroup-relations problems is the establishment of reliable and meaningful information about these problems.[22] Mr. Schermer has observed that the assembly of this information by a human-relations commission is "the most certain, least risky, least controversial, least expensive means of gaining the respect, good will, and cooperation of the press and mass media, responsible civic organizations and local government officials."[23] One of the most important persons on the staff of a commission is for that reason an information and research specialist. I think that Mr. Schermer underrates the ease with which a human-relations commission, even one with fairly representative citizens sitting on it and supported by an adequate budget, can obtain and publish reliable and meaningful information about serious intergroup problems in a community. Austin is a good example. In January 1967, the planning department of the city of Austin had had in its hands for many months, according to the most reliable of sources, the results of a survey of human-relations matters in the city. Some of this information had even been released to preferred individuals in city.[24] The report, however, could not be obtained from the city planning department.[25] The rumor was that

---

[22] Schermer, *Guidelines*, pp. 26–27; National Association of Intergroup Relations Officials, *A Memorandum to Municipalities*, pp. 12–13.

[23] Schermer, *Guidelines*, p. 26.

[24] See the information on the St. John's satellite slum released to the executive director of the University YMCA–YWCA, set forth in text at note 24 of Chapter 2.

[25] One member of the department, who has since left it, promised to provide me

the City Council would not permit its release. Moreover, the obtaining of sound information about human-relations problems in a community depends heavily upon the willingness of the majority and minority groups in that community to talk about these problems. What human-relations problems are in a community depends to a considerable extent upon what the majority and minority groups consider the important problems to be. While this should be perfectly obvious from its very statement, it is also almost universally overlooked. The riot in Watts in August 1965 is one of the more unfortunate examples of this. While it had been known for a very long time that Negroes had been walled up in Los Angeles central city ghettos due to discrimination in housing segregation and that they were excluded from a great many areas of employment opportunities due to discrimination by employers and unions, there were a whole series of specific grievances, summarized by the McCone Report, which the Watts community felt were important and that had gone unheeded by the majority group for a very long period of time.[26] What was true and may still be true in Watts is true of most communities in the nation today. It is not enough to publish the usual statistics, tailored to the local scene, on lack of housing and job opportunities. The information about human-relations that is meaningful to a local community is information that grows out of the exchange between members of local majority and minority groups. It must relate in the most specific ways to the difficulties which members of these groups see as being present in their community.

PROMOTING INTERGROUP INVOLVEMENT WITH HUMAN-RELATIONS PROBLEMS

The foregoing remarks suggest that the most important step a human-relations commission can take in a community is to initiate a series of exchanges between members of the majority- and minority-group communities.[27] One obvious way is to establish committees to study various human-relations problems in the community. By carefully selecting their members from the majority and minority groups

---

with a copy in July, 1966, but later found it necessary to give an excuse for not making it available.

[26] State of California, Governor's Commission on the Los Angeles Riots, *Violence in the City—An End or a Beginning?* (Los Angeles: December 2, 1965) (Commission Report).

[27] Schermer, *Guidelines*, pp. 27–28. National Association of Intergroup Relations Officials, *A Memorandum to Municipalities*, pp. 20–23.

in the community, the commission can assure that they will begin to discuss a specific area of these problems, their causes, and the means of resolving them. Out of their dialogue can emerge the first real involvement of the community with the problem assigned the committees. It is possible for committee members to experience a personal educational process and to pass on to other members of the community the benefit of their exchange. Usually this will be in the form of a committee report containing an assessment of what the problem really is that was assigned to them to study and what should be done about it. Probably, the first committees that will be established will concern community education, intergroup tensions and conflicts, police–minority-group relations, housing opportunities, employment opportunities, business opportunities, social changes in neighborhoods and communities, assistance services to minority groups, public schools, municipal and county policies and laws, and public accommodations.

Committee work of a human-relations commission can be very valuable in initiating communication between majority and minority groups in a community and in developing a consensus within the commission and its committees about what needs to be done about specific integroup-relations problems. It also can be of great importance in the execution of programs adopted for this purpose. Still committee work is of limited value in moving a whole community to confront its human-relations problems. A community process of change needs to be initiated. Obviously, that process, at best, is likely to be an uneven and diffused matter. Still it must go on. While publicity about human relations in the news media will facilitate the process of change, it is not the process itself. The problem for a human-relations commission is to adopt techniques that will cause that community change to begin and mature. I am inclined to think that the greatest contribution that a human-relations commission can make to a community is to transmit organizational know-how in dealing with human-relations matters to the majority and minority groups of a community.[28] Americans have organizations galore. Their problem is to make a good use of them. This problem is especially a problem in the minority-group areas. In Austin, Texas, for example, it is fair to say that the Latin American community is largely without effective internal group organization although there are numerous ethnic-group or-

[28] Schermer, *Guidelines*, pp. 29–30; National Association of Intergroup Relations Officials, *A Memorandum to Municipalities*, pp. 11–12, 22–23.

ganizations. The Negro community abounds with strong ethnic- and religious-group organizations but most do not really concern themselves with intergroup problems and those that do are most ineffective. The Anglo community has many strong organizations of every kind but almost none of them truly focus upon the intergroup-relations problems in the community. The question for the human-relations commission is either how to help these organizations to become motivated to look into human-relations problems and to devote a substantial amount of their activities to doing significant work with these problems or to assist in bringing new organizations into being which will be so motivated and work in this way. There are a number of devices that have been utilized by human-relations commissions for accomplishing this purpose. One of these calls for commission members on its staff to make talks before various organizations about the purpose of the commission and its work. Another is to hold workshops and institutes with various organizations and interested groups upon various roles that have to be performed in a city with regard to handling human-relations problems. Still another is the assistance provided in neighborhoods and communities within a city or county with regard to setting up organizations that can focus primarily upon human- and intergroup-relations problems. The objective in each of these methods is to secure and help talented persons at each level and within each major segment of the city or county to provide leadership to the area or segment they serve so that it will confront and resolve its human-relations problems.

DEVELOPING MINORITY-GROUP LEADERSHIP RELATIVE TO INTERGROUP-RELATIONS PROBLEMS

Of special importance are commission programs directed toward developing minority-group leaders, representing a fourth type of constructive action function. The premise of these programs is that if a minority group is to advance its status in society, it must actively work for this purpose and take advantage of the programs developed for equalizing the opportunities for achieving this result. On the other hand, before a minority group will begin to do this it requires welltrained and inspired leaders at the community level, who recognize the importance of this premise. Two kinds of leadership programs have emerged in the work of local commissions. One is the general development of community leaders among members of minority groups. Another is the preparation of these community leaders for holding appointive office in local government or membership in civic organizations.[29] Typical of the first type of commission program are the leadership-training institutes sponsored by the Pittsburgh Commission since 1961.[30] The purpose of these institutes has been to prepare from three to five members of each participating church to become human-relations consultants and to serve on a human-relations committee for the church. The function of these consultants, when trained, is to assist members of the congregation in taking advantage of the new opportunities in housing, employment, education, hospitalization, public accommodations, and other areas made possible by the local and state human-relations commissions and the basic laws under which they operate. They also refer to the local commission persons who have encountered discrimination or problems of group tension or conflict, blockbusting, police administration, school administration, or other similar human-relations problems. As members of the human-relations committee for their churches, they provide guidance and leadership to the committee in developing programs to funnel information to members of the congregations concerning their responsibilities and rights under civil-rights legislation and their preparation for and seeking of available opportunities of various types. A key feature in the development of community leaders was the role of the clergy in selecting members of their congregations to enter the training institutes and to accept the responsibilities of becoming a human-relations consultant. The institutes consisted of three two-hour sessions with one session being held each week for three successive weeks. In 1961 and 1962, 24 churches and 121 persons participated in the institutes.[31] Following the institute, as a regular procedure, a Commission staff member meets with the chairmen of the human-relations committees in the 24 churches. In this meeting the chairmen have an opportunity to exchange ideas, discuss programs and problems, and receive advice as to methods and techniques to be used in their communities. During 1963 a series of clinics about housing, employment, and law enforcement were held by the human-relations committees of each of the 24 churches participating in this program.[32] The clinics were devices for

---

[29] Philadelphia Commission on Human Relations, *Annual Report* (1962), pp. 2, 16; New York City Commission on Human Rights, *Annual Report* (1963), p. 26.

[30] Pittsburgh Commission on Human Relations, "Report on Civil Rights Leadership Training Institutes" (1962) (mimeographed).

[31] *Id.*, p. 2.

[32] *Pittsburgh Human Relations Review,* Vol. 6, No. 6 (December, 1963), p. 3.

assisting individuals to prepare for successful efforts in obtaining housing and employment.

Of course, a program for developing leadership within the minority-group community among its existing leadership stands or falls in light of the possibilities for leadership and change that exist within that group. In Austin, Texas, the Pittsburgh program would be most difficult to implement. Probably the situation in Austin would be more or less typical of what can be expected throughout the South and Southwest and probably in many, if not most, Negro communities throughout the rest of the country. In Austin, it is sadly true that by and large neither ministers, nor teachers, nor business and professional men of the Negro community have been willing to concern themselves with working for human rights.[33] It would almost be accurate to describe the apathy within the Negro community as being especially prevalent in these groups. Apathy is not, however, an accurate term to use in describing the great mass of Austin's Negroes. Reverend J. E. Obey, a member of the board of directors of the Citywide Committee for Human Rights, became in 1966 the first of over fifty Negro pastors to involve himself actively and continuously in a program to resolve intergroup and human-relations problems in Austin. Throughout five years of activity beginning in 1963 Negro ministers largely have kept themselves outside the arena in which the confrontation on human rights was taking place in this city. The first two ministers to participate withdrew early. Another minister made an *ad hoc* contribution in 1967. But beyond this, Negro ministers, the traditional leaders of their people, have not been willing to explore or pursue courses of action that would improve intergroup relations in the community. Reverend Obey in 1966 described the situation as resulting from the belief entertained by most Negro ministers that progress for their people could come only from supporting white politicians who would promise specific advances in jobs or other opportunities.[34] They were willing, he observed, to travel two hundred miles to a political barbecue but unwilling to travel two blocks to help a person seriously in need of help in solving his individual problem in obtaining a job or medical attention or in dealing with police or other authorities.[35] Another Negro, a

[33] See Chapter 2.

[34] Interview with Reverend J. E. Obey, pastor of David Chapel Baptist Church, second largest church in East Austin, in October, 1966.

[35] Reverend Obey also stated that many of the older Negro Baptist ministers will not collaborate with Negro Methodist ministers even in religious matters. A trend toward cooperation is, however, evident among the younger ministers.

businessman, stated that Negro ministers received frequent "hand-outs" from Anglo businessmen and were sometimes reminded by bankers and others that the ministers had been helped by loans for their churches and that they should be friendly to political friends of the lenders.[36] The political approach, as indicated in Chapter 2, has also been utilized by a leading group of Negro business and professional men in Austin.[37] This has consisted in supporting the political efforts of the governor of the state who has in turn opened over five hundred jobs to Negroes throughout the state for the first time in history.[38] The great mass of Negroes have, however, continued in much the same status as before with their pressing human-relations problems going unsolved and untended. A pamphlet on the role of Negro ministers or Negro business and profession men, such as have been published by the Pittsburgh Commission on Human Relations, is likely to have only minimal effect in Austin. In this and other cities in the South and Southwest, a human-relations commission should, of course, attempt to energize these elements of Negro community. In the main, however, they must seek to assist a new Negro leadership to emerge. The most likely sources of this leadership are teachers, small businessmen, and young people. They must be trained in the role of minority-group leadership and provided with specific opportunities to exercise leadership roles within their local communities. This can be done in a number of ways. Some can be employed by the human-relations commission itself. Others can be assisted in forming and operating appropriate neighborhood and subcommunity organizations. Public forums can be sponsored by the commission on pressing problems in the minority-group communities.

The problem of lack of leadership in the Latin American communities of the Southwest is a very special and complex problem.[39] There are far fewer human and material resources in these communities than among the Negro communities of the same area. There are fewer business and professional leaders. There are far fewer teachers. The educational attainment of the entire ethnic group, as earlier indicated, is about half that of the entire Negro group. Probably the greatest resource for leadership of this group, strangely enough, lies outside of it

[36] Interview with Mr. Jasper Glover, Austin real-estate broker, in June, 1966.
[37] See Chapter 2.
[38] Interview with Mr. and Mrs. M. J. Anderson, Austin Negro leaders, in December, 1965.
[39] See text in Chapter 2, pp. 00–00.

in the Negro and Anglo groups. Moreover, the Roman Catholic Church is in a position to pour great human resources into the war upon lack of leadership among Latin Americans, most of whom belong to this church. It is in a far more secure position than the individual Negro pastors of small Protestant churches. It can open the doors of its cathedrals, as Archbishop Robert E. Lucey of San Antonio recently did, for a group of Rio Grande Valley farm workers who were striking and marching for a $1.25 minimum wage law.[40] Its priests can, as did the priests of the San Antonio archdiocese, go into a farm area seething with intergroup-relations problems and guide poor and ill-educated Latin Americans in an unprecedented "March for Justice" to the state capital.[41] A major problem from one community to the next in the Southwest, as it is for other areas of the country, concerns the Christian and Jewish churches themselves. Perhaps the most significant job in human relations for a human-relations commission to accomplish in each community is moving its churches to put their teachings into actual practice regarding minority groups.

PROMOTING AND ASSISTING COMMUNITY AND NEIGHBORHOOD ORGANIZATIONS

Some local human-relations commissions have demonstrated considerable ability in performing a fifth constructive function: the development of new community and neighborhood organizations having the objective of self-help in meeting intergroup problems. The lessons learned in this field of activity should be put to work in a more thorough-going and wide-spread way. An example of this activity has concerned the situation in which a minority group, such as Negroes or Latin Americans, begin to move into an area in which none or few of their group had previously moved and the on-going social process of neighborhood change becomes greatly accelerated as a result. Usually the neighborhood is an older one in which there is a higher percentage of dilapidated and substandard housing than in other neighborhoods. As the minority group moves into the neighborhood, there is a tendency for Anglo residents to move out of it. The prior failure of the neighborhood or community leadership in reversing any process of physical or social deterioration already underway becomes even more telling at this point. If residents have been backward previously in

[40] *San Antonio Express News* (Nov. 6, 1966), Sec. H., pp. 1–2.
[41] *Ibid.*

taking care of their property or in seeking ways to improve community facilities, what efforts have been made to overcome these difficulties
may end as fear over the future of the community becomes the dominant force. If the community has not been prepared for the fact of
ethnic change so as to understand it and how to meet it, community
tensions may arise quickly, discrimination against the minority group
may expand, and acts of violence and vandalism occur. While a local
commission must deal quickly and well with particular instances of
group tensions and conflicts as they arise, it must do much more for
the community undergoing ethnic change. In the first place, the commission must be on its guard to identify areas of racial transition under
its jurisdiction before group tensions arise. Whether these areas are
identified before or after this event, the commission must then institute programs for maintaining or restoring stability in the community
on a long-range basis. The New York, Philadelphia, Pittsburgh, Chicago, and Detroit Commissions, among others, have done outstanding
jobs in this respect. The usual technique is to organize a community
council or intergroup-relations committee so as to reach the leadership
structure of a wide geographic area surrounding the specific neighborhood which has received its first minority-group families. The underlying premise of this technique is that this wider area will be vitally
affected by the transitional neighborhood and that its physical and
social deterioration can be prevented and its present conditions stabil-
ized and later improved only when its citizens face up to the problems
of ethnic change and become involved in formulating the goals of a
community-stabilization program and in executing actions designed to
implement these goals.[42] The function of the community council is to
promote a harmonious and productive democratic process in the community in which persons of all racial, religious, and nationality groups
may freely participate, to maintain property values by preventing the
resident white families from becoming panic-stricken and fleeing from
the community, to improve the physical facilities and quality of education in the public schools, to promote widespread participation in
activities that contribute to the improvement and general welfare of
the community, and to obtain the enactment and observance of city
ordinances bearing closely upon the stabilization and improvement of
the community.[43]

Organizing a community council consumes an inordinate amount of

[42] *Pittsburgh Human Relations Review*, Vol. 6, No. 4 (August, 1963), p. 3.
[43] *Ibid.*

the time and energy of a local commission. The commission must first determine whether a council is needed in a community, and, if so, search for persons within it who are interested, qualified, and willing to work on the council.[44] Depending on the vitality of the community involved and the quality of its leadership, this may take many days or even weeks of interviews and conferences. When a sufficient number of citizens have been moved to commit themselves to serve on the council, still further meetings are necessary in order that the individuals may develop the spirit, know-how, and momentum necessary for them to become an effective group. Their first effort as a group is directed toward a study of the human-relations problems of their community and a consideration of the types of community action that may help solve them. The process followed by a commission in determining whether a community council should be organized, in planning its organization, and in holding the necessary preliminary discussions and conferences for bringing it into being can easily cover the period of a whole year. Where councils can be built on a membership base provided by existing groups, such as the Parent Teacher Association or churches, a shorter period of gestation is possible. In Chicago during 1963 the Commission assisted seven communities in organizing their councils.[45] During the same year the Los Angeles County Commission assisted approximately twelve communities in this task.[46] By 1967 the work of the Los Angeles County Commission had been greatly expanded in this area.[47]

When a council has finally been formally organized through commission efforts, the next task is to provide its members with the necessary assistance, information, and training for performing their leadership function in their community. To accomplish a major portion of this task the commission assigns a staff consultant to each council it organizes.[48] The consultant arranges programs, exhibits films, and generally seeks to inform the council he serves concerning current

[44] Los Angeles County Commission on Human Relations, "Notes on the History and Activities of the Human Relations Commission" (July, 1963), pp. 4–5 (mimeographed).

[45] Chicago Commission on Human Relations, *Annual Report, 1963*, p. 14.

[46] Los Angeles County Commission on Human Relations, "Notes on the History," p. 4.

[47] Los Angeles County Commission on Human Relations, "Resumé of Staff Organization, Assignments, Programs and Projects, Personnel Needs, and Workload" (December, 1966) (mimeographed), pp. 1–8, 10–13.

[48] Los Angeles County Commission on Human Relations, "Notes on the History," pp. 5–6.

human-relations problems. He also provides it with expert advice and assistance when it undertakes to plan remedial action for community problems. Experience has demonstrated that most community councils rely heavily upon the consultant assigned to them and require him to confer at least once a month with their chairman and to attend both the meetings of the council's executive committee and regular council meetings. The Los Angeles Commission estimates that servicing an active community council requires one week per month of its consultant's time.

To provide community-council members with the basic knowledge and training they require in order to perform their leadership function, some commissions have organized study courses and institutes. A basic study course organized by the Los Angeles County Commission, for example, consists of six two-hour weekly sessions.[49] The Commission staff assists the council in obtaining speakers, assembling course material, and making the various necessary arrangements. In a somewhat broader educational approach, the New York City Commission held an all-day workshop in 1962 in which thirty-four community or neighborhood councils participated.[50] The purpose of this workshop was to stimulate wider participation in programs designed to build a spirit of community among the residents of each neighborhood. By 1965 the Commission was conducting its workshops in Spanish in Puerto Rican areas.[51]

Typical of the community councils organized by a local commission is the KABB Community Council in Pittsburgh organized by the local commission in early 1962 to deal with problems of community stabilization presented in four neighborhoods in the south area of the city.[52] One of these neighborhoods, Beltzhoover, was located in a census tract which in 1960 had 50 per cent or more housing units occupied by nonwhite persons, who were principally Negroes.[53] This tract was surrounded by four census tracts in which no housing units were occupied by nonwhites and a fifth census tract in which fewer than 5 per cent of its housing units were occupied by nonwhites. The Beltz-

---

[49] *Ibid.*

[50] New York City Commission on Human Rights, *1962 Annual Report*, p. 16.

[51] New York City Commission on Human Rights, *Annual Report for 1965*, p. 9.

[52] *Pittsburgh Human Relations Review*, Vol. 6, No. 4 (August, 1963), pp. 2–3; Vol. 6, No. 6 (December, 1963), pp. 3–4; Vol. 7, No. 3 (June, 1964), p. 3.

[53] Pittsburgh Commission on Human Relations, *Report of the Status of Housing of Negroes in Pittsburgh* (May, 1962), p. 7. Much of the statistical information which follows was drawn from this report.

hoover neighborhood is one of two neighborhoods and three larger areas of high nonwhite concentration in Pittsburgh in which more than 100,000 Negroes live. The remaining much larger areas of the city and the suburbs outside the city have almost no Negro families due to the practice of discrimination against the Negro in the sale and rental of housing. Prior to 1950 Beltzhoover had more than 10 per cent but less than 25 per cent nonwhite occupied dwelling units. By 1960, as indicated above, nonwhite occupation of dwelling units had increased to 50 per cent of the total. As in other areas occupied by Negroes in any great numbers, most of the dwellings and buildings in Beltzhoover were much older than in other sections of the city: 95 per cent of the new dwellings built in Pittsburgh between 1950 and 1957 had been built outside the three large areas with the highest Negro concentration.[54] Many of the dwellings in Beltzhoover were in need of painting and cleaning. It was one of the city's neighborhoods in which less than 50 per cent of the total housing units could be classified as "sound, nondefective" in 1960 as compared with the average of 80 per cent "sound, nondefective" units in census tracts having less than 1 per cent of the housing units occupied by nonwhites.[55] A 1960 survey of the units occupied by nonwhites in Pittsburgh revealed that out of every 10 of these units only 4.4 were "sound, nondefective" while 4.3 were in need either of plumbing to provide adequate sanitation or of structural repair to remove conditions of deterioration; 1.3 were completely dilapidated; and 2 were overcrowded.[56] In Beltzhoover, in addition, there were a considerable number of abandoned dwellings, abandoned cars, and ugly vacant lots. Many public improvements were also needed in the area. A process of both physical and social deterioration was likely to engulf Beltzhoover and to spread to adjacent neighborhoods in light of the prior universal experience not only in Pittsburgh and Pennsylvania but in other similar areas throughout the country. This experience demonstrates that when minority groups are sharply confined in their movement in the housing market, any breach in this pattern in a given neighborhood causes the overall pent-up pressure for housing in that city to be focused upon that neighborhood. The rapid racial change that follows brings widespread tension that is deeply disturbing both to the white residents and to the newly arrived

[54] Commonwealth of Pennsylvania Department of Labor and Industry, *Report of Governor's Committee on Discrimination in Housing* (1959), p. 8.
[55] *Id.*, pp. 13, 18 (Table 8).
[56] *Id.*, p. 16.

nonwhite immigrants. The case history of a move-in in the Pittsburgh area has already been recounted earlier in connection with our examination of the local commission's function in taking care of tension incidents. Beyond the factor of tensions, prior experience had amply demonstrated that as the receiving neighborhood is hard pressed by new nonwhite families seeking better living conditions than in their central city ghettos, many of the older homes are converted into smaller units causing conditions of overcrowding similar to that in areas from which the immigrants had come. When the receiving area becomes overcrowded it soon begins to deteriorate. As the nonwhites move into the neighborhood, the whites move to the suburbs. Between 1950 and 1960, 91,000 whites moved to the Pittsburgh suburbs while 18,500 Negroes moved into the city.[57]

To avoid the usual process of social and physical deterioration in Beltzhoover and three other nearby neighborhoods, the KABB Community Council was organized by the Pittsburgh Commission in early 1962.[58] At the present time the council has about 115 members representing either themselves or one of thirty-three agencies, institutions, and civic or social groups in the community. The council has provided vital service, with the assistance of the local commission, in resolving tension incidents in the community. It has sponsored a program involving the painting of buildings and cleaning up of the area. It has obtained a number of public improvements such as the installation of traffic lights at critical points. It has studied the extent of juvenile misbehavior and the need for establishing special programs for juveniles. It has met with the Department of City Planning to determine the needs of the community, its resources for meeting these needs, and a long-term plan for its renewal. Working together with an organization of residents composed of members of Jewish, Protestant, Catholic, and other religious congregations, the council has sought to establish a climate in which racial integration of the community will be facilitated through a solution of the various problems arising in connection with this ethnic change. It is the judgment of council members that they have provided, with the assistance of the local commission, a channel of communication through which residents and community groups can make their views on public issues known to others in the community. As a result of the discussion it makes possible, the council is able to develop and direct unified community efforts for solving

[57] *Id.*, p. 7.
[58] See note 52 above.

various problems of human relations. Its members know that deterioration of the community's neighborhoods can be prevented by the pride its residents take in keeping up their homes and by their insistence upon observance of zoning laws and building codes. They know and convey to their fellow residents that moving away from the community simply to avoid contact with minority group families is an unwise choice. The value of their homes can be preserved. The desirability of the community can remain intact irrespective of the ethnic group of new neighbors. This depends upon what its residents do to keep it a desirable community. This applies to the public schools in the community as well. If they are presently good schools, they will remain in that status and can be improved if parents take an active interest in them and provide the faculty and administrators full cooperation. Moreover, running away from the communities will simply delay, and not for very long, the eventual problem of having to adjust to minority group families entering each city and suburban neighborhood.

In addition to organizing and assisting community councils each year the local commissions in New York, Philadelphia, Pittsburgh, Detroit, Baltimore, Chicago, and Los Angeles conduct literally scores of conferences, institutes, and workshops for different interest groups in the localities they serve.[59] The purpose of these meetings remains the same however much they may differ in length, depth of coverage, or type of program. This purpose is to stimulate the participants in these meetings to think about human-relations problems presently at large in each of their fields or areas and then, in returning to their work, to provide the requisite leadership for getting these problems solved, with commission assistance whenever needed. These meetings, varying from one day to ten weeks in length, have been held for the clergy; bankers; builders; mortgage companies; real-estate managers, brokers, and operators; members of the various mass media; hospital administrators; labor leaders, senior executives for major commercial and industrial firms; civil-rights organizations; educators; and civic organizations. In addition to holding meetings on human relations

---

[59] The *Annual Report* (1964) of the Philadelphia Commission on Human Relations reports a series of meetings that were conducted in both the Puerto Rican community and the fast growing Northeast area where racial change of neighborhood is underway [pp. 15–18]. The 1965 annual report tells of the opening of the agency's first field office to expand its usual community services [Philadelphia Commission on Human Relations, *1965 Annual Report*, pp. 10–11].

problems and the proper role of various persons in the city's power structure for dealing with them, the local commission through its research and public information divisions channels a veritable river of human-relations publications of great usefulness and interest to these persons.

PROMOTING RESPONSIBILITY IN MASS-MEDIA REPORTING
OF INTERGROUP-RELATIONS MATTERS

It would be difficult to single out any one group as peculiarly important in providing leadership on human-relations problems in local areas. Nevertheless, it is certainly true that for the good and evil that can be done for human relations in a locality, no group is more important than the executives of mass-media organizations.[60] Most of the educational, informational, and action programs of a local human-relations commission depend heavily upon the mass media serving the local area for their success. In order to perform most of its basic functions the local commission must create lines for systematic communication between government and the citizenry as well as between the various ethnic groups in the community, build intergroup understanding and goodwill, and elicit specific responses to commission programs. Due to the importance of mass media in accomplishing these three objectives, the local commission through its public-relations or information division usually makes special efforts to establish and strengthen personal contacts with representatives of all mass media. It seeks to help them understand the work of the commission and the vital dependence of this work, for its success, upon their interpretation and presentation of the commission's programs and positions to the public. In 1961 the Philadelphia Commission held the first seminar for executives of the press, radio and television stations, and intergroup agencies to discuss the handling of news having intergroup significance.[61] The purpose of the seminar, conducted over a period of five meetings, was to create a more direct and productive communication between the agencies and mass media. One result of the seminar was the adoption of a set of guidelines or a code relative to handling news with intergroup significance.[62] Over the years most local commissions have held regular conferences with mass media with the same objec-

---

[60] See Schermer, *Guidelines*, pp. 31–32.
[61] Philadelphia Commission on Human Relations, *Annual Report* (1962), p. 15; *1965 Annual Report*, p. 5.
[62] Schermer, *Guidelines*, Appendix E, pp. 82–84.

tives in mind. By and large, these conferences, as in Chicago, have resulted in the responsible handling of stories of racial tension.[63] They
have also led to the commissions' being afforded regular broadcast
time to present programs concerning job opportunities, housing, and
various human-relations problems. Members of the local commissions' staffs are also frequently invited to appear on regular news and
public affairs programs produced by radio and television stations.

The significance of the work of a local human-relations commission
in helping its community to turn the corner in human relations is
never better illustrated than it is by their moving mass media to provide substantial assistance in establishing effective lines of communication between the government and the citizenry and between ethnic
groups. One has only to compare the performance of mass media in
handling the reporting of human-relations news in communities in
states having neither state nor local human-relations commissions. In
the South, even in the more advanced areas like Austin, Texas, the
absence of an effective local human-relations commission usually
means that the mass media have badly failed to live up to the role they
can and should be performing.

CONTROL OF INTERGROUP TENSIONS AND CONFLICTS

We have examined so far the roles a human-relations commission
can perform at the local level in becoming an effective agency for assisting a community in beginning to confront and to work to resolve
its serious intergroup-relations problems. It serves as an official body
which, in being truly representative of the whole community, has the
only real opportunity of all agencies in the community to serve as the
focal point for efforts on the part of all interested groups and segments
of the community to deal effectively with these problems. It can serve
to establish reliable information about these problems and to communicate that information to all the people. It can involve citizens within
the majority and minority groups in the work of commission committees and thereby accomplish the goals both of educating them in human-relations matters and of securing from them the performance of
leadership roles in the community in proposing and executing programs for resolving intergroup-relations problems. It can develop new
leadership within the minority-group communities where the mere
existence of competent leadership is especially a problem. It can also

---

[63] Chicago Commission on Human Relations, *Annual Report, 1962*, p. 23.

direct efforts toward involving various interest groups and individuals and organizations within them in the process of dealing with human-relations matters.

We next turn to some specific tasks performed by an able human-relations commission operating within a community. One of these is concerned with the management and resolution of particular instances of intergroup friction arising out of various kinds of tension incidents and conflicts which occur at the neighborhood or community level. This function is usually administered as part of what is called the "community-relations" program of a commission. One commission has described the purpose of this type of program to be "to promote a peaceful and secure community in which dignity and mutual respect, equal opportunity, law and order and a sense of civic responsibility among peoples of all races, religions, and national origins."[64]

The history of cities across the country having minority groups within them indicates that the problem of community-tension incidents is a large and growing one in the field of intergroup relations. In Philadelphia in 1962, a total of 495 tension incidents were reported to its local commission.[65] During a twelve-month period ending September 3, 1962, the Los Angeles County Commission reported the occurrence of at least four serious clashes between minority-group persons and police agencies.[66] Three of these involved Negroes while the fourth involved Latin Americans. In New York there has been a gradual increase of tension incidents between police and members of minority groups in the 1960's. In the month of July 1961 alone over 290 of these incidents had occurred and during 1965 a growing number of interpersonal situations were escalating into community situations.[67] In 1963 the Detroit Commission processed over 160 tension incidents.[68] In 1964 and 1965 the Pittsburgh Commission reported an unprece-

---

[64] Philadelphia Commission on Human Relations, *Annual Report* (1962), p. 35.

[65] *Id.*, p. 4. The annual reports of the Commission for 1963 and 1965 do not list the number of tension incidents but do indicate that they are increasing rapidly both in number and potentiality for disaster [Philadelphia Commission on Human Relations, *Annual Report* (1963), pp. 15–17; *Annual Report* (1964), pp. 5–8; *1965 Annual Report*, pp. 2, 11–13].

[66] Los Angeles County Commission on Human Relations, *1960–2 Biennial Report*, pp. 8–9. In the two-year period, 1960–1961, in the City of Los Angeles alone, a 188 per cent increase was reported in intergroup conflict at the juvenile level.

[67] New York City Commission on Intergroup Relations, *1961 Annual Report*, p. 31; New York City Commission on Human Rights, *Annual Report for 1964*, p. 3.

[68] Detroit Commission on Community Relations, *Report "Geared for Action"* (1964), p. 4.

dented number of tension cases.[69] Once in a while a particular tension incident erupts into extraordinarily serious violence.[70] This occurred in New York in the summer of 1964 following the killing of a Negro youth by a New York policeman. In 1965 there were numerous outbreaks, the most serious of these being the one that occurred in Watts.[71] In 1966 and 1967 the outbreaks continued in 104 additional cities including those in Cleveland, Newark and Detroit. The largely peaceful, nonviolent actions for open housing in Northern city suburbs carried out by the separate forces led by Reverend Martin Luther King and Reverend James L. Groppi met with extreme hostility and sometimes violence from white groups.[72] Most of these incidents, however, were satisfactorily resolved through commission action.

Tension incidents fall into certain well-defined categories. With the Pittsburgh Commission, the largest group of tension incidents were those connected with housing. The typical housing tension incident arises when a white person owning a home desires to sell or lease it and a Negro desires the home.[73] When the Negro visits the house to determine its desirability, he and his family are seen by neighbors. Panic seizes some of the latter. Various unfounded comments are expressed and begin to circulate concerning the probable loss of housing values, activity of the NAACP, and the social habits of the Negro family involved. Neighbors call the white owner and the Negro potential buyer or lessee to harangue and discourage them. One neighbor, usually a professional man, circulates a petition opposing the transaction. The white owner becomes the target of various types of pressure. His employer is asked to fire him. One group of neighbors tries to buy his house. Other neighbors express their intention to sell their own property immediately. One neighbor proposes having the neighborhood children boycott the new Negro children as a means of causing the family to move out of the neighborhood. Some white teenagers, spurred on by their elders, begin to drive up and down the street asking where the Negro family is going to live.

[69] *Pittsburgh Human Relations Review*, Vol. 7, No. 6 (December, 1964), p. 2; Vol. 8, No. 2 (April, 1965); Vol. 9, No. 4 (August, 1966).
[70] *The New York Times* (July 17, 1966), sec. 4, p. 1; *The National Observer* (July 25, 1966), p. 4.
[71] See note 26 above.
[72] *The National Observer* (August 15, 1966), p. 5; *Time* (August 19, 1966), pp. 20–21; *The Christian Science Monitor* (September 16, 1967), p. 3.
[73] See, *e. g.*, Pittsburgh Commission on Human Relations, "Hastings Street Move-In, A Case History" (1961) (mimeographed).

A second type of tension incident arises in connection with police activity, examples of which have frequently been in the news since 1964. The police represent the most easily identifiable official authority in a community.[74] They are frequently the only authority with which the Negro minority comes in contact. When tension and dissatisfaction of the Negro community with its lot reaches unbearable levels, the police become the most obvious authority against which this minority group elects to rebel. The social isolation and the general group dissatisfactions of the Negro have operated to stimulate the less stable elements of the minority group to engage in increased criminal and delinquent activities. This is especially true of the youth who are now accounting for a large proportion of increased criminal and delinquent activity. The majority white group of our society has a number of important freedoms not as substantially available to the subordinated and segregated nonwhite group. The socially enforced segregation by which this has been accomplished has led to frustrations, and these in turn have led to tensions and finally, aggressions and hostilities. Negro and Latin American youths especially find it unrealistic to hold any allegiance to moral standards and ways of proceeding toward the normal objectives of young people, held also by the dominating white persons, when the latter reject them at one or more points of contact deemed important by these youth—employment or public accommodations, for instance. It is an undeniable fact that the minority-group communities consider the police a part of the dominant society that rejects them. They view the police as "a conspirator with the official and unofficial authority of the dominant society to deprive them of their rights as citizens and as human beings."[75]

A third type of tension incident arises in connection with public-school activities. In 1961, for example, it was generally charged that discrimination was being practiced in a New York City public school.[76] This led to a "cold war" situation of long duration in which Negro and white students manifested exceptionally bad intergroup attitudes likely to lead to violence. More recently, tension incidents involving public schools have arisen as a result of the effort by the Negro and other sections of the community to eliminate *de facto* segregation in those

[74] John Y. Buggs, "Police–Community Relations: A Critique on Issues That Tend to Divide Us" (Los Angeles County Commission on Human Relations, 1962) (mimeographed). This is one of the best brief analyses of the problem discussed in this paragraph.

[75] *Id.*, p. 17.

[76] New York City Commission on Human Rights, *1962 Annual Report*, pp. 12–13.

schools and the response of cities to this effort. In 1961, for example, the Detroit Commission had to deal with a white parent boycott of a Board of Education program to transfer by bus children, a majority of whom were Negro, from seriously crowded center-district schools to the three nearest schools with capacity to handle the overflow.[77] Up to 60 per cent of the white children were kept at home during the boycott and attempts were made by some white parents to organize picket lines to prevent the entry of Negro children into their new schools. In 1965 the major tension producing incident in Philadelphia concerned the bussing policy of the local Board of Education.[78]

A fourth type of tension incident involves teenage groups. A pattern of animosity developed in 1962, for example, between Jewish and Italian youths in a Philadelphia neighborhood area.[79] Beatings of local Jewish boys occurred with regularity on Friday and Saturday evenings and sometimes on dismissal of a public school in the area, resulting in the Jewish youth beginning to talk of retaliation with weapons.

A fifth type of tension incident frequently occurs when a minority group misunderstands the purpose of official action that affects them as, for example, in 1962 when a group of Philadelphia city agencies jointly conducted a community rehabilitation program.[80] The group, Puerto Rican in origin, believed rumors to the effect that the purpose of the program was to displace all of that group from the area. The situation became complicated when a Negro was killed by a Puerto Rican and rumors circulated that Negro gangs were forming for the purpose of retaliation. This was followed by the organization of defensive groups by the Puerto Ricans.

To deal with tensions like the types just reviewed and many others, commissions depend upon an expert staff to make the day-to-day decisions on the neighborhood scene of the incidents, since any other form of administration would be impracticable.[81] Emotions of the par-

[77] Detroit Commission on Community Relations, *1961 Annual Report*, p. 2.

[78] Philadelphia Commission on Human Relations, *1965 Annual Report*, p. 13.

[79] Philadelphia Commission on Human Relations, *Annual Report* (1962), p. 63; *Annual Report* (1963), pp. 15–16. The latter reported a rash of physical attacks and clashes, involving Negro and white students triggered by a group of white youths attacking Negro youths.

[80] *Id.* (1962), p. 61.

[81] Los Angeles County Commission on Human Relations, "Notes on the History and Activities of the Human Relations Commission," (July, 1963), pp. 3–4, 6 (mimeographed).

ticipants in these incidents usually run very high. Moreover, since these incidents occur at the neighborhood level, each incident is a highly individuated group problem consisting of many unwieldy elements spread over a considerable area and involving numerous persons. It has generally been recognized that in no other area of intergroup relations is expertise so essential as in that of tension incidents. If a false step is taken in attempting to resolve one of these incidents, it will often cause the situation to become worse. Action must be taken rapidly and accurately. Of course, a first objective in processing these cases is to prevent each tension incident from erupting into violence and spreading into other areas. The long-range objective is to prevent completely their occurrence. Local commissions have accumulated a considerable body of knowledge concerning the causes of these incidents as well as the appropriate techniques for handling them. Typically, the community-relations division of a local commission will organize a tension-control center to receive and to process its tension and conflict incidents.[82] Some of these incidents will be handled by commission personnel, who will perform the essential steps of resolution with the help, where necessary, of other officials and private persons and organizations. Other tension incidents, perhaps the greater number, will be referred to organized groups of dedicated private individuals to whom the professional staff of the commission have communicated their know-how based on experience concerning the appropriate methods to be used for resolving the tension presented. The organization of these community groups for the purpose of dealing with tension problems is basic to the work of the commission, so necessarily much of the commission's time is consumed with organizing, instructing, and servicing these groups. The approach of the commission in processing cases of tension then becomes one of moving the available leadership in a neighborhood to work with the commission, other officials, and private organizations in alleviating the tension involved.

The housing incident previously summarized actually occurred in Pittsburgh. The Negro family in question consisted of a doctor, his wife and three children. The parents desired a home rather than an apartment for raising their children and they also wanted better school

---

[82] New York City Commission on Human Rights, *Annual Report* (1963), pp. 22–23; *Pittsburgh Human Relations Review*, Vol. 8, No. 2 (April, 1965), p. 1; Los Angeles County Commission on Human Relations, "Resume of Staff Organization," pp. 14–16.

facilities than were presently available to them. The house they wished to buy was in a neighborhood consisting of a mixture of Catholic, Jewish, and Protestant families. Jewish families predominated in the immediate vicinity of the house. Although the Pittsburgh Commission was aware of the rising tension in the neighborhood, it waited until a request for assistance was made by the white owner and the potential Negro buyer. An experienced professional human-relations worker was immediately assigned to the case. After contacting the two families, she asked both the churches and the real-estate agencies related to the situation to counsel caution to the objecting citizens with respect to their expressed purposes of selling their homes and moving out of the neighborhood. She met with people across the street who were friends of the white owner and agreeable to the move-in. From this family she learned the characteristics of the people in the neighborhood and their reactions to the sale. She then made personal contacts with the various families in the immediate neighborhood. When one woman began to agitate for violence against the Negro family, teenagers in a lower income area drove up and down the street asking where the Negro doctor was planning to move. At this point the worker contacted the police. An officer and the worker then called on the woman to advise her that her activities under certain circumstances would result in her arrest. The worker requested a regular check on the house in the interim between the time the white owner vacated it and the Negro family moved in. At a subsequent point, neighbors who objected to the Negro family called a meeting which the commission worker attended. They asked her to help them solve their problem of keeping the Negro family out of the neighborhood. The worker informed them of the right of the Negro family to move in and to obtain protection from authorities. She pointed out other cases of Negro move-ins which had worked out successfully. She explained that it was pure myth that property values went down when a Negro moves into a white neighborhood. This was one of the great reasons for the opposition that had developed. The truth is, she explained, that property values will remain the same and behave as they normally would if white owners refuse to succumb to rumors and fears and sell their properties out of panic. The only reasons property values depreciate in the long run are common to property in white, Negro, or mixed neighborhoods: failure of homeowners to keep up their property, neglect by municipal government to perform its responsibilities, and encroachment of industrial property upon the neighborhood. She discussed the rumor that had also bothered this group of neighbors, to the effect that Negroes are careless and untidy, with the result that the neighborhood would become run down. She pointed out the fact that experience in their city and other cities showed that Negroes have maintained the standards of the formerly all-white neighborhoods into which they move and have often worked with white neighbors to improve these neighborhoods through home-owner associations and similar organizations. At the meeting, some support developed for the move-in of the Negro family. After the meeting, the worker counseled the families agreeable to the move-in on what action would facilitate the acceptance of the Negro family by the neighborhood. This information was passed on by these families to others. By the time of the move-in, four families were ready to accept the new family and the situation. When the Negro family did move in, they were counseled to stay in the house at night during the first two weeks in order to discourage vandalism. Police patrol cars were assigned to keep watch over the house during the same period. As things worked out, the children of the Negro family readily made friends with the white children of the neighborhood. This event led to the gradual acceptance of the Negro family by all of the younger families in the area. Eventually only two families remained hostile. One of these moved out of the neighborhood. As things progressed, the new Negro family started remodeling its home. Others followed suit, to the point that every home was given some improvement. While four houses were sold in the following year, they were sold to young Jewish families at prices comparable to those obtained in all-white areas. The peaceful, constructive result of this tension incident was to a very considerable extent made possible by the valuable work of the human-relations worker of the Pittsburgh Commission. Other tension incidents arising out of the activities of the public schools, police department, official agencies, teenage groups, and other sources will, of course, call for similar types of procedures on the part of commission personnel and of those cooperating with them.

As each additional year rolls by since the advent of the Civil-Rights Revolution it becomes increasingly evident that those human-relations commissions operating at the local level must become far more effective in detecting the specific grievances that trigger community tensions and conflicts. They must also become far more effective in conveying to the leadership of both majority and minority groups within the community the absolute necessity for them to secure an adjustment of these grievances. Unfortunately, no federal commission has been assigned a role in this area of prime importance in the human-relations area. By and large no state human-relations commission has been assigned or assumed a regular role in this area. Group tension and conflict incidents are likely to increase rather than decrease in the cities throughout this country. Only by a maximum effort from federal, state, and local commissions operating at the local level can there be hope that the period of adjustment that must now begin will be as free as possible from the unfortunate kind of outbreaks of violence that have been occurring throughout the nation.

CONTROL OF EXPLOITATION OF INTERGROUP-RELATIONS PROBLEMS

An eighth "constructive-action" function of a local human-relations commission is to control activities designed to exploit intergroup-relations problems and to unreasonably obstruct members of minority groups in seeking employment, housing, and other things which they need. A good example of an activity of this sort is the practice of "blockbusting," engaged in by unscrupulous real-estate operators. Real-estate operators in the 1960's fixed upon a scheme for profiting from urban racial problems.[83] They decided to induce persons owning property in all-white neighborhoods to sell their properties at the lowest possible prices for them, followed by their resale of this same property to Negroes or Puerto Ricans at exorbitant prices and interest rates. On the one hand, they utilized deception, manipulation, and the creation of conditions to cause fear and anxiety in order to move white persons to sell their property at low prices. On the other, they depended upon the very desperate need of Negroes to find better housing in order to move them to buy the property on unfairly high terms. When a community was selected by these real-estate operators as the target for their scheme, they would flood it with postcards and flyers telling homeowners that they could get cash for their homes if they decided to sell them in a hurry. They also made telephone calls around the clock warning homeowners that Negroes were moving into the area and would cause their property values to collapse shortly. These operators also made personal calls on owners in their homes to warn them that their wives and children would no longer be safe in the streets. They placed "For Sale" signs on both publicly-owned plots and private

[83] New York City Commission on Human Rights, *Report on Blockbusting* (1963). The material in this paragraph is largely drawn from this excellent study of the problem.

property without authorization. Some operators employed Negroes to parade up and down a street in order to give the appearance of being prospective buyers looking at property being offered for sale. The use of these and similar practices over a period of several months in a target community usually produced the desired panic sale of properties at prices well below market value. In an East New York section, for example, there was an extensive turnover in homeownership with the new buyers being either Negro or Puerto Rican. A study of a random selection of properties sold during one blockbusting melee showed that the average cash price paid to white owners was about $12,000 and the average resale price paid shortly thereafter by Negro purchasers was $20,000. Resale prices exceeded fair market value all the way from 28.5 per cent to 118 per cent. Furthermore, interest rates paid by Negroes for mortgages taken by these operators were far higher than those obtaining in FHA, VA, or conventional loans. To deal with this situation, commissions in various affected areas across the country helped to organize and cooperated closely with neighborhood and block organizations to combat the effects of blockbusting.[84] The New York City Commission held public investigative hearings to publicize dramatically the sordid practices being utilized. While these hearings were being held, the practice diminished. After the hearings ceased, the practices resumed.[85] As a result of the hearings by commissions or city councils in various cities, recommendations were made for legislation to curb exploitation by real-estate operators and others engaged in the practice, who, as speculators operating as principals, were not covered by existing laws applicable to real-estate agents.

This problem has been dealt with recently by ordinances in a number of cities. Several major cities, in addition to prohibiting specific practices associated with blockbusting, have given to their local commissions the function of investigating complaints of violation of these prohibitions and of seeking to eliminate by conciliation any violations they found to exist.[86] They were authorized to hold hearings and to issue subpoenas in this connection. If the commissions in these cities

[84] Chicago Commission on Human Relations, *Selling and Buying Real Estate in a Racially Changing Neighborhood* (1962). The work of this Commission is typical of the official response.

[85] New York City Commission on Human Rights, *1962 Annual Report*, p. 3.

[86] Chicago, Illinois, Ordinance 198.7B, *Race Relations Law Reporter*, Vol. 8, (1963), p. 1208; Detroit, Michigan Ordinance 753-F, *Race Relations Law Reporter*, Vol. 7 (1962), p. 1260; and St. Louis, Missouri Ordinance 52328, *Race Relations Law Reporter*, Vol. 9 (1964), p. 372.

are not successful with their efforts at conciliation, they may refer the case to an appropriate official with a recommendation that it be prosecuted in the courts or that an administrative sanction be imposed. In Detroit and St. Louis a fine may be imposed on violators after conviction. In Chicago, in the case of a real-estate broker licensed by the city, the mayor is authorized to suspend or revoke his license if the Commission find him to be violating the ordinance. In the case of a real-estate broker licensed by the state, the mayor is authorized to direct, after appropriate Commission action, that a complaint be filed with the relevant state agency seeking a suspension or revocation of the license. The Detroit and St. Louis ordinances reach the activities of persons acting as principals as well as real-estate brokers. The Detroit Commission, which has had the longest experience (nearly two years) in administering this type of ordinance, has achieved great success in disposing of complaints. In the first six months of 1963, 378 complaints of violation were filed.[87] The Commission vigorously processed these cases and conducted a rigorous surveillance of the degree of compliance with the law. As a result, the number of complaints filed dropped to 285 in the second half of 1963. In the majority of these cases, the Commission was able to obtain conciliation agreements to cease blockbusting activities. The New York Commission has taken the position that in addition to enactment and enforcement of antiblockbusting legislation, a number of other steps are necessary to enable it to deal adequately with the underlying problem.[88] One of these is motivating banks and lending institutions to reevaluate and examine their whole operation so as to extend their mortgage finance services to minority-group persons. Another is motivating brokers, managers, and investors in housing to encourage the opening of neighborhoods to minority-group persons. In 1962 the New York City Commission established a Housing Division separate from its Compliance Division.[89] While both deal with the problem of housing for minority groups, the purpose of the new division is to employ "constructive-action" methods, in contrast to the complaint-processing method of the older division, much along the lines used since 1960 by the Philadelphia Commission in dealing with employment discrimination. During 1965, the

[87] Detroit Commission on Community Relations, *Report "Geared for Action"* (1964), p. 3.
[88] New York City Commission on Human Rights, *Report on Blockbusting* (1963), pp. 10–15.
[89] New York City Commission on Human Rights, *1962 Annual Report*, pp. 8–9.

Philadelphia Commission also vigorously extended this technique to problems of housing discrimination when it became clear that the 1963 fair-housing ordinance was being largely ignored. It held public investigative hearings and filed twenty-four times more complaints than it had initiated in 1964.[90] The complaints had been generated through use of a new and unique testing procedure.

It is appropriate at this point to remark that with the enactment of local legislation to deal authoritatively with the problem of blockbusting, several of our major local commissions have turned an important corner in the evolution of human-relations agencies. Commissions in cities like Detroit and Chicago were among the earliest established.[91] They had, however, mainly been confined to handling tension incidents, advising local officials on appropriate remedial measures for various human-relations problems, and utilizing educational and informational techniques. With this new legislation, Detroit and Chicago joined cities that had, beginning in 1947, established commissions to deal authoritatively with problems of discrimination in employment and later in housing and public accommodations.

PROMOTING BETTER POLICE-COMMUNITY RELATIONS

A ninth "constructive-action" function is, like the last one discussed, closely related to the duties of tension control performed by local commissions. This is the function of processing complaints concerning police administration. These complaints may allege brutality, illegal arrest, illegal searches or seizures, harassment, disrespect, or other mistreatment of the citizen by the police. While complaints of discrimination in housing, employment, or public accommodations are filed by or in behalf of a minority-group person, complaints about police administration, like information concerning tension incidents and blockbusting, may come from either a member of the white majority group or a minority group. Of course, police maladministration may derive from discrimination against a person because of his race, religion, or nationality. Moreover, this discrimination may inflict injuries upon the minority-group person that takes different forms from that inflicted upon majority-group persons, as, for example, the failure to protect a person or his property from the aggressive action of other persons. As yet only a few cities have established effective agencies

---

[90] Philadelphia Commission on Human Relations, *1965 Annual Report*, pp. 4–6.
[91] See Appendix C of this book.

that are independent of the police department to receive and investigate complaints of police maladministration. Among those which have such agencies are Philadelphia and Rochester, New York.[92] In other cities, these complaints are handled by the police department.[93]

The problem of abuse of police authority has been in existence for a very long period. In Philadelphia during the six-year period prior to the creation of its Police Advisory Board in 1958 many persons had complained of this type of abuse to the police commissioner.[94] This official usually agreed to conduct an investigation. In some cases he ordered a special investigation and in others he referred the complainant to the Police Board of Inquiry, a body composed exclusively of members of the police department. This agency had been set up originally not to hear complaints by civilians, but to try cases of alleged violations of departmental rules and regulations such as those proscribing neglect of duty and insubordination. The findings and recommendations of this Board are submitted to the commissioner, who possesses the only authority under the city charter to discipline a police officer. An example of its regard for complaints by civilians was presented in a case of a policeman charged in 1956 under a civilian's complaint with striking the civilian without any provocation and under a departmental complaint with striking his commanding officer. The Board did not consider the civilian's complaint, but recommended that the patrolman be disciplined for his offense against his superior. Between 1952 and 1958 no civilian complaint of police abuse of authority was successful in obtaining discipline of the police officer involved. In 1957 the Philadelphia branch of the American Civil Liberties Union concluded, on the basis of the previous several years experience, that the police department's handling of civilian complaints had failed to accord substantial justice to the complainants. It proposed that a civilian administrative tribunal be established to hear these complaints. When the city council failed to enact an ordinance embodying the essence of this proposal, the mayor established a body, called the Police Advisory Board, in October 1958 by an executive order.[95] This Board is organized and operates much the same way that a

[92] Comment, "The Administration of Complaints by Civilians against the Police," *Harvard Law Review*, Vol. 74 (1964), p. 511.

[93] *Id.*, p. 499.

[94] Spencer Coxe, "Police Advisory Board: The Philadelphia Story," *Connecticut Bar Journal*, Vol. 35 (1961), pp. 138–155.

[95] Philadelphia Police Advisory Board, *Annual Report* (1963), p. 1.

more fully structured state or local human-relations commission operates in processing complaints of discrimination against minority-group members.[96] It does not possess the subpoena power nor the authority to issue cease and desist orders. It does, however, have authority to investigate complaints against the police, to settle them through conciliation, to hold public hearings when it deems this necessary, and to recommend to the mayor sanctions where appropriate, such as suspensions, departmental reprimands, and letters of apology. During the fourth year of its operation, the agency received ninety-eight complaints: thirty-five alleging brutality, twenty-one illegal arrests or searches, thirty-nine harassments, and three other forms of maladministration.[97] In the fifth and six years of its operation, the category of "other" forms of maladministration was numerically almost as large as any other category, indicating that new forms of maladministration were being discovered by the Board.[98] With its carry-over from the previous year, the Board disposes of an average of 100 complaints each year. In the fourth year of its operation, it closed 96 cases satisfactorily without a hearing.[99] These included cases in which, after a thorough investigation, the agency concluded the complaints were not justified and the complainants, having been given an opportunity to request a public hearing, elected not to file this request; cases in which the complainants withdrew their complaints after expressing their satisfaction with the manner in which their grievances were adjusted by the city; and cases in which the agency determined informally that the police officer respondent had engaged in conduct involving maladministration. In the latter type of case, the Board with the cooperation of the chief inspector of the police department and police captains arranged for apologies by the police officer and a statement that the citizen's rights would be respected in the future.[100] Beyond these cases are those in which the Board determines that a public hearing should

[96] Note, "The Administration of Complaints by Civilians against the Police," *Harvard Law Review*, Vol. 77 (1964), pp. 512–516.

[97] Philadelphia Police Advisory Board, *Fourth Annual Report* (1962), Appendix A.

[98] Philadelphia Police Advisory Board, *Annual Report* (1963), "Status of Cases," p. 1; American Civil Liberties Union, *45th Annual Report* (New York: 1966), p. 71.

[99] Philadelphia Police Advisory Board, *Fourth Annual Report* (1962), p. 3, Appendix "A." It has been reported that, as of February 1966, the Board had reviewed from its inception in October 1958 a total of 725 complaints, held 116 hearings, and recommended that 15 suspensions and 23 reprimands be assessed by the police commissioner [*New York Times* (February 20, 1966), p. 36].

[100] Philadelphia Police Advisory Board, *Fourth Annual Report* (1962), p. 4.

be held or in which the complainant requests a public hearing. In the fourth year of its operations the Board held eleven of these hearings rendering a decision for the complainant in six cases and for the police officer respondent in five cases.[101] At the conclusion of the hearing, if the Board concluded the police officer had been guilty of maladministration, it sent its recommendations to the mayor relative to the disciplinary action deemed appropriate in the case.[102] Copies of this were sent to the police commissioner.

A recent study has compared the efficacy of independent agencies and police departments in handling complaints of police maladministration.[103] It demonstrates that the independent agency or commission has several distinct advantages over a police department in processing such complaints. The leading advantage is the guarantee that "command influence," so well understood by those who have studied administration of military justice through courts-martial, will be avoided. A second important advantage is the gain in public acceptance of the resolution of complaints when favorable, as they usually are, to the police. A third advantage is that the civilian interest and point of view in fair administration of the law can best be safeguarded by civilian administration of review procedures. Even the most impartial police department, in handling of complaints of police maladministration, suffers in this respect. The need for knowledge and experience in evaluating police actions and the effect of official board decisions upon police operations can be built into the structure of independent commissions by placing one or more police officers on the commission. This interest is already guaranteed to a considerable extent by the fact that the accused officer and his attorney are accorded full opportunity to provide guidance to the commission. Moreover, the police department itself through its chief officers can always file a brief or make on oral presentation of its own point of view. The argument that an independent agency will destroy the morale of a police force deserves little credit. The same is true of the argument that an independent agency in overseeing police administration will move police officers to be less effective in performing their duties. Both arguments have been fully demonstrated to be in error in light of the experience of the Philadelphia Board during its five year of operation. A high police official has

---

101 *Id.*, Appendix "A."
102 *Id.*, p. 3.
103 Comment, "The Administration of Complaints by Civilians against the Police," p. 499.

observed that the morale of the police force has not been affected in any way.[104] Moreover, Philadelphia enjoys both the lowest crime rate per hundred thousand people and the highest rate of arrests for crimes committed of the five major cities in the country.[105]

Mr. George Schermer, formerly executive director of the Detroit and the Philadelphia Human-Relations Commissions, has given his assessment of the work of the Philadelphia Board in processing complaints of police maladministration.[106] He makes the point that while the Philadelphia Human-Relations Commission has jurisdiction to receive and investigate complaints of police maladministration, it did not exercise this jurisdiction extensively and never held a public hearing involving a complaint concerning police action. It preferred to emphasize the development of a working relationship with the police department in handling tension and conflict incidents. The Commission welcomed the creation of the Philadelphia Board since it deemed the function of investigating complaints against the police as not coinciding well with its other functions. Asked about the rumor circulated by police departments in cities considering the creation of human-relations commissions, such as Austin, Texas, to the effect that Philadelphia police are harassed by the operations of the Philadelphia Board and that extensive police time is wasted in investigations and hearings, Mr. Schermer stated that any objective observer will state that the allegation is ridiculous. In the first place, the Board has utilized the chief inspector of the police department to investigate the complaints made. These investigations are no more elaborate under the independent board system than they would be if the police commissioner were conducting his own investigation. He further pointed out that there is a shameful waste of police man hours at magistrate hearings. He stated: "Literally hundreds of thousands of police man-hours are lost as officers make their appearance to testify concerning arrests they have made only to have the matter continued or discharged by the politically oriented magistrates who have little concern for the proper enforcement of the law."[107] In his view the Philadelphia Police Review Board and the Philadelphia Human-Relations Commission are important buffers that protect the police from unjust charges and help them in the performance of their duties. To this it may be

[104] *Id.*, p. 517.
[105] Philadelphia Police Advisory Board, *Fourth Annual Report* (1962), p. 2.
[106] Letter dated November 4, 1963, to author from Mr. George W. Schermer.
[107] *Ibid.*

added that they make it possible for the citizen who considers he has been wronged by police actions to resort to an independent agency to secure a resolution of his problem in a constructive, impartial manner. He is now much less likely to harbor resentment, to spread his hostile feelings throughout the community, and to breed contempt for the city government.

The experience of Philadelphia with a specialized human-relations agency to process complaints about police maladministration is now being studied by city authorities across the nation.[108] In 1965–1966 New York City debated the creation of a police review board similar to the Philadelphia one. In July 1966 Mayor Lindsay created a Civilian Complaint Review Board, building upon a departmental complaint review system.[109] Under the latter, lower echelons of the department had conducted investigations of complaints of police maladministration filed by citizens and a civilian complaint supervisor reviewed investigation reports with a view to determining whether he should recommend the filing by higher authority of charges against the accused policeman.[110] A Civilian Complaint Review Board, consisting of nonuniformed officials of the department connected with its Community Relations Division, subsequently reviewed his recommendation. As of May 1966 this Board could conduct hearings for the purpose of determining whether to recommend the filing of charges against the accused officer. If a charge was filed, a deputy police commissioner then conducted the trial of the officer. The Board reviewed 555 complaints of police maladministration during 1964–1965 and had acted on 385 of them by March 22, 1966. It rejected 325 of the latter as either unfounded or unsubstantiated. The Police Commissioner filed charges relative to only thirty-eight of the fifty-seven policemen involved in the 60 complaints which the Board deemed to warrant official disciplinary action. By March 22, 1966, the deputy police commissioner had acted on the basis of seventeen trials to direct three

[108] Coxe, "Police Advisory Board," p. 138; American Civil Liberties Union, *45th Annual Report,* (1966), pp. 69–72; Ed Cary, "Annotated Bibliography on Police Review Boards," *Law and Transition Quarterly,* Vol. III (1966), p. 197.

[109] *The National Observer* (October 24, 1966), p. 4.

[110] Note, "The Administration of Complaints by Civilians against the Police," pp. 499, 503, 504, 507–511; Walter Gellhorn, *When People Complain* (Cambridge, Mass.: Harvard University Press, 1966), pp. 180, 190; Herman Goldstein, "Administrative Problems in Controlling the Exercise of Police Authority," *The Journal of Criminal Law, Criminology and Police Science,* Vol. 58, No. 2 (June, 1967), pp. 166–170.

dismissals, five acquittals, and the assessment of nine fines. Without the filing of charges, nineteen policemen were given reprimands.[111]

The Civilian Complaint Review Board created by Mayor Lindsay was basically a continuation of the earlier departmental board utilizing four additional civilian members and an executive director not connected with the department but operating under the aegis of the Mayor.[112] Its creation was the result of an effort to respond to the pressures for a more acceptable review system. In its three months of operation prior to November 8, 1966, the new board had received complaints from 140 whites and 113 Negroes.[113] Of 113 cases investigated, only 3 recommendations were made for disciplinary action against the respondent officer. In no case had the new civilian members, who were a majority of the members of the Board, outvoted the police department members.

Despite the performance of the Mayor's new board the Patrolmen's Benevolent Association secured a referendum on whether to prevent the police commissioner or any other officer of New York City from establishing or maintaining any board for the review of civilian complaints concerning abuse of authority or use of unnecessary force by policemen unless each member of the board is a deputy police commissioner. On the other hand, the police commissioner of New York City, Mr. Howard R. Leary, approved the Mayor's new board and supported it in the referendum campaign and election.[114] So also did Senator Robert F. Kennedy, and Senator Jacob K. Javits,[115] and the Association of the Bar of the City of New York. After a campaign much affected by emotionalism and misunderstanding, promoted by policemen and the American Legion, the New York City electorate defeated the Mayor's board and made useless any future effort to establish a similar board unless by a law of the same level as the referendum law.[116]

The New York City experience with civilian review of complaints

---

[111] Gellhorn, *When People Complain*, p. 180. That there was considerable fire underneath this smoke of complaints is indicated by the action of the New York courts. In 1965, *e.g.*, when New York City was a defendant in 237 lawsuits in which its policemen were charged with brutality, 33 claims were settled or won on trial for a total of $169,482. In the previous fiscal year the comparable figures were 72 claims and $232,424 [Gellhorn, *When People Complain*, p. 184 n. 89].

[112] *Id.*, pp. 171–172, 190–191.

[113] *The National Observer* (October 24, 1966), p. 4.

[114] *The New York Times* (October 23, 1966), Sec. 4, p. 5.

[115] *The National Observer* (October 24, 1966), p. 4; Gellhorn, *When People Complain*, pp. 171–172.

[116] *The New York Times* (November 9, 1966), pp. 1, 23.

concerning police brutality and other forms of maladministration simply confirmed that one of the most sophisticated cities in the world and its police have much to learn about human-relations matters and that, while the Deep South has its difficulties with according voting rights to Negroes, Northern cities have their difficulties in according to members of minority groups the same rights they accord to anyone else protesting the legality of administrative action generally. At least New York City had the dubious merit of denying this right in question not only to Negroes but also to Puerto Ricans and others who have complained about the abuse of authority by police. There is almost universal opposition by policemen to independent review of complaints alleging their abuse of their authority.[117] Fraternal orders of policemen have sought to secure elimination of police review boards in Rochester and Philadelphia. The same opposition has kept similar boards from being activated in York, Pennsylvania, and Minneapolis, Minnesota. Professor Walter Gellhorn, a national authority on administrative law, has taken the position in his Holmes Lectures that the civilian review board is not a suitable instrumentality for getting at the underlying problem of police brutality and other forms of maladministration.[118] The reasons he gives are that this type of board fails to focus upon administrative derelictions of a similar nature by administrative agencies equally harmful to the persons affected by them and that the complaint process is an extremely burdensome and inapt tool for dealing with an arena "in which citizens and policemen fight one another."[119] He recommends the adoption of an *ombudsman* type of official who would call derelictions to the attention of police heads who would be made "unremittingly responsible for what all their subordinates do."[120] The *ombudsman*, following the Scandinavian model, would be the instrument of the legislature although functioning independently, would have unlimited access to government records in investigating alleged administrative derelictions, and could express opinions concerning the existence of maladministration injuring the citizen with explanations of his reasons for so thinking.[121] Although some *ombudsmen*, as in Sweden and Finland, are given the power to prosecute

[117] Gellhorn, *When People Complain*, p. 170; American Civil Liberties Union, *45th Annual Report*, pp. 70–72.
[118] Gellhorn, *When People Complain*, pp. 170–185.
[119] *Id.*, pp. 185–187, 192–193.
[120] *Id.*, p. 193.
[121] *Id.*, pp. 9–10.

officials in the courts, they proceed principally by seeking to persuade the offending official what should be done. They are the unhidden persuaders in essence.

This is not the place to examine with the fullness required the fitness of the *ombudsman* concept for the American scene. Some comments are, however, pertinent at this point. In the first place, no modern nation of Western Society has had a comparable experience to that of the United States in failing on such a huge scale and for so long to solve the festering and burgeoning problem of relations between its majority group and its ethnic, religious, and social minorities. The problem of relations between the police and the community, particularly its minority-group elements and its poor is one of the major parts of this problem. It is fair and necessary to say that the intergroup-relations problem is America's greatest internal problem and that its recent manifestations have shaken the very foundations of the social fabric. Since this human-relations problem certainly ranks with the greatest problems encountered in our nation's history, it is essential that each of our major institutions of government be heavily involved in resolving it. Admittedly, as Professor Gellhorn points out, "ombudsmen have dealt with small illnesses, not with major diseases . . . , prescribing for discomforts not likely to become disasters, and pointing paths to healthful living."[122] While the *ombudsman* concept undoubtedly has merit for the smaller problems, the problem of police-community relations is not one of the latter. With riots having occurred in the ghettos of over a hundred cities during the summers of 1966 and 1967, it is important to recognize that failure to solve this problem is a major contributing factor in producing them. Following the Watts riot of 1965 the McCone Commission investigated charges of police abuse and, without taking a position as to the exent of the practice, recommended the establishment of a system for reviewing these charges.[123] In 1965 a sociological study was conducted in the Los Angeles Negro ghettos covering, among other things, the reactions of Negroes to the Los Angeles violence.[124] When they were asked, "What do you think caused the riot?" 42 per cent of heads of households interviewed stated that police brutality was one of the causes while an

---

[122] *Id.*, p. 40.

[123] State of California, Governor's Commission on the Los Angeles Riots, *Violence in the City*, pp. 31–34.

[124] H. Edward Ransford, "Attitudes of Negroes toward the Los Angeles Riots," *Law in Transition Quarterly*, Vol. III (1966), pp. 191–196.

additional 24 per cent said that police methods were a cause. While 66 per cent thus mentioned police activity as a cause, 48 per cent named additional causes such as unemployment, low-paying jobs, housing, and poverty. The percentage of Negro heads of households mentioning police brutality or methods as a cause was considerably higher in Watts and in a similar ghetto area in Los Angeles. The elements of a community are inevitably on a collision course when one of them entertains such an overwhelming consensus about its mistreatment by the guardians of the law. The riots of 1966 and 1967 continue to give evidence that the problem of police-community relations is one of the major human-relations problems toward the solution of which the full resources of governmental activity must be directed. Even if Professor Gellhorn's suggestion for an *ombudsman* approach is useful as an auxiliary tool, it must be rejected as the exclusive formal approach to the problem's solution.

In the second place, it must be emphasized that the problem of police-community relations is a human-relations problem and reflects the existence of a larger human-relations problem at the local and national levels. As was shown in Chapter 2 a human-relations problem involving majority-minority group relations has considerably different dimensions from the more typical problems of government. It calls for different techniques and approaches in order to achieve a satisfactory solution. While the *ombudsman* concept could be viewed as a human-relations technique, it certainly was not born in the context of a nation confronting and attempting to solve the type of human-relations problem that has so long plagued the United States. Professor Gellhorn does not discuss nor even note in his Holmes Lectures the development of the human-relations commission in the United States since 1945. This institution has emerged gradually as our nation finally has had to confront and attempt to solve its human-relations problem, involving the unfair treatment of minority groups by its majority group and most of the private and public institutions controlled by the majority group. While the human-relations commission at its best is an imperfect institution, it is a far cry from the weak-sister civilian review boards which Professor Gellhorn takes to task. When it is well-adapted to the performance of its task, the human-relations commission, particularly at the local level, has none of the imperfections of the civilian review board. Moreover, it has strengths to which no *ombudsman* could ever ascend. Indeed, it avoids the central weakness of the *ombudsman* concept which is essentially the notion that one expert or even many experts can get an administrative agency head to do what he ought to do by way of ceasing to inflict unwarranted harm upon citizens. It can be safely predicted that, so far as human-relations problems between major ethnic groups are concerned, the *ombudsman* concept has little to offer as a solution. Not the least of the techniques of the human-relations commission is "going to the country" where necessary, putting the administrative agency on the spot, and letting the public bring pressure to bear where it most needs to be felt. Human-relations problems require an airing as well as a contact and a dialogue between members of the in-majority group and the out-minority group. The sweet reasoning of the *ombudsman,* which a good human-relations commission has long been an expert in using, needs to be supplemented by more vigorous techniques where necessary. What these are and how they can be improved have been the major foci of this book.

There are a number of weaknesses in the Philadelphia type of human-relations agency, established by executive order rather than by ordinance and limited to dealing only with a narrow area of human-relations problems.[125] On the other hand, local governments would do well to create locally based and locally manned human-relations commissions to administer the law calling for administrative review of charges of abuse of police authority and to utilize the full spectrum of human-relations techniques. This is true because what is at stake is a local human-relations problem having its causes, accompanying conditions, and harmful results centered in the local community and in its majority and minority groups. The experience in New York City and similar cities with police review boards demonstrates as well as any experience could how intertwined human-relations matters are with the life of the community in which they occur and how difficult it is to separate the handling of them from the local level. It is inevitable that our country, which has always placed confidence in independent review of administrative action when challenged as being unlawful, should subject police administration to that review. If cities will not do this, then either the state or the federal government must do it. But the better resolution calls for the local community to become

---

[125] Two obvious procedural weaknesses are the lack of authority to compel witnesses to attend and to testify and the lack of authority to issue and to obtain judicial enforcement of orders. Another basic defect is the absence of the structure, personnel, and techniques of the well-established, broad-gauged human-relations commission having community-wide acceptance of its role and a considerable involvement of the citizenry in the performance of its functions.

involved in effectuating the necessary resolution. The Pittsburgh Human-Relations Commission has regularly handled police–community-relations problems and is thus able, as a well-established and recognized official agency, to bring all of its extensive authority and influence in the human-relations field to bear upon the case of alleged police maladministration.[126] In light of the Commission's experience the Alpha Model Laws set forth in Chapters 8 through 9 assign jurisdiction to the human-relations commissions created or regulated by them to handle this type of problem.

COOPERATION WITH LOCAL GOVERNMENT AGENCIES

A tenth principal "constructive-action" function of official local human-relations agencies is their close cooperation with other local governmental agencies which have to deal with human-relations problems in the course of their overall operations. One of the primary forms of this cooperation is the provision of information and training for governmental-agency personnel who are assigned responsibilities in this area. The police department is a good example. A basic problem of the police department is to maintain good lines of communication with each element of the community it serves, particularly minority groups. Since the police department is often the only official local authority with whom many minority-group members come into contact, it is the target for much of the frustration and tension felt by these persons with respect to the majority group in the community. For this reason it is important that this department understand human-relations problems and know how to deal with them, know the current trouble spots in human relations, plan specifically for dealing with particular problems as they arise, and have a working relationship with minority-group leaders for cooperative efforts in solving these problems.

As late as 1960 in Detroit, for example, despite the awful lesson of the 1943 race riot, Negroes and city officials were hardly on speaking terms and group tensions were running high.[127] Although Negroes formed about 30 per cent of the city's population, only 136 Negroes served as police officers on a force of 4,200.[128] This was small relative improvement over the situation in 1943 when, although Negroes formed 10 per cent of the population, only 40 of them served on the

---

[126] James J. Dillon, "The Police Department and CHR . . . A Code of Cooperation," *Pittsburgh Human Relations Review*, Vol. 7, No. 3 (June, 1964), pp. 1–2.

[127] *The Wall Street Journal* (August 12, 1964), p. 1, col. 6.

[128] Detroit Commission on Community Relations, *1961 Annual Report*, p. 3.

police force then numbering 3,600.[129] In 1960 the Baptist Ministerial Alliance, voicing the belief of most of the Negro community, complained in its petition to the Common Council that the department discriminated against Negroes in its employment policies.[130] In early 1961 a departmental "crack-down on crime" in the Negro community added fuel to the fire and divided the city into two racial communities.[131] Hundreds of Detroit Negroes were arrested or questioned on the street as "suspicious persons" in connection with a spate of street crimes. The arrests and questionings took place in what police called "high crime areas." Police and press reports identified Negroes as being suspected of committing many of these crimes. The issue was publicly raised and debated whether Negroes as a group were responsible for these criminal acts. Negro and civil-rights organizations protested these charges and police tactics, insisting that the problem of crime be recognized for what it was, a community problem and responsibility. Negro leadership began to question the fairness and the purpose of city government toward their element of the community.

The city Community-Relations Commission, faced with one of the most serious problems during its existence, set about moving the city and its police department to re-establish lines of communication with civic, business, labor, church, and Negro leadership. It insisted upon the principle that crime is a community problem rather than a racial one and that defamation of people because of their race would continue to divide the community. After some frustrating efforts to act in a decisive way to re-establish communication between city officials and the Negro community, a basic change in Commission structure was secured and implemented in late 1961.[132] Seven city officials who had served on the fifteen-member Commission were replaced by citizen members pursuant to an ordinance enacted in that year. This change eliminated a situation in which city officials as members proved themselves reluctant to support Commission actions that might infringe upon the authority of another official to handle his department's affairs. In 1962 a new city administration entered office and appointed a new police commissioner. This official adopted the Commission's point of view and ordered both the recruiting of Negro

---

[129] George Brown, "The Truth About the Detroit Riot," *Harper's*, Vol. 187 (1943), p. 493.
[130] Detroit Commission on Community Relations, *1961 Annual Report*, p. 3.
[131] *Id.*, pp. 3–4.
[132] *Id.*, p. 6.

policemen and the halting of certain police tactics used against Negroes. He directed the holding of meetings between neighborhood residents and precinct police. The commissioner himself invited Negro leaders to meet with him on various problems. In 1964 it was asserted that great improvements had occurred in the relations between the police and members of the Negro community.[133] The Detroit riots in the summer of 1967 indicate these improvements were insufficient.

In Philadelphia the cooperation between the local Human-Relations Commission and the police department has been more structured.[134] The department designated certain police officers as community-relations officers and assigned them on the basis of one to a district. These officers were given the responsibility for developing a good relationship between the police department and each element of the districts. Each month the Philadelphia Commission holds a briefing session with these special officers to provide them with information concerning intergroup problems. In 1962, for example, these sessions focused upon the role of the American Civil Liberties Union and the activities of the American Nazi Party and the Black Muslim movement. The Commission has also provided staff services to police–community-relations teams. These organizations are composed of representatives of public and private agencies serving particular parts of the city. The agency members in team sessions exchange information on intergroup-relations problems and seek to determine what methods and programs will best resolve these problems. Paralleling these Commission services, the executive director of the Philadelphia Police Advisory Board conducts a course at the Police Academy for police recruits, on the Board's functions and procedures relative to complaints concerning police maladministration.[135] The Philadelphia Commission has now designed a comprehensive human-relations program for all members of the police force at the request of police department officials.[136] The Pittsburgh Commission and Bureau of Police in 1966 jointly instituted a similar program.[137] The Philadelphia Commission

---

[133] *The Wall Street Journal*, August 12, 1964, p. 8.

[134] Philadelphia Commission on Human Relations, *Annual Report* (1962), p. 39; *1965 Annual Report*, p. 11.

[135] Philadelphia Police Advisory Board, *Fourth Annual Report* (1962), p. 6.

[136] Philadelphia Commission on Human Relations, *Annual Report* (1962), p. 16. A similar program has been utilized in Chicago [Chicago Commission on Human Relations, *Annual Report* (1966), p. 4].

[137] *Pittsburgh Human Relations Review*, Vol. 9, No. 1 (February, 1966), pp. 1, 4; Vol. 10, No. 1 (February, 1967), p. 3. This program is one of the most ambitious

also was instrumental in securing the creation of the office of police inspector of human relations.[138] In a more specific type of cooperation the Philadelphia Commission and the police department have developed a working paper establishing the responsibilities of the Commission, the police department, and other public agencies relative to dealing with riots, conflicts, and other forms of intimidation. In New York City the local Commission has aided the police department in establishing a departmental library of human-relations materials.[139] In November of 1962 the tables were turned when, through the cooperation of the police commissioner, instructors at the Police Academy presented to the staff of the Commission a special course on techniques of police investigation. In Los Angeles County the local Commission has acted somewhat more broadly in developing its six-weeks human-relations institute. It presents this institute in cities within its jurisdiction for both police and other city officials. In 1966 the county Commission reviewed its recommendations to law-enforcement agencies and other bodies covering police-community relations during the previous three years, to learn the extent of their implementation. It also designed a series of workshops involving youths and law-enforcement personnel to increase the opportunity for communication between them.[140]

Other city departments also require assistance of a local human-relations commission. A good example is the city recreation department. In Pittsburgh in 1963 the local Commission and the Bureau of Recreation jointly planned and carried out two in-service training sessions.[141] The object of the sessions was to produce a greater understanding of the problems both agencies are encountering in attempting to meet the many changes occurring in Pittsburgh's minority-group communities with regard to residential patterns, economic status, levels of education, and aspiration. Particular emphasis was given to problems of the minority-group teenager. Case materials on recreation programming were specially prepared for group discussion sessions.

---

undertaken and contemplates training five hundred policemen to deal with inter-group situations and incidents.

[138] Philadelphia Commission on Human Relations, *Annual Report* (1962), p. 16.

[139] New York City Commission on Human Rights, *1962 Annual Report*, pp. 2, 14.

[140] Los Angeles County Commission on Human Relations, *1960–2 Biennial Report*, p. 9; "Resume of Staff Organizations, Assignments, Programs and Projects, Personnel Needs, and Workload" (December, 1966), p. 14.

[141] *Pittsburgh Human Relations Review*, Vol. 6, No. 2 (April, 1963), p. 2.

Still another good example of a city department requiring the assistance of a local commission is the local board of education. The New York, Philadelphia, Pittsburgh, Detroit, Chicago, and Los Angeles County Commissions have worked very closely with school boards in their respective jurisdictions.[142] The central problem in public education in Northern and Western urban communties is *de facto* segregation of minority-group children, principally Negro, Puerto Rican, and Mexican American. This segregation is the product not of official school policy, but of private discrimination in housing and employment that walls up these minority groups in central-city ghettos which usually contain the city's poorest schools. This private discrimination has also been mightily aided by public measures relative to housing in previous years. The New York City government was one of the first to commit itself to a policy of integrated education. On June 26, 1963, its Board of Education issued a statement reaffirming its endorsement of the view "that public education in a racially-restricted setting is socially unrealistic and blocks the attainment of the goals of democratic education."[143] Between 1963 and 1967, by way of contrast, the Boston School Board was unwilling even to admit that it was confronted with a problem of *de facto* segregation, much less that it should direct its official efforts toward eliminating it.[144] On the other hand, Philadelphia in 1963 and Chicago and Cleveland in 1964 adopted policies calling for desegregation of their *de facto* segregated public schools.[145] Although some of Cleveland's Negro children had been transported daily from their ghettos to previously all-white schools in outlying districts prior to adoption of this new policy, they had largely been kept segregated in the classrooms and playgrounds of these schools.[146] Detroit as early as 1961 had instituted a program of bussing

---

142 See, *e. g.*, Detroit Commission on Community Relations, *1961 Annual Report,* p. 2; Los Angeles County Commission on Human Relations, *1960–2 Biennial Report,* pp. 4–6.

143 See note 147 below.

144 *The New York Times,* February 10, 1964, p. 15, col. 1; James S. Doyle, "Cut-Off in Boston," *The New Republic* (August 27, 1966), p. 8. This refusal was in the teeth of a recently enacted state law forbidding more than 50 per cent nonwhite enrollment in any public school [*Mass. Gen. Laws Ann.*, ch. 15, sec. 1; ch. 71, sec. 37D (Supp. 1966)].

145 W. R. Odell, "Educational Survey Report for the Philadelphia Board of Education," (1965), p. 29; *The New York Times* (February 10, 1964), p. 31, col. 1; *The New York Times* (February 14, 1964), p. 33, col. 2.

146 *The New York Times* (February 10, 1964), p. 15, col. 1; *Massachusetts State Advisory Committee to the United States Commission on Civil Rights, Report on*

Negro children from its seriously overcrowded central district schools to nearby schools with pupil capacity, which had been attended predominantly by white children. Yet in 1966 demonstrations revealed widespread discontent with the progress made by city authorities in dealing with this problem.[147] Prior to 1963 the New York City Commission on Human Rights had confined its activities to cooperating with the Board of Education in specific cases in which decisions had to be made bearing upon the problem of integration. For example, in 1961, when sites had been proposed for a new public school to replace two older ones, the Commission had studied both the Board's choice and the alternative proposals made by civil-rights organizations.[148] The Commission's study was directed to determining which site would provide the best possible balance between Negro, Puerto Rican, and white students. Similarly, when a school integration request was filed with the Board by a community organization, the Commission studied the proposal. Its studies in both instances contributed to the Board's eventual decision. The Commission also cooperated with the Board in its "open enrollment" program involving the transfer of pupils from schools in minority-group areas to schools in outlying areas on request of their parents. It worked closely with the Board's newly formed human-relations unit in developing materials dealing with problems encountered by "receiving" schools including overcrowding, bussing schedules, remedial-reading problems, and resentment by receiving communities over the inflow of pupils who were "underachievers." The Commission also conducted training sessions for the Board's school-community coordinators and assisted them in setting up in-service human-relations courses for each school district.[149]

Racial Imbalance in the Boston Public Schools (Washington, D.C.: U.S. Government Printing Office, January, 1965), pp. 24–30, 51–52.

[147] Detroit Commission on Community Relations, *1961 Annual Report*, p. 3. The unsolved problem of *de facto* segregation continued in 1966–1967 to plague Detroit and unquestionably was one of the basic factors leading to the unrest and riots of 1967. The Detroit Commission lent its assistance to community groups seeking fundamental changes in the public policy in this area. Its efforts, however, fell far short of those of the New York City Commission reviewed in the next section [Detroit Commission on Community Relations, *Annual Report* (1966), pp. 12–14].

[148] New York City Commission on Intergroup Relations, *1961 Annual Report*, p. 27.

[149] New York City Commission on Intergroup Relations, *Report of Progress* (1960), pp. 12–13, 28. The Commission has widened its areas of cooperation with school authorities and parent groups in subsequent years [New York City Commission on Human Rights, *Annual Report for 1964*, pp. 7–9; *Annual Report for 1965*, p. 9].

Promoting Official Solutions of Intergroup-Relations Problems: Lobby for the People

In 1963 and 1964 the work of the New York City Commission relative to *de facto* segregation assumed another dimension which will serve to illustrate an eleventh main function of local human-relations commissions. This function is the conducting of research concerning local human-relations problems, the recommendation of solutions for them to local government officials, and the active working for adoption of these solutions.[150]

In 1963, as the Civil-Rights Revolution was gaining momentum, it became evident that the Negro and Puerto Rican communities in New York City were deeply concerned about lack of official progress in solving the city's problem with *de facto* segregation in the public schools: 54 per cent of the city's elementary school children and 39 per cent of its junior high school children attended segregated white or Negro and Puerto Rican schools. The 165 segregated schools attended by the latter children were double the figure attended by them only six years earlier. By 1975 it was expected that population growth and other factors would cause the proportion of Negro and Puerto Rican children attending segregated schools to increase at least 25 per cent. Beyond the social disvalue in a democracy of segregated schools for a highly disadvantaged minority group lay the dismal fact that the quality of education in ghetto schools suffered greatly by comparison with other schools in the city's system. In 1961 the members of the city's Board of Education had been removed from office by state authorities after an investigation of certain school construction scandals. The carefully selected new members inherited along with many other problems the problem of *de facto* segregation which the Board had done so little to resolve in the past. Neither these new blue ribbon members nor the new superintendent whom they appointed in 1962 made much progress in dealing with this problem. Thus, despite New York City's early recognition of its responsibility to eliminate *de facto* segregation in its public schools, a New York state education agency

[150] The report of the New York City problem with *de facto* segregation and the role of the city Commission on Human Rights in dealing with it is largely based upon news accounts published in the *New York Times* between July 1, 1963, and September 1, 1964, concerning the significant developments during that period relative to these matters. In addition, the report draws upon the following: Fred M. Hechinger, "The City Schools—A Mixed Report Card," *The New York Times Magazine*, June 14, 1964, p. 24; Fred Powledge, "Mason-Dixon Line in Queens," *The New York Times Magazine*, May 10, 1964, p. 12.

was forced to report that nothing the city's Board of Education had undertaken since 1954 had contributed in any meaningful degree to desegregating the public schools.

In this state of affairs and with the evident mounting of tension in Negro and Puerto Rican communities over the problem, the local Commission in 1963 undertook to provide sorely needed official leadership to help the city get off dead center in handling this problem. The need for this was highlighted in the summer of 1963 by the state commissioner of education who directed all of the state's school boards to examine their racial policies and to ensure that integration was being genuinely effectuated. After devoting a careful study to the problem of *de facto* segregation, the Commission on July 25 of that year elaborated a six-point integration policy which it urged the Board of Education to adopt and implement. The Commission first of all suggested that the Board formulate a long-range master plan, together with a time-table for its execution, for integrating pupils, teachers, curriculum, and administrative staff of city schools into an educational whole. It also proposed that the Board assign pupils to schools with the specific objective of producing integration; to adopt a combination of appropriate integration techniques including those employing site selection, rezoning, pairing of schools, exchange of school populations, and transportation of children from one district to another; to establish a coordinated integration policy committee consisting of high officials of relevant city agencies; and to institute in collaboration with the Commission a program of informing and involving the community.

Having made its proposal, the Commission turned to the task of insuring its adoption and implementation. Its educational department had earlier served as a consultant to a number of private groups on school matters. This department now met with the Citywide Committee for Integrated Schools as well as with its component groups consisting of parent's and civil-rights organizations. The Citywide Committee had been formed to coordinate efforts of all interested groups to obtain significant progress with school integration. The department sought to develop means of bringing these groups and the Board together in order that they might work out realistic plans for peaceful and orderly integration. Negotiations were begun between school authorities and civil-rights groups. When they ended in a stalemate, civil-rights leaders announced they would call for a city-wide boycott of public schools on the opening day for the fall term, September 9, to protest the racial imbalance in them. They concluded that this drastic step was necessary in the New York situation to dramatize that the time for official action had come. Intervening as a mediator in the negotiations, the Commission held two sessions in its offices with the contending parties and was successful in moving them to enter into an agreement upon a method of proceeding for the immediate future. The agreement called for the Board to prepare a master plan for integration of the schools, together with a time-table for its complete execution. The plan was to be submitted in two stages with an interim plan to be made available by December 1 and a final one by February 1. Along with the proposals made by the Commission for establishing an overall integration policy, the Board received some fifteen plans for integration from various private groups. When the interim plan prepared by the school superintendent was submitted on December 9, civil-rights groups, after studying it, took the position that it failed at every point to meet the criteria they had set down for a master plan in agreeing to postpone their boycott the previous September and that the Board had virtually ignored the various proposed plans previously submitted to it by them. The president of the Citywide Committee representing various private organizations expressed the special concern of these groups with the failure of the Board to produce either a master plan for the whole city system or a time-table for implementing it. The local Commission took the position that city school officials were not doing enough, and, indeed, were heading in the wrong direction in tackling the problem of school segregation. The Commission offered to sit down with the city Board "to assist in constructive planning" for integration. It took the position that the interim plan and the Board chairman's support of the neighborhood school concept ran counter to the Board's reaffirmation in June of its responsibility to achieve integration.

When, by January 5, the Board had made no public response to these private and official criticisms of its interim proposal, all major civil-rights organizations under the aegis of the Citywide Committee announced their intention to join in a boycott of the public schools on February 3 to protest the Board's failure to live up to its agreement of the previous September. The Commission met with the Board to present its comments and suggestions concerning the Board's interim proposal for integration and sought to bring the Board and civil-rights groups together for further discussions. The superintendent did meet with these groups in the presence of the Commission chairman and Board members. On January 20 these meetings bore some fruit. The

Board instructed the superintendent to prepare a master plan having city-wide application, together with a time-table, incorporating as its chief feature the pairing of schools on the model of the Princeton plan. The superintendent submitted his plan in late January. Its chief feature was the proposal to pair twenty elementary and junior high schools primarily attended by Negro and Puerto Rican children with an equal number of similar schools primarily attended by white children. While the proffered proposal did constitute a plan of sorts, it was hardly a master plan for the whole system. It comprehended only a small number of the segregated schools attended by Negroes and Puerto Ricans. Moreover, only four segregated schools were scheduled for pairing in the first year of the plan's operation. Even if all the schools scheduled for pairing under the plan were in fact paired, this would reduce the proportion of minority segregated schools by only 1 per cent.

Civil-rights organizations, after studying the plan, decided that it was so insufficient as to warrant finally taking the drastic step of staging a boycott of the school system to dramatize the need for more realistic planning. The Commission again attempted to mediate the controversy between the Board and the private organizations but in a negotiating session, the chairman of the Commission found the contending parties so far apart at that time as to make negotiation impossible. The Commission chairman in recognition of the usefulness at this point of a boycott for clearing the air and creating a more realistic approach by the Board stated that the boycott "would be a very effective demonstration." He also praised the Board plan as a step in the right direction but nevertheless unrealistic in its piecemeal and limited approach to the problem of school segregation. In particular, the Commission renewed its proposals, made the previous July, calling for the Board to integrate whole school districts rather than merely to pair schools. Following the boycott in which 360,000 school children, representing 45 per cent of the total enrollment, stayed home, the Commission secured city approval and funds to create a new top-level post of director of an education division to be filled by an educational specialist. The purpose of this move was to strengthen the Commisson's leadership in educational matters involving human-relations problems. Upon establishment of this division, it initiated a study of the Board's school construction program to determine its bearing upon the problem of integration.

It was alleged that this program was creating segregated schools.

Meanwhile, the Board was faced with new opposition from an organization primarily of white parents who wished to avoid pairing of schools. This organization conducted a demonstration at the Board's headquarters on March 13 in which some 15,000 persons participated. To counter the possible effect of this action and to maintain the momentum in the Board's effort to develop a more comprehensive integration plan, several of the organizations which had participated in the February 3rd boycott conducted a second boycott on March 16. When it was reported at the end of March that the Board was preparing to water down its late January plan, the Commission stated publicly that a retreat by the Board would be very destructive. Civil-rights organizations which had divided on the wisdom of the second boycott now reunited in the face of this new threat. On May 4th they asked for round-the-clock negotiating sessions with the Board. Stating their criteria for an acceptable master integration plan, they announced that massive demonstrations would be held before the Board headquarters and city hall if these criteria were not accepted. Shortly thereafter field studies conducted under Board auspices revealed that the chief feature of its late January plan—the pairing of schools—was highly impracticable since it would probably produce racially imbalanced schools, the very condition it was seeking to eliminate through its use of the device. This self-reappraisal was followed up by the release of two studies of the Board's plan by the local human-relations commission and the state commissioner of education. On May 11 the local Commission released the results of its study of the Board's school building program. It confirmed earlier fears that the building program was creating segregated schools faster than the Board would be ending racial imbalance under its integration plan. On the following day the state commissioner of education released a report on a study of the Board's plan. It was highly critical of the plan and confirmed the position earlier taken by the Commission and civil-rights groups that the plan was too limited in scope to stimulate "even slight progress toward desegregation." The state report made proposals, among others, for site selection of all high schools to provide integration, creation of middle (four-grade schools) to replace junior high schools so located as to provide maximum integration, retention of the neighborhood concept for primary level schools, and equalizing of facilities so that schools continuing to be segregated would not be older, more overcrowded, and in greater need of essential facilities than other schools. The issuance of these two critical reports was followed by the promised demonstration of civil-rights organizations on May 18th. These, together with the Board's own reappraisal of the efficacy of its plan, created a new climate for negotiation. Between May 18 and the end of the month the school superintendent made a series of announcements of changes in the Board's plan. The chief elements of change were a proposal for transferring 40,000 students to vacancies in integrated schools, pairing of but four schools, and re-examination of the school construction program. When civil-rights organizations insisted on still further modifications of the plan, the superintendent held a series of five meetings with them. These meetings finally produced an agreement on both sides upon a master integration plan on June 15. The chief modification of the new Board plan was the provision for transfer of ninth grade minority group students to thirty-six designated integrated high schools.

The dimensions of the achievement to which the New York City Commission contributed are reflected in a 1965 memorandum stating the policy of the New York City Board of Education relative to excellence for the city's schools.[151] This policy was put partially into force with the 1966–1967 school year and is to be fully realized by the 1972–1973 school year. It guarantees each child the right to choose any high school which fits his particular needs in a program that will culminate in four-year comprehensive high schools. It inaugurates a system for the intermediate years of schooling under which children will be introduced to other children who are different from those they associated with in elementary school. They are to associate with children of different races, nationalities, and economic status. The policy provides for a full day's instruction for each child and for transfer to underutilized schools to achieve this objective. It utilizes the concept of pre-kindergarten and kindergarten programs and seeks to have 30,000 to 40,000 children receiving this education annually by 1970. It institutes programs for gifted students. It insures that each school will receive a fair share of experienced and competent instructors. It provides for massive teacher retraining programs in the field of human relations. Handicapped children will receive additional special services. Another major objective is the development of public understanding of the essentiality of integration as a component of excel-

---

[151] City of New York Board of Education, "Implementation of Board Policy on Excellence for the City's Schools" (Memorandum submitted to the Board by Dr. Bernard E. Donovan, Acting Superintendent of Schools, April 28, 1965) (mimeographed).

lence in education. Finally, summer school will be made available to all students as funds permit with the objective of having a year round academic program.

This example of a local human-relations commission performing the function of studying a human-relations problem of the city government, recommending a specific solution to the local government authorities, and working for its adoption reveals many subtleties concerning the techniques used in performing the function. One stammers in seeking an appropriate characterization of these techniques. In this example, a central technique was to fix upon a practicable solution and to insist upon a substantial adoption of it. Also involved was an adroit use of public argument and support of efforts of responsible leaders of groups seeking to effectuate change in the human-relations situation. One must also note a skillfulness in assisting negotiations between contending parties through continually bringing them together at the crucial times, suggesting middle courses, and reminding both of their responsibilties for agreeing upon a practicable solution. Finally, one must observe how the natural requirements for appropriate performance of this function called for a local agency to perform it rather than a state or federal agency. Although the state had a state human-relations agency and a state education agency, the former performed no role whatsoever and the latter a considerably smaller one in producing the final solution. The requisite knowledge of the local situation, the possession of the crucial working relationships with city government that could provide leverage in pressing for a solution, the prestige enjoyed in public argument on human-relations issues, and the confidence with which private groups seeking solutions regarded the acting agency all belonged singularly to the city's Human-Relations Commission. No other agency could have performed adequately this eleventh constructive-action function of a local human-relations commission. In an eleven-month period, this agency had been the central figure in substantially reversing a ten-year history of successive failure on the part of the nation's largest city in solving one of its major human-relations problems.

Sometimes in the performance of the eleventh function of local human-relations agencies, the remedy the commission must recommend is new legislation rather than, as in the case just examined, the creative use of the existing framework of the law. A good example of the latter type has already been noted in another connection. When the blockbusting tactic appeared on local scenes in 1961–1962, it had to be dealt with immediately and effectively by local government since the tactic was inherently capable of causing rapid and widespread havoc with the stability of neighborhoods in large cities. There could be no waiting for the slow processes of state government while a decision was made whether to act, with the possibility that no action would be taken or that a general approach would be selected not adequately tailored to resolve the local problem. In New York City, Detroit, Philadelphia, Pittsburgh, St. Louis, and other cities, the problem presented was immediately studied by local human-relations commissions either on their own motion or by direction of the mayor or city council. Some of the local commissions held public hearings. All either prepared, reviewed, or submitted drafts of remedial legislation and recommended their passage. These recommendations resulted in new legislation in a number of cities and the legislation has apparently been successfully administered by these agencies.[152] Similarly in Detroit, Chicago, and Pittsburgh, a very considerable problem developed in private hospitals and medical institutions relative to the availability of equal hospital services, of appointment and employment of physicians, and of training for the medical and nursing professions. In the 1958–1960 period studies were conducted by local commissions of one or more of these matters. In 1956, for example, Negro physicians held staff appointments at only nine of the fifty-odd private hospitals in Chicago.[153] This situation greatly affected the opportunity of Negroes to gain admission to private hospitals serving the general public since most patients enter hospitals only as a result of their physicians' being on the hospital staff and making the arragement for their admission. In addition, there were very few Negro patients in Chicago private hospitals and the evidence indicated that there was considerable discrimination against them. Moreover, some medical and nursing schools would not admit Negroes for training. In Pittsburgh, although Negroes were admitted to private hospitals, there was discrimination in according them the full facilities of these institutions.[154] In Detroit in all three areas—bed utilization, appointments of physicians and nurses to hospital staffs, and admission to medical and nursing training—the local Commission found there was a significant degree

[152] See note 86 above.

[153] Chicago Commission on Human Relations, *Annual Report, 1962*, p. 17.

[154] Pittsburgh Commission on Human Relations, *Racial Practices in Pittsburgh Hospitals* (1959), pp. 4–6, 9–11.

of discrimination against Negroes.[155] As a result of studies and recommendations made by human-relations commissions in these cities remedial action was taken in them. In Chicago this action took the form of appointment of a mayor's committee on staff appointments for Negro physicians.[156] The committee, assisted by a full-time Commission staff member, by a process of publicity and negotiation obtained significant improvements in hospital staff appointments for Negro physicians and consequently admissions of Negro patients to private hospitals. Its work culminated in enactment of a city ordinance in April 1962 forbidding discrimination by private hospitals in employment or appointment of physicians.[157] By the beginning of 1963, forty-three Negro doctors held sixty-one appointments in thirty-one of Chicago's sixty-nine hospitals.[158] Moreover, the Commission obtained from sixty-six of these hospitals a new commitment to, or a reaffirmation of, a policy of nondiscrimination in admission of patients, room assignment, quality of treatment, and use of hospital facilities. By a similar process in Detroit in 1958 the local Commission secured elimination of discrimination in admissions to medical and nursing training.[159] Between 1958 and 1961 the Commission worked with a private hospital building-fund organization and city officials to bring pressure to bear on private hospitals still not following the principle of equal accessibility to facilities and services for all persons. The private organization was asked to deny funds to hospitals who would not agree to follow this principle and the city was asked to refuse to approve redevelopment plans involving hospitals who would not similarly agree. The Commission effort to obtain compliance with the principle was reasonably successful. Finally, the Commission was granted in 1963 the jurisdiction to eliminate discrimination in all phases of the operations of hospitals and medical institutions.[160] By 1966 it was able to repeat substantial elimination of discrimination in this area.[161]

155 Detroit Commission on Community Relations, *1961 Annual Report*, p. 10.
156 Chicago Commission on Human Relations, *Annual Report, 1962*, p. 17.
157 Chicago Code § 137-13.2, *Race Relations Law Reporter*, Vol. 7 (1962), p. 605.
158 Chicago Commission on Human Relations, *Annual Report, 1962*, pp. 17–18. Conformance to this commitment has been regularly investigated by the Commission on Human Relations, *Annual Report, 1963*, p. 12.
159 Detroit Commission on Human Relations, *1961 Annual Report*, p. 10.
160 Detroit Ordinance 813-F (October 8, 1963), *Race Relations Law Reporter* (1963), p. 1693.
161 Detroit Commission on Community Relations, *Annual Report* (1966), pp. 5–6.

ASSISTANCE SERVICES

The twelfth major constructive-action function of local human-relations commissions is to provide either directly or through collaboration with private and public agencies various types of assistance services to minority-group members. The services directed to individual persons are designed to help them with various difficult problems encountered by them as newcomers to a city, as persons needing to borrow money, as searchers for more adequate housing, as young people, and as leaders and representatives of their minority groups. The services directed to communities in which minority-group members live are designed to assist these communities with various difficult problems such as stabilization of the community to prevent further deterioration and to begin its improvement.

One of the most interesting services of a local commission is provided to the newcomer to the city, who is, usually, in some sense, a member of a minority group. In Chicago, for example, around 250,000 of the present population are persons who have migrated to Chicago since the end of World War II.[162] These persons consist, in the order of their group size, of Southern Negroes, Southern whites, Mexican Americans and Puerto Ricans, American Indians, and Cubans. Most of these newcomers are very needy, poorly educated, low in literacy, unskilled, and lacking in sufficient knowledge of health and sanitation measures. Due to their ignorance of urban ways, these immigrants are likely to be preyed upon by unscrupulous people, particularly the money lenders. Unless these newcomers are provided with assistance in adjusting to their new environment and in obtaining needed training and jobs, many of them will remain or become unemployed, heavily indebted, and alienated. To meet this problem the mayor of Chicago set up a committee on new residents, under the guidance of the local Commission, to help these residents solve their problems of adjustment to urban living. Each year this committee provides assistance services to 4,000 newcomers in communities that are "ports of entry" for the city. In 1963, for example, more than 800 of these persons were helped to obtain employment.[163] Many other newcomers were given specific assistance with problems concerning health, credit, language, and housing. In addition, nearly 800 adults and 3,500 children were provided tutoring services by volunteer tutors working un-

[162] Chicago Commission on Human Relations, *Annual Report, 1962*, p. 6.
[163] Chicago Commission on Human Relations, *Annual Report, 1963*, pp. 17–18.

der the auspices of the committee. The purpose of this service was to help these persons to develop greater educational skills. The committee also helped in establishing credit unions in two public-housing projects similar to those already formed in New York City. These unions serve particularly important functions by providing counsel to tenants on installment buying, income management, budgeting, and saving as well as providing a source of loans at low interest rates. Of course, the credit unions serve both minority-group newcomers and those who have lived in the city for a long period.

Other commissions have extended some of the service rendered newcomers by the Chicago Commission to all minority-group members. In some cities the local commissions have developed employment counselling programs either for young persons or adults or both. In Philadelphia the local Commission's employment-counselling program consisted of training sessions concerning preparation for employment and job hunting.[164] These were attended by persons all the way from the teenage group to the retirement-age group. The subjects explored in the sessions included problems peculiarly affecting persons in the minority-group community relative to their job opportunities, techniques of interview and appropriate behavior and appearance on the part of the applicant, availability of scholarships and requirements for admission to colleges. Training sessions were held on the premises of sponsoring organizations such as church, fraternal, social, and civic groups. In addition to the general sessions, an effort was made to provide individual counselling to trainees desiring it in the area of their special needs. In all, about 2,670 persons were reached by the Philadelphia Commission's program during 1962. Of the 1,200 who participated in the training sessions, 600 were awarded certificates of merit. Another 1,370 persons participated in employment-information programs conducted by the Commission's staff in public and private schools. In Chicago and New York the local Commissions have also recruited applicants for apprenticeship programs from minority groups.[165]

Another service rendered to newcomers and recently extended to all minority-group members by the Chicago Commission is assisting those persons, who are financially able to obtain housing outside of

[164] Philadelphia Commission on Human Relations, *Annual Report* (1962), pp. 48–49.

[165] Chicago Commission on Human Relations, *Annual Report, 1962*, p. 12; New York City Commission on Human Rights, *Annual Report for 1965*, pp. 13–14.

central city ghettos, to prepare for taking this step and then to find the housing they desire in all-white or integrated areas. In recent years private organizations have provided a housing service of this sort in several parts of the country. In the suburban areas adjacent to Boston, for example, Fair Housing, Inc., acting through representatives of local committees, or housing aides, has helped home-seekers in contacting cooperative realtors, accompanied them in their activity of seeking housing, and assisted them in appropriate situations to verify that discrimination in housing is being practiced and to file a complaint with the state Human-Relations Commission.[166] Between 1961 and 1963 this organization was able to assist fifty-three minority group (principally nonwhite) families in obtaining housing in all-white or integrated communities. A housing office of Fair Housing, Inc., located in the central Boston area acts as a liaison between minority-group families in that area who need and seek housing and local housing committees who discover or develop nonsegregated housing opportunities and then accompany these families in their search for housing. The housing office maintains a monthly open occupancy listing service on homes and apartments. It also provides minority-group families with information concerning transportation, price ranges, education and services in suburban communities. A similar organization was formed in Pittsburgh in November 1963 under the name Clearing House of Open Occupancy Selection (CHOOSE).[167] Its achievements in assisting minority-group families to find suitable housing have formed the subject of a recent study.[168] In February 1964 the New York City Commission initiated a similar official program in collaboration with four major civil-rights organizations.[169] This program, like the unofficial programs, is based on the proposition that the keystone supporting all discrimination and segregation is housing segregation.[170] The problem of discrimination is based upon a lack of mutual acceptance on the part of persons belonging to different racial, religious, and nationality groups. The necessary mutual acceptance at the community level cannot come into existence unless mem-

---

[166] Massachusetts Advisory Committee to the United States Commission on Civil Rights, *Report on Massachusetts: Housing in Boston*, (Washington, D.C.: U.S. Government Printing Office, December 1963), pp. 31–34, 54–67.

[167] *Pittsburgh Human Relations Review*, Vol. 7, No. 2, (April, 1964), pp. 2–3.

[168] *Pittsburgh Human Relations Review*, Vol. 9, No. 6 (December, 1966), p. 3.

[169] *The New York Times* (February 1, 1964), p. 26.

[170] Los Angeles County Commission on Human Relations, *1960–2 Biennial Report*, p. 6.

bers of each of these groups acquire knowledge of the others. This mutual knowledge and acceptance can develop only when these people
are in substantial communication with each other. While lifting the
barriers to employment for minority racial, religious, and nationality
groups will assist this process, the necessary communication cannot
develop until these persons and persons in the majority group are in
situations of continuous physical proximity in a community.[171] Under
the New York City program, one private organization concentrates in
developing support for integrated living in communities where no
minority-group families now live.[172] Another organization establishes
contact with Negro and Puerto Rican families who, being financially
able to do so, wish to purchase or rent housing in a presently integrated or all white community. A third organization provides the
service of instructing the family heads about how and where to look
for available integrated housing and of providing housing aides to
accompany the families in examining the premises. It also assists the
families to verify discrimination in housing if it is encountered and to
file complaints with the city Human-Rights Commission if this proves
necessary. The fourth civil-rights organization performs the function
of conducting an educational campaign for integrated living through
mass media and other means of communication. The local Commission, in addition to organizing this official program for execution
through private civil-rights organizations, acts as a consultant to these
organizations and as a coordinating agency. It seems clear that the
active intervention in this area of assistance services by an official
commission should make the service considerably more effective than
when it is performed by private organizations alone.

Under the New York program more than three hundred Negro
families secured new houses in previously all white or in mixed neighborhoods in 1966.[173] In addition, a number of real estate firms operating apartment buildings signed conciliation agreements opening
their facilities to minority-group families and establishing a working
relationship between them and two of the civil-rights organizations
cooperating with the Commission.[174]

There are many types of assistance services needed by the poor

[171] New York City Commission on Human Rights, *Annual Report for 1965,*
pp. 4–6.
[172] *The New York Times* (February 1, 1964), p. 26.
[173] *The New York Times* (November 6, 1966), sec. 1, p. 31.
[174] New York City Commission on Human Rights, *Annual Report for 1965,* p. 6.

and the disadvantaged among both the minority and majority groups. One area relates to assistance in learning about and utilizing available welfare services. One of the numerous typical problems in Austin, Texas, relates to an indigent Negro or Latin American requiring medical services. The Austin private organization referred to earlier, the Citywide Committee for Human Rights (CCHR), has during 1966–1967 provided help to these persons in their efforts to obtain clinic cards designed by the city-owned hospital authorities for monitoring the provision of medical and hospital services to the indigent.[175] One 64-year-old Negro had been trying to obtain a clinic card for two years. Authorities had denied the application on the ground that he had not satisfied them concerning his disposition of the proceeds—less than $2,000—obtained from the sale of his property to the Austin Urban Renewal Agency over two years earlier. When CCHR was asked in August 1966 to help this man its representatives found him in bed with pneumonia and terribly swollen limbs resulting either from liver trouble or heart trouble or both. He could hardly speak and seemed extraordinarily weak. The CCHR team concluded that he needed immediate medical attention. It secured the donation of an ambulance from a friendly funeral home, but when he was presented to hospital authorities they objected that he did not have a clinic card. When issuance of a card was requested, authorities stated the man had not made the necessary disclosure about the funds mentioned above. CCHR's representatives contended that they had learned the money had been spent principally for another home and that the remainder, less than $500, had been used to support the patient and his wife during a two-year period, since neither worked. Both had an income only from welfare-assistance sources. Authorities still insisted that hospital services would only be rendered on the basis of a card and that the patient had not shown his need for one. After six hours of negotiation they finally agreed that he would be permitted to stay at the hospital and receive medical attention while CCHR assisted his family in securing the necessary documentation to show disposition of the funds he had received for his home. Even after they had agreed to treat the patient, authorities at first wanted simply to give him a shot and send him home over the weekend to await a home call by a doctor attached to the hospital. CCHR explained to the family what was nec-

[175] The following examples of assistance-services were either directed by or participated in by myself as director of the CCHR.

essary in order to obtain a clinic card for him and then helped them secure the necessary documentation. The next day a clinic card was issued. Another case involved a 63-year-old Negro woman whose sole income was $34.00 a month in welfare assistance. Her son, apparently handicapped in some serious way, lived with her. He received approximately $60.00 a month in welfare assistance. Their monthly rental was $30.00. In September 1966, the mother was admitted to the city hospital. After twenty-two days hospitalization, she was presented with a bill for over $900 and asked to pay $10.00 per month on the account. She had been denied a clinic card. When CCHR was asked to help, it discovered that she was a diabetic and had nearly exhausted the supply of insulin that she had obtained while at the hospital. She needed both medical attention and medicine. The hospital, when contacted, stated that they had denied her a clinic card because she had said she had several pieces of property outside the city but that she had no income from them. CCHR proposed that an OEO supported legal assistance office be called into the picture, that an investigation be conducted to determine if the property existed, and that a temporary clinic card be issued until the investigation had been completed. If it turned out that there was property, it was agreed that she should then sell her out-of-the-city property to satisfy the charges.

Another area of difficulty is the relationship between minority-group families and the public-school authorities. Two examples on the Austin, Texas, scene will suffice. Many children of these families can bring only ten or fifteen cents to school to pay for their lunch. Under a local program the remaining twenty-five or twenty cents to pay for a lunch is provided for these children. Sometimes a child cannot bring even the ten or fifteen cents when the father is temporarily out of work. When this occurs there may be difficulties in assuring the principal that the child really is in a situation of need. The child may be sent home at lunchtime instead of being provided with a free lunch. In October 1966 CCHR encountered one Latin American family in which such a child was being sent home and was suffering from malnutrition due to the fact that it was difficult for her to travel the distance both ways between school and home and to eat what was available at home during a thirty-minute period. Representatives of CCHR informed the principal of its concern in the matter and was assured that a new Spanish-speaking staff member would call on the family and ascertain the latter's needs. Meanwhile the organization paid for lunches for the child. Other Latin American families could afford to pay for the lunch of their children in October 1966, but complained that the children were not given time to eat what they purchased at lunch time. The parents were reluctant to tell school authorities about the problems. Representatives of CCHR called on the school principal who, although quite hostile at the outset, admitted she had received a directive from the school superintendent to look into the problem of children not having enough time to eat. She agreed to look further into the matter. Representatives of CCHR checked out the lunch lines to see whether the children were able to eat their food during the time allotted.

One of the most unfortunate situations in Austin and throughout the state is the sale of real property to Negroes and Latin Americans on the basis of what is called a contract of sale. This contract is not a conveyance but merely an agreement to convey title to the property when all or a large portion of the purchase price has been paid. Most of these contracts provide that title to the property will not be conveyed until the last penny of the purchase price has been paid. It has been estimated that as high as 90 per cent of all real-estate transactions in Austin with members of minority groups are conducted upon the basis of these conditional sales contracts.[176] If the purchaser defaults under the contract before that time, and the installment due is not paid within a very short period, often no more than five days, the contract provides that the contract of sale is extinguished and the relationship thereafter is one between the property owner and a mere tenant at will. In August 1965, for example, a Latin American was unable to pay his installment due under a contract of sale of real property. He had regularly paid these installments prior to this time. He had also improved the property to the extent of $4,000. After the installment was five days overdue, the seller filed suit to evict the purchaser from the property as the contract payments had been forfeited. I was asked to assist the family.[177] With the assistance of two other lawyers, negotiation was begun with the property owner and he was assured that the theory of the validity of this contract with respect to a forfeiture, one generally accepted among local sellers, would be tested in the courts. The result was that suit was dropped and the Latin American allowed to resume his installment payments.

[176] This is the opinion of Mr. Jasper Glover, an Austin real estate broker since 1946. A similar estimate was made by the Austin Urban Renewal Agency in a memorandum furnished me by a staff member of the agency.

[177] This case was referred by Catholic Charities of the Austin Diocese, Inc.

This result was not the usual one simply because Negroes and Latin Americans are largely uninformed concerning what their rights are or might be. Usually members of these minority groups faced with this situation simply accept the new status of tenant at will or move or are evicted from their homes, suffering in each instance forfeiture of the existing value of the home less the amount still owing to the seller. It has been authoritatively estimated that the average life of a contract of sale in Austin is but four years.[178] Most Negroes and Latin Americans do not know there is another way of buying a home such as by securing a deed either at the outset or after the payment of a reasonable down payment under a contract of sale. There are many other disadvantages to purchases under a contract of sale. Purchasers may not borrow money upon the "equity" they have in their home. They are not usually in a position to know whether the seller has good title or, in the alternative, to purchase title insurance. There are instances of several homes purchased in Austin in the period 1949–1951 for about $6000 under contracts of sale where the taxes have not been paid by the seller and property owner. The seller-owner, who continued to be liable for taxes, provided in some contracts for payment of the taxes by the purchaser. Taxes, however, were not paid although it was sometimes contended by the purchaser that he did pay money to the owner to cover taxes. In other instances the stipulated payments have included an amount for taxes which the owner did not pay to the tax authorities. Many of these purchasers still owe $3000 or more under their contracts. Should the city sue for taxes and have the homes sold to satisfy a judgment, what will be the status of purchasers under the contracts of sale? It seems clear that they will lose all claim to the property being purchased since their claim to it is only against the seller who now has no title to the property. It is obvious that most Negroes and Latin Americans badly needed counselling concerning proper methods of purchasing real property so as to avoid such pitfalls as these.

Recently in Austin CCHR acted to deal with the problem just described. It learned from a staff member of the Austin Urban Renewal Agency that twelve hundred families would face removal from a certain project area and the necessity for purchasing new or replacement homes. In order to inform them about better ways of purchasing

[178] This is the opinion of Mr. Jasper Glover. A similar estimate was made by the Austin Urban Renewal Agency in the memorandum mentioned in note 176.

homes than the contract of sale, CCHR held a public forum at a church in the project area at which two able real estate brokers made the necessary explanations. It also distributed a small publication summarizing these explanations.

Many other forms of assistance services have been rendered by CCHR. These have been briefly described in Chapter 2.[179] As its directors and members became acquainted with the needs of minority-group families and individuals, they then proceeded to recruit the necessary material and human resources for the purpose of rendering specialized services to respond meaningfully to those needs. In the process CCHR has developed into a facility through which persons and organizations, not now doing so, can begin to make meaningful contributions of services and money for resolving human relations problems regularly encountered by minority and other disadvantaged groups in Austin, Texas. Without question the most important contribution is that of devoted service by local citizens. Any careful observer of the human-relations scene in any city must report that this is the contribution which is the crucial missing dimension in the life of that city. When it is added, even in relatively small amounts, it is the dimension most productive of needed change in human relations.

It is unquestionably true that local human-relations commissions have touched only the very surface in organizing and assisting others to organize programs of assistance services for members of minority groups. The whole war on poverty contemplated by the Economic Opportunity Act,[180] particularly in its community action program, obviously has relevance to this problem.[181] One commentator has observed that "seen in the perspective of our country's great accomplishments in education, training, and welfare, the Office of Economic Opportunity (OEO) for all its strident publicity, is small potatoes."[182] The comments of the proponents of "A Freedom Budget for All Americans" seem more just than the latter: it is "clear that the major aspects of a full-scale war against poverty cannot be found within the confines of the Economic Opportunity Act . . . nor are these aspects

[179] See pp. 78–81, above.

[180] 42 U.S.C.A. §§ 2701–2967, *as amended* (Supp. 1966).

[181] Office of Economic Opportunity, *Community Action Program Guide* (Washington, D.C.: U.S. Government Printing Office, February, 1965), p. 7; Richard H. Leach, "The Federal Role in the War on Poverty Program," *Law and Contemporary Problems*, Vol. 31 (1966), p. 28.

[182] Carl H. Madden, "The War on Poverty," *Law and Contemporary Problems*, Vol. 31 (1966), p. 55.

supported adequately by other national policies or programs."[183] The proponents of this budget place great emphasis upon improved educational opportunity. But they place even greater emphasis upon improved employment opportunity and upon training and education of parents as well as their children, for this purpose, in contrast to the current program which emphasizes training of the latter.[184]

Nevertheless, the great untapped source of relief for the poor and the disadvantaged at the local level—even after full account is taken of the federal poverty programs—are local programs for education and assistance. There are countless churches and other organizations with space and people to devote to many kinds of special assistance services so greatly needed by the poor. There are countless businesses and unions which could offer training programs in various skills on or off the job and with or without pay. The great opportunity for human-relations commissions in the future years will be to move the majority and minority groups of all communities across the nation to utilize their very considerable local resources for providing education, training, and other forms of assistance services to members of minority and other disadvantaged groups. The great problem in mobilizing these local resources is one of human relations. This is the problem upon which the current poverty program does not really focus and which requires a human-relations program and an official human-relations agency for its resolution.

[183] A. Philip Randolph Institute, *A "Freedom Budget" for All Americans* (New York: A. Philip Randolph Institute, October, 1966), p. 39.
[184] *Id.*, pp. 38–64, 25–33.

Allocation of Optimum Roles for Implementation of Civil Rights in Our Federal System

The examination we have made of the experience of local and state commissions on human relations and of the federal courts and administrative agencies concerned with civil rights problems permits us to draw certain significant conclusions relative to the effectiveness of civil-rights legislation and its administration in resolving problems of relations between the majority and minority groups throughout the nation. The last chapter demonstrates beyond any shadow of a doubt that it is essential to the effectiveness of any civil-rights legislative program, whether established by the federal, state, or local government, that its primary focus be upon intergroup relations taking place at the local level where are to be found most of the causes, conditions accompanying, and results flowing from discrimination and other harmful activity directed against minority and other disadvantaged groups. The central task that must be performed by some government in each community with serious problems of intergroup relations is the reconstruction of those relations so as to eliminate the causes of this harmful activity, to ameliorate the conditions flowing from it, and to overcome the results and scars that have been inflicted upon the community and its minority groups. With regard to the majority group, performance of this task means the reorganization and reformation of majority-group actions, habits, customs, and private and official arrangements that have produced and continue to maintain the conditions so seriously affecting the opportunities of minority and other disadvantaged groups in the community. With regard to the minority and other disadvantaged groups performance of this task requires the development of leaders within these groups who will concentrate upon matters of human rights and relations, the provision of various kinds of assistance to these groups and leaders in preparing for and obtaining various needed opportunities, and the protection of these groups against certain typical kinds of exploitation and abuse. This central task of reconstruction of intergroup relations calls for the assembly and redirection of the maximum human and material resources within each community. It demands that each community acknowledge the performance of this task to be its own responsibility and that each of its groups become genuinely involved in discharging it. The necessary institution for guiding the performance of this task and providing the appropriate leadership is a human-relations commission whose members are drawn, where at all feasible, in large part from the citizens of the community itself. This commission must be given a comprehensive civil-rights legislative program to administer together with ample procedural authority, staff, and budget for carrying out this program. Three kinds of functions must be assigned the commission: (a) the processing of individual complaints about all forms of harmful discrimination, through investigation, conciliation, hearings, issuance of cease and desist orders, and judicial-enforcement actions where necessary; (b) the negotiation from a position of strength with wide sectors of business, union organizations, professions, government agencies, and private organizations for the taking of action by them to improve opportunities available to minority groups; and (c) the engagement in constructive official action designed to create the attitudes, conditions, and actions essential in each community for moving its majority and minority groups to confront and to resolve all of its serious problems of intergroup relations. This latter function involves, as we saw in the last chapter, numerous types of official programs directed toward both officials and private persons and institutions.

Turning to existing civil-rights legislative programs and conditions in which they are operative, we see, in the first place, that our state and federal programs focus merely upon one aspect of intergroup problems, discrimination against minority groups. They do so through employing the single technique of processing individual complaints of discrimination. They have not attempted to perform either the second or third functions needed for adequately dealing with problems of intergroup relations. These programs are highly unrealistic and, in light of the tremendous scope of the task that has to be performed throughout the country, almost ridiculously inadequate. It is clear today that through these programs little has been or will be accomplished in turning the great tide of discrimination against minority groups or in removing unreasonable obstacles, not necessarily discriminatory in nature, that block their access to all needed opportunities in the public life of our communities.[1] Obviously, the processing of individual complaints of discrimination under laws prohibiting that activity is essential to any adequate civil-rights legislative program. The point here is that it is only a very small part of an adequate program.

In the second place, our state and federal programs are defective even in their performance of the function of processing individual complaints of discrimination. The defects relate to their limited jurisdiction over discriminatory transactions, lack of jurisdiction over other unreasonable impediments preventing members of minority groups from securing opportunities, procedures in processing complaints, institutional structures, operational concepts, and funding. In the case of the federal government, the defects include all these plus the fact that the courts rather than a human-relations commission have been selected as the primary agency for enforcing prohibitions against discrimination. Chapter 5 was concerned with examining these various defects and making recommendations for their elimination.

In the third place, our state and federal programs are defective due to the fact that they do not really operate in or involve the citizenry of communities having serious intergroup problems. There are, as we have seen, well over two thousand of these local communities at the present time although probably no more than ten to fifteen of them have the needed comprehensive official human-relations program at work within them. The state programs seek to eliminate discriminatory activity through processing individual complaints by a central admin-

---

[1] The most recent confirmation of the position of this study is to be found in University of Michigan–Wayne State University Institute of Labor and Industrial Relations, *A Study of Patterns of Discrimination in Employment for the Equal Employment Opportunity Commission* (Report submitted to Equal Employment Opportunity Commission, Dr. Frances R. Counsens, Project Director, September, 1966). "Existing laws have accomplished little in breaking established patterns of employment" [*Id.*, p. 242(a)]. Owners of businesses and managers in the top echelons of business have a "limited knowledge of a commission's very existence, to say nothing of its program" [*Id.*, p. 242(a)]. "More than 50 percent of those interviewed claimed to have no knowledge of the existence of any public civil rights agency in their community. When the answers to several related questions are treated together, there is some doubt even about the 21 percent who claimed to know about the agency but had no contact with it prior to the interview" [*Id.*, p. 242(b)]. "If the agencies involved in this study are representative, there is a lesson here for all state and municipal commissions, namely, need for modification of orientation and program. . . . agencies need to consider shifting from past and

istrative agency, usually called a human-relations commission, whose personnel are drawn largely, if not wholly, from areas outside the community in which the complaint of discrimination originates. They do not conceive that their function is to redo or reconstruct intergroup relations in a community. They do not seek to involve the citizenry with the very process of administering the basic statute under which they operate or in dealing broadly with intergroup relations in their community. There is no close relationship maintained between the enforcement activity of the state commissions and the official agencies in the local communities which may have similar jurisdiction as well as other duties with regard to intergroup-relations problems. As a matter of fact, their jurisdiction does not clearly extend to many problems concerning these relations. The federal program under the Civil Rights Acts of 1964–1968 is even more attenuated than that of the typical state program operating through human-relations commissions with power to enforce administratively statutory prohibitions against discrimination. It does not utilize a human-relations commission for such enforcement but relies upon the remedy of civil enforcement actions filed in the federal courts by private persons and the Attorney General, a remedy which history has demonstrated to be woefully ineffective in the civil-rights field. There is no attempt to build a viable locally administered federal program for dealing with the intergroup problems at the local level. The Community Relations Service established by Title X of the 1964 act is a very poor substitute for such a program.[2] Its operation is directed only toward threats to peaceful relations among the citizens of the community. The provision establishing the Service speaks to no other of the manifold and pervasive problems of intergroup relations that smolder and damage minority-group opportunities without breaking into the heat of violence or constituting a threat of doing so.

In the fourth place, as implied by the foregoing observations, there is no adequate place in existing state and federal civil-rights legislative programs for a human-relations commission operating at the local level, involving the local citizenry in its administration, or performing the two most important of the three functions that have to be per-

---

present preoccupation with complaints in order to concentrate on broader spheres of activity which might reach larger numbers of employers and others" [*Id.*, 242(b)].

[2] 42 U.S.C. §§ 2000g—2000g-3 (1964).

formed in order to make real headway in resolving serious intergroup-relations problems in our communities.

Given the appropriate conditions in a community, a local government human-relations commission is the ideal agency for performing the three functions that government must perform for dealing effectively with intergroup-relations problems at the local level. This has been amply demonstrated by the performances of the human-relations commissions in the cities of Philadelphia, Pittsburgh, Erie, New York City, Baltimore, St. Louis, Kansas City, Detroit, Chicago, and perhaps one or two other cities. The difficulty, however, is that over two thousand other cities, towns, and counties have not yet established official human-relations commissions to deal with serious intergroup-relations problems existing within them. Some few have established official commissions with grossly inadequate conceptions of the functions that have to be performed to adequately solve intergroup-relations problems and without giving them adequate enforcement and other necessary authority, staff, or funds with which to operate. It is essential that local governments be apprized of the necessity of creating these human-relations commissions, empowering them as they should be, and staffing and funding them properly. Chapter 11 sets forth the Alpha Model Local Civil-Rights Ordinance. This ordinance is designed for the local government whose leadership is willing to institute a comprehensive civil-rights program involving performance of the three basic functions relating to intergroup-relations problems by an official human-relations commission. Chapter 11 contains comments upon the reasons for the various provisions and adopts the approaches suggested in Chapters 5 and 6.

It is, however, highly unlikely that many local governments are going to be moved in the near future to create official human-relations commissions of the type envisaged by the Model Local Ordinance set out in Chapter 11. These first efforts, when taken, are also likely to fall far short of a comprehensive program. Moreover, we can no longer wait for local governments to undertake the task of reconstructing the status of intergroup relations within their communities. This task must be undertaken now either by the state or federal governments. Let us first examine the optimum program of a state government in the civil-rights field that would encompass the performance of this task. In the first place, each state should adopt civil-rights legislation that would allocate to its state human-relations commissions effective authority to perform the first type of commission task—the processing individual complaints of discrimination. Jurisdiction should be extended to the maximum area of harmful discrimination and procedures should be reformed to eliminate all the weaknesses examined in Chapter 5. In addition, the authority and the duty to perform the second and third functions relative to intergroup relations previously discussed should be assigned to the state commission. All of these functions should be performed to the extent necessary in each community that does not have its own well-established human-relations commission performing them under a comprehensive civil-rights program.

In the second place, in performing its three functions in a local community, the state commission should utilize the device of a state-local human-relations commission. This commission would in effect be a division or section of the state commission operating only in the community in which it is created. It should be a microcosm of the state commission and exercise all of its authority within the community for which it is established subject of course to such direction and review of its work as the state commission determines to be appropriate. Just as the members of the state commission should be selected so as to be generally representative of the various groups in the state implicated in the problem of intergroup relations, so too should the members of each state-local commission be selected principally from those who reside or work in the community served so as to be generally representative of the various groups within it.

In the third place, states should assign to their state human-relations commission the task of promoting the creation of human-relations commissions by local governments and the enactment of comprehensive civil-right laws for these commissions to administer which cover the three necessary functions relative to intergroup relations. They should also be given the task of assisting local governments in setting up these commissions in the best possible way and in achieving the greatest possible effectiveness in administration of their civil-rights programs.

In the fourth place, as the state commissions implement the role in human relations outlined above, they should move to emphasize as their special function the preventing of discriminatory and other harmful action directed toward minority and other disadvantaged groups by state and local government. They should also try to reach the same kind of action in programs receiving any form of state financial assistance. They should in addition concentrate upon the major businesses, unions, professions, and other private institutions whose activities cut across the jurisdictional lines of local governments.

Chapter 8 sets forth the provisions of the Alpha Model State Civil-Rights Act which speaks to each of the four considerations set out above as essential components of a comprehensive state civil-rights program. One additional state statute is needed, however—to empower local governments to create human-relations commissions, to regulate their creation of these commissions so that they will be effective for handling intergroup relations problems, and finally to provide for their subordination to and coordination with the work of the state commissions. Many states have precluded cities and counties from combining the first function of a human-relations commissions regarding enforcement of law prohibiting discrimination and other conduct seriously harming minority and other disadvantaged groups with the other two essential functions of such a commission. This is obviously true of the substantial number of states in which cities and counties do not have and cannot obtain home-rule status that would enable them to regulate this kind of harmful activity.[3] In these states local governments only have those specific powers that have been granted to them.[4] The specific authority to deal with discrimination and other practices affecting minority and other similar disadvantaged groups has not been granted to cities and counties in these states and their existing grants of authority have generally been construed not to comprehend this authority.[5]

Some local governments in states recognizing the principle of local home rule have also been precluded from regulating discriminatory and other harmful practices affecting minority groups. This preclusion has occurred in several ways. In the first place counties in these states are usually not permitted to achieve home-rule status as cities are.[6] In the second place, when some of the states of the North and West have established state human-relations commissions they have either occupied *pro tanto* the field of civil-rights regulation within the

---

[3] Charles S. Rhyne, *Municipal Law* (Washington, D.C.: National Institute of Municipal Law Officers, 1957), pp. 18, 62.

[4] *Id.*, pp. 70–72.

[5] See, *e.g.*, Attorney General of State of Kansas, Letter of February 19, 1957, to Kansas Anti–Discrimination Commission, *Race Relations Law Reporter*, Vol. II (1957), pp. 557–558.

[6] Rhyne, *Municipal Law*, p. 18.

state to the exclusion of local governments[7] or, with just about the same effect in excluding local governments, have left it doubtful whether the latter can regulate either in the same or related areas in which the state is operating.[8] In the third place, state human-relations commissions in other Northern and Western states have been slow to recognize the exceptional value of well-established local government commissions with comprehensive civil-rights programs. They have not encouraged and sometimes have even discouraged their creation and operation. Prior to 1964 only one state commission, the one in Pennsylvania, had actively pursued the policy of encouraging local governments to organize commissions for administration of civil-rights legislation at the local level instead of administration of this legislation itself as a statewide agency operating from outside of these local governments.[9] In May 1964 the Connecticut Commission adopted the

---

[7] Cal. Labor Code, § 1431 (1964). Most states have taken as their model the New York statute, which was the first in the field, as previously noted. The latter contains a provision reading: "Nothing contained in this article shall be deemed to repeal any of the provisions of the civil rights law of this state relating to discrimination because of race, creed, color, or national origin . . ." [N. Y. Exec. Law, § 300 (1951)]. The attorney general of the State of Michigan took the position that the Michigan civil-rights statute containing a provision closely similar to this superseded civil-rights ordinances in four Michigan cities which had established local commissions to administer a prohibition of employment discrimination [Attorney General of the State of Michigan, Opinion No. 2880, May 22, 1958, *Race Relations Law Reporter*, Vol. III (1958), pp. 798–801]. The opposite position was taken by the attorney general of Minnesota with reference to a Minneapolis ordinance concerning the Minnesota civil-rights statute containing a similar provision [Attorney General of the State of Minnesota, Opinion No. 271, October 20, 1955, *Race Relations Law Reporter*, Vol. 1 (1956), pp. 803–807].

[8] In New York a lower court has held that the state civil-rights statute, which created its state commission against discrimination, did not vest exclusive jurisdiction over housing discrimination in that commission so as to supersede a New York City ordinance granting jurisdiction to the city commission over the same field [*City of New York v. Clafington, Inc.*, 40 Misc. 2d 547, 243 N.Y.S. 2d (Sup. Ct., N.Y. Co., 1963)]. When the New York legislature had first granted jurisdiction in 1961 to its state commission over housing discrimination, it had not amended the basic statute to make it clear that cities could continue to enforce or could enact local legislation dealing with the same area. For this reason in October of that year, the state Commission and the New York City Commission entered into a cooperative agreement concerning the receipt and processing of housing discrimination complaints by the two agencies and allocating the work load between them for the New York City area [New York City Commission on Intergroup Relations, *1961 Annual Report*, pp. 15–18].

[9] Pennsylvania Human Relations Commission, *Sixth Annual Report* (1962), p. 19; *Seventh Annual Report* (1963), pp. 32, 3–6; *Pittsburgh Human Relations Review*, Vol. 5, No. 5 (October, 1962), p. 4. There was a statutory base supporting this action. [Pa. Stat. Ann. Lit. 43, §§ 962 (1964)].

same policy.[10] In 1965 the New York legislature expressly granted authority to the New York City Commission to administer all state civil-rights law administered by the state Commission.[11] In 1966 and 1967 other legislatures applied this principle to all local governments.[12]

It is essential that any statutory preclusion of local governments from enacting civil-rights law and administering it through local human-relations commissions be eliminated. In states not granting home-rule authority to cities and counties it will be essential that a state statute be enacted granting the necessary specific authority to local governments to enact civil-rights laws and to create human-relations commissions with appropriate authority, functions, procedures, staffs, and budgets to administer these laws. In states that do accord home-rule authority to cities and counties, it is first of all essential to make it clear that the statute creating the state human-relations commission does not bar local governments having home-rule authority from exercising that authority in the same area as that administered by the state commission. It will also be important to enact in these states the same kind of legislation previously recommended for states not according home-rule authority to cities and counties. The mere existence of general authority to regulate matters in the civil-rights field does not assure that local governments will exercise that authority or that, if they do, their exercise will be adequately responsive to the need for local civil-rights legislation. The enactment of a general state statute authorizing and regulating the creation of human-relations commissions by local governments having home-rule authority will serve the function of guiding the making of choices by local governments as to the type and degree of involvement it wishes to make initially and subsequently in dealing with civil-rights matters. It will serve to inform these local governments about the interest of these states in local civil-rights programs, to remove any doubt about their original authority to act in this field, to urge them to exercise this authority, and to provide guidelines to be followed in enacting this form

---

[10] New Haven Human Rights Committee, *Report to Mayor of New Haven, Connecticut* (1964), pp. 34–37 (offset print).

[11] N.Y. Gen. Municipal Law, Art. 12-D, Sec. 239-s (Supp. 1966).

[12] Ky. Rev. Stat. §§ 344.300-.350 (Supp. 1966); Ann. Ind. Stat. § 40.2317a (Supp. 1967); Minn. Stat. Ann. §§ 363.115–116 (Supp. 1967); West. Va. Code § 5-11-12 to -13 (Supp. 1967). Pennsylvania also strengthened its policy in the latter year. [Pa. Stat. Ann. Lit. 43, § 962.1 (Supp. 1967)].

of legislation. Beyond these functions, this legislation will serve to prepare the way for coordination of the work of local human-relations commissions with that of the state human-relations commission.

Chapter 9 sets forth the Alpha Model State Act on Local Human-Relations Commissions. It is designed to speak to the various problems involved in allocating to local government a primary role, if it elects to perform it, in resolving problems of intergroup relations. It also speaks to the special problem of eliminating any existing statutory preclusion of local governments from performing this role and of coordinating their performance of it with the work of a state human-relations commission.

We may now turn to a consideration of the optimum role of the federal government with regard to intergroup-relations problems. Putting aside for a moment the lessons indicated by Chapters 1, 5, and 6 with respect to difficulties with the existing federal program, it is first of all clear that one primary role of the federal government must be to prevent every form of misuse of federal authority to support or promote discrimination and other harmful activity directed toward minority and other disadvantaged groups. This includes the preclusion of the use of federal financial assistance or powers derived from the federal government for discriminatory or other harmful activities directed toward these groups. The very pervasiveness and size of the federal government operations make its leadership in the area of intergroup relations of vital significance in the total national picture. Beyond this, the federal government, due to its supreme position in the federal system, should specially monitor the operations of state and local government to assure the elimination of discrimination and other unreasonable burdens placed by them upon minority and other disadvantaged groups. It should also preclude the use of state and local government financial assistance or powers derived from these sources to support discrimination and other harmful activities toward these groups. The federal government should finally reach the operations of large businesses and unions engaged in industries affecting interstate commerce. The vehicle for performing the many-faceted function so far described should be a federal human-relations commission. It should be empowered to perform both the first intergroup-relations function of processing complaints of discrimination and the second function of wide spectrum negotiation with business, unions, private institutions, and government for opening opportunities to minority groups. This commission should be given the procedural authority, staff, and budget that would enable it to perform these functions in the most effective way.

In the second place, the federal human-relations commission should be assigned the function of moving state and local governments to take action in conformance with the optimum roles of these governments in the civil-rights field. Where state and local governments now have human-relations commissions, the federal commission should seek to get them to undertake the performance of the second and third functions relative to intergroup relations along with the first function and to move these states to utilize state-local commissions in those communities where this becomes necessary. Similarly, where states and local governments do not now have human-relations commissions, the federal commission should seek to move them to establish these agencies and to adopt a comprehensive civil-rights program as previously outlined. To facilitate these changes the federal government should institute a federal-state and federal-local human-relations program similar, in its institutional aspects, to its urban-renewal,[13] civil-defense,[14] and economic-opportunity programs.[15] Each of these programs provides for a federal agency to supervise the making of either loans and capital grants or financial contributions to cities or states for the carrying out of a program in which both the grantor and grantee governments have a major interest. Each of these programs is designed to encourage the operation of local public agencies for the carrying out of a plan upon which the participating governments or parties agree. A similar arrangement is essential to the proposed program. Indeed, financial contributions to states participating in the civil-defense program are conditioned upon each state providing, by state law, that the plan agreed upon shall be in effect in all political subdivisions of the state and be mandatory on them.[16] Financial contributions under the latter program are also available for personnel and administrative expenses, which would be the major item in financial aid to local human-relations commissions.[17] Under the Civil Defense Program, the federal agency administering it is authorized to provide for training or instruction of local and state officials in the

---

[13] 42 U.S.C. §§ 1441–1497 (Supp. II, 1965–1966).
[14] 50 App. U.S.C.A. §§ 2251–2286 (1964).
[15] 42 U.S.C. §§ 2701–2991e (Supp. II, 1965–1966).
[16] 50 App. U.S.C. § 2286(a) (1964).
[17] 50 App. U.S.C. § 2286 (1964).

organization, operation, and techniques of civil defense.[18] It is also authorized to create a national civil-defense college and three civil-defense technical schools.[19] A provision of this sort is especially needed in a federal-state and a federal-local human-relations program. As previously indicated, there are only some ten to fifteen well-established local commissions now in existence while there are over two thousand cities and counties that should establish a commission. When these governments establish their commissions, there will be a very great need for trained human-relations personnel to serve on their staffs. There are now only a limited number of these personnel available and additional personnel will have to be trained to fill the need for them. In addition, the chairmen and members of these commissions could profitably engage in seminars and training programs conducted by the federal agency. Under the Urban Renewal Program, the administrator of the federal agency is authorized to furnish to local governments, at their request, a service designed to assist them in the preparation of a workable urban renewal program and to provide them with technical and professional assistance for planning and developing local programs.[20] A similar provision is contained in the Public Health Service Act of 1944 under which the Public Health Service details its officers or employees to a local or state government for the purpose of assisting the latter in work related to the functions of the Service.[21] The provision of services in planning programs and the detailing of personnel to local and state governments to assist them in human-relations work are likely to be invaluable devices in a federal-state and federal-local human-relations program. In this way some assurance can be had that a new commission will put its best foot forward and avoid initial mistakes that could prejudice its later effectiveness. In addition, the federal agency should funnel to state and local commissions information concerning new techniques found by experience in various parts of the country to be useful in solving human relations problems.

The federal-state and federal-local human-relations program conceived along lines just suggested would undoubtedly be efficacious in many Northern and Western states and perhaps also in some Southern states. It would not be efficacious, however, in Southern states un-

[18] 50 App. U.S.C. § 2281(3) (1964).
[19] *Ibid.*
[20] 42 U.S.C. § 1451(d) (Supp. II, 1965–1966).
[21] 42 U.S.C. § 215(b), (d) (1964).

willing to establish state commissions or in Southern and other communities unwilling to establish local commissions. Even with the bait of federal financial contribution, it is unlikely that state and local governments in much of the South will establish their own human-relations commissions for a number of years (no one can guess how long). Moreover, the first official commissions established are likely to be rather ineffective, milquetoastish institutions. Meanwhile, the need for effective human-relations commissions in state and communities is as great in the South as elsewhere, perhaps even greater. To meet this situation the federal-state and federal-local human-relations program proposed should be modified so as to provide that the federal human-relations commission administering it may establish federal-state and federal-local commissions with authority to administer federal civil-rights law. Each of these commissions would be assigned the duty to perform all three functions that are required for dealing adequately with intergroup-relations problems. These commissions would have the full authority of the federal human-relations commissions. For the purpose of this part of its program this commission and its local and state counterparts should be provided with authority to administer law proscribing all forms of discriminatory and other unreasonable activity directed against minority and other disadvantaged groups. The great function of a federal-state and federal-local human-relations commission would be to provide leadership at the state and local levels, respectively, in getting communities moving toward confronting and solving their human-relations problems. Due to the nature of most of their functions, no serious constitutional law problem would be presented. Most of its functions would not be regulatory in the strict sense, and insofar as they are regulatory, a federal-state commission and a federal-local commission could perform as validly under the Constitution as a federal commission located in Washington, D.C.

We have many analogies for the creation of a federal-state and federal-local human-relations commission whose members are drawn from the locality served by the commission. One is the local Selective Service Board, which consists of three or more members appointed by the President on the basis of recommendations made by the governor of the state for which appointed.[22] Another analogy is provided by the local, county, and state committees utilized by the Secretary of Agriculture for administering the federal agricultural-adjustment and soil-

[22] 50 App. U.S.C. § 460(b)(3) (1964).

conservation programs.[23] While members of the state and local review committees used in these programs are appointed to their positions, members of the local and county committees are elected to their positions by farmers within local administrative areas who participate or cooperate in programs administered by these committees.[24] Still another analogy is the federal jury commissioner who alternates with the clerk of the federal district court in selecting qualified citizens for potential jury service by placing their names in the jury box.[25] This commissioner, who is required to be a citizen of good standing residing in the district in which he functions, serves to ensure a local participation in the jury-selection process. The federal-local human-relations commission proposed above would, like the federal-local agencies just noticed, depend heavily for its effectiveness upon the fact that local citizens would be members of the administrative body. Citizens would be selected either by the President or by the head of the supervising federal agency. They would be selected from those members of each community who are in a position to provide leadership in their community if given proper backing and authority. These commissions would, of course, need to be adequately financed and staffed. They should in addition be provided with the advice and assistance of the federal supervising agency to the extent needed. These commissions would assure that, on local scenes, the vicious circle which propagates discrimination against minority groups would be broken. Given time, it would probably lead to local and state governments' assuming the responsibility they had previously refused to shoulder.

Chapter 10 sets forth the Alpha Model Federal Civil-Rights Act establishing a human-relations commission and assigning to it the various functions essential to the achievement of an optimum role for the federal government in resolving problems of intergroup relations. Chapter 11 completes the circle by presenting the Alpha Model Local Civil-Rights Ordinance. If the series of laws outlined in this chapter and more fully explained in subsequent chapters were to be placed in effect at their respective levels of our federal system, we would be in a position to make maximum progress in solving our pressing intergroup-relations problems.

The discussion in this and previous chapters cannot be properly closed without some comment on the relation of the comprehensive

[23] 16 U.S.C. § 590h(b) (1964); 7 U.S.C. § 1388 (1964).
[24] *Ibid.*
[25] 28 U.S.C. § 1864 (1964).

human-relations program outlined in this chapter to the federal war-on-poverty program. The basic policies of the latter programs were left poorly defined in the Economic Opportunity Act of 1964.[26] Neither the Council of Economic Advisers, Hubert Humphrey, nor Professor John Kenneth Galbraith, who urged the President to promote adoption of such a program, outlined the basic guidelines for conducting it. Nor did the President enunciate a philosophy concerning the basic methods through which the program was to be effectuated in proposing its adoption. Congress also failed to clarify the role that the federal government was to play in fighting poverty. This role was instead left to be defined administratively by Sargent Shriver in conjunction with executive guidance provided by President Johnson. The act did provide that there be a maximum feasible participation by the residents of the areas and the members of the groups served.[27] Shriver later stated that his administration of the act was designed to change institutions as well as people, especially the "hostile or uncaring or exploitive institutions," whether governmental or private.[28] The special target was said to be the local governments which had ignored "the views of the poor and of representative community groups."[29] It has been observed that this administrative policy casts the federal government in a role it has never before played so directly: "in effect, . . . reshaping local government."[30] These statements plus the administrative policy of requiring "the involvement of the whole community in the planning and operation of the [community-action] program" all seemed to point to the relevance of a goal for ameliorating human-relations or intergroup-relations problems existing at the community level such as has been advocated in this book. This relevance is reinforced by the stated purpose of the Office of Economic Opportunity community action program. The purpose of federal assistance to community-action programs has been stated to be to help urban and

---

[26] See Richard H. Leach, "The Federal Role in the War on Poverty Program," *Law and Contemporary Problems,* Vol. 31 (1966), pp. 18–38.

[27] *Id.,* p. 27.

[28] *Hearings on Examination of the War on Poverty Program Before the Committee on the War on Poverty Program of the House Committee on Education and Labor,* 89th Cong., 1st Sess. (Washington, D.C.: U.S. Government Printing Office, 1965), pp. 16–17.

[29] Office of Economic Opportunity, "Congressional Presentation," I, p. 83 (1965).

[30] A. Philip Randolph Institute, *A Freedom Budget for All Americans* (New York: A. Philip Randolph Institute, October, 1966), p. 39.

rural communities to mobilize their resources to combat poverty.[31] One of these great resources, as demonstrated in this book, is the healthy status of intergroup relations.

As the war-on-poverty program has actually been administered, however, it is distinctively clear that it is not a program dealing with the causes of poverty grounded in human-relations or intergroup-relations problems. No phase of it is even remotely comparable to any of the three basic phases of a comprehensive official human-relations program. The war on poverty, despite the objectives articulated by Shriver, does not really deal with "hostile or uncaring or exploitive institutions" at the community level; with the discriminatory and other unreasonable actions by which their hostility and exploitation of the poor among minority groups takes place; with the underlying causes of and conditions accompanying these actions; nor with the methods for enabling members of majority and minority groups to work together for harnessing community resources for eliminating them. Moreover, judged by the experience in Texas and in Austin, its capital, it seems clear that the goal of "reshaping local government" is not really being implemented and that there has been no substantial effect upon the usual way in which local government operates. Things are substantially what they have always been. It also seems clear that the great fabric of poverty has only been altered very slightly. Most Southerners and Southwesterners in the majority group believe that minority groups are enmeshed in poverty due to their own fault, lack of motivation, lack of ability, and moral deficiencies. They believe that the remedy for this situation, to the extent one can exist, involves the use of measures such as are presently incorporated into the war-on-poverty program. They do not feel that the majority group is at all responsible for the existence of the poverty conditions in which minority groups largely live, or that it needs to make any basic changes in its existing attitudes and actions toward these groups. Judged by programs and actions rather than expressions of goals, the official war-on-poverty program largely accords with their point of view. There is no program of human or intergroup relations incorporated into the overall war-on-poverty program. Many participants in the community-action programs are without experience in inter-

[31] Carl H. Madden, "The War on Poverty," *Law and Contemporary Problems,* Vol. 31 (1966), p. 55.

group relations. They do not realize the importance of programs directed toward problems of intergroup relations. Those who have experience or training in handling these problems have no official arena in which to put these assets to work. The official outlines of eligible activities for community-action programs do not focus upon the majority group at all and upon minority groups only with regard to certain kinds of assistance services.[32] Important as the latter are, they are primarily of the type that do not relate to enabling minority groups to become effective in resolving intergroup-relations problems. The very mode of operation of the community-action program stifles every orientation for dealing effectively with these problems. The power structure is deep in the saddle in its operation. The poor are not adequately represented in the local agencies through which the program is administered. Negroes and Latin Americans indeed sit on these agencies but they are power-structure oriented. There is no central agency program for moving local community-action programs to focus on intergroup-relations problems. OEO emphasis upon "local initiative" in proposing community-action programs is important for many phases of any federal program to relieve poverty. Sole reliance upon "local initiative" in a federal program designed to relieve poverty by attacking its causes grounded in majority-group actions of a hostile and exploitive character toward minority groups, however, is utterly unrealistic. A community that has not been doing anything about its intergroup-relations problems is not likely to propose meaningful community-action programs to deal with these problems. The fundamental assumption of the war-on-poverty program that communities of this kind will commit their ideas and resources and assume responsibility for developing and carrying out local-action programs[33] relative to intergroup-relations problems is demonstrably erroneous. A sound federal intergroup-relations program, such as has been suggested in this chapter, is one of the most necessary steps in federal programming for dealing adequately with poverty.

[32] Office of Economic Opportunity, *Community Action Program Guide*, Vol. 1, Part C (Washington, D.C.: U.S. Government Printing Office, (February, 1965), pp. 21–30.

[33] Leach, "The Federal Role in the War on Poverty Program," *Law and Contemporary Problems*, Vol. 31, p. 24.

PART II

The Alpha Model State Civil-Rights Act, with Comments

THE ALPHA MODEL STATE CIVIL-RIGHTS ACT

Table of Contents

The Alpha Model State Civil-Rights Act

AN ACT

To promote and protect the welfare of the people of this state by prevention and elimination of certain unreasonable practices and policies, including discrimination based upon race, color, religion, ancestry, national origin, age, or sex; to create a state human-relations commission, providing for local sections thereof and defining the functions, powers, and duties of the commission; to regulate the relation between the state commission and local commissions; and for other purposes.

PART I. SHORT TITLE: FINDINGS AND DECLARATION OF POLICIES; LIBERAL CONSTRUCTION; GENERAL DEFINITIONS

Section 101. Short title. This Act shall be known, and may be cited, as the "[name of state] Civil Rights Act."

Section 102. Findings and policies. (a) The population of this state consists of people of many races, colors, religions, ancestries, and national origins as well as of different sexes and age groups, and economic status. It is essential to the public health, safety, welfare, peace, and progress of the state and of each community within it that this diversity serve to strengthen individual and collective efforts to achieve man's enduring goals and not be used to weaken these efforts. The latter result occurs when members of one group practice, through private or governmental institutions, discrimination and other harmful activity against members of another group in any phase of community life merely on account of their race or other normal group characteristics. Practices of this kind and the conditions accompanying them undermine the freedom and justice essential to genuine democracy. Among other things, they prevent full development and utilization of the capacities of many persons; cut them off from various kinds of economic, social, cultural, and political opportunities; deny them adequate education and training; cause among them widespread unemployment and underemployment; deprive them of earnings necessary to maintain decent standards of living; require them to resort to public relief; and produce segregated residential areas which, through their *de facto* segregated schools and typical substandard, unsafe, and unsanitary living conditions, support the whole structure of discrimination and disadvantages suffered by their inhabitants. These practices also cause or contribute to intergroup tensions and conflicts, school drop-outs, crime, juvenile delinquency, disease, fire hazards, higher welfare costs, and loss of tax revenues.

(b) It is the policy of this state to ensure that all persons enjoy the full benefits of citizenship or residence and be afforded equal opportunity to participate, on the basis of personal merit, in the social, cultural, economic, political and other phases of community life within the state, free from any discrimination on account of race, color, religion, ancestry, or national origin and from any unreasonable restrictions on account of sex, age, or economic status. In order to implement this policy it is essential that the state government assume the initiative for repairing the consequences of past denials of equal opportunities to particular groups, for preventing denials of these opportunities in the future, and for controlling and eliminating the underlying causes of intergroup-relations problems. Government initiative for accomplishing these purposes must be exercised within each community. Human-relations problems cannot be adequately solved until the government and citizenry of each community throughout the state honestly face these problems and with good will and industry work together for their solution. It is a central purpose of this Act to encourage the institution of adequate human-relations programs by each political subdivision having serious intergroup-relations problems. Where a political subdivision faced with these problems has established and maintains an adequate human-relations program administered by an effective local human-relations commission, the state government will, through the [name of state] State Human Relations Commission created by this Act, cooperate in every possible way with that local government and will confine its operations in that political subdivision to handling human-relations problems falling properly within state cognizance or not being handled by the local commission. Where a political subdivision has not established or does not maintain an adequate human-relations program to handle serious problems of intergroup relations, the state commission will administer the human-relations program established by this Act within that community through one of its local sections.

Section 103. Liberal construction. This Act shall be construed liberally to further its purposes and, more generally, to promote justice in human relations.

Section 104. General definitions. In this Act, unless the context otherwise requires,

(1) "Person" means an individual, partnership, association, corpo-

ration, joint-stock company, labor union, mutual company, trustee in bankruptcy, receiver or other fiduciary or the agent, legal representative or employee thereof, and the state, any of its political or civil subdivisions, or any agency thereof;

(2) "Commission" means the [name of state] State Human Relations Commission created by this Act;

(3) "Commissioner" means a member of the Commission;

(4) "Local section" means a section of the Commission established for a political subdivision by the Commission pursuant to Section 301.

(5) "Political subdivision" means a [city, county . . .] and any combination of two or more of these determined by the Commission to be appropriate for the purpose of establishing a local section;

(6) "Local section commissioner" means a member of a local section;

(7) "Local commission" means a human-relations commission established by a political subdivision;

(8) "Cooperative agreement" means a cooperative agreement made by the Commission under Section 402;

(9) "Negotiation function" means the function assigned to the Commission and its local sections, respectively, under Subsection (a) (3) of Section 502 and Subsection (a) (2) of Section 503;

(10) "Constructive-action function" means the function assigned to the Commission and its local sections, respectively, under Subsection (a) (5) of Section 502 and Subsection (a) (3) of Section 503;

(11) "Community" refers to either a local or a state community, or to both depending on the context;

(12) "Discrimination" means any direct or indirect exclusion, distinction, segregation, limitation, refusal, denial, or any other differentiation or preference in the treatment of a person or persons on account of race, color, religion, ancestry, national origin, age, sex, or economic status, and any denial of any right, privilege, or immunity secured or protected by the Constitution or laws of the United States.

PART II. STATE HUMAN-RELATIONS COMMISSION

Section 201. Establishment of State Human-Relations Commission. There is hereby created the [name of state] State Human Relations Commission. The membership of the Commission consists of seven commissioners to be appointed by the Governor by and with the advice of the [Senate]. The chairman of the Commission shall be designated by the Governor from its membership. The Commission may designate one of its commissioners to act as chairman during the absence or incapacity of the chairman.

Section 202. Commissioners' terms of office. The term of office of each commissioner is six years and until the appointment and qualification of his successor. Of these commissioners first appointed two shall be appointed for a term of two years, two for a term of four years, and three for a term of six years. A person appointed to fill a vacancy occurring prior to expiration of a term shall be appointed only for the unexpired part of that term.

Section 203. Quorum. Four commissioners constitute a quorum. Vacancies on the Commission do not impair the authority of the remaining commissioners to exercise the powers of the Commission.

Section 204. Outside employment; salary. No commissioner may engage in any other business or employment. The salary of each commissioner is [   ] a year. Each commissioner may obtain compensation for all expenses actually and necessarily incurred by him in the performance of his duties.

Section 205. Removal from office. The Governor may remove a commissioner for inefficiency, neglect of duty, misconduct, or malfeasance in office, after giving him a written statement of the charges against him and an opportunity to be heard concerning them.

PART III. LOCAL SECTIONS OF THE COMMISSION

Section 301. Establishment of local sections of the Commission.

(a) The Commission shall establish a local section of the Commission in each political subdivision determined by it to have serious intergroup-relations problems and not to have established and to be maintaining an adequate human-relations program administered by an effective human-relations commission.

(b) A political subdivision is conclusively presumed to have serious intergroup-relations problems if at least one thousand (1,000) Negroes, Latin Americans, or both Negroes and Latin Americans are resident or employed within it. "Latin American" means any person who has a Spanish surname.

(c) In determining whether a political subdivision has established and is maintaining an adequate human-relations program administered by an effective local commission, the Commission is to be guided by the nature of the program and powers entrusted to it under this Act.

(d) Each local section shall be known as the "[name of political subdivision]-State Human Relations Commission."

(e) The membership of each local section consists of seven local section commissioners to be appointed by the Commission, one of whom is to be designated as chairman. Each local section may designate one of its local section commissioners to act as chairman during the absence or incapacity of its chairman. A person is eligible for appointment as a local section commissioner if he lives or works in the political subdivision. The Commission is authorized to make appointments of local section commissioners on the basis of an election conducted by it within the political subdivision served by a local section. Persons over the age of seventeen who reside or work in the political subdivision are entitled to vote in an election for this purpose, which shall be conducted pursuant to regulations promulgated by the Commission.

Section 302. Authority of a local section. Each local section shall exercise all of the authority and be subject to all of the duties of the Commission within its political subdivision subject to such supervision and review of its decisions as the Commission shall provide.

Section 303. Local section commissioners' terms of office; quorum; removal from office. The provisions of Sections 202, 203, and 205 apply to local section commissions, except that the Commission shall perform the functions assigned to the Governor under those sections.

Section 304. Compensation for expenses. Each local section commissioner may obtain compensation for all expenses actually and necessarily incurred by him in the performance of his duties.

PART IV. RELATION OF THIS ACT TO SIMILAR STATE LAW;
    COOPERATIVE AGREEMENTS WITH LOCAL COMMISSIONS

Section 401. Non-repealer. Except as expressly provided, nothing in this Act shall be deemed to repeal or supersede any of the provisions of any other law of this state or of any of the political subdivisions of this state relating to regulation of intergroup-relations problems, including discrimination on account of race, color, religion, ancestry, national origin, age, sex, or economic status.

Section 402. Making of cooperative agreements with local commissions. The Commission may cooperate with a local commission established to administer laws comparable to this Act. To further such cooperation and to achieve more adequate administration of this Act, the Commission may enter into written agreements with these local commissions under which the local sections of the Commission will refrain from performing the whole or part of any one or more of their three basic functions set out in Section 503.

Section 403. Complaints covered by a cooperative agreement. Any complaint filed with or by the Commission or a local commission falling within the coverage of a cooperative agreement shall be processed by the local commission with which the agreement was made unless the chairman or a majority of the commissioners of the local commission requests the Commission to process it or unless the Commission directs that the complaint be retained by or referred to it. The request or direction that a complaint be processed by the Commission may be made after the local commission has rendered its decision, and, in this event, the Commission shall, except as it may limit the issues upon notice or by rule, exercise all the authority it would have had in making the initial decision. The rule stated in this section also applies to complaints filed with or by a local section.

Section 404. Rescission of a cooperative agreement. The Commission may rescind a cooperative agreement whenever it determines that the agreement no longer serves the interest of promoting effective achievement of the purposes of this Act.

Section 405. Effect of resort to procedure of this Act. In the absence of a cooperative agreement between the Commission and a local commission, the procedure provided by this Act shall, when invoked by an individual aggrieved relative to action covered by this Act, be exclusive and the final determination of the case shall exclude any other action of a civil nature based upon the same matter of which complaint has been made by that person.

Section 406. Effect of resort to procedure of another law. If a person institutes an action relative to conduct covered by this Act without resorting to the procedure provided by it, he may not subsequently resort to that procedure. The Commission may, however, direct a local commission receiving or filing a complaint alleging discrimination covered by this Act to refer the complaint to it for initial decision or a review of the decision of that commission in a similar manner to the procedure for complaints covered by cooperative agreements.

Section 407. Conflict between this Act and the law of political subdivisions. In the event of an alleged conflict between the interpretation of a provision of this Act and the interpretation of a similar provision contained in the law of any political subdivision, the interpretation of the provision in this Act shall apply to the latter law.

PART V. THE CENTRAL TASK, FUNCTIONS, GOALS, AND POLICIES
OF THE COMMISSION AND ITS LOCAL SECTIONS

Section 501. The central task of the Commission and its local sections. (a) The central task of a local section of the Commission is the reconstruction of intergroup relations within the community served by it so as to eliminate the causes of, ameliorate the conditions accompanying, and overcome the results flowing from discrimination and other harmful activity directed against minority and other disadvantaged groups. Performance of this task of reconstruction calls for the assembly and redirection of the maximum human and material resources within each community having serious intergroup-relations problems and bringing them to bear upon those problems in the most effective way. It demands that each of these communities be persuaded to acknowledge that the performance of this task is ultimately its own responsibility and that each of its groups become genuinely involved in discharging it.

(b) The local section is to be the major institution within a political subdivision for guiding the performance of this task and for providing as well as eliciting the appropriate leadership to secure its realization until the political subdivision undertakes its performance in an effective manner. With regard to the majority or controlling group, the local section must seek to obtain reorganization and reformation of all group actions, habits, customs, and private and official arrangements that have produced and continue to maintain the conditions adversely affecting the opportunities of minority and other disadvantaged groups. With regard to the latter, the local section must seek to move its members to confront problems of group actions, habits, customs, and private arrangements that hamper them in obtaining and maximizing upon needed opportunities; to provide them with various kinds of assistance services calculated to help them prepare for and obtain needed opportunities, and to protect them against certain typical types of exploitation and abuse. Persons within the majority or controlling group must be found who will provide wise leadership within that group so as to move it to begin to confront and resolve its intergroup-relations problems. Within minority and other disadvantaged groups leaders must be found or developed who will help these persons to perform the kinds of actions that are calculated to start and facilitate the process of dialogue and negotiation between the various groups looking to an improvement in their relations and in the opportunities available to minority and other disadvantaged groups.

(c) The central task of the Commission is analogous to that of its local sections. It is concerned with the reconstruction of intergroup relations within the entire statewide community. In addition to over-seeing and supervising the work of its local sections, the Commission is especially concerned with problems of intergroup relations that cannot be adequately handled by a local section or a local commission.

Section 502. Basic functions of the Commission. (a) The Commission shall perform the following basic functions:

(1) supporting, supervising, and reviewing the operation of its local sections so as to ensure their adequate performance of their central task with regard to reconstructing intergroup relations within the political subdivisions served, exercise of their three assigned basic functions, achievements of the goals of this Act, and implementation of the policies established for this purpose;

(2) promoting the creation of local commissions by political subdivision, and supporting, supervising, and reviewing their operation with a view to moving them to perform effectively a role essentially comparable to that assigned the Commission's local sections;

(3) negotiating with governing bodies and agencies of political subdivisions, with state agencies, and with persons and organizations having statewide operations for the taking of action by them to improve opportunities available to minority and other disadvantaged groups and utilizing of inspections, surveys, private conferences, public hearings, reports, and enforcement actions to assure the effectiveness of negotiation.

(4) processing individual complaints relative to denials of any right, privilege, or immunity secured or protected by the Constitution or laws of the United States and relative to all forms of discrimination and other harmful activity directed against minority and other disadvantaged groups by persons whose activities can be dealt with more effectively through action of the Commission than through action of its local sections or of local commissions; and

(5) undertaking various types of constructive action designed to eliminate the causes of intergroup-relations problems insofar as they have their source outside local communities, to deal with actions and conditions affecting the public welfare that result from the continued

existence of these problems, and to move the statewide community and its groups to direct the maximum resources of that community, both human and material, to the accomplishment of these objectives.

(b) It is the sense of the Legislature that the processing of individual complaints should be relegated as far as possible to local sections and that the negotiation and constructive-active functions of the Commission should receive the greatest emphasis in its administration of the Act.

Section 503. Basic functions of the local sections. (a) Each local section shall perform, within the political subdivision it serves, three basic functions:

(1) processing individual complaints relative to denials of any right, privilege, or immunity secured or protected by the Constitution or laws of the United States and relative to all forms of discrimination and other harmful activity directed against minority and other disadvantaged groups;

(2) negotiating with wide sectors of businesses, unions, professions, official agencies, and private organizations for the taking of action by them to improve opportunities available to minority and other disadvantaged groups and utilizing inspections, surveys, private conferences, public hearings, reports, and enforcement actions to assure the effectiveness of negotiation; and

(3) undertaking various types of constructive action designed to eliminate the causes of intergroup-relations problems within the local community, to deal with action and conditions affecting the public welfare that result from the continued existence of these problems, and to move the local community and its groups to direct the maximum resources of that community, both human and material, to the accomplishment of these objectives.

(b) It is the sense of the Legislature that the negotiation and constructive-action functions of each local section should receive the greatest emphasis in its administration of the Act.

Section 504. Goals of the Commission and its local sections. The Commission and its local sections shall seek to achieve the following goals in performing their basic tasks and functions:

(a) Economic opportunity:

(1) complete equality of economic opportunity, unrestricted by considerations of race, color, religion, ancestry, or national origin or by unreasonable considerations of sex or age, affirmatively implemented in all areas and all levels of economic enterprise; in employ-

ment, including supervisory and executive levels; in the professions and trades; in proprietorship and management; in purchasing or renting land or building space for business purposes; in obtaining financial credit; and in dealing with places of public accommodations; and

(2) full encouragement of aspirations, motivation, initiative, persistence in job hunting, and development of requisite skills among all elements of the population, so that equality of opportunity will not be subverted by adherence to traditional patterns of employment or by ignorance, cynicism, and indolence.

(b) Housing opportunity:

(1) complete equality of opportunity to select and purchase, or rent and occupy, a home, or to finance the purchase of a home in accordance with the interests of the individual or family, ability to pay, and such other reasonable standards as may be applied equally to all others regardless of race, color, religion, ancestry, or national origin, or unreasonable considerations of sex, age, or economic status; and

(2) purposeful, open encouragement to persons and families of all groups to seek homes in the general market on an ethnically and religiously decentralized pattern; promotion of racially and religiously inclusive communities; and encouragement of real-estate practices conducive to such neighborhood patterns.

(c) Educational and training opportunities:

(1) an educational system that provides all children and adults with adequate opportunity to obtain education and training for responsible citizenship and for economic productivity in accordance with their needs and potentialities, without handicap because of race, color, religion, ancestry, national origin, age, sex, or economic status;

(2) special educational programs to compensate for the cultural deprivation of particular segments of the population resulting from the history of discrimination based upon race, color, ancestry, national origin, or other similar factors;

(3) an educational system that gives each child the right to choose any high school that fits his particular need;

(4) an educational system that gives each child the experience of shared learning experiences and life values with other children of different races, nationalities, and economic status;

(5) an educational system that provides each child with a full day's instruction;

(6) an educational system that distributes the talents of its in-

structional staff so as to allocate a fair share of experience and compe-
tence to each school;

(7) an educational system whose teachers have received adequate training in human relations and in the history and culture of
minority groups;

(8) an educational system that employs a building program and
a system of school zones designed to secure an integrated student body
at the high school and junior high school levels.

(d) Associational opportunities:

(1) freedom for all persons of all races, colors, religions, ancestries, or national origins to form and maintain voluntary associations
without interference, fear, or shame either with persons belonging to
the same ethnic or other groups, or with persons belonging to different
ethnic groups, for personal, religious, social, cultural, economic, or
political purposes.

(2) recognition and respect from persons of all groups for the
worth and dignity of all others regardless of race, color, religion,
ancestry, national origin, age, sex, or economic status; and

(3) prohibition of any efforts on the part of any persons or
groups to act against or limit the rights and privileges of persons of
different race, color, religion, ancestry, national origin, age, sex, or
economic status.

(e) Community-relations status:

(1) a community-wide public awareness, shared by persons of
all races, colors, religions, ancestries, national origins, ages, sexes, and
economic brackets, and in all neighborhoods, that all citizens of the
community share an interdependence and mutuality of concern for
the general safety, health, and welfare, and that intercommunication
and cooperation are essential for the good of each individual and for
the common good.

(f) Administration of law:

(1) full and equal protection of the law to all persons, equal
treatment and due courtesy to, and respect for, all persons by all law-
enforcement officers, regardless of race, color, religion, ancestry,
national origin, age, sex, or economic status;

(2) respect for the law; respect for, and cooperation with, law-
enforcement officers by all persons of all races, colors, religions, ancestries, national origins, ages, sexes, and economic brackets; and

(3) equal opportunity to obtain the services, facilities, benefits,

advantages, assistance, or licenses generally available to other persons under any governmental program.

Section 505. Implemental policies of the Commission and its local sections. The following implemental policies are to be pursued by the Commission and its local sections in performing their negotiation and constructive-action functions:

(1) establishment and dissemination of reliable information about the nature and status of intergroup-relations problems within the community served;

(2) initiation of continuing discussion and negotiation between members of the majority or controlling group and members of minority and other disadvantaged groups concerning intergroup-relations problems within the community served, with a view to their achieving growing agreement upon appropriate actions to resolve the problems through

(A) formation of Commission committees with representatives from both types of groups to assist the Commission in achieving this objective;

(B) stimulation of community organizations to perform this function;

(C) conduct of public forums, conferences, and similar discussions concerning intergroup-relations problems; and

(D) persuasion of government agencies to utilize advisory committees made up of members of minority and other disadvantaged groups as well as members of the majority or controlling group;

(3) development of leaders within each group in the community served to provide leadership within the group for study and discussion of and action to resolve intergroup-relations problems and provision of various kinds of assistance to them in performing this function;

(4) definition of the optimum role in dealing with intergroup-relations problems for particular individuals and institutions, such as ministers, lawyers, physicians, bankers, builders, real-estate agents, mass media, police department, public schools, public hospitals, churches, and associations of a business, professional, educational, trade, civic, or religious nature;

(5) establishment and maintenance on a continuing basis of a system for anticipating, handling, and preventing intergroup tensions and conflicts and dealing with their underlying causes that will involve the participation of all needed elements of the local and state community and government served;

(6) organization of and assistance to local community and neighborhood councils designed for study, discussion, and action with regard to resolving problems of the community and neighborhood, such as change in ethnic composition, deterioration of property, failure to enforce law, lack of adequate public facilities and government services, intergroup tensions and conflicts, inadequate economic opportunities, juvenile delinquency, crime, and similar matters;

(7) organization of programs to deal with activities designed to exploit and abuse members of minority and other disadvantaged groups or to exploit the existence of intergroup-relations problems, such as blockbusting, sharp-credit practices, unfair methods of selling or renting real property, selling of personal property below normal quality and above going market prices, and similar practices;

(8) processing of complaints of abuse of authority by law-enforcement officers and taking of appropriate action to eliminate abuses;

(9) provision of services to governmental departments and agencies with regard to intergroup-relations problems, such as the training of agency personnel assigned responsibility in this area, holding of institutes and workshops to explore the proper agency role and policies in dealing with intergroup-relations problems, and development of materials on intergroup relations for agency use;

(10) development and proposal of governmental programs to deal with matters contributing to poor intergroup relations, working for their adoption, and provision of assistance in their implementation. A good example of one of the matters with regard to which this function can be profitably exercised is a *de facto* segregated public school system;

(11) provision of various kinds of assistance services to members of minority and other disadvantaged groups, and cooperation with private agencies in providing these services, including, among others, the following:

(A) assistance to newcomers in understanding and adjusting to their new community environment;

(B) organization of tutorial services and classes for children and adults seeking to upgrade their education and skills;

(C) examination of refusals of government agencies to grant various forms of welfare assistance to indigents, assisting applicants for this assistance to conform to agency requirements, and securing redress for unwarranted refusals;

(D) securing assistance for indigents from private organizations desiring to be helpful but lacking personnel or contacts to facilitate their desire;

(E) assistance to members of minority groups desiring to obtain housing in areas occupied principally or solely by members of the majority or controlling group, by developing support in those areas for integrated living, contacting members of minority groups financially able to move to these areas, instructing the latter on how and where to look for integrated housing, providing housing aides to accompany a minority-group family seeking housing, and conducting an educational campaign in mass media in favor of integrated living;

(F) conduct of various kinds of counselling services for members of minority and other disadvantaged groups relative to purchase of property, securing of loans, applying for employment, and budgeting of family income; and

(G) investigation and resolution of complaints about the operation and policies of governmental agencies.

PART VI. POWERS AND DUTIES OF THE COMMISSION
AND ITS LOCAL SECTIONS

Section 601. General powers and duties of the Commission. The Commission has the following powers and duties:

(1) to establish and maintain in office in the city of [   ], an office for each of its local sections within the political subdivision for which it is established, and such other offices within the state as it may deem necessary;

(2) to meet and function at any place within the state.

(3) to appoint an executive director and any attorneys, hearing examiners, clerks, and other employees and agents for itself and its local sections as it may deem necessary, and to fix the compensation of these officers, employees, and agents;

(4) to accept outside funds, gifts, or bequests, public or private, to help finance the activities of itself or of its local sections;

(5) to enter into cooperative working arrangements with federal agencies having related responsibilities when these agreements will aid in carrying out the purposes and provisions of this Act;

(6) to adopt, promulgate, amend, and rescind rules and regulations to effectuate the purposes and provisions of this Act;

(7) to submit at least once a year to the Legislature and to the

Governor a report concerning the activities of itself and its local sections and its recommendations.

Section 602. Implemental powers and duties of the Commission and its local sections. The Commission and its local sections have the following implemental powers and duties in performing their basic tasks and functions and in carrying out their implemental policies:

(1) to make or arrange for studies in any field of human relationship that will promote the purposes of this Act;

(2) to investigate by means of public hearings or otherwise any particular or general conditions having an adverse effect upon intergroup relations, including alleged violations of the law of the state or of a political subdivision;

(3) to publish the results of research, studies, and investigations and other materials that will promote the purposes of this Act;

(4) to work with interested citizens, with federal, state, and local agencies, and with civic, community, racial, religious, ethnic, business, industrial, labor, and civil-rights organizations;

(5) to establish advisory committees, when this will aid in effectuating the purposes of this Act, for

(A) studying and reporting upon problems of discrimination based upon race, color, religion, ancestry, national origin, age, or sex, and other harmful activity directed toward minority and other disadvantaged groups;

(B) fostering, through community effort or otherwise, goodwill and cooperation among the groups and elements of the population; and

(C) making recommendations for the development of policies and procedures that will aid the Commission or its local sections in carrying out the purposes of this Act;

(6) to reimburse members of advisory committees for expenses incurred in the rendering of services by them and to provide them with technical and clerical assistance for the performance of their duties;

(7) to use such voluntary and uncompensated services of private persons and institutions and officials as may from time to time be offered and needed to perform the functions and duties described in Subsections (1), (2), (3), and (5);

(8) to initiate or receive, investigate, and act upon complaints of discrimination or other harmful activity directed toward minority

and other disadvantaged groups, whether or not specifically prohibited by this Act;

(9) to refer to a federal agency any complaints specified for reference in a cooperative working arrangement with that agency or otherwise specifically directed by that agency to be referred to it as well as any complaint that the Commission determines should be referred to that agency for initial action or review;

(10) in processing any complaint, as appropriate, to utilize methods of persuasion, conciliation, and mediation or informal adjustment of grievances, to hold public hearings, and, in the case of complaints of alleged unlawful discriminatory acts, to make findings of fact, issue orders, and publish its findings of fact and orders in accordance with this Act;

(11) in holding public hearings for the purpose of investigation or for processing complaints to subpoena witnesses, compel their attendance, administer oaths, take the testimony of any person under oath, and in connection with this to require the production for examination of any books or papers relating to any matter under investigation or in question; and

(12) to obtain upon request and to use the services of all departments and agencies of the State and its political subdivisions.

Section 603. Powers and duties of local sections. Each local section has the following powers and duties in performing its basic task and functions and in carrying out its implemental policies:

(1) to meet and function at any place within the political subdivision for which it was established; and

(2) to submit at least once a year to the Commission a report concerning its activities and recommendations.

PART VII. PROCEDURES RELATIVE TO COMPLAINTS;
REMEDIES; JUDICIAL REVIEW; RECORDS

Section 701. Definitions. In this part

(1) "Commission" means either the Commission or a local section, as these terms are defined in Section 104, depending on which is handling a charge or complaint of a discriminatory act. In Sections 714, 715, 716, 717, 718, and 719 "Commission" means either the Commission, as just defined, or a hearing panel;

(2) "Commissioner" means either a commissioner or a local section commissioner, as these terms are defined in Section 104, de-

pending on whether the Commission or a local section is handling a charge or complaint of a discriminatory act;

(3) "Civil-rights organization" means an organization which, under its articles of incorporation or association, is organized to deal with intergroup-relations problems;

(4) "Chairman" means either the chairman of the Commission or the chairman of a local section, as these terms are defined in Section 104, depending on whether the Commission or a local section is handling a charge or complaint of a discriminatory act;

(5) "Discriminatory act" means any act or practice of discrimination, including an unlawful discriminatory act;

(6) "Discrimination" means any direct or indirect exclusion, distinction, segregation, limitation, refusal, denial, or any other differentiation or preference in the treatment of a person or persons on account of race, color, religion, ancestry, national origin, age, sex, or economic status, and any denial of any right, privilege, or immunity secured or protected by the Constitution or laws of the United States;

(7) "Charge" means an initial complaint filed under Section 702 of this Act;

(8) "Party or parties" means the complainant, individual aggrieved, respondent, and any person admitted as a party, or properly seeking and entitled as of right to be admitted as a party in a proceeding under this part;

(9) "Complainant" means a person who, with authority to file a charge under Section 702 or to request the filing of a complaint under Section 711, does so;

(10) "Individual aggrieved" means the individual aggrieved by an alleged discriminatory act that is the subject of a charge filed under Section 702 or of a complaint filed under Section 711. The individual aggrieved is also a complainant when he exercises the authority to file a charge or to request the filing of a complaint;

(11) "Respondent" means the person whose action is alleged to be a discriminatory act in a charge or a complaint; it also includes an official agency made a party respondent to a proceeding in which an official or employee of that agency is alleged to have committed a discriminatory act;

(12) "Investigating commissioner" means the commissioner designated by the chairman under Section 704 to assume responsibility for investigation of a charge;

(13) The statements "probable cause exists" or "probable cause

does not exist" refer to the presence or absence, respectively, of *prima facie* evidence that a discriminatory act has been committed as judged in accordance with the criterion for determining the existence of probable cause stated in Subsection (c) of Section 705;

(14) "Unlawful discriminatory act" means a discriminatory act made unlawful under Part VIII of this Act;

(15) "Hearing panel" means one or more commissioners or staff members of the Commission appointed by the chairman under Subsection (a) of Section 712;

(16) "Review hearing" means a hearing on review of a finding of no probable cause to believe a charge conducted under Section 708;

(17) "Review hearing panel" means one or more commissioners or staff members of the Commission appointed by the chairman under Subsection (b) of Section 708 to conduct a review hearing;

(18) "Complaint" means a formal complaint filed under Subsection (a) of Section 711;

(19) "Conciliation agreement" means an agreement reached between the parties to a proceeding for the purpose of adjusting a charge or complaint of the Commission of a discriminatory act under Section 709.

Section 702. Filing a charge. (a) Any individual aggrieved by an alleged discriminatory act or his agent may file a charge complaining of that act with the Commission.

(b) A commissioner, the Attorney General, or any civil-rights organization having reason to believe that a discriminatory act has been committed may file a charge complaining of that act with the Commission.

Section 703. Form, filing time, and contents of a charge. A charge is sufficient for the purpose of Commission action if the charge

(1) is filed on or before one year after the alleged discriminatory act allegedly occurred;

(2) is in writing;

(3) states the names and addresses of the respondent and the individual aggrieved or sufficient information to permit identification of those persons;

(4) states the particulars concerning the allegedly discriminatory act; and

(5) is in the form prescribed by the Commission and contains any other information that the Commission may require.

Section 704. Designation of investigating commissioner; service of charge. Upon the filing of a charge the chairman shall

(1) designate one of the commissioners to assume responsibility for investigating its allegations, and

(2) furnish the parties with a copy of the charge.

Section 705. Probable-cause investigation. (a) The investigating commissioner, upon being designated, shall investigate promptly the allegations of the charge and determine whether or not probable cause exists for believing the allegations are true.

(b) In making his investigation, the investigating commissioner may

(1) use the commission staff, and

(2) issue subpoenas to the respondent to furnish information, records, or other documents relating to the allegations in the charge.

(c) Probable cause exists for believing that a discriminatory act has occurred if there is *prima facie* evidence of the discriminatory act in the sense that, when considered by itself and without regard to evidence to the contrary, the evidence is of a substantial nature in support of the allegations of the charge. Otherwise probable cause does not exist for a belief of this kind. The determination relative to probable cause is not to be made by regarding and weighing the evidence not supporting the charge against the evidence supporting it.

Section 706. Temporary judicial restraining orders. (a) If the investigating commissioner finds that probable cause exists for believing the allegations of a charge complaining of an unlawful discriminatory act, the chairman may, at that or any subsequent time prior to final disposition of the case, direct the Commission's lawyer to sue in a court of competent jurisdiction for appropriate injunctive relief against the respondent to prevent any conduct by him tending to render ineffectual any steps that the Commission, a hearing panel, or the courts may take to eliminate or remedy the unlawful discriminatory act, and seek orders restraining and enjoining the respondent from disposing to another or otherwise making unavailable the subject matter with regard to which the discriminatory act allegedly occurred.

(b) The court may grant temporary relief or a restraining order upon terms and conditions that it deems just and proper pending the final determination of the proceedings under this Act.

(c) If the court grants relief or an order under Subsection (b), the Commission shall finally dispose of the case on or before the thirtieth day after the effective date of the court's order, unless the time for rendering this decision is extended by the court upon terms and conditions that it deems just and proper. If the Commission dismisses or a court directs dismissal of the charge or complaint after the court has granted relief or an order under Subsection (b), the respondent may recover from the state damages and costs sustained by reason of this relief or order in an action in that court.

Section 707. Action on a finding of no probable cause. (a) If the investigating commissioner finds that probable cause does not exist for believing the allegations in the charge, he shall give written notice to the parties

(1) of his finding and the reasons for it; and

(2) that the charge will be dismissed on the tenth day after the notification is made unless a request for a review hearing is made earlier than that time.

(b) The investigating commissioner shall state in the written notice to the parties a brief, simple explanation of the procedure for obtaining a review hearing.

(c) The investigating commissioner shall send the notice within ten days after he makes the finding of no probable cause.

(d) If no party files a timely request for a review hearing, the Commission shall issue an order dismissing the charge and serve it upon the parties. This order is not reviewable in the courts.

Section 708. Review of a finding of no probable cause. (a) After a finding that probable cause does not exist for believing the charge, the chairman shall grant a request by a party for a review hearing if

(1) the request is made on or before the tenth day after the day the investigating commissioner gave notice of this finding; and

(2) the request is in the form and contains the information required by a rule of the Commission.

(b) If the chairman grants a request for a review hearing, he shall appoint a review-hearing panel consisting of one or more commissioners or staff members unless the Commission itself elects to conduct the hearing *en banc*. No commissioner or staff member who assisted him in investigating the charge is eligible for appointment or service.

(c) After appointment of a review-hearing panel or election of the Commission to conduct the review hearing, the chairman shall cause to be issued and served upon the parties a notice of hearing stating the place and time of the hearing and the review-hearing panel, if any, which will conduct the hearing.

(d) At the review hearing, any party may present any information supporting the allegations of the charge.

(e) If the Commission or review-hearing panel finds that probable cause does not exist for believing the charge, as this criterion is defined in Subsection (c) of Section 704, the Commission shall issue an order dismissing the charge and cause it to be served upon the parties.

Section 709. Conciliation efforts before and after finding of probable cause. (a) If the investigating commissioner determines that probable causes exists for believing the charge, he shall give written notice of the determination to the parties and of a date and time for them to appear at a conciliation meeting with him for the purpose of attempting to adjust the matter charged.

(b) At any time after the filing of a charge or a complaint involving an unlawful discriminatory act, the respondent may request a reasonable time within which to permit negotiation of a conciliation agreement containing a consent cease and desist order disposing of the whole or any part of the proceeding. The allowance of negotiation, and its duration, subject to Section 710(c), shall be at the discretion of the chairman or the official or officials in charge of the case at the time the request is made.

(c) The allowance of negotiation under Subsection (b) does not operate to interfere with the processing of a charge. The investigating commissioner shall, at the conciliation meeting called under Subsection (a), try to reach an adjustment of the matters charged, that in his judgment is a satisfactory one, utilizing persuasion, conciliation and mediation for this purpose. He shall also seek, where appropriate, to obtain incorporation of the adjustment into a conciliation agreement containing a consent cease and desist order.

Section 710. Conciliation agreements and action upon them. (a) A conciliation agreement including a consent cease and desist order may be accepted by the investigating commissioner or other official or officials in charge of the case only if it

(1) embodies an adjustment of the matters complained of in the charge or complaint that is judged to be satisfactory; and

(2) contains

(A) an admission by the respondent of jurisdictional facts;

(B) a provision that the charge or complaint may be used to construe the terms of the consent cease and desist order;

(C) a provision that the consent cease and desist order has the same force and effect as if entered after a full hearing;

(D) a provision that the agreement does not become a part of the official record of the proceeding until its acceptance becomes final;

(E) a provision that the entire record on which the consent cease and desist order is based consists solely of the charge or complaint and the agreement;

(F) a waiver of the requirement that the order be accompanied by a statement of findings of fact and conclusions;

(G) a waiver of further procedural steps before the investigating commissioner, the hearing panel, or the Commission;

(H) a provision that the order may be altered, modified, or set aside in the manner provided by law for other orders; and

(I) a waiver by the respondent of any right to challenge or contest the validity of the consent cease and desist order entered in accordance with the agreement.

(b) A conciliation agreement including a consent cease and desist order may contain a statement that signing the agreement is for settlement purposes only and does not constitute an admission by the respondent that he has violated the Act as alleged in the charge or complaint. It may cover only part of the matters of which complaint is made. Any part of those matters not covered by the agreement is to be treated as if no agreement had been reached.

(c) On or before the thirtieth day after giving notice that probable cause exists or, in the case of allowance of negotiation after the filing of a complaint, on or before the expiration of the time granted for negotiation, the investigating commissioner or other official or officials in charge of the case shall either accept any agreement reached and submitted by the parties or reject it. If the decision is to accept the agreement, that decision shall constitute an order of the Commission on the thirtieth day after its service upon the parties unless the Commission issues an order staying the effective date of the decision or places the case on its own docket for review. If the decision is to reject the agreement, that decision shall constitute an order of the Commission immediately upon its service upon the parties.

Section 711. Filing of complaint upon failure of conciliation; right to hearing. (a) If the investigating commissioner fails to obtain a satisfactory adjustment of a charge concerning a discriminatory act on or before the thirtieth day after his finding that probable cause exists for believing its allegations, he may, and upon request of the complainant or individual aggrieved in the case of a charge of an unlawful discriminatory act he shall, cause to be issued and served upon the respondent a formal complaint, in the name of the Commission, concerning that act. He shall also send copies of the complaint to all parties.

(b) At any time after his determination that probable cause exists to believe a charge, if he judges circumstances so warrant, the investigating commissioner may cease his efforts to obtain a satisfactory adjustment by conciliation and follow the procedure in Subsection (a).

(c) A formal complaint is sufficient if it meets the requirement of Section 703 for a charge.

(d) If the investigating commissioner issues a formal complaint, he shall also immediately issue to the respondent a notice of hearing stating the place and time of the hearing, the hearing panel, if any, that will conduct the hearing, and the requirement that the respondent appear to answer the complaint. He shall also send copies of the notice to all parties.

(e) A failure or refusal to issue a complaint upon request of the complainant or individual aggrieved in accordance with Subsection (a) is deemed to be an order of the Commission.

(f) The Commission, hearing panel, or complainant may amend a complaint at any time prior to issuance of an order based on the complaint.

Section 712. Designation of hearing panel, presiding officer, and person to present complainant's case. (a) The chairman shall appoint one or more commissioners or staff members as a hearing panel to conduct the hearing of a formal complaint. The Commission also may, at its election, conduct the hearing *en banc.* No commissioner or any staff member who assisted him on the case in processing the charge prior to filing that complaint is eligible for appointment and neither may participate in the hearing of the complaint except as a witness nor in the decision of the case.

(b) If the chairman appoints two or more members of a hearing panel, he shall designate one of them to serve as presiding officer at the hearing. The presiding officer shall rule on all matters of practice and procedure.

(c) The chairman shall designate either one or more of the Commission's attorneys or other staff members to present the complainant's case. The chairman may also designate an attorney representing the complainant or individual aggrieved as assistant to the attorney or staff member designated under this subsection.

(d) The respondent may file an answer in person or by registered or certified mail in accordance with rules of the Commission. The Commission shall furnish a copy of the answer to all parties. The respondent may amend an answer at any time prior to issuance of an order based on the complaint.

Section 713. Procedure at hearing. (a) Rules stated in this section and in Sections 714, 715, 716, 717, 718, and 719 as being applicable to the Commission are also applicable to a hearing panel.

(b) A party may appear at the hearing in person or otherwise, with or without counsel.

(c) The Commission is not bound by the strict rules of evidence prevailing in courts of law or equity. Any evidence may be received, but the Commission, as a matter of policy, shall exclude irrelevant, immaterial, and unduly repetitious evidence.

(d) Any party and, at the discretion of the Commission, any person may present oral and documentary evidence, submit rebuttal evidence, and conduct whatever examination or cross-examination may be required for a full and true discourse of the facts.

(e) All testimony is to be given under oath.

(f) The Commission may subpoena witnesses, compel their attendance, administer oaths, take testimony under oath, and receive or require the production of documentary evidence relating to the matter in question.

(g) The Commission, on request, shall issue subpoenas on behalf of any party if he shows the general relevance and reasonable scope of the evidence sought.

(h) The hearing is open to the public.

Section 714. Transcripts and records. (a) The presiding officer shall have the testimony taken at the hearing recorded either by a stenographer or by a mechanical recorder.

(b) If a stenographer records the testimony, the presiding officer shall have the testimony transcribed. If the testimony is recorded on a mechanical recorder, only those parts of it designated by the parties need be transcribed.

(c) The transcript of testimony and exhibits and all papers and requests filed in the proceeding constitute the exclusive record for decision.

(d) The presiding officer shall make the record available to any party if he pays lawfully prescribed costs.

(e) If decision rests on official notice of a material fact not appearing in the record evidence, the presiding officer shall afford any party, on timely request, an opportunity to show the contrary.

Section 715. Findings and decision. (a) After the hearing is completed, the presiding officer shall give the parties a reasonable opportunity to submit proposed findings of fact and conclusions and supporting reasons for the proposals.

(b) After the time allowed for submitting proposals has expired, the Commission shall make a tentative decision. The Commission shall include in this decision its findings of fact and conclusions and the reasons supporting them.

(c) The presiding officer shall cause a copy of the tentative decision to be served on the parties.

(d) On or before twenty (20) days after the day the tentative decision is served on the parties, any party may file with the Commission exceptions to the findings of fact and conclusions, with a brief supporting its exceptions, or may file a brief supporting the findings of fact and conclusions.

(e) If exceptions are filed under Subsection (d) of this section, the Commission shall grant the party filing them an opportunity to present argument in support of them. If no exceptions are filed or, after hearing argument on exceptions filed, the Commission shall proceed to make its final decision. The Commission shall include in this decision its findings of fact and conclusions and the reasons supporting them.

(f) The Commission may not make its final decision or issue an order based upon it unless

(1) the respondent has had the opportunity to be heard on the complaint, as amended, on which the decision and order are based;

(2) every member of the Commission participating in the decision or issuance of the order has considered the whole record or such parts of it as may be cited by any party; and

(3) the decision or order is supported by and is in accordance with the reliable, probative, and substantial evidence in the record.

Section 716. Order on a finding of a violation. (a) If the Commission in its final decision determines that the respondent has committed an unlawful discriminatory act, it shall issue an order requiring the respondent

(1) to cease and desist from committing that act; and

(2) to take affirmative action that will effectuate the purposes of this Act and be just and proper.

(b) The order may include a requirement that the respondent file with the Commission a report of the manner in which it complies with the order.

(c) The affirmative action that may be required under Subsection (a) (2) of this section includes, but is not limited to,

(1) hiring, reinstatement, or upgrading of employees with or without pay;

(2) admission or restoration of individuals to union membership, admission to or participation in a guidance program, apprenticeship training program, on-the-job training program, or other occupational training or retraining program, with the utilization of reasonable criteria in an objective manner in the admission of individuals to such programs;

(3) institution of occupational training programs so as to give one group of employees as fair an opportunity for advancement as any other group of employees;

(4) admission of individuals to a place of public accommodation or an educational institution;

(5) sale, exchange, lease, rental, assignment or sublease of real property to an individual;

(6) extension to all individuals of the full and equal enjoyment of the accommodations, advantages, facilities, benefits, privileges, services, or goods of the respondent;

(7) posting notices in conspicuous places in the respondent's business, place of public accommodation, educational institution, organizational offices, or other offices and places of operation in the form prescribed by the Commission and inclusion of such notices in advertising material;

(8) cancellation, rescission or revocation of a contract, deed, lease or other instrument transferring real property, which is the subject of a complaint of an unlawful discriminatory act, to a person who had actual knowledge or record notice, prior to the transfer or the execution of the legally binding obligation to make the transfer, that a determination of probable cause had been made with respect to the discriminatory act;

(9) payment to the individual aggrieved of profits obtained by

the respondent through a violation of Section 845, subject to the principles of equity; and

(10) payment to the individual aggrieved of damages for an injury caused by an unlawful discriminatory act and costs, including a reasonable attorney's fee. Unless greater damages are proven, damages may be assessed at $500 for each violation.

(d) The affirmative action that may be required of an official agency under Subsection (a)(2) of this section, in a case involving a respondent official or agency employee who has committed an unlawful discriminatory act, also includes, but is not limited to

(1) suspension of respondent from office or employment for such period of time as the Commission may deem necessary;

(2) removing of respondent from office or employment;

(3) disqualifying respondent from holding the office or employment through which the unlawful discriminatory act was accomplished or any other government office or employment for such period of time not to exceed ten years as in the judgment of the Commission may be necessary to effectuate the policies of this Act;

(4) demotion of the respondent;

(5) reduction of the respondent's pay;

(6) reprimand of the respondent; and

(7) any other disciplinary action that might be taken against the respondent by the official agency that he serves as a sanction for a violation of law in the carrying out of his office or employment.

(e) The affirmative action that may be required of an official agency under Subsection (a)(2) of this section, in a case involving an official or employee of that agency who has committed an unlawful discriminatory act, also includes, but is not limited to

(1) expunction and destruction of the criminal record made concerning the individual aggrieved by that act on the basis of a report by that official or employee in connection with the transaction in which that act was performed; and

(2) payment of any damages and costs assessed against that official or employee.

(f) The presiding officer shall cause a copy of the final decision and order to be served upon all parties.

Section 717. Binding effect of decision on other agencies. (a) The finding of the Commission that a respondent has committed an unlawful discriminatory act is binding on any official agency of the state or a political subdivision thereof that issued a license or provided official financial assistance to a program of activity under which the act was committed.

(b) The finding of the Commission that a respondent committed an unlawful discriminatory act is binding on any official agency of the state or political subdivision thereof that awarded the contract in the performance of which the act was committed.

(c) The presiding officer shall cause a copy of the final decision and order to be furnished to an official agency subject to Subsections (a) and (b) of this section.

Section 718. Order on a finding of no violation. (a) If the Commission in its final decision determines that the respondent has not committed an unlawful discriminatory act, it shall state its findings of fact and conclusions and issue an order dismissing the complaint as to the respondent.

(b) The presiding officer shall furnish all parties with a copy of the final decision and order.

Section 719. Decision and report on a finding of a discriminatory act that is not unlawful. (a) If the Commission in its final decision determines that the respondent has committed a discriminatory act that is not unlawful, it shall issue a report recommending to the respondent that he

(1) cease and desist from committing that act; and

(2) take affirmative action that will effectuate the purposes of this Act and be just and proper.

(b) The affirmative action that may be recommended under Subsection (a)(2) of this section includes, but is not limited to, any of the actions set out in Subsections (c), (d), and (e) of Section 716.

Section 720. Judicial review; enforcement. (a) Any party to the proceeding and any person aggrieved by an order of the Commission may obtain judicial review of the order and the Commission may obtain an order of court for its enforcement in a proceeding under this section.

(b) The proceeding for review or enforcement shall be filed in the [court in a county (insert appropriate intermediate appellate court)] in which the alleged unlawful discriminatory act which is the subject of the order occurred or in which a respondent resides or transacts business.

(c) The proceeding for review or enforcement is initiated by filing a petition in the court. Copies of the petition shall be served upon all parties of record. Within thirty (30) days after service of the petition upon the Commission or its filing by the Commission, or within such further time as the court may allow, the Commission shall transmit to the court the original or a certified copy of the entire record upon which the order is based, including any transcript of testimony, which need not be printed. By stipulation of all parties to the review proceeding, the record may be shortened.

(d) Upon initiation of a review or enforcement proceeding, the court may

(1) grant such temporary relief or restraining order as it deems just and proper; and

(2) make and enter upon the pleadings, testimony, and proceedings set forth in the transcript an order enforcing, modifying and enforcing as so modified, or setting aside in whole or in part the order of the Commission.

(e) The findings of the Commission as to the facts shall be conclusive if supported by reliable, probative, and substantial evidence on the record considered as a whole.

(f) No objection that has not been urged before the Commission shall be considered by the court unless the failure to urge the objection is excused for good cause shown. Any party may move the court to remit the case to the Commission in the interest of justice for the purpose of adducing additional specified and material evidence and seeking findings thereon, provided that he shows reasonable grounds for the failure to adduce such evidence before the Commission.

(g) The jurisdiction of the [   ] court shall be exclusive and its final judgment or decree shall be subject to review by the [   ] court in the same manner and form and with the same effect as in appeals from a final judgment or decree in a [special proceeding].

(h) The Commission's copy of the testimony shall be available at all reasonable times to all parties for examination without cost, whether or not in connection with judicial review of the order of the Commission.

(i) A proceeding under this section must be initiated within thirty (30) days after a copy of the order of the Commission is received, unless the Commission is the petitioner. A party is deemed to have received a copy of an order of the Commission, in the case of refusal to issue a complaint under Section 711, on the seventh day following the party's request for its issuance. If no proceeding is initiated by a party or other aggrieved person under this section within the permitted period, the Commission may obtain a decree of the court for enforcement of its order upon showing that a copy of the petition for enforcement was served on the respondent and that the respondent is subject to the jurisdiction of the court.

Section 721. Inspection; records. (a) The Commission and any designated representative of the Commission shall have access at any reasonable time to premises, records, and documents relevant to a charge or complaint and the right to examine, photograph, and copy evidence upon presenting written authorization of the chairman.

(b) Every employer, employment agency, labor organization, and [the state official agency performing the function of a public employment office under a cooperative agreement with the United States Employment Service] shall make and keep such records relating to race, color, ancestry, national origin, sex, or age as the Commission may prescribe from time to time by rule, after public hearing, as reasonably necessary for the purpose of showing compliance with this Act.

(c) The Commission, by regulation, shall require each person subject to this Act who controls an apprenticeship or other training program to keep all records reasonably necessary to carry out the purpose of this Act, including, but not limited to, a list of applicants who wish to participate in such program, including the chronological order in which such applications were received, and shall furnish to the Commission upon request, a detailed description of the manner in which persons are selected to participate in the apprenticeship or other training programs.

(d) Every person subject to this Act shall

(1) make and keep such records relevant to the determination of whether discriminatory acts have been or are being committed;

(2) preserve such records for such periods; and

(3) make such reports therefrom

as the Commission shall prescribe by regulation or order as reasonable, necessary, or appropriate for the enforcement of this Act or the regulations or orders thereunder.

(e) Witnesses whose depositions are taken or who are summoned before the Commission or its agents shall be entitled to the same witness and mileage fees as are paid to witnesses in the courts of the state.

Section 722. Posting notices of pending proceedings. If the investigating commissioner finds that probable cause exists for believing the allegations of a charge complaining of an unlawful discriminatory act relative to real property, the chairman may cause a notice to be posted on all entrances to the real property which is the subject of the complaint, for a period not to exceed ten days, stating that prospective transferees will take the real property subject to the rights of the complainant or individual aggrieved and to the power of the Commission to nullify a transfer of the real property.

PART VIII. UNLAWFUL DISCRIMINATORY ACTS

Subpart A. Definitions

Section 801. Definitions. In this Act

(1) "Official agency" means an authority of the government of [name of state], or a political subdivision thereof, or their members and employees;

(2) "Official financial assistance" means financial assistance provided by an official agency;

(3) "License" means the whole or any part of any official agency permit, certificate, approval, registration, charter, membership, or other form of permission;

(4) "Age" refers to the age of a person between thirty-five and sixty-five years of age;

(5) "Police officer" means any police officer of any official agency.

Subpart B.   Unlawful Discriminatory Acts in General: Discrimination by Police Officers, Official Agencies, and Programs and Activities Operating under Official Financial Assistance or by a License

Section 811. Unlawful discriminatory acts in general. It is an unlawful discriminatory act for one or more persons conducting a business; professional activity; employees', business, or professional organization; institution, program, or activity operating under official financial assistance or a license; or governmental activity to utilize a method of doing business or operating that, considered either by itself or in conjunction with similar action of other persons, unfairly or unreasonably restricts the economic, housing, educational, training, associational, public accommodations, political, or governmental opportunities of members of any race, color, religion, ancestry, national origin, age, sex, economic status, or any other group from which it is unreasonable to base such restrictions.

Section 812. Abuse of authority by a police officer. (a) It is an unlawful discriminatory act for any police officer to deny any person equal protection of the laws under the Constitution or laws of the United States on account of race, color, religion, ancestry, national origin, age, sex, economic status, or any other basis that is unreasonable.

(b) It is an unlawful discriminatory act for any police officer to deprive any person of any rights, privileges, or immunities secured or protected by the Constitution or laws of the United States or to misuse or abuse his official powers by any of the following acts:

(1) subjecting any person to physical injury or death or his property or business to physical damage or destruction for any unlawful purpose;

(2) subjecting any person to unnecessary force during the course of an arrest or performance of any duty or while the person is being held in custody;

(3) subjecting any person to violence or unlawful restraint in the course of eliciting a confession to a crime or any other information;

(4) subjecting any person to undue harassment or gross personal indignity or insult;

(5) subjecting any person to an illegal search or seizure or arrest;

(6) refusing to provide protection to any person or his property or business from unlawful violence knowing that such violence was planned or was then taking place;

(7) subjecting any person to violence or unlawful restraint for the purpose of obtaining anything of value;

(8) aiding or assisting private persons in any way to carry out acts of unlawful violence; and

(9) threatening to do any of the above acts.

Section 813. Abuse of authority by an official agency. (a) It is an unlawful discriminatory act for any official agency to deny any person equal protection of the laws under the Constitution or laws of the United States by denying that person, among other things, on account of race, color, religion, ancestry, national origin, economic status, or other basis that is unreasonable:

(1) equal access to or utilization of any public school or other public facility;

(2) equal opportunity to obtain and utilize a license generally obtainable from that agency;

(3) equal opportunity to obtain and to enjoy services, loans,

grants, insurance, loan guarantees, welfare assistance, or any other thing or action generally available to other persons from that agency.

(b) It is an unlawful discriminatory act for any official agency to deprive any person of any rights, privileges, or immunities secured or protected by the Constitution or laws of the United States.

Section 814. Official condonation of abuse of authority. It is an unlawful discriminatory act for any official agency to permit, authorize, or condone a violation of Sections 811, 812, or 813.

Section 815. Discrimination in programs and activities operating under official financial assistance or a license. (a) It is an unlawful discriminatory act for any person conducting any program or activity operating under any form of official financial assistance or a license, on the ground of race, color, religion, ancestry, national origin, age or sex, to act with regard to another person so as to cause him to be excluded from participation in, or be denied the benefits of, or be subjected to discrimination under that program or activity, or to violate any rule, regulation, or order issued under Subsection (b) of this section.

(b) Every official agency which is empowered to extend official financial assistance to any program or activity, by way of grant, loan, or contract, or to issue a license, is authorized and directed to effectuate the provisions of Subsection (a) of this section with respect to such program or activity or license by issuing rules, regulations, or orders of general applicability which shall be consistent with achievement of the objectives of the statute authorizing extension of the financial assistance or issuance of the license in connection with which the action is taken. No such rule, regulation, or order shall become effective unless and until approved by the Commission.

Subpart C. Discrimination in Employment

Section 821. Definitions. In this Act

(1) "Employer" means a person employing one or more employees within the state, exclusive of parents, spouse, or children of that person, and including the state, any political subdivision, or official agency of either.

(2) "Labor organization" means any organizational person that exists for the purpose, in whole or in part, of representing employees in collective bargaining. Collective bargaining includes any negotiation or dealing with employers concerning grievances, terms or con-

ditions of employment, or other aid or protection for one or more employees.

(3) "Employment agency" means any person regularly undertaking, with or without compensation, to procure employment opportunities for individuals or to procure, refer, or place individuals as employees.

(4) "Individual" means any individual other than one employed or seeking employment by his parents, spouse, or child, or employed or seeking employment in the domestic service of or in a personal or confidential capacity by any person.

Section 822. Unlawful discriminatory acts by an employer. It is an unlawful discriminatory act for any employer to refuse to hire or otherwise to discriminate against any individual with regard to hire, tenure, promotions, terms, conditions, or privileges of employment, or any matter related to employment, on account of the race, color, religion, ancestry, national origin, sex, or age of the individual.

Section 823. Unlawful discriminatory acts by an employment agency. It is an unlawful discriminatory act for any employment agency to fail or to refuse to classify properly, procure, recruit, refer or place for employment, or otherwise to discriminate against any individual on account of the race, color, religion, ancestry, national origin, sex, or age of the individual.

Section 824. Unlawful discriminatory acts by a labor organization. It is an unlawful discriminatory act for a labor organization to discriminate against any individual or to limit, segregate, or classify its membership in any way that would tend to deprive the individual of employment opportunities, limit his employment opportunities, or otherwise affect adversely his status as an employee or as an applicant for employment, or that would affect adversely his wages, hours, or conditions of employment, on account of the race, color, religion, ancestry, national origin, sex, or age of the individual.

Section 825. Unlawful discriminatory acts concerning quotas, information, and publicity on employment. It is an unlawful discriminatory act for any employer, employment agency, or labor organization, prior to employment, admission to membership, or admission to participation in any occupational training or retraining program,

(1) to establish, announce, or follow a policy of denying or limiting, through a quota system or otherwise, the employment, membership, or participation opportunities of any individual or group on

account of race, color, religion, ancestry, national origin, age, or sex;

(2) to make any inquiry, cause inquiry to be made concerning, or make any record of the race, color, religion, ancestry, national origin, age, or sex of any applicant for employment, membership, or participation;

(3) to use, or cause to be used, any form of application for employment, membership, or participation containing questions or entries regarding race, color, religion, ancestry, or national origin;

(4) to cause to be published, circulated, or displayed any notice or advertisement relating to employment, membership, or participation indicating any preference, limitation, specification or discrimination based upon race, color, religion, ancestry, national origin, age, or sex;

(5) to utilize, or cause to be utilized, in the recruitment or hiring of individuals, any employment agency or labor organization known by the person utilizing them to discriminate against individuals on account of race, color, religion, ancestry, national origin, age, or sex; or

(6) to penalize or discriminate in any manner against any individual because he has opposed any act forbidden by this subpart or because he has made a charge, testified, or assisted in any manner in any investigation, proceeding, or hearing concerning such act.

Section 826. Advertisements by individuals seeking employment. It is an unlawful discriminatory act for any individual seeking employment to publish, or cause to be published, any advertisement that specifies or indicates his race, color, religion, ancestry, or national origin or expresses or indicates a limitation or preference concerning the race, color, religion, ancestry, or national origin of any prospective employer.

Section 827. Exemptions relating to occupational qualification, retirement or insurance plans, religious organizations, and plans dealing with imbalance. (a) It is not an unlawful discriminatory act for an employer to hire, a labor union to classify its membership or refer an individual for employment, or an employer, employment agency, or labor organization to request information, or an individual seeking employment to publish an advertisement that expresses a personal quality or preference on the basis of what would otherwise be prohibited under this subpart when this basis is a bona fide occupational qualification reasonably necessary to the normal operation of that particular business or enterprise.

(b) It is not an unlawful discriminatory act for an employer, employment agency, or labor organization to select a person to be a participant in any occupational training or retraining program on the basis of the ability to complete the required training and the industry average period of employment thereafter before attaining the age of sixty-five (65) years of age.

(c) It is not an unlawful discriminatory act for an employer to terminate employment or otherwise deal with an individual under the terms of any bona fide retirement or pension plan or under the terms of any bona fide group or employee insurance plan.

(d) It is not an unlawful discriminatory act for a religious or denominational institution or organization, or any organization operated for charitable or educational purposes which is operated, supervised, or controlled by or in connection with a religious or denominational organization or group, from limiting employment or membership of the same religion or denomination, or from making a selection of employees or members that is reasonably calculated to promote the religious principles for which it is established or maintained.

(e) It is not an unlawful discriminatory act for an employer to adopt or to implement a plan to fill vacancies or hire new employees designed to eliminate or reduce imbalance with respect to race, color, religion, ancestry, national origin, sex, or age, if the plan has been filed with the Commission and the Commission has not disapproved the plan.

Subpart D. Discrimination in Public Accommodations and Educational Institutions

Section 831. Definitions. In this Act

(1) "Place of public accommodations" means any place in or through which any business or professional activity is conducted that is open to, accepts, or solicits the patronage of or offers goods or services to the general public. It does not include those clubs, associations, corporations, or other organizations that

(A) are organized by and for a regular dues-paying membership;

(B) are formed for noncommercial, nonprofit purposes;

(C) have policies determined by their members; and

(D) have facilities and services that are available only to their members and their bona fide guests or to similar organizations;

(2) "Educational institution" means any nursery; kindergarten; elementary or secondary school; academy; college; university; exten-

sion course; or nursing, secretarial, business, vocational, technical, trade, or professional school.

Section 832. Discrimination in public accommodations. (a) It is an unlawful discriminatory act for any person, being the owner, proprietor, or lessee of any place of public accommodations, to refuse, withhold from, or deny to any individual any of the accommodations, advantages, facilities, benefits, privileges, services, or goods of that place on account of race, color, religion, ancestry, national origin, age, or sex.

(b) It is an unlawful discriminatory act for any person, being the owner, proprietor, or lessee of any place of public accommodations, to circulate, issue, display, post, mail, or otherwise to publish a statement, advertisement, or sign that indicates that any of the accommodations, advantages, facilities, benefits, privileges, services or goods of that place will be denied to any individual on account of race, color, religion, ancestry, national origin, age, or sex, or that the patronage of, or presence at that place of, any individual is objectionable, unwelcome, unacceptable, undesirable, or unsolicited on account of race, color, religion, ancestry, national origin, age, or sex.

(c) It is an unlawful discriminatory act for any person, being the owner, proprietor, or lessee of any place of public accommodations, to make any written or oral inquiry concerning, or keep any record of, the race, color, religion, ancestry, age, or sex of any individual in connection with the solicitation, reservation, booking, sale, or dispensing of any of the accommodations, advantages, facilities, benefits, privileges, services, or goods of that place.

Section 833. Exemption of places of public accommodation serving individuals of one sex. The Commission may exempt by rule any kind of place of public accommodation from the provisions of Section 832 relative only to serving individuals only of a single sex if it finds that that type of operation is customary in the business or profession concerned.

Section 834. Discrimination in educational institutions. (a) It is an unlawful discriminatory act for any person, being the owner, proprietor, or lessee of any educational institution

(1) to refuse to admit or otherwise to discriminate against any individual with respect to the terms, conditions, accommodations, advantages, facilities, benefits, privileges, or services of that institution on account of race, color, religion, ancestry, or national origin;

(2) to make or use a written or oral inquiry or form of applica-

tion for admission that elicits or attempts to elicit information, or to make or keep a record, concerning the race, color, religion, ancestry, or national origin of an applicant for admission;

(3) to require, or cause to be required, that a photograph of any applicant for admission be submitted with any form of application for admission;

(4) to publish, circulate, or display, or cause to be published, circulated, or displayed, any written, printed, oral, or visual communication, advertisement, catalogue, or any other form of publicity relating to admission, that expresses or indicates any preference, limitation, specification, or discrimination on account of the race, color, religion, ancestry, or national origin of any applicant for admission;

(5) to establish, announce, or follow a policy of denial or limitation through a quota system or otherwise of educational opportunities of the members of any group on account of race, color, religion, ancestry, or national origin; or

(6) to use in the recruitment of potential applicants for admission any service or agency known by the person to discriminate against individuals on account of race, color, religion, ancestry, or national origin.

(b) As used in this section "person" does not include the United States, a state, or any political subdivision of the latter, or any official agency of the foregoing.

Section 835. Exception of religious organizations and certain organizations related to them. It is not an unlawful discriminatory act for a religious or denominational institution or organization, or any organization operated for charitable or educational purposes, which is operated, supervised, or controlled by or in connection with a religious or denominational institution or organization from limiting admission to, or giving preference in, its accommodations, advantages, facilities, benefits, services, or goods of a place of public accommodations or an educational institution to persons of the same religion or denomination, or from making a selection of applicants or individuals that is reasonably calculated to promote the religious principles for which it is established or maintained.

Subpart E.   Discrimination in Real-Estate Transactions
Section 841. Definitions. In this Act

(1) "Real-estate transaction" means the sale, exchange, rental, lease, or other similar transaction relative to real property.

(2) "Real property" means buildings, structures, real estate, lands, tenements, leaseholds, interests in real-estate cooperatives, condominiums, and hereditaments, corporeal and incorporeal, or any interest therein.

(3) "Real-estate broker or salesman" means a person, whether licensed or not, who, for or with the expectation of receiving a consideration, lists, sells, purchases, exchanges, rents, or leases real property, or who negotiates or attempts to negotiate any of these activities, or who holds himself out as engaged in these activities, or who negotiates or attempts to negotiate a loan secured or to be secured by mortgage or other encumbrance upon real property, or who is engaged in the business of listing real property in a publication; or a person employed by or acting on behalf of any of these.

(4) "Owner" includes the lessee, sublessee, assignee, trustee, trustor, beneficiary, mortgagee, mortgagor, or any person having any legal or equitable right of ownership or possession or the right to lease, rent, or assign any real property, or any agent, employee, or legal representative therof, and the state or any of its political subdivisions, or any agency thereof.

Section 842. Discrimination in real-estate transactions. It is an unlawful discriminatory act for an owner or any other person engaging in a real-estate transaction, or for a real-estate broker or salesman, on account of race, color, religion, ancestry, national origin, sex, or economic status

(1) to refuse to engage in a real-estate transaction with a person;

(2) to discriminate against a person in the terms, conditions, or privileges of a real-estate transaction or in the furnishing of facilities or services in connection therewith;

(3) to refuse to receive or transmit any bona fide offer to engage in a real-estate transaction from a person;

(4) to refuse to negotiate relative to a real-estate transaction with a person;

(5) to represent to a person that real property is not available for a real-estate transaction or for inspection for this purpose when in fact it is so available, or to fail to bring a listing for a real-estate transaction to his attention, or to refuse to permit him to inspect real property that is available for a real-estate transaction;

(6) to establish, announce, or follow, or cause to be established, announced, or followed, a policy of denying or limiting, through a quota system or otherwise, a real-estate transaction to any person;

(7) to offer, solicit, accept, use or retain a listing of real property with the understanding that a person may be discriminated against in a real-estate transaction in the furnishing of facilities or services in connection therewith;

(8) to make or use a written or oral inquiry or form of application, contract, or any other document, in a real-estate transaction, or in the furnishing of facilities and services thereto, that elicits or attempts to elicit information, or to make or keep a record, concerning any person or any present or prospective owner, occupant, or tenant of the property that is the subject of that transaction; or

(9) to publish, circulate, or display, or cause to be published, circulated, or displayed, any written, printed, oral, or visual communication, advertisement, catalogue, or any other form of publicity relating to a real-estate transaction, that expresses or indicates any preference, limitation, specification, or discrimination concerning a person.

Section 843. Discrimination in financial assistance on real estate transactions. It is an unlawful discriminatory act for any person to whom application is made for financial assistance in connection with a real-estate transaction or for the construction, rehabilitation, repair, maintenance, or improvement of real property

(1) to discriminate against the applicant on account of race, color, religion, ancestry, national origin, or sex; or

(2) to use a form of application or contract for that assistance or to make a written or oral inquiry that elicits or attempts to elicit information, or to make or keep a record, concerning the race, color, religion, ancestry, national origin, or sex of the applicant or that indicates, directly or indirectly, an intent to make a limitation, specification, or differentiation on one of these bases.

Section 844. Restrictive covenants and conditions. (a) Every provision in an oral agreement or a written instrument relating to a real-estate transaction that purports to forbid or restrict a subsequent real-estate transaction involving the same property to individuals of a specified race, color, religion, ancestry, national origin, or sex is void.

(b) Every condition, restriction, or prohibition, including a right of entry or possibility of reverter, in a written instrument relating to a real-estate transaction that directly or indirectly limits the use or occupancy of real property on the basis of race, color, religion, ancestry, national origin, or sex is void.

(c) It is an unlawful discriminatory act to insert in a written instrument relating to a real-estate transaction a provision that is void under this section or to honor or attempt to honor that provision in the chain of title.

Section 845. Discrimination by blockbusting. It is an unlawful discriminatory act for any person, for the purpose of inducing a real-estate transaction, or a listing of real property for this purpose, from which he may benefit financially

(1) to represent that a change has occurred or will or may occur in the composition with respect to race, color, religion, ancestry, or national origin of the owners or occupants in the block, neighborhood, or area in which the real property is located; or

(2) to represent that this change will or may result in the lowering of property values, an increase in criminal or antisocial behavior, or a decline in the quality of schools in the block, neighborhood, or area in which the real property is located;

(3) to make any misrepresentations concerning the listing for sale or the anticipated listing for sale or the sale of any real property designed to initiate or facilitate a change in the ethnic composition of a block, neighborhood, or area in which the property is located; or

(4) to place a sign purporting to offer for sale any real property that is not in fact offered for sale, providing that any sign remaining on the property within seventy-two hours after the execution of a purchase agreement shall not be considered a violation of this section.

Section 846. Exemption of religious organization. It is not an unlawful discriminatory act for a religious or denominational institution or organization, or any organization operated for charitable or educational purposes which is operated, supervised, or controlled by or in connection with a religious or denominational institution or organization, from limiting, or giving preference in, a real-estate transaction to persons of the same religion or denomination, or from making a selection of buyers, tenants, lessees, assignees, or sublessees that is reasonably calculated to promote the religious principles for which it is established or maintained.

Subpart F. Other Unlawful Discriminatory Acts

Section 851. Discrimination by business and professional organizations. It is an unlawful discriminatory act for any organization of businessmen, tradesmen, or professional men in which membership is valuable or essential to an individual for the purpose of engaging or advancing in a business, trade or profession to exclude or otherwise discriminate against any individual on account of race, color, religion, ancestry, national origin, age, or sex.

Section 852. Discrimination by retaliation, coercion, obstruction, and attempt. It is an unlawful discriminatory act for a person, or for two or more persons to conspire,

(1) to retaliate or discriminate against a person because he has opposed an unlawful discriminatory act, or because he has made a charge, testified, assisted, or participated in an investigation, proceeding, or hearing under this Act;

(2) to aid, abet, incite, or coerce a person to engage in an unlawful discriminatory act;

(3) wilfully to interfere with the performance of a duty or the exercise of a power by the Commission or one of its members or representatives;

(4) wilfully to obstruct or prevent a person from complying with the provisions of this Act or an order issued thereunder; or

(5) wilfully to fail to obey a rule, regulation, or order promulgated under Section 721.

Section 853. Attempts. An attempt to commit, directly or indirectly, an unlawful discriminatory act is an unlawful discriminatory act.

Section 854. Violation of conciliation agreements containing a consent cease and desist order. It is an unlawful discriminatory act for a party to a conciliation agreement containing a consent cease and desist order made under this Act to violate the terms of the agreement.

Section 855. Action to relieve imbalance. It is not an unlawful discriminatory act for a person subject to Part VIII to adopt and carry out a plan to eliminate or reduce imbalance with respect to race, color, religion, ancestry, national origin, age, or sex if the plan has been filed with the Commission or its appropriate local section and the plan has not been disapproved.

PART IX. CRIMINAL SANCTIONS; OTHER REMEDIES; MISCELLANEOUS.

Section 901. Wilful violation of Commission order; wilful interference. Any person who wilfully violates any order of the Commission or this Act or who wilfully resists, prevents, impedes, or interferes with the performance of a duty or the exercise of a power by the Commission or one of its commissioners or representatives, is guilty of a misdemeanor and shall be fined not more than [   ], or imprisoned for not more than [   ], or both.

Section 902. Jurisdiction and venue of [   ] courts over civil actions; statute of limitations. (a) Each [   ] court shall have jurisdiction of civil actions brought under this part, and shall exercise the same without regard to whether the aggrieved party shall have exhausted any administrative or other remedies that may be provided by law.

(b) A civil action under this part may be brought in any [county or judicial district] in the state

(1) in which the alleged unlawful discriminatory act occurred;

(2) in which the records relevant to such act are maintained and administered; or

(3) in which the respondent resides, transacts business, or has his principal office.

(c) A civil action under this part must be filed on or before one year after the alleged discriminatory act occurred.

Section 903. Civil actions for prevention of unlawful discriminatory acts; complaint; legal representation; commencement of action without payment of fees, costs, or security; intervention by the Attorney General. (a) Any individual aggrieved by an unlawful discriminatory act or a civil-rights organization on behalf of that individual, may, instead of seeking redress by the administrative procedure provided in Part VII of this Act, bring a civil action in the appropriate [   ] court of the state, without regard to the amount in controversy, by filing with it a complaint

(1) signed by the complainant;

(2) setting forth facts pertaining to such act; and

(3) requesting damages and such other relief, including an application for a permanent or temporary injunction, restraining order, or other equitable remedies or affirmative relief as may be deemed necessary to undo or mitigate the effects of, or prevent the continuation of any unlawful discriminatory acts; and shall be entitled to recover threefold the damages sustained or $500, or whichever is larger.

(b) Upon application by the complainant and in such circumstances as the court may deem just, the court may appoint an attorney for such complainant and may authorize the commencement of the action without the payment of fees, costs, or security.

(c) Upon timely application, the court may, at its discretion, permit the Attorney General to intervene in such civil action if he certifies that the case is of general public importance.

Section 904. Civil actions by the Attorney General; complaint;

expedition of action. (a) Whenever the Attorney General has probable cause to believe that any person has performed or is engaged in an unlawful discriminatory act, the Attorney General may bring a civil action in the appropriate [   ] court by filing with it a complaint

(1) signed by him (or in his absence by the Acting Attorney General);

(2) setting forth facts pertaining to such act; and

(3) requesting such relief, including an application for a permanent or temporary injunction, restraining order, or other equitable remedies or affirmative relief as may be deemed necessary to undo or mitigate the effects of, or prevent the continuation of, any unlawful discriminatory acts.

(b) Upon the filing of a complaint under subsection (a) of this section, the chief judge of the [   ] (or in his absence, the acting chief judge) in which the case is pending shall immediately designate a judge in such [   ] to hear and determine the case. In the event that no judge in the [   ] is available to hear and determine the case, the chief judge, or the acting chief judge, as the case may be, shall certify this fact to the chief judge of the [   ] (or in his absence, to the acting chief judge) who shall then designate a judge to hear and determine the case. The judge designated pursuant to this subsection shall assign the case for hearing at the earliest practicable date and cause the case to be in every way expedited.

Section 905. Injunction; appropriate affirmative action; appeals. (a) If the court finds in an action under Sections 903 or 904 that the respondent has engaged in or is engaging in an unlawful discriminatory act charged in the complaint, the court may enjoin the respondent from engaging in such act and order such affirmative action as may be appropriate, which may include any affirmative action that the Commission might order under Section 716 of this Act.

(b) In any action under Sections 903 or 904 the court, in its discretion, may allow the prevailing party, other than the Commission or the United States, a reasonable attorney's fee as part of the costs, and the Commission and the state shall be liable for costs the same as a private person.

(c) An appeal from the final judgment of the court in any civil action brought under Section 903 shall lie to the [insert name of appropriate intermediate appellate court].

Section 906. Termination and other action relative to official finan-

cial assistance and licenses. (a) Upon receiving a copy of the final decision and order of the Commission under Section 717, an official agency of the state or political subdivision thereof that extended official financial assistance to a program or activity of a respondent or issued a license to a respondent is bound by the finding of discrimination and may take appropriate action

(1) to terminate or refuse to grant or continue assistance under such program or activity or to revoke or suspend such license, but such termination, refusal, revocation, or suspension shall be limited in its effect to the particular program, license, or part thereof, in which such noncompliance has been so found; or

(2) to utilize any other means authorized by law.

(b) In the case of any action terminating or refusing to grant or continue assistance, or revoking or suspending a license because of failure to comply with Section 815, the head of the official agency shall file with the committees of the [House and Senate] having legislative jurisdiction over the program or activity or license involved a full written report of the circumstances and the grounds for such action. No such action shall become effective until thirty days have elapsed after the filing of such report.

Section 907. Public contractors. (a) Upon receiving a copy of the final decision and order of the Commission under Section 717, an official agency of the government of the state or of a political subdivision thereof that awarded a contract to the respondent public contractor is bound by the finding of discrimination and may take appropriate action

(1) to terminate a contract or a portion thereof on condition that the respondent carry out a program of compliance with the provisions of this Act; and

(2) refrain from entering into further contracts, or extensions or other modifications of existing contracts, with the respondent until the Commission is satisfied that the respondent will carry out policies in compliance with the provisions of this Act.

(b) Any person who has been the subject of a final decision and order of the Commission under Section 717 may be deemed by an official agency of the government of the state or of a political subdivision thereof as ineligible for award of a public contract until the Commission is satisfied that the respondent will carry out policies in compliance with the provisions of this Act.

Section 908. Prima facie evidence. In a proceeding under this Act, a written, printed, or visual communication, advertisement, or other form of publication, or written inquiry, or record, or other document purporting to have been made by a person is prima facie evidence that it was authorized by him.

Section 909. Jurisdiction for issuance of compliance orders; petition for order to modify or set aside demand or specification of grounds. (a) If a person fails to permit, upon a demand by the Commission, access to premises and examination, photographing, or copying of evidence, or fails to make, keep, or preserve records or make reports in accordance with Section 721 or if a person fails to comply with a subpoena issued by the Commission or a commissioner, the [court of the county] in which such person is found, resides, or transacts business, shall, upon application of the Commission, have jurisdiction to issue to such person an order requiring him to comply with Section 721 or to comply with the subpoena.

(b) In any proceeding brought by the Commission under Subsection (a) of this section, the defendant may petition the court for an order modifying or setting aside the demand or subpoena of the Commission.

Section 910. Relation of criminal to administrative or civil proceedings under this Act. The pendency or final determination of a criminal proceeding is not a bar to an administrative or civil proceeding arising from the same act or situation. The pendency or final determination of an administrative proceeding is not a bar to a criminal proceeding arising from the same act or situation.

Section 911. Repeal. The following acts and parts of acts are repealed:

(1)   ;
(2)   ;
( )   .

Section 912. Effective date; initial appointment of officers. (a) This Act shall take effect ninety days after the day that all of the seven commissioners first take office, or on such prior date after enactment of this Act as the Governor shall prescribe and file with the Secretary of State.

(b) Any of the officers provided for in this Act may (notwithstanding Subsection (a)) be appointed in the manner provided for in this Act, at any time after the date of enactment of this Act. Such officers shall be compensated from the date they first take office, at the rates provided for in this Act.

[*Section 913. Savings provisions.* The provisions of this Act, so far as they are the same as those of acts repealed by this Act, are intended as a continuation of such acts and not as new enactments. The provisions of this Act shall not affect any act done or any complaint or proceeding pending under authority of the repealed acts. All rules and regulations adopted pursuant to any act repealed by this Act shall continue with the same force and effect as if such Act had not been repealed.]

COMMENTS

PREFATORY NOTE

1. History. The Alpha Model State Civil-Rights Act was drafted in response to the felt need for uniform guidelines relative to state civil-rights legislation.[1] The Alpha Model Act draws heavily upon a similar model act drafted by the author and included as an appendix to a law review article published in June 1965.[2] Two additional similar model acts have been prepared since that time: the "Harvard" Model State Civil Rights Act and the Uniform Model State Anti-Discrimination Act. The first was prepared by the Harvard Student Legislative Research Bureau of Harvard Law School in December 1965.[3] The second was prepared for and adopted in August 1966 by the National Conference of Commissioners on Uniform State Laws.[4] These earlier model acts may be consulted profitably in evaluating choices of content made in drafting the Alpha Model Act.

The state statutes establishing human-relations commissions that deal with discrimination in employment may be found in two convenient loose-leaf services.[5] State statutes on discrimination in places of public accommodations are collected in hearings held in 1963 by the United States Senate Committee on Commerce.[6] State statutes on

[1] Norman Dorsen, "The Prospects for a Model or Uniform Civil Rights Act" (study prepared for the Special Committee on Civil Rights of the National Conference of Commissioners on Uniform State Laws, 1965), pp. 21–39.

[2] Joseph P. Witherspoon, "Civil Rights Policy in the Federal System: Proposals for a Better Use of Administrative Process," *Yale Law Journal,* Vol. 74 (1965), pp. 1175–1244.

[3] Harvard Student Legislative Research Bureau, "A Proposed Model State Civil Rights Act," *Harvard Journal of Legislation,* Vol. 3 (1965), pp. 64–102.

[4] National Conference of Commissioners of Uniform State Laws, "The Model [State] Anti-Discrimination Act: The Comprehensive Act," *Harvard Journal of Legislation,* Vol. 4 (1967), pp. 224–278.

[5] Commerce Clearing House, Inc., *Labor Law Reports: Employment Practices;* Bureau of National Affairs, Inc., *Labor Relations Reporter: State Labor Laws,* Binders 4 and 4A.

[6] *Hearings before the Senate Committee on Commerce on S. 1732,* 88th Cong., 1st Sess. (Washington, D.C.: U.S. Government Printing Office, 1963), p. 1315.

discrimination in housing are assembled in a 1964 publication of the
United States Housing and Home Finance Agency.[7] Statutes enacted
in the public-accommodations and housing fields subsequent to the
last two publications and in other fields since 1956 may be found in
the *Race Relations Law Reporter* published by the Vanderbilt University School of Law.

2. Reorientation of State Civil-Rights Policy. The Alpha Model State
Civil-Rights Act presents a thoroughgoing reorientation of the typical
state civil-rights law. Every careful study of the approximately twenty
years' experience in administering this type of legislation concludes
that it has been far less effective than desired or needed in light of the
immense regulatory problems presented.[8] The reorientation proposed
in the Alpha Model Act to achieve greater effectiveness involves
wholly new tasks, functions, and goals for the state human-relations
commission, new methods for its operation, and much new substantive
law. These changes are designed to elaborate the idea, developed in
the preceding chapters, that in order to achieve any sufficient rectification of the status of intergroup relations in this country, official action must take place at the local level and that such action can only
be secured through an administrative agency operating within a community, that is authorized to deal with the full spectrum of human-
relations problems existing at that level.

3. Structure of the Act. The Alpha Model State Civil-Rights Act is
one of four Alpha Model Acts, the remaining being the Alpha Model State Act on Local Human-Relations Commissions, the Alpha
Model Federal Civil-Rights Act, and the Alpha Model Local Civil-
Rights Ordinance. Each of these acts is constructed to parallel and
dovetail with the others. Each act consists of nine parts. The first
three parts relate to findings and policies, general definitions, and the
establishment of a human-relations commission to administer the act
in question. The fourth part deals with the relationship between the
commission established and other similar commissions at other levels
of government. The fifth part concerns the task, functions, goals, and
implemental policies of the commission. The sixth part relates to its
procedural powers and duties. The seventh part concerns procedures
to be followed in processing complaints of discriminatory acts, admin-

[7] U.S. Housing and Home Finance Agency, *Fair Housing Laws* (Washington,
D.C.: U.S. Government Printing Office, September, 1964).
[8] See Chapters 1, 5 and 6, above; also see note 1, Chapter 7, above.

istrative hearings, remedies, judicial review, and similar matters. The eighth part sets forth certain substantive law concerning unlawful discriminatory acts. The final part covers criminal sanctions and other remedies.

PART I.   SHORT TITLE; FINDINGS AND POLICIES; LIBERAL CONSTRUCTION; GENERAL DEFINITIONS

This part contains findings and a declaration of policy. Both of these sound the central note, to be heard throughout the Act, that the focus of governmental action is to be not only upon discrimination, in whatever form, against minority groups but also upon other equally harmful activity directed toward all disadvantaged groups in the community, the underlying causes of this activity, and the various forces that can be mustered for eliminating these causes and opening up equal opportunities for all. In each of these respects the Alpha Model State Act is to be radically different from existing state legislation, and from the Harvard and Uniform Model Acts which largely do no more than adopt the threadbare concept incorporated into most of this legislation. The Alpha Model Act deals both with the outer edge and the inner core of denials of equal opportunity. The declaration of policy also signals the responsibility of local communities and their citizens for dealing with these denials and the projected operation of the state human-relations commission at the local level.

This part contains only those definitions that are particularly relevant to the provisions concerning establishment of a state human-relations commission, relation of its work to that of local commissions, and assignment of its central task, functions, goals, implemental policies, and procedural powers and duties. Other definitions are set out in subsequent parts to which they principally relate. Definitions relevant to the processing of complaints of discriminatory acts appear in Section 701. Definitions pertaining to each of the different kinds of unlawful discriminatory acts are set forth in the various subparts of Part VIII, such as Sections 801, 821, 831, and 841.

PART II.   STATE HUMAN-RELATIONS COMMISSIONS

All existing state civil-rights acts and the Harvard and Uniform Model State Acts utilize as their centerpiece substantive law proscribing discriminatory acts against minority groups in specified fields such as employment, public accommodations, housing, and education. The principal function of the state human-relations commissions spoken to in these acts is the processing of individual complaints of discrimination. All else in these acts is keyed to these two principal parts of them. In order to avoid duplicating the history of these acts and to emphasize the new approach of the Alpha Model State Act, the statement of the substantive law dealing with unlawful discriminatory acts is placed toward the very end of the Act, in its Part VIII. The procedure for processing and hearing complaints of discriminatory acts is also placed in the latter part of the Act, in its Part VII. This placement relative to other provisions does not, of course, affect the great importance of this substantive civil-rights law—indeed, some of this law is quite new in the field and especially important for implementing the new approach incorporated into the Act. What this placement does permit, however, is the statement at the outset of the principal tasks, functions, goals, and implemental methods of the state human-relations commission, only one of whose functions involves the processing of individual complaints. A proper administrative perspective is thus somewhat better assured.

Part II has no statutory innovations, as compared with existing statutes, in creating a state human-relations commission. The principal difference concerns the salary of commissioners. The workload contemplated for the state commission will easily make it the busiest official agency of the state. It is incomprehensible that a state could expect to obtain the performance required of commissioners under this Act from those who serve on a part-time basis and who are compensated, as is true under many state statutes, by a per diem allowance for days of actual service. Salaried officials are distinctly needed. Moreover, salaries should be set at such a level that the very finest and most capable of career administrators will be attracted to the agency. Salaries should be fixed at least at the level fixed for the highest paid state officials such as the governor, judges of the supreme court, president of the state university, or coach of the university football team. Indeed, salaries should be comparable to those paid by private enterprise for top management officials although this is clearly an unrealistic objective as matters stand today.

In establishing a seven-member human-relations commission, Section 201 follows the practice of many states, including California, Colorado, and New Jersey. The use of nine commissioners as in New York and Maryland, of ten as in Connecticut, and of eleven as in Pennsylvania has, however, worked well in these states. On the other hand, three commissioners (as in Wyoming) or four (as in Massachusetts) seem entirely too few for a populous state with numerous and serious human-relations problems. In light of the added responsibilities cast upon the state commission under Part III for operating through local sections in each of numerous political subdivisions of the state, as compared with existing commissions, at least seven commissioners should be appointed. Some of these commissioners will undoubtedly be required to assume responsibility for supervision of administration at the local level for particular areas of the state.

The mode of appointment depends, of course, on constitutional and other legal requirements within each state. Most states provide for appointment as in Section 201. In view of the critical importance of this commission it seems wise to require appointment of commissioners to be by and with consent of the senate. Nevertheless, the term "Senate" is bracketed so that the legislature may indicate the appropriate body for approval of appointments.

PART III. LOCAL SECTIONS OF THE COMMISSION

This part has no counterpart in existing state law or in the Harvard and Uniform Model Acts. Some few commissions, as in Massachusetts and New York,[9] have established a few regional and field offices but these are quite different from the concept of a local section. The former are primarily offices for minor administrative work such as receiving complaints and investigating them. The latter, in light of Part V of the Act, is in effect a microcosm of the Commission itself and performs in its assigned political subdivision with the full authority of the Commission. Indeed, it will perform certain functions at the primary level of administration that the Commission cannot itself perform but can only supervise.

Under existing circumstances Subsections (a), (b), and (c) of Section 301 will operate so as to require the Commission to establish local sections in most of the populous cities and counties of each state. If the Alpha Model Act were universally adopted, the criteria of the section would automatically require establishment of local sections in about 2,000 political subdivisions of the country.[10] These are the localities in which experience has demonstrated that serious intergroup-relations problems exist. The criteria governing establishment of local sections

---

[9] See, *e.g.*, New York State Commission against Discrimination, *Report of Progress* (1960), pp. 85–87; New York State Commission for Human Rights, *Annual Report, 1962*, pp. 51, 3, 30.

[10] See Chapter 6, at note 11 and following.

will, however, require their establishment in political subdivisions having within them a lesser number of Negroes or Latin Americans than specified in Subsection (b) of Section 301 or having within them other disadvantaged groups, if the Commission concludes these criteria are satisfied under the particular circumstances existing within them.

The term "political subdivision" is defined in Section 104 to mean a "[city, county . . .]." Each political subdivision of a state should be listed in this definition, if under state law it is accorded a substantial general governmental role within the state. It is possible that in some jurisdictions, such as Massachusetts, the designation of a county as a comprehended political subdivision would be deleted due to the nominal governing functions performed by counties within these states. Moreover, political subdivision is defined in Section 104 to include "any combination of two or more political subdivisions determined by the Commission to be appropriate for the purpose of establishing a local section." This means the Commission can overlook the usual boundaries of existing political subdivisions to reach through a single local section what are the integral communities of the state.

A most important facet of the local section concept is the requirement spelled out in Subsection (e) of Section 301 with regard to eligibility for appointment as a local section commissioner. Eligibility turns on residence or employment within the political subdivision. The principal purpose of this requirement is to secure community involvement in the human-relations program of the state and to enhance the acceptability and practicability of the program. Some will question how this requirement would operate in such areas as the Deep South where the controlling group of whites in many political subdivisions are strongly opposed to legislation of this sort. The answer to this objection is threefold. The Alpha Model State Act is feasible only for a state that at the state level is willing to implement in a bona fide manner the purposes and policies of this Act. If this willingness exists at the state level, members of minority groups and other sympathetic persons in a political subdivision can be appointed local section commissioners in such numbers as to guarantee an effective local section operation. If this willingness at the state level does not exist, another Alpha Model Act is the appropriate device for dealing with the situation presented. One of these is the Alpha Model Federal Civil-Rights Act that authorizes, like this Part, the establishment of a local section of a federal human-relations commission and appointment of local section commissioners from a broader base, utilizing, if necessary, personnel from out of the political subdivision or, in extreme cases, from out of the state. Other relevant Alpha Model Acts are the Alpha Model State Act for Local Human-Relations Commissions and the Alpha Model Local Civil-Rights Ordinance. These will permit willing political subdivisions within a state, even in the Deep South, to deal with intergroup-relations problems even when the state as a whole and other political subdivisions are not willing.

The device of an election provided for in Subsection (e) of Section 301 may become appropriate when the Commission wishes to select local leaders as local section commissioners who are not aligned with a hostile power structure. Who these persons are, however, is not always ascertainable. The electoral principle can be a salutary device for permitting these persons to emerge as local leaders and for involving disadvantaged groups with the improvement of their situation in the community. Much of the value of the representation principle may also be secured through the use of this device.

Section 304 relative to compensation for local section commissioners, contrary to the similar section for commissioners of the Commission (Section 204), does not provide for payment of a salary. Most local commissions operate on this basis. It is more possible to utilize part-time commissioners at the local level when they are provided with a competent and ample staff. Each local section would have, under Subsection (1) of Section 601, its own executive director, attorneys, hearing examiners, and other staff members deemed necessary by the Commission.

PART IV.　RELATION OF THIS ACT TO SIMILAR STATE LAW; COOPERATIVE AGREEMENTS WITH LOCAL COMMISSIONS

The purpose of this Part is to preserve the effectiveness of any existing human-relations commission of political subdivisions and to provide for the problems involved in the coexistence of these local commissions and the Commission created by this Act. A fundamental principle underlying each of the Alpha Model Acts is that a local commission can be, if its political subdivision wills and acts prudently for this result, the most effective agency for dealing with human-relations problems at the local level. It is in order better to promote this local development that the Alpha Model State Act on Local Human-Relation Commissions and the Alpha Model Local Civil-Rights Ordinance have been drafted. The problems of providing for state authorization for creation of local human-relations commissions by political subdivisions are far too complex to be dealt with wisely in the same statute creating and empowering a state human-relations commission. For this reason the Alpha Model State Civil-Rights Act, unlike the Uniform Model Act,[11] only deals with the problem of the coexistence of local commissions and the Commission created by it.

The approach taken in this part rejects the extraordinarily limited role which the Uniform Model Act would accord to local commissions. That Act devitalizes local commissions by precluding them from holding public hearings, issuing subpoenas, issuing cease and desist orders, and enforcing such orders in the courts.[12] At the same time that it effectuates this debasement, the Uniform Model Act provides no sufficient substitute at the local level such as a local section of the Commission as has been done in the Alpha Model State Act. The Uniform Model Act thus fails to honor one of the most important lessons taught by twenty years of experience with state human-relations commissions. To the great credit of the Harvard Model State Civil Rights Act, it recognizes the need for the state commission created by it to promote the creation of local commissions having the necessary authority to be fully effective.[13] Unfortunately that Act contains no specific provision implementing that recognition.

Section 401 simply assures, so far as political subdivisions are concerned, that they may continue to enforce local law in the same field with this Act subject, necessarily, to this and other parts of the Act.

Section 402 provides for cooperation agreements between the Commission and local commissions. The Commission may vest local commissions with the whole or only a very small part of its authorized operations at the local level under these agreements. Complete flexibility is intended so as to comprehend the great variety in local commissions and their capacity to do effective work. Section 402 is to be read in connection with Subsection (a) (2) of Section 502. The latter provision assigns to the Commission the function of promoting the creation of local commissions and of supporting, supervising, and reviewing their operation. The cooperative agreement is a central device for accomplishing the latter objectives. The agreement could relate not only to the kind of function to be performed by the local commission that would otherwise be performed by the Commission

---

[11] §§ 901–906. See note 4, above.

[12] §§ 904–905. See note 4, above.

[13] Harvard Student Legislative Research Bureau, "A Proposed Model State Civil Rights Act," p. 100.

through its local section, but also to other forms of supervision and of review, as well as to financial support, personnel loans, and technical assistance. Section 404 is a safeguard under which the Commission could by terminating the agreement resume performance of the Commission role in a political subdivision through its local section.

Section 403 relates only to the complaint-processing function and defines the intended role for local commissions relative to this function.

Sections 405 and 902 are to be read together in determining the exclusive nature of the administrative procedure under this Act. When an individual aggrieved by an unlawful discriminatory act, the Attorney General, or a civil-rights organization utilizes this procedure, that complainant is precluded under both sections from utilizing any other available remedy either before local commissions (in absence of a cooperative agreement), the courts, or other state administrative agencies. On the other hand if a commissioner of the Commission utilizes the procedure of the Act, the persons listed in section 902 may utilize other available remedies, such as civil action in the courts. Similarly if an individual aggrieved utilizes the procedure of the Act, no other person is precluded from utilizing remedies available elsewhere such as one provided by a licensing agency for revoking the license of one who is a respondent in a proceeding under this Act.

Section 406 makes the procedure of the Act unavailable to a complainant who has resorted to another remedy except where the other remedy is that provided by a local commission and the Commission directs the complaint to be referred to it. This provision preserves the interest in good relations between the Commission and local commissions without inflicting any undue disadvantage upon a complainant who resorted to a local commission.

Section 407 is a necessary provision for "in-lining" local substantive civil-rights law with this Act. This provision has reference only to provisions about the same subject matter. It would not, for example, mean that a local provision covering employers of twenty-five or more employees is to be read to mean an employer of one or more employees, as that term is defined in this Act. On the other hand, the employees of an employer might be determined both under local law and this Act by excluding domestic employees. What the term "domestic employees" means under both local law and this Act must be determined, in the event of conflict of interpretations, by the interpretation of the term in this Act.

PART V. THE CENTRAL TASK, FUNCTIONS, GOALS, AND POLICIES OF
THE COMMISSION AND ITS LOCAL SECTIONS

The heart of the Alpha Model State Civil-Rights Act is this part. In
stating the central task of the local sections of the Commission, Section
501 simply makes explicit what careful students of intergroup-relations problems have been articulating for years as the task which has
to be performed at the local level by well-organized local human-relations commissions. In expressing the similar task to be performed by
the commission itself as contrasted with its local sections an analogy
has been drawn to the function of local commissions. By and large the
operation of the New York State Commission for Human Rights has
most closely approximated what is described in Subsection (c) of Section 501. But even that able Commission has failed to see the value of
local sections as proposed in this Act and has certainly heavily over-
emphasized the individual-complaint–processing function.

Section 502 serves to outline the various functions of the Commission. The section is unprecedented in state civil-rights acts which, as
already indicated, are monolithically designed to invest commissions
with the complaint-processing function. These functions outlined in
Section 502 are (1) supporting and supervising of the work of its local
sections; (2) promoting the creation of local commissions and supporting and supervising their operation; (3) "wide-spectrum" negotiation; (4) "constructive action"; and (5) the processing of individual complaints. Even the last function is different in quality from the
usual complaint-processing function given state commissions. In the
first place, the focus of the function is quite different since the Commission deals primarily with discrimination by large concerns, unions,
and other organizations with state-wide operations, and by state and
local government agencies. In the second place, the Commission is
concerned not only with the discrimination usually reached by the
more advanced state statutes but also with many forms of harmful
action not formally discriminatory in nature but nevertheless just as
effective in closing opportunities to minority groups. This coverage
will be more particularly examined in the comment on Part VIII of
the Act. Moreover, the whole concept of abuse of authority by police
officers and official agencies involving invasions of constitutional
rights, privileges, and immunities is brought into the field of state
civil-rights law. But what really distinguishes this section is the inclusion of the remaining functions. Each of them carries the Commission

into areas of operation not yet traversed by state commissions and only barely touched by a few local commissions. The support and supervision of its local sections and of local commissions will require quite a different form of operation from the one historically and currently utilized. In addition to selecting commissioners and staff for its local sections, the Commission will have to formulate and execute policies for supporting and supervising the work of its local sections and the local commissions. The very different nature of the work of these agencies, especially the former under this Act, causes the supporting and supervising of their work by state commissions to be different also from their usual work. This leads us to the two widely different functions shared at different levels of performance by the Commission and its local sections: the "wide-spectrum"–negotiation function and the constructive-action function. The descriptions of these functions contained in Sections 502 and 503 are quite general and stated in terms of the immediate objects dealt with in their performance. These general descriptions, however, take on important additional meaning in light of the central task defined for both the Commission and its local sections in Section 501, the general goals of their work stated in Section 504, the general prohibition of unlawful discriminatory acts in Section 811, the implemental policies stated in Section 505, and the procedural powers stated in Section 602.

Section 504 states the basic goals to be pursued as the Commission and its local sections perform each of the functions assigned them. This section is modelled to a large extent upon a statement of human-relations goals formulated by the Philadelphia Commission on Human Relations in 1963[14] after well over a decade of experience in the field. In the statement of education and training goals the section is modelled upon the policy for promoting excellence in the public schools adopted in 1965 by the City of New York Board of Education.[15] The statement of the administration of law goals includes a goal that underlies much of the legislation proposed in the Congress of the United States between 1963 and 1967 seeking to ensure respect for individual constitutional rights by official agencies.[16]

[14] George Schermer, *Guidelines: A Manual for Bi-Racial Committees* (New York: Anti-Defamation League of B'nai B'rith, 1964), pp. 71–73.

[15] Bernard E. Donovan, *Implementation of Board Policy on Excellence for the City's Schools* (report submitted to the City of New York Board of Education, April 28, 1965) (mimeographed).

[16] *Hearings on S. 3296, etc., before the Subcommittee on Constitutional Rights of the Senate Committee on the Judiciary*, 89th Cong., 2nd. Sess. (Washington, D.C.:

The "wide-spectrum"–negotiation function referred to in Sections 502 and 503 is supported by a new form of substantive civil-rights law stated in Section 811. The need for and nature of this law has been examined in Chapter 5. The law is designed to reach any form of activity that unfairly or unreasonably restricts the availability of any of the various classes of basic opportunities generally available to others to members of any race, color, religion, ancestry, national origin, age, sex, or economic status. It is also directed against this activity when it forms part of an industrial, professional, governmental, union, or private-organizational pattern of conduct, even in the absence of strictly conspiratorial conduct. This law means that the Commission and its local sections can negotiate from great strength with wide sectors of business, government, and private organizations in the state-wide and local communities. It means that there is an "instant law" available to deal with new and subtle forms of activity that cripple efforts of disadvantaged groups to improve their status in these communities. Section 602 provides the Commission and its local sections with numerous procedural devices short of class-enforcement actions to push a sector of the business world or other group of institutions firmly into line with its interpretations of Section 811. But ultimately the Commission and its local sections have available an administrative class action and the issuance of cease and desist orders that apply to the entire class. The series of Sections 502, 503, 602, and 811 probably provide the single most potent weapon in the new Act for dealing through traditional administration of legal rules with activity causing serious harm to minority and other disadvantaged groups. It introduces a new era in law enforcement at state and local levels, which is most closely approximated by some of the administrative class actions of the Federal Trade Commission.

The constructive-action function referred to in Sections 502 and 503 is elaborated by the statement of implemental policies contained in Section 505 and supported by the procedural powers and duties provided by Section 602. These implemental policies when applied constitute forms of constructive action that experience of some well-organized local commissions has amply demonstrated are useful for accomplishing the essential task committed to them, as restated in Sec-

---

U.S. Government Printing Office, June 6, 1966); *Hearings before the Subcommittee No. 5 of the House Committee on the Judiciary on Miscellaneous Proposals regarding the Civil Rights of Persons*, 89th Cong., 2nd Sess. (Washington, D.C.: U.S. Government Printing Office, May 5–26, 1966).

tion 501. Chapter VI contains a detailed study of these policies in actual operation. This function, unlike the individual-complaint–processing function and the "wide-spectrum"–negotiation function, is not performed through either formal or informal administration of legal rules. It is essentially an "action-proposing" or "action" function on the part of the Commission and its local sections. It involves the insertion by these agencies into the local and state-wide communities of action that is calculated to produce change for the better in the status of their human relations.

PART VI. POWERS AND DUTIES OF THE COMMISSION AND ITS LOCAL SECTIONS

This part is quite similar to sections of existing state civil-rights statutes and to Section 706 of the Harvard Model Act and Section 702 of the Uniform Model Act. It contains a series of what can properly be called auxiliary powers. Some of them are procedural in nature and designed to facilitate the performance of one or more functions allocated to the Commission and its local sections under Part V of this Act.

The last sentence of Subsection (3) of Section 601 allows the Commission to fix the compensation of the executive director and other members of the Commission or local section staffs. This sentence will have to be deleted in a state whose constitution or laws preclude a commission from doing this.

Subsections (4) and (5) of Section 601 are designed to permit the Commission to receive financial aid from and to cooperate with the federal government relative to the handling of intergroup-relations problems. The Civil Rights Act of 1964 in the area of employment discrimination provides that the Equal Employment Opportunity Commission may utilize the services of state and local agencies charged with administration of fair-employment-practices laws and reimburse them for the services rendered. It also provides that that Commission may enter into written agreements with these agencies in the interest of effective enforcement of the federal prohibition against employment discrimination. The Alpha Model Federal Civil-Rights Act contemplates far more extensive federal assistance to state and local commissions pursuant to written agreements for cooperation. These subsections make it possible for the Commission to make these agreements and to receive this important aid.

The rule-making power stated in Subsection (6) of Section 601 is "legislative" in nature rather than "interpretative" so far as procedural rules and rules promulgated under Section 721 relative to record-keeping are concerned.

Subsection (2) of Section 602 is an important procedural authority granted to the Commission that is not contained in either the Harvard Model Act or the Uniform Model Act. It is, however, a provision found in the better local civil-rights ordinances, such as the one establishing the Pittsburgh Commission on Human Relations.[17] The provision permits the Commission to hold hearings for study and investigation purposes wholly apart from the filing of complaints. The authority thus backs up what has been called in this book the "wide-spectrum"–negotiation function although it also has many other uses relative to individual and general situations involving human relations. It permits the Commission to operate in the various ways that congressional committees and agencies (such as the Federal Trade Commission and the Interstate Commerce Commission) do.

Subsection (8) of Section 602 also is of special significance. We have previously noted the wide-spectrum"–negotiation function and the new substantive law in Section 811 that backs up effectively the use of formal and informal techniques of negotiation with large segments of the community. There remain, however, considerable areas of activity in the community that may not rise to the level of a law violation, either of Section 811 or of the more usual forms of civil-rights law. Nevertheless, it may be vitally important to process a complaint concerning this activity and even to hold a formal hearing concerning it and perhaps to issue a formal recommendation for solving the dispute. This subsection and the whole array of procedural authority relative to complaints contained in Part VII are linked together. They permit the Commission to deal formally, as well as informally, with complaints concerning activity that is not a violation of law but that presents a dispute that the Commission should attempt to resolve. Subsection (11) permits the Commission to utilize the subpoena power and other typical hearing powers even with regard to this class of complaints.

PART VII. PROCEDURES RELATIVE TO COMPLAINTS;
REMEDIES; JUDICIAL REVIEW; RECORDS

The procedure under Part VII relates to three main kinds of ac-

[17] See Appendix C.

tions: (1) Commission actions for enforcement of Section 811 against a whole class of respondents representing a segment of the business community, a whole profession, unions as a whole, or a group of private organizations; (2) actions against individual respondents for enforcement of those sections of Part VIII proscribing specific kinds of unlawful discriminatory acts; and (3) actions to resolve disputes concerning discriminatory activity that does not violate any section of Part VIII of the Act.

The full panoply of rules provided by this part applies to the first two classes of actions. Some of these rule are obviously inapplicable to the third class of actions, such as those relating to judicial review or enforcement of orders.

The procedure for all three classes of actions is in general as follows: certain designated persons may file a charge with the Commission or one of its local sections complaining of a discriminatory act. The chairman of the Commission or local section then designates a commissioner, called the investigating commissioner, to assume responsibility for investigating the charge, with the help of the commission staff. If this commissioner finds from evidence gathered that there is probable cause for believing the allegations of the charge, he must attempt to adjust the matter through conciliation unless he judges this process to be inadvisable under the circumstances. His objective, in the case of an unlawful discriminatory act, is a conciliation agreement between the parties, that contains a consent cease and desist order. If the commissioner attempts conciliation and a conciliation agreement containing a consent cease and desist order is reached on or before the thirtieth day following his service on the parties on his probable-cause determination, he must either accept or reject it within that period. If he accepts an agreement, that decision will constitute an order of the Commission thirty days after its service upon the parties unless the Commission acts to the contrary. If no agreement is reached or if an agreement reached is rejected within the permitted time, the investigating commissioner is required upon request of the complainant or aggrieved individual (if different from the former), to issue to the respondent a formal complaint in the name of the Commission or local section together with a notice of hearing and to provide copies to the other parties. The hearing is conducted usually by a panel of one or more commissioners or staff members who must be other than those associated with the investigation of the complaint. The Commission or local section may also elect to conduct the hearing *en banc* as would undoubtedly be the case in most actions against large segments of an industry, all the members of a profession, and similar respondents. After the hearing is completed, the parties are given an opportunity to submit proposed findings of fact and conclusions before the panel hands down a tentative decision and to file exceptions to and present argument concerning that decision after it has been made. Final decision that an unlawful discriminatory act has been committed requires the panel to issue an order to cease and desist. This order may include one or more of a whole range of sanctions. The order is subject to judicial review upon petition of the parties and to judicial enforcement upon petition of the Commission or its local sections.

The procedure in Part VII contains correctives for each of the problems discussed at length in Chapter 5 relative to weaknesses in existing state civil-rights acts. The first corrective relates to the matter of who may file a charge. Under Section 702 an individual aggrieved by a discriminatory act may file a charge as well as a commissioner, the attorney general, or any civil-rights organization having reason to believe that a discriminatory act has been committed. The need for granting authority to the Commission or to a commissioner to file a charge of discrimination was discussed in Chapter 5. The principal gain from this change, over many existing acts, is the ability it gives to the Commission to shape its business and to emphasize in its enforcement of the Act areas and matters most needing to be reached. Moreover, the Act permits the single commissioner to file a complaint rather than confining that permission to the Commission acting as a whole on the ground that the Commission has other important work to do and this work can be adequately performed by a single commissioner. The premission to file a complaint has also been extended to civil-rights organizations to assure that difficult problems of discrimination will more certainly be brought to the Commission's attention. Many of these organizations are in far closer touch with the harmful activity being directed against minority groups than is the Commission. The hand of these organizations needs to be strengthened within the ethnic and similar groups which they serve. They can be made more serviceable not only to these groups but also to the community at large if they are given this privilege. Complaints by commissioners are more likely to arise as a result of general investigations conducted by the Commission or local sections as a side product of investigations of charges being investigated by single commissioners. Several state and local laws now permit both individual commissioners (in Colorado for instance[18]) and civil-rights organizations (Rhode Island[19]) to file charges. Section 702 also adopts the practice of many states in permitting the Attorney General to file a complaint. This authority has not been utilized extensively by this official where it exists. Nevertheless, there may be special reasons for utilizing the value of a complaint filed by this official relative to some respondents and for this reason the authority is included in Section 702.

It has previously been noted that Section 703 establishes a one-year statute of limitations for the filing of a charge. The filing of a formal complaint by an investigating commissioner who has failed to secure adjustment of the subject-matter of a charge by conciliation must also be done, under Subsection (c) of Section 711, on or before one year after the discriminatory act allegedly occurred. This follows the precedent of New York which in 1965, after twenty years' experience with a ninety-day limitation period, adopted the one-year period.[20] A discussion of the issues relative to an appropriate statute of limitation in a civil-rights statute may be found in Chapter 5.

Sections 704–711 and 712 operate to effectuate an internal separation of functions for the Commission. Sections 704–711 require the chairman of the Commission to designate a commissioner to perform the function of gathering evidence in order to exmine the allegations of a charge, to determine whether probable cause exists, to seek to adjust a probable violation by conciliation, and to file a complaint and notice of hearing in the name of the Commission if conciliation fails to produce a satisfactory adjustment. Section 712 requires the chairman of the Commission to designate a hearing panel of one or more commissioners or staff members to conduct a hearing on a formal complaint of discriminatory act. The investigating commissioner and those staff members who assisted him in investigating the charge from which the formal complaint emerged are made ineligible for appointment by this section. In this way the functions of the Commission prior to filing a formal complaint are carefully separated from the functions of the Commission in a formal adjudication relative to that complaint. The technique of internal separation of the functions of investigating a charge, determining existence of probable cause, negotiating settlements, and instituting proceedings from the function of

---

[18] *Colo. Rev. Stat. Ann.* 80-21-6 (1964).

[19] *R.I. Gen. Laws Ann.* 28-5-17 (1957); Pittsburgh Ordinance No. 237 § 8(a) (1955), *Race Relations Law Reporter,* Vol. 1 (1956), p. 750.

[20] N.Y. Exec. Law, § 297(3), *as amended* (Supp., 1967).

adjudication serves to preclude the performance of inconsistent functions by the same person that might prevent impartial performance of the latter function. This technique was adopted in the Federal Administrative Procedure Act in 1946 and has worked out well in practice.[21]

The problems created by the concept of reasonable or probable cause in existing state civil-rights statutes for determining whether to believe the allegations of a complaint have been fully examined in Chapter 5. The problem is essentially one of undue delay in making the determination, the unfairness to complainants of the method of making the determination, the unevenness in application of the concept of probable cause, and the absence of an adequate remedy for incorrect determinations. The undue delay in making the determination has been due to the practice of commissions in gathering evidence in the investigation relative to the allegations of the complaint as if it were preparing for presenting both sides of a case and then weighing the evidence as if making a final decision rather than conducting an investigation. The unfairness to complainants of this method of determining probable cause is that they have no opportunity to participate in the *ex parte* process of making the determination and, when it is adverse to them, no opportunity to have a hearing on the charge against the respondent although the respondent upon being faced with an adverse determination always has the right to a hearing. The uncertainty as to the correctness of the determination and the unevenness in applying the probable-cause concept stems basically from the lack of objective administrative criteria for making the determination or from the lack of a decisional method developing these criteria. The absence of an adequate method for avoiding these problems results from the fact that neither the complainant nor the aggrieved person is permitted to challenge the determination of no probable cause before the agency or the courts. A good example of this situation is provided by the Massachusetts Civil-Rights Act. The only Commission "order" explicitly provided for by that act is one issued by that Commission after a formal hearing of a complaint and only "such order" is made subject to judicial review on petition of a complainant.[22] The dismissal of a complaint after investigation on the ground that there is a lack of reasonable cause for believing its allegations

---

[21] 5 U.S.C. § 55(d) (Supp. II, 1965–1966); see, Kenneth C. Davis, *Administrative Law Text* (St. Paul, Minnesota: West Publishing Co. (1959), pp. 225–244).
[22] *Mass. Gen. Laws Ann.*, ch. 151B, § 6 (1965).

may be a Commission "order" but it is clearly not the "such order" referred to in the judicial review section of the Massachusetts statute.

The Alpha Model Act seeks to remedy each of these defects. The undue delay due to the method of evaluating evidence gathered in the investigation is distinctly precluded by specifying how the determination is to be made. This method or definition is spelled out in Subsection (c) of Section 705. It requires the investigating commissioner, and, in conjunction with Section 708, the review hearing panel, to determine if probable cause exists or not by regard only for evidence supporting the charge and by ascertaining if that evidence is of a substantial nature. If regard for that evidence alone indicates that it is of substantial nature, a finding that probable cause exists is mandatory. This provision also remedies in part the problem of the unfairness of a final determination of no probable cause based upon a weighing of the evidence without giving the complainant a hearing. It does so by eliminating the weighing of evidence and substituting a test of evidence more favorable to the complainant without prejudicing the respondent in any way. The unevenness with which the probable-cause concept has been administered and the uncertainty concerning the correctness of these determinations is spoken to by providing for both agency and judicial review of these determinations. This is done through Section 708 which governs the availability of agency review and through Section 720 which provides for review of Commission orders without limitation. Subsection (e) of Section 708 directs the Commission to issue an order dismissing the charge if the review hearing panel finds that probable cause does not exist for believing the charge. This is a reviewable order. Unless the complainant requests and participates in a review hearing, however, the order dismissing the complaint for lack of probable cause to believe it under Subsection (d) of Section 707 is not reviewable.

Sections 709–711 are concerned with efforts of the Commission to use conciliation to enforce the Act, with conciliation agreements, and with rendering them enforceable. All state civil-rights statutes administered by human-relations commissions call for a commission effort through conciliation to persuade a respondent to undo the effects of unlawful conduct which it has probable cause to believe he has been performing. Several of the problems presented by these statutes have been discussed in Chapter 5. Most contain no limitation on the length of the period during which conciliation may continue. Due to a misguided reliance upon conciliation as almost the sole basis for enforcement of civil-rights laws, many human-relations commissions have delayed resort to public hearings of complaints for grossly unreasonable periods. Conciliation efforts have sometimes been continued for periods of a year or more. In the second place civil-rights statutes generally preclude a disclosure of any information concerning efforts in a particular case to eliminate a discriminatory practice by conciliation. The lack of pressure by the public resulting from its knowledge and disapproval of respondents' conduct simply enhances the probability that a respondent will do nothing to change his ways. Even if conciliation agreements are reached, moreover, they are usually not enforceable in the courts. Even if technically enforceable, as in a few states, most statutes do not speak to the content of conciliation agreements which to a large extent determines their value.

Section 711 effectively resolves the problem of undue delay in conducting an effort at conciliation to eliminate an unlawful discriminatory act by requiring the investigating commissioner to issue a complaint and set a hearing on it within thirty days after his probable-cause determination if the complainant or individual aggrieved requests this action. The according of this right to a hearing is the best possible remedy for undue delay in conciliation. Section 709 adds a new dimension to conciliation efforts by providing that a respondent may at any time after the filing of a charge request time in which to work out a conciliation agreement containing a consent cease and desist order disposing of the proceeding. Existing statutes leave conciliation efforts entirely up to the commissions. This provision may encourage efforts of complainants and respondents to act earlier, particularly in light of the certainty that a public hearing under Section 711 will be held within thirty days after the probable-cause determination. Section 710 provides for the necessary and permissible content of conciliation agreements containing consent cease and desist orders. It also provides in its Subsection (c) that a decision accepting a conciliation agreement in accordance with the section by the investigating commissioner becomes an order of the Commission automatically on the thirtieth day after its service on the parties. This means that, as an order of the Commission, it is enforceable in the courts under Section 720. In spelling out the necessary content of a conciliation agreement Section 710 follows the settlement procedure developed after long experience by the Federal Trade Commission, as explained in Chapter 5. It requires an agreement, for example, to contain an express waiver of any right to challenge the validity of the consent cease and desist order entered in accordance with it and an agreement that the order has the same force and effect as if entered after a full hearing.

Section 711 relates to the filing of a complaint upon the failure of conciliation efforts. The purpose of this section in granting the complainant or individual aggrieved a right to a hearing has been explained previously. One important related feature of this section is the privilege it accords to the investigating commissioner to issue a formal complaint at any time after making his probable-cause determination that he concludes conciliation efforts no longer are feasible. Another feature is the protection the section accords to the complainant or the individual aggrieved by deeming a refusal or failure of the investigating commissioner to issue a complaint upon request by either of them an order of the Commission. Since Section 720 makes orders of the Commission subject to judicial review, this makes the failure or refusal to issue a formal complaint also subject to judicial review.

Section 712, 713, and 714 governing designation of a hearing panel, procedures at the hearing, and transcript and records follow modern administrative procedure statutes.

Section 715 relative to findings and decisions has no counterpart in existing state civil-rights statutes, except those few subject to general administrative procedure statutes. Section 715 also has no counterpart in the Harvard Model Act or the Uniform Model Act. In most instances under the Alpha Model Act a hearing panel of one or two commissioners or staff members will be designated to conduct a hearing on a complaint. Upon concluding the hearing the panel is required under this section (the term "Commission" in the section includes a hearing panel) to give the parties a reasonable opportunity to submit proposed findings of fact, conclusions, and supporting reasons. After considering these the panel then enters a tentative decision. At this point, the parties are given the opportunity to consider this decision, to file exceptions to it as well as a brief, and to present argument. The approach utilized here resembles the one utilized by the Federal Administrative Procedure Act in the situation in which the agency rather than one of its hearing examiners decides the case initially. The greater opportunity to influence decision accorded to the parties seems desirable in light of the lessened period for conciliation and the usefulness of a fuller hearing of the parties in obtaining an understanding of the reasons for the decision and its meaning. The section also specifies the status of the evidence that must exist before the

Commission may make a final decision and issue an order on the basis of it. Most state civil-rights statutes and the Uniform Model Act fail to do this. The Harvard Model Act specifies that "a preponderance of evidence in the record considered as a whole" is required.[23] The Alpha Model Act follows the Federal Administrative Procedure Act[24] in specifying that the decision and order may be issued only after a consideration of "the whole record or those parts of it as may be cited by any party and supported by and in accordance with the reliable, probative, and substantial evidence." This is a standard that has worked reasonably well with federal agencies. In the civil-rights field this standard seems especially appropriate where proof of discrimination is so difficult and the likelihood of its existence so great.

Section 716 resembles existing state statutes in authorizing orders that direct a respondent not only to cease and desist from unlawful conduct but also to take affirmative action to provide an adequate corrective for the violation. It does, however, contain a larger series of permissible forms of affirmative action than most of these statutes. Some are made necessary by the institution of the new form of civil-rights law contained in Section 811. This section covers a vast range of potential conduct the correction of which will require many new forms of affirmative conduct in Commission orders. One example of needed new remedies is spelled out in Subsection (a) (3) of this section: the institution by the respondent of occupational-training programs to equalize opportunities for advancement between different classes of employees. Others are made necessary to provide remedies against discriminatory conduct of official agencies, agency heads, and their employees. The suspension or removal from or disqualification for public office and public employment permitted by Subsection (d) of this section may be essential to move some official agencies, public officers, and public employees to stop discriminating against minority and other disadvantaged groups. A special sanction has been devised for official agencies whose officials or employees perform unlawful discriminatory acts. In Subsection (e) of this section the agency is made liable for payment of any damages and costs assessed against those officials or employees.[25] Subsection (c) (8) of the section is patterned

---

[23] § 707 (g). See note 3 above.

[24] 5 U.S.C. § 556(d) (Supp. II, 1965–1966).

[25] This type of remedy was proposed in Section 3 of S. 1497, which was introduced in the first session of the 89th Congress [*Hearings . . . on S. 3296, S. 1497*, p. 30].

after Subsection (b) (8) of Section 706 of the Uniform Model Act.[26] This provision permits the Commission to order the respondent to cancel, rescind, or revoke a contract, deed, or other instrument transferring real property, which is the subject of a complaint of an unlawful discriminatory act, to a person who had knowledge prior to the transfer or creation of a legally binding obligation that a determination of probable-cause had been made with respect to a discriminatory act by the respondent concerning that property. Subsection (c) (9) of the section permits the Commission to order the respondent to pay the aggrieved individual any profits obtained by the former through a violation of Section 845, subject to the principles of equity. Section 845 relates to blockbusting activities, a practice whose principal aim is profit from exploiting the foibles and fears of whites who own property that Negroes or other minority groups may be interested in buying. The approach in this section is superior to that utilized in the similar provision, Subsection (b) (9) of Section 706, of the Uniform Model Act.[27] In the first place, the latter gives the profits to the "complainant" in all instances without limitation although the complainant may be a commissioner, the attorney general, or a non-profit organization chartered to combat discrimination. There is no justification for such a provision. Only the individual aggrieved by the unlawful discriminatory act should be entitled to these profits. In the second place, the provision of the Uniform Model Act is generalized to reach any violation of the act. There may well be other situations in which the remedy of taking away profits obtained from an illegal act would be appropriate but they are not easy to surmise in advance. While this remedy can hardly be called drastic, it is an unusual remedy for what amounts to a tort. Limiting the provision to a violation of Section 845 will not preclude the use of it as a model in other situations since the provision is not a limiting one. On the other hand, this form of statement indicates that care should be taken in extending it to other violations. The provision is modelled after a similar provision in the Lanham Act relating to recovery for violation of a trade mark registered in the United States Patent Office.[28] Subsection (c) (10) follows both the Harvard Model Act and the Uniform Model Act in allowing at least $500 for any injury caused by an unlawful discriminatory act. Subsection (e) (1) allows the Commission to direct a

[26] See note 4, above.
[27] *Ibid.*
[28] 15 U.S.C. § 1117 (1964).

police department or like agency to expunge and destroy a criminal record made concerning an individual aggrieved by a discriminatory act of a police officer. This remedy is essential to correct the damage done by a police officer in violating the Act. This type of remedy has been utilized in the form of recommended action by the Philadelphia Police Advisory Board and its experience clearly indicates the need for it.[29]

Section 717 makes a Commission finding that a respondent has committed an unlawful discriminatory act binding on an official agency that issued the license or awarded the contract under which the act was committed. This seems a superior approach to that of either the Harvard Model Act or the Uniform Model Act. The former authorizes the Commission to suspend or revoke the license.[30] It does not speak to the contract problem. The Uniform Model Act makes its finding relative to the respondent binding on the licensing or contract agency only when it finds that the respondent's board of directors or a high management official authorized, recklessly tolerated, or performed the discriminatory act.[31] The first approach errs by giving the Commission a task that can best be performed by the licensing or contract agency in light of competing considerations involved in the administration of its statutory program and of the civil-rights act. The latter errs by casting on the Commission a determination that is relevant not to the appropriate binding quality of a determination by the Commission but to whether a license or contract should be terminated or other remedial action taken by the licensing or contract agency in light of the violation. The approach in Section 717 of the Alpha Model Act more properly allocates between disparate agencies the two basic functions: one concerning determination of whether a violation of the Civil-Rights Act has occurred and the other its relevance or application to administration of another program. If the contract or licensing agency proves to be reluctant to apply severe enough sanctions for violations of the Civil-Rights Act, then will be the time to take corrective action. It should not be assumed that either type of agency will fail to do its work well in this regard. The situation is to be distinguished from official agencies whose own performance or that of their employees is in question under this Act, as in the case of police de-

[29] Philadelphia Police Advisory Board, *Annual Report* (1963), "Report of Complaints," pp. 5–22.

[30] § 707(g). See note 3, above.

[31] § 706(c), (d). See note 4, above.

partments. In the latter situation the department is sitting in judgment on itself in effect and we already have a history of the typical results obtained in this situation and the public reaction to the department's performance of the adjudicative task.[32]

Section 720 deals with judicial review and enforcement of orders of the Commission. Most state civil-rights statutes permit only a complainant or a respondent to secure judicial review of an order of a human-relations commission. Section 720 of the Alpha Model Act accords the right to secure judicial review to any party or to any person aggrieved by the order. The definition of "party" in Section 701 includes a complainant, individual aggrieved by an unlawful discriminatory act, respondent, and any person admitted as a party or properly seeking and entitled as of right to be admitted as a party. This corresponds to the definition contained in the Federal Administrative Procedure Act.[33] The concept of a "person aggrieved" will extend the right to other persons such as a union or business competitive to the respondent who have legitimate interests in the equal enforcement of the Act. This section is patterned upon the New York Law Against Discrimination.[34] It makes any order of the Commission reviewable except an order dismissing a complaint under Section 707 for lack of probable cause to believe it where a review hearing of this determination is not requested under Section 708. Subsection (f) of Section 720 also simplifies the process to be followed by the Commission in obtaining enforcement of its order where it is not challenged by any party to the hearing. Under these circumstances the Commission does not need to support its finding in court by a showing that substantial evidence exists on the record considered as a whole. Otherwise the court must determine that such evidence does exist to support the Commission's findings in order to sustain them on judicial review or to enforce the order based on them.

PART VIII   UNLAWFUL DISCRIMINATORY ACTS

This part contains six subparts. Subpart A contains definitions especially relevant to Subpart B but also relevant to other subparts and other parts of the Act. Subpart B contains what may be called the general prohibition of unlawful discriminatory acts. This subpart also contains specific prohibitions of discrimination by official agencies,

[32] See Chapter 6, at note 92 and following.
[33] 5 U.S.C. § 551(3) (Supp. II, 1965–1966).
[34] See Appendix A.

their heads, and employees. It finally speaks to persons who discriminate in conducting programs and activities operating with official financial assistance or a license. Subpart C deals with discrimination in employment, Subpart D with discrimination in public accommodation and private educational institutions, Subpart E with discrimination in real-estate transactions, and Subpart F with certain other types of discrimination.

Section 811 is designed to do for the field of civil rights what Section 5 of the Federal Trade Commission Act of 1914 was designed to do for federal antitrust policy. It is an omnibus prohibition designed to include as well as go beyond any specific prohibitions of discrimination against minority groups by establishing a fundamental principle. It does this in several ways. In the first place, it applies to a person engaging in almost any form of human activity affecting the participation of other persons in the public life of a community: a business, a professional service; an organization of employees, businessmen, or professional men; a program or activity operating under a license or official financial assistance; or a government activity. In the second place, it is addressed to any unfair or unreasonable restriction upon the opportunities of others and not merely to discrimination against them. In the third place, the opportunities to be protected are arrayed in the broadest kind of way: that is, as economic, housing, educational, training, associational, public-accommodations, political, and governmental opportunities. In the fourth place, the persons to be protected are those suffering from unreasonable restrictions created by others relative to obtaining and taking advantage of opportunities due not only to race, color, religion, ancestry, and national origin, as with most state civil-rights statutes, but also to age, sex, economic status and any other basis that is unreasonable. Protection of persons against age discrimination in employment has been adopted by numerous states. The federal government and several states have also protected persons against sex discrimination in employment. The protection of persons in a low economic status from discrimination and other unreasonable restrictions based upon their low economic status is one of the most needed of protections in the field of civil rights. This type of activity is one of the more obvious facts of life in American society both in private and official activity and it does incalculable damage. The choice of the term "economic status" follows the pattern set in Title II of the proposed Civil Rights Act of 1966 relative to discrimination in according the right to serve on grand and petit juries in state courts.[35] The problem of discrimination based upon economic status should be reached in all areas. The coverage of discrimination upon "any other basis that is unreasonable" is new and especially appropriate to an omnibus provision like Section 811. It will permit the Commission to examine other bases of discrimination in light of their effect upon the person and his opportunities. If the effect is substantially the same as in the case of the specified bases of discrimination, it may be attacked by the Commission as unlawful. The final point about Section 811 is that it reaches restrictions which considered by themselves alone may not be unreasonable but which are, nevertheless, unreasonable due to the fact that they are practiced by a group of persons even though their action is the product of separate decisions and in no sense conspiratorial in nature.

The great value of Section 811 is that it will permit the Commission to study the various facets of community life and evaluate which of them are creating the unreasonable and unfair restrictions upon the opportunities of minority and other disadvantaged groups. In light of these studies the Commission can then conduct negotiation on a wide scale looking to their elimination and where necessary hold hearings for whole classes of respondents engaging in the prohibited conduct. It can, where warranted, issue administrative orders to eliminate the harmful activity and to direct the performance of affirmative action so as to open up many opportunities for many disadvantaged groups. It establishes a principle that should be adequate to permit effective remedial action against most forms of harmful activity that have been or may in the future be directed against the perennially disadvantaged groups of our country.

Section 812 is patterned after a number of bills introduced during the first and second sessions of the 89th Congress to deal with abuse of authority by police officers. Subsection (a) of the section was suggested by Title VI of H. R. 14770 introduced on May 2, 1966, by Representative Jacob H. Gilbert, Democrat, of New York.[36] This title provided for suspension or removal from or disqualification for office of a police officer under circumstances similar to those contained in this section. Subsection (a), however, speaks to all denials of equal protection by police officers when based not only on race or color, as in Title VI of H. R. 14770, but also on religion, ancestry, national origin, age,

[35] *Hearings . . . on S. 3296, S. 1497*, p. 23.
[36] *Hearings before the Subcommittee No. 5*, No. 16, pp. 725, 760.

sex, economic status, or any other basis that is unreasonable. Subsection (b) of the section is similar to H. R. 5427 which was introduced in the first session of the 89th Congress by Representative William F. Ryan, Democrat, of New York.[37] This bill sought to reach the prohibited conduct only through the vehicle of criminal sanctions, a notoriously inadequate remedy in the civil rights field. Subsection (b), like subsection (a), provides a far more effective administrative remedy. It also specifies additional unlawful acts for which the remedy is available. These additional unlawful acts include the subjecting of any person to undue harassment or gross personal indignity or insult, to an illegal search or seizure or arrest; and to refusals to provide protection to any person as well as his property or business against unlawful violence. These additional acts have been dealt with satisfactorily by the Philadelphia Police Advisory Board and should be included in legislation of this sort in order to cover the full range of harmful conduct now in evidence. Violations of Section 812 will subject both the respondent police officer and his public employer to the duty of paying damages for the injury or death caused another under Section 716. In this respect the section operates in much the same way as Title V of H. R. 14770 previously mentioned.[38] This title related to "civil indemnification."

Of course, the proposal of Section 812 at the state or local level will set up a hue and cry from local police departments and state law-enforcement agencies if we are to judge by the fate of proposals for police review boards noted in Chapter 6. It is believed that part of the problem has been the fact that under these proposals a specialized kind of human-relations agency to deal only with police-community relations was to be created. It seems clear that where an established human-relations commission with general jurisdiction over matters of discrimination has performed the same task, there has been relatively good reception for its work. It is true that in Pittsburgh, where we find the chief example of this, the Commission has not had regulatory jurisdiction over cases of abuse of authority by police officers. Nevertheless, it is essential that the matter be dealt with through regulatory authority in an independent agency particularly in southern states where the worst forms of abuse of police authority have been taking place. The absence of an independent agency with this authority simply means that we can expect the situation to continue as it has for

[37] *Id.*, pp. 3–4.
[38] *Id.*, pp. 753–760.

so long. Moreover, in principle, an independent agency is justified in the sense that no agency is above the law nor removed from independent judgments as to whether it is abiding by the law, particularly in the case of such gross violations as are covered by Section 812. For the purposes of processing complaints of abuse of police authority, the Commission could utilize a police officer as a member of the hearing panel to hear a complaint. This might make the proposed section somewhat more acceptable to police departments which claim that the use of independent agencies to try cases of this sort means that they will lack understanding of the police "point of view" and of police problems.

Subsection (a) of Section 813 deals with denials of equal protection of the laws under the Constitution or laws of the United States on a more generalized basis than Subsection (a) of Section 812, which applies such a prohibition only to police officers, and than the Civil Rights Act of 1964, which applies only to school boards (Title III), public colleges (Title III), and authorities operating other governmental facilities (Title IV). In the first place, Subsection (a) reaches all agencies of the State and of its political subdivisions. This includes, of course, their members or heads and employees, by virtue of the definition of agency contained in Section 812. In the second place, Subsection (a) specifies some of the trouble areas in which denial of equal protection is occurring but without limiting the coverage of the provision as is the case with Titles III and IV of the Civil Rights Act of 1964. The first specification relates to public schools and other governmental facilities. The second concerns licenses through which official agencies control entry into vast areas of economic opportunities. License here, by virtue of the definition in Section 801, covers the whole range of governmental permissions, including a charter, a registration, and a certificate. The third trouble area specified relates to welfare-assistance, services, loans, grants, insurance, loan guarantees, and any other thing generally available to other persons from a given agency. This will be especially valuable to members of minority groups who have experienced, due either to their minority-group or low-income status great difficulties with regard to welfare assistance. Both Sections 812 and 813, like the general provision in Section 811, prohibit discrimination based upon the economic status of a person.

Subsection (a) of Section 813 specifies that denials of equal protection by official agencies are unlawful when based on a person's race, color, religion, ancestry, national origin, or other basis that is unreasonable. Obviously not mentioned here as previously, is discrimination on the basis of sex or age. Nevertheless, discrimination on one of these bases may be prohibited in a particular situation or class of situations under the concept "other basis that is unreasonable." For example, it might not be unreasonable to bar a girl or an older person respectively, from admission to a public high school conduted only for boys or only for younger persons. On the other hand, it would be unreasonable ordinarily to bar a person of female sex or an older person from attending a community college.

Subsection (b) of Section 813 simply extrapolates on Subsection (b) of Section 812 so as to apply the prohibition of deprivations or rights, privileges, or immunities secured by the Constitution or laws of the United States to any official agency. One example of the application of this subsection would be the utilization of inspection ordinances by local government agencies so as to harass a homeowner in an unreasonable manner.

Section 814 applies to official condonation of violations of Section 811, 812, or 813. The agencies of the state and its political subdivisions already are subjected to liability for payment of damages assessed against a respondent agency head or employee found to have committed some form of unlawful discriminatory act. This liability applies without regard to the agency of the state or of the political subdivision having permitted, authorized, or condoned the violation. The effect of this section will be to permit a respondent agency to be subjected to other remedies available to the Commission under Section 716.

Section 815 builds upon the lessons derived from enactment and administration of Title VI of the Civil Rights Act of 1964 relative to discrimination in programs and activities receiving federal financial assistance. In the first place, this title, despite certain deficiences, has proved to be the most significant part of the 1964 act. In the second place, the title left uncovered vast areas of discrimination by organizations operating under federal charters and licenses. It also specifically exempted several forms of federal financial assistance which constitute the locus of most discrimination in the fields of real-property transactions and financing of real-property transactions. These difficulties are fully explained in Chapter 1. Section 815 adopts the basic principle of Title VI of the 1964 act and extends it in the needed directions by covering official and private action under all forms of official financial assistance and under licenses. As earlier indicated, the latter term is defined in Section 801 to reach the widest possible area of governmental permissions.

Subpart C in dealing with discrimination in employment follows the pattern utilized in most state civil-rights acts. The chief difference is that the term "employer" covers persons employing one or more employees within the state. As explained in Chapter 5, several major industrial states, such as New Jersey, Minnesota, and Wisconsin, have found it feasible to apply their statutes to such employers. In addition, there is great need to cover these employers since they frequently have operations in which members of minority groups are more able to perform well. Finally, the ability to enter into employment in these smaller businesses may operate to hasten the time in which members of minority groups will gain the necessary know-how to start comparable businesses of their own.

The term "individual," which is used to refer to the person who is the target of alleged discrimination in employment, is defined in Section 821 to exclude any individual employed by or seeking employment by his parents, spouse, or child, or employed or seeking employment in the domestic service of any person. This provision follows a commonly stated exemption in state civil-rights acts. It seeks to protect interests deemed more important than the interest in civil rights.

The third feature of this subpart is that its prohibitions apply to discrimination in employment on account of race, color, religion, ancestry, national origin, sex, or age of the individual. Discrimination in employment based on sex was prohibited by the Civil Rights Act of 1964 and discrimination based on sex or age or both have been prohibited by numerous states, as of January 1967. The 1964 federal act and many of the state acts include these prohibited bases of discrimination along with the other bases without special treatment. This indicates that no special statute is needed to deal with discrimination in employment on the basis of sex or age. Any peculiarities of these types of cases can be handled though definition or statement of special conditions or provisos. In defining "age" the Alpha Model Act follows the lead of the Michigan Civil Rights Act in including the age bracket beginning at thirty-five and proceeding up from that point. Most statutes on age discrimination set an age bracket beginning at an older age, usually forty or forty-five. The cut-off point is usually sixty-five and that is the cut-off point selected in the definition of age contained in Section 801. The central purpose of prohibitions of discrimination on the basis of age is to protect the middle-aged and older groups of persons who, although thoroughly able to perform the duties of various positions, are frequently denied employment solely or principally due to their age. This purpose was emphasized by the President's Executive Order No. 11141 of 1964 which states the federal policy that contractors and subcontractors shall not discriminate in employment on account of age in the performance of their federal contracts.[39] Middle-age is a relative term, but it seems clear that many persons are not regarded favorably for positions if over thirty-five. For this reason the age thirty-five has been utilized in defining the term "age" in Section 801. Discrimination on the basis of persons of younger age can be handled under Section 811.

The Uniform Model Act suggests that it is wise policy for a state to make its first civil-rights statute strictly correspond to the provisions of the Civil Rights Act of 1964. It does this by marking certain provisions and parts of them as "basic" parts. On the other hand, it suggests that another version should be enacted as either initial or subsequent legislation if the state really wants to go beyond the federal approach. The latter version differs not merely in, for example, the number of employees required for an employer to be covered but also in the very construction of many foundational provisions. Sometimes the two alternative proposals call for quite different versions of the same section of the Act. This is not only a confusing way to suggest legislation. It is also believed to be an unwise suggestion. A state should be presented with a model that by and large is good for today as well as tomorrow and that can by simple amendment be built upon so as to be made more or less inclusive. This is not possible if a state selects what in the Uniform Model Act is called its "basic" parts. For this reason, the Alpha Model Act is proffered in but one version. Its coverage can be scaled down, kept at its present suggested level of comprehension, or expanded still further. But the change in coverage detail does not require a change in the underlying model. At the same time, the Alpha Model Act does cover the full range of violations presently covered by Title VII concerning employment in the Civil Rights Act of 1964. Moreover, it applies to transactions in interstate commerce as well as intrastate commerce. For these reasons the Alpha Model Act possesses the distinct advantage of serving not only as a good model for a foreshortened initial effort in the civil-rights field but also for a long-range, pervasive operation.

[39] *Federal Register*, Vol. 29 (Washington, D.C.: U.S. Government Printing Office, February 14, 1964), p. 2477.

Section 826 spells out several exceptions to coverage under Subpart C. Subsection (a) provides for an exception in the circumstance where race, color, religion, ancestry, national origin, age, or sex is a bona fide qualification necessary to the normal operation of a business. This is a fairly typical type of provision in existing statutes. Subsection (b) provides for an exception relative to occupational training programs where one is required to be of no greater age than would permit him, after training, to complete the industry average period of employment before age sixty-five. The slanting of this exception toward younger persons may be warranted in light of the outlay involved in maintaining a training program. So long as older persons are able to obtain training through other means no serious harm is done. This exception is contained in Section 659.024(4) of the Oregon Civil Rights Act by virtue of a recent amendment to that act.[40] As more experience is gained with its operation, it can be further evaluated. If it were to be judged that older persons are unduly hampered by it in obtaining employment, Section 811 will be available to the Commission for providing a corrective. The third exception in Subsection (c) applies to employer actions, otherwise challengeable under Section 826, that are based upon provisions in bona fide retirement, pension, and group or employee insurance plans. This provision is patterned after Subsection (a) of Section 5 of the Pennsylvania Human Relations Act.[41] One of the obvious purposes of this provision is to honor the value of retirement, pension, and like plans even though they involve forced retirements under the age of sixty-five or other action violative of the prohibition against age discrimination. Since a *quid pro quo* is provided under these plans, which intrinsically have great value, the exception is justified. The fourth exception in Subsection (d) relates to religious organizations. It is similar to a provision of the Washington act that is applicable to housing.[42]

Subpart D covers discrimination in both public accommodations and educational institutions. The definition of "place of public accommodations" is designed to cover virtually all business and professional activity. It should be the rare business or profession that can claim exemption. For this reason, this subpart rejects the method either of partial specification of kinds of places of public accommodations covered or of statement of a general formula followed by such partial

[40] See Appendix A.
[41] *Ibid.*
[42] *Ibid.*

specification. Each is likely to suggest less than the fullest possible coverage. The provision in Section 103 calling for a liberal interpretation of the Act should be sufficient to move a fair-minded court to give Section 831 its intended widest possible coverage consistent with its purpose. In addition the very content of the definition demonstrates and is consistent with this purpose. It specifically covers any professional activity as well as any business activity. Neither the Harvard nor the Uniform Model Acts apply to professional activities. Yet it is clear that no professional person can justify denying access to his professional services merely on the basis of race, color, religion, ancestry, national origin, age, or sex. The condition precedent to coverage of either a professional or a business activity is that it be conducted upon the basis that it is open to, accepts, or solicits the patronage or offers goods or services to the general public. To make this point clear the definition excludes private clubs, associations, corporations, or other private organizations. The definition of these organizations is closely patterned upon the criteria proposed by Professor Van Alstyne.[43] The only modification of his criteria is in the last one listed in the definition. A club that is otherwise private under the definition remains so although it permits its facilities to be used by another private club. This is to cover the practice of such private clubs as country clubs in permitting their facilities to be used on occasion for social activities solely by another private organization. This exception should not undercut the purpose of the subpart.

Section 833 is an attempt to deal with a problem of discrimination based upon sex in public accommodations. It is designed to preserve the custom in a business or in a profession of catering to but one of the sexes. An obvious example is a woman's beauty shop or a health spa operating on the basis of alternative periods for serving each of the sexes.

Section 834 applies to discrimination in privately owned or privately operated educational institutions and closely follows the existing law on the subject.[44] Subsection (5) does not preclude a school from using a quota system for the purpose of obtaining a geographical representativeness in its student body. If this system were, as a side matter, to result in one racial, religious, or similar group being preferred, this does not fall within the prohibition of the subsection.

[43] William W. Van Alstyne, "A Critique of the Ohio Public Accommodations Law," *Ohio State Law Journal*, Vol. 22, pp. 201, 208.
[44] See Appendix A.

Under Section 834, Sections 832 and 834 are subject to an exception in favor of religious organizations similar to the exception contained in Section 826.

Subpart E deals comprehensively with discrimination in real-estate transactions, including those dealing with dwellings and commercial spaces, and in the financing of these transactions. It is based upon the Minnesota and New Jersey statutes and the Uniform Model Act, except that it rejects the exemptions of these acts which greatly water down their effectiveness. For example, the "tight-living" exemptions contained in Section 602 of the Uniform Model Act in favor of owner-occupied single and two-family units exempts nearly two-thirds of the available housing in large urban areas like Philadelphia.[45] No justification can be given for an exemption that creates such an obstacle upon a policy of open housing. It may be politically required in order to secure any legislation, but it cannot be justified in terms of the policy of civil-rights acts.

If a state desires to reach real-estate transactions involving only multiple, contiguously located, and publicly assisted housing accommodations, it is suggested that the formulas contained in the Harvard Model Act are well designed for that purpose. These formulas could be utilized in the Alpha Model Act simply by modifying the definition of real property as follows:

Section 841. Definitions.

In this Act

. . .

(2) "Real property" means buildings, structures, real estate, lands, tenements, leaseholds, interests in real-estate cooperatives, condominiums, and hereditaments, corporeal and incorporeal, or any interest therein which constitutes a multiple dwelling, contiguously located housing accommodation or publicly assisted housing accommodation.

. . .

(5) "Multiple dwelling" means [insert definition in Section 201 (g) of the Harvard Model Act].

(6) "Housing accommodation" means [insert definition in Section 201 (f) of the Harvard Model Act].

(7) "Publicly assisted housing accommodation" means [insert definition in Section 201 (h) of the Harvard Model Act].

[45] Philadelphia Commission on Human Relations, *Annual Report* (1964), p. 22.

(8) "Contiguously located housing accommodation" means [insert definition in Section 201(i) of the Harvard Model Act].

Section 843 is similar to provisions of many state civil-rights acts (for example, New York, Minnesota, and California).[46] It is based upon the proposition that discrimination in providing financial assistance is a key factor in maintaining residential segregation of minority groups. This problem is discussed in Chapter 1.

Section 845 is designed to deal effectively with the problem of "blockbusting," a practice that is inherently capable of causing rapid and widespread havoc with the stability of neighborhoods in large cities. This practice, and the efforts to deal with it, have been described in Chapter 6. The section is patterned after the Detroit "antiblockbusting" ordinance.[47]

Section 846 contains an exemption for religious organizations similar to those set forth in Sections 826 and 835.

Subpart F deals with a miscellaneous group of unlawful discriminatory acts. Section 851 is an important new form of civil-rights law. It seeks to protect certain aspects of the freedom to associate. It directs certain organizations of businessmen, tradesmen, or professional men not to exclude or otherwise discriminate against an individual on account of race, color, religion, ancestry, national origin, age, or sex. The organizations reached are those "in which membership is valuable or essential to an individual for the purpose of engaging or advancing in a business, trade, or profession." A provision of this kind has been adopted by Connecticut.[48] Section 851 is as important as any other type of civil-rights provision and further secures valuable economic opportunities.

The Civil Rights Act of 1968 is less extensive in covering discriminatory transactions involving real property, financing of real property, participation in business and professional organizations, and services than is this Alpha Model State Act. Title VIII of the 1968 act provides, in its Section 810(c), for the Secretary of Housing and Urban Development to notify the appropriate state or local agency of a complaint of discrimination in housing where the state or local fair housing law "provides rights and remedies for alleged discriminatory housing practices which are substantially equivalent to the rights and

---

[46] See Appendix A.
[47] Detroit Ordinance 753-F, *Race Relations Law Reporter*, Vol. 7 (1962), p. 1260.
[48] See Appendix A.

remedies provided in this title." Subparts E and F of Part VIII and Part VII of the model state act satisfy the requirements of Section 810(c) relative to substantially equivalent rights and remedies. Indeed, Sections 902–905 of the Alpha Model State Act provide for a complete alternative to administrative process in the form of civil actions to be filed in the courts. Thus, a state government enacting this model act will be able to ensure that its human relations commission will be able to handle complaints of discrimination in housing covered by the Civil Rights Act of 1968.

The only value of Section 854, which is directed to violations of conciliation agreements containing a consent cease and desist order, may be to enable the Commission to devise a more stringent set of sanctions. Ordinarily, one would suppose that the Commission would simply seek to enforce the conciliation agreement in the courts under Section 720.

Section 855 is designed to preserve the operation of any state statute authorizing or directing the elimination of imbalance in a particular area of operation and to encourage persons subject to this Act to take positive action to open opportunities to minority and other seriously disadvantaged groups. Massachusetts, for example, has a statute directing the submission of plans for elimination of racial imbalance in the public schools.[49]

PART IX.   CRIMINAL SANCTIONS; OTHER REMEDIES; MISCELLANEOUS

Section 901 providing criminal penalties for certain actions is properly confined to wilful violations of Commission orders and wilful interference with performance of Commission functions. This is in line with modern notions concerning appropriate use of criminal sanctions, notions that are especially appropriate for the area of regulation dealing with civil-rights matters. The section is based upon Section 714 of the 1964 Civil Rights Act.

Sections 902–905 provide for original enforcement of the substantive provisions of this act through the courts by civil actions filed either by aggrieved parties or by the attorney general. This mode of enforcement of the act is a complete alternative to its enforcement by the Commission. A similar dual mode for enforcement has been utilized successfully in the administration of the federal antitrust laws.[50]

[49] *Mass. Gen. Laws Ann.*, ch. 71, § 37D; ch. 76, § 12A, *as amended* (Supp. 1966).
[50] See, generally, Phillip Areeda, *Antitrust Analysis* (Boston: Little, Brown and Co., 1967), pp. 27–49.

These laws are in many ways similar to civil-rights laws and the prior experience in enforcement of the former is instructive concerning what may prove effective in enforcement of the latter. Both private persons and the U.S. Attorney General may enforce the federal antitrust laws through civil actions in the federal courts. The Federal Trade Commission may also enforce the policy of the basic Sherman Antitrust Act through adjudication under Section 5 of the Federal Trade Commission Act. It may further enforce the Clayton Antitrust Act directly in administrative proceedings as well as under Section 5 of the Federal Trade Commission Act, relative to action causing injury to competition but falling short of a violation of the Sherman or Clayton Acts. Both the U.S. Attorney General and the Federal Trade Commission have made substantial contributions to the enforcement of federal antitrust policy. Moreover, since 1950, private antitrust actions have proved a very effective weapon for enforcement of federal antitrust laws. The number of these actions has grown from 62 filed in 1947[51] to 722 filed in 1966.[52] In 1962 alone 2,105 of these suits were commenced. Many of these actions have been filed following prior successful actions brought by the U.S. Attorney General.

Following the analogy of the federal antitrust laws, Section 903 provides that the aggrieved person may recover treble damages for injuries sustained or $500, whichever is larger, by the filing of a civil action in a designated state court. This provision parallels Section 716 providing for the damages that may be awarded by the Commission in a proceeding before it. The complainant may also obtain in his civil action various forms of equitable or affirmative relief as needed for dealing with a violation that has been found to exist. Section 905(a) defines the affirmative remedies that may be ordered by the court in appropriate cases. These remedies are precisely similar to those that may be utilized by the Commission under Section 716. Section 703 is basically similar to Sections 4 and 16 of the Clayton Antitrust Act providing, respectively, for treble damage and equitable actions by private parties to enforce the federal antitrust policy.[53] It is thus far

[51] Comment, "Antitrust Enforcement by Private Parties: Analysis of Developments in the Treble Damage Suit," *Yale Law Journal*, Vol. 61 (1952), pp. 1010, 1063.

[52] *Annual Report of the Director of the Administrative Office of the United States Courts 1966* (Washington, D.C.: U.S. Government Printing Office, 1966), p. 103.

[53] 15 U.S.C. §§ 15, 26 (1964).

superior, as a practicable mode of private enforcement, to Section 706(e) of the 1964 Civil Rights Act. The latter does not provide for dual enforcement of federal civil-rights policy and remits an aggrieved person to a series of administrative and judicial steps before he is permitted to proceed in a court to obtain an adjudication of his charge. Moreover, that person can obtain no administrative adjudication of his charge and judicial enforcement of an administrative order designed to correct a violation of the law.

Section 904 in according the right to the attorney general to bring a civil action permits him to file the action on substantially the same basis that a private person may. For this reason the section is greatly superior to Section 707 of the 1964 Civil Rights Act. The latter severely limits the U.S. Attorney General in filing a civil action or in obtaining relief against existing discrimination violatve of the act. For these reasons Section 904 of the Model Act is more nearly akin to Section 4 of the Sherman Antitrust Act[54] and Section 15 of the Clayton Antitrust Act,[55] which authorizes U.S. district attorneys under the direction of the U.S. Attorney General to file equitable actions to prevent violations of these respective acts.

The allocation of dual responsibility for administration of this Act, as between the attorney general and the Commission, should work as well as dual responsibility for administration of federal antitrust policy has worked. The attorney general and the Commission can allocate between themselves appropriate areas of law enforcement much as their federal counterparts have done in the administration of federal antitrust policy.

Section 902 grants jurisdiction to an appropriate court to determine civil actions filed under Sections 903 and 904, regulates venue for filing these actions, and specifies the time within which an action must be filed. The section also makes clear that the court shall exercise its jurisdiction without regard to whether the aggrieved party shall have exhausted any administrative or other remedies that may be provided by law. This provision clearly signals the completely alternative character of Sections 902–905 as a mode of enforcement of the act.

Section 905, in addition to defining the permissible forms of affirmative remedies, gives the court the discretion to allow a reasonable attorney's fee to the prevailing party.

[54] *Id.*, § 4 (1964).
[55] *Id.*, § 25 (1964).

Sections 906 and 907 deal with the problem of responsive action by official agencies other than the Commission when the latter finds a respondent has violated the act. The former section relates to recipients of official financial assistance and licenses and the latter to holders of official contracts. Both sections leave it to the discretion of these official agencies what is to be done by them relative to a respondent who, being also either a recipient of official financial assistance or a license or a holder of an official contract, has been found by the Commission to have violated the act. These agencies are bound, however, by the Commission's finding of discrimination. The total result is that the official agencies are accorded a discretion that can be best handled by them in light of the various interests of the state in the matter. Ordinarily, action short of cancellation of the assistance, licenses, or contract will be effective in eliminating discrimination. Where this drastic remedy is needed, it can be used. The effect of these provisions will be to hasten the time when the policy of the act is generally observed.

Section 908 is a rule of evidence modeled after similar provisions of certain state civil-rights acts.[56] It shifts the burden to the respondent to show that a communication or publication indicating on its face that the respondent follows a discriminatory policy was unauthorized.

Section 909 provides that the Commission may obtain enforcement of its right to obtain access to a respondent's premises for investigatory purposes or of its subpoena by an appropriate court. This section is modelled after Section 710(b) of the 1964 Civil Rights Act.

Since this Act is comprehensive in nature and provides for its enforcement both by the courts and the Commission, Section 911 provides blanks for filling in the existing civil-rights laws that are to be repealed. Many states have civil-rights laws providing for their enforcement only by courts.

[56] *E.g.*, Colo. Rev. Stat. § 25-2-2 (1963).

9

The Alpha Model State Act on Local Human-Relations Commissions, with Comments

THE ALPHA MODEL STATE CIVIL-RIGHTS ACT ON LOCAL HUMAN-RELATIONS COMMISSIONS

Table of Contents

*The Alpha Model State Civil-Rights Act
on Local Human-Relations Commissions*

AN ACT

To promote and protect the welfare of the people of this state by prevention and elimination of certain unreasonable practices and policies, including discrimination based upon race, color, religion, ancestry, national origin, age, sex, or economic status; to authorize political subdivisions to create and empower local human-relations commissions, assigning local commission tasks, functions, and policies, regulating their procedures, and providing for judicial review of their determinations; and for other purposes.

PART I. SHORT TITLE; FINDINGS AND DECLARATION OF POLICIES; CONSTRUCTION

Section 101. Short Title. This Act shall be known, and may be cited, as the [name of state] Act on Local Human-Relations Commissions.

Section 102. Findings and Declaration of Policies. (a) The population of this state consists of people of many races, colors, religions, ancestries, and national origins as well as of different sexes, age groups, and economic brackets. It is essential to the public health, safety, welfare, peace, and progress of the state and of each community within it that this diversity serve to strengthen individual and collective efforts to achieve man's enduring goals and not be used to weaken these efforts. The latter result occurs when members of one group practice, through private or governmental institutions, discrimination and other harmful activity against members of another group in any phase of community life merely on account of their race or other normal group characteristics. Practices of this kind and the conditions accompanying them undermine the freedom and justice essential to genuine democracy. Among other things, they prevent full development and utilization of the capacities of many persons; cut them off from various kinds of economic, social, cultural, and political opportunities; deny them adequate education and training; cause among them widespread unemployment and underemployment; deprive them of earnings necessary to maintain decent standards of living and require them to resort to public relief; and produce segregated residential areas which, through their *de facto* segregated schools and typically substandard, unsafe, and unsanitary living conditions, support the whole structure of discrimination and disadvantages suffered by their inhabitants. These practices also cause or contribute to intergroup tensions and conflicts, school drop-outs, crime, juvenile delinquency, disease, fire hazards, higher welfare costs, and loss of tax revenues.

(b) It is the policy of this state to ensure that all persons enjoy the full benefits of citizenship or residence and be afforded equal opportunity to participate, on the basis of personal merit, in the social, cultural, economic, political, and other phases of community life within the state, free from any discrimination on account of race, color, religion, ancestry, or national origin and from any restrictions on account of sex, age, or economic status that are unreasonable. In order to implement this policy it is essential that the state and local governments assume the initiative for repairing the consequences of past denials of equal opportunities to particular groups, preventing denials of these opportunities in the future, and controlling and eliminating the underlying causes of intergroup-relations problems. Government initiative for accomplishing these purposes must be exercised within each community. Human-relations problems cannot be adequately solved until the government and citizenry of each community throughout the state honestly face these problems and with good will and industry work together for their solution. It is a central purpose of this Act to encourage the institution of adequate human-relations programs by each political subdivision having serious intergroup-relations problems. [Where a political subdivision faced with these problems has established and maintains an adequate human-relations program administered by an effective local human-relations commission, the state government will, through the [name of state] State Human-Relations Commission created by the [name of state] Civil Rights Act, cooperate in every possible way with that local government and will confine its operations in that political subdivision to handling intergroup-relations problems falling properly within state cognizance or not being handled by the local commission. Where a political subdivision has not established or does not maintain an adequate human-relations program to handle serious problems of intergroup relations, the state commission will administer the human-relations program established by the [name of state] Civil Rights Act within that community through one of its local sections.]

(c) It is the purpose of this Act to create the full and necessary authority in each political subdivision of this state to deal adequately with all of its human-relations problems and to supplement through official local action the implementation of state policy relative to promoting and assuring equality of opportunity for all residents of each community.

(d) It is not the purpose of this Act to limit the existing authority of any political subdivision to enact substantive legislation addressed to human-relations problems.

Section 103. Liberal Construction. This Act shall be construed liberally to further its purposes and, more generally, to promote justice in human relations.

PART II. GENERAL DEFINITIONS

Section 201. General Definitions. In this Act, unless the context otherwise requires,

(1) "Person" means an individual, partnership, association, corporation, joint-stock company, labor union, mutual company, trustee in bankruptcy, receiver or other fiduciary, or the agent, legal representative, or employee thereof, and a political subdivision or any agency, officer, or employee thereof;

(2) "Local commission" means a local human-relations commission established by one or more political subdivisions under Section 301;

(3) "Commissioner or commissioners" refers to a commissioner or commissioners of a local commission;

(4) "Governing board" means the governing board or boards of a political subdivision;

(5) "Political subdivision" means a [city, county . . .] of this state and any combination of two or more of these which, by joint action under Section 301, create a local commission;

(6) "Local civil-rights law" means any legislation enacted by a governing board pursuant to Section 802 and the duties imposed on and authority granted under this Act to a local commission created under Section 301;

(7) "Cooperative agreement" means a cooperative agreement made by a local commission under Section 403 with another human-relations commission;

(8) "Negotiation function" means the function assigned to a local commission under Subsection (b) of Section 502;

(9) "Constructive-action function" means the function assigned to a local commission under Subsection (c) of Section 502;

(10) "Community" refers to the community or communities within the political subdivision served by a local commission;

(11) "Discrimination" means any direct or indirect exclusion, distinction, segregation, limitation, refusal, denial, or any other differentiation or preference in the treatment of a person or persons on account of race, color, religion, ancestry, national origin, age, sex, or economic status, and any denial of any right, privilege or immunity secured or protected by the Constitution or laws of the United States.

PART III. LOCAL HUMAN-RELATIONS COMMISSION

Section 301. Authority to establish a local commission. (a) The governing board of any political subdivision, or the governing boards of two or more political subdivisions acting jointly, may, by appropriate legislative action, establish a local human-relations commission for the purpose of administering local civil-rights law.

(b) A local commission created under this section shall be known as the [name of political subdivision] Human-Relations Commission.

(c) Any local commission established under this section is subject to the provisions of this Act.

Section 302. Authority to determine number, terms, appointment, compensation, quorum, and removal of commissioners. The governing board may determine the number of commissioners of a local commission at any figure not less than seven; their terms, which shall be given a staggered order; manner of appointment and filling of vacancies; mode of compensation, if any; method of selecting a chairman and acting chairman; number constituting a quorum; and method of removal.

Section 303. Appointment of commissioners and chairmen. Upon creating a commission under Section 301 the governing board shall appoint the commissioners and select a chairman.

Section 304. Authority to appropriate funds for local commission. The governing board may appropriate funds for the salaries of commissioners and staff of a local commission and for other expenses of the commission.

Section 305. Authority to accept outside funds for local commission. The governing board may accept outside funds, gifts or bequests, public or private, to help finance the activities of a local commission.

Section 306. Relations between political subdivisions. The establishment of a local commission by one political subdivision under Section 301 does not preclude establishment of a local commission by another political subdivision under the same section. A county shall not, however, exercise its jurisdiction in a political subdivision located in the same county if the latter has established a commission pursuant to Section 301 with similar jurisdiction.

Section 307. Applicability of this Act. All existing local human-relations commissions are deemed to be local commissions established under Section 301. No new local human-relations commission may be established except under Section 301.

PART IV. RELATION BETWEEN A LOCAL COMMISSION AND OTHER HUMAN-RELATIONS COMMISSIONS

Section 401. Non-repealer. Except as expressly provided, nothing in this Act shall be deemed to repeal or supersede any of the provisions of any other law of this state or any of its political subdivisions relating to regulation of intergroup-relations problems, including discrimination on account of race, color, religion, ancestry, national origin, age, sex, or economic status, unless such provision is inconsistent with any of the purposes of this Act, or any provision of it.

Section 402. Right of a local commission to exercise its jurisdiction under a local civil-rights law. Unless specifically ousted from exercising jurisdiction under local civil-rights law by administrative action of a state or federal commission having similar jurisdiction over intergroup-relations problems, a local commission may exercise that jurisdiction.

Section 403. Authority to make cooperative agreements with other human-relations commissions. A local commission may cooperate with other local commissions or with a state or a federal human-relations commission established to administer civil-rights law. In furtherance of such cooperation and to achieve more adequate administration of this Act, the commission may enter into written agreements with one or more of these commissions.

Section 404. Rescission of a cooperative agreement. A local commission may rescind a cooperative agreement whenever it determines that the agreement no longer serves the interest of promoting effective achievement of the purposes of this Act.

Section 405. Effect of resort to procedure of this Act. In the absence of a cooperative agreement between the commission and another human-relations commission, the procedure provided by this Act to be utilized by a local commission shall, when invoked by an individual aggrieved relative to action covered by local civil-rights law, be exclusive and the final determination of the case shall exclude any other action of a civil nature filed by that person.

Section 406. Effect of resort to procedure of another law. If a person institutes an action relative to conduct covered by local civil-rights law without resorting to the procedure provided by this Act, he may not subsequently resort to that procedure. A local commission may, however, at the direction of a state or federal human-relations commission, process a complaint alleging discrimination covered by local civil-rights law referred to it for that purpose by the latter.

Part V. The Central Task, Functions, Goals, and Policies of a Local Commission

Section 501. The central task of a local commission. (a) The central task of a local commission is the reconstruction of intergroup relations within the community served by it so as to eliminate the causes of, ameliorate the conditions accompanying, and overcome the results flowing from discrimination and other harmful activity directed against minority and other disadvantaged groups. Performance of this task of reconstruction calls for the assembly and redirection of the maximum human and material resources within that community and bringing them to bear upon intergroup-relations problems in the most effective way. It demands that the community be persuaded to acknowledge its own responsibility for the performance of this task, and that each of its groups become genuinely involved in discharging it.

(b) The local commission should be the major institution within a political subdivision for guiding the performance of this task and for providing as well as eliciting the appropriate leadership to secure its realization. With regard to the majority or controlling group, the local commission must seek to obtain reorganization and reformation of all group actions, habits, customs, and private arrangements that have produced and continue to maintain the conditions adversely affecting the opportunities of minority and other disadvantaged groups. With regard to the latter, the local commission must seek to move the group members to confront problems of group actions, habits, customs, and private arrangements that hamper them in obtaining and maximizing needed opportunities; to provide them with various kinds of assistance services calculated to help them prepare for and obtain needed opportunities, and to protect them against certain typical types of exploitation and abuse. Persons within the majority groups must be found who will provide wise leadership within that group so as to move it to begin to confront and resolve its intergroup-relations problems. Within minority and other disadvantaged groups leaders must be found or developed who will help these groups to perform the kinds of actions that are calculated to start and facilitate the process of dialogue and negotiation between the various groups looking to an improvement in their relations and in the opportunities available to minority and other disadvantaged groups.

Section 502. Basic functions of a local commission. (a) A local commission shall perform the following basic functions:

(1) processing of individual complaints relative to denials of any right, privilege, or immunity secured or protected by the Constitution or laws of the United States and relative to all forms of discrimination and other harmful activity directed against minority or other disadvantaged groups;

(2) negotiating with wide sectors of businesses, unions, professions, government agencies, and private organizations for the taking of action by them to improve opportunities available to minority and other disadvantaged groups and utilizing of inspections, surveys, private conferences, public hearings, reports, and enforcement actions to assure the effectiveness of negotiation; and

(3) undertaking of various types of constructive action designed to eliminate the causes of intergroup-relations problems within the community, to deal with actions and conditions affecting the public welfare that result from the continued existence of these problems, and to move the community and its groups to direct the maximum resources of that communty, both human and material, to the accomplishment of these objectives.

(b) It is the sense of the Legislature that the negotiation and constructive-action functions of each local commission should receive the greatest emphasis in its administration of local civil-rights law.

Section 503. Goals of a local commission. A local commission shall seek to achieve the following goals in performance of its basic task and functions:

(a)–(f)

[Subsections (a)–(f) of this section are the same as the corresponding subsections of Section 504 of the Alpha Model State Civil-Rights Act.]

Section 504. Implemental policies of a local commission. The following implemental policies are to be pursued by a local commission in performing its negotiation and constructive-action functions:

(1)–(11)

[Subsections (1)–(11) of this section are the same as the corresponding subsections of Section 505 of the Alpha Model State Civil-Rights Act.]

Part VI. Powers and Duties of a Local Commission

Section 601. General powers and duties of a local commission. A local commission has the following general powers and duties:

(1) to establish and maintain an office in the place designated by the governing board and such other offices within the political subdivision it serves as it may deem necessary;

(2) to meet and function at any place with the political subdivision it serves;

(3) to appoint an executive director and any attorneys, hearing examiners, clerks, and other employees and agents as it may deem necessary, and to fix their compensation;

(4) to adopt, promulgate, amend, and rescind rules and regulations to effectuate the purposes and provisions of this Act;

(5) to submit at least once a year to the governing board a report concerning its activities and its recommendations.

Section 602. Implemental powers and duties of a local commission. A local commission has the following implemental powers and duties in performing its basic task and functions and in carrying out its implemental policies:

(1)–(12)

[Subsections (1)–(12) of this section are the same as the corresponding subsections of Section 602 of the Alpha Model State Civil-Rights Act.]

Part VII. Procedures Relative to Complaints; Remedies; Judicial Review; Records

Section 701. Definitions. In this part

(1) "Commission" means a local commission, as defined in Section 201. In Sections 714, 715, 716, 717, 718, and 719 "commission" means either a commission or a hearing panel of that commission;

(2) "Commissioner" means a commissioner of a commission; "attorney general" includes the chief legal officer of a political subdivision.

(3) "Civil-rights organization" means an organization which, under its articles of incorporation or association, is organized to deal with intergroup-relations problems;

(4) "Chairman" means the chairman of a commission;

(5) "Discriminatory act" means any act or practice of discrimination, including an unlawful discriminatory act;

(6) "Discrimination" means any direct or indirect exclusion, distinction, segregation, limitation, refusal, denial, or any other differentiation or preference in the treatment of a person or persons on account of race, color, religion, ancestry, national origin, age, sex, or economic status, and any denial of any right, privilege, or immunity secured or protected by the Constitution or laws of the United States;

(7)–(19)

[Subsections (7)–(19) of this section are the same as the corresponding subsections of Section 701 of the Alpha Model State Civil-Rights Act.]

Sections 702–722. [Sections 702–722 of this Act are the same as the corresponding sections of the Alpha Model State Civil-Rights Act.]

PART VIII. UNLAWFUL DISCRIMINATORY ACTS

Section 801. Definitions. (a) In this Act

(1) "Unlawful discriminatory act" means an act made unlawful, through appropriate legislative action, by a political subdivision under the authority granted in Section 802;

(2) "Official agency" means an authority of the political subdivision and its members and employees;

(3) "Official financial assistance" means financial assistance provided by an official agency;

(4) "License" means the whole or any part of any official-agency permit, certificate, approval, registration, charter, membership, or other form of permission;

(5) "Age" refers to the age of a person between thirty-five and sixty-five years of age;

(6) "Employer" means a person employing [   ] or more employees within a political subdivision, exclusive of parents, spouse, or children of that person, and including a political subdivision itself or an official agency of it;

(7) "Employment agency" means any person regularly undertaking, with or without compensation, to procure employment opportunities for individuals or to procure, refer, or place individuals as employees;

(8) "Individual" means any individual other than one employed

or seeking employment by his parents, spouse, or child or employed or seeking employment in the domestic service of or in a personal or confidential capacity by any person;

(9) "Place of public accommodations" means any place in or through which any business or professional activity is conducted that is open to, accepts, or solicits the patronage of or offers goods or services to the general public. It does not include those clubs, associations, corporations, or other organizations that

(A) are organized by and for regular dues-paying memberships;

(B) are formed for noncommercial, nonprofit purposes;

(C) have policies determined by their members; and

(D) have facilities and services that are available only to their members and their bona fide guests or to similar organizations.

(10) "Educational institution" means any nursery; kindergarten; elementary or secondary school; academy; college; university; extension course; or nursing, secretarial, business, vocational, technical, trade, or professional school;

(11) "Real-estate transaction" means the sale, exchange, rental, lease, or other similar transaction relative to real property;

(12) "Real property" means buildings, structures, real estate, lands, tenements, leaseholds, real-estate cooperatives, condominiums, and hereditaments, corporeal and incorporeal, or any interest therein;

(13) "Real-estate broker or salesman" means a person, whether licensed or not, who, for or with the expectation of receiving a consideration, lists, sells, purchases, exchanges, rents, or leases real property, or who negotiates or attempts to negotiate any of these activities, or who holds himself out as engaged in these activities, or who negotiates or attempts to negotiate a loan secured or to be secured by mortgage or other encumbrance upon real property, or who is engaged in the business of listing real property in a publication; or a person employed by or acting on behalf of any of these;

(14) "Owner" includes the lessee, sublessee, assignee, trustee, trustor, beneficiary, mortgagee, mortgagor, or any person having any legal or equitable right of ownership or possession or the right to lease, rent, or assign any real property, or any agent, employee, or legal representative thereof, and a political subdivision or any agency thereof.

(b) The definitions of terms in Subsection (a) of this section are to be utilized by the governing board in exercising its authority under Section 802 to prohibit unlawful discriminatory acts.

Section 802. Authority of a political subdivision to prohibit unlawful discriminatory acts. (a) The governing board is authorized, by appropriate legislative action, to prohibit as an unlawful discriminatory act, any of the following:

(1) any act by one or more persons conducting a business; professional activity; employees', business, or professional organization; institution, program, or activity operating under official financial assistance or a license; or governmental activity involving the utilization of a method of doing business or operating that, considered by itself or in conjunction with similar action of other persons, unfairly or unreasonably restricts the economic, housing, educational, training, associational, public-accommodations, political, or governmental opportunities of members of any race, color, religion, ancestry, national origin, age, sex, economic status, or any other group upon which it is unreasonable to base such restrictions;

(2) an act of any police officer or official agency of a political subdivision denying any person equal protection of the laws under the Constitution or laws of the United States on account of race, color, religion, ancestry, national origin, age, sex, economic status, or any other basis that is unreasonable, including denials of equal access or utilization of any public school or other public facility, equal opportunity to obtain and utilize a license generally obtainable by others, or equal opportunity to obtain and to enjoy services, loans, grants, insurance, loan guarantees, welfare assistance, or any other thing or action generally available to other persons;

(3) an act of any police officer or official agency of a political subdivision depriving any person of any right, privilege, or immunity secured or protected by the Constitution or laws of the United States;

(4) an act by any official agency permitting, authorizing, or condoning an act described in paragraphs (2) or (3) of this subsection;

(5) an act of any person conducting any program or activity operating under any form of official financial assistance or license that involves discrimination under that program or activity on account of race, color, religion, ancestry, national origin, age, or sex;

(6) an act of any employer, labor organization, or employment agency against an individual in the conduct of the former's activities

on account of race, color, religion, ancestry, national origin, age, or sex of the individual;

(7) an act of any person operating a place of public accommodations that discriminates against any individual on account of race, color, religion, ancestry, national origin, age, or sex;

(8) an act of any person, other than a political subdivision or an official agency of it, in the operation of an educational institution that discriminates against any individual on account of race, color, religion, ancestry, national origin, age, or sex;

(9) an act of any owner, any other person engaging in a real-estate transaction, or any real-estate broker or salesman relative to any person involving a refusal to engage in a real-estate transaction; discrimination in the terms, conditions, or privileges of a real-estate transaction; refusal to transmit any bona fide offer to engage in a real-estate transaction; refusal to negotiate relative to a real-estate transaction; representation that real property is not available for a real-estate transaction; or utilization of a quota system for denying or limiting a real-estate transaction on account of race, color, religion, ancestry, national origin, sex, or economic status;

(10) an act of any person to whom application is made for financial assistance in connection with a real-estate transaction or for construction, rehabilitation, repair, maintenance, or improvement of real property involving discrimination against the applicant on account of race, color, religion, ancestry, national origin, or sex;

(11) an act of any person for the purpose of inducing a real-estate transaction or a listing of real property for this purpose from which he may benefit financially, involving a representation that a change has occurred or will occur in the composition with respect to race, color, religion, ancestry, or national origin of the owners or occupants in the block, neighborhood, or area in which the real property is located; a representation that this change will or may result in the lowering of property values, an increase in criminal or antisocial behavior, or a decline in the quality of schools in the block, neighborhood, or area in which the real property is located; or misrepresentation concerning the listing for sale or sale of any real property that is calculated to initiate or facilitate a change in the ethnic composition of a block, neighborhood, or area in which the property is located;

(12) an act of any organization of businessmen, tradesmen, or professional men in which membership is valuable or essential to an

individual for the purpose of engaging or advancing in a business, trade, or profession that involves exclusion or other discrimination against any individual on account of race, color, religion, ancestry, national origin, age, or sex;

(13) an act of retaliation or discrimination against a person because he has opposed an unlawful discriminatory act or because he has made a charge, testified, assisted, or participated in an investigation, proceeding, or hearing under this Act;

(14) an act of aiding, abetting, inciting, or coercing a person to engage in an unlawful discriminatory act;

(15) an act of wilfully interfering with the performance of a duty or exercise of power by a local commission or one of its commissioners or representatives;

(16) an act of wilfully obstrucing a person from complying with the provisions of local civil-rights law;

(17) an act of wilfully failing to obey a rule, regulation, or order promulgated under Section 721;

(18) an act of a party to a conciliation agreement containing a consent cease and desist order made under this Act involving a violation of the terms of the agreement; and

(19) any act that might reasonably be judged to support and facilitate the commission of the foregoing acts.

(b) The governing board may exercise in its discretion all or a portion of each authority granted in Subsection (a) of this section and it may incorporate by reference into local civil-rights law any state law administered by a state commission performing a function comparable to a local commission under this Act.

Section 803. Exceptions to coverage of local civil-rights law. The governing board may make reasonable exceptions to the coverage of local civil-rights law prohibiting unlawful discriminatory acts under Subsection (a) of Section 802 and shall make the following exceptions where a local civil-rights law would otherwise apply:

(a) It is not an unlawful discriminatory act for an employer to hire, a labor union to classify its membership or refer an individual for employment, or an employer, employment agency, or labor organization to request information, or an individual seeking employment to publish an advertisement that expresses a personal quality or preference on the basis of what would otherwise be prohibited under local civil-rights law when this basis is a bona fide occupational qualification reasonably necessary to the normal operation of a particular business or enterprise;

(b) It is not an unlawful discriminatory act for an employer, employment agency, or labor organization to select a person to be a participant in any occupational training or retraining program on the basis of the ability to complete the required training and the industry average period of employment thereafter before attaining the age of sixty-five (65) years of age;

(c) It is not an unlawful discriminatory act for an employer to terminate employment or otherwise deal with an individual under the terms of any bona fide retirement or pension plan or under the terms of any bona fide group or employee insurance plan; and

(d) It is not an unlawful discriminatory act for a religious or denominational institution or organization, or any organization operated for charitable or educational purposes which is operated, supervised, or controlled by or in connection with a religious or denominational organization or group to limit employment, membership or admission; to give preference in its accommodations, advantages, facilities, benefits, privileges, services, or goods; to limit or give preference in the sale, lease, rental, assignment, or sublease of real property to persons of the same religion; or to make a selection of employees, members, applicants, buyers, tenants, lessees, assignees, subleases, or persons that is reasonably calculated to promote the religious principles for which it is established or maintained.

PART IX. CRIMINAL SANCTIONS; OTHER REMEDIES; MISCELLANEOUS

[This part is the same as Part IX of the Alpha Model State Civil-Rights Act with the following addition to Section 904.]

Section 904. (c) The term "attorney general" includes the chief legal officer of a political subdivision.

COMMENTS

PREFATORY NOTE

1. History. The Alpha Model State Act on Local Human-Relations Commissions was drafted in response to the need demonstrated earlier in this book for uniform guidelines relative to a state statute authorizing and empowering political subdivisions to create local human-relations commissions and to enact local civil-rights law. This second Alpha Model State Act draws even more heavily than the first one upon a similar model act drafted by the author and included as an appendix to a law review article published in June 1965.[1] One additional model act bearing upon this problem has been prepared since that time: the Uniform Model State Anti-Discrimination Act (mentioned in the "Comments" section of Chapter 8. Chapter 9 of that Act deals with the matter in a brief manner.

2. Reorientation of state civil-rights policy. The Alpha Model State Civil-Rights Act, as previously stated, presents a thoroughgoing reorientation of the typical type of state civil-rights law. It assigns to the state commission created by it, wholly new tasks, functions, and goals; new methods for its operation; and much new substantive law. It is premised upon the proposition that in order to achieve any sufficient rectification of intergroup relations in this country, official action must take place at the local level whether the action be taken by the federal, state, or local government. It puts a state commission "into business" at the local level through its local sections. The latter are designed to be microcosms of the statewide commission exercising the full authority of the latter in each political subdivision in which they operate.

The Alpha Model State Act on Local Human-Relations Commissions is designed to be the counterpart of the Alpha Model State Civil-Rights Act. The latter Act looks to the time when political subdivisions will adequately discharge their responsibilities through comprehensive human-relations programs administered by effective local human-relations commissions. This second Alpha Model Act provides guide-

---

[1] Joseph P. Witherspoon, "Civil Rights Policy in the Federal System: Proposals for a Better Use of Administrative Process," *Yale Law Journal*, vol. 74 (1965), pp. 1175–1244.

lines and directives for local governments that decide to undertake the performance of these responsibilities.

3. Structure of the Act. The Alpha Model State Act on Local Human-Relations Commissions consists of nine parts. The first three parts relate to findings and declarations of policies, general definitions, establishment of local human-relations commissions to administer local civil-rights law, and applicability of the Act. The fourth part deals with the relation between a local commission and other similiar commissions at various levels of government. The fifth part concerns the task, functions, goals, and implemental policies of a local commission. The sixth part relates to its general and implemental duties. The seventh part concerns procedures to be followed relative to complaints of discriminatory acts, administrative hearings, remedies, judicial review, and similar matters. The eighth part sets forth the authority of a political subdivision to enact local civil-rights law prohibiting unlawful discriminatory acts. The final part covers criminal sanctions and other remedies.

4. Analysis of Existing Similar State Law. Four states—Kentucky,[2] New York,[3] Pennsylvania,[4] and Wisconsin[5]—have enacted statutes in the last few years to address the problem to which the second Alpha Model Act speaks. The first statute, Article 12-D of the New York General Municipal Law, which was enacted in 1963, represents one possible approach. It authorizes the governing board of a political subdivision to establish a human-relations commission and allocates to a local commission, when created, the duty of performing some parts of two functions previously described as properly belonging to human-relations commissions: the individual-complaint-processing function and the constructive-action function. On the other hand, the political subdivision is given no authority to enact local civil-rights law and to empower its commission to enforce either local or state civil-rights law through the holding of public hearings, issuance of cease and desist orders, and securing enforcement of these orders in the courts. Moreover, the act does not specifically recognize that local commissions should have a "wide-spectrum"-negotiation function nor does the act back up this function with substantive law needed to make its

---

2 Ky. Rev. Stat. §§ 344.300–.990 (Supp. 1966).
3 N.Y. Gen. Munic. Law, §§ 239o–239s, *as amended* (McKinney Supp. 1967).
4 Pa. Stat. Ann. tit. 43, §§ 959–963 *as amended* (1965).
5 Wis. Stat. Ann. § 66.433 (1965).

exercise effective by prohibiting unreasonable and unfair restrictions placed upon members of minority and other disadvantaged groups. Indeed, the local commissions are directed to refer complaints of violations of state civil-rights laws to the state human-relations commission for processing by the latter when they fall within its jurisdiction. The New York statute, consequently, maintains the unconditional primacy of the state human-relations commission in dealing with violations of state civil-rights law in all political subdivisions. The latter law, on the other hand, does not speak to the problem created when political subdivisions fail to respond to the need for their performance of the "wide-spectrum"-negotiation function and of the constructive-action function. It is true that New York is a state granting home rule to cities and counties. But it is also true that most of these political subdivisions are not exercising their authority to create human-relations commissions with full authority to deal with human-relations problems at the local level.[6] Moreover, and perhaps one of the principal factors contributing to this, is the fact that the state civil-rights law has clouded the issue of their authority to act in the same field as the state Commission. For example, until 1965 New York City, which had previously created a local commission with enforcement authority only in the housing field, operated alongside the state Commission in New York City. The state Commission continued to exercise a substantial jurisdiction over local housing discrimination over which the local commission would otherwise be exercising its own jurisdiction. When the New York legislature had first granted jurisdiction over housing discrimination to its state Commission in 1961, it had not amended the basic statute to make it clear that cities could continue to enforce or could enact local legislation dealing with the same area. For this reason in October of that year, the state Commission and the New York City Commission entered into a cooperative agreement concerning the receipt and processing of housing-discrimination complaints by the two agencies and allocated the work load between them for the New York City area.[7] Since the state Commission had substantially full jurisdiction over other areas of discrimination in public accommodations and employment, it continued to exercise its jurisdic-

6 See Charles S. Rhyne, *Municipal Law* (Washington, D.C.: National Institute of Municipal Law Officers, 1957), p. 18. Only 7 out of 119 eligible cities in New York had adopted home rule charters in 1949 [Rodney L. Mott, *Home Rule for America's Cities* (Chicago: American Municipal Association, 1949), Appendix Two, p. 62].

7 New York City Commission on Intergroup Relations, *1961 Annual Report*, pp. 15–16.

tion in these areas and the New York City Commission was given no similar jurisdiction. In 1965 the state legislature provided that "nothing in Art. 12-D of its General Municipal Law shall be deemed to limit or reduce the powers of the New York City Commission of Human Rights, and with respect to such powers, the jurisdiction of the Commission in relation to matters within the city of New York shall be deemed to be concurrent with the jurisdiction of the New York State Commission for Human Rights."[8] In late December of the same year the New York City Council responded to this grant of authority by adopting its first comprehensive civil-rights ordinance creating a new human-relations commission and giving it jurisdiction over discrimination in education, employment, public accommodations, housing, and commercial space.[9] The authority of political subdivisions in New York in the civil-rights field is affected by four statutes: a state home-rule statute,[10] a state civil-rights act, a state act on local human-relations commissions, and the recent state act giving the New York City Commission concurrent jurisdiction with the New York State Commission. These statutes produce the following anomalous results: the state Commission has full and exclusive jurisdiction over discrimination in all regulated fields except in New York City; political subdivisions, even though possessing home-rule powers, are excluded from exercising regulatory jurisdiction over discrimination in all fields in which the state Commission has jurisdiction; the state Commission probably has grossly inadequate jurisdiction to perform the "wide-spectrum"-negotiation and the constructive-action functions in any political subdivisions; although political subdivisions have the authority to perform part of the last two functions, many of them are not doing so and there is no agency of state government available to perform these functions; political subdivisions that are performing these functions are greatly hampered in being effective due to the lack of adequate substantive civil-rights provisions to back them up and the authority to enforce them.

The Wisconsin statute,[11] also enacted in 1963, has the distinct merit of authorizing local governments both to create human-relations com-

---

[8] N.Y. Gen. Munic. Law, § 239s, *as amended* (McKinney Supp. 1967).

[9] New York City Charter and Code Ann. §§ B1-1.0–6.0 (Supp. 1966); *Race Relations Law Reporter*, Vol. 11 (1966), p. 467.

[10] N.Y. Munic. Home Rule Law, Art. 1–6 (McKinney Book 35c); N.Y. Statute of Local Governments, Art. 1–3, 10–13, 20–21 (McKinney Book 35c, 1967).

[11] Wis. Stat. Ann. § 66.433 (1965).

missions and to enact prohibitions of discrimination against minorities for administration by these commissions. Despite these and other meritorious features added by its subsequent admendment, the statute embodies a number of policy choices that deeply cut into its effectiveness for achieving the purpose of promoting local administration of civil-rights law. One major, if not overriding, deficiency in the statute is its undercutting of the principle of local responsibility. Wisconsin is a "local home-rule" state.[12] Its cities and villages have for several decades enjoyed a "home-rule" status by virtue of constitutional and statutory provisions.[13] Counties, among other local governments, have not been granted this status.[14] The latter local governments rather than the former should have been, one would think, the primary focus of a statute creating new authority in local government to deal with the civil-rights problem of minority groups. Instead the statute is made to apply without differentiation both to home-rule cities and villages and to counties, towns, and other local governments not having this status. The result is apparently a curious and severe limiting of the authority of the former to legislate in the civil-rights field and an inadequate grant of initial authority in the same field to the latter. One basic lesson to be learned from the Wisconsin effort is that a state should not enact a local human-relations-commission statute without carefully preserving the full pre-existing authority of local governments having a home-rule status to deal with the civil-rights problem of minority groups. In terms of the current great need for local administration of civil-rights law by larger cities one may even view the statute as a backward step.

That the Wisconsin statute has the effect just described may be discerned in several ways. In the first place, unless the subject matter of discrimination against minority groups occurring at the local level was one of "statewide concern," admitting only of state regulation, it was a matter of local or mixed concern which prior to the 1963 statute both cities and villages had authority to regulate extensively under their "home-rule" status.[15] The very enactment of the 1963 statute and making it applicable to "home-rule" cities and villages tends to support the thesis that the subject matter is now designated by the

---

[12] See Note, "Municipal Corporations—Home Rule in Wisconsin," *Wisconsin Law Review* (1955), p. 145.

[13] Wis. Stat. Ann., Const., Art. XI, sec. 3 *as amended*; § 61.34(1), § 62.11(5) (1957).

[14] Rhyne, *Municipal Law*, p. 18.

[15] *Cf., Muench v. Public Service Commission*, 261 Wis. 492, 515 (1952).

legislature to be one of "statewide concern" and that the authority of these local governments, like that of local governments not possessing "home-rule" status, is only that conferred by this statute. In the second place, the statute clearly confers only limited authority to regulate discrimination upon local government whether or not enjoying "home-rule" status. The limited character of this authority is manifested in a number of ways and constitutes an additional reason for avoiding the example of the Wisconsin statute. In the first place, the local commission is authorized by the statute to recommend enactment of, and by implication the local government's governing body is authorized to enact, local legislation designed to eliminate discrimination only in the areas of employment and housing accommodations and only when this discrimination is based upon race or color. Harmful discrimination against minority groups, however, occurs not only in these fields but also in many others. Moreover, this discrimination is directed at many other minority groups besides racial groups: such as, religious, nationality, ancestral, age, and sex groups. Other provisions of the Wisconsin statute indicate that the local commission can "act" to improve, as contrasted with recommending local legislation to deal with, intergroup relations by urging elimination of discrimination based upon race, color, or creed in real-estate transactions and the conduct of places of public accommodations; and of discrimination based on race, color, or national origin in other transactions.[16] The statute appears, therefore, to preclude home-rule cities and villages from exercising authority they formerly possessed to reach this additional harmful area of discrimination just as it falls short of granting initial authority to counties and other non-"home-rule" local governments to meet the full scope of current discrimination in these and other fields where they desire to do this.

The very limited character of the authority conferred upon local governments by the 1963 statute, as amended, is manifested in a second way. When local commissions are set up by local governments under this statute they cannot be authorized to hold public hearings to try respondents charged with discrimination, or to issue administrative orders, enforceable in the courts, for effectively eliminating discrimination. The authority to use this and other modern administrative civil sanctions is denied local governments. Their commissions are permitted to use only the technique of conciliation to eliminate

[16] Sections 9 and 7(b) of the statute as amended in 1965: Wisc. Stat. Ann. §§ 66.433 (1965).

violations of local civil-rights law. When conciliation fails, the commissions can only remit the matter to other competent authority. That local governments are so limited is indicated in several ways. There is no provision in the statute specifically authorizing a local commission to conduct hearings to determine whether a violation of local civil-rights law has occurred, to issue cease and desist orders, and to seek their enforcement in the courts. Indeed, the 1963 statute, as originally enacted, contained a provision specifically authorizing receipt of complaints of discrimination in public accommodations violative of a state criminal statute, in housing, and in employment.[17] Under this provision, if the complaints believed to be justified could not be resolved by conciliation, the commission was directed to refer them to the proper local law enforcement officer or agency. This provision clearly withdrew authority to enforce any state or local law prohibiting discrimination from the commission. Even this slight concession to local administrative process in the field of civil rights was eliminated in a 1965 amendment of the act although the commission was given the authority to hold public hearings to "study, analyze, and recommend solutions for major social problems and discrimination in housing, employment and public accommodations" on the basis of race, religion, or ethnic status.[18] All of this points toward a minimal authority in local governments to deal with discrimination through effective administrative process and sanctions. This view is further confirmed by the practical construction given the state act by the capital city of the state, Madison, when it enacted a civil-rights ordinance in late 1963.[19] This ordinance deals comprehensively with various forms of troublesome discrimination practiced against minority groups but employs only criminal sanctions for their enforcement in the courts despite its creation of a local human-relations commission. In light of the general knowledge in Wisconsin, before and after enactment of the state law, concerning the gross inadequacy of criminal and civil actions in the courts for enforcement of civil-rights statutes,[20] it was most unlikely

[17] *Wis. Stat. Ann.* §§ 66.433(3)(d) (1963).
[18] Wis. Stat. Ann. §§66.433(3)(a),–(c)4.
[19] Madison, Wisconsin Ordinance No. 1568 (December 13, 1963), *Race Relations Law Reporter*, Vol. 8 (1963), p. 1672.
[20] Pamela H. Rice and Milton Greenberg, "Municipal Protection of Human Rights," *Wisconsin Law Review* (1952), p. 678. Recommendations similar to those found in this work eventually persuaded the Wisconsin Legislature when it established and empowered a state commission [Wis. Stat. Ann. §§ 111.31–.37 (Supp. 1967)].

that Madison city fathers, having spoken so extensively against various forms of discrimination, would have chosen such sanctions unless it was believed by them that there was no authority under the existing statute to utilize administrative sanctions and to enforce them in the courts. A final indicator of the limited authority granted to local governments under the state statute in question came to the surface in 1965 when the state legislature gave its industrial commission jurisdiction over housing discrimination in addition to its existing jurisdiction over employment discrimination.[21] The state Commission was authorized to hold hearings, to issue cease and desist orders, and to secure their enforcement in the courts. There was no provision reserving the authority of local governments to issue local administrative orders concerning these matters as was the case in conjunction with local administrative orders relating to the safe and hygienic conditions of places of employment.[22] All of this strongly indicates that the Wisconsin legislature has vested exclusive jurisdiction in its industrial commission to utilize the techniques of modern administrative process to eliminate discrimination in employment and housing. If there is jurisdiction in local government to utilize this process, it would appear to be available only in areas of discrimination not yet assigned to the industrial commission, such as in places of public accommodation. The injunction in the 1963 act, as amended in 1965, that the purpose of the local commission is to study, analyze, and recommend to the governing body of a political subdivision local legislation to eliminate discrimination in housing, employment and public accommodations on the basis of class, race, religion or ethnic or minority status, must, therefore, be taken to mean recommendation of legislation using methods other than the administrative process which has been assigned to the state industrial commission, such as criminal or civil penalties. This approach is contrary to the almost universal modern legislative judgment concerning appropriate enforcement procedure when administration of civil-rights law is entrusted to a human-relations commission.

In addition to weaknesses resulting from limiting the authority of home-rule local governments and in withholding both adequate regulatory authority and adequate enforcement techniques from all local government, the Wisconsin statute suffers from a number of additional defects. The statute fails to confer on local commissions created

[21] Wis. Stat. Ann. § 111.32(5)(a) *as amended* (Supp. 1967).
[22] Wis. Stat. Ann. § 101.16 (1957).

under the act the full range of authority previously discussed as essential for adequate resolution of the civil-rights problem of minority groups at the local level. Neither the negotiation nor the constructive-action function is specifically conferred upon these commissions. This type of authority is certainly as important as, if not ultimately more important than, the usual type of regulatory authority exercised by local commissions. The statute, for example, does not specify the authority to process and to control incidents of group tension and conflict. It does not authorize the local commission to investigate by means of public hearings general conditions bearing adversely upon human relations in the community. It does not grant the commission the authority to issue subpoenas in order to secure essential testimonial and documentary evidence for probing into general problems at investigations conducted through public hearings or to enable it to process effectively specific complaints of law violation. The local commission is not authorized to provide the various kinds of assistance services to minority groups and their members relative to their adjustment to living in a community. The Wisconsin statute also fails to speak to the specifics concerning the many problems of coordinating the work of the local commission with that of similar state and federal commissions. Finally, the statute fails to authorize local governments to deal with problems other than discrimination, that bear just as heavily and harmfully upon minority groups. One of these problems concerns complaints of police brutality and other forms of police maladministration. Another concerns the technique of "blockbusting."

The Kentucky statute, enacted in 1966, is a considerable improvement over the New York or Wisconsin statutes authorizing creation of local human-relations commissions. It adopts certain suggestions made by the author in 1965. Kentucky does not accord home-rule powers to its cities and counties[23] with the exception of Louisville. The statute specifically authorizes cities and counties to adopt ordinances prohibiting discrimination on the basis of race, color, religion, or national origin. It also specifically authorizes them to permit local commissions to receive, initiate, and investigate complaints; to hold hearings; to adjudicate charges of violation; to obtain subpoenas compelling attendance of witnesses and production of evidence; and to issue remedial orders, which may include requirements for affirmative action. It provides for joint action by political subdivisions in creating a single local

---

[23] Ky. Rev. Stat. §§ 81.010, 83.010 (Supp. 1966).

commission. It also authorizes political subdivisions to provide for execution of policies embodied in the 1966 state and 1964 federal civil-rights acts but does not compel this action.

One principal deficiency of the Kentucky statute is its failure to speak to two of the three essential functions of effective human-relations commissions, particularly those operating at the local level. These are the "wide-spectrum"-negotiation function backed up by appropriate substantive law, and the constructive-action function. These functions are not only ignored; they are also not made mandatory upon local commissions. Experience has demonstrated that many political subdivisions think of correction of local human-relations problems wholly in terms of an individual-complaint-processing function. They need guidelines and directions to move them to perform the far more important human-relations functions just mentioned. Even as to the function to which the statute does speak, the effect is to limit the authority of political subdivisions. They have only the authority provided by the statute and the statute does not give them authority to deal with discrimination upon other unreasonable bases than race, color, religion, or national origin. It does not, for example, permit political subdivisions to proscribe discrimination on the basis of sex, age, economic status, physical handicap, or other bases that may, under many circumstances, be unreasonable. Moreover, the Kentucky statute does not provide definitions of concepts basic to the construction of a good civil-rights law, such as "employer" and "places of public accommodations." Definitions are essential to avoid the creation of harmful loopholes in coverage or to avoid the infliction of needless harm in accomplishing the objectives of this type of legislation. Definitions are also essential to ensure some measure of coordination between the operation of a state civil-rights act and local civil-rights laws.

A third principal deficiency of the Kentucky statute relates to remedial powers and duties of local commissions and their procedures for processing a complaint of discrimination. While the statute authorizes a political subdivision to give a local commission certain appropriate remedial powers and duties and to enjoin upon them certain procedures in processing complaints, it also permits them not to provide for these matters. But this is precisely the area in which local option is not needed and can be disastrous relative to assuring effective local action. The necessary remedial powers and duties and procedures should be spelled out in a statute authorizing creation of local human-relations commissions. This is the approach in state civil-rights acts and, if essential there to assure fairness and effectiveness, that approach is, *a fortiori*, essential in dealing with political subdivisions when regard is had both to their reluctance to discharge their responsibilities and their lack of experience in this area. While they are likely to know the extent to which laws against discrimination can be effectively enforced by local officials and should be given fairly full discretion in this regard, they are not likely to know what remedial powers and duties and procedures are necessary for effective operation of a human-relations commission. It is here that the guideline and directive function of a state statute can be well served.

One final deficiency of the Kentucky statute is that it does not authorize a political subdivision to appropriate funds necessary for the purpose of supporting the operation of a local commission. While it authorizes a local commission to accept grants, gifts, or bequests, either public or private, these sources of funds may not be available either with regularity or in sufficient amount. Besides, local government should foot the bill, to the extent possible, of a human-relations program. Both the New York and Wisconsin statutes previously reviewed, and the Pennsylvania statute next to be examined, do authorize political subdivisions to appropriate funds for supporting local human-relations commissions.

The Pennsylvania statute speaks in a more adequate way to the authority of a political subdivision for the structure of a local commission than the statutes examined so far. Otherwise it is subject to the same criticisms as the Kentucky statute although it also shares the superiority of that statute over the New York and Wisconsin statutes.

The New York statute granting the New York City Human Relations Commission concurrent jurisdiction with the New York State Commission under the state civil-rights act[24] suggests a third alternative to the two general approaches utilized in existing legislation just examined. If the third alternative were generalized, it would speak to each of the difficulties pointed out so far with regard to the four general statutes examined. It would do this by providing a comprehensive uniform statute for administration by both the state and any local commission that is so authorized. The difficulty is that such an approach could be appropriate only where a state and a political subdivision have reached a considerable degree of sophistication concern-

---

[24] N.Y. Gen. Munic. Law, § 239s, *as amended* (McKinney Supp. 1967).

ing human-relations matters and their regulation. In fact, the New York special statute was enacted only after twenty years of experience in the field by the state Commission and about ten years by the New York City Commission. Moreover, it was made applicable to but one political subdivision. The communities served by each were roughly equivalent in sophistication relative to human-relations problems and each of the commissions had reached a high level of performance in dealing with these problems. In the South and Southwest it is likely that some local governments are far in advance of the state government in readiness to proceed with solution of civil-rights problems. In this situation, no state statute presently exists or is likely to be enacted to serve as a framework for common use by a state commission and local commissions. If a state statute is enacted it will probably be inadequate for use as a framework by a city willing to utilize greater sophistication in dealing with its human-relations problems. A state statute of some sort, certainly at least one granting home-rule powers, is essential to permit a city to proceed to act in this way. In other states, the very opposite in state-local relations may obtain and the state government may be far more able to deal with human-relations problems than are local governments. This, apparently, is the case in Massachusetts, as well as in California. Moreover, there can be a wide variation among local governments in their readiness to deal with intergroup-relations problems. One recalls to mind the large difference in this respect in the Commonwealth of Pennsylvania between Chester, on the one hand, and Pittsburgh or Philadelphia, on the other.[25]

PART I. SHORT TITLE; FINDINGS AND DECLARATION OF POLICIES; CONSTRUCTION

This part contains findings and a declaration of policy. Both of these sound the central note, to be heard throughout the Act, that the focus of governmental action is to be not only upon discrimination, in whatever form, against minority groups but also upon other equally harmful activity directed toward all disadvantaged groups in the community, upon the underlying causes of this activity, and upon the various forces that can be mustered for eliminating these causes and opening up equal opportunities for all. This second Alpha Model State Act is the counterpart of the first which was directed to the establishment of

---

[25] *The Community and Racial Crises*, edited by David Stahl, Frederick B. Sussman, and Neil J. Bloomfield (New York: Practicing Law Institute, 1966), pp. 58–71.

a state policy for administration by a state commission. Like the first it signals the responsibility of local communities and their citizens for dealing with denials of equal opportunity. The first Alpha Model State Act provided in part for the operation of the state human-relations commission at the local level. The second Alpha Model State Act provides for the operation of local human-relations commissions at the same level with a view to their substitution for or replacement of the state-commission operation to that extent.

Subsection (b) of Section 102 contains a series of provisions in brackets concerning the basis upon which the state commission will permit a local commission to replace its operation at the local level. These provisions should be inserted in this Act if the state has enacted into law the first Alpha Model State Act or a similar statute.

Subsection (c) states the central purpose of this Act: to provide political subdivisions with full and necessary authority to deal adequately with all of their human-relations problems and to supplement through official local action the implementation of state civil-rights policy.

Subsection (d) is designed to avoid the result produced by the New York, Wisconsin, and Kentucky acts, cutting down any pre-existing authority of political subdivisions to enact substantive legislation addressed to human-relations problems. The disclaimer is limited to substantive civil-rights law due to the fact that this Act does limit the authority of political subdivisions with regard to remedial powers and duties and procedures for processing complaints.

Part II. General Definitions

This part contains only those definitions that are particularly relevant to the provisions concerning the establishment of a local commission by political subdivisions, the relation of the work of a local commission to that of other similar commissions at all governmental levels, and assignment of the central task, functions, implemental policies, and remedial powers and duties of local commissions. Other definitions are set out in the subsequent parts to which they principally relate.

Part III. Local Human-Relations Commissions

Section 301 is one of the fundamental parts of the statute. It authorizes one or more political subdivisions to create a human-relations commission for the purpose of administering local civil-rights law.

The "political subdivision" is defined in Subsection (5) of Section 201 to mean a "[city, county . . .] of this state . . ." Other particular types of political subdivisions can be added to these in order to comprehend the various forms of political subdivisions utilized in a particular state. Moreover, it is possible in some jurisdictions, such as Massachusetts,[26] that the designation of a county as a comprehended political subdivision would be deleted due to the nominal governing functions performed by counties within these states. The principle for including any form of political subdivision within this definition should be the performance by it of a substantial general regulatory role within the state. For convenience of terminology, the term "political subdivision" is also defined to include "any combination of two or more designated subdivisions which, by joint action under Section 301, create a local commission."

The authority of a political subdivision under Section 301 is to create a local human-relations commission "for the purpose of administering local civil-rights law." The term "local civil-rights law" is defined in Subsection (6) of Section 201. It includes any legislation enacted by the governing board of a political subdivision under Section 802 of the Act. It also includes the duties imposed on and the authority granted to a local commission created under Section 301. Section 802, as will be more fully explained below, authorizes a governing board to regulate or prohibit a number of activities adversely affecting human relations in a political subdivision. Most of the local legislation authorized under this section calls for the local commission to exercise what has been called here the individual-complaint-processing function with a view to determining if discrimination has been directed against a particular individual. Other parts of the Act allocate other functions to and impose additional duties upon local commissions. Section 501 states the central task of a local commission. Section 502 requires a local commission also to perform a "wide-spectrum" negotiation function and a constructive-action function. Section 503 states the goals that a local commission must pursue in performing each of its three principal functions. Section 504 outlines certain implemental policies to be utilized by a local commission in performing its "wide-spectrum"-negotiation and constructive-action functions. Sections 601 and 602 grant certain remedial powers and impose certain remedial duties upon a local commission as it carries out its functions.

[26] Elwyn E. Mariner, *This Is Your Massachusetts Government* (Arlington Heights, Mass.: Mariner Books, 1967), pp. 125–129.

By the approach just outlined the Alpha Model Act speaks to one of a number of knotty problems that have to be resolved in formulating an adequate state statute authorizing and regulating the creation of human-relations commissions by the political subdivisions of a state. This is the problem previously mentioned, of the variety of situations in which local governments are to be found relative to their readiness to deal with the civil-rights problem of minority and other disadvantaged groups. The Act takes cognizance both of the initial variety of situations to which it is likely to be addressed in different political subdivisions and the subsequent uneven growth in the exercise of local responsibility across the state that is likely to take place over a considerable period of years. Its central approach in this respect is to provide local governments full authority to deal effectively with all human-relations problems without, however, requiring them to act in any way whatsoever. They are not required to set up local commissions nor are they required, if they do establish these commissions pursuant to the Act, to prohibit or regulate any particular conduct adversely affecting the civil rights of minority or disadvantaged groups. A local government may elect merely to use the authority granted by Section 301 of the Act to create a human-relations commission without giving it any regulatory authority. If this alone is done, however, the commission is required to perform, to the extent of its ability, the "wide-spectrum"-negotiation and constructive-action functions under Section 502 and to do this in accordance with the goals and implemental policies outlined in Sections 503 and 504. By and large there should be little, if any, opposition to the performance of these functions since they are not regulatory in character in the usual sense of the word. Moreover, the degree and manner of their implementation is largely a matter for local discretion. If a political subdivision elects to do no more than simply create a commission, there is also a third effect of its decision. While it will not have created any local civil-rights law under Section 802 in the form of prohibitions of unlawful discriminatory acts, it will be under the duty of processing complaints of discrimination by virtue of Section 501. This section instructs a commission to process complaints relative to denials of any right, privilege, or immunity secured or protected by the Constitution or laws of the United States and relative to all forms of discrimination or other harmful activity directed against minority or other disadvantaged groups. Part VII sets up a procedure that must be followed by the commission in the processing of complaints of discriminatory acts. These acts are defined in Section 701 to mean any act or practice of discrimination, including unlawful discriminatory acts. Discrimination is defined in the same section to comprehend in the broadest possible way every form of differentiation or preference by one person in the treatment of another person on account of race, color, religion, ancestry, national origin, age, or economic status, and any denial of any right, privilege, or immunity secured or protected by the Constitution or laws of the United States. This means that a local commission, once created under Section 301, has the obligation under Section 501 to process according to the procedure outlined in Part VII of this Act both complaints of discriminatory acts made unlawful by its political subdivision under Section 802 and complaints of harmful discriminatory acts not yet made unlawful under the latter section. The result is that a political subdivision in creating a human-relations commission, although it does not prohibit any form of discrimination as an unlawful discriminatory act, establishes an agency that must under the Act receive complaints of many forms of discriminatory acts in whatever fields they occur, investigate these complaints, determine whether probable cause exists to believe them to be true, utilize methods of conciliation to attempt to move a respondent to cease discrimination which it believes him to be committing, and even hold public hearings with a view to ascertaining more formally whether discrimination is occurring and making, where appropriate, recommendations to the parties and others for correcting discrimination found to exist together with public disclosure of its recommendations. Thus, as a result of Section 501, the definition of "discrimination" in Section 701, and the procedure for processing complaints in Part VII, the Act ensures that each political subdivision which begins to act at all in the field of human relations through creating a human-relations commission will have a commission with the authority and duty to confront all of the community's current problems of discrimination, whatever they are. The weapons it will have fall short of the authority to issue cease and desist orders and to seek their enforcement in the courts but they are considerable and can be effective in many situations. They are also substantially greater in scope than those which many political subdivisions allocate to their first commissions. Many political subdivisions confine their first official efforts in dealing with human-relations problems to giving their new human-relations commissions the authority to investigate complaints of discrimination and to utilize conciliation to eliminate it in some one or few areas (for example, in government employment, public accommodations, or employment by government contractors). It is important, however, for a political subdivision to direct its first effort in this field, although it authorizes its commission to use only the weapons of receiving, investigating, and conciliating complaints of discrimination, to the full spectrum of discrimination. This at least ensures that the community will become aware of the extent of discrimination within the community, its social costs, and possible methods of dealing with it. This also ensures that the local commission will gain valuable experience as well as make a greater initial contribution to the amelioration of the civil-rights problem of minorities and other disadvantaged persons. It is also important for a political subdivision directing its first official efforts to human-relations problems to give its commission the authority to compel testimony and production of evidence, to hold public hearings, and to make and publicize findings and recommendations for elimination of discrimination. This brings the pressure of public opinion in the community to bear upon a respondent even when no law exists to prohibit his conduct. Section 501 and Part VII assure that both of these optimum approaches will be followed by any political subdivision when it first begins to deal with human-relations problems through a commission.

If a political subdivision does elect to do more than simply create a human-relations commission and determines to prohibit conduct bearing adversely upon human relations (such as, discrimination against minority groups in employment, or public accommodations, or housing), it is free to proceed as narrowly or as broadly as persons on the local scene deem prudent and appropriate. The local government may direct its first effort in dealing with human-relations problems only to prohibiting discrimination in some of the more greatly needed public accommodations. It is authorized, however, to act comprehensively and to prohibit discrimination, if it so desires, in all forms of public accommodations and of employment, but not to do so in any forms of housing or activities operating with governmental financial assistance or under a license. It may wish to go still further and authorize its commission to try alleged violations of prohibitions of discrimination in all areas in which discrimination against minorites occurs. Section 802 of the Act authorizes a political subdivision to prohibit all this and much more when it addresses itself to problems of human relations in the community it serves. The central theory of this as well as the first Alpha Model Act is that whatever state official effort is immediately directed to the resolution of these problems at the local level, the ultimate and necessary approach for adequately resolving them must involve leaving room for each community to make the initial momentous decision to begin to deal officially with these problems; to do this in its own way, in its own time, and with its own rate of progress; and should it extend its effort to the fullest possible extent and do this in an effective manner, to replace state and federal activity in this field at the local level. The comment on Section 802 below will explain somewhat more fully the kinds of choices available to a political subdivision in enacting a local civil-rights law.

Some of the specifics of Part III may now be noted. One problem it is necessary to deal with in an Act of this sort is the existence of prior commissions. Another is the problem of bringing under the aegis of this Act any political subdivision that seeks to deal with human-relations problems in the future. Section 307 deals with these two problems. All existing local human-relations commissions are deemed to be "local commissions" established under Section 301. Any new local human-relations commission must be established under the same section. Since Subsection (c) of Section 301 makes any commission created under that section subject to the provisions of the Act, this means that the Act effectively controls the operations of all local human-relations commissions. Most state civil-rights acts have failed to deal with these problems and, thereby, have left a large loophole for existing commissions and future ones to remain or be ineffective expedients in th human-relations field.

Section 302 follows the Pennsylvania statute in spelling out the matters of commission structure that must be dealt with but leaving the way of handling them up to the political subdivisions. The section does require that the number of commissioners not be less than seven. The reason for this figure is basically the same as the one given in the comment upon the requirement of the same figure in the case of state commissions under the first Alpha Model Act. A local commission should be large enough to permit some allocation of functions among its members. Some commissioners should be free to deal with overall commission policy while others should perform the role of investigating commissioners or make up a hearing panel as seems appropriate under Part VII.

Section 306 permits a city commission to operate within the jurisdiction of the city and excludes a commission of a county in which the city is located from operating in that city to the extent that the former has jurisdiction over a particular matter under is local civil-rights law.

If city jurisdiction over a particular matter of human relations is lacking, the county commission may speak to that particular matter in that city.

PART IV.   RELATION BETWEEN A LOCAL COMMISSION AND
OTHER HUMAN-RELATIONS COMMISSIONS

Section 402 emphasizes that a local commission may exercise its jurisdiction under local civil-rights law within its political subdivision unless prohibited from doing this by specific administrative action of a state or federal commission having similar jurisdiction. This has reference to all three functions enjoined upon a local commission by the provisions of Section 502. Ordinarily, a state or federal commission could, under the Alpha Model Act, be performing the "wide-spectrum"-negotiation function and the constructive-action function in a given political subdivision and not be at all discomfited by a local commission performing the same two functions in the same political subdivision. Each could be working on different problems. Only where there was an attempt by the local commission to handle the same specific problem as a state or federal commission would there be any necessity for the latter to act to protect its jurisdiction. With respect to the individual-complaint function, however, if the state or federal human-relations commission were operating in a political subdivision, it is not at all unlikely that it would want to replace efforts of the local commission altogether. The only reason the state or federal commission would be operating locally would be the fact that it deemed the local commission to have an inadequate human-relations program or an ineffective local commission for enforcing it. This section ties in with Section 301 of the Alpha Model State Civil-Rights Act. The latter section states the conditions under which the state commission shall establish a local section of the state commission in a political subdivision to perform the role a local commission should be performing.

Sections 403 and 404 deal with the matter of cooperative agreements between a local commission and other commissions at all levels of government in the federal system. The first section authorizes the making of these agreements, and the second permits them to be terminated under certain conditions. It seems better to spell out the guidelines and directives concerning their content in state and federal civil-rights acts since the commissions operating under those acts will be the prime movers and certainly the ultimate decision makers concerning any agreements made. Sections 402 and 403 of the Alpha Model State Civil-Rights Act, for example, speak to these matters.

Sections 405 and 406 are almost precisely comparable to the same numbered sections of the Alpha Model State Civil-Rights Act. The comment made on those sections is applicable here.

PART V. THE CENTRAL TASKS, FUNCTIONS, GOALS, AND POLICIES OF A LOCAL COMMISSION

The heart of the Alpha Model State Act on Local Commissions is Part V. In stating the central task of a local commission Section 501 simply makes explicit what careful students of intergroup-relations problems have been articulating for years as the task which has to be performed at the local level by well-organized local human-relations commissions. By and large the operation of the Philadelphia Commission on Human Relations has closely approximated, at least since 1960, the performance of the task outlined in this section. Political subdivisions need to be told what their task is in the integroup-relations field. They are not likely otherwise to understand this task soon enough.

Section 502 outlines the basic functions of a local commission. At present, of the existing state laws speaking to establishment of local commissions, only the New York statute previously examined does this. Moreover, the Uniform Model Act completely fails to appreciate the necessity for doing this. Section 502 has its counterparts in some local ordinances but even in these a sharp delineation of commission functions is usually lacking. The absence of this formulation is of no consequence with local commissions, such as those in Philadelphia and Pittsburgh, that have just "growed," like Topsy, and learned from experience their necessary lessons about functions to be performed. The statement of functions is of crucial consequence, however, in a state statute seeking to set guidelines and directives for political subdivisions about to set sail in a far rougher sea than the political subdivisions who entered it some years ago. The functions outlined in this section are (1) the processing of individual complaints relative to denials of rights, privileges, and immunities secured by the Constitution or laws of the United States and relative to all forms of discrimination and other similar activity directed toward minority groups; (2) the "wide-spectrum"-negotiation function; and (3) the constructive-action function. The description of these functions contained in Section 502 is quite general and stated in terms of the immediate objects dealt with in their performance. These general descriptions, however, take on important additional meaning in light of the central task defined for a local commission in Section 501, the general goals of its work stated in Section 503, the general outline of acts that a political subdivision is authorized to prohibit contained in Section 802, the implemental policies in performing commission functions stated in Section 504, and commission procedural powers and duties stated in Section 602.

The Comment on the Alpha Model State Civil-Rights Act concerning its Sections 504 and 505 are applicable to Sections 503 and 504 of this Act and should be consulted.

PART VI. POWERS AND DUTIES OF A LOCAL COMMISSION

The comments on the Alpha Model State Civil-Rights Act relative to its Part VI are applicable to Part VI of this Act and should be consulted.

PART VII. PROCEDURES RELATIVE TO COMPLAINTS; REMEDIES; JUDICIAL REVIEW; RECORDS

The comments on the Alpha Model State Civil-Rights Act relative to its Part VII are applicable to Part VII of this Act and should be consulted.

PART VIII. UNLAWFUL DISCRIMINATORY ACTS

Section 802 outlines the kinds of acts that a political subdivision may prohibit by appropriate legislative action as unlawful discriminatory acts. If the political subdivision does prohibit these acts, this forms part of the local civil-rights law that must be enforced by its commission pursuant to the procedure set out in Part VII of the Act.

One problem presented in constructing Section 802 concerning the authority of local governments to regulate activities bearing adversely upon human relations was created by the very scope of the freedom it was necessary to grant to these governments to formulate the content of their prohibitions of this type of conduct. Since the ultimate aim of the statute is the best and most practicable exercise of local responsibiliy over the civil-rights problem of minorities at any time in each of the communities throughout the state, it is necessary that the authority of a local government to act extend from an authority to do less than the state is in fact doing in the civil-rights field to an authority to do more than the state might at some time be doing in this field. Thus, in regard to employment discrimination, it is desirable to permit a local government to deal only with employers of twenty-five or more employees if it so desires although the state government deals with employers of ten or more employees. Similarly it is desirable to permit a local government, if it so desires, to regulate employers of one or more employees although the state has not as yet advanced to that level of regulation. This type of difference between local and state law creates no problems in view of the commitment of the statute to permitting and facilitating administration of civil-rights law by local agencies. On the other hand, most state statutes have exempted certain employers from coverage of the state prohibition of employment discrimination. One example is the employer of his own spouse, parent, or child. Another is the employer of domestic servants. The policy of the state relative to this exemption seeks to implement an interest deemed more valuable, in this context, than preventing employment discrimination. For this reason, Section 802 in granting authority to local government to regulate discrimination in, for example, employment has been modified by the definitions of "employer" and "individual" set forth in Section 801. The first term is defined as meaning "a person employing [   ] or more employees" within a political subdivision, exclusive of parents, spouse, or children of that person.

The term "individual," which has reference under Subsection (6) of Section 802 to a person against whom an employer may be prohibited from discriminating, is defined to exclude a person employed or seeking employment by his parents, spouse, or child, or employed or seeking employment in the domestic service of or in a personal or confidential capacity by any person. Similarly, Subsection (8) of Section 801 in defining "place of public accommodations," with reference to which a political subdivision may prohibit discrimination under Subsection (7) of Section 802, excludes from its compass clubs, associations, corporations, or other organizations which have the characteristics, there defined, of a private, nonprofit organization operating in a specified manner. An exemption of this kind is usually contained in statutes granting jurisdiction to state human-relations commissions over public-accommodations discrimination. No policy of local autonomy would warrant overriding the interest protected, so long as the state protects it. On the other hand, the term "place of public accommodations" is defined in the broadest possible sense in Section 801, probably more broadly than it is defined in any state statute. For example, its definition also comprehends any place of rendering professional services which is open to, accepts, or solicits the patronage of the general public. Many state statutes do not comprehend this activity with the result that discrimination on the basis of race and color practiced by physicians and dentists (among other professional persons) is not prohibited. Certainly, a local government should have authority to prohibit this discrimination if it desires to do so, even if the state government does not.

In states like New York and New Jersey, which have for many years had well-established state commissions with jurisdiction over most of the area of discrimination against minorities, it is likely that many local governments, if given the option contained in Section 802 to enact local civil-rights law, would simply incorporate the provisions of the state law into the local law enacted. This is precisely what New Haven did in creating its human-relations commission in May 1964. In states like Massachusetts, which have a strong orientation to use of state rather than local government to resolve public problems of an inherently local nature, Section 802, however necessary it may be in principle in the civil-rights context, will seem to many people a bitter and perhaps even a foolish pill to swallow. These states, if they permit local government to administer civil-rights law at all, are most likely to designate the state law as the law to be administered by local commissions. To resolve the problem of local unreadiness to administer the full range of state civil-rights law, it would be necessary for the state commission to be given the duty of monitoring the degree to which a local commission would be permitted to administer the state law. This could be done through the requirement that a local commission have entered into a cooperative agreement with the state commission before it could administer any portion of the state law. Much would be lost by this approach but it would be considerably better than the situation that presently obtains in states like Massachusetts and California.

The general acts which a political subdivision may prohibit as unlawful discriminatory acts, spelled out in Section 802, follow chronologically the order of provisions prohibiting unlawful discriminatory acts contained in the Alpha Model State Civil-Rights Act for enforcement by a state commission. The comment upon these sections following that Act in Chapter 8 should be consulted. A political subdivision can obtain guidance in formulating a prohibition of a particular kind of unlawful discriminatory act in exercising its authority under Section 802 of this Act simply by consulting Part VIII of the Alpha Model State Civil-Rights Act.

Section 803 requires a political subdivision to make certain exceptions from its local civil-rights laws. These include the exception of situations in which a group characteristic is a bona fide occupational qualification, in which certain age requirements are established for occupational-training programs, in which age requirements are enforced under bona fide retirement and other similar plans, and in which a religious organization is involved. Section 803 also permits a political subdivision to make reasonable exceptions from the coverage of its prohibitions. A number of exceptions may be reasonably made in regard to regulation of discrimination based upon sex, age, and economic status.

PART IX.   CRIMINAL SANCTIONS; OTHER REMEDIES; MISCELLANEOUS

This part is, with one slight exception, the same as Part IX of the Alpha Model State Civil-Rights Act and the comments upon the former are applicable to this part.

10

The Alpha Model Federal Civil-Rights Act, with Comments

THE ALPHA MODEL FEDERAL CIVIL-RIGHTS ACT

Table of Contents

The Alpha Model Federal Civil-Rights Act

AN ACT

To prevent unreasonable practices directed against minority and other seriously disadvantaged groups in the nation's communities, including discrimination based upon race, color, religion, ancestry, national origin, age, sex, or economic status, in law enforcement and public administration, in activities operating with government financial assistance or a license, in employment, in the operation of places of public accommodations and of education institutions, in real-estate transactions, in financing of transactions relating to real property, and in the functioning of business and professional organizations, and other activities.

Be it enacted by the Senate and House of Representatives of the United States of America in Congress assembled, That:

This Act may be cited as the "Civil Rights Act of [year of enactment]."

TITLE I. FINDINGS AND DECLARATION OF POLICIES; CONSTRUCTION; GENERAL DEFINITIONS

Section 101. Findings and declaration of policies. (a) The population of this nation, its states, and their political subdivisions consists of people of many races, colors, religions, ancestries, and national origins, as well as of different sex, age, and economic groups. It is essential to the public health, welfare, peace, and progress of the nation, each state, and each political subdivision that this diversity serve to strengthen individual and collective efforts to achieve man's enduring goals and not be used to weaken these efforts. The latter result occurs when members of one group practice, through private or governmental institutions, discrimination and other harmful activity against members of another group in any phase of community life merely on account of their race or other normal group characteristics. Practices of this kind and the conditions accompanying them undermine the freedom and justice essential to genuine democracy. Among other things, they prevent full development and utilization of the capacities of many persons; cut them off from various kinds of economic, social, cultural, and political opportunities; deny them adequate education and training; cause among them widespread unemployment and underemployment; deprive them of earnings necessary to maintain decent standards of living and require them to resort to public relief;

and produce segregated residential areas which, through their *de facto* segregated schools and typical substandard, unsafe, and unsanitary living conditions, support the whole structure of discrimination and disadvantages suffered by their inhabitants. These practices also cause or contribute to intergroup tensions and conflicts, school drop-outs, crime, juvenile delinquency, disease, fire hazards, higher welfare costs, and loss of tax revenues.

(b) It is the policy of the United States to ensure that all persons enjoy the full benefits of citizenship or residence and be afforded equal opportunity to participate, on the basis of personal merit, in the social, cultural, economic, political, and other phases of life within the national, state, and local communities, free from any discrimination on account of race, color, religion, ancestry, or national origin, and from any restrictions on account of sex, age, or economic status that are unreasonable. In order to implement this policy it is essential that each governmental element in the federal system assume the initiative for repairing the consequences of past denials of equal opportunities to particular groups, preventing denials of these opportunities in the future, and controlling and eliminating the underlying causes of intergroup-relations problems. Government initiative for accomplishing these purposes must be exercised within each community. Human-relations problems cannot be adequately solved until the government and citizenry of each community and of each state honestly face these problems and with good will and industry work together for their solution.

Section 102. Policy of Act Relating to Local and State Human-Relations Problems. It is a central purpose of this Act to encourage the institution and maintenance of adequate human-relations programs by each state and by each political subdivision within a state having serious intergroup-relations problems. Where a political subdivision faced with these problems has established and maintains an adequate human-relations program administered by an effective local human-relations commission, the United States government will, through the Federal Human-Relations Commission established by this Act, cooperate in every possibly way with the local government and will confine its operations in that political subdivision to handling human-relations problems falling properly within federal cognizance that are not being handled by either the local commission or a state commission.

Where a political subdivision has not established or does not maintain an adequate human-relations program administered through an effective human-relations commission to handle serious intergroup-relations problems in that political subdivision, and the state in which it is located does not establish such a program administered by an effective local section of a state commission operating in that political subdivision, the Federal Human-Relations Commission will administer the human-relations program established by this Act within that community through one of its local sections. Moreover, where a state has not established or does not maintain an adequate state human-relations program administered by a state human-relations commission, the Federal Human-Relations Commission may establish a state section for the purpose of better promoting the purposes of this Act. If a state does maintain an adequate state human-relations program administered by an effective state human-relations commission, the Federal Human-Relations Commission will cooperate in every possible way with that commission and will confine its operations to handling matters falling properly within federal cognizance that are not being handled by the state commission.

Section 103. Liberal Construction. This Act shall be construed liberally to further its purposes and, more generally, to promote justice in human relations.

Section 104. General Definitions. In this Act, unless the context otherwise requires,

(1) "Person" means an individual, partnership, association, corporation, joint-stock company, labor union, mutual company, trustee in bankruptcy, receiver, or other fiduciary, or the agency, legal representative, or employee thereof; and the United States, any state, or any of its political subdivisions, or any agency, officer, or employee thereof.

(2) "Commission" means the Federal Human-Relations Commission established by Section 201 of this Act.

(3) "Commissioner" means a member of the Commission.

(4) "Local section" means a section of the Commission established by the Commission pursuant to Section 301 of this Act.

(5) "Political subdivision" means a city or other political subdivision of a state having a substantial general regulatory authority and any combination of two or more of these determined by the Commission to be appropriate for the purpose of establishing a local section.

(6) "State" means a state, territory, or possession of the United

States, the District of Columbia, Puerto Rico, the Virgin Islands, American Samoa, Guam, Wake Island, the Canal Zone, and Outer Continental Shelf lands defined in the Outer Continental Shelf Lands Act.

(7) "State section" means a section of the Commission established by the Commission pursuant to Section 302 of this Act.

(8) "Local section commissioner" means a member of a local section.

(9) "State section commissioner" means a member of a state section.

(10) "Local commission" means a human-relations commission established by a political subdivision.

(11) "State commission" means a human-relations commission established by a state.

(12) "Cooperative agreement" means a cooperative agreement made by the Commission under Section 402.

(13) "Discriminatory act" means any act or practice of discrimination, including an unlawful discriminatory act.

(14) "Discrimination" means any direct or indirect exclusion, distinction, segregation, limitation, refusal, denial, or any other differentiation or preference in the treatment of a person or persons on account of race, color, religion, ancestry, national origin, age, sex, or economic status, and any denial of any right, privilege, or immunity secured or protected by the Constitution or laws of the United States.

(15) "Negotiation function" means the function assigned to the Commission and its local and state sections, respectively, under Subsection (a)(3) of Section 502, Subsection (a)(2) of Section 503, and Section 504.

(16) "Constructive-action function" means the function assigned to the Commission and its local and state sections, respectively, under Subsection (a)(4) of Section 502, Subsection (a)(3) of Section 503, and Section 504.

(17) "Community" refers to either the local, state, or national community or all of these, depending on the context.

(18) "Annual contribution" means annual contributions by the Commission to a local or state commission under Section 603.

(19) "Official plan of action" means a plan submitted by a political subdivision or a state to the Commission under Section 603.

TITLE II. Federal Human-Relations Commission

Section 201. Establishment; appointment; political representation; chairman. There is hereby created the Federal Human-Relations Commission. The membership of the Commission consists of seven commissioners to be appointed by the President, by and with the advice and consent of the Senate. No more than four of these commissioners may be members of the same political party. The chairman of the Commission shall be designated by the President from its membership. The Commission may designate one of its commissioners to act as chairman during the absence or incapacity of the chairman.

Section 202. Commissioners' terms of office; vacancies. The term of office of each commissioner is six years and until the appointment and qualification of his successor. Of those commissioners first appointed two shall be appointed for terms of two years, two for terms of four years, and three for terms of six years. A person appointed to fill a vacancy occurring prior to expiration of a term shall be appointed only for the unexpired part of that term.

Section 203. Quorum; exercise of powers during vacancy. Four commissioners constitute a quorum. Vacancies on the Commission do not impair the authority of the remaining commissioners to exercise the powers of the Commission.

Section 204. Seal; judicial notice. The Commission shall have an official seal which shall be judicially noticed.

Section 205. Legal representation. Attorneys appointed under this Act may, at the direction of the Commission, appear for and represent the Commission in any case in court.

Section 206. Personnel subject to Section 118i of Title 5, U.S.C. All officers, agents, attorneys, and employees of the Commission shall be subject to the provisions of Section 118i of Title 5 of the United States Code, notwithstanding any exemption contained in such section.

Section 207. Outside employment; salaries. No commissioner may engage in any business, vocation, or employment other than that of serving as a member of the Commission. The salary of each commissioner is [   ] a year. Each commissioner may obtain compensation for all expenses actually and necessarily incurred by him in the performance of his duties.

Section 208. Removal from office. The President may remove a commissioner for inefficiency, neglect of duty, misconduct, or malfeasance in office, after giving him a written statement of the charges against him and an opportunity to be heard.

TITLE III. Local and State Sections of the Commission

Section 301. Establishment of local sections; name, appointment; eligibility for; chairman, elections; authority. (a) The Commission shall establish a local section of the Commission in each political subdivision determined by it to have serious intergroup-relations problems and not to have established and maintained within it an adequate human-relations program effectively administered by a local human-relations commission or a local section of a state commission.

(b) A political subdivision is conclusively presumed to have serious intergroup-relations problems if at least one thousand (1,000) Negroes, Latin Americans, or both Negroes and Latin Americans are resident or employed within it. "Latin American" means any person who has a Spanish surname.

(c) In determining whether a political subdivision or a state has established and is maintaining an adequate human-relations program effectively administered by a local commission or a local section within that political subdivision, the Commission is to be guided by the nature of the program and powers entrusted to it under this Act.

(d) Each local section shall be known as the "[name of political subdivision]-Federal Human-Relations Commission."

(e) The membership of each local section consists of seven local section commissioners to be appointed by the Commission, one of whom is to be designated as chairman. Each local section may designate one of its local section commissioners to act as chairman during the absence or incapacity of its chairman. A person is eligible for appointment as a local section commissioner if he is a citizen of the United States. The Commission should seek to find qualified commissioners who live or work in the political subdivision served by the local section on which they sit, who live in the state in which that political subdivision is located, or who live in another state, in that order of preference. The Commission is authorized to make appointments of local section commissioners on the basis of an election conducted by it within the political subdivision served by a local section. Persons, over the age of seventeen, who reside or work in the political subdivision, are entitled to vote in an election for this purpose, which shall be conducted pursuant to regulations promulgated by the Commission.

(f) Each local section shall exercise all of the authority and be subject to all of the duties of the Commission within its political subdivision subject to such supervision and review of its decisions as the Commission shall provide.

Section 302. Establishment of a state section; name; appointment; and eligibility for; chairman. (a) The Commission may establish a state section of the Commission in any state determined by it not to have established and to be maintaining within it an adequate human-relations program, effectively administered by a state human-relations commission.

(b) In determining whether a state has established and is maintaining an adequate human-relations program, effectively administered by a state human-relations commission, the Commission is to be guided by the nature of the program and powers entrusted to it under this Act.

(c) Each state section shall be known as the "[name of state]-Federal Human-Relations Commission."

(d) The membership of each state section consists of seven state section commissioners to be appointed by the Commission, one of whom is to be designated as chairman. Each state section may designate one of its state section commissioners to act as chairman during the absense or incapacity of its chairman. A person is eligible for an appointment as a state section commissioner if he is a citizen of the United States. The Commission should seek to find qualified commissioners who live in the state for which a state section is established or who live in another state, in that order of preference.

(e) A state section has such authority as the Commission delegates to it. The Commission may delegate to a state section any of its functions that it would otherwise perform relative to the state for which it is established.

Section 303. Section commissioners' terms; quorum; removal from office. The provisions of Sections 202, 203, and 208 of Title II apply to local and state section commissioners, except that the Commission shall perform the functions assigned to the President under those sections.

Section 304. Outside employment; compensation. No local or state section commissioner may engage in any other business, vocation, or employment while serving as a member of his section. The salary of local and state section commissioners shall be determined by the Commission. Each local and state section commissioner may obtain compensation for all expenses actually and necessarily incurred by him in the performance of his duties.

TITLE IV.   RELATION OF THIS ACT TO SIMILAR STATE AND LOCAL LAW; COOPERATIVE AGREEMENTS WITH STATE AND LOCAL COMMISSIONS

Section 401. Construction of Act not to exclude operation of state and local laws and not to invalidate consistent state and local law. Nothing contained in any title of this Act shall be construed as indicating a purpose on the part of Congress to occupy the field in which any such title operates to the exclusion of state or local laws on the same subject matter, nor shall any provision of this Act be construed as invalidating any provision of state or local law unless such provision is inconsistent with any of the purposes of this Act, or any provision thereof.

Section 402. Cooperation with local and state human-relations commissions; utilization of services; reimbursement; cooperative agreements. The Commission may cooperate with local and state human-relations commissions established to administer laws comparable to this Act. The Commission, with the consent of these commissions, may, for the purpose of carrying out its functions and duties under this Act and within the limitation of funds appropriated specifically for such purpose, utilize the services of these commissions and their employees and, notwithstanding any other provision of law, may reimburse these commissions and their employees for services rendered to assist the Commission in carrying out its functions and duties. In furtherance of such cooperation and to achieve more adequate administration of this Act, the Commission may enter into written agreements with these commissions under which, among other things, the local or state sections of the Commission will refrain from performing the whole or part of any one or more of their assigned or delegated functions. The Commission may rescind a cooperative agreement whenever it determines that the agreement no longer serves the interest of promoting effective achievement of the purposes of this Act.

Section 403. Complaints covered by a cooperative agreement. (a) Any complaint filed with or by the Commission or a local commission falling within the coverage of a cooperative agreement shall be processed by the local commission unless its chairman or a majority of its commissioners request the Commission to process the complaint or unless the Commission directs that the complaint be retained by or referred to it. The request or direction that a complaint be processed by the Commission may be made after the local commission has rendered its decision, and, in this event, the Commission shall, except as it may limit the issues upon notice or by rule, exercise all the authority it would have had in making the initial decision.

(b) Any complaint filed with or by the Commission or a state commission falling within the coverage of a cooperative agreement shall be processed in accordance with its terms. The agreement may provide for its processing by a local section of the Commission, a local commission, or the state commission, as appropriate. The local and state commissions may request the Commission to process the complaint and the Commission may direct that the complaint be retained by or referred to it as in Subsection (a).

Section 404. Effect of resort to procedure of this Act. In the absence of a cooperative agreement between the Commission and a local or state commission, the procedure provided by this Act shall, when invoked by an individual aggrieved relative to action covered by this Act, be exclusive and the final determination of the case shall exclude any other action of a civil nature based upon the same matter of which complaint has been filed by that person.

Section 405. Effect of resort to procedure of another law. If a person institutes an action relative to conduct covered by this Act without resorting to the procedure provided by it, he may not subsequently resort to that procedure. The Commission may, however, direct a local or state commission receiving or filing a complaint alleging discrimination covered by this Act to refer the complaint to it for initial decision or a review of the decision of that commission in a similar manner to the procedure for complaints covered by cooperative agreements.

TITLE V. THE CENTRAL TASK, FUNCTIONS, GOALS, AND POLICIES OF THE COMMISSION AND ITS LOCAL AND STATE SECTIONS

Section 501. The central task of the Commission and its local and state sections. (a) The central task of a local section of the Commission is the reconstruction of intergroup relations within the community served by it so as to eliminate the causes of, ameliorate the conditions accompanying, and overcome the results flowing from discrimination and other harmful activity directed against minority and other disadvantaged groups. Performance of this task of reconstruction calls for the assembly and redirection of the maximum human and material resources within each community throughout the nation having serious intergroup-relations problems and bringing them to bear upon those problems in the most effective way. It demands that each community be persuaded to acknowledge that the performance of this task is ultimately its own responsibility and that each of its groups become genuinely involved in discharging it.

(b) The local section is to be the major institution within a political subdivision for guiding the performance of this task and for providing as well as eliciting the appropriate leadership to secure its realization until the political subdivision or state undertakes its performance in an effective manner. With regard to the majority or controlling group, the local section must seek to obtain reorganization and reformation of all group actions, habits, customs, and private and official arrangements that have produced and continue to maintain the conditions adversely affecting the opportunities of minority and other disadvantaged groups. With regard to the latter, the local section must seek to move its members to confront problems of group actions, habits, customs, and private arrangements that hamper them in obtaining and maximizing upon needed opportunities; to provide them with various kinds of assistance services calculated to help them prepare for and obtain needed opportunities, and to protect them against certain typical exploitation and abuse. Persons within the majority or controlling group must be found who will provide wise leadership within that group so as to move it to begin to confront and resolve its intergroup-relations problems. Within minority and other disadvantaged groups, leaders must be found or developed who will help these groups to perform the kinds of actions that are calculated to start and facilitate the process of dialogue and negotiation between the various groups, looking to an improvement in their relations and in the opportunities available to minority and other disadvantaged groups.

(c) The central task of a state section is analogous to that of local sections of the Commission. It is concerned with the reconstruction of intergroup relations within the entire statewide community. In addition to overseeing and supervising the work of local sections when this function is assigned it, a state section is especially concerned with problems of intergroup relations that cannot be handled adequately by a local section or a local commission within the state.

(d) The central task of the Commission is analogous to those of its local and state sections. It is concerned with the reconstruction of intergroup relations within the entire nationwide community. In addition to overseeing and supervising the work of local and state sections, the Commission is especially concerned with problems of intergroup relations that cannot be adequately handled by local sections or commissions and state sections or commissions.

Section 502. Basic functions of the Commission. (a) The Commission shall perform the following basic functions:

(1) supporting, supervising, and reviewing the operation of its local and state sections so as to ensure adequate performance of their respective central tasks with regard to reconstructing intergroup relations within the political subdivisions and states served; exercise of their basic functions; achievement of the goals of this Act; and implementation of the policies established for this purpose;

(2) promoting of the creation of local commissions by political subdivisions and state commissions by states, and supporting, assisting, and reviewing their operation with a view to moving them to perform effectively a role essentially comparable to that assigned its local and state sections;

(3) negotiating with governing bodies and agencies of political subdivisions, with states and state agencies, with federal agencies, and with persons and organizations having statewide and nationwide operations for the taking of action by them to improve opportunities available to minority and other disadvantaged groups and utilizing inspections, surveys, private conferences, public hearings, reports, and enforcement actions to assure the effectiveness of negotiation.

(4) undertaking various types of constructive action designed to eliminate the causes of intergroup-relations problems insofar as they have their source outside local communities and beyond state lines, to deal with actions and conditions affecting the public welfare that result from continued existence of these problems, and to move the statewide and nationwide communities and their groups to direct the maximum resources of those communities, both human and material, to the accomplishment of these objectives.

(5) processing individual complaints relative to denials of any right, privilege, or immunity secured or protected by the Constitution or laws of the United States and relative to all forms of discrimination and other harmful activity directed against minority and other disadvantaged groups by persons whose activities can be dealt with more effectively through action of the Commission rather than by action of local sections or commissions and state sections or commissions.

(b) It is the sense of Congress that the processing of individual complaints should be relegated as far as possible to local and state sections and that the negotiation and constructive-action functions of the Commission should receive the greatest emphasis in its administration of the Act.

(c) Each local section shall perform three basic functions within the political subdivision it serves:

(1) processing individual complaints relative to denials of any right, privilege, or immunity secured or protected by the Constitution or laws of the United States and relative to all forms of discrimination and other harmful activity directed against minority or other disadvantaged groups.

(2) negotiating with wide sectors of businesses, unions, professions, official agencies, and private organizations for the taking of action by them to improve opportunities available to minority and other disadvantaged groups and utilizing inspections, surveys, private conferences, public hearings, reports, and enforcement actions to assure the effectiveness of negotiation;

(3) undertaking various types of constructive action designed to eliminate the causes of intergroup-relations problems within the local community, to deal with actions and conditions affecting the public welfare that result from the continued existence of these problems, and to move the local community and its groups to direct the maximum resources of that community, both human and material, to the accomplishment of these objectives.

(b) It is the sense of the Congress that the negotiation and constructive-action functions of each local section should receive the greatest emphasis in its administration of the Act.

Section 504. Basic functions of state sections. State sections shall exercise such basic functions of the Commission as it shall delegate to them.

Section 505. Goals of the Commission and its local and state sections. The Commission and its local and state sections shall seek to achieve the following goals in the performance of their basic tasks and functions:

(a)–(f)

[Subsections (a) through (f) of this section are the same as the corresponding subsections of Section 504 of the Alpha Model State Civil-Rights Act.]

Section 506. Implemental policies of the Commission and its local and state sections. The Commission and its local and state sections shall pursue the following implemental policies in performing their negotiation and constructive-action functions:

(1)–(11)

[Subsections (1) through (11) of this section are the same as the corresponding subsections of Section 505 of the Alpha Model State Civil-Rights Act.]

TITLE VI. POWERS AND DUTIES OF THE COMMISSION AND ITS LOCAL AND STATE SECTIONS

Section 601. General powers and duties of the Commission. The Commission has the following general powers and duties:

(1) to establish its principal office in or near the District of Columbia, an office for each of its local sections within the political subdivision for which it is established, an office for each of its state sections within the state for which it is established and such other regional or state offices as it deems necessary to accomplish the purposes of this Act;

(2) to meet and function at any place;

(3) to appoint in accordance with the civil-service laws an executive director and any attorneys, hearing examiners, clerks, and other employees and agents for itself and its local and state sections as it may deem necessary to assist it in the performance of its functions, and to fix their compensation in accordance with the Classification Act of 1949;

(4) to accept outside funds, gifts, or bequests, public or private, to help finance the activities of itself or of its local and state sections;

(5) to adopt, promulgate, amend, and rescind rules and regulations to effectuate the purposes and provisions of this Act; and

(6) to submit at least once a year to the Congress and to the President a report concerning the activities of itself and its local and state sections, and its recommendations.

Section 602. Implemental powers and duties of the Commission and its local and state sections. The Commission and its local and state sections have the following implemental powers and duties in performing their basic tasks and functions and in carrying out their implemental policies:

(1)–(11)

[Subsections (1) through (11) of this section are the same as the corresponding subsections of Section 602 of the Alpha Model State Civil-Rights Act.]

(12) with the consent of the agency concerned, to utilize or employ the services or personnel of any government agency of any state or political subdivision thereof to perform such functions on its behalf as may appear desirable.

Section 603. Authorization for annual contributions for local and state commissions and contracts concerning; limitations on amount; official plan of action; minimum civil-rights law; proposal for activities and projects; necessary agreements; review of application; payments; aggregate amount available; withholding of payment. (a) The Commission has the authority to make annual contributions to local and state commissions in order to assist them in achieving and maintaining an adequate and effectively administered human-relations program and to make provision for such annual contributions in a contract with a local or state commission providing for their payment and stipulating the conditions under which the contributions are to be made. Annual contributions shall be limited to the amounts and periods necessary, in the determination of the Commission, to assure the adequacy and effective administration of an applicant's human-relations program.

(b) No contract may be entered into for any annual contributions to an applicant under this section unless

(1) there is presented to the Commission a workable human-relations program for administration by a human-relations commission and an official plan of action that shall provide

(A) by law that, in the case of the state, the program and plan shall be in effect in all political subdivisions of the state and effectively administered within them through local sections comparable to those of the Commission except in a political subdivision that has a local commission effectively administering an adequate human-relations program;

(B) that the state or the political subdivision, as the case may be, will enact, if it does not now have, the necessary legislation to provide a minimum civil-rights law comparable to this Act, which is deemed adequate by the Commission to subserve the needs and possibilities for progress of the jurisdiction presenting the program;

(C) that the state or the political subdivision, as the case may be, will match contributions provided by the Commission to support its human-relations commission at least equal to the total of one third of the aggregate cost of operation for its commission;

(D) that the state or the political subdivision, as the case may be, will review its official human-relations program and official plan of action at least once annually, and whenever it revises the plan, resubmit it to the Commission;

(2) the governing board of the political subdivision or the Legislature has approved the human-relations program and official plan of action;

(3) there is presented to the Commission a proposal for activities and projects for execution by a local or state commission that are designed to meet human-relations problems within the jurisdiction to be served and that are of sufficient size, scope and quality to give reasonable promise of substantial progress toward resolving those problems;

(4) on the basis of its review of such program, plan, and proposed activities under them, the Commission determines that they meet the requirements of this section; and

(5) the contract contains an agreement by the applicant

(A) that payments of annual contributions will be used only in carrying out its human-relations program and activities and projects which have been approved by the Commission;

(B) that it will in all respects comply with the provisions of this Act;

(C) that it will adopt adequate procedures for evaluating the effectiveness of the human-relations program and activities and projects conducted under that program; and

(D) that it will make to the Commission periodic reports evaluating the effectiveness of its human-relations program and such other reports as may be required by the Commission as reasonably necessary to enable it to perform its duties under this Act.

(c) In determining whether to make a contract for annual contributions to an applicant under this section and in fixing the amount thereof and the terms and conditions on which it will be made, the Commission shall take into consideration the amount available for annual contributions under this section and the other applications which are pending before it; the financial condition of the applicant and other resources available to it; the nature, extent, and gravity of the human-relations problems faced by it, and such other factors as it finds to be relevant for determining whether the granting of an application will promote the purposes of this Act.

(d) All payments of annual contributions pursuant to this section shall be made out of any funds available to the Commission when such payments are due.

(e) The Commission is authorized to enter into contracts for annual contributions under this section aggregating not more than [   ] per annum.

(f) In the case of any official plan of action for a human-relations program and any activities or projects under it that have been approved by the Commission, if the Commission after reasonable notice and opportunity for hearing to the local or state commission administering the plan, finds

(1) that the plan has been so changed as not to constitute an adequate human-relations program; or

(2) that the administration of the plan is not effective or fails to comply substantially with the contract for annual contributions, the Commission shall notify the agency that further payments will not be made to it until the Commission is satisfied that the plan has been changed so as to constitute an adequate human-relations program or that there is no longer any such failure to comply or that administration has become effective. Until the Commission is so satisfied, it shall withhold payment of annual contributions to the agency.

Section 604. Grants and contracts for training its personnel or local and state commissions. The Commission is authorized, upon application of any political subdivision or state or the commission thereof to render technical assistance to the applicant in the preparation, adoption, and implementation of a human-relations program. Such technical assistance may, among other activities, include making available to such applicants information regarding effective methods of coping with human-relations problems and making available to such applicants personnel of the Commission or other persons specially equipped to advise and assist them in coping with such problems.

Section 605. Grants and contracts for special training of local and state commission personnel. The Commission is authorized to arrange, through grants or contracts with institutions of higher learning, for the operation of short-term or regular-session institutes or courses for special training of commissioners and staff and committee members of a local or state commission to deal effectively with human-relations problems. Individuals who attend such an institute may be paid stipends for the period of their attendance in amounts specified by the Commission in regulations, including allowances for travel to attend such institutes.

Section 606. Grants for employment of specialists by local and state commissions. The Commission is authorized upon application of a local or state commission to make grants to that commission to pay, in whole or in part, the cost of employing specialists to advise on problems of human relations.

Section 607. Scientific and humanistic research and basic studies in human-relations problems; services of specialists; contracts; grants for research and development work. (a) In order to accomplish the purposes of this Act, the Commission is authorized to conduct, encourage, and promote fundamental scientific and humanistic research and basic studies to develop the most effective methods for resolving human-relations problems through official and private action.

(b) In carrying out its function under this section the Commission may

(1) acquire the services of social scientists, psychologists, public-administration specialists, human-relations specialists, and other personnel, by contract or otherwise;

(2) enter into contracts with educational institutions and scientific organizations;

(3) make research and training grants; and

(4) conduct research and development work in the field in order to test the effectiveness of methods of dealing with human-relations problems.

TITLE VII. Procedures Relative to Complaints; Remedies; Judicial Review; Records

Section 701. Definitions. In this part

(1) "Commission" means either the Commission or a local or state section, as these terms are defined in Section 104, depending on which is handling a charge or complaint of a discriminatory act. In Sections 714, 715, 716, 717, 718, and 719 "Commission" means either the Commission, as just defined, or a hearing panel.

(2) "Commissioner" means either a commissioner or a local or state section commissioner, as these terms are defined in Section 104, depending on whether the Commission or a local or state section is handling a charge or complaint of a discriminatory act.

(3) "Civil-rights organization" means an organization which,

under its articles of incorporation or association, is organized to deal with intergroup-relations problems.

(4) "Chairman" means either the chairman of the Commission or the chairman of a local or state section, as these terms are defined in Section 104, depending on whether the Commission or a local or state section is handling a charge or complaint of a discriminatory act.

(5) "Discriminatory act" means any act or practice of discrimination, including an unlawful discriminatory act.

(6) "Discrimination" means any direct or indirect exclusion, distinction, segregation, limitation, refusal, denial, or any other differentiation or preference in the treatment of a person or persons on account of race, color, religion, ancestry, national origin, age, sex, or economic status, and any denial of any right, privilege, or immunity secured or protected by the Constitution or laws of the United States.

(7)–(19)

[Subsections (7)–(19) of this section are the same as the corresponding subsections of Section 701 of the Alpha Model State Civil-Rights Act. Where the term "Part" is used, substitute "Title."]

Sections 702–719. [Sections 702–719 of this Act are the same as the corresponding sections of the Alpha Model State Civil-Rights Act. Where the term "Part" is used, substitute the term "Title."]

Section 720. Judicial review; enforcement. (a) Any party to the proceeding and any person aggrieved by an order of the Commission may obtain judicial review of the order and the Commission may obtain an order of court for its enforcement in a proceeding under this section.

(b) The proceeding for review or enforcement shall be filed in the district court of the United States for the district

(1) in which the alleged unlawful discriminatory act occurred;

(2) in which the records relevant to such act are maintained and administered;

(3) in which a respondent resides, transacts business, or has his principal office. For the purposes of Sections 1404 and 1406 of Title 28, of the United States Code, the judicial district in which the respondent has his principal office shall in all cases be considered a district in which the action might have been brought;

(c) The proceeding for review or enforcement is initiated by filing a petition in the court. Copies of the petition shall be served upon all parties of record. Within thirty (30) days after service of the petition upon the Commission or its filing by the Commission, or within such further time as the court may allow, the Commission shall transmit to the court the original or a certified copy of the entire record upon which the order is based, including any transcript of testimony, which need not be printed. By stipulation of all parties to the review proceeding, the records may be shortened.

(d) Upon initiation of a review or enforcement proceeding, the court

(1) may grant such temporary relief or restraining order as it deems just and proper; and

(2) may make and enter upon the pleading, testimony, and proceedings set forth in the transcript an order enforcing, modifying and enforcing as so modified, or setting aside in whole or in part the order of the Commission.

(e) The findings of the Commission as to the facts shall be conclusive if supported by reliable, probative, and substantial evidence on the record considered as a whole.

(f) No objection that has not been urged before the Commission shall be considered by the court unless the failure to urge the objection is excused for good cause shown. Any party may move the court to remit the case to the Commission in the interest of justice for the purpose of adducing additional specified and material evidence and seeking findings thereon, provided that he shows reasonable grounds for the failure to adduce such evidence before the Commission.

(g) The jurisdiction of the district court of the United States shall be exclusive and an appeal from the final judgment or decree shall lie to the court of appeals, as provided in Sections 1291 and 1292, Title 28, of the United States Code.

(i) A proceeding under this section must be initiated within thirty (30) days after a copy of the order of the Commission is received, unless the Commission is the petitioner. A part is deemed to have received a copy of an order of the Commission, in the case of refusal to issue a complaint under Section 711, on the seventh day following the party's request for its issuance. If no proceeding is initiated by a party or other aggrieved person under this section within the permitted period, the Commission may obtain a decree of the court for enforcement of its order upon showing that a copy of the petition for enforcement was served on the respondent and that the respondent is subject to the jurisdiction of the court.

Sections 721–722. [Sections 721–722 of this Act are the same as the corresponding sections of the Alpha Model State Civil-Rights Act.]

TITLE VIII. UNLAWFUL DISCRIMINATORY ACTS

Subpart A. Definitions

Section 801. Definitions. In this Act

(1) "Official agency" means an authority of the government of the United States, of any state, a political subdivision of the latter, or their officers and employees;

(2) "Official financial assistance" means financial assistance provided by an official agency;

(3) "License" means the whole or any part of any official agency permit, certificate, approval, registration, charter, membership, or other form of permission;

(4) "Age" refers to the age of a person between thirty-five and sixty-five years of age;

(5) "Police officer" means any police officer of any official agency.

Subpart B. Unlawful Discriminatory Acts in General; Discrimination by Police Officers, Official Agencies, and Programs and Activities Operating under Official Financial Assistance or a License

Sections 811–815. [Sections 811–815 are identical with the corresponding sections of the Alpha Model State Civil-Rights Act.]

Subpart C. Discrimination in Employment

Section 821. Definitions. In this Act

(1) "Employer" means a person employing one or more employees, exclusive of parents, spouse, or children of that person, and including the United States, a corporation wholly owned by the government of the United States, a state or political subdivision thereof, or an official agency;

(2) "Labor organization" means any organizational person, including any employee-representation committee, group, association, or plan in which employees participate, that exists for the purpose, in whole or in part, of representing employees in collective bargaining and includes any conference, general committee, joint or system board, or joint council existing for this purpose which is subordinate to a national or international organization;

(3) "Employment agency" means any person regularly undertaking, with or without compensation, to procure employment opportunities for individuals or to procure, refer, or place individuals as employees and includes an agency of the United States, of a state, and of a political subdivision of the latter;

(4) "Individual" means any individual other than one employed or seeking employment by his parents, spouse, or child, or employed or seeking employment in the domestic service of or in a personal or confidential capacity by any person;

Sections 822–826. [Sections 822–826 are the same as the corresponding sections of the Alpha Model State Civil-Rights Act.]

Subparts D–F

[Subparts D–F are the same as the corresponding subparts of Part VIII of the Alpha Model State Civil-Rights Act.]

TITLE IX.   CRIMINAL SANCTIONS; OTHER REMEDIES;
            MISCELLANEOUS

Section 901. Wilful violation of Commission order; wilful interference. Any person who wilfully violates any order of the Commission or this Act or who wilfully resists, prevents, impedes, or interferes with the performance of a duty or the exercise of a power by the Commission or one of its commissioners or representatives, is guilty of a misdemeanor and shall be fined not more than [   ], or imprisoned for not more than [   ], or both.

Section 902. Jurisdiction and venue of United States courts over civil actions; statute of limitations, inapplicability of sections 101–115 of Title 29, U.S.C. (a) Each United States district court and each United States court of a place subject to the jurisdiction of the United States shall have jurisdiction of civil actions brought under this title, and shall exercise the same without regard to whether the aggrieved party shall have exhausted any administrative or other remedies that may be provided by law.

(b) A civil action under this title may be brought in any judicial district in the state

(1) in which the alleged unlawful discriminatory act occurred;

(2) in which the records relevant to such an act are maintained and administered; or

(3) in which the respondent resides, transacts business, or has his principal office. For the purposes of Sections 1404 and 1406 of Title 28 of the United States Code, the judicial district in which the respondent has his principal office shall in all cases be considered a district in which the action might have been brought.

(c) A civil action under this title must be filed on or before one year after the alleged discriminatory act occurred.

(d) The provisions of Sections 101–115 of Title 29 of the United

States Code shall not apply with respect to civil actions brought under this title.

Section 903. Civil actions for prevention of unlawful discriminatory acts; complaints; legal representation; commencement of action without payment of fees, costs, or security; intervention by the Attorney General. (a) Any individual aggrieved by an unlawful discriminatory act or a civil-rights organization on behalf of that individual, may, instead of seeking redress by the administrative procedure provided in Title VII of this Act, bring a civil action in the appropriate district court of the United States, without regard to the amount in controversy, by filing with it a complaint

(1) signed by the complainant;

(2) setting forth facts pertaining to such act; and

(3) requesting damages and such other relief, including an application for a permanent or temporary injunction, restraining order, or other equitable remedies or affirmative relief as may be deemed necessary to undo or mitigate the effects of, or prevent the continuation of any unlawful discriminatory acts; and shall be entitled to recover threefold the damages sustained or $500, whichever is larger.

(b) Upon application by the complainant and in such circumstances as the court may deem just, the court may appoint an attorney for such complainant and may authorize the commencement of the action without the payment of fees, costs, or security.

(c) Upon timely application, the court may, in its discretion, permit the Attorney General to intervene in such civil action if he certifies that the case is of general public importance.

Section 904. Civil actions by the Attorney General; complaints; three-judge district court for cases of general public importance; hearing, determination, and expedition of action; single-judge district court. (a) Whenever the Attorney General has probable cause to believe that any person has performed or is engaged in an unlawful discriminatory act, the Attorney General may bring a civil action in the appropriate district court of the United States by filing with it a complaint

(1) signed by him (or in his absence by the Acting Attorney General);

(2) setting forth facts pertaining to such act; and

(3) requesting such relief, including an application for a permanent or temporary injunction, restraining order, or other equitable remedies or affirmative relief as may be deemed necessary to undo or

mitigate the effects of, or prevent the continuation of any unlawful discriminatory acts.

(b) In such proceeding the Attorney General may file with the clerk of the district court a request that a court of three judges be convened to hear and determine the case. Such request by the Attorney General shall be accompanied by a certificate that, in his opinion, the case is of general public importance. A copy of the certificate and request for a three-judge court shall be immediately furnished by such clerk to the chief judge of the circuit (in his absence, the presiding circuit judge of the circuit) in which the case is pending.

(c) Upon receipt of a request for a court of three judges, the chief judge of the circuit or the presiding circuit judge of the circuit, as the case may be, shall designate immediately three judges in such circuit, of whom at least one shall be a circuit judge and another of whom shall be a district judge of the court in which the proceeding was instituted, to hear and determine such case, and the judges so designated shall assign the case for hearing at the earliest practicable date, participate in the hearing and determination thereof, and cause the case to be in every way expedited.

(d) If the Attorney General does not file a request that a court of three judges be convened in a proceeding under this section, the chief judge of the district (or in his absence, the acting chief judge) in which the case is pending, shall immediately designate a judge in such district to hear and determine the case. In the event that no judge in the district is available to hear and determine the case, the chief judge of the district, or the acting chief judge, as the case may be, shall certify this fact to the chief judge of the circuit (or in his absence, to the acting chief judge) who shall then designate a district or circuit judge of the circuit to hear and determine the case. The judge designated pursuant to this subsection shall assign the case for hearing at the earliest practicable date and cause the case to be in every way expedited.

Section 905. Injunction; appropriate affirmative action; appeals.
(a) If the court finds in an action under Sections 903 or 904 that the respondent has engaged in or is engaging in an unlawful discriminatory act charged in the complaint, the court may enjoin the respondent from engaging in such act and order such affirmative action as may be appropriate, which may include any affirmative action that the Commission might order under Section 716 of this Act.

(b) In any action under Sections 903 or 904 the court, at its discretion, may allow the prevailing party, other than the Commission or the United States, a reasonable attorney's fee as part of the costs, and the Commission and the United States shall be liable for costs the same as a private person.

(c) An appeal from the final judgment of a three-judge district court in any civil action brought under Section 903 will lie to the Supreme Court. An appeal from the final judgment of a single-district court in any civil action brought under Section 903 or Section 904 shall lie to the court of appeals, as provided in Sections 1291 and 1292, Title 28, of the United States Code.

Section 906. Termination and other action relative to official financial assistance and licenses. (a) Upon receiving a copy of the final decision and order of the Commission under Section 717, an official agency of the government of the United States that extended official financial assistance to a program or activity of a respondent or issued a license to a respondent is bound by the finding of discrimination and may take appropriate action

(1) to terminate or refuse to grant or continue assistance under such program or activity or to revoke or suspend such license, but such termination, refusal, revocation, or suspension shall be limited to the particular political entity, or part thereof, or other recipient as to whom such finding has been made and shall be limited in its effect to the particular program, license, or part thereof, in which such non-compliance has been so found, or

(2) to utilize any other means authorized by law.

(b) In the case of any action terminating, or refusing to grant or continue, assistance or revoking or suspending a license because of failure to comply with Section 815, the head of the official agency shall file with the committees of the House and Senate having legislative jurisdiction over the program or activity or license involved a full written report of the circumstances and the grounds for such action. No such action shall become effective until thirty days have elapsed after the filing of such report.

Section 907. Public contractors. (a) Upon receiving a copy of the final decision and order of the Commission under Section 717, an official agency of the government of the United States that awarded a contract to the respondent public contractor is bound by the finding of discrimination and may take appropriate action

(1) to terminate a contract or a portion thereof on condition that

the respondent carry out a program of compliance with the provisions of this Act, and

(2) refrain from entering into further contracts, or extensions or other modifications of existing contracts, with the respondent until the Commission is satisfied that the respondent will carry out policies in compliance with the provisions of this Act.

(b) Any person who has been the subject of a final decision and order of the Commission under Section 717 may be deemed by an official agency of the government of the United States as ineligible for award of a public contract until the Commission is satisfied that the respondent will carry out policies in compliance with the provisions of this Act.

Section 908. Prima facie evidence. In a proceeding under this Act, a written, printed, or visual communication, advertisement, or other form of publication, or written inquiry, or record, or other document purporting to have been made by a person is *prima facie* evidence that it was authorized by him.

Section 909. Jurisdiction for issuance of compliance orders; petition for order to modify or set aside demand or specification of grounds; waiver of objections. (a) If a person fails to permit, upon a demand by the Commission, access to premises and examination, photographing, or copying of evidence, or fails to make, keep, or preserve records or make reports in accordance with Section 721, or if a person fails to comply with a subpoena issued by the Commission or a commissioner, the district court of the United States for the district in which such person is found, resides, or transacts business, shall, upon application of the Commission, have jurisdiction to issue to such person an order requiring him to comply with Section 721 or to comply with the subpoena.

(b) Within twenty days after the service upon a person of a demand by the Commission for the production of documentary evidence or for permission to examine, photograph, or copy evidence in conformity with Section 721, such person may file in the district court of the United States for the judicial district in which he resides, is found, or transacts business, and serve upon the Commission a petition for an order of such court modifying or setting aside such demand. The time allowed for compliance with the demand in whole or in part as deemed proper and ordered by the court shall not run during the pendency of such petition in the court. Such petition shall specify each ground upon which the petitioner relies in seeking such relief, and may be based upon any failure of such demand to comply with the provisions of Section 721 or with the limitations generally applicable to compulsory process or upon any constitutional or legal right or privilege of such person. No objection which is not raised by such petition may be urged in the defense to a proceeding initiated by the Commission under Subsection (a) of this section for enforcement of such a demand unless such proceeding is commenced by the Commission prior to the expiration of the twenty-day period, or unless the court determines that the defendant could not reasonably have been aware of the availability of such ground of objection.

(c) In any proceeding brought by the Commission under Subsection (a) of this section, the defendant may petition the court for an order modifying or setting aside the demand or subpoena of the Commission.

Section 910. Relation of criminal to administrative or civil proceedings under this Act. The pendency or final determination of a criminal proceeding is not a bar to an administrative or civil proceeding arising from the same act or situation. The pendency or final determination of an administrative proceeding is not a bar to a criminal proceeding arising from the same act or situation.

Section 911. Criminal contempt proceedings; trial by jury, criminal practice, penalties, exceptions, intent; civil contempt proceedings. (a) In any proceeding for criminal contempt arising under this Act, the accused, upon demand therefor, shall be entitled to a trial by jury, which shall conform as nearly as may be possible to the practice in criminal cases. Upon conviction, the accused shall not be fined more than $1,000 or imprisoned for more than six months.

(b) This section shall not apply to contempts committed in the presence of the court, or so near thereto as to obstruct the administration of justice, nor to the misbehavior, misconduct, or disobedience of any officer of the court in respect to writs, orders, or process of the court. No person shall be convicted of criminal contempt hereunder unless the act or omission constituting such contempt shall have been intentional, as required in other cases of criminal contempt.

(c) Nothing in this section shall be construed to deprive courts of their power, by civil contempt proceedings, without a jury, to secure compliance with or to prevent obstruction of, as distinguished from punishment for violations of, any lawful writ, process, order, rule, decree, or command of the court in accordance with the prevailing usages of law and equity, including the power of detention.

Section 912. Repeal. The following acts and parts of acts are repealed:

(1) Titles II, III, VI, VII, X, Sections 407–410 of Title IV, Sections 1101–1104 of Title XI of the Civil Rights Act of 1964, the Age Discrimination in Employment Act of 1967, and Title VIII of the Civil Rights Act of 1968;

Section 913. Savings provisions. (a) All orders, determinations, rules, and regulations shall continue in effect according to their terms until modified, terminated, superseded, set aside, or repealed by the Commission, by any department or agency, by any court of competent jurisdiction, or by operation of law, if they

(1) have been issued, made, granted, or allowed to become effective under any provision of law amended by this Act by any department or agency or any court of competent jurisdiction, and

(2) are in effect at the time this Act takes effect.

(b) The provisions of this Act shall not affect any proceedings pending at the time this section takes effect before any department or agency (or component thereof), having functions replaced by functions allocated to the Commission; but such proceedings, to the extent that they relate to such functions, shall be continued before the Commission. Such proceedings, to the extent they do not relate to such functions, shall be continued before the department or agency before which they were pending on the effective date of this Act. In either case, orders shall be issued in such proceedings, appeals shall be taken therefrom, and payments shall be made pursuant to such orders, as if this Act had not been enacted; and orders issued in any such proceedings shall continue in effect until modified, terminated, superseded, or repealed by the Commission (in the exercise of any authority vested in it by this Act), by a court of competent jurisdiction, or by operation of law.

(c) (1) No suit, action, or other proceeding commenced by or against any officer in his official capacity as an officer of any department or agency, functions of which are replaced by functions allocated to the Commission, shall abate by reason of the enactment of this Act. No cause of action by or against any department or agency, functions of which are replaced by functions allocated to the Commission, or by or against any officer thereof in his official capacity shall abate by reason of the enactment of this Act. Causes of actions, suits, actions, or other proceedings may be asserted by or against the United States or such official of the Commission as may be appropriate and, in any litigation pending when this section takes effect, the court may at any time, on its own motion or that of any party, enter an order which will give effect to the provisions of this subsection.

(2) Except as provided in paragraph (3)

(A) the provisions of this Act shall not affect suits commenced prior to the date this section takes effect, and

(B) in all such suits proceedings shall be had, appeals taken, and judgments rendered, in the same manner and effect as if this Act had not been enacted.

(3) If before the date on which this Act takes effect, any department or agency, or officer thereof in his official capacity, is a party to a suit, and such department or agency performs a function replaced by a function allocated to the Commission under this Act, then such suit shall be continued by the Commission (except that in the case of a suit not involving such a function the suit shall be continued by the department, agency, or officer which was a party to the suit prior to the effective date of this Act).

(d) Reference in any other federal law to any department or agency, officer or office performing any function, power, or duty replaced by a function, power, or duty allocated to the Commission by this Act and exercised after the effective date of this Act shall be deemed to mean the officer or agency in which this Act vests the function, power, or duty.

Section 914. Severability. If any provision of this Act or its application to any person or situation is held invalid, that invalidity does not affect, impair, or invalidate other provisions or applications of the Act that can be given effect independently of the invalid provision or application, and for this purpose the provisions of this Act are severable.

Section 915. Effective date; initial appointment of officers. (a) This Act shall take effect ninety days after the day that all of the seven commissioners first take office, or on such prior date after enactment of this Act as the President shall prescribe and publish in the Federal Register.

(b) Any of the officers provided for in this Act may—notwithstanding Subsection (a)—be appointed in the manner provided for in this Act, at any time after the date of enactment of this Act. Such officers shall be compensated from the date they first take office, at the rates provided for in this Act. Such compensation and related expenses of their offices shall be paid from funds available for the functions similar to those allocated to the Commission pursuant to this Act.

COMMENTS

PREFATORY NOTE

1. History. The Alpha Model Federal Civil-Rights Act was drafted in response to the need demonstrated earlier in this book for a federal statute that would relate federal efforts to resolve civil-rights problems more effectively to local and state efforts and more effectively to the conditions existing at the local and state levels of our federal system. It was also drafted to meet the need also demonstrated earlier in this book for the utilization of the modern tools of administrative process in the administration of federal civil-rights law. This third Alpha Model Act draws heavily upon the Alpha Model State Civil-Rights Act and for this reason represents a diametrically opposite approach to that utilized by the draftsmen of the Uniform Model State Anti-discrimination Act who largely took as their model the Civil Rights Act of 1964. It is a model act whose underlying assumption is that what is necessary to be done at local and state levels must largely shape what can be done effectively at the federal level.

2. Reorientation of Federal Civil-Rights Policy. The Alpha Model Federal Civil-Rights Act presents a thoroughgoing reorientation of the existing federal civil-rights law just as the Alpha Model State Civil-Rights Act presents a thoroughgoing reorientation of the typical type of state civil-rights law. It creates a Federal Human-Relations Commission. This agency differs fundamentally from the United States Commission on Civil Rights,[1] which is a nonregulatory agency designed to conduct investigations and studies largely for the purpose of informing the Congress concerning action that might be necessary to deal with civil-rights problems. It differs also from the Equal Employment Opportunity Commission,[2] which not only is an administrative agency lacking the authority of most major federal regulatory agencies but also is an agency conceived along the lines of the typical state civil-rights agency that functions primarily by processing complaints of discrimination. Every careful study of the approximately twenty years' experience in administering this type of legislation concludes that it has been far less effective than desired or needed in light of the

---

[1] 42 U.S.C. §§ 1975–1975e (1964).
[2] 42 U.S.C. §§ 2000e–2000e15, *as amended* (Supp. II, 1965–1966).

immense regulatory problems presented.[3] Just as the Alpha Model
State Act on Local Human-Relations Commissions was designed to be
the counterpart of the Alpha Model State Civil-Rights Act at the local
level of our federal system, so the Alpha Model Federal Civil-Rights
Act is designed to be its counterpart at the national level of our federal
system. The reorientation proposed in this third Alpha Model Act to
achieve greater effectiveness in the administration of civil-rights law
involves the creation of the first genuine federal human-relations or
human-rights regulatory commission; the allocation to it, as compared
with similar existing federal and state agencies, of wholly new tasks,
functions, goals, and operational methods; and a far broader span of
substantive civil-rights law for administration by it. These changes
are designed to elaborate the idea developed in preceding chapters
that in order to achieve any sufficient rectification of the status of intergroup relations in this country, official action must largely take
place at the local level and can only be secured through an administrative agency, operating within a community, that is authorized to deal
with the full spectrum of human-relations problems existing at that
level. These changes are also designed to provide for the unique contribution that the federal government can make to the solution of
human-relations problems not only by providing support for local and
state efforts in the civil-rights field and by performing the local and
state role where necessary, but also by bringing to bear throughout
the nation the extraordinarily pervasive influence that federal action
can have upon patterns of action that are so harmful to the nation's
minority and other seriously disadvantaged groups.

3. *Structure of the Act.* The Alpha Model Federal Civil-Rights Act
is the third of four Alpha Model Acts, as previously mentioned. Each
of these Acts is constructed to parallel and dovetail with the others.
This Act, like the others, consists of nine parts. The first three titles
relate to findings and declaration of policies, general definitions, and
establishment of a human-relations commission to administer the Act.
The fourth title deals with the relationship between the commission
established and other similar commissions at other levels of government. The fifth title concerns the task, functions, goals, and implemental policies of the commission. The sixth title relates to its procedural powers and duties as well as to its power to provide several
forms of assistance to local and state human-relations commissions.

---

[3] See Chapters, 1, 5, 6 and note 1 of Chapter 1 of this book.

The seventh title concerns procedure to be followed in processing complaints of discriminatory acts, administrative hearings, remedies, judicial review, and similar matters. The eighth title sets forth certain substantive law concerning unlawful discriminatory acts. The final title covers criminal sanctions, other remedies, and a series of miscellaneous matters.

TITLE I. FINDINGS AND DECLARATION OF POLICIES; CONSTRUCTION; GENERAL DEFINITIONS

This title contains findings and a declaration of policies. Both of these sound the central note, to be heard throughout the Act, that the focus of governmental action is to be not only upon discrimination, in whatever form, against minority groups but also upon other equally harmful activity directed toward all disadvantaged groups in the community, the underlying causes of this activity, and the various forces that can be mustered for eliminating these causes and opening up equal opportunities for all. In each of these respects the Alpha Model Federal Civil-Rights Act is radically different from the existing federal civil-rights acts, state civil-rights acts, and the Harvard and Uniform Model State Acts relating to civil rights, that do little more than adopt the threadbare concept incorporated into most of this legislation. This Alpha Model Act, like the previous ones, is designed to deal both with the outer edge and the inner core of denials of equal opportunity. The Alpha Model State Civil-Rights Act provided in part for the operation of the state human-relations commission at the local level. The Alpha Model State Act on Local Human-Relations Commissions provided for the operation of local human-relations commissions at the same level with a view to their eventual substitution for or replacement of the state commission to that extent. The Alpha Model Federal Civil-Rights Act provides for a Federal Human-Relations Commission to operate both at the local level through local sections and the state level through state sections of that Commission under certain conditions to be explained subsequently.

This title contains only those definitions that are particularly relevant to the provisions concerning the establishment of the Federal Human-Relations Commission, action by the Commission in setting up local and state sections, the relation of its work to that of local and state commissions, and the assignment to the Commission and its sections of their central tasks, functions, goals, implemental policies, and procedural powers and duties. Other definitions are set out in subsequent titles to which they principally relate. Definitions relevant to the processing of complaints of discriminatory acts appear in Section 701. Definitions pertaining to each of the different kinds of unlawful discriminatory acts are set forth in the various subparts of Title VIII, such as Sections 801, 821, 831, and 841.

TITLE II. FEDERAL HUMAN-RELATIONS COMMISSION

Section 201 establishes a Federal Human-Relations Commission. The new Commission will administer a large new area of civil-rights law, part of which replaces most of the titles of the Civil Rights Act of 1964. The EEOC is phased out of existence by Section 912 while the United States Commission on Civil Rights, which is operating largely as a legislative research and investigative staff for the Congress, is left untouched. The new civil-rights substantive law is to be administered not only by the new Commission, but also by the federal courts. A number of classes of complainants are authorized to file complaints either with the Commission or with the courts. One of the authorized complainants is the Attorney General who may file complaints in the courts in much the same way that government complaints are now filed in them with regard to violations of federal antitrust laws. Individuals aggrieved by unlawful discriminatory acts and civil-rights organizations in their behalf may also file complaints either with the Commission or with the courts. The purpose of the provisions in Title IX, which create a concurrent jurisdiction in the United States district courts to enforce the Model Act, is to promote the same kind of enforcement of the Act as is now obtained with regard to the federal antitrust laws.

All existing state civil-rights acts enforced by human-relations commissions,[4] the Civil Rights Act of 1964,[5] and the Harvard[6] and Uniform Model State Acts[7] utilize as their centerpiece substantive law proscribing discriminatory acts against minority groups in specified fields such as employment, public accommodations, housing, and education. The principal function of the human-relations commission (or, in the case of the federal government, both the human-relations commission and

---

[4] See Appendix A of this book.

[5] 42 U.S.C. §§ 2000a–2000h-6, *as amended* (Supp. II, 1965–1966).

[6] See Harvard Student Legislative Research Bureau, "A Proposed Model State Civil Rights Act," *Harvard Journal of Legislation*, Vol. 3 (1965), pp. 63–102.

[7] National Conference of Commissioners of Uniform State Laws, "Model [State] Anti-Discrimination Act," *Harvard Journal of Legislation*, Vol. 4 (1967), pp. 224–278.

the courts) spoken to in these acts is the processing of individual complaints of discrimination. All else in these acts is keyed to these two principal parts. In order to avoid this history and to emphasize the new approach of the Alpha Model Federal Civil-Rights Act, the statement of the substantive law dealing with unlawful discriminatory acts is placed toward the end of the Act in its Title VIII. The procedure for processing and hearing complaints of discriminatory acts is also placed in the latter part of the Act in its Title VII. This placement relative to other provisions does not, of course, affect the great importance of this substantive civil-rights law—indeed, most of this is new law relative to existing federal law and some of it is new to the civil-rights field and especially important for implementing the new approach incorporated into the Act. What this placement does permit, however, is the statement at the outset of the principal tasks, functions, goals, and implemental policies of the Federal Human-Relations Commission, only one of whose functions involves the processing of individual complaints. A proper administrative perspective is thus somewhat better assured.

Title II involves no statutory innovations, as compared with existing state statutes or the Civil Rights Act of 1964, in creating a human-relations commission. In establishing a seven-member Federal Human-Relations Commission, Section 201 follows the practice of many states with long experience in the civil-rights field.

TITLE III.   LOCAL AND STATE SECTIONS OF THE COMMISSION

This title has no counterpart in existing state law or in the Harvard and Uniform Model Acts. Some few states such as New York, Ohio, Pennsylvania, and Michigan, have established a few regional or branch offices but these are quite different from the concept of a local section of the federal Commission.[8] The former are primarily offices for minor administrative work such as receiving complaints and investigating them. The latter, in light of Title V, is in effect a microcosm of the Commission itself and performs in its assigned political subdivision with the full authority of the Commission. Indeed, it will perform certain functions at the primary level of administration that the Commission through its commissioners, cannot itself perform, but only supervise.

---

[8] See Appendix A of this book; also see Commerce Clearing House, *Employment Practices Guide* (1966), para. 170, pp. 375–379.

Under existing circumstances Subsections (a), (b), and (c) of Section 301 will operate so as to require the Commission to establish local sections in most of the populous cities and counties of each state. If the Alpha Model Federal Act were to be adopted, the criteria of the section would automatically require establishment of local sections in about 2,000 political subdivisions of the country.[9] These are the localities in which experience has demonstrated that serious intergroup-relations problems exist. The criteria governing establishment of local sections will, however, require their establishment in political subdivisions having a lesser number of Negroes or Latin Americans than specified in Subsection (b) of Section 301 or having other disadvantaged groups within them if the Commission concludes these criteria are satisfied under the particular circumstances existing within them.

The term "political subdivision" is defined in Section 104 to mean "a city, county, or other political subdivision of a state having a substantial general regulatory authority and any combination of two or more of these determined by the Commission to be appropriate for the purpose of establishing a local section." This definition permits the Commission to utilize its judgment in selecting not only what kind of political subdivisions are suitable for the establishment of a local section but also what combination of them is appropriate for being serviced by a single local section. It is possible that in some jurisdictions, such as Massachusetts, the designation of a county as a comprehended political subdivision would not be made due to the nominal governing functions performed by counties within these states. It is also possible that a single local section can do a superior job to several with regard to human-relations problems of closely related political subdivisions in large metropolitan areas.

A most important facet of the local section concept is the requirement spelled out in Subsection (3) of Section 301 with regard to eligibility for appointment as a local-section commissioner. While a person is eligible for appointment if he is a citizen of the United States, the Commission is directed to seek to find qualified commissioners who live or work in the political subdivision to be served by them and then to resort to persons who live in the state in which the political subdivision is located or in other states, in that order of preference. The purpose of this directive is to maximize whatever enlightened leadership exists in the political subdivision and the state relative to civil-

9 See Chapter 6, pp. 221–223.

rights problems. In the South and Southwest, and particularly the Deep South, the problem of finding this leadership will be more difficult than in other areas of the nation. It may be necessary to utilize substantial numbers of out-of-political subdivision personnel in some areas and perhaps in some instances substantial numbers of out-of-state personnel. But as the local section becomes more effective and accepted in a political subdivision the Commission should move to replace them by able and devoted persons selected from within the political subdivision. The Commission should also utilize the local sections as a training ground for leaders of minority groups. There are many Negro and Latin American persons in the Southwest, for example, who, while not now active in politics or holding public office, have considerable potential for serving as local-section commissioners. The ultimate purpose of Subsection (3) is to secure community involvement in an adequate human-relations program for the political subdivision and to enhance the acceptability and practicability of the program.

The device of an election provided for in Subsection (3) of Section 301 may become appropriate when the Commission wishes to select local leaders as local section commissioners who are not aligned with a hostile power structure. Who these persons are, however, is not always readily ascertainable. The electoral principle can be a salutary device for permitting these persons to emerge as local leaders and for involving disadvantaged groups with the improvement of their situation in the community. Much of the value of the representation principle may also be secured through the use of this device.

The establishment of state sections by the Commission is provided for in Section 302. There are now thirty state human-relations commissions. There is a great need for leadership at the state level in the civil-rights field not only in these states but also in the twenty states not having these commissions. The section would require the Commission to establish at least twenty state sections immediately, and probably several more. The state section would perform a function essentially different from local sections of the Commission. Each would be operative with regard to different problem areas within the state. The former would be naturally focused upon problems arising or occuring within a political subdivision while the latter would be examining problems that cut across the geographical lines of political subdivisions and especially with problems presented by action of state agencies.

Subsection (3) of Section 302 is designed, like its parallel in Section 301, to direct appointment of qualified persons within the state to the state sections, if they are available. Subsection (e) of the section gives the Commission considerable flexibility in determining how best to deal with human-relations problems within each state. As we see in Title V, the Commission may not usurp the role of its local sections. It may appoint and remove commissioners, but it may not run the affairs of a local section as it may a branch or regional office. The local section is, to a considerable extent, an independent authority not dissimilar in some respects to a local human-relations commission. This is also true of a state section. The major difference between them is that the Commission, rather than the Model Act, determines what functions are to be delegated to a state section.

TITLE IV.   Relation of This Act to Similar State and Local
            Law; Cooperative Agreements with State and
            Local Commissions

The purpose of Title IV is to preserve the effectiveness of any existing human-relations commission of a political subdivision or of a state and to provide for the problems involved in the coexistence of these local and state commissions on the one hand, and the Federal Human-Relations Commission on the other. A fundamental principle underlying each of the Alpha Model Acts is that a local commission can be the most effective agency for dealing with human-relations problems at the local level, if its political subdivision wills and acts prudently for this result and is permitted to do so by the state. The Alpha Model State Act for Local Human-Relations Commissions and the Alpha Model Civil-Rights Ordinance have been drafted in order better to promote this local development. For the same reason the Alpha Model State Civil-Rights Act directs the state commission created by it to operate at the local level through local sections.

Section 301 states the conditions under which it would be necessary for the Federal Human-Relations Commission to establish a local section to operate in a political subdivision. If that Commission determines that a political subdivision has established and maintains an adequate human-relations program and that it is effectively administered by a local human-relations commission, Section 402 provides that the Commission may utilize the services of this commission with its consent and make cooperative agreements with it relative to handling human-relations problems within the political subdivision. The section deals with the problem of existing state commissions in the same way.

Section 403 provides for the handling of complaints by local and state commissions under agreements made with them by the Commission. Ordinarily complaints relative to acts occurring within a political subdivision would be handled by the local commission and complaints relative to acts cutting across geographical lines of political subdivisions would be handled by a state commission under these agreements and the operation of this section. On the other hand, the section preserves the right of the Commission to direct that a complaint be retained by or referred to it for processing. A given complaint may have implications for national policy that require this handling.

Section 404 in effect gives an individual an election between the remedy provided by this Act and the remedy provided by the law administered by a local or state human-relations commission that does not have an agreement with the Commission. Section 405 excludes a person from utilizing the procedure of this Act relative to conduct covered by it when he has previously resorted to other procedure under other law relative to the same conduct. Implemented here is the interest in honoring prior official settlements of a controversy. This provision saves to the Commission the right to direct a local or state commission receiving a complaint with regard to action covered by the Act to refer the complaint to it.

TITLE V.   The Central Task, Functions, Goals, and Policies of the Commission and Its Local and State Sections

The heart of the Alpha Model Federal Civil-Rights Act, in so far as it relates to human-relations problems at the local and state levels, is Title V. In stating the central task of the local sections of the Commission, Section 501 simply makes explicit what careful students of intergroup-relations problems have been articulating for years as the task which has to be performed at the local level by well-organized local human-relations commissions. In making clear what the task of state sections of the Commission is, as contrasted with that of its local sections, an analogy has also been drawn to the task of local commissions. The task of the Commission itself has been described on the basis of an analogy to the task of a state commission conceived along lines described in the Alpha Model State Civil-Rights Act.

Section 502 serves to outline the various functions of the Commission. This section in unprecedented either in state or federal civil-rights law, which, as already indicated, are monolithically designed to invest commissions with the complaint-processing function. The functions outlined in Section 502 are (1) supporting and supervising the work of its local and state sections; (2) promoting the creation of local and state human-relations commissions and supporting and reviewing of their operation; (3) "wide-spectrum" negotiation; (4) "constructive action"; and (5) processing of individual complaints. Even the last function is different in quality from the usual complaint processing function given state commissions and the Equal Employment Opportunity Commission. In the first place, the focus of the function is quite different since the Commission deals primarily with discrimination on the part of large concerns, unions, and other organizations having nationwide or regionwide operations, and of state and local government agencies. In the second place, the Commission is concerned not only with the discrimination usually reached by the more advanced state statutes and the Civil Rights Act of 1964 but also with many forms of harmful action not formally discriminatory in nature but nevertheless just as effective in closing opportunities to minority and other seriously disadvantaged groups. This coverage will be more particularly examined in the comment upon Title VIII of the Act. Moreover, the whole concept of abuse of authority by police officers and official agencies involving invasions of constitutional rights, privileges, and immunities is brought into the field of federal civil-rights law. But what really distinguishes the section is the inclusion of the remaining functions. Each of them carries the Commission into areas of operation not yet traversed by any state or federal agency dealing with human-relations problems and only barely touched by a few local commissions. The support and supervision of its local commissions will require quite a different form of operation from the one historically and currently utilized at either the state or federal levels. In addition to selecting commissioners and staff for its local sections, the Commission will have to formulate and execute policies for supporting and supervising or reviewing the work of these sections and of local commissions. The very different nature of the work of these agencies, especially the former under this Act, causes the supporting and supervising of their work by the Commission to be different from the usual work of a federal agency. This leads us to the two widely different functions shared at different levels of performance by the

Commission and by its local and state sections; the "wide-spectrum"-negotiation function and the constructive-action function. The descriptions of these functions contained in Sections 502 and 503 are quite general and stated in terms of immediate objects dealt with in their performance. These general descriptions, however, take on important additional meaning in light of the central task defined for both the Commission and its local and state sections in Section 501, the general goals of their work stated in Section 505, the general prohibition of unlawful discriminatory acts in Section 811, the implemental policies stated in Section 506, and the procedural powers stated in Section 602.

The comments on the Alpha Model State Civil-Rights Act concerning its Sections 504 and 505 are applicable, respectively, to Sections 505 and 506 of this Act and should be consulted for a full explanation of them.

TITLE VI.   POWERS AND DUTIES OF THE COMMISSION AND ITS LOCAL AND STATE SECTIONS

The Comment on the Alpha Model State Civil-Rights Act relative to its Part VI is applicable to Title VI of this Act and should be consulted. Title VI of this Act, however, contains Sections 603 and 604 for which there are no counterparts in the Alpha Model State Civil-Rights Act. Comments on these sections follow.

Section 603 is patterned to a considerable extent upon the program of annual contributions to public-housing agencies under the federal low-cost housing policy.[10] The merit of this approach is that it enables the Commission to move those sections of the country that are ready for it more rapidly toward achievement of the purposes of this Act. The distinctive feature of the section is its requirement that a workable human-relations program and official plan of action be submitted by a political subdivision or state and approved by the Commission before it will consider entering into a contract for annual contributions with its human-relations commission. This concept is patterned after the workable program concept utilized in the federal slum-clearance and urban-renewal program.[11] The workable program and plan must provide for several kinds of things: its mandatory operation throughout

---

[10] 42 U.S.C. §§ 1410, 1415, 1421a (1964), *as amended* (Supp. II, 1965–1966).
[11] 42 U.S.C. §§ 1451(c), (d), 1453–1455 (1964), *as amended* (Supp. II, 1965–1966).

the state, where it is a state plan; enactment of a minimum civil-rights law comparable to the Model Federal Act; support by the political subdivision or state for its commission's operation equal to one-third of its aggregate cost; and annual review of the adequacy of the human-relations program. Beyond the plan of action, a local or state commission must propose to the Commission specific activities and projects for the implementation of the plan in order to place itself in a position to obtain a contract for annual contributions. This requirement is similar to the requirement of proposal of specific projects in the federal slum-clearance and urban-renewal program.[12] The requirement for submission of a workable human-relations program and an official plan of action serves the purpose of assuring an adequate general framework of law, general policy, and a well-organized commission for work in the human-relations field by a political subdivision or a state. The further requirement for submission of a specific proposal of activities and projects serves the purpose of bringing a workable program and plan of action down to earth for a specific period of time. It is essential for evaluating the amount of annual contributions that should be made and for how long. It also helps the Commission to assure that a truly effective human-relations program will be supported by its funds.

The devices utilized in Section 603 mean that the Commission will be able to guide many states immediately to the institution of far more effective human-relations programs and interlace their work and that of the Commission in the most effective way. One good feature of this approach is that the annual contributions contract may be made for an extended period of years. There is no reason why a ten-year contract might not be made if the official plan of action is sufficiently developed and its specifics are adequately spelled out through proposals of particular activities and projects. Contracting for an extended period of years will permit local and state commissions to free themselves to a considerable extent of the restraints imposed by limited budgets. Since the Commission will foot two-thirds of the cost of local- or state-commission operations when they are acceptable to the Commission, this means that present programs throughout the country can be expanded threefold. Moreover, the fact that a contract for annual contributions has been made between the Commission and a local or state commission for a number of years does not preclude an increase

[12] 42 U.S.C. § 1453 (1964), *as amended* (Supp. II, 1965–1966).

in the amount of the annual contributions by an additional agreement or change in the existing contract to reflect new needs.

If the overall plan and specific proposals for activities and projects are approved by the Commission, then a contract becomes the vehicle for spelling out the obligations of both parties. It serves the purpose of securing from the local or state commission the proper action to carry out specific tasks essential to the accomplishment of the purposes of the section and of the Act. One important feature of the section is the requirement that the contract contain an agreement that the local or state commission will adopt effective procedures for evaluating the effectiveness of the human-relations program and activities conducted under it and file reports concerning this effectiveness. Subsection (c) of the section contains valuable guidelines for determining the amount of the annual contributions to be paid under a contract. If a local community has very great human-relations problems but is willing to do only a minimally effective job in dealing with them, it will get less than a similar community that is willing to do more about them.

The requirement of Section 603 that the official plan of action be resubmitted along with specific proposals of supporting activities each time additional contributions are sought means that the official plan is regularly up for review and re-evaluation by the Commission. This is likely to have a salutary effect upon applicants for annual contributions. It will likely motivate the applicant to add to the scope of the overall program and plan and to seek to accomplish more on the home front in the way of promoting better human relations.

Subsection (f) of Section 603 is patterned after a similar provision contained in many phases of the federal social-security policy.[13] Although a contract has been entered into, this provision allows the Commission to cut off payment of annual contributions upon the occurrence of either of two conditions after giving the local or state commission reasonable notice and opportunity for a hearing. These conditions are a fundamental defect in the plan of action, due to changes in it, and a substantial failure in its administration.

Sections 604 through 607 provide considerable flexibility to the Commission in tailoring various forms of additional financial assistance, through contractual arrangements and grants, to the needs of local and state commissions. Section 604 speaks to technical assistance, Section 605 to provision of institutes and courses for training

---

[13] See, *e.g.*, 42 U.S.C. § 604 (1964).

commission personnel, and Section 606 to payments for needed human-relations specialists on particular problems. Section 607 could prove to be one of the most valuable arms of a Federal Human-Relations Commission in providing guidance to local and state commissions on effective methods for resolving human-relations problems. Much research has been done concerning the facts of human-relations problems; very little has been done concerning the appropriate methods for resolving them.

TITLE VII. PROCEDURES RELATIVE TO COMPLAINTS; REMEDIES; JUDICIAL REVIEW; RECORDS

TITLE VIII. UNLAWFUL DISCRIMINATORY ACTS

The sections of these two titles are the same as the corresponding sections of the Alpha Model State Civil-Rights Act set out in Chapter 8, with four minor exceptions. For this reason the Comment on the sections of the latter Act corresponding to the sections of this Act should be consulted. They are fully applicable here. Only Sections 701, 720, 801, and 821 are slightly different from the corresponding sections in the Alpha Model State Civil-Rights Act. Sections 701, 801, and 821 contain definitions that have been altered to fit the circumstance that it is the federal government, rather than a state or a local government, which is administering the procedural and substantive law included in these titles. Section 720 needed a slight modification due to the fact that a federal court needed to be designated, rather than a state court, to exercise the power of judicial review of Commission action.

There is no serious question about the constitutionality of the provisions in this Act in reaching discriminatory transactions. In the first place, two of the three functions allocated to the Federal Human-Relations Commission—the "wide-spectrum"-negotiation and constructive-action functions—operate at the local and state levels without the utilization of regulatory provisions. They are primarily concerned with producing consensus, consent, and motivation on the part of persons in private and public life with respect to remedial action to be taken voluntarily by them. There is no constitutional provision which excludes the federal government from coming to any village, city, county, or state and utilizing executive leadership to get people and organizations to do what they ought to be doing relative to human-relations problems. The utilization of effective informal tools of persuasion, such as public hearings, subpoenaing of witnesses and evidence, investigations, and surveys, does not convert these functions into regulatory measures. The third function concerns the processing of complaints of denials of equal protection and of discrimination. There can be no question that the federal government can protect against denials of equal protection at the local and state levels through locally operating sections of a federal agency. As pointed out in Chapter 7, the pattern has long since been established for operation at the local level of a federal regulatory program.[14] So far as discrimination against persons, based upon race, color, religion, ancestry, national origin, sex, age, or economic status is concerned, the question of federal authority to reach this area of activity is very extensive. In the Senate hearings on the proposed Civil Rights Act of 1966 Nicholas de B. Katzenbach, while serving as Attorney General, stated the fundamental bases for federal legislation reaching discrimination on these bases when practiced by the owner even of a single dwelling in any place in the United States. After outlining the terrible dimensions of discrimination in housing and home financing and its impact upon the Negro ethnic group and other ethnic groups, he stated:

it should be plain that scattered State and local laws are not enough. The work of private volunteer groups is not enough. Court decisions are not enough. The limited authority now available to the executive branch is not enough. The time has now surely come for decisive action by Congress. Only Congress can fully commit the Nation to begin to solve the problem on a national scale. That is the purpose of Title IV (applicable to the housing described above).[15]

He based his arguments concerning constitutionality of this proposed legislation on the commerce clause and the Fourteenth Amendment of the Constitution of the United States. With respect to the applicability of the former he stated:

The commerce clause makes Congress responsible for the protection and promotion of interstate commerce in all its forms. The construction of homes and apartment buildings and the production and sale of building materials and home furnishings take place in or through the channels of interstate commerce. When the total problem is considered, it is readily

[14] See Chapter 7, pp. 298–301, above.
[15] *Hearings on S. 3296, etc. before the Subcommittee on Constitutional Rights of the Senate Committee on the Judiciary*, 89th Cong., 2nd Sess. (Washington, D.C.: U.S. Government Printing Office, June 6, 1966), p. 84.

apparent that interstate commerce is significantly affected by the sale of even single dwellings, multiplied many times in each community.[16]

After reviewing the various ways in which interstate commerce was involved with even single dwellings, he recognized the point that it is difficult to determine the extent to which discrimination by individual homeowners affects interstate commerce. With regard to this he replied:

But each part of the pattern of discrimination affects, and is affected by, the whole. And to eliminate the clear and substantial effect that patterns of discrimination have on commerce, Congress can and must deal with separate parts.[17]

He then reviewed the cases settling the point that the reach of the commerce clause is not exceeded by virtue of the fact that a particular activity regulated is local or is quantitatively unimportant where considered in isolation—such as the sale of a single dwelling.[18] From this point of view, it seems clear that discrimination in the sale of single dwellings is easily within the reach of that clause. It restricts the movement of building materials and home furnishings from one state to another. It confines Negroes to older homes in the ghettos and consequently restricts the number of new homes that are built to satisfy their demand for housing and still further reduces the amount of building material moving in interstate commerce to build new homes needed by them. This discrimination in housing also prevents many Negroes from being as mobile as other elements of our population in moving to new areas across the country where there are opportunities of various kinds that they would like to utilize. Since they are deterred from moving to seek these opportunities, interstate commerce is impeded and new homes are not built to take care of the demand that would be present if it were possible for them to move and to obtain them.[19]

Attorney General Katzenbach then examined the support of the Fourteenth Amendment for the prohibition of discrimination in the sale of a single dwelling. The right to acquire property without discrimination dates from the Civil War. The first Civil Rights Act (of

[16] *Ibid.*
[17] *Id.*, p. 85.
[18] *Mabee v. White Plains Publishing Co.*, 327 U.S. 178 (1964); *Wickard v. Filburn*, 317 U.S. 111 (1942); also see *United States v. Sullivan*, 332 U.S. 689 (1948).
[19] *Hearings on S. 3296*, p. 86.

1866) provided that all citizens of the United States, whatever their race or color, had the same right to inherit, purchase, lease, sell, hold, and convey real and personal property as enjoyed by white persons irrespective of any existing law or custom.[20] This statutory right to purchase and rent real property, still on the books today, can be enlarged since it is one of the privileges of national citizenship that Congress may protect even from wholly private action of a hostile nature.[21] Beyond this, and of particular relevance to the applicability of the Fourteenth Amendment, is the fact that government action, both state and federal, has been largely responsible for and indeed, still currently supports existing patterns of discrimination in residential property.[22] This means that present practices cannot be fairly viewed as the result of purely private choice. Beyond this is the fact that the Fourteenth Amendment contains a clause granting to Congress the authority to enact legislation containing remedies to promote civil and political equality for all citizens. Attorney General Katzenbach concluded that this last clause "surely provides a constitutional basis for Title IV. The authority for the legislation is clear."[23]

If the reasoning of Attorney General Katzenbach is sound, as it certainly must be conceded to be, so far as it applies to housing, it is also just as sound as applied to discrimination by an employer of one or more persons against a single applicant for a job or a single existing employee. This view has been well stated by Congressman John H. Dent of Pennsylvania:

Certainly, if a man is entitled to protection for his welfare, his physical and personal welfare by unemployment compensation, workmen's compensation, and social security, when he gets a job, he certainly ought to be as entitled to the fundamental right of getting that job, with no arbitrary restrictions on him, except, for protection.[24]

Unless the channels for employment are open to Negroes, Latin Americans, and other minority groups, they cannot obtain jobs when and where jobs become available that will enable them to purchase and lease real property. They cannot provide adequately for their families,

---

[20] 14 Stat. 27 (1866), 42 U.S.C. 1982 (1964).
[21] Civil Rights Cases, 109 U.S. 3, 22 (1883).
[22] See Chapter 1, pp. 19–21, above.
[23] *Hearings on S. 3296*, p. 88.
[24] *Hearings on H.R. 8998 and H.R. 8999 before the General Subcommittee on Labor of the House Committee on Education and Labor*, 89th Cong., 1st Sess. (Washington, D.C.: U.S. Government Printing Office, July 21, 1965), p. 107.

educate their children properly, and prepare for the day when they will be old and unemployable. If Negro ghettos and the discrimination in housing that creates them deter people from moving to take advantage of jobs and other economic opportunities that are available across state lines, how much more must discrimination in employment against Negroes deter them in moving across state lines to seek jobs that will be denied them on account of their race or color. How much more must this discrimination cause Negroes to feel that it is not worthwhile to prepare themselves to hold jobs that will not be opened to them however qualified they may be. Moreover, if the Fourteenth Amendment permits Congress to enact legislation to protect Negroes, Latin Americans, and other minority groups against discrimination in the sale of a single dwelling so as to ensure their fundamental right to purchase or rent property, how much more applicable it is to permit Congress to enact legislation to protect the same persons in their fundamental right to obtain employment from an employer of one or more persons with no arbitrary restriction being directed against them, based upon race, color, religion, ancestry, national origin, sex, age, or economic status. For without meaningful protection of this right the other rights become illusory and, indeed, a mockery. If it be said that this discrimination does not in itself involve governmental action, it must be replied that governmental action supports the whole area of private action involving discrimination in employment. One of the notorious aiders and abetters of private discrimination in employment has been the national system of public employment offices.[25] Although state agencies operate local public employment offices, the federal government pays the entire cost of operating them. It has been thoroughly documented that these employment services do accept and comply with employer requests for workers specifying "whites only" and in the Southwest frequently specifying "Anglos only."[26] Although the federal government can exercise thoroughgoing control of the operations of these employment services, it has not made substantial efforts to secure observance of policies for elimination of employment discrimination. Moreover, the federal government has contributed and continues to contribute large sums of money to support programs of local and state governments which have discriminated and

[25] Paul H. Norgren and Samuel E. Hill (Assisted by F. Ray Marshall), *Toward Fair Employment* (New York: Columbia University Press, 1964), pp. 36–39, 132–146.

[26] *Ibid.*; also see Chapter 2, pp. 46–49, above.

continue to discriminate against Negroes, Latin Americans, and other minority groups in employment.[27] One cannot say of private-employment discrimination practices against minority groups that they are the result of purely private choice. They have been tolerated, supported, and even suggested as a model of behavior by governmental action.

The reasoning reviewed so far as supporting the constitutionality of federal legislation prohibiting discrimination in the sale of single dwellings and discrimination in employment by employers of one or more persons is, *a fortiori*, applicable to support federal legislation with regard to other areas of discrimination covered by this Alpha Model Act. With regard to discrimination by privately owned educational institutions it seems clear that this practice operates to deter movement across state lines by young people seeking educational opportunities needed to prepare themselves for a useful and satisfactory life as a citizen. Also the refusal of business colleges and similar schools to train Negroes or Latin Americans can seriously affect the flow of applicants for positions to businesses engaged in interstate commerce or in areas affecting interstate commerce. The right to an education, more generally, has been recognized in the context of our modern times to be one of the great fundamental rights. With so many of our young people failing to graduate from public high schools or to continue past the first year of college the demand for privately owned educational and training facilities is especially great. Many of these institutions are licensed by government and many enjoy substantial tax advantages and other forms of governmental financial assistance. This indicates the degree of governmental involvement in support of these activities.

In the case of public accommodations, which, as defined in the Alpha Model Acts, covers most business and professional activities, one can mark innumerable effects upon interstate commerce flowing from discrimination practiced by their owners against members of minority groups. Our nation's people are very mobile. It would be difficult to find a business or professional office that an interstate traveler might not need to utilize at some point or other in his travels. A physician's office, a private hospital, a drug store, a department store, an automobile repair shop, an automated laundry, and an automobile dealer are some of the more obvious examples. All of these and many others are

[27] 42 U.S.C. § 2000e-6(b) (1964).

often needed by and should be open to all interstate travelers. Moreover, the failure of any business or professional office to service members of minority groups who live in the vicinity of them inevitably has substantial effects upon interstate business by cutting down the volume of business done by them. When dental work is required by a Negro in a city whose dentists will not treat him, he must either travel to some other part of the state or out of the state to obtain that work or else do without it. In either event interstate commerce is indirectly affected in the area where discrimination is taking place due to the fact that some service is not being performed there that is more or less supported by the arteries of interstate commerce.

TITLE IX.   CRIMINAL SANCTIONS; OTHER REMEDIES;
            MISCELLANEOUS

This title contains some provisions that are more complex than their counterparts in the Alpha Model State Acts. They represent in large part the retention of the method of enforcement through the courts now contained in most federal civil-rights laws. On the other hand, this method of enforcement has been greatly strengthened to increase its effectiveness as an alternative to enforcement through administrative process rather than as the single mode of enforcement of federal civil-rights laws. Section 902 grants jurisdiction over civil actions to United States district courts and spells out liberal venue provisions. It also maintains the same statutory limitation of one year on assertion of causes of actions utilized with regard to filing of complaints with the Federal Human-Relations Commission. Section 903 permits either an individual aggrieved by an unlawful discriminatory act or a civil-rights organization to file such a civil action. Section 904 gives the same right to the Attorney General when he has probable cause to believe a person has performed or is engaged in an unlawful discriminatory act. The provision of the Civil Rights Act of 1964 allowing a three-judge district court on request of the Attorney General and expedition of the case is retained. Under Section 905 the district court may employ any remedy in its decree that is available to the Federal Human-Relations Commission in framing a cease and desist order under Section 716 of the Act.

The allocation of dual responsibility for administration of federal civil-rights policy should work as well as dual responsibility for administration of federal antitrust policy has worked.

The Commission can handle, particularly through its local and state sections and agreements with local and state commissions, the more usual run of enforcement cases. The Commission and the Attorney General can allocate between themselves appropriate areas of law enforcement in the cases of nationwide importance.

Sections 906, 907, 908, and 909 correspond closely with the same section of the Alpha Model State Civil-Rights Act. The comment on the latter Act is also applicable to these sections and should be consulted for explanation of them.

Section 911 on contempt proceedings is based on Section 1101 of the Civil Rights Act of 1964.

Section 912 repeals Titles II, III, VII, X, Sections 407–410 of Title IV and Sections 1101–1104 of Title XI of the Civil Rights Act of 1964. This action is made necessary since Title VIII of the Alpha Model Federal Act is a complete package of substantive law, covering, in part, the area to which the repealed titles and sections of titles are applicable. The repeal is also made necessary due to the fact that the Federal Human-Relations Commission is made the principal agency for the enforcement of the Act while, under the Civil Rights Act of 1964, the federal courts are the principal agency for its enforcement. The community-relations-service function is allocated to the new Commission in a far more effective way and for this reason Title X of the 1964 Act is eliminated. The law-enforcement function of federal administrative agencies provided for under Title VI of the 1964 Act relative to certain federal financial assistance to programs and activities is allocated to the new Commission so that the title may be eliminated also. For similar reasons Section 912 also repeals the Age Discrimination in Employment Act of 1967 and Title VIII of the Civil Rights Act of 1968. The rule-making function of these agencies is spelled out anew in Subsection (b) of Section 815 of the new Act. Other federal law can be added to the repeal section if its provisions are added to the Model Act.

Section 913 relates to comprehensive-savings provisions made necessary by the fact that existing business before federal courts and administrative agencies under the Civil Rights Acts of 1964–1968 is being replaced by the Alpha Model Federal Civil-Rights Act. These provisions are patterned after similar provisions in the Department of Transportation Act.[28]

---

[28] Department of Transportation Act, § 12, 80 Stat. 931 (1966).

CHAPTER

The Alpha Model Local Civil-Rights Ordinance, with Comments

THE ALPHA MODEL LOCAL CIVIL-RIGHTS ORDINANCE

Table of Contents

The Alpha Model Local Civil-Rights Ordinance

PART I. SHORT TITLE; FINDINGS AND DECLARATION OF POLICIES; CONSTRUCTION

Section 101. Short title. This Ordinance shall be known, and may be cited, as the "[name of political subdivision] Civil-Rights Ordinance."

Section 102. Findings and declaration of policies. (a) The population of this political subdivision consists of people of many races, colors, religions, ancestries, and national origins as well as of different sexes, age groups, and economic brackets. It is essential to the public health, safety, welfare, peace, and progress of this political subdivision and the communities within it that this diversity serve to strengthen individual and collective efforts to achieve man's enduring goals and not be used to weaken these efforts. The latter result occurs when members of one group practice, through private or governmental institutions, discrimination and other harmful activity against members of another group in any phase of community life merely on account of their race or other normal group characteristics. Practices of this kind and the conditions accompanying them undermine the freedom and justice essential to genuine democracy. Among other things, they prevent full development and utilization of the capacities of many persons; cut them off from various kinds of economic, social, cultural, and political opportunities; deny them adequate education and training; cause among them widespread unemployment and underemployment; deprive them of earnings necessary to maintain decent standards of living and require them to resort to public relief; and produce segregated schools and typical substandard, unsafe, and unsanitary living conditions, support the whole structure of discrimination and disadvantages suffered by the graduates of these schools and the inhabitants of these homes. These practices also cause or contribute to intergroup tensions and conflicts, school drop-outs, crime, juvenile delinquency, disease, fire hazards, higher welfare costs, and loss of tax revenues.

(b) It is the policy of this political subdivision to ensure that all persons enjoy the full benefits of citizenship or residence and be afforded equal opportunity to participate, on the basis of personal merit, in the social, cultural, economic, political, and other phases of community life within the political subdivision, free from any discrimination on account of race, color, religion, ancestry, or national origin, and from any unreasonable restrictions on account of sex, age, or economic status. In order to implement this policy it is essential that the government of this political subdivision assume the initiative for repairing the consequences of past denials of equal opportunities to particular groups, preventing denials of these opportunities in the future, and controlling and eliminating the underlying causes of intergroup-relations problems. Government initiative for accomplishing these purposes must be exercised within each community. Human-relations problems cannot be adequately solved in this political subdivision until its government and citizenry honestly face these problems and with good will and industry work together for their solution. It is a central purpose of this Ordinance to institute an adequate human-relations program and to secure its effective administration by the human-relations commission created by this Ordinance.

Section 103. Liberal construction. This Ordinance shall be construed liberally to further its purposes and, more generally, to promote justice in human relations.

PART II. GENERAL DEFINITIONS

Section 201. General Definitions. In this Ordinance, unless the context otherwise requires,

(1) "Person" means an individual, partnership, association, corporation, joint-stock company, labor union, mutual company, trustee in bankruptcy, receiver, or other fiduciary, or the agent, legal representative, or employee thereof; and the political subdivision, or any agency, officer, or employee thereof;

(2) "Commission" means the [name of political subdivision] Human-Relations Commission created by this Ordinance.

(3) "Commissioner" means a member of the Commission.

(4) "Cooperative agreement" means a cooperative agreement made by the Commission under Section 402.

(5) "Negtiation function" means the function assigned to the Commission under Subsection (a) (2) of Section 502.

(6) "Constructive-action function" means the function assigned to the Commission under Subsection (a) (3) of Section 502.

(7) "Discrimination" means any direct or indirect exclusion, distinction, segregation, limitation, refusal, denial, or any other differentiation or preference in the treatment of a person or persons on account of race, color, religion, ancestry, national origin, age, sex, or economic status, and any denial of any right, privilege, or immunity secured or protected by the Constitution or laws of the United States.

(8) "Governing body" means the governing body of the political subdivision.

PART III. LOCAL HUMAN-RELATIONS COMMISSION

Section 301. Establishment of human-relations commission. There is hereby created the [name of political subdivision] Human-Relations Commission. The membership of the Commission consists of seven commissioners to be appointed by the [city council, city commission, or the mayor by and with the consent of the city council, city commission]. The chairman of the Commission shall be designated by the [same authority as the appointing authority] from its membership. The Commission may designate one of its commissioners to act as chairman during the absence or incapacity of the chairman.

Section 302. Commissioners' terms of office. The term of office of each commissioner is six years and until the appointment and qualification of his successor. Of those commissioners first appointed two shall be appointed for a term of two years, two for a term of four years, and three for a term of six years. A person appointed to fill a vacancy occurring prior to expiration of a term shall be appointed only for the unexpired part of that term.

Section 303. Quorum. Four commissioners constitute a quorum. Vacancies on the Commission do not impair the authority of the remaining commissioners to exercise the powers of the Commission.

Section 304. Compensation. Each commissioner may obtain compensation for all expenses actually and necessarily incurred by him in the performance of his duties.

Section 305. Removal from office. The [same authority as appointing authority] may remove a commissioner for inefficiency, neglect of duty, misconduct, or malfeasance in office, after giving him a written statement of the charges against him and an opportunity to be heard concerning them.

PART IV. COOPERATIVE AGREEMENTS WITH OTHER COMMISSIONS; EFFECT OF RESORT TO PROCEDURE OF OTHER LAW

Section 401. Making of cooperative agreements with other human-relations commissions. The Commission may cooperate with another human-relations commission established to administer laws comparable to this Ordinance. In furtherance of such cooperation and to achieve more adequate administration of this law, the Commission may enter into written agreements with these other commissions under which it will perform the whole or part of any one or more of the three basic functions set out in Section 503 rather than the other commission which may have jurisdiction to perform the same functions within the political subdivision.

Section 402. Rescission of a cooperative agreement. The Commission may rescind a cooperative agreement whenever it determines that the agreement no longer serves the interest of promoting effective achievement of the purposes of this Ordinance.

Section 403. Effect of resort to procedure of another law. If a person institutes an action relative to conduct covered by this Ordinance without resorting to the procedure provided by it, he may not subsequently resort to that procedure. The Commission may, however, process a complaint referred to it by a state or federal commission.

PART V. THE CENTRAL TASK, FUNCTIONS, GOALS, AND POLICIES OF THE COMMISSION

Section 501. The central task of the Commission. (a) The central task of the Commission is the reconstruction of intergroup relations within the political subdivision so as to eliminate the causes of, ameliorate the conditions accompanying, and overcome the results flowing from discrimination and other harmful activity directed against minority and other disadvantaged groups. Performance of this task of reconstruction calls for the assembly and redirection of the maximum human and material resources within each community of the political subdivision and bringing them to bear upon those problems in the most effective way. It demands that each of these communities be persuaded to acknowledge that the performance of this task is ultimately its own responsibility and that each of its groups become genuinely involved in discharging it.

(b) The Commission is to be the major institution within the political subdivision for guiding the performance of this task and for providing as well as eliciting the appropriate leadership to secure its realization. With regard to the majority or controlling group, the local section must seek to obtain reorganization and reformation of all group actions, habits, customs, and private and official arrangements that have produced and continue to maintain the conditions adversely affecting the opportunities of minority and other disadvantaged groups. With regard to the latter, the Commission must seek to move its members to confront problems of group actions, habits, customs, and private arrangements that hamper them in obtaining and maximizing upon needed opportunities; to provide them with various kinds of assistance services calculated to help them prepare for and obtain needed opportunities, and to protect them against certain typical types of exploitation and abuse. Persons within the majority or controlling group must be found who will provide wise leadership within that group so as to move it to begin to confront and resolve its intergroup-relations problems. Within minority and other disadvantaged groups, leaders must be found or developed who will help these groups to perform the kinds of actions that are calculated to start and facilitate the process of dialogue and negotiations between the various groups looking to an improvement in their relations and in the opportunities available to minority and other disadvantaged groups.

Section 502. Basic functions of the Commission. (a) The Commission shall perform within the political subdivision three basic functions:

(1) processing individual complaints relative to denials of any right, privilege, or immunity secured or protected by the Constitution or laws of the United States and relative to all forms of discrimination and other harmful activity directed against minority or other disadvantaged groups;

(2) negotiating with wide sectors of business, unions, professions, official agencies, and private organizations for the taking of action by them to improve opportunities available to minority and other disadvantaged groups, and utilizing inspections, surveys, private conferences, public hearings, reports, and enforcement actions to assure the effectiveness of negotiation; and

(3) undertaking various types of constructive action designed to eliminate the causes of intergroup-relations problems within the local community, to deal with actions and conditions affecting the public welfare that result from the continued existence of these problems, and to move the local community and its groups to direct the maximum resources of the community, both human and material, to the accomplishment of these objectives.

(b) It is the sense of the governing body that the negotiation and constructive-action functions of the Commission should receive the greatest emphasis in its administration of the Ordinance.

Section 503. Goals of the Commission. The Commission shall seek to achieve the following goals in performing its basic task and function:

(a)–(f)

[Subsections (a)–(f) are the same as the corresponding subsections of Section 504 of the Alpha Model State Civil-Rights Act set out in Chapter 8.]

Section 504. Implemental policies of the Commission. The following implemental policies are to be pursued by the Commission in performing its negotiation and constructive-action functions:

(1)–(11)

[Subsections (1)–(11) are the same as the corresponding subsections of Section 505 of the Alpha Model State Civil-Rights Act set out in Chapter 8.]

PART VI. POWERS AND DUTIES OF THE COMMISSION

Section 601. General powers and duties of the Commission. The Commission has the following general powers and duties:

(1) to establish its principal office in the [name of political subdivision] or of a place within it;

(2) to meet and function at any place within the political subdivision;

(3) to appoint for itself an executive director and any attorneys, hearing examiners, clerks, and other employees and agents as may seem necessary, and to fix the compensation of these officers, employees, and agents;

(4) to accept outside funds, gifts, or bequests, public or private, to help finance its activities;

(5) to enter into cooperative working arrangements with local, state, and federal agencies having related responsibilities, when these agreements will aid in carrying out the purposes and provisions of this Ordinance;

(6) to adopt, promulgate, amend, and rescind rules and regulations to effectuate the purposes and provisions of this Ordinance; and

(7) to submit at least once a year to the governing body a report concerning its activities and its recommendations.

Section 602. Implemental powers and duties of the Commission. The Commission has the following implemental powers and duties in performing its basic tasks and functions and in carrying out its implemental policies:

(1)–(11)

[Subsections (1)–(11) are the same as the corresponding subsections of Section 602 of the Alpha Model State Civil-Rights Act set out in Chapter 8.]

(12) to obtain upon request and use the service of all departments and agencies of the political subdivision.

PART VII.   PROCEDURES RELATIVE TO COMPLAINTS; REMEDIES; JUDICIAL REVIEW; RECORDS

Section 701. Definitions. In this part

(1) "Commission" means the Commission, as defined in Section 201. In Sections 714, 715, 716, 717, 718, and 719 "Commission" means either the Commission or a hearing panel of the Commission.

(2) "Commissioner" means a commissioner of the Commission.

(3) "Civil-Rights organization" means an organization which, under its articles of incorporation or association, is organized to deal with intergroup-relations problems.

(4) "Chairman" means the chairman of the Commission.

(5) "Discriminatory act" means any act or practice of discrimination, including an unlawful discriminatory act.

(6) "Discrimination" means any direct or indirect exclusion, distinction, limitation, refusal, denial, or any other differentiation or preference in the treatment of a person or persons on account of race, color, religion, ancestry, national origin, age, sex, or economic status, and any denial of any right, privilege, or immunity secured or protected by the Constitution or laws of the United States.

(7)–(19)

[Subsections (7)–(19) of this section are the same as the corresponding subsections of Section 701 of the Alpha Model State Civil-Rights Act set out in Chapter 8. Where the term "Act" is used, substitute the term "Ordinance."]

Sections 702–719. [Sections 702–719 are the same as the corresponding sections of the Alpha Model State Civil-Rights Act set out in Chapter 8. Where the term "Act" is used, substitute the term "Ordinance."]

Section 720. Judicial review; enforcement. (a) If the respondent refuses or fails to comply with any order of the Commission or violates any of the provisions of this Ordinance, the Commission shall certify the case and the entire record of its proceedings to the [chief legal officer of the political subdivision], who shall invoke the aid of an appropriate court to secure enforcement or compliance with the order or to impose the penalties set forth in Section 901.

(b) The Commission's copy of the testimony shall be available at all reasonable times to all parties for examination without cost, whether or not in connection with judicial review of the order of the Commission.

Sections 721–722. [Sections 721–722 are the same as the corresponding sections of the Alpha Model State Civil-Rights Act set out in Chapter 8. Where the term "Act" is used, substitute the term "Ordinance."]

PART VIII.   UNLAWFUL DISCRIMINATORY ACTS
Subpart A.   Definitions

Section 801. Definitions. In this Ordinance

(1) "Official agency" means an authority of the government of the political subdivision and its members and employees.

(2) "Official financial assistance" means financial assistance provided by an official agency.

(3) "License" means the whole or any part of any official-agency permit, certificate, approval, registration, charter, membership, or other form of permission.

(4) "Age" refers to the age of a person between thirty-five and sixty-five years of age.

(5) "Police officer" means any police officer of any official agency.

Subpart B.   Unlawful Discriminatory Acts in General; Discrimination by Police Officers, Official Agencies, and Programs and Activities Operating under Official Financial Assistance or a License

Sections 811–815. [Sections 811–815 are the same as the corresponding sections of the Alpha Model State Civil-Rights Act set out in Chapter VIII.]

Subpart C.   Discrimination in Employment

Section 821. Definitions. In this Ordinance

(1) "Employer" means a person employing one or more employees within the political subdivision, exclusive of parents, spouse, or children of that person, and including the political subdivision and any official agency thereof.

(2) "Labor organization" means any organizational person that exists for the purpose, in whole or in part, of representing employees in collective bargaining. Collective bargaining includes any negotiation or dealing with employers concerning grievances, terms, or conditions of employment or other aid or protection for one or more employees.

(3) "Employment agency" means any person regularly under-

taking, with or without compensation, to procure employment opportunities for individuals or to procure, refer, or place individuals as employees.

(4) "Individual" means any individual other than one employed or seeking employment by his parents, spouse, or child, or employed or seeking employment in the domestic service of or in a personal or confidential capacity by any person.

Sections 822–826. [Sections 822–826 are the same as the corresponding sections of the Alpha Model State Civil-Rights Act set out in Chapter 8.]

Subparts D–F

[Subparts D–F are the same as the corresponding subparts of Part VIII of the Alpha Model State Civil-Rights Act set out in Chapter 8.]

PART IX.   CRIMINAL SANCTIONS; OTHER REMEDIES; MISCELLANEOUS

Section 901. Wilful violation of Commission order; wilful interference. Any person who wilfully violates any order of the Commission or this Ordinance or who wilfully resists, prevents, impedes, or interferes with the performance of a duty or the exercise of a power by the Commission or one of its commissioners or representatives, is subject to a fine of not more than [   ], and in default of payment of the fine and costs shall be subject to imprisonment for a period not exceeding ninety [90] days.

Section 902. Termination and other action relative to official financial assistance and licenses. (a) Upon receiving a copy of the final decision and order of the Commission under Section 717, an official agency of the political subdivision that extended official financial assistance to a program or activity of a respondent or issued a license to a respondent may take appropriate action

(1) to terminate or refuse to grant or continue assistance under such program or activity or to revoke or suspend such license, but such termination, refusal, revocation, or suspension shall be limited in its effect to the particular program, license, or part thereof, in which such noncompliance has been so found; or

(2) to utilize any other means authorized by law.

(b) In the case of any action terminating, or refusing to grant or continue, assistance, or revoking or suspending a license because of failure to comply with Section 815, the head of the official agency shall file with the governing body a full written report of the circumstances and the grounds for such action. No such action shall become effective until thirty days have elapsed after the filing of such a report.

Section 903. Public contractors. (a) Upon receiving a copy of the final decision and order of the Commission under Section 717, an official agency of the government of the political subdivision may deem the respondent ineligible for award of a public contract until the Commission is satisfied that the respondent will carry out policies in compliance with the provisions of this Ordinance. The final decision of the Commission, as to the fact of discrimination by the respondent, is binding on all other agencies for all purposes.

Section 904. Prima-facie evidence. In a proceeding under this Ordinance a written, printed, or visual communication, advertisement, or other form of publication or written inquiry or record, or other document purporting to have been made by a person is prima-facie evidence that it was authorized by him.

Section 905. Securing compliance with record-keeping requirements and subpoenas. If a person fails to permit, upon a demand by the Commission, access to premises and examination, photographing, or copying of evidence, or fails to make, keep, or preserve records, or make reports in compliance with Section 721 or if a person fails to comply with a subpoena issued by the Commission or a commissioner, the Commission shall certify the case and the entire record of its proceedings to the [chief legal officer of the political subdivision], who shall invoke the aid of an appropriate court to secure enforcement or compliance with the order or to impose the penalties set forth in Section 901.

Section 906. Relation of criminal to administrative or civil proceedings under this act. The pendency or final determination of a criminal proceeding is not a bar to an administrative or civil proceeding arising from the same act or situation.

Section 907. Repeal. The following ordinances and parts of ordinances are repealed:

   [(1)   ;

    (2)   ;

    ( )   .]

Section 908. Severability. If any provision of this Ordinance or its application to any person or situation is held invalid, that invalidity does not affect, impair, or invalidate other provisions or applications of the Ordinance that can be given effect independently of the invalid provision or application, and for this purpose the provisions of this Act are severable.

Section 909. Effective date; initial appointment of officers. (a) This Ordinance shall take effect ninety days after the day that all of the seven commissioners first take office, or on such prior date after enactment of this Ordinance as the mayor shall prescribe and file with [the chief legal officer of the political subdivision].

(b) Any of the officers provided for in this Ordinance may, notwithstanding Subsection (a), be appointed in the manner provided for in this Ordinance at any time after the date of enactment of this Ordinance. Such officers shall be compensated from the date they first take office.

Section 910. Savings provisions. The provisions of this Ordinance, so far as they are the same as those of ordinances repealed by this Ordinance, are intended as a continuation of such ordinances and not as new enactments. The provisions of this Ordinance shall not affect any act done or any complaint or proceeding pending under authority of the repealed ordinances. All rules and regulations adopted pursuant to any ordinance repealed by this Ordinance shall continue with the same force and effect as if such ordinance had not been repealed.

COMMENTS

PREFATORY NOTE

1. History. The Alpha Model Local Civil-Rights Ordinance was drafted in response to the felt need for guidelines relative to local civil-rights legislation.[1] The model ordinance draws heavily upon the three Alpha Model Acts set out in Chapters 8, 9, and 10 above and upon a model act drafted by the author and included as an appendix to a law review article published in June, 1965.[2] There has been surprisingly little scholarly effort directed toward the problem of model local civil-rights ordinances. The National Association of Intergroup Relations Officials does not include in its 1965 *Memorandum to Municipalities* a model ordinance.[3] It does refer to a number of cities having civil-rights ordinances—such as Louisville, Kentucky; Toledo, Ohio; Philadelphia, Pennsylvania; and Kalamazoo, Michigan—as illustrating "what a human relations agency can do."[4] The dean of America's human-relations consultants, George Schermer, takes the position that "it may not be advisable to risk a major legislative contest for an ordinance during the formative period"[5] in which local efforts are being made to involve local government in human-relations activities. In-

[1] National Association of Intergroup Relations Officials, *A Memorandum to Municipalities: Guidelines for Municipal Human Relations Committees* (Washington, D.C.: pamphlet, 1964); U.S. Department of Commerce, Community Relations Service, *How to Turn Talk into Action: A Guide for an Effective Commission on Human Relations* (Washington, D.C.: U.S. Government Printing Office, June, 1965); George Schermer, *Guidelines: A Manual for (Urban) Bi-Racial Committees* (New York: Anti-Defamation League of B'nai B'rith, 1964). Also see Norman Dorsen, "The Prospects for the Model or Uniform Civil Rights Act" (study prepared for the Special Committee on Civil Rights of the National Conference of Commissioners on Uniform State Laws, 1965), pp. 21–39 (mimeographed).

[2] Joseph P. Witherspoon, "Civil Rights Policy in the Federal System: Proposals for a Better Use of Administrative Process," *Yale Law Journal*, Vol. 74 (1965), pp. 1175–1244.

[3] National Association of Intergroup Relations Officials, *A Memorandum to Municipalities.*

[4] *Id.*, pp. 5–9.

[5] Schermer, *Guidelines*, p. 26.

stead, he feels "a mayor's committee may do very well for the first year or two."[6] He does, however, insist that a local official human-relations agency should have a statutory base and an adequate budget to begin with. He also includes in his *Guidelines: A Manual for Bi-Racial Committees* what he calls a "Model Ordinance."[7] This manual was published in 1964 by the Anti-Defamation League of B'nai B'rith. The "Model Ordinance" included in it is the Topeka, Kansas, Civil Rights Ordinance. Mr. Schermer views it as a model ordinance "because it is the most complete of the more than two dozen reviewed, except for those ordinances prohibiting discrimination in employment and/or housing . . . "[8] The Federal Community Relations Service in 1965 issued a pamphlet entitled *How to Turn Talk into Action.*[9] This pamphlet also eschews setting forth a suggested civil-rights ordinance but does speak to some of the items that should be included in any "proper local ordinance."[10] It insists upon delegating to the local commission the power both "to initiate investigations into potential or actual areas of trouble and tension" and "to hold public hearings and to request and summon the presence of citizens."[11] It also states that the Commission should have substantive civil-rights law to enforce that is "at least as broad as the 1964 Civil Rights Act and prevailing state law."[12]

I take the position that the situation in 1968 is a vastly different one from the situation that obtained prior to that time. The status of human relations in most major cities of the country has become extraordinarily serious and will become more so in future years until the problems involved are adequately met by official government action. It is no longer appropriate to view what a city or other political subdivision with serious human-relations problems should do, even as an initial effort, from the standpoint of what is politically expedient. It is important for every one of these political subdivisions to be made aware of what it is minimally necessary for them to do in order to begin the reconstruction of human relations in an adequate manner. Prior to the time they undertake to perform their responsibilities, offi-

---

[6] *Ibid.*
[7] *Id.*, p. 60.
[8] *Ibid.*
[9] U.S. Department of Commerce, Community Relations Service, *How to Turn Talk into Action.*
[10] *Id.*, pp. 5–6.
[11] *Id.*, p. 6.
[12] *Ibid.*

cial efforts in the civil-rights area falling short of what is minimally adequate should be supplied by either the state or the federal governments. The Alpha Model Local Civil-Rights Ordinance is a response to the need for a statement of requirements to be met by a minimally adequate human-relations ordinance. It gives effect to the recommendations previously noted made by the Federal Community Relations Service as to what should be in any proper civil-rights ordinance. But it also goes well beyond these recommendations and implements the suggestions contained in earlier chapters of this book about minimally adequate law in the civil-rights field.

2. *Reorientation of local civil-rights policy.* The Alpha Model Local Civil-Rights Ordinance presents a thoroughgoing reorientation of the typical local and state civil-rights law. Every careful study of the approximately twenty years' experience in administering this type of legislation concludes that it has been far less effective than desired or needed in light of the immense regulatory problems presented.[13] The reorientation proposed in the Alpha Model Local Ordinance to achieve greater effectiveness involves wholly new tasks, functions, and goals for most local human-relations commissions now in existence, new methods for their operation, and much new substantive law. These changes are designed to elaborate the idea developed in preceding chapters that in order to achieve any sufficient rectification of the status of intergroup relations in this country, official action must take place at the local level and can only be secured through an administrative agency operating within a community, that is authorized to deal with the full spectrum of human-relations problems existing at that level.

3. *Structure of the Ordinance.* The Alpha Model Local Civil-Rights Ordinance is the fourth of the four Alpha Model Acts, as previously mentioned. Each of these is constructed to parallel and dovetail with the others. This Ordinance, like the prior Acts, consists of nine parts. The first three parts relate to findings and declaration of policies, general definitions and establishment of a local human-relations commission to administer the Ordinance. The fourth part deals with the relationship between the commission established and other similiar commissions at other levels of government. The fifth part concerns the task, functions, goals, and implemental policies of the Commission. The sixth part relates to its procedures to be followed in processing

[13] See Chapters 1, 5, 6 and note 1 of Chapter 7 of this book.

complaints of discriminatory acts, administrative hearings, remedies, enforcement of commission orders, and similar matters. The eighth part sets forth certain substantive law concerning unlawful discriminatory acts. The final part covers criminal sanctions, other remedies, and a series of miscellaneous matters.

PART I. SHORT TITLES; FINDINGS AND DECLARATION
         OF POLICIES; CONSTRUCTION

PART II. GENERAL DEFINITIONS

[The Comment on Parts I and II of the Alpha Model State Civil-Rights Act in Chapter 8 is fully applicable here and should be consulted.]

PART III. LOCAL HUMAN-RELATIONS COMMISSION

[The Comments on Part II of the Alpha Model State Civil-Rights Act in Chapter 8 and on Part III of the Alpha Model State Act on Local Human-Relations Commissions in Chapter 9 are fully applicable here and should be consulted.]

PART IV. COOPERATIVE AGREEMENTS WITH OTHER
          HUMAN-RELATIONS COMMISSIONS; EFFECT OF RESORT
          TO PROCEDURE OF OTHER LAW

This part differs considerably from the corresponding parts of the other Alpha Model Acts. This is due to the fact that a local commission is in a subordinate position relative to a state commission and to the Federal Human-Relations Commission created by the Alpha Model Federal Civil-Rights Act or a similar federal agency. The earlier acts had to provide for the coexistence of a local human-relations commission with a superior commission under a variety of circumstances. Part IV of this ordinance need only provide for its entering into and termination of cooperative agreements with superior agencies. Section 403 continues the policy of the other Alpha Model Acts in precluding resort to the procedure of this Ordinance where the person seeking to do so has already resorted to the procedure of other statutes covering the same conduct. The section does, however, preserve the right of the local commission to process a complaint referred to it by a state or a federal commission.

PART V. THE CENTRAL TASK, FUNCTIONS, GOALS, AND
POLICIES OF THE COMMISSION

A fundamental principle underlying each of the Alpha Model Acts is that a local commission can be, if its political subdivision wills and acts prudently for this result, the most effective agency for dealing with human-relations problems at the local level. The approach taken in this Part rejects the extraordinarily limited role which the Uniform Model State Anti-Discrimination Act[14] would accord to local commissions. That Act denudes local commissions by precluding them from holding public hearings, issuing cease and desist and other remedial orders where violations are discovered, and enforcing these orders in the courts.[15] The Uniform Model Act fails to honor one of the most important lessons taught by twenty years of experience with state human-relations commissions as primary administrators of civil-rights law at the local level.[16] In order to achieve necessary room for operation on the part of well-organized local human-relations commissions, it is necessary that state and federal legislation be enacted similar to that suggested by the three Alpha Model Acts set forth in Chapters 8, 9, and 10.

The heart of the Alpha Model Local Civil-Rights Ordinance is this part. In stating the central task of the Commission created by this Ordinance, Section 501 simply makes explicit what careful students of intergroup-relations problems have been articulating for years as the task which has to be performed at the local level by well-organized local human-relations commissions. By and large the operations of the Philadelphia and Pittsburgh Human-Relations Commissions[17] most closely approximate what is described as the task of a local human-relations commission.

Section 502 serves to outline the various functions of the Commission. The Comments on Part V of both the Alpha Model State Civil-Rights Act in Chapter 8 and the Alpha Model State Act on Local Human-Relations Commissions in Chapter 9 have fully set forth the

---

[14] See Chapter 9 of that act. See National Conference of Commissioners of Uniform State Laws, "Model [State] Anti-Discrimination Act," *Harvard Journal of Legislation*, Vol. 4 (1967), pp. 224–278.

[15] *Ibid*. See Chapters 904 and 905 of that act.

[16] Harvard Student Legislative Research Bureau, "A Proposed Model State Civil Rights Act," *Harvard Journal of Legislation*, Vol. 3 (1965), p. 100.

[17] See Appendix C.

nature of this and the remaining sections of this part and should be consulted.

PART VI. POWERS AND DUTIES OF THE COMMISSION

PART VII. PROCEDURES RELATIVE TO COMPLAINTS; REMEDIES; JUDICIAL REVIEW; RECORDS

These parts are identical for most of their extent with the corresponding parts of the Alpha Model State Acts set forth in Chapters 8 and 9. The Comments on these parts are fully applicable and should be consulted. Section 720 is the only section that differs fundamentally from the comparable section in the Alpha Model State Acts. This is due to the fact that political subdivision must, so far as state courts are concerned, depend upon their existing jurisdiction for obtaining enforcement of the orders of its Commission. For the same reason, there is no necessity to provide for judicial review of these orders. State statutes or other state law will speak to this matter either generally or specifically.

PART VIII. UNLAWFUL DISCRIMINATORY ACTS

The substantive law concerning discrimination against minority and other seriously disadvantaged groups contained in this part is identical with the substantive law set forth in the Alpha Model State Civil-Rights Act in Chapter 8 and the Alpha Model Federal Civil-Rights Act in Chapter 10. It is believed that any political subdivision that is genuinely serious about the resolution of serious human-relations problems within it would be willing to enact each of the provisions of Part VIII. On the other hand, it is also recognized that the enactment of substantive civil-rights law is a matter for political resolution and that what is essential for resolving a problem, even on a minimally adequate basis, may not be possible at some given time as compared with another. The Comments on Part VIII contained in the Alpha Model State Civil-Rights Act set out in Chapter 8 and in the Alpha Model State Act on Local Human-Relations Commissions set out in Chapter 9 will be helpful in guiding choices of substantive civil-rights law that fall short of the compass included in Part VIII of this Act.

Title VIII of the Civil Rights Act of 1968 provides, in its Section 810(c), for the Secretary of Housing and Urban Development to notify the appropriate state or local agency of a complaint of discrimination in housing where the state or local fair housing law "provides rights and remedies for alleged discriminatory housing practices which are substantially equivalent to the rights and remedies provided in this title." Subparts E and F of Part VIII and Part VII of the Alpha Model Ordinance satisfy the requirements of Section 810(c) relative to substantially equivalent rights and remedies. Thus, a local government enacting this ordinance will be able to handle complaints of discrimination in housing covered by the Civil Rights Act of 1968.

PART IX. CRIMINAL SANCTIONS; OTHER REMEDIES; MISCELLANEOUS

The Comments on Part IX of the Alpha Model State Civil-Rights Act and on the Alpha Model State Act on Local Human-Relations Commissions are largely applicable to this part and should be consulted.

Appendix A

State Human-Relations Commissions or Agencies Operating under Statutes Giving Them Authority to Enforce Civil-Rights Law

1. Alaska: State Commission for Human Rights (members: 5)
Room 24, Reed Building   Willard L. Bowman, Exec. Dir.
Anchorage, Alaska 99501   Established: 1963
      1968 budget: $53,000
Alaska Stat. *as amended* (Michie Supp. 1967).

The Commission	
established	secs. 18.80.010-.020
jurisdiction over employment, housing, financing of housing, and public accommodations	sec. 18.80.060(4)
powers and duties	secs. 18.80.030 to .070
procedure	secs. 18.80.100 to .130,-.150,-.160
judicial enforcement, review	sec. 18.80.135

Employment (Covers employers of one or more persons, employment agencies, and labor organizations; covers discrimination on account of race, color, religion, national origin, age, or sex.)

definitions	sec. 18.80.300(2)–(5)
unlawful practices	sec. 18.80.220

Real Property (Covers all housing transactions, all real estate transactions of real estate brokers and salesmen; covers discrimination on account of race, color, religion, or national origin.)

definitions	sec. 18.80.300(8)
unlawful practices	sec. 18.80.240

Financing of Real Property (Covers all financial institutions; covers discrimination on account of race, color, religion, national origin.)

definitions	sec. 18.80.300(9)
unlawful practices	sec. 18.80.250

Public Accommodations (Covers public accommodations broadly and then specifies certain types; covers discrimination on account of race, color, religion, or national origin.)

definitions	sec. 19.80.300(7)
unlawful practices	sec. 18.80.230, .255

---

2. California: State Fair Employment Practice Commission (members: 7)
P. O. Box 603   Edward Howden, Exec. Dir.
San Francisco, Calif. 94101   established: 1959
      1967 budget: $700,356

Cal. Ann. Code, Labor, *as amended* (West Supp. 1967); Health and Safety
(West Supp. 1967).

The Commission

established	Labor, secs. 1414–1415, 1417
jurisdiction over employment	Labor, sec. 1419.5
jurisdiction over housing and financing of housing	H & S, sec. 35730
exclusive jurisdiction over housing relative to political subdivisions	H & S, sec. 35743
powers and duties	Labor, secs. 1418–1419, 1416; 1421
procedure	Labor, secs. 1421.1, 1422–1427, 3096
	H & S, secs. 35731–35738
judicial enforcement, review	Labor, secs. 1428–1429

Employment (Covers employers of five or more persons, the state, and
political subdivisions, employment agencies, labor organizations; covers
discrimination on account of race, color, religious creed, ancestry, or
national origin.)

definitions	Labor, sec. 1413(b)–(e)
unlawful practices	Labor, sec. 1420

Real Property (Covers transactions relative to multiple dwellings of five
or more units and publicly assisted housing accommodations; covers discrimination on account of race, color, religion, ancestry, or national
origin.)

definitions	H & S, sec. 35710
unlawful practices	H & S, sec. 35720(1)–(6)

Financing of Real Property (Covers any person or "other financial
institutions"; covers discrimination on account of race, color, religion, or
national origin.)

definitions	H & S, sec. 35710(2)
unlawful practices	H & S, sec. 35720(7)

Cal. Ann. Code, Civil, secs. 51–53, *as amended* (Supp. 1967).

Public Accommodations (Judicially enforced only.)

---

3. Colorado: Civil Rights Commission (members: 7)

306 State Services Bldg.	James F. Reynolds, Director
1525 Sherman St.	Ruth Steiner, Acting Asst. Dir.
Denver, Colorado 80203	established: 1951
	reconstituted: 1955
	1966–1967 budget: $128,920

Colo. Rev. Stat. Ann. (Supp. 1965).

The Commission

established	art. 80-21-4
jurisdiction over employment, real property, financing of real property, and public accommodations	arts. 69-7-2, 25-3-1
powers and duties	arts. 80-21-5, 25-3-3, 69-7-4, 25-3-2 to -4

procedure   arts. 80-21-8, 69-7-7

judicial enforcement, review   arts. 80-21-8, 69-7-7, 25-3-5

judicial remedy   art. 69-7-8

Employment (Covers employers of six or more persons, the state, political subdivisions, employment agencies, and labor organizations; covers discrimination on account of race, color, creed, or national origin.)

definitions   art. 80-21-2

unlawful practices   art. 80-21-6

Real Property (Covers all housing transactions except those involving rooms in single-family dwellings maintained and occupied by owner or lessee as a household, all commercial space, and all brokers and builders; covers discrimination on account of race, color, creed, ancestry, national origin, or sex.)

definitions   art. 69-7-3

unlawful practices   art. 69-7-5

Financing of Real Property (Covers any person; covers discrimination on account of race, color, creed, ancestry, national origin, or sex.)

definitions   art. 69-7-3(c)

unlawful practices   art. 69-7-5(1)(c)

Public Accommodations (Covers specified public accommodations and then others through a general clause; covers discrimination on account of race or color.)

unlawful practices   arts. 25-1-1 to -2-3

---

4. Connecticut: Commission on Human Rights and Opportunities (members: 11)

92 Farmington Ave.   Arthur L. Green, Dir.

Hartford, Connecticut 06115   Angelo T. Serluco, Asst. Dir.

     established: 1947

     1965–1967 budget: $368,683

Conn. Gen. Stat. Ann. Rev., *as amended* (Supp. 1967).

The Commission

established   sec. 31-123

jurisdiction over employment, real property, public accommodations, and membership in certain associations   sec. 53-56

powers and duties   sec. 31-125

procedure   secs. 31-127; 53-56

judicial enforcement, appeals   sec. 31-128

Employment (Covers employers of three or more persons, the state, political subdivisions, employment agencies, and labor organizations; covers discrimination on account of race, color, creed, ancestry, national origin, or age [40–65].)

definitions   sec. 31-122

unlawful practices   sec. 31-126

state contractors   sec. 4-114a

Real Property (Covers all transactions relative to commercial property, public housing, publicly assisted housing, and all housing accommodations and lots intended for housing except rentals in one- or two-family, owner-occupied housing accommodations; covers discrimination on account of race, color, creed, ancestry, or national origin.)

unlawful practices	sec. 53-35

Public Accommodations (Covers public accommodations generally; covers discrimination on account of race, color, creed, ancestry, or national origin.)

unlawful practices	sec. 53-35

Associations of Licensed Persons (Covers any association having purpose of furthering professional or occupational interests of its members when its members are required by the state to have a license; covers discrimination on account of race, color, or creed.)

unlawful practices	sec. 53-35a

---

5. Delaware: State Human Relations Commission (members: 28)

2407 Lancaster Ave.	Mrs. Hallie H. Tybout, Exec. Sec.
Wilmington, Delaware 19805	established: 1962
	1965–1966 budget: $12,600

Del. Code Ann., *as amended* (Supp. 1967).

The Commission

established	tit. 31, sec. 3001
jurisdiction over public accommodations	tit. 31, sec. 3003
powers and duties	tit. 31, sec. 3004; tit. 6, secs. 4505, 4507–4509
procedure	tit. 6, secs. 4506, 4512
action for specific enforcement of order, appeal	tit. 6, secs. 4516, 4513

Public Accommodations (Covers public accommodations generally but excludes housing; covers discrimination on account of race, color, creed, or national origin.)

definitions	tit. 6, sec. 4501
unlawful practices	tit. 6, sec. 4504

---

6. Hawaii: Enforcement Division, Department of Labor and Industrial Relations

825 Mililani St.	Alfred Laureta, Director
Honolulu, Hawaii 96813	Antone Rodrigues, Administrator
	established: 1963
	1967 budget: not separately stated

Hawaii Rev. Laws, *as amended* (Supp. 1967).

The Division

designated as administrator	sec. 90A-2
jurisdiction over employment powers	sec. 90A-7

procedure   secs. 90A-2 to -6

Employment (Covers all employers, employment agencies, and labor organizations; covers discrimination on account of race, color, religion, ancestry, age, or sex.)

definitions   sec. 90A-1.5
unlawful practices   sec. 90A-1

Real Property: legislation too recent to be included on this list may be found in Hawaii Rev. Laws, *as amended* (Supp. 1965), and Hawaii Sess. Laws, 1967, Act. 193.

---

7. Illinois: Fair Employment Practices Commission (members: 5)
160 N. LaSalle St.   Walter J. Ducey, Exec. Dir.
Chicago, Illinois 60601   established: 1961
                                             1965–1967 budget: $197,500

Ill. Ann. Stat., *as amended* (Supp. 1967).
    The Commission
established   ch. 48, sec. 855
jurisdiction over employment, pow-
    ers and duties   ch. 48, secs. 856, 859, 867
procedure   ch. 48, sec. 858
judicial enforcement   ch. 48, secs. 860–862
    Private Business Schools State Board
jurisdiction over private business
    schools   ch. 144, sec. 137
    Director of Department of Conservation
jurisdiction over state parks con-
    cessions   ch. 105, sec. 468.1
    Illinois Liquor Control Commission
jurisdiction over liquor establish-
    ments   ch. 43, secs. 97, 149

Employment (Covers employers of fifty or more persons (twenty-five or more after July 1, 1968), the state, political subdivisions, employment agencies, and labor organizations; covers discrimination on account of race, color, religion, ancestry, or national origin.)

definitions   ch. 48, sec. 852
unlawful practices   ch. 48, sec. 853

Public Accommodations (Covers discrimination on account of race, color, or creed.)

unlawful practices (private business
    schools)   ch. 144, secs. 138, 151(11)
unlawful practices (state park con-
    cessions)   ch. 105, sec. 468.1
unlawful practices (liquor estab-
    lishments)   ch. 43, sec. 133

Public Accommodations, Public Employment, Public Facilities (Judicially enforced only. Covers discrimination on account of race, color, or religion; allows suit for damages, suit for abatement of discrimination in public accommodations as a public nuisance, civil action for injunction by attorney general, and discharge of discriminating official by head of department or other proper official.)

unlawful practices	ch. 38, secs. 13-1 to -4

8. Indiana: Civil Rights Commission (members: 5)

1004 State Office Bldg.	Harold O. Hatcher, Exec. Dir.
100 N. Senate Ave.	Osma D. Spurlock, Deputy Dir.
Indianapolis, Indiana 46204	established: 1961
	1965–1966 budget: $65,880
	1966–1967 budget: $70,810

Ind. Stat. Ann., *as amended* (Supp. 1967).

The Commission

established	secs. 40-2310 to -2311
jurisdiction over employment, real property, financing of real property, and public accommodations	sec. 40-2312(e)
powers and duties	sec. 40-2312
procedure	secs. 40-2309(k), 40-2312(k)–(l)
judicial review	sec. 40-2312(l)
local commissions	sec. 40-2317a

Employment (Covers employers of six or more persons, the state, political subdivisions, employment agencies, and labor organizations; covers discrimination on account of race, color, creed, ancestry, or national origin.)

definitions	sec. 40-2309(d)–(g)
unlawful practices	sec. 40-2308

Real Property (Covers transactions involving all housing, commercial space, and brokers; covers discrimination on account of race, color, creed, ancestry, national origin.)

definitions	secs. 40-2308, -2309(h), (l)
unlawful practices	sec. 40-2308

Financing of Real Property (Covers public accommodations generally; covers discrimination on account of race, color, creed, ancestry, or national origin.)

definitions	sec. 40-2309(i)
unlawful practices	sec. 40-2308

9. Iowa: Civil Rights Commission (members: 7)

State Capitol Bldg.	James A. Thomas, Exec. Dir.
Des Moines, Iowa 50319	established: 1965
	1965–1966 budget: $30,000
	(approximate)

Iowa Code Ann., *as amended* (Supp. 1967).

The Commission

established	sec. 105A.3-4
jurisdiction over employment and public accommodations	
powers and duties	sec. 105A.5(2)

procedure   sec. 105A.9
judicial enforcement, review   sec. 105A.10
concurrent jurisdiction of political
    subdivisions   sec. 105A.12

Employment (Covers employers of one or more employees, the state, political subdivisions, employment agencies, and labor organizations; covers discrimination on account of race, color, creed, religion, or national origin.)

definitions   sec. 105A.2(3)–(6)
unlawful practices   sec. 105A.7

Real Property (Covers all sales, rentals, and leases of real property other than rentals or leases of housing accommodations in owner-occupied, two-family homes, rentals or leases of fewer than six rooms in owner-occupied homes, and sales, rentals, and leases of property owned by religious institutions; covers discrimination on account of race, color, creed, religion, or national origin.)

definitions   sec. 105A.2
unlawful practices   sec. 105A.13

Public Accommodations (Covers public accommodations generally; but excludes all housing accommodations except for transients; covers discrimination on account of race, color, creed, religion, or national origin.)

definitions   sec. 105.A.2(10)
unlawful practices   sec. 105A.6

---

10. Kansas: Commission on Civil Rights (members: 5)
State Office Bldg.   Homer C. Floyd, Exec. Dir.
Topeka, Kansas 66612   established: 1953
                                       1966 budget: $66,395
                                       1967 budget: $84,097

Kan. Stat. Ann., *as amended* (Supp. 1967).

The Commission
established   sec. 44-1003
jurisdiction over employment and
    public accommodations   sec. 44-1004(4)
powers and duties   sec. 44-1004
procedure   secs. 44-1005, -1010
judicial enforcement, review   sec. 44-1011

Employment (Covers employers of four or more persons, the state, political subdivisions, employment agencies, and labor organizations; covers discrimination on account of race, color, religion, ancestry, or national origin.)

definitions   sec. 44-1002(b)–(e)
unlawful practices   sec. 44-1009

Public Accommodations (Covers only a very limited number of public accommodations; covers discrimination on account of race, color, religion, ancestry, or national origin.)

definitions   sec. 44-1002(h)–(i)
unlawful practices   sec. 44-1006(b)

11. Kentucky: Commission on Human Rights (members: 11)

172 Capitol Annex Bldg.　　　　　Galen Martin, Exec. Dir.
Frankfort, Kentucky 40601　　　　James C. Hicken, Asst. Dir.
　　　　　　　　　　　　　　　established: 1962
　　　　　　　　　　　　　　　1965–1966 budget: $59,400
　　　　　　　　　　　　　　　1966–1967 budget: $156,788

Ky. Rev. Stat. (Supp. 1966).
　　The Commission
established　　　　　　　　　　　secs. 344.150 to -.160
jurisdiction over employment and
　　public accommodations　　　　sec. 344.190(8)
powers and duties　　　　　　　　secs. 344.170 to -.190, 344.250
procedure　　　　　　　　　　　　secs. 344.200 to -.300
judicial enforcement, review　　　sec. 344.240
concurrent jurisdiction of cities and
　　counties　　　　　　　　　　　secs. 344.300 to -.350
　　Employment (Covers employers of eight or more persons, employment agencies, and labor organizations; covers discrimination on account of race, color, religion, or national origin.)
definitions　　　　　　　　　　　sec. 344.030
unlawful practices　　　　　　　　secs. 344.040 to -.100
　　Public Accommodations (Covers public accommodations generally; covers discrimination on account of race, color, religion, or national origin.)
definitions　　　　　　　　　　　sec. 344.130
unlawful practices　　　　　　　　secs. 344.120, -.140

---

12. Maryland: Commission on Interracial Problems and Relations
　　　(members: 9)

State Office Bldg.　　　　　　　　Parren J. Mitchell, Exec. Dir.
301 West Preston St.　　　　　　　established: 1951
Baltimore, Maryland 21201　　　　1966 budget: $63,503
Md. Ann. Code Art. 49B, *as amended* (Supp. 1967).
　　The Commission
established　　　　　　　　　　　secs. 1–2
jurisdiction over employment and
　　public accommodations　　　　secs. 12–14, 25
powers and duties　　　　　　　　sec. 3
procedure　　　　　　　　　　　　secs. 12–14
judicial enforcement　　　　　　　sec. 15(a)–(c)
alternative judicial remedy　　　　sec. 15(d)
local commissions　　　　　　　　sec. 26
　　Employment (Covers employers of twenty-five or more persons [after July 1, 1968] other than the state or bona fide private membership club; covers discrimination on account of race, color, creed, national origin, or sex.)
definitions　　　　　　　　　　　sec. 18

unlawful practices   sec. 19

Real Property (Covers all transactions related to dwellings except those fully constructed prior to June 1, 1967 or those completed, under certain conditions, prior to June 1, 1968; covers discrimination based upon race, color, religious creed, or national origin.)

definitions   sec. 21
unlawful practices   sec. 22

Financing of Real Property (Covers all financing of transactions relative to dwellings by persons regularly engaged in business of financing such transactions; covers discrimination on account of race, color, religious creed, or national origin.)

definitions   sec. 21
unlawful practices   sec. 23

Public Accommodations (Covers only a very limited number of public accommodations; covers discrimination on account of race, color, creed, or national origin.)

definitions   sec. 11
unlawful practices   sec. 11

---

13.   Massachusetts: Commission against Discrimination (members: 4)
41 Tremont St.   Walter H. Nolan, Exec. Sec.
Boston, Massachusetts 02108   established: 1946
                                        1965 budget: $169,651
Mass. Gen. Laws Ann., *as amended* (Supp. 1967).

The Commission

established   ch. 6, sec. 56
jurisdiction over employment, real
   property, financing of real property, public accommodations and
   education   ch. 151B, sec. 5
powers and duties   ch. 151B, sec. 3; ch. 151C, sec. 5
procedure   ch. 151B, sec. 5; ch. 151C, sec. 3
judicial enforcement, review   ch. 151B, sec. 6; ch. 151C, sec. 4

Employment (Covers employers of six or more persons, the Commonwealth, political subdivisions, employment agencies, and labor organizations; covers discrimination on account of race, color, creed, ancestry, national origin, sex, age [40–65].)

definitions   ch. 151B, sec. 1(2)–(6), (8)
unlawful practices   ch. 151B, sec. 4

Real Property (Covers publicly assisted housing accommodations, multiple dwellings, contiguously located housing, all other housing offered for sale or rent to public except owner-occupied two-family houses; and commercial space; covers discrimination on account of race, creed, color, or national origin.)

definitions   ch. 151B, sec. 1(9)–(12)
unlawful practices   ch. 151B, sec. 4(6)–(7)
special sanctions   ch. 112, sec. 87AAA

Financing of Real Property (Covers any person engaged in business of granting mortgage loans; covers discrimination on account of race, color, religious creed, ancestry, or national origin.)
unlawful practices   ch. 151B, sec. 4(3B)

Public Accommodations (Covers broad span of specified public accommodations; covers discrimination on account of race, color, class, religious sect, creed, denomination, or nationality.)
unlawful practices   ch. 272, secs. 92A, 98

Education (Covers any institution for instruction or training accepting applications from public generally except religious educational institutions; covers discrimination on account of race, religious creed, color, or national origin.)
definitions   ch. 151C, sec. 1(b)–(c)
unlawful practices   ch. 151C, sec. 2

---

14. Michigan: Civil Rights Commission (members: 8)
900 Cadillac Square Bldg.   Burton I. Gordin, Exec. Dir.
Detroit, Michigan 48226   Arthur L. Johnson, Deputy Dir.
                                   established: 1955
                                   reconstituted: 1963
                                   1965–1966 budget: $634,441
                                   1966–1967 budget: $900,000

Mich. Stat. Ann., *as amended* (Supp. 1967).
   The Commission
established   Const., Art. 5, sec. 29,
                                   sec. 3,548(1)–(3)
jurisdiction over employment, housing, financing of real estate transactions, public accommodations   Const., Art. I, sec. 2,
                                   secs. 3,548(4); 17.458(7)
powers and duties   Const., Art. 5, sec. 29
procedure   secs. 3,548(4); 17.458(7)
judicial enforcement, review   sec. 3, 548(4)

Employment (Covers employers of eight or more persons, the state, political subdivision, employment agencies, and labor organizations; covers discrimination on account of race, color, religion, ancestry, national origin, age [35–60], or sex.)
definitions   sec. 17,458(2)
unlawful practices   sec.17,458(3)–(3a)
special sanction   sec. 17,458(4a)

Real Property (Covers all housing transactions; covers discrimination on account of race, color, religion, or national origin.)
unlawful practices   Const., Art. I, sec. 2

Financing of Real Property (Covers all mortgage lending institutions; covers discrimination on account of race, color, religion, or national origin.)
unlawful practices   Const., Art. I, sec. 2

Public Accommodations (Covers all public accommodations; covers discrimination on account of race, color, religion, or national origin.)
unlawful practices   Const., Art. I, sec. 2

---

15. Minnesota: State Department of Human Rights (Commissioner of Human Rights and Board of Human Rights) (members: 9)

55 State Office Bldg.   Mrs. Viola M. Kanatz, Exec. Dir.
St. Paul, Minnesota 55101   predecessor established: 1955
            reconstituted: 1961, 1967
            1965–1967 budget: $160,690
            1967–1969 budget: $401,660
            (requested)

Minn. Stat. Ann., *as amended* (Supp. 1967).

The Department, Commissioner, and Board
established   sec. 363.04
jurisdiction over employment, real property, financing of real property, and public accommodations   sec. 363.06 subdiv. 1
duties of commissioner of human rights   sec. 363.05
procedure   secs. 363.06, -.07
judicial enforcement, review   secs. 363.072, -.091
local commissions   secs. 363.115, -.116

Employment (Covers employers of one or more persons, the state, political subdivisions, labor organizations, and employment agencies; covers discrimination on account of race, color, creed, religion, or national origin.)
definitions   secs. 363.01 subdivs. 4–5, 15;
            363.02
unlawful practices   sec. 363.03 subdiv. 1

Real Property (Covers any real property transaction except one involving rental of part of two-family, owner-occupied house or of room of one-family, owner-occupied house; covers discrimination on account of race, color, creed, religion, or national origin; also covers real estate brokers, salesmen, and their employees.)
definitions   secs. 363.01 subdivs. 12–13;
            363.02 subdiv. 2
unlawful practices   sec. 363.03 subdiv. 2

Financing of Real Property (Covers any form of financial service; covers discrimination on account of race, color, creed, religion, or national origin.)
definitions   sec. 363.01 subdiv. 18
unlawful practices   sec. 363.03 subdiv. 3

Public Accommodations (Covers wide spectrum of public accommodations; covers discrimination on account of race, color, religion, or national origin.)
definitions   sec. 363.01 subdiv. 18

unlawful practices	sec. 363.03 subdiv. 3

Public Services (Covers any service rendered by any public agency operated by the state or a political subdivision; covers discrimination on account of race, color, creed, religion, or national origin.)

definitions	sec. 363.01 subdiv. 20
unlawful practices	sec. 363.03 subdiv. 4

Education (Covers any public or private educational institutions except religious institutions; covers discrimination on account of race, color, creed, religion, or national origin.)

definitions	sec. 363.01 subdiv. 20
unlawful practices	sec. 363.03 subdiv. 5

---

16. Missouri: Commission on Human Rights (members: 11)

P. O. Box 1129   Peter C. Robertson, Exec. Dir.
Jefferson City, Missouri 65101   (on leave)
                                     Richard E. Risk, Acting Exec. Dir.
                                     established: 1961
                                     1965–1966 budget: $164,812
                                     1966–1967 budget: $217,746

Mo. Rev. Stat., *as amended* (Supp. 1967).

The Commission

established	sec. 213.020
jurisdiction over employment and	
public accommodations	sec. 213.030
powers and duties	secs. 296.030; 314.050
procedure	secs. 296.040; 314.060, -.070
judicial enforcement, review	secs. 296.050; 314.070

Employment (Covers employers of twenty-five or more persons, the state, political subdivisions, employment agencies, and labor organizations; covers discrimination on account of race, color, creed, religion, ancestry, national origin, or sex.)

definitions	sec. 296.010
unlawful practices	sec. 206.020

Public Accommodations (Covers public accommodations generally and specific public accommodations; covers discrimination on account of race, color, creed, religion, ancestry, or national origin.)

definitions	secs. 314.020, -.040
unlawful practices	sec. 314.030

---

17. Nebraska: Equal Employment Opportunity Commission
     (members: 7)

c/o Chairman
227 No. 9th St.   established: 1965
Lincoln, Nebraska 68501   1966 budget: not available
Neb. Rev. Stat., *as amended* (Supp. 1967).

The Commission

established	sec. 48-1116

jurisdiction over employment   secs. 48-1101, -1117(a)
powers and duties   sec. 48-1117
procedure   secs. 48-1118, -1119
judicial enforcement, review   sec. 48-1120
   Employment (Covers employers of twenty-five or more employees [after July 2, 1968] but excluding a bona fide private membership club, employment agencies, and labor organizations; covers discrimination on account of race, color, religion, national origin, or sex.)
definitions   secs. 48-1102, -1103
unlawful practices   secs. 48-1104 to -1115
   Public Accommodations (Judicially enforced only.)
unlawful practices   sec. 20-101

---

18.   Nevada: Commission on Equal Rights of Citizens (members: 5)
215 East Bonanza Rd.   James H. Anderson, Exec. Sec.
Las Vegas, Nevada 89101   established: 1961
                                      reconstituted: 1965
                                      1965–1967 budget: $18,400
Nev. Rev. Stat., *as amended* (Supp. 1967).
   The Commission
established   secs. 233.030 to -.050
jurisdiction over employment and
   public accommodations   secs. 613.410, 651.110
powers and duties   secs. 233.060, -.080, 613.410, 651.110
procedure   secs. 233.070, 613.410, -.430, 651.110
civil action by commission to en-
   force statute   secs. 613.420, 651.110
local commissions   sec. 651.100
   Employment (Covers employers of fifteen or more employees, employment agencies, and labor organizations; covers discrimination on account of race, color, religion, national origin, or sex.)
definitions   secs. 613.310, -.350 to -.400
unlawful practices   sec. 613.330
   Public Accommodations (Covers only a few specified public accommodations; covers discrimination on account of race, color, religion, or national origin.)
definitions   secs. 651.050, -.060
unlawful practices   sec. 651.110

---

19.   New Hampshire: Commission for Human Rights (members: 5)
State House   Richard W. Day, Chrm.
Concord, New Hampshire 03301   established: 1965
                                      1967–1968 budget: $2,500
N.H. Rev. Stat. Ann. (1966).
   The Commission
established   sec. 354-A:4
jurisdiction over employment, hous-

ing, and public accommodations   sec. 354-A:7 VI
powers and duties   secs. 354-A:5–7
procedure   sec. 354-A:9
judicial enforcement, review   sec. 354-A:10

Employment (Covers employers of six or more persons, the state, political subdivisions, employment agencies, and labor organizations; covers discrimination on account of race, color, or national origin.)
definitions   sec. 354-A:3(2)–(6)
unlawful practices   sec. 354-A:8 I–III

Real Property (Covers all housing transactions except rentals in owner-occupied housing with three or less units and rentals of rooms in owner-occupied housing accommodations; covers discrimination on account of race, color, creed, national origin.)
definitions   sec. 354-A:3(10–11)
unlawful practices   sec. 354-A:8 V

Public Accommodations (Covers very few public accommodations; covers discrimination on account of race, color, creed, or national origin.)
definitions   sec. 354-A:3(9)
unlawful practices   sec. 354-A:8 IV

---

20. New Jersey: State Division of Civil Rights, Department of Law and Public Safety

175 West State Street   George S. Pfaus, Dir.
Newark, New Jersey 08608   established: 1945
   1966 budget: $250,146

N.J. Stat. Ann., *as amended* (Supp. 1967).

The Commission
established   sec. 18: 25-6, -7
jurisdiction over employment, housing, financing of real property, public accommodations, and education   sec. 18: 25-9.1
powers and duties   sec. 18: 25-8, -10, -18
procedure   sec. 18: 25-13 to -17
judicial enforcement, review   sec. 18: 25-19 to -21

Employment (Covers employers of one or more persons, the state, political subdivisions, employment agencies, and labor organizations; covers discrimination on account of race, color, creed, ancestry, national origin, age, or liability for service in armed forces of the United States.)
definitions   sec. 18: 25-5 b–g
unlawful practices   sec. 18: 25-12 a–d

Real Property (Covers all housing transactions except rentals of apartments in owner-occupied, two-family houses and of rooms in owner-occupied, one-family houses; covers real estate broker and salesmen transactions; covers discrimination on account of race, color, creed, ancestry, or national origin.)
definitions   sec. 18: 25-5 m–p

unlawful practices   sec. 18: 25-12 g–h
Financing of Real Property (Covers any person or "other financial institution"; covers discrimination on account of race, color, creed, ancestry, or national origin.)
definitions   sec. 18:25-5 n
practices   sec. 18: 25-12 i
Public Accommodations (Covers fairly wide range of public accommodations, including educational institutions under jurisdiction of State Board of Education or Commissioner of Education.)
definitions   sec. 18: 25-5 l
unlawful practices   sec. 18: 25-12 f

---

21. New Mexico: Fair Employment Practices Commission (members: 5)
173 E. De Vargas St.   John F. Otero, Dir.
Santa Fe, New Mexico 87501   established: 1949
                                       1965–1966 budget: $3,000
                                       1966–1967 budget: $27,295
                                            (requested)

N.M. Stat. Ann. (1960).
The Commission
established   sec. 59-4-6
jurisdiction over employment   sec. 59-4-8(f)
powers and duties   secs. 59-4-7, -8, -9
procedure   sec. 59-4-10
judicial enforcement, review   sec. 59-4-11
Employment (Covers employers of four or more persons, the state, political subdivisions, employment agencies, and labor organizations; covers discrimination on account of race, color, religious creed, ancestry, or national origin.)
definitions   sec. 59-4-3
unlawful practices   sec. 59-4-4
Public Accommodations (Judicially enforced only.)
unlawful practices   secs. 49-8-1 to -7

---

22. New York: State Commission for Human Rights (members: 9)
270 Broadway   George H. Fowler, Chairman
New York City, New York 10007   Jesse Kleinman, Exec. Dir.
                                       established: 1945
                                       1965 budget: $1,693,010
N.Y. Law, *as amended* (McKinney Supp. 1967).
The Commission
established   Exec. Law, secs. 293, 293a
jurisdiction over employment, real
   property, financing of real property, public accommodations, ed-
   ucation   Exec. Law, sec. 295.6(a)
powers and duties   Exec. Law, secs. 294, 295

procedure   Exec. Law, sec. 297
judicial enforcement, review   Exec. Law, sec. 298
local commissions   Gen. Munic. Law, sec. 239 o–t
Commissioner of Education and Board of Regents
jurisdiction over education   Educ. Law, sec. 313(5)
powers and duties   Educ. Law, sec. 313(7)–(8), (5)(g)
procedure   Educ. Law, sec. 313
judicial enforcement, review   Educ. Law, sec. 313(6)

Employment (Covers employers of four or more persons, the state, political subdivisions, employment agencies, and labor organizations; covers discrimination on account of race, color, creed, national origin, sex, or age [40–65].)
definitions   Exec. Law, sec. 292
unlawful practices   Exec. Law, sec. 296.1, -.1a, -.3a

Real Property (Covers transactions involving publicly assisted housing accommodations, all housing except rental of units in owner-occupied two-family dwellings and of rooms in dwelling by occupants, and commercial space; covers discrimination on account of race, color, creed, or national origin.)
definitions   Civil Rights Law, sec. 18-b
                                        Exec. Law, sec. 292.10–15
unlawful practices   Civil Rights Law, sec. 18-c
                                        Exec. Law, sec. 296.3, -5(a)–(c)

Financing of Real Property (Covers any person or "other financial institution or lender" relative to financing of transactions concerning any housing accommodation or commercial space; covers discrimination on account of race, color, creed, or national origin.)
definitions   Exec. Law, sec. 292.10, -.13
unlawful practices   Exec. Law, sec. 296.5(d)

Public Accommodations (Covers only specific places, but quite a number are listed; covers discrimination on account of race, creed, color, or national origin.)
definitions   Exec. Law, sec. 292.9
unlawful practices   Exec. Law, sec. 296.2

Education (Administered by the Commission; covers any educational corporation or association holding itself out to public to be nonsectarian and exempt from taxation; covers discrimination on account of race, color, or religion.)
definitions   Exec. Law, sec. 292
unlawful practices   Exec. Law, sec. 296.4

Education (Administered by Commissioner of Education and Board of Regents; covers any educational institution of post-secondary grade and any business or trade school subject to jurisdiction of Commissioner of Education or Board of Regents; covers discrimination on account of race, color, creed, or religion.)
definitions   Educ. Law, sec. 313(2)
unlawful practices   Educ. Law, sec. 313(3)

Associations (Covers discrimination on account of race, creed, color, national origin, or sex by a real estate board with respect to admission of persons to membership.)
unlawful practices   Exec. Law, sec. 296.5(d)

---

23.   Ohio: Civil Rights Commission (members: 5)
24 Parsons Ave., Room 234   Ellis L. Ross, Exec. Dir.
Columbus, Ohio   established: 1959
                                      1966 budget: $211,750
                                      1967 budget: $302,419

Ohio Rev. Code Ann., *as amended* (Supp. 1967).

The Commission
established   sec. 4112.03
jurisdiction over employment, hous-
   ing, financing of housing transactions, and public accommoda-
   tions   sec. 4112.05(A)
powers and duties   sec. 4112.04
procedure   sec. 4112.05
judicial enforcement, review   sec. 4112.06

Employment (Covers employers of four or more persons, the state, political subdivisions, employment agencies, and labor organizations; covers discrimination on account of race, color, religion, ancestry, or national origin.)
definitions   sec. 4112.01(B)–(E)
practices   sec. 4112.02(A)–(F)

Real Property (Covers all housing transactions except sales and rentals of owner-occupied, one- and two-family buildings; covers discrimination on account of race, color, religion, ancestry, or national origin.)
definitions   sec. 4112.01(J)–(M)
unlawful practices   sec. 4112.02(H)–(K)

Financing of Housing Transactions (Covers any lending of money for housing transactions; covers discrimination on account of race, color, religion, ancestry, or national origin.)
definitions   sec. 4112.01(A)
unlawful practices   sec. 4112.02(H)(3)

Public Accommodations (Covers only a few specified public accommodations; covers discrimination on account of race, color, religion, ancestry, or national origin.)
definitions   sec. 4112.01(I)
unlawful practices   sec. 4112.02(G)

---

24.   Oregon: Labor Commissioner, Civil Rights Division, Bureau of Labor
466 State Office Bldg.   Norman D. Nilsen, Commissioner

Portland, Oregon 97201   Mark A. Smith, Administrator
                                 established: 1949
                                 1965–1967 budget: $118,913
                                 1967–1969 budget: $192,666
                                      (requested)

Ore. Rev. Stat. (1965).
  The Division
designated to administer law
  against discrimination   sec. 659.100
jurisdiction over employment, real
  property, public accommodations sec. 659.100
powers and duties   secs. 659.103, -.115
procedure   secs. 659.040, -.060
judicial enforcement, review   secs. 659.070, -.080
  Real Estate Commissioner
designated to administer certain aspects of law against discrimina-
  tion in housing   sec. 696.300(1)(v)
administrative sanction   sec. 696.300(1)

  Employment (Covers employers of six or more persons, the state, designated political subdivisions, employment agencies, and labor organizations; covers discrimination on account of race, color, religion, national
origin, or age [25–65].)
definitions   secs. 659.010(5)–(10), (13)–(14)
unlawful practices   secs. 659.024 to -.030

  Real Property (Covers any person engaged in business of selling, leas-
ing, or renting real property; covers discrimination on account of race,
color, religion, or national origin.)
definitions   secs. 659.010(14), -.031
unlawful practices   sec. 659.033

  Public Accommodations (Covers certain specified public accommodations and then all public accommodations generally; covers discrimination on account of race, color, religion, or national origin.)
definitions   secs. 30.675, 345.240(2)
unlawful practices   secs. 659.037, 659.010(4),
                                       345.240(1)

---

25. Pennsylvania: Human Relations Commission (members: 11)
1401–03 Labor and Industry Bldg.   Elliot M. Shirk, Exec. Dir.
Harrisburg, Pennsylvania 17105   established: 1955
                                   1965 budget: $655,878
                                   1967–1968 budget: $877,631
                                        (requested)

Pa. Stat. Ann., *as amended* (Supp. 1967).
  The Commission
established   tit. 43, sec. 956
jurisdiction over employment,

Employment (Covers employers of six or more persons, the state, political subdivisions, employment agencies, and labor organizations; covers discrimination on account of race, color, religious creed, ancestry, national origin, or age [40–62].)

Real Property (Covers transactions involving housing accommodations offered for sale or rent other than residence of owner; covers discrimination on account of race, color, religion, creed, ancestry, or national origin.)

Financing of Real Property (Covers any person; covers discrimination in financing of housing on account of race, color, religious creed, ancestry or national origin.)

Public Accommodations (Covers public accommodations generally and then specifies certain public accommodations; covers discrimination on account of race, color, religious creed, ancestry, or national origin.)

Education (Covers any post-secondary school; covers discrimination on account of race, color, religious creed, ancestry, or national origin.)

---

26. Rhode Island: Commission against Discrimination (members: 5)
State House Arthur L. Hardge, Exec. Sec.
Providence, R.I. 02903 established: 1949
 1965–1966 budget: $45,119
 1966–1967 budget: $54,224

R.I. Gen. Laws. Ann., *as amended* (Supp. 1967).

The Commission

  Employment (Covers employers of four or more persons, employment
agencies, and labor organizations; covers discrimination on account of
race, color, religion, or country of ancestral origin.)

  Employment (Covers employers of one or more persons, the state, political subdivisions, employment agencies, and labor organizations; covers
discrimination on account of age [45–65].)

  Real Property (Covers all housing transactions except rentals of apartments in owner-occupied, two- and three-family houses and of rooms in
private residences; covers discrimination on account of race, color, religion, or country of ancestral origin.)

  Financing of Real Property (Covers any person; covers discrimination
in financing of housing on account of race, color, religion, or country of
ancestral origin.)

  Public Accommodations (Covers wide range of specified public accommodations; covers discrimination on account of race, color, religion, or
country of ancestral origin.)

---

27. Utah: Anti-Discrimination Division, Industrial Commission of Utah
      (members: 3)

State Capitol, Room 418   M. Phyl Poulson, Exec. Sec.
Salt Lake City, Utah 84114   established: 1965
                                     1965–1967 budget: $51,000
                                     1967–1969 budget: $56,000
Utah Code Ann., 1953 (Replacement Vol. 1966).
  The Division

powers and duties	sec. 34-17-5
procedure	sec. 34-17-7
judicial enforcement, review	sec. 34-17-8

Employment (Covers employers of twenty-five or more persons, the state, political subdivisions, employment agencies, and labor organizations; covers discrimination on account of race, color, religion, ancestry, national origin, or sex.)

definitions	sec. 34-17-2
unlawful practices	sec. 34-17-6

Public Accommodations (Judicially enforced only.)

unlawful practices	sec. 13-7-1–13-7-4

---

28. Vermont: Commission on Human Rights (members: 5)
established: 1967
1967 budget: not available

Vt. Stat. Ann., tit. 13, *as amended* (1967).

The Commission

established	sec. 1461
jurisdiction over public accommodations and real property	sec. 1463(a)
powers and duties	sec. 1462
procedure	secs. 1463–1464
judicial enforcement, review	secs. 1466–1467

Public Accommodations (Covers a broad spectrum of public accommodations; covers discrimination on account of race, creed, color, or national origin.)

definitions	sec. 1451(b)
unlawful practices	sec. 1451(a)

Real Property (Covers all transactions in real property except those involving lease of housing accommodations in owner-occupied, two-family buildings, rental of four or less rooms in owner-occupied family building, and homes for elderly, ill, or disabled operated by religious organizations; covers discrimination on account of race, color, religious creed, or national origin.)

definitions	sec. 1452(a)(1)–(2), -(b)
unlawful practices	sec. 1452(a)

---

29. Washington: State Board against Discrimination (members: 5)
1411 Fourth Ave. Bldg.   Alfred E. Cowles, Exec. Sec.
Seattle, Washington 98101   established: 1949
1965–1967 budget: $152,182
1967–1969 budget: $263,624

Wash. Rev. Code Ann., *as amended* (Supp. 1967).

The Board

established	secs. 49.60.050, -.060
jurisdiction over employment, real property, financing of real prop-	

erty, and public accommodations   sec. 49.60.120(4)
powers and duties   secs. 49.60.070 to -.140
procedure   secs. 49.60.230 to -.255
judicial enforcement, review   secs. 49.60.260 to -.270
  Employment (Covers employers of eight or more persons; employment agencies; and labor organizations; covers discrimination on account of race, color, creed, national origin, or age.)
definitions   sec. 49.60.040 para. 2–5
unlawful practices   secs. 49.60.180 to -.200
  Real Property (Covers publicly assisted housing only; covers discrimination on account of race, creed, color, or national origin.)
definitions   sec. 49.60.040 para. 8–9
unlawful practices   sec. 49.60.217(1)–(4)
special sanctions applicable to real
  estate brokers   sec. 18.85.230
  Financing of Real Property (Covers any person or financial institution relative to transactions concerning publicly assisted housing; covers discrimination in financing of housing on account of race, color, creed, or national origin.)
definitions   sec. 49.60.040
unlawful practices   sec. 49.60.217(5)
  Public Accommodations (Covers wide range of specified public accommodations including educational institutions; covers discrimination on account of race, color, creed, or national origin.)
definitions   sec. 49.60.040 para. 7
unlawful practices   secs. 49.60.215 to -.216, -.175

---

30. West Virginia: Human Rights Commission (members: 9)
W-202 State Capitol Bldg.   Carl W. Glatt, Exec. Dir.
Charleston, W. Va. 25305   established: 1961
                                     reconstituted: 1967
                                     1967 budget: not available
W. Va. Code, *as amended* (Supp. 1967).
  The Commission
designated to administer the
  human-rights act   sec. 5-11-4
jurisdiction over employment and
  public accommodations   sec. 5-11-4
powers and duties   sec. 5-11-8
procedure   sec. 5-11-10
judicial enforcement   sec. 5-11-11
local commissions and exclusiveness
  of remedy   sec. 5-11-12
  Employment (Covers employers of twenty-five or more persons, the state, political subdivisions, employment agencies, and labor organizations; covers discrimination on account of race, color, religion, national origin, or ancestry.)

definitions   sec. 5-11-3(d)–(i)
unlawful practices   sec. 5-11-9(a)–(e), (g)
   Public Accommodations (Covers broad spectrum of public accommodations; covers discrimination on account of race, color, religion, national
origin, or ancestry.)
definitions   sec. 5-11-3(i)–(j)
unlawful practices   sec. 5-11-9(f)

---

31. Wisconsin: Equal Opportunities Division, Industrial Commission
       (members: 3)
819 North 6th St.   Joseph C. Fagan, Chairman
Milwaukee, Wisconsin 53203   Virginia Huebner, Dir.
                                     Walter S. Zetlau, Asst. Dir.
                                     established: 1945
                                     1965–1967 budget: $168,455
                                     1967–1969 budget: $329,999
                                          (proposed)

Wis. Stat. Ann. (Supp. 1968).
   The Division
designated to administer law
   against discrimination   sec. 111.33
jurisdiction over employment, hous-
   ing, and financing of housing   sec. 101.60(3)
power and duties   secs. 111.34 to -.35, 101.60(4)
procedure   sec. 111.36
judicial enforcement, review   secs. 111.36(3), -.37, 101.60(5)
   Employment (Covers employers of one or more persons, employment
agencies, and labor organizations; covers discrimination on account of
race, color, creed, ancestry, national origin, age [40–65], sex, or handicap.)
definitions   sec. 111.32
unlawful practices   sec. 111.36
   Real Property (Covers transactions involving all residential property
except one-family, owner-occupied houses, owner-occupied apartment
houses with four or less units, and owner-occupied rooming houses with
four or less units; covers discrimination on account of race, religion,
ancestry, or national origin.)
definitions   sec. 101.60(1)
unlawful practices   sec. 101.60(2)(a), (b), (d)
   Financing of Real Property (Covers financing of transactions relative to
residential property lots or home construction; covers discrimination on
account of race, color, religion, ancestry, or national origin.)
definitions   sec. 101.60(1)(c)
unlawful practices   sec. 101.60(2)
   Governor's Commission on Human Rights (Has jurisdiction to investigate discrimination in public accommodations and to seek to eliminate it
by conciliation only.)
created   sec. 15.85

Public Accommodations (Judicially enforced only.)
unlawful practices   sec. 942.04

---

32.   Wyoming: Fair Employment Commission (members: 3)
304 Capitol Bldg.   established: 1965
Cheyenne, Wyoming 82001   1967 budget: no appropriation
Wyom. Stat. Ann. (Supp. 1965).
   The Commission
established   sec. 27-259
jurisdiction over employment   sec. 27-260(3)
powers and duties   sec. 27-260
procedure   sec. 27-262
judicial enforcement, review   sec. 27-263, -264
   Employment (Covers employers of two or more persons, the state, political subdivisions, employment agencies, and labor organizations; covers
discrimination on account of race, color, creed, ancestry, national origin,
or sex.)
definitions   sec. 27-258
unlawful practices   sec. 27-261
   Public Accommodations (Judicially enforced only.)
unlawful practices   sec. 6-83.1

---

33.   District of Columbia: Commissioner's Council on Human Relations
      (members: 11)
208 District Bldg.   Paul M. Rilling, Exec. Dir.
14th and E Sts., N.W.   Ruth B. Harris, Assoc. Exec. Dir.
Washington, D.C. 20004   established: 1961
                                       1967 budget: $63,639
                                       1967 Foundation grant: 15,000
                                                               $78,639
D.C. Code, 1967 ed., tit. 1 App., Org. Ord. No. 125, 1961, *as amended*; D.C.
Police Regulations, Ord. No. 65-768, 1965, Art. 47.
   Commission
established   D.C. Code, tit. 1, Org. Ord. No. 125
jurisdiction over employment   D.C. Police Regs., Art. 47, sec. 6
powers and duties   ″   ″   ″   ″   ″ sec. 7
procedure   ″   ″   ″   ″   ″ secs. 6,
                                       8–9
judicial review, enforcement   ″   ″   ″   ″   ″ secs. 9–10
   Employment
definitions   D.C. Police Regs, Art. 47, secs. 2–3
unlawful practices   ″   ″   ″   ″   ″ sec. 4

Appendix B

State Human-Relations Commissions or Similar Agencies Operating under Statutes or Executive Orders without Authority to Enforce Civil-Rights Law through Issuance of Orders Enforceable in the Courts

1. Arizona: Arizona Civil Rights Commission

Philip S. Malinsky, Exec. Dir.   1966–1967 budget: $40,062
1623 West Washington St.
Phoenix; 85007

Arizona Rev. Stat. Ann., §§ 41-1401 to -1483 (Supp. 1967).

Jurisdiction over discrimination in employment, public accommodations, and voting rights. While statute prohibits this discrimination, it is enforced through criminal sanctions in actions before a justice of the peace on complaint of the aggrieved party.

---

2. Delaware: Division against Discrimination, Department of Labor and Industrial Relations

C. Robert Burns, Div. Chief
506 W. 10th St.
Wilmington; 19801

Del. Code Ann., tit. 19 §§ 710–713, 106, 125, *as amended* (Supp. 1966).

Jurisdiction over discrimination in employment. While statute prohibits this discrimination, it is enforced through criminal sanctions in court actions brought by the state attorney general on request of the Division.

---

3. Maine: Commissioner of Labor and Industry

Marion E. Martin, Comm.
Augusta; 04330

Me. Rev. Stat. Ann., tit. 26, §§ 861–864 (Supp. 1967).

Jurisdiction over discrimination in employment. While statute prohibits this discrimination, it is enforced through criminal sanctions only.

4. Oklahoma: Oklahoma Human Rights Commission
William Y. Rose, Dir.
State Capitol, Rm. 221
Oklahoma City; 73105

Okla. Stat. Ann., tit. 74, §§ 951–954 (1965).	Jurisdiction over any form of discrimination on the basis of race, color, creed, ancestry, or national origin. Statute only prohibits discrimination in employment by a state agency and is enforced not by the Commission but by the State Personnel Board.

5. Tennessee: Tennessee Commission for Human Development

Cornelius Jones, Exec. Dir. 305 Cordell Hull Bldg. Nashville Tenn. Code Ann., §§ 4-2102 to 2105 (1967).	Has general functions of promoting better human relations, assisting local human-relations commissions, conducting studies of human-relations problems, and making reports on studies.

Appendix C

A Selected List of Local Human-Relations Commissions Operating under Ordinances or Laws Giving Them Authority to Enforce Prohibitions against Discrimination, as Well as Other Authority

1. Baltimore, Maryland: Community Relations Commission
    (members: 10, staff: yes)

Samuel T. Daniels, Dir.
210 N. Calvert St.; 21202

established: 1956
reconstituted: 1964
1966–1967 budget: $117,864

Baltimore Code, Art. 14A; *Race Relations Law Reporter*, Vol. 9 (1964–1965), p. 354.

Jurisdiction over employment, public accommodations, city services, and education.

---

2. Chicago, Illinois: Commission on Human Relations (members: 15, staff: yes)

Edward Marciniak, Exec. Dir.
211 W. Wacker Dr.; 60606

established: 1943
reconstituted: 1947
1965 budget: $386,540

Chicago Municipal Code, chs. 21, 137, 198. 7A–B, 199.

Jurisdiction over employment (city contracts), housing, city services, hospital services, and public accommodations.

---

3. Cleveland, Ohio: Community Relations Board (members: 17, staff: yes)

Bertram E. Gardner, Exec. Dir.
Stanley J. Lechowic, Asst. Exec. Dir.
211 Cts. Building
1404 E. Ninth St.; 44114
Ordinance No. 1479-48, *Labor Relations Reference Manual*, Vol. 25 (1950), p. 3030.

established: 1945
1967 budget: $93,427

Jurisdiction over employment.

---

4. Corpus Christi, Texas: Human Relations Committee (members: 9)

Charles J. McManus, Admin. and
   Ass't City Att'y
City Hall; 78403

established: 1963
1967 budget: no separate item

Ordinance 7053 (1963); Ordinance 7421 (1964), *Race Relations Law Reporter,* Vol. 10 (1965–1966), p. 1897.

Jurisdiction over public accommodations.

---

5. Des Moines, Iowa: Commission on Human Rights (members: 9, staff: yes)

Perry W. Hooks, Exec. Dir.
Armory Bldg.
E. 1st and Des Moines Sts.; 50309
Ordinance (1956) *Race Relations Law Reporter,* Vol. 2 (1957–1958), p. 225; Ordinance 7079 (1964), *id.,* Vol. 9 (1964–1965), p. 990; Ordinance 7362 (1966), *id.,* Vol. 12 (1967–1968), p. 488.

predecessor established: 1951
reconstituted: 1954
1966 budget: $36,586
Jurisdiction over employment and housing.

---

6. Detroit, Michigan: Commission on Community Relations (members: 15, staff: yes)

Richard V. Marks, Sec.-Dir.
Joseph C. Coles, Asst. Dir.
150 Mich. Ave., 4th fl.; 48226
Ordinance 19-1963, *Race Relations Law Reporter,* Vol. 8 (1963–1964), p. 1666.

established: 1944
reconstituted: 1953
1966–1967 budget: $248,513
Jurisdiction over employment, housing, and public accommodations.

---

7. Duluth, Minnesota: Fair Employment and Housing Practices Commission (members: 5, staff: yes)

Mrs. Benjamin F. Cornelius, Exec. Sec.
City Hall; 55802
Ordinance (1953), *Labor Relations Reference Manual,* Vol. 33 (1954), p. 3012; Ordinance (1956); Ordinance 7260 (1963), U.S. Housing and Home Finance Agency, *Fair Housing Legislation* (Washington, D.C.: U.S. Government Printing Office, Sept., 1964), p. 270.

established: 1953
reconstituted: 1956
1966 budget: $984
Jurisdiction over employment and housing.

---

8. Erie, Pennsylvania: Community Relations Commission (members: 11, staff: yes)

Leonard L. Karter, Exec. Dir.
508 Municipal Bldg.; 16501
Ordinance 19-1963, *Race Relations Law Reporter,* Vol. 8 (1963–1964), p. 1666.

established: 1954
1967 budget: $31,630
Jurisdiction over employment, public accommodations, and housing.

9. Gary, Indiana: Commission on Human Relations (members: 15, staff: yes)

Charles H. King, Jr., Exec. Dir.	predecessor established: 1950
City Hall; 46402	reconstituted: 1964
	1967 budget: $60,120
Gary Municipal Code §§ 7-103, -104	Jurisdiction over employment, hous-
(1960); Ordinance 4050 (1965),	ing, and home financing.
Race Relations Law Reporter, Vol.	
10 (1965–1966), p. 906.	

10. Indianapolis, Indiana: Commission on Human Rights (members: 25, staff: yes)

J. Griffin Crump, Exec. Dir.	established: 1960
1742 City-County Bldg.; 46204	1967 budget: $32,665
Ordinance (1964)	Jurisdiction over housing.

11. Kalamazoo, Michigan: Department of Human Relations (staff: yes)

Edward E. Ferguson, Exec. Dir.	established: 1957
241 West South St.; 49006	1967 budget: $15,384
Ordinance 750 (1966), *Race Rela-*	Jurisdiction over housing.
tions Law Reporter, Vol. 11 (1966–	
1967), p. 1580.	

12. Kansas City, Kansas: Commission on Human Relations (members: 15, staff: yes)

Todd H. Pavela, Exec. Dir.	established: 1962
805 N. 6th St.; 66101	1966 budget: $16,300
Ordinance 43510 (1962) and Ordi-	Jurisdiction over employment (city
nance 44155 (1963), *Race Relations*	contracts) and public accommoda-
Law Reporter, Vol. 8 (1963–1964),	tions.
p. 1682; Ordinance (1966) amend-	
ing §§ 2-209, -210, -212 to -219 of	
the Kansas City Code of Ordinances.	

13. Kansas City, Missouri: Advisory Commission on Human Relations (members: 7, staff: yes)

Robert W. MacNeven, Exec. Dir.	established: 1960
City Hall, 26th fl.; 64106	1967 budget: $32,606
Ordinance 31118 (1965) adding	Jurisdiction over employment (city
Art. XXXIV to K.C., Mo. Adminis-	contractors and city franchise hold-
trative Code, *Race Relations Law*	ers), public accommodations, and
Reporter, Vol. 10 (1965–1966), p.	housing.
925 (administered by contract offi-	
cer); Ordinance 24250 (1960), add-	
ing § 39-26 to K.C., Mo. Rev. Ordi-	
nances, *id.*, Vol. 5 (1960–1961), p.	

248; Pub. Accom. Ordinance
(1963), adding §§ 39-262 to -269 to
K.C., Mo. Rev. Ordinances, *id.*, Vol.
8 (1963–1964), p. 1684; Ordinance
(1967), *New York Times* (July 22,
1967), p. 10, col. 7.

---

14.   Lexington and Fayette County, Kentucky: Commission on Human
      Rights (members: 15, staff: yes)
George E. Shinert, Exec. Dir.   established: 1963
City Hall Annex   1966 budget: $21,536
227 North Upper St.
Lexington; 40507
New York Times (August 2, 1967),   Jurisdiction over housing.
p. 16, col. 7.

---

15.   Louisville and Jefferson County, Kentucky: Human Relations Com-
      mission (members: 11, staff: yes)
J. Mansir Tydings, Exec. Dir.   established: 1962
3 City Hall   1964 budget: $29,987
Louisville; 40202
Ordinance No. 23 (1965), *Race*   Jurisdiction over employment, pub-
Relations Law Reporter, Vol. 10   lic accommodations, and housing.
(1965–1966), p. 913; Ordinance No.
231 (1963), *id.*, Vol. 8 (1963–1964),
p. 719; Ordinance No. 192 (1965),
Louisville Human Relations Commission, *Third Annual Report*
(1965–1966), p. 13.

---

16.   Madison, Wisconsin: Equal Opportunities Commission (members: 9,
      staff: yes)
James Stern, Sec.   established: 1964
413 City-County Bldg.; 53709   1967 budget: $10,335
Ordinance 1568, *Race Relations*   Jurisdiction over employment, hous-
Law Reporter, Vol. 8 (1963–1964),   ing, public accommodations, and
p. 1672; Ordinance 1997 (1966).   city facilities.

---

17.   a.   Minneapolis, Minnesota: Fair Employment Practices Commis-
           sion (members: 5, staff: yes)
Louis H. Ervin, Exec. Dir.   established: 1947
51 Public Health Center   1967 budget: $19,060
250 South 4th St.; 55415
Ordinance (1947), as amended,   Jurisdiction over employment.
Labor Relations Reference Manual,
Vol. 28 (1951), p. 3087.

b.   Minneapolis, Minnesota: Mayor's Commission on Human Relations

Ordinance 89-33 (1963), *Race Relations Law Reporter*, Vol. 8 (1963–1964), p. 1651.

No enforcement powers, but authority to seek settlement of complaints concerning discrimination in employment, public services, and education.

---

18.   Montgomery County, Maryland: Commission on Human Relations
      (members: 9, staff: yes)

S. W. Parrish, Exec. Sec.
County Office Bldg.
Rockville; 20850
Ordinance 2-120 (1962), *Race Relations Law Reporter*, Vol. 7 (1962–1963), p. 263; *New York Times* (July 21, 1967), p. 35, col. 2.

established: 1962
1964 budget: $550

Jurisdiction over public accommodations and housing.

---

19.   New Haven, Connecticut: Commission on Equal Opportunities
      (members: 7, staff: yes)

Richard Belford, Exec. Dir.
John C. Daniels, Deputy Dir.
147 Court St.; 06510
Equal Opportunities Ordinance (1964), *Race Relations Law Reporter*, Vol. 9 (1964–1965), p. 1877.

established: 1964
1967 budget: $48,715

Jurisdiction over employment, housing, and public accommodations.

---

20.   New York City, New York: Commission on Human Rights (members: 15, staff: yes)

William B. Booth, Chairman (salaried)
80 Lafayette St.; 10013
Local Law (1965) amending title B and repealing titles C and D of Ch. 1 of N.Y. City Administrative Code, *Race Relations Law Reporter*, Vol. 11 (1966–1967), p. 467.

established: 1955
1966–1967 budget: $716,165

Jurisdiction over employment, housing, commercial space, public accommodations, and financing of real property.

---

21.   Oklahoma City, Oklahoma: Community Relations Commission
      (members: 9, staff: yes)

Orra G. Compton, Exec. Dir.
Municipal Center Bldg.
331 W. Main; 73102
Ordinance 10,539 (1964), *Race Relations Law Reporter*, Vol. 9 (1964–1965), p. 998.

established: 1964
1966–1967 budget: $27,015

Jurisdiction over public accommodations.

22. Omaha, Nebraska: Human Relations Department (staff: yes)

Joe N. Williams, Exec. Dir.
Interim City Hall, 4th fl.
18th and Dodge Sts.; 68102
Home Rule Charter of City of
Omaha (1956); Ordinance (1962),
adding title 14 to Omaha Munic.
Code, *Race Relations Law Reporter,*
Vol. 7 (1962–1963), p. 600.

established: 1956
reconstituted: 1965
1967 budget: $25,346
Jurisdiction over employment.

23. Peoria, Illinois: Commission on Human Relations (members: 21, staff: yes)

Valeska S. Hinton, Exec. Dir.
404 City Hall Bldg.; 61602

App. D, Peoria Munic. Code, *Race
Relations Law Reporter*, Vol. 9
(1964–1965), p. 1885.

predecessor established: 1942
reconstituted: 1961
1966 budget: $11,319
Jurisdiction over housing.

24. Philadelphia, Pennsylvania: Human Relations Commission (members: 9, staff: yes)

Terry C. Chisholm, Exec. Dir.
Larry Groth, Deputy Dir.
601 City Hall Annex; 19107
Bill No. 2256 (1963), *Race Relations Law Reporter*, Vol. 8 (1963–
1964), p. 1203.

established: 1948
1967 budget: $448,669

Jurisdiction over employment, housing, and public accommodations.

25. Pittsburgh, Pennsylvania: Commission on Human Relations (members: 5, staff: yes)

David V. Washington, Exec. Dir.
908 City-County Bldg.; 15219

Omnibus Ordinance (February 28,
1967).

established: 1946
1964 budget: $99,018
additional 1967 funds for
government-contract-compliance
investigation and police
training: $63,000
Jurisdiction over employment, housing, and public accommodations.

26. Phoenix, Arizona: Human Relations Commission (members: 15, staff: yes)

Henry A. Cabirac, Jr., Exec. Dir.
135 N. 2nd Ave., Suite 315; 85003
Resolution No. 11461 (1963); Ordinance G-587 (1964).

established: 1963
1967–1968 budget: $67,721
Jurisdiction over public accommodations.

27. Rockville, Maryland: Human Relations Commission (members: 7, staff: yes)

Bernard L. Tetreault, Exec. Dir.
111 South Perry St.; 20850
Ordinances 43-64 and 44-64, *Race Relations Law Reporter*, Vol. 9 (1964–1965), pp. 1881, 1895.

established: 1964
1967–1968 budget: $14,000
Jurisdiction over public accommodations.

28. St. Louis, Missouri: City Council on Human Relations (members: 15, staff: yes)

William J. Decatur, Exec. Dir.
200 Municipal Courts Bldg.; 63103
Ordinance 45184 (1950); Ordinance 50151 (1962), *Race Relations Law Reporter*, Vol. 7 (1962–1963), p. 1257; Ordinance 50553 (1961), *id.*, Vol. 6 (1961–1962), p. 881; Ordinance 52328 (1964), *id.*, Vol. 9 (1964–1965), p. 372.

established: 1950
1967–1968 budget: $51,715
Jurisdiction over employment, housing, and public accommodations.

29. St. Paul, Minnesota: Human and Civil Rights Commission (members: 11; staff: yes)

1745 City Hall; 55802

established: 1955
reconstituted: 1964
1964 budget: $29,000

Ordinance 10456 (1955), *Race Relations Law Reporter*, Vol. 2 (1957–1958), p. 702; Ordinance (1964), *id.*, Vol. 9 (1964–1965), p. 1481.

Jurisdiction over employment, housing, public accommodations, education, and public services.

30. San Antonio, Texas: Community Relations Commission (members: 15, staff: yes)

City Hall
Post Office Box 9066; 78204
Resolution (1964); Ordinances 33863 (1965) and 34383 (1966).

established: 1964
1966–1967 budget: $12,000
Jurisdiction over public accommodations. Only criminal sanctions.

31. San Francisco, California: Human Rights Commission (members: 15, staff: yes)

William Becker, Exec. Dir.
1254 Market St., Suite 305; 94102

predecessor established: 1957
reconstituted: 1964
1966–1967 budget: $209,379

Ordinance No. 209-64 (1964), *Race Relations Law Reporter*, Vol. 9 (1964–1965), p. 1489; Ordinance (1966).

Jurisdiction over neighborhood practices and employment (city contracts).

32. South Bend, Indiana: Human Relations and Fair Employment Practices Commission (members: 9, staff: yes)

George V. Neagu, Exec. Dir.	established: 1956
226 West Colfax Ave.; 46601	reconstituted: 1965
	1967 budget: $20,280
Ordinance 4820 (1965).	Jurisdiction over employment.

33. Springfield, Illinois: Human Relations Commission (members: 21, staff: yes)

Farries H. Morrison, Jr., Exec. Dir.	established: 1948
202 Municipal Bldg.; 62701	reconstituted: 1954
Ordinance (1964).	Jurisdiction over employment, housing, and public accommodations.

34. Toledo, Ohio: Board of Community Relations (members: 25; staff: yes)

G. Nelson Smith, Exec. Dir.	established: 1946
Ted S. Cooper, Assoc. Dir.	1967 budget: $50,000
565 North Erie St.; 43624	1967 federal funds administered for youth program: $500,000
Toledo Mun. Code, Art. XLI, *Labor Relations Reference Manual*, Vol. 35 (1955), p. 137; Ordinance (1963), U.S. Housing and Home Finance Agency, *Fair Housing Legislation* (Washington, D.C.: U.S. Government Printing Office, September, 1964, p. 299; Ordinance (1967).	Jurisdiction over employment, housing, and neighborhood practices.

35. Tulsa, Oklahoma: Community Relations Commission (members: 9, staff: yes)

Lois H. Gatchell, Exec. Dir.	established: 1961
613 Kennedy Bldg.; 74103	1966–1967 budget: $16,561
Ordinance (1964), *Race Relations Law Reporter*, Vol. 9 (1964–1965), p. 1001.	Jurisdiction over public accommodations.

36. Youngstown, Ohio: Mayor's Human Relations Commission and Fair Employment Practices Committee (members: 7, staff: yes)

J. Ronald Pittman, Exec. Dir.	established: 1950
City Hall; 45503	1967 budget: $20,015
	federal funds for on-the-job training program in 1966–1967: $144,351
Ordinance (1950), *Labor Relations Reference Manual*, Vol. 27 (1950), p. 3039; Ordinance (1967).	Jurisdiction over employment and housing.

Appendix D

A Selected List of Local Human-Relations Agencies Which Have Principally Operated without Enforcement Authority

See Charles S. Rhyne and Brice W. Rhyne, *Civil Rights Ordinances* (Washington, D.C.: National Institute of Municipal Law Officers, 1963); George L. Schermer, *Guidelines: A Manual for Bi-Racial Committees* (New York: Anti-Defamation League of B'nai B'rith, 1964); and *Race Relations Law Reporter*, Vols. 1–12 (1956–1967), for examples of ordinances employed by these cities.

1. Atlanta, Georgia: Community Relations Commission (members: 14, staff: yes)

Eliza K. Paschall, Exec. Dir.
1203 City Hall; 30303

established: 1966
1967 budget: $25,000

---

2. Austin, Texas: Human Relations Commission (members: 15, staff: yes)

City Hall; 78701

predecessors established: 1964, 1966
established: 1967
1966 budget (for private-corporation predecessor): $25,000

---

3. Buffalo, New York: Department of Community Relations (members: 35, staff: yes)

Sidney Harris, Exec. Dir.
1502 City Hall; 14202

established: 1945
1966–1967 budget: $78,945

---

4. Cambridge, Massachusetts: Civic Unity Committee (members: 9, staff: yes)

Zoya Slive, Exec. Dir.
57 Inman St.; 02139

established: 1945
1967 budget: $10,000

---

5. Cincinnati, Ohio: Human Relations Commission (members: 9, staff: yes)

Clinton L. Reynolds, Acting Exec. Dir.
158 City Hall; 45202
The Cincinnati ordinance designating this corporation as a city agent is found in *Race Relations Law Reporter*, Vol. 10 (1965–1966), p. 911.

predecessor established: 1945
reconstituted: 1965
1967 budget: $69,700
This is a nonprofit private corporation designated to investigate and conciliate disputes concerning discrimination. Only a few cities

which have experimented with this device have retained it. Austin, Texas, is a recent example of a city abandoning its use.

---

6. Dayton, Ohio: Human Relations Council (members: 17, staff: yes)
Edward A. King, Exec. Dir.   established: 1963
11 West Monument Bldg.; 45402   1967 budget: $35,087

---

7. Denver, Colorado: Commission on Community Relations (members: 15, staff: yes)
Helen L. Peterson, Exec. Dir.   established: 1948
Richard I. Peterson, Consultant   reconstituted: 1959
260 West Side Annex Bldg.   1967 budget: $79,900
West Colfax at Kalamata; 80204

The Commission has subpoena power.

---

8. Evansville, Indiana: Mayor's Commission on Human Relations (members: 62, staff: yes)
Janet R. Walker, Exec. Dir.   established: 1960
City Hall; 47708   1967 budget: $14,580

---

9. Fort Wayne, Indiana: Mayor's Commission on Human Relations (members: 13, staff: yes)
Alvin E. Wesley, Exec. Dir.   established: 1952
City Hall   1967 budget: $17,732
300 Berry St.; 46802

---

10. Greensboro, North Carolina: Commission on Human Relations (members: 25, staff: yes)
Louis Brooks, Exec. Dir.   established: 1966
Drawer W-2; 27402   1967 budget: $14,685

---

11. Los Angeles County, California: Commission on Human Relations (members: 25, staff: yes)
John A. Buggs, Exec. Dir.   established: 1944
John P. Lyons, Asst. Exec. Dir.   1966–1967 budget: $504,648
1184 Hall of Records; 90012

---

12. Milwaukee, Wisconsin: Commission on Community Relations (members: 36, staff: yes)
Calvin W. Beckett, Exec. Dir.   predecessor established: 1944
706 City Hall; 53202   reconstituted: 1960
                                      1967 budget: $40,219

---

13. Rochester and Monroe County, New York: Human Relations Commission (members: 15, staff: yes)

Loftes C. Carson, Exec. Dir.   established: 1960
39 Main St.; 14614   1967 budget: $79,400

14. Saginaw, Michigan: Human Relations Commission (members: 15, staff: yes)
Kenneth J. Augustine, Exec. Sec.   established: 1958
City Hall Annex   1966–1967 budget: $13,906

15. St. Petersburg, Florida: Community Relations Commission (members: 9, staff: yes)
Alexander A. Kawkins, Exec. Sec.   predecessor established: 1965
City Hall; 33733   reconstituted: 1967
     1967 budget: $20,000 (estimated)

16. Syracuse, New York: Mayor's Commission on Human Rights (members: 26, staff: yes)
Millicent Allewalt, Exec Dir.   established: 1963
211 City Hall; 13202   1967 budget: $22,240

17. Stamford, Connecticut: Human Rights Commission (members: 8, staff: yes)
Charles H. Durant III, Exec. Dir.   established: 1964
Town Hall, Atlantic Square; 06901   1967–1968 budget: $33,455

18. Topeka, Kansas: Human Relations Commission
Thomas A. Ebendorf, Exec. Sec.   established: 1963
City Hall; 66601   1967 budget: $16,970

19. Waterbury, Connecticut: Human Relations Commission (members: 11, staff: yes)
Rev. Charles W. Lanham, Chrm.   established: 1966
City Hall   1967 budget: none
     The Commission has subpoena power.

20. Waterloo, Iowa: Commission on Human Rights
Ronald J. James, Dir.
City Hall Annex   established: 1966
400 East 6th St.; 50703   1967 budget: not available

Appendix E

A Timetable of Passage of Civil-Rights Laws Enforced by Human-Relations Commissions or Divisions of Agencies

Year	Employment	Private Housing	Public Accommodations
1945	N.Y., N.J.		
1946	Mass.		
1947	Conn.		
1948			
1949	N.M., Ore., R.I., Wash.		Conn., N.J.
1950			
1951			
1952			N.Y., R.I.
1953			Mass., Ore.
1954			
1955	Mich., Minn., Pa.		
1956			
1957	Wis., Colo.		Wash., Colo.
1958			
1959	Cal., Ohio	Mass., Conn., Colo., Ore.	
1960			
1961	Ill., Kan., Mo.	N.J., Minn., N.Y., Pa.	Ohio, Pa.
1962			
1963	Alaska, Ind., Haw.	Alaska, Cal., Mich.	Alaska, Ind., Kan., Mich.
1964			Del., Md.
1965	Utah, Iowa, Md., Nev., Wyo., Neb., N.H.	Ind., R.I., N.H., Ohio, Wis.	Iowa, Nev., N.H., Minn., Mo.
1966	Ky.		Ky.
1967	W.Va.	Haw., Iowa, Md., Vt., Wash.	Vt., W.Va.

Appendix F

States with Civil-Rights Laws Enforced Only by the Courts

Employment
1. Arizona: Ariz. Rev. Stat., §§ 41-1401 to 1483 (Supp. 1967)
2. Delaware: Del. Code Ann. tit. 19, §§ 710–713 (Supp. 1967)
3. Idaho: Idaho Code, §§ 18-7301 to 7303, *as amended* (Supp. 1967)
4. Georgia: Code of Ga. Ann., §§ 54-1001 to 1007 (Supp. 1967)
5. Louisiana: La. Rev. Stat. Ann., §§ 23:892 to 893 (1964)
6. Maine: Me. Rev. Stat. Ann. tit. 26, §§ 861–864 (Supp. 1967)
7. Montana: Mont. Rev. Codes Ann., §§ 64-301 to 303 (Supp. 1967)
8. North Dakota: N.D. Cent. Code, §§ 34-06.1-01 to 09 (Supp. 1967)
9. Oklahoma: Okla. Stat. Ann. tit. 40, § 198.1, -.2 (Supp. 1967)
10. South Dakota: S.D. Laws 1966, H.B. No. 594, §§ 1–4
11. Texas: Tex. Ann. Rev. Civ. Stat., arts. 6825, 6252-14 (Supp 1966); ch. 72 [S.B. No. 185] Texas Laws 1967

Public Accommodations
1. Arizona: Ariz. Rev. Stat., §§ 41-1441, -1442 (Supp. 1967)
2. California: Cal. Civil Ann. §§ 51–53 (Supp. 1967)
3. Idaho: Idaho Code Ann. §§ 18-1703 to 7303 (Supp. 1967)
4. Maine: Me. Rev. Stat. Ann. tit. 17, § 1301, *as amended* (Supp. 1967)
5. Montana: Mont. Rev. Codes Ann., §§ 64-301 to 303 (Supp. 1967)
6. North Dakota: N.D. Cent. Code, § 12-22-30 *as amended* (Supp. 1967)
7. South Dakota: S.D. Laws 1963, ch. 58, §§ 1–2 (1963)

Housing
1. Maine: Me. Rev. Stat. Ann. tit. 17, § 1301, *as amended* (Supp. 1967)

INDEX

access, right of: 394
adjudication: by human-relations commissions, 105
administrative agencies: SEE agencies, administrative
administrative hearings. SEE hearings, formal
administrative jobs: Negroes in, 120
administrative orders: by human-relations commissions, 381, 415. SEE ALSO cease and desist orders
Administrative Procedure Act, Federal: civil-rights ordinances modeled on, 60, 372; Alpha Model Acts modeled on, 375, 376, 379
administrative processes: attacks of, on discrimination, 9, 12, 14, 17, 24, 30, 31, 60, 138, 382, 417, 464; inadequacy of, 14; backed up by judicial process, 138; enforcement authority of, 139; nature of: 363; use of, by human-relations commissions, 366, 483
administrative trial. SEE trial, administrative
affirmative action: ordered by human-relations commissions, 376, 381; in civil-rights cases, 392, 393
age, discrimination because of: human-relations commissions attack, 107, 163 n.–164 n., 415, 419; prohibition of, 366, 380–390 *passim*, 425, 478, 481; definition of, 385, 433; mentioned, 7, 206
Age Discrimination in Employment Act of 1967: 10, 23
agencies, administrative: role of, in human relations, 12, 212, 288–304; need enforcement authority, 97
——, civil-rights: lack of, 17; need enforcement authority, 97; and other federal programs, 474–476

——, enforcement: EEOC as, 14; and civil-rights policy, 9, 27;
——, federal: discrimination by, 20–21, 210, 216–217; enforcement of civil-rights laws by, 84–85; proposed by Norgren-Hill study, 124
——, government: discrimination by, 55, 166, 213, 364, 366, 379–380, 384, 473; Negroes employed by, 120; nature of, 206; wide-spectrum negotiations with, 289
——, independent: to handle police maladministration, 255
——, local: agreements of, with EEOC, 67; cooperation of human-relations commissions with, 263–268
——, state: discrimination by, 30; agreements of, with EEOC, 67
agency review: of human-relations commission determinations, 185–190, 373; various model acts on, 188–189
Agriculture, Secretary of: 300
Agriculture committees: compared to human-relations commissions, 300–301
air force. SEE armed forces
airlines: discrimination by, 172
Akin, Harry: 57–58, 61–62, 82 n.
Alaska civil-rights law: on housing discrimination, 144–145
Alaska Commission for Human Rights: jurisdiction of, 147, 150; filing of complaints with, 166; outline of, 505
Alpha Model Federal Civil-Rights Act: on federal human-relations commission, 212–213; nature of, 301, 465–466; reasons for, 360–361, 464; and other civil-rights laws, 464, 466, 467, 468, 473, 483, 484; and Alpha Model State Act, 464, 465, 471, 472, 474; and Alpha Model State-Local Act,